REAL ESTATE
LAW
THIRD EDITION

FRANK GIBSON
JAMES KARP
ELLIOT KLAYMAN

**Real Estate
Education Company**
a division of Dearborn Financial Publishing, Inc.

While a great deal of care has been taken to provide accurate and current information, the ideas, suggestions, general principles and conclusions presented in this text are subject to local, state and federal laws and regulations, court cases, and any revisions of same. The reader is thus urged to consult legal counsel regarding any points of law—this publication should not be used as a substitute for competent legal advice.

© 1983, 1987, 1992 by Dearborn Financial Publishing, Inc.

Published by Real Estate Education Company/Chicago,
Dearborn Financial Publishing, Inc.

93 94 10 9 8 7 6 5 4 3 2

Acquisitions Editor: Margaret M. Maloney
Cover Design: Mary Kushmir

Library of Congress Cataloging-in-Publication Data

Gibson, Frank F.
    Real estate law / Frank Gibson, James Karp, Elliot Klayman. — 3rd ed.
        p.   cm.
    Includes indexes.
    ISBN 0-7931-0121-2 : $33.25
      1. Real property—United States.   I. Karp, James.   II. Klayman, Elliot I.
III. Title.
KF570.G5   1992
346.7403'3—dc20
[347.30643]   92-4103
                                       CIP

Contents

Part 3
Sales of Ownership Interest

Part 6
Leasehold Interests and Alternatives

Preface

The fundamental principles of real estate law were developed because of land's historic importance as a source of wealth. These principles are more difficult for people to grasp because they were created under different social and economic conditions than exist today. Additionally, the vocabulary includes terms that are hardly household words. These characteristics often foster in the uninitiated a lack of confidence and a negative attitude toward the subject matter.

In order to overcome these obstacles to understanding, we have provided the reader with a solid foundation and useful review of key terms and concepts.

Changes in the Third Edition

Organization

The text has been reorganized into six parts with chapters covering similar transactions grouped together. Part one covers the fundamentals of real estate law; part two discusses the transferring of real estate; part three addresses the sale of ownership interests; part four discusses the financing of a transaction; part five deals with the regulation of ownership interests; and part six addresses leasehold interests and alternatives.

Content

We have added or expanded discussions of several areas that have become increasingly important to real estate practitioners, including the growing importance of environmental regulation in real estate (Chapter 23), time-shares (Chapter 27) and buyer agency (Chapter 11).

Pedagogy

- *Key Terms* are integrated into the body of the text with definitions highlighted in boldface type.

- *Case Examples* are primarily hypothetical cases that exemplify key concepts within the chapter.

- *Case Studies* are abstracts of actual cases designed to help the reader understand the intricacies of key cases affecting real estate law. Background information for each case is provided to help the reader focus on the key issues of the case.

- *Review and Discussion Questions* test the reader's understanding and mastery of key chapter concepts. Answers are provided in the Instructor's Manual (IM). The IM provides chapter purpose, learning objectives, lecture outlines, multiple-choice questions, and answer key for multiple-choice questions.

- *Case Problems* challenge the reader to apply key concepts to hypothetical situations. Answer are provided in the instructor's manual (IM).

- The *Alphabetical Index of Cases* allows for quick reference to particular cases.

- The *Subject Index of Cases* refers readers to cases relating to a particular area of study.

- The *Glossary* provides the reader convenient review of the terms introduced in the text.

Each of us received help from many people, and for this we thank them. We would like to acknowledge the following reviewers for their helpful suggestions and recommendations on several drafts of the manuscript: Barbara J. Beatty, J.D., Green River Community College and Seattle Central Community College; Maurice Boren, National Institute of Real Estate; Richard L. Coffinberger, George Mason University; Gerard Halpern, professor emeritus, University of Arkansas; Hans R. Isakson, University of Northern Iowa; Wayne R. Michelsen, J.D.; Paula C. Murray, University of Texas-Austin; Leo Kearney O'Drudy, Jr., University of Virginia; George N. Plavac, Cuyahoga Community College, Metro Campus; Ron Stark, Northwest Mississippi Community College; Barry L. Wittenkeller, J.D. The end-of-chapter summaries were originally written by Eleanor McConnell.

About the Authors

Frank F. Gibson, J.D., M.A.

Professor and Chair of the Finance Department in the College of Business, The Ohio State University

James P. Karp, J.D.

Professor and Chairman of the Department of Law and Public Policy, The School of Management, Syracuse University

Elliot I. Klayman, J.D., L.L.M.

Associate Director of the Center for Real Estate Education and Research; Professor in the College of Business, Department of Finance, The Ohio State University

Part 1

Nature and Ownership of Real Estate

1

Introduction to Law and Legal Systems

Law and the Real Estate Business

Many aspects of the real estate business are closely associated with law. In fact, only the world of finance may be more closely controlled by law. Almost any professional activity of a broker, salesperson, appraiser or investor involves certain legal restrictions. For this reason, people employed to do these jobs, as well as people employed to do many other jobs in real estate, have a genuine need to know about the law and legal systems. The more extensive their knowledge, the more effectively will they be able to do their jobs.

Real estate professionals deal not only with lawyers but also with recording clerks, building inspectors, tax officials, zoning board employees and personnel from state and federal housing agencies. All of these people have specialized functions in the legal system. Understanding what they do and some of the responsibilities of their jobs increases the real estate professional's ability to work effectively with them. Many private individuals with whom salespeople and brokers come in contact also have specialized knowledge of the law; loan officers and appraisers are examples. Real estate professionals who have similar knowledge will be able to work more effectively with other specialists and improve their professional image at the same time.

Legal knowledge is especially important to people who sell real estate. They are involved in the real estate transaction at a critical point as far as legal input is concerned. Clients and customers will often question them about legal matters or the advisability of consulting an attorney. Although sales personnel should never give legal advice, a knowledge of law will help them develop an awareness of situations in which a lawyer should be consulted. Because legal knowledge is considered so important, some states require salespeople and brokers engaged in selling real estate to complete a formal course in real estate law.

Although this book is devoted to a study of real estate law, to some extent that designation is misleading. Real estate law cannot really be separated from other types of law. A famous jurist once said, "Law is a seamless web"; nevertheless, because of the complexity of law, people who want to understand it often consider it in small segments. The boundaries of these segments are never exact, nor is there general agreement on what each segment includes. So, initially, the reader must realize that, although much of what is said about real estate law applies to law in general, some strands of the "seamless web" are more important to the real estate business than others. This book deals primarily with these strands.

Most of this book discusses specific rules important to real estate people. In this first chapter, however, the book takes a broader look at law and the legal system. This chapter attempts to clarify the law by looking at where law is found and the structure in which it operates.

Sources of Law

The answer to many legal questions comes from life's experiences. As a person learns in school, on the job or through daily living, laws important to that person become part of his or her knowledge of the manner in which things operate. Sometimes legal questions arise that are not answerable from experience. How does one find the answers to these questions? To what source does the student, the real estate professional, the lawyer or the judge turn to find out what the law is?

One of the prevailing myths about law is that all laws are found in nicely indexed, officially published volumes of statutes enacted by a legislative body. According to this belief, all a person has to do to answer a legal question is to locate the correct page in the right book, and the law will be there in clear black letters. Unfortunately, few legal questions are answered this simply.

Thousands of cases, statutes and administrative regulations are published each year. As a result, determining what the law is has become increasingly difficult. Computers have, during the past twenty-five years, provided a tool that enhances the potential for legal professionals and the general public to access the sources of law more effectively. The speed and manipulative power of the computer allow increased control over the burgeoning quantities of legal information.

Two major computer-assisted legal research systems exist. Both services contain the full text of more than one million documents. These systems include information about cases, statutes, administrative regulations, attorney general opinions, law review articles, treaties, administrative decisions and citation indexes. A researcher who locates relevant information stored in the data bases can obtain a copy of this information via the printer in a matter of seconds.

Although computers are used effectively in many real estate offices both large and small, little use is made of the legal data bases that are available. Access to this information is expensive. Charges range from $50 to $150 for each hour of use. Additionally, the information cannot be accessed effectively unless the operator has some background in legal analysis and research. Some authorities predict that computer assisted legal information will become more readily available in the near future, but as of 1992 effective use of this information seems remote for real estate professionals.

In order to answer a legal question involving real estate, a person might have to examine one source or a number of different sources. Sometimes an answer will be found in a state constitution or the federal Constitution. Most often, however, people find the answer to real estate law questions in court opinions, often referred to as *precedents*, in statutes and in the regulations of administrative agencies. The different sources of law are discussed in the paragraphs that follow.

Constitutions

A basic source of law, constitutions provide the framework within which the federal and state governments must operate. Ordinarily one does not associate real estate law with constitutional problems, but at least two functions of constitutions are important to the real estate business. First, the U.S. Constitution allocates power between the states and the federal government. Because the states generally have retained power over local matters, most real estate law is state law. However, as the states have given the federal government power to regulate businesses affecting interstate commerce, numerous federal statutes apply to the real estate business. At present, many people in the field are concerned about how federal statutes such as the Sherman Act and the Clayton Act are affecting real estate. Bankruptcy statutes and consumer protection laws such as "Truth-in-Lending," the Real Estate Settlement Procedures Act and environmental protection legislation are other examples of federal law that apply to real estate.

A second function of constitutions—both state and federal—is the protection of individual rights, including private property. Constitutional provisions require that the law be applied equally to all; in addition, they prohibit government from depriving a person of life, liberty or property without due process. This means that an individual's property can be taken by government only under limited circumstances. But the protection accorded the individual is far from absolute. Both the power of eminent domain and the police power allow government to acquire private property.

Precedent

A published opinion of an appellate court that serves as authority for determining a legal question in a later case with similar facts.

A distinctive feature of the law of English-speaking countries is its reliance upon cases decided by appellate courts as a source of law. Reports of these cases are published as opinions, which provide the answers to many legal questions.

Case Example

Clayborne and his adult daughter lived in a house that Clayborne owned. At the request of the daughter, Dexter painted the house. Clayborne did not authorize the work, but he knew that it was being done and raised no objection. Clayborne refused to pay Dexter, arguing that he had not contracted to have the house painted.

Dexter asked his attorney if Clayborne was legally liable to pay him. The attorney told Dexter that in their state several published appellate court decisions had established that, when a homeowner allows work to be done on his home by a person who would ordinarily expect to be paid, a duty to pay exists. The attorney stated that, based on these *precedents*, it was advisable for Dexter to bring a suit to collect the reasonable value of the work that he had done.

In the legal system of English-speaking countries, judges are obligated to follow principles established by prior cases (precedents). This obligation is ingrained in our system. The extent to which a court is governed by precedent is difficult to assess. Although the practice of following precedent is not a legal duty, it is definitely more than a tradition. A judge who failed to follow precedent would not be convicted of a crime, but he or she ordinarily would be reversed and in extreme cases censured or possibly impeached. People trained in our system generally consider reliance upon precedent an effective and fair way to reach a decision, and the concept is fundamental to American law.

The obligation to follow precedent is limited by a number of factors. A court need not follow precedent established in another state, although in reaching decisions courts sometimes consider precedent from other states when their own state has no case law on the subject. Lower courts are bound to follow decisions rendered by higher courts of their state. Again, failure to do so may result merely in the lower court's decision being reversed. The highest appellate court in a state can overrule its own precedent. Although this occurs on occasion, most state appellate courts overrule reluctantly because they believe that certainty is a desirable characteristic of law. The reluctance to overrule is often seen in private areas such as real estate law, for certainty is deemed very important where property rights are involved. A court will overrule a prior decision when the rule of law was applied incorrectly in the first place or when the rule is not considered applicable because of a change in circumstances.

Courts and attorneys frequently avoid the effect of a previous case by distinguishing it from the case under consideration. A case is distinguished when a significant factual difference can be pointed out between the two situations. For example, assume that, in defending Clayborne in a suit brought by Dexter, Clayborne's attorney asks the court to dismiss the case, because she has found the published decision of a case with like facts where the appellate court held that the homeowner was not required to pay. Dexter's attorney argues that in that case the homeowner was on vacation and did not know that the work was being done. As Clayborne knew that his house was being painted, the two cases are different and can be distinguished. If the court agrees that the two cases are significantly different, *i.e.,* can be distinguished, it will decide that the earlier decision is not precedent and therefore not controlling in deciding the case before it.

Law that evolves from published opinions of appellate courts or precedent is often called *judge-made law* or *decisional law*. In England, reliance upon previous decisions and upon custom and tradition created a law that was common to the entire country. Therefore, the law based upon prior opinions is often referred to as *common law*. Sometimes people have difficulty accepting the idea that in these opinions statutes are not involved in any manner. In fact, often no statute exists that can be used to settle the dispute.

A modern example of judge-made law is found in those appellate decisions that impose responsibility upon builders of defective homes. Before World War II, the builder of a defective home had little legal responsibility for injury or property damage once the home was sold. The buyer was required to make his or her own inspection of the premises. On the basis of this inspection, the buyer accepted responsibility for all defects, relieving the builder of responsibility for any defective construction. The courts were applying the ancient doctrine of *caveat emptor*—"let the buyer beware."

During the 1950s and the 1960s, courts began to recognize the unfairness of this rule. They began to allow buyers of new homes to recover for personal injury and property damage resulting from defective construction. In numerous states, this modification of the law from *caveat emptor* to *caveat venditor* ("let the seller beware") was accomplished without legislation. As one state court commented:

> If at one time . . . the rule of caveat emptor had application to the sale of a new house by a vendor-builder, that time is now past. The decisions and legal writings herein referred to afford numerous ex- amples and situations illustrating the harshness and injustice of the rule when applied to the sale of a new house by a builder-vendor. . . . Obviously, the ordinary purchaser is not in a position to ascertain when there is a defect in a chimney flue, or vent of a heating apparatus, or whether the plumbing work covered by a concrete slab foundation is faulty.
>
> The caveat emptor rule as applied to new houses is an anachronism patently out of harmony with modern home buying practices. It does a disservice not only to the ordinary prudent purchaser but to the industry itself by lending encouragement to the unscrupulous, fly-by- night operator and purveyor of shoddy work. *Humber v. Morton, 426 S.W.2d 554 (Tex. 1968).*

Statutory Law

Law enacted by local and state legislative bodies and by Congress.

The Role of Statutes

Although for many years the opinions of courts were the chief source of real estate law in English-speaking countries and for the legal system generally, during the past 100 years statutes have gradually assumed this role. Among the many reasons for this trend are that statutes are more comprehensive, statutes can modify the law more rapidly, statutes can treat an entire problem rather than just a part and statutes are usually more understandable than cases.

During the past 75 years, statutes have been used to bring greater uniformity to state law. Economic expansion after the Civil War has been characterized by the growth of regional and national markets. States, however, have often adopted different laws to solve common problems occurring in these markets. This practice has increased the cost of doing business and caused confusion and uncertainty.

Uniform Laws

In 1890, the National Conference of Commissioners on Uniform State Law was established to alleviate this problem. The commission is charged with determining what uniform laws are necessary, drafting a uniform statute and trying to get states to adopt it. More than 100 uniform laws have been recommended, although few have been adopted by all or even a majority of the states.

The commission's most conspicuous success has been the Uniform Commercial Code. This statute has been adopted in all of the states. In some instances it applies to transactions involving real property. This limited application will be discussed more fully later in the book.

The commission has recently proposed a number of laws that deal with real estate. These include a uniform condominium act, a uniform residential landlord-tenant act, a uniform simplification of land transfers act and a uniform eminent domain code. As of 1992, however, the impact of these uniform laws on real estate has been minimal.

Court Interpretation of Statutes

Despite the growing importance of statutes as a source of law, court opinions continue to play a significant role in determining what the law is. Many statutes are broadly written. Often their meaning is not clear until they have been interpreted by a court. It is probably safe to say that, in a majority of instances, a lawyer looking for the answer to a legal question will first check for an appropriate statute and then review relevant court opinions interpreting that statute.

Codification of Appellate Judge-made Law

Another reason that court opinion continues to be important is that statutes often are merely a codification of the cases dealing with a particular legal problem. When a legislative body codifies the law, it adopts a statute that reflects the decisional law. For example, when the courts in some states decided that the act of selling real property implied a warranty of fitness for habitation, the state legislature passed statutes mirroring the court's decisions.

Administrative Rules and Regulations

In our dynamic, complex society, much of the work of government is done by administrative agencies. Both Congress and state legislatures create administrative agencies as part of legislation that aims to cure some social ill. The agency is empowered to enforce and implement the goals of the legislation. A substantial number of administrative agencies significantly influence the real estate business. Among such federal agencies are the Department of Housing and Urban Development, the Environmental Protection Agency and the Federal Home Loan Bank Board. State administrative agencies also have a far-reaching influence on the real estate business. They are the source of rules pertaining to such matters as licensing and disciplining real estate sales personnel, zoning, safeguarding the environment, and landlord and tenant rights.

Administrative agencies perform several functions. They are authorized to settle disputes and, in doing so, act like courts; this is called *administrative adjudication*. The procedures used in administrative adjudication are generally much less formal than those used by the courts, making reaching a settlement less time-consuming and costly. Another benefit of administrative adjudication is that the agency personnel resolving the dispute are experts in the subject area of the dispute and can therefore resolve the case more effectively than is sometimes possible in a court.

Many agencies also have the power to make rules and regulations that have the force of law. In this respect they act like legislatures. An agency's authority to make rules and regulations is granted in the legislation that created the agency. If the rule or regulation issued by the agency is constitutional, proper procedures have been followed and the agency has not exceeded the power and authority granted to it by the legislature, the rule or regulation is immune from modification or invalidation by the courts.

Court Structure

People in the real estate business sometimes become involved in litigation, so it is helpful for them to know something about the structure of the system that applies the law.

Trial and Appellate Courts

Two types of courts are fundamental to the operation of the legal system. They are trial and appellate courts.

Trial Courts

The function of a trial court is to determine the facts and to apply the relevant law to these facts. A jury usually makes the factual determination, but in some cases the parties are not entitled to a jury, or they waive this right. Disputed facts are then decided by the judge. Whether a judge or jury makes the factual determination, findings are based upon evidence. In most instances evidence is the oral testimony of witnesses who are questioned by attorneys for the parties.

The testimony of most witnesses is valuable because the witness has personal knowledge of the facts. One important type of witness often does not have personal knowledge of the situation, but does have expertise related to a disputed fact. This person is the expert witness. The testimony of the expert witness is not permitted until the trial court judge is convinced that the witness is qualified. When qualified, the expert witness answers a hypothetical question that covers technical aspects of a disputed fact. Real estate brokers and appraisers often testify as expert witnesses in cases involving disputed land values.

Appellate Courts

If either party thinks that a legal error has been made by the trial court judge, the party may ask a higher court to review the case. This procedure is called an *appeal*, and the court hearing the case is an appellate court. The function of the appellate court is quite different from that of the trial court. This court is not concerned with deciding disputed facts; rather, it corrects legal mistakes. For this reason, there is no jury in an appellate court; rather, there is a panel of judges. The judges do not listen to the testimony of witnesses. Instead, they read briefs in which the parties explain what they believe the law to be, and they may hear oral arguments presented by attorneys. Later the judges decide which party is correct. One of the judges will then write an opinion presenting the views of the majority. If the court finds that an error has been made, the opinion will order the lower court to correct its mistake. These opinions are the judge-made law as explained earlier.

Federal and State Courts

A first step in understanding the American legal structure is to recognize that the federal government and each of the states have their own system of trial and appellate courts. Each of the systems—state and federal—in most instances is the final authority within its own jurisdiction. One exception to this principle is that federal courts do have authority over state courts in questions involving the U.S. Constitution.

Jurisdiction of State Courts

The authority of state courts is extensive. It includes cases involving violations of the state's criminal statute as well as statutes that involve matters as diverse as divorce, education, public health and social welfare. Most contract cases and those involving personal injuries are also heard in state courts. In fact, state courts have jurisdiction over all matters except those the Constitution or Congress has given exclusively to the federal courts or has denied to the states.

Jurisdiction of Federal Courts

The jurisdiction of federal courts is limited to that given to them by the Constitution and the federal statutes that create them. As a result federal courts hear only cases that involve the Constitution, treaties between the U.S. and a foreign nation, federal statutes, and citizens of different states. In the following case, the jurisdiction of the federal courts to decide a case brought against New Orleans real estate brokers is questioned.

McLain v. Real Estate Board of New Orleans, Inc.
U.S. Supreme Court
444 U.S.232 (1980)

Background: McLain and others (petitioners) brought a class action on behalf of real estate purchasers and sellers. The action was against real estate trade associations, firms and brokers (respondents). The complaint stated that the respondents had engaged in a price-fixing conspiracy in violation of the Sherman Act, a federal statute.

The petitioners' complaint alleged the following: (1) that respondents' activities were "within the flow of interstate commerce and have an effect upon that commerce"; (2) that respondents assist their clients in securing financing and insurance involved with the purchase of real estate and that much of this financing and insurance comes from outside the state.

The U.S. District Court dismissed the complaint, finding that respondents' activities involving real estate were purely local in nature and did not substantially affect interstate commerce. The U.S. Court of Appeals affirmed, and the petitioner appealed.

Decision: The U.S. Supreme Court vacated and remanded the case for trial.

Mr. Chief Justice Burger delivered the opinion of the Court.

The question in this case is whether the Sherman Act extends to an agreement among real estate brokers in a market area to conform to a fixed rate of brokerage commissions on sales of residential property.

A

The broad authority of Congress under the Commerce Clause has, of course, long been interpreted to extend beyond activities actually *in* interstate commerce to reach other activities, while wholly local in nature, nevertheless substantially *affect* interstate commerce. During the near century of Sherman Act experiences, forms and modes of business and commerce have changed along with changes in communication and travel, and innovations in methods of conducting particular businesses have altered relationships in commerce. Application of the Act reflects an adaptation to these changing circumstances.

The conceptual distinction between activities "in" interstate commerce and those which "affect" interstate commerce has been preserved in the cases, for Congress has seen fit to preserve that distinction in the antitrust and related laws by limiting the applicability of certain provisions to activities demonstrably "in commerce." It can no longer be doubted, however, that the jurisdictional requirement of the Sherman Act may be satisfied under either the "in commerce" or the "effect on commerce" theory.

Although the cases demonstrate the breadth of Sherman Act prohibitions, jurisdiction may not be invoked under that statute unless the relevant aspect of interstate commerce is identified; it is not sufficient merely to rely on identification of a relevant local activity and to presume an interrelationship with some unspecified aspect of interstate commerce. To establish jurisdiction a plaintiff must allege the critical relationship in the pleadings and if these allegations are controverted must proceed to demonstrate by submission of evidence beyond the pleadings either that the defendants' activity is itself in interstate commerce or, if it is local in nature, that it has an effect on some other appreciable activity demonstrably in interstate commerce.

To establish the jurisdictional element of a Sherman Act violation it would be sufficient for petitioners to demonstrate a substantial effect on interstate commerce generated by respondents' brokerage activity. Petitioners need not make the more particularized showing of an effect on interstate commerce caused by the alleged conspiracy to fix commission rates, or by those other aspects of respondents' activity that are alleged to be unlawful. The validity of this approach is confirmed by an examination of the case law. If establishing jurisdiction required a showing that the unlawful conduct itself had an effect on interstate commerce, jurisdiction would be defeated by a demonstration that the alleged restraint failed to have its intended anticompetitive effect. This is not the rule of our cases. A violation may still be found in such circumstances because in a civil action under the Sherman Act, liability may be established by proof of *either* an unlawful purpose or an anticompetitive effect.

Nor is jurisdiction defeated in a case relying on anticompetitive effects by plaintiff's failure of quantify the adverse impact of defendant's conduct. Even where there is an inability to prove that concerted activity has resulted in legally cognizable damages, jurisdiction need not be impaired, though such a failure may confine the available remedies to injunctive relief.

C

On the record thus far made, it cannot be said that there is an insufficient basis for petitioners to proceed at trial to establish Sherman Act jurisdiction. It is clear that an appreciable amount of commerce is involved in the financing of residential property in the Greater New Orleans area and in the insuring of titles to such property. The presidents of two of the many lending institutions in the area stated in their deposition testimony that those institutions committed hundreds of millions of dollars to residential financing during the period covered by the complaint. The testimony further demonstrates that this appreciable commercial activity has occurred in interstate commerce. Funds were raised from out-of-state investors and from interbank loans obtained from interstate financial institutions. Multistate lending institutions took mortgages insured under federal programs which entailed interstate transfers of premiums and settlements. Mortgage obligations physically and constructively were traded as financial instruments in the interstate secondary mortgage market. Before making a mortgage loan in the Greater New Orleans area, lending institutions usually, if not always, required title insurance, which was furnished by interstate corporations. Reading the pleadings, as supplemented, most favorably to petitioners, for present purposes we take these facts as established.

At trial, respondents will have the opportunity, if they so choose, to make their own case contradicting this factual showing. On the other hand, it may be possible for petitioners to establish that, apart from the commerce in title insurance and real estate financing, an appreciable amount of interstate commerce is involved with the local residential real estate market arising out of the interstate movement of people, or otherwise.

To establish federal jurisdiction in this case, there remains only the requirement that respondents' activities which allegedly have been infected by a price-fixing conspiracy be shown "as a matter of practical economics" to have a not insubstantial effect on the interstate commerce involved. It is clear, as the record shows, that the function of respondent real estate brokers is to bring the buyer and seller together on agreeable terms. For this service the broker charges a fee generally calculated as a percentage of the sale price. Brokerage activities necessarily affect both the frequency and the terms of residential sales transactions. Ultimately, whatever stimulates or retards the volume of residential sales, or has an impact on the purchase price, affects the demand for financing and title insurance, those two commercial activities that on this record are shown to have occurred in interstate commerce. Where, as here, the services of respondent real estate brokers are often employed in transactions in the relevant market, petitioners at trial may be able to show that respondents' activities have a not insubstantial effect on interstate commerce.

* * *

We therefore conclude that it was error to dismiss the complaint at this stage of the proceedings. The judgment of the Court of Appeals is vacated, and the case is remanded for further proceedings consistent with this opinion.

Vacated and remanded.

The power of federal courts to hear cases that arise under the Constitution, treaties and federal statutes is called *federal question* jurisdiction. Most federal question matters involve the application or interpretation of one of the many federal statutes, such as the Environmental Protection Act, the Civil Rights Act or the Internal Revenue Code.

The power of federal courts to hear cases involving citizens of different states is called *diversity jurisdiction.* Diversity jurisdiction exists because when the Constitution was adopted many people believed that a citizen of one state would not get a fair trial if sued in another state. Consequently, those who drafted the Constitution included in it a provision extending federal judicial power to disputes between citizens of different states. Because diversity jurisdiction places a substantial burden on the federal courts as they are often applying state law, Congress has limited the diversity jurisdiction of these courts to cases in which the dispute involves more than $50,000.

Case Example

Able was a resident of New Hampshire and Baker a resident of New York. The two entered into a contract in which Baker agreed to purchase a large resort hotel in New Hampshire from Able. Baker breached the contract, and Able sued her in the New Hampshire courts for $75,000 damages. Baker may transfer the case to the federal district court since the parties are residents of different states and the amount in controversy exceeds $50,000.

Most real estate litigation is brought in state courts because the dispute does not involve a federal statute or U.S. Constitutional question, and the parties are usually residents of the same state. In addition, most real estate legal disputes concern land located within the state, and there is no basis whatsoever for a federal court's taking jurisdiction.

State Court System

As there are 51 independent court systems operating within the United States, understanding the structure of American courts might seem an impossible task. The task is, however, simplified by the existence of a pattern common to both the federal and the 50 state systems. This structure can be visualized as a pyramid with two or sometimes three levels.

State Trial Courts

Trial courts are at the base of the structural pyramid. Trial courts can be classified into three brcad groups. This classification is based upon the court's power to hear a case, which is termed its *jurisdiction*.

Courts of general jurisdiction   Each state usually has a trial court of general jurisdiction. In some states these are called *superior courts*. Other states call them *county courts, district courts, circuit courts* or *courts of common pleas*. These courts have the power to hear a wide variety of civil and criminal cases. Ordinarily, there are no limits on the court's monetary jurisdiction, and the court has the power to grant extraordinary remedies, such as the injunction and specific performance. An injunction is an order forbidding a person to do a particular act. Conversely, an order for specific performance commands that a particular act be performed.

In a number of states these courts hear appeals from administrative agencies and courts of limited jurisdiction (see Figure 1.1). Trial by jury is available for most cases. The court generally has statewide jurisdiction but is organized on a district basis. These courts are generally considered the cornerstones of judicial administration.

Courts of limited jurisdiction   Many of the more populous states have created trial courts that are limited to hearing cases in which the damages are less than a certain amount, fixed by statute. Depending upon the state, this amount ranges from a few hundred to thousands of dollars. These courts also generally have criminal jurisdiction over cases involving petty crimes and misdemeanors. *Municipal courts* is a common name for these courts. Other states call them *justice courts, magistrates courts* or *district courts.*

Generalizations about courts of limited jurisdiction are difficult to make. Their authority differs widely from state to state. In metropolitan areas their monetary jurisdiction is sometimes extensive, and the courts are manned by full-time judges with large staffs. In some rural areas these courts hear only the most trivial cases and may be presided over by part-time judges with no legal training. Courts of limited jurisdiction are important to the legal system because they take some of the pressures off the courts of general jurisdiction.

Courts of special jurisdiction   Either because of tradition or because of the peculiar needs of judicial administration, in many states special courts have been

Figure 1.1: A Typical State Judicial System

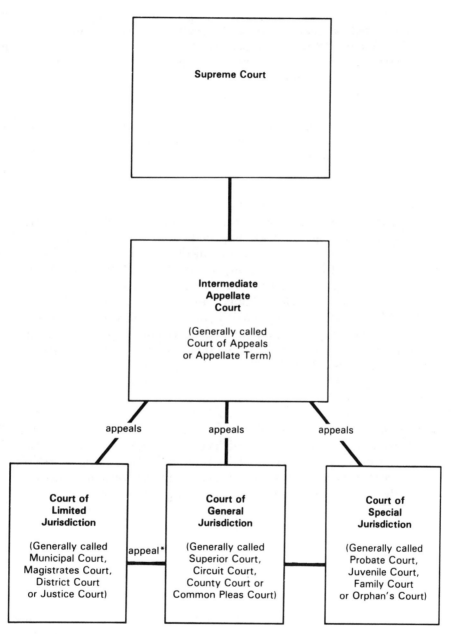

* In a number of states, courts of general jurisdiction consider appeals from courts of limited jurisdiction.

established to resolve a wide variety of disputes. Traffic offenses are one type of case often tried in a court of special jurisdiction. Traffic cases are generally tried in a special court or a special division of a trial court as so many traffic offenses are processed that they would clog the regular judicial machinery.

Juvenile and domestic relations cases are also heard by a special court. These courts provide privacy and informal procedures that are effective in dealing with juvenile and family matters.

Numerous states also have separate probate courts. These courts exercise jurisdiction over the administration of decedents' estates. When a real estate broker or sales associate is involved in a transaction that has to do with a decedent's real property, the broker or sales associate often has to deal with a probate court. In some states, probate courts have jurisdiction in guardianship, adoption, and competency proceedings.

State Intermediate Appellate Courts

About half the states have, by constitution or statute, established an intermediate level of appellate courts. The purpose of these courts is to lighten the burden of the state's supreme court. Some intermediate appellate courts have limited powers to act as trial courts. Usually this involves the power to issue extraordinary writs. However, the primary function of these courts is to provide appellate review. Although the extent of appellate jurisdiction is generally broad, some states place limits on the appeals that can be heard, possibly on the type of case or the maximum monetary amount. An intermediate appellate court might be permitted to hear civil appeals or civil appeals only in cases wherein the amount in controversy is under $30,000.

State Supreme Courts

At the apex of a state's judicial system is the state supreme court, which in most states hears appeals in all civil and criminal matters. This jurisdiction is often concurrent with that of the intermediate appellate court. Because of the extensiveness of the review process and the large number of appeals, most states allow their court of last resort to accept for review only cases that the justices or judges consider important. Appeals as a matter of right may, however, often be taken in important cases, such as those that involve constitutionality of a state or federal statute or the death penalty.

Federal Court System

U.S. District Courts

The U.S. District Courts are the trial courts of the federal system. The United States is divided into 94 districts, each with a single district court. Almost all federal cases are initiated in these courts as they have the power to hear all types of federal cases except those assigned by Congress to special courts such as the tax court.

U.S. Courts of Appeal

The federal intermediate appellate courts are called *U.S. Courts of Appeal*. In 1985 the United States was divided into 12 geographic areas called *circuits*, with a court of appeals for each. These courts hear appeals from the federal district courts that are included in their circuit. They also hear appeals from administrative agencies. They do not have the power to act as trial courts.

U.S. Supreme Court

The United States Supreme Court is the final appellate court in the federal system. Most of the cases the Supreme Court reviews come from the U.S. Courts of Appeal and from the state supreme courts. The Supreme Court may review state supreme court decisions involving the federal Constitution or a federal statute.

In certain cases the Supreme Court must hear an appeal. One example is a case in which a U.S. Court of Appeals has held a state statute unconstitutional. Another is when a lower federal court has held a federal statute unconstitutional and the United States is a party. In most cases the party seeking review must first ask the Supreme Court to hear the case by petitioning for a writ of certiorari. This is a writ in which a superior court orders an inferior court to supply a record of a particular case. The Supreme Court denies most petitions for certiorari as it does not consider the case important enough to hear. Denial of certiorari does not mean that the petitioner has been denied an appeal. All of these cases have been heard by at least one appellate court and sometimes more.

Summary

People employed in the real estate field have a genuine need to know about the law and the legal systems that regulate the profession. In fact, licensing requirements in some states include a course in real estate law.

Law has several sources: published appellate court opinions or *precedents*, statutes (*statutory law*), rules and regulations issued by regulatory agencies, and the provisions of the federal and various state constitutions. Judges have a fundamental obligation to follow precedent. The body of law that has evolved as appellate judges base their written decisions on precedent is called common law.

Much law today results from appellate courts' interpretations of statutes. These interpretations become precedent, which establishes the meaning of the statute. In the past half century, administrative agencies have become an increasingly important source of law as they are empowered to make rules and regulations.

The court system, consisting of several types and levels of courts, is established to settle disputes or apply penalties when laws are broken. In trial courts, judges or jury panels decide the facts based on evidence and apply the relevant law. If either party feels that a legal error has been made, he or she may appeal to a higher court, called an appellate court. Cases here are decided not by juries but by judges who hear the arguments presented by both sides. Most real estate disputes are decided at the state level in trial courts.

Review and Discussion Questions

1. Name the courts in your state having (a) general jurisdiction, (b) limited jurisdiction and (c) final jurisdiction.

2. (a) Define the doctrine of precedent. (b) Indicate limitations on the use of precedent.

3. During the past 50 years, statutory law has gradually replaced judge-made or decisional law. Explain the reasons for this.

Case Problems

1. Sorensen, a licensed real estate broker, entered into a listing agreement with Schomas. Sorensen located a buyer who submitted a purchase offer. Schomas refused to accept the offer or to pay Sorensen the commission that was clearly owed. Enraged, Sorensen threatened to "take the case to the United States Supreme Court, if necessary." Explain why Sorensen probably would be unable to do this.

2. Taylor was involved in litigation involving a real estate problem. Taylor's friend Bennett testified in Taylor's behalf at the trial. Bennett's testimony was critical to the outcome of the case. Taylor lost the case and decided to appeal. When Taylor informed Bennett of his intention to appeal, Bennett told him that he could not testify a second time as the experience had drained him emotionally. Taylor told Bennett that it would not be necessary for him to testify again. Explain why.

3. Stanley Beck purchased a remote farm to which he moved with his family. After living there for a time, Beck became disturbed because his children had a long walk to the school bus. The walk was especially dangerous during the winter, because there were no sidewalks and the road was often icy. Beck asked an attorney whether the purchase could be rescinded on the grounds of fraud. Beck contended that the seller, knowing Beck had school-age children, should have informed him that the walk to the bus stop could be dangerous in winter.

    The attorney told Beck that, in their state, silence could not be the basis for fraud unless the seller, knowing of a hidden defect in the property that could cause injury, failed to disclose it. The attorney stated that there was no precedent for the proposition that a long walk on an icy road to a school bus is a hidden defect that a seller is bound to reveal. Explain what the attorney meant by *precedent* and why the fact that no precedent existed was significant.

4. The City of Lubbock, Texas, under the Texas Urban Renewal Act, designated a particular area for slum clearance. The land was to be cleared and sold for private development. The sales would be subject to restrictions to prevent the future growth of slums. Johnson owned property within the designated area. Although his structures met all requirements of the city's building code, they were to be demolished along with substandard buildings. What arguments might Johnson raise against the condemnation? Would he be successful? *Davis v. City of Lubbock, 326 S.W.2d 699 (Tex. 1959).*

5. Ed Freeman, who lives in Michigan, enters into an agreement to construct a building for Bartley Bros. Inc., a New York corporation. The contract price is $250,000. The building is to be built on land owned by Bartley Bros. in Pennsylvania. The agreement was signed in Freeman's office in Michigan. Freeman defaults, and Bartley Bros. sues in federal court. Does the federal court have jurisdiction? Support your answer.

2

Land and
Related Concerns

Land

The solid surface of the earth and the natural elements (water and minerals) associated with it.

Until recently, the idea that people could exist for any length of time apart from land was inconceivable. Even today, when the idea of human beings living out their lives on islands in space is a possibility accepted by serious scientists, human destiny remains linked with land. Whenever humans have survived, they have taken their living directly or indirectly from the land. Because land and people have always been inseparable, the ways in which land has been viewed are as diverse as the world's communities.

Much of the conflict between the American Indians and Europeans who settled this hemisphere resulted from attitudes toward land. The Indians regarded land differently than did the Europeans who settled North and South America after 1500. Land, to the Indians, was a resource possessed by the tribe. It was not subject to individual ownership. Some native groups in Africa, Australia and South America hold similar views today. In western Europe during the late Middle Ages the idea of community ownership in some lands existed, but by the time major colonization occurred in North America, the concept of individual property rights prevailed. Most settlers who came to this country after 1700 wanted to own their own land. Although themes other than individual ownership can be discerned in the way Americans regard land, a majority, especially those living in the United States, continue to consider it a commodity to be owned individually.

A number of factors account for this view. Probably the most important is historic. Our pioneer ancestors were individualistic in economic matters. The men and women who wrested the land from the great forests of the East and from the prairies of the West were acquiring wealth for themselves and their families.

They saw land, like any commodity, as something that could be bought and sold or passed on to their children. These people also believed in personal freedom. They regarded private ownership of land as a bulwark against both the intrusion of the state and the inquisitiveness of their neighbors. Finally, traditional economic theory in the Western world includes land as an important factor of production. Although land—like labor and capital—is not productive on its own, a price has to be paid for it because it is both necessary and scarce. Land is an important good that, with labor and capital, can be put to work to provide profit for the owner.

Real Estate

Land and its improvements; mines, minerals and quarries under the land; air and water rights associated with land; and other rights and privileges related to land.

Although it is a commonly used term, the meaning of *real estate* varies from place to place and from situation to situation. For example, in a number of states, leases are not considered real estate. In some states the duration of the lease determines whether the tenant's interest is real estate; in other states it does not. In addition, *real estate* sometimes has more than one statutory definition within a single state, some definitions being broader than others. It is difficult to give *real estate* one definition, because the sense in which it is used in everyday speech does not always correspond to its specific legal meaning.

In some contexts the terms *real estate* and *land* are used interchangeably; however, the meaning of *real estate* is generally broader than the meaning of *land*. Real estate includes not only land but also improvements on the land, such as a house, a barn and other structures. Many rights and privileges associated with land are considered to be real estate as well. For example, if one has a right of way from his or her own land across the land of a neighbor to reach a road, that right-of-way is real estate and can be sold or transferred as such in many instances. Water rights, mines, minerals and quarries are also considered real estate for most purposes.

Real property is a term lawyers and judges often use as a synonym for *real estate*. This chapter discusses real estate, or real property, principles in greater detail.

Land as a Natural Resource

Although the view of land as a commodity has been dominant in the United States, this is but one view of land. A contrasting view of land as a social resource that must be preserved for future generations has gained increasing acceptance in recent years. As a result of this trend, vast areas of our nation have been set aside as a public domain, and governments at all levels have adopted legislation to control land use for the benefit of society. Land has become the subject of a large body of law as our nation tries to cope with the problems involved with its use and disposition.

As traditionally defined by courts and commentators, land encompasses the surface of the earth, everything above that surface and all that is below. Land has been described as an inverted pyramid extending upward indefinitely into space and downward to the center of the earth. Many items such as water, minerals, oil and gas can be separated from the land. Because these things are both scarce and desirable, they, along with space, are often severed and treated as independent commodities. The result has been that detailed laws regulating their use have developed throughout the United States. These laws differ from place to place as they reflect the needs of people in a particular area.

Water

Water is an element essential to human survival. Without water, land is of little value. Consequently, lands adjacent to water or having water readily available are usually more valuable than other lands. Because of water's importance, disputes sometimes develop between property owners attempting to take advantage of this valuable resource. Efforts to solve these disputes have led to an extensive law of water rights.

Whatever the legal system, several factors appear to have a major influence on water rights law. The most significant is water's scarcity or abundance. The influence of this condition is clearly evident in American law. Another important factor is the type of economy prevailing in the area. Climate and technology are also significant in determining rights of individuals to water. Water rights law in the United States has been involved mainly with problems involving surface water, primarily because of technological inability to use underground water effectively. More recently, however, legal questions have also arisen concerning water that flows underground and water that percolates, or rises to the surface of the earth.

Surface Water
Water upon the surface of the earth in flowing streams and lakes.

Lakes and streams that are the subject of water rights can be navigable or nonnavigable. A navigable body of water is one that has the capacity to be useful for commerce or travel. The U.S. Constitution allocates power to Congress to regulate navigable waters, but until Congress acts, the states also may regulate. Although Congress frequently has taken actions that involve navigable waters, it has not, except in limited instances, restricted the rights of owners of land along these waterways. As Congress has not asserted all its powers over navigable waters, the power of the state over waters within its jurisdiction is paramount, just as it is for nonnavigable waters.

Riparian Land
Riparian lands are those that border on a stream or watercourse. Riparian lands extend away from the stream, including the stream's drainage area or watershed, although all of the drainage area is not necessarily riparian land. The riparian area of the watershed is only that portion under ownership of a person whose property fronts on the waterway. A landowner's property might be in the

watershed of a stream, but the landowner is not a riparian owner unless his or her property fronts on the stream.

Littoral Land

Littoral lands are those that border on an ocean, a sea, or a lake. In some states *littoral* applies only to lands that border on a tidal body such as an ocean or a sea. Other states use the term to describe lands that border on lakes as well. In many states the term is not used at all: *riparian* is used to designate lands bordering on lakes, oceans and seas as well as those bordering on flowing streams.

In general, the rights of owners of littoral lands are the same as those of the owners of riparian lands. These rights are discussed in the paragraphs that follow. However, at least one difference exists between riparian owners and littoral owners. Littoral owners do not own the land to the water. They own only to the line to which the high tide rises. This is called the *high-water mark*. From the high-water mark to the water (the *low-water mark*), the property is owned by the state. Therefore, the states have the power to control and regulate from the high-water mark to the low-water mark.

Surface Water Rights Theories

At present, two distinct theories of surface water rights exist in the United States. They are *riparianism* and *prior appropriation*. The riparian rights doctrine is the foundation of water rights law in most of the eastern United States. All states east of the Mississippi follow this theory to some extent, although the theory has been greatly modified by statute in Mississippi. Riparian rights are also the basis of water rights law in a number of states west of the Mississippi. Generally, these states, such as Minnesota, Arkansas and Louisiana, have an abundance of water.

Prior appropriation is the basis of water rights law in the more arid regions of the western United States. A number of the western states, however, use both doctrines. This is generally the case in those large states that are arid in certain sections but have sufficient water in others, such as California, Washington, Oregon, Texas and Oklahoma.

Riparianism (Riparian Rights Eastern States)

> *Water rights doctrine based upon the idea that all owners of riparian lands are entitled to share equally in the use of water.*

Riparianism has two basic principles. First, ownership of the land bordering on water establishes a right to use the water equally. This right cannot be lost by disuse, but it is clearly limited to use, not ownership.

Case Example

Kerley owned land on the upper end of a lake. The upper and lower ends of the lake were connected by a narrow neck of water about 18 inches deep. Wolfe, who owned the land on both sides of this passage, erected a fence to prevent rowboats and other small craft from passing through. Kerley, claiming that he was a riparian owner, brought an action to have the fence removed. The court ordered Wolfe to remove the fence as it interfered with the rightful use of the lake by other riparian owners. *Kerley v. Wolfe, 349 Mich. 350, 84 N.W.2d 748 (1957).*

Second, as the abutting land owner has no proprietary right in the water itself, any control over flowing water is lost once it passes the riparian tract. Conflicts concerning right of use that sometimes arise between upstream and downstream owners have generally been solved in one of two ways: natural flow doctrine or reasonable use doctrine.

Natural flow   The riparian rights principle that each riparian owner possesses the right to the ordinary flow of water along his or her land undiminished in quantity and unimpaired in quality is called the *natural flow doctrine.* In a natural flow jurisdiction, a downstream or lower riparian owner can limit the use of water by the upper riparian owner if the upper riparian owner interferes with the stream's natural flow. This doctrine developed in England at a time when the English economy was primarily agrarian. Rainfall was abundant, and even extensive use of water by farm owners did not ordinarily decrease the natural flow of the stream. In the United States the natural flow principle was adopted in eastern states with abundant rainfall when they were primarily agrarian. The natural flow principle, however, is not conducive to effective use of water in an industrialized economy. Thus, in most states the principle is greatly modified by legislation and judicial decision. It is doubtful that the original principle exists in pure form anywhere in the United States today.

Reasonable use   The riparian rights principle that allows a riparian owner to make reasonable use of the water that flows by his or her land is called the *reasonable use doctrine.* The doctrine of reasonable use dominates water rights law in the riparian states. It permits the riparian owner to make any use of water that does not unreasonably harm a lower riparian owner. The upper owner thus may reduce the natural flow of the stream as long as this does not unreasonably injure the lower owner. The test of reasonable use turns on the circumstances of each case. Many factors are considered, including the intended use, its extent, its duration and the necessity for it. Other factors that courts consider are the needs of other riparian owners, climate conditions, the nature of the stream and the customs of the area.

The doctrine of reasonable use thus does not concern itself with impairment of the natural flow or quality of the water but allows full use of the water in any beneficial manner, provided it does not unreasonably interfere with the beneficial use by others. In some states the riparian owner's beneficial use of water is restricted to riparian lands; others permit the use on or off the land if this does not cause damage to other riparian owners.

Most jurisdictions following the reasonable use doctrine have established a hierarchy of uses as a means of determining reasonable use. Domestic uses have priority over agricultural uses, and agricultural uses have priority over industrial and commercial uses.

Case Example

Deetz and Carter owned land along the Cold Creek. The creek followed a natural course through the Carter ranch down to the Deetz property. Cold Creek, although small, had a steady year-round flow, and the Deetz family obtained all its domestic supply of water from it. Carter diverted water from the creek for irrigation and livestock. This action so lowered the level of the creek that the Deetz family could not use the water for domestic purposes. An appellate court affirmed a decree restricting Carter's agricultural use of the water to permit Deetz's domestic use. *Deetz v. Carter, 232 Cal. App. 2d 851, 43 Cal. Rpr. 321 (1965).*

Riparian rights are subordinate to navigation and to regulation by state and federal governments. Where the public has access to navigable streams or lakes, most states permit the use of these waters without obstruction or restriction by abutting landowners.

Prior Appropriation (Western States)

A water rights doctrine giving primary rights to the first users of water.

The doctrine of riparianism is not suited to the conditions in the arid states of the West, especially where irrigation is necessary. In these states the principle of prior appropriation developed. In general, a system of prior appropriation creates a superior right in the person who is the first to use a body of water for economic purposes.

Prior appropriation was originally based upon custom and necessity and eventually became a part of the positive law. Today, prior appropriation is recognized in either the constitutions or statutes of all the western states. Several of these states have rejected riparian rights completely. Colorado was the leader in this move, and absolute rejection of riparianism is referred to as the *Colorado doctrine.* California and other states with areas of abundant water combine riparian rights with prior appropriation principles.

Case Example

Hunter was the first settler in a valley in Washington. A sizable creek flowed through the valley, but Hunter's land was not on the creek. Sogle settled in the valley shortly after Hunter. In 1882, the two began construction of an irrigation ditch from the creek to Sogle's land. Later the ditch was to be extended to Hunter's land, but the two had a dispute and the ditch was not extended.

In 1883, Hunter began to construct his own ditch. This ditch was finally completed in 1885. In litigation during the 1920s involving conflicting claims to water rights from the creek, the court held that owners with title through Sogle had superior rights to those holding title through Hunter. The court also held that Hunter's claim commenced from 1883, when he started his own ditch. It ruled that the time of diversion relates back to the beginning of work when the work has been pursued with reasonable diligence. *Hunter Land Co. v. Laungenour, 140 Wash. 558, 250 P. 41 (1926).*

Beneficial use   The right of prior appropriation is limited to the extent that the water can be used beneficially. However, once an appropriator has established priority, the right to have water exists except for changes that are the result of natural causes. Like the riparian system, prior appropriation does not create title but merely invests a right to use the water.

The foundation of the system of prior appropriation is the beneficial use of water. In order to obtain a permit, intent to apply the water to a beneficial use must be established.

Case Example

Lake Shore Duck Club (Lake Shore) obtained a permit to divert all water from Dix Creek. The water was to be used to improve the habitat for wildfowl on public lands. The club constructed the necessary dams and ditches to divert the water from the creek. The Lake View Duck Club (Lake View), which had been using water from the creek for many years, continued to do so. Lake View contended that the permit received by Lake Shore was invalid because the use of the water was not beneficial.

Lake Shore sued to quiet its title to the water, and Lake View moved to dismiss. The trial and appellate courts held for Lake View. Both courts agreed that a beneficial use must inure to the exclusive benefit of the appropriator and be subject to that person's complete dominion and control. Diverting water onto public lands to aid in the propagation of wildlife did not meet this requirement. *Lake Shore Duck Club v. Lake View Duck Club, 50 Utah 76, 166 P. 309 (1917).*

Generally, "beneficial use" is construed liberally, and ordinarily one beneficial use is not preferred over others. There may, however, be constitutional or statutory guidelines for determining preferential uses. Where such guidelines exist, domestic use is invariably preferred. A change of beneficial use is permissible but cannot be used as an excuse for enlarging an appropriation.

In addition to beneficial use, the applicant for a permit must

- establish that the water is subject to appropriation;

- show that it can be taken without injury to others;

- actually divert water by means of an artificial structure; or

- apply the water to a beneficial use within a reasonable time.

Statutory Permit Systems

The prior appropriation systems of the western states evolved through local customs and regulations. As population increased, states replaced local regulations with comprehensive state legislation. This legislation, although based on the prior appropriation principle, treats water resources as a public trust. Today in the West, state agencies allocate water resources through permit systems that attempt to insure the orderly distribution of water so that the public interest is served.

Statutory permit systems require a person seeking to obtain unappropriated water to file an application for a permit with a state agency. The application includes the information necessary to determine if granting the permit is in the public interest. Notice of the application is provided to the public so that people who object to granting the permit have an opportunity to present their arguments. A public hearing is held if there are objections to granting the permit.

Evidence at the hearing is provided by a state official, often the state engineer, who has reviewed the facts stated in the application. Objectors also have a right to present their case against issuing the permit. All state statutes provide for judicial review of the agency's determination.

A number of eastern states have also adopted statutory permit systems. Permit systems in the eastern states limit the rights of riparian owners. These systems are based upon the riparian principle of reasonable use of water. Administrative officials who issue permits consider factors such as the purpose of the use, the suitability of the use to the watercourse or lake, and the harm the use might cause as well as its economic and social values. The future development of real estate in the East will be increasingly affected by permit systems.

Subterranean Water

Subterranean water is an important resource in many areas of the United States. In recent years litigation involving subterranean water has increased. One reason is that methods for obtaining it have improved. Another is that population has expanded in many areas of the country that lack adequate supplies of surface water. This has led to increased dependence on subterranean waters in these areas. Subterranean water is divided into two classes: percolating waters and underground streams.

Percolating Waters

Water that passes through the ground, not flowing in a clearly defined underground stream or supplied by streams flowing on the surface.

Percolating waters may be rainwater infiltrating the soil or water from a stream that has seeped or oozed from the streambed and is no longer part of the flow. Percolating waters include underground lakes, artesian basins and veins and rivulets that flow in a course not discoverable from the surface without excavation.

Percolating waters are involved in more legal disputes than underground streams. The reason is that underground streams are difficult to identify as such, and courts in many states presume that the water is percolating unless it can be shown to flow in a clearly defined channel.

Common law rule In the traditional English common law of subterranean water rights, percolating waters belong absolutely to the owner of the land in which they are found. This traditional English rule is followed in many areas of the United States. Where this common law rule is followed, the landowner may deal with percolating water without regard to the manner in which his or her actions affect others. For example, the landowner may divert the percolating waters completely to the detriment of adjoining landowners. Conversely, if an owner does something on his or her property that inhibits the drainage of percolating waters, he or she is not responsible for damage caused to neighbors by the backup.

Reasonable use rule   Because of injustices resulting from the application of the common law rule, a number of state courts and legislatures have modified it. The most common modification is the substitution of a rule based on reasonable use. This rule has been recognized in states as diverse as Florida, Minnesota, New Jersey and Washington.

According to this rule, each owner of land has the right to use the percolating waters to fulfill the reasonable needs and necessities of the land.

Case Example

The City of Shawnee purchased 20 acres of land about eight miles from the city. It drilled 12 wells on the tract and transported the water in pipelines to the city. This action caused wells on farms to dry up, and the residents sought an injunction. The trial court refused to grant the injunction. Upon appeal relief was granted, the appellate court stating "the rule of reasonable use is that each landowner is restricted to a reasonable . . . use of his own property, in view of the similar rights of others." *Canada v. City of Shawnee, 179 Okla. 53, 64 P.2d 694 (1937).*

Reasonable use does not prevent the proper use of percolating waters by landowners in manufacturing, agriculture or irrigation. The landowner is immune from liability to the extent that the use of the water was reasonably necessary in connection with the use or improvement of the land. The reasonable use rule does prohibit, as the previous case illustrates, the withdrawal of percolating waters for distribution or sale for uses not connected with property ownership if this use damages neighboring owners.

Correlative rights doctrine   California courts have rejected both the common law and reasonable use rules as they apply to percolating waters. Instead these courts have adopted a doctrine that requires landowners to share percolating waters in proportion to their ownership of the surface area. A property owner may not extract more than his or her share even if the water is being used beneficially on the land. This *correlative rights doctrine,* as it is known, is similar to that applied by some states to the extraction of oil and gas. However, because the correlative rights doctrine is hard to apply, it has not been accepted outside of California.

Underground Streams
   Subterranean waters that flow in a clearly defined channel discoverable from the earth's surface.

Water rights in subterranean streams are relatively less important than those involving percolating waters, for the two reasons previously mentioned. First, establishing that an underground stream exists is difficult. The person asserting that water is flowing in an underground stream must establish from the surface the direction and course of the stream and that the stream has a definite bed, bank and current. Excavation to prove this is not permitted. Second, the courts in most cases presume that subterranean water is percolating water.

Legal disputes involving underground streams are ordinarily solved by applying the surface water law of the jurisdiction. If the state applies riparian rights to surface water problems, riparian rights will be applied to underground streams. When prior appropriation is the rule for surface water, it will be applied to underground streams as well.

Mineral Rights

The right to extract minerals from under the land, which may be legally assigned to or owned by someone other than the surface owner.

The common law envisioned the surface owner's rights as extending upward indefinitely into the sky and downward to the center of the earth. Until the industrial revolution, this definition was adequate to solve most legal questions. Except for a limited number of metals such as gold and silver, minerals were not of great concern to society. Consequently, problems involving subsurface rights were rare. The industrial and technological revolutions changed this situation. The demand expanded for many minerals found below the surface. This led to an increase in the value of these minerals and the subsurface in which they were found.

Early industrialization depended upon coal as a source of energy. Metals such as iron, copper, tin and lead also contributed to commercial growth. Technological developments of the 20th century have further increased dependence upon these and other minerals as well as gas and oil. As these resources become more valuable, real property law must adapt to provide solutions for legal problems created by their increased use.

Land was recognized as a commodity that could be divided horizontally for the purposes of ownership. One person could own the surface while others had rights in the subsurface. An owner could grant the right to extract minerals, lease land with the right to take minerals or convey title to the subsurface in which valuable resources were located. American law clearly allows a surface estate and one or more subsurface estates to be carved separately out of a single tract and held in entirely separate ownership.

Acquisition of Mineral Rights

Mineral rights may be acquired in four different ways: by (1) mineral deed, (2) mineral reservation, (3) mineral lease and (4) mineral rights option.

Mineral Deed

A *mineral deed* is similar to a deed used to transfer title to surface estates, which is discussed in Chapter 7. Although the mineral deed transfers only title to mineral rights, the law relating to the two has many of the same features. The person acquiring mineral rights by deed ordinarily acquires absolute title just as one would who acquired a surface estate. The deed grants in express terms a mineral estate, describing the size and kinds of minerals acquired. The deed or other document conveying the mineral rights should also grant all rights necessary to conduct a mining operation. These would include rights related to access, development, processing and transportation.

Mineral Reservation

Absolute title to mineral rights is often acquired by a *mineral reservation* in a deed. In this situation the owner, upon disposing of the surface, retains the mineral rights. In each instance, the grant or the reservation, the owner of the mineral rights has an interest that can be conveyed without regard to surface ownership.

Mineral Lease

Mineral rights are often acquired by *mineral lease*. The lessee obtains an exclusive right to carry out mining operations and title to the ore. Unlike the absolute sale of mineral rights, the lessor usually retains a present or future right in the mineral estate. In a lease arrangement the owner of the property is compensated by royalty payments. These payments are based on a fixed percentage of the value of extracted minerals. A mineral lease should contain provisions setting forth the duration of the lease, renewal rights of the lessee, any rights to suspend lease provisions and responsibilities of the lessee relative to the surface condition of the property.

Mineral Rights

A *mineral rights option* provides the holder, usually a mining company, with the right to explore the property for the presence of minerals. The agreement establishes a period of time within which the exploration must take place. Before the period ends, the mining company must decide whether to lease or purchase the land at the price stated in the option.

Ownership of Oil and Gas

American courts have not been consistent in their treatment of the nature of the landowner's interest in oil and gas under the surface. Some courts have attempted to solve legal disputes involving oil and gas ownership by applying principles developed in cases involving ownership and mining of solid minerals. The theory that evolved is known as the *ownership theory*. Other courts recognized that oil and gas migrate under the ground from high-pressure to low-pressure areas. These courts applied rules similar to those applied to questions involving the ownership of wild animals and migratory birds. This theory is called the *nonownership theory.* The two theories are discussed below.

Ownership Theory

The theory under which oil and gas are minerals and are therefore as subject to absolute ownership as coal or any other solid mineral.

"Absolute" is the key to this theory. In fact, the term *absolute* is often used in place of *ownership*. The ownership theory is not applicable logically to gas and oil because they are migratory within the earth. However, many states apparently have adopted this theory. In addition to Texas (see the following Case Example), states following this principle include Arkansas, Colorado, Kansas, Pennsylvania, Tennessee and West Virginia.

Case Example

S.R. Hill executed a lease of oil and gas rights to Mid-Kansas Oil and Gas Co. The county assessed a tax against the company based on the lease. At the time, no oil or gas had been taken from the ground. The company argued that it could not be taxed, because oil and gas in place cannot be owned. This argument was based on the premise that, until oil or gas is brought to the surface, owners of adjacent land may lawfully appropriate the oil or gas.

The question of tax liability was decided in favor of the county. The court stated: "[G]as and oil in place are minerals and realty, subject to ownership, severance, and sale while embedded in the sands or rocks beneath the earth's surface, in like manner and to the same extent as coal or any other mineral." *Stephens County vs. Mid-Kansas Oil and Gas Co., 113 Tex. 160, 254 S.W. 290 (1923).*

Under the ownership theory, the landowner may sever oil and gas by deed just as he or she would sever solid minerals or a portion of the surface itself. The person who acquires the oil or gas gets the same property rights that are acquired when buying a lot on the surface.

Nonownership Theory

The theory that oil and gas are not the subject of ownership because of their migratory nature.

Under this theory, the landowner has no ownership of oil and gas in place. Each landowner has an exclusive right to drill on the land and becomes the owner when the oil is brought to the surface. The right can be transferred by sale or otherwise. Although the right to search for oil and gas is an interest in land, it is not real property. Some states by statute attribute to this interest many rules applying to real property. Ohio, Louisiana, New York, Alabama, Indiana and Kentucky are among the states in which courts generally adhere to the nonownership theory.

Although the nature of oil and gas ownership differs under these two theories, many significant aspects of oil and gas law are the same under both. For example, although drilling near the boundary line of one's land in most states is not an illegal interference with the rights of owners of adjoining land, a slanted well that goes under the surface of another's land is a trespass. Under both theories, government has the power to regulate operating and production practices, waste is not permitted and no driller may unreasonably injure the reservoir. Additionally, the important *rule of capture* is recognized under both.

Rule of Capture

The rule that states that the owner of the surface has the right to appropriate all oil and gas from wells on his or her land, including oil and gas that have migrated from the land of another.

Whether a jurisdiction recognizes the ownership or the nonownership theory, as oil and gas migrate under the ground, the person whose wells produce the oil and gas owns it. This principle is applied in jurisdictions accepting the ownership doctrine even though oil brought to the surface does not always originate beneath the land of the driller. Similarly, ownership of oil and gas that migrate away from the surface owner's lands is lost. The rule of capture is a logical approach to ownership of oil and gas. It is impossible to distinguish oil that has seeped from under the land of another from that originally under the surface on which the well is located.

Case Example

Hastings owned 165 acres of land in northern Ohio. The Ohio Oil Co. owned oil and gas rights in several large parcels of land partially surrounding Hastings's acreage. Although the company had ample space to locate wells elsewhere, it drilled several wells at 400-foot intervals 25 feet from the Hastings property line. Hastings sought an injunction prohibiting the company from operating oil wells at any point within 200 feet of Hastings's farm. He argued that much of the oil produced from the company's wells percolated from under his land. Ohio courts refused to grant the injunction, thus recognizing the rule of capture. *Kelley v. The Ohio Oil Co., 57 Ohio St. 317 (1897).*

The rule of capture allows each landowner to appropriate oil and gas produced by all wells on his or her property. Early cases even permitted the wasteful disposal of whatever these wells produced. In some states an operator may increase flow from wells by pumping, although this practice draws oil from adjoining land. The only protection available to a neighbor is to drill and pump on his or her own land.

State Statutes

During the past 25 years, court opinions and statutes in a number of states have extended the rights of all landowners to share in a common source of oil and gas. Waste is prohibited, and each landowner is permitted a reasonable opportunity to obtain a just and equitable share of the oil or gas in the pool. This is known as the doctrine of *correlative rights.* The gas under the ground may go wherever it will, but an operator may not draw off gas from a neighbor's land in a manner that will unnecessarily deplete a common pool.

A few states have adopted legislation defining the amount of land that must surround a well or requiring a specific distance between wells. These are known as *spacing statutes.* Their purpose is to prevent waste and to give each surface owner an opportunity to take from the common pool.

Other states attempt to control production so that each owner has a reasonable opportunity to recover a fair share of the oil and gas under his or her tract by pooling or prorating the allowable production of oil. Extensive regulation by the state is a fact of life where oil is involved.

Air Rights

Until recently, the traditional theory that whoever owns the soil owns to the heavens was sufficient to solve most disputes involving invasion of airspace. Airspace problems, which usually concerned overhanging branches, bushes or eaves, were important to the parties but of little significance to society. With the advent of the airplane as a major means of transportation, courts and legislative bodies had to reconsider the old concept of absolute control of airspace. The early English rule that airspace was an appurtenance to land, giving absolute and exclusive right to the owner "to the highest heavens," was repudiated. In general, the courts recognize that the public interest in efficient transportation outweighs any theoretical trespass in airspace. As long as air flight does not interfere with the owner's right to the effective use of the space above his land, airplanes passing through this space are not trespassing. In brief, a landowner's exclusive domain extends at least to a height that makes it possible for the land to be used in a reasonable manner. To this extent the owner of the surface has absolute ownership of the space above his or her land.

Recently some important developments in real estate have been possible because the ownership of airspace may be separated from ownership of the surface. As population has expanded, investors have turned to space above land to satisfy both commercial and residential needs. When an individual purchases a high-rise condominium, that person is acquiring title to airspace. In metropolitan areas such as New York City and Chicago, railroads owning downtown property have separately conveyed airspace above the tracks to be used for commercial buildings. The purchaser acquires that space above the area needed by the railroad for its trains and a surface easement sufficient to support construction and facilities.

Summary

Land is fundamental to human survival. Throughout much of history, land was considered a resource of the tribe or social group, to be cultivated for the general good. By the time North America was opened for colonization, individual property rights prevailed. Now land was viewed as wealth—a major factor of production to be controlled according to the prevailing economic and political theory of the nation in which it lies.

Real estate, or real property, is defined differently according to the situation and the place and usually includes more than land. Improvements and rights and privileges associated with land are also considered real estate.

Of growing significance to environmentalists is the view of land as a social resource to be preserved for future use. This view currently influences the passage of laws affecting land use and development. Large areas have been set aside for public use. Land has become the topic of a large body of environmental law.

The value of land is increased by its closeness to water or by the presence of mineral deposits underneath it. Extensive law serves to resolve disputes and regulate usage when water or *mineral rights* are at issue.

Water rights law, which pertains mainly to surface water, falls into two categories: *riparianism* and *prior appropriation*. Under riparian rights, generally, all users of adjacent water have equal rights to it. Riparian principles apply generally in states where water is abundant, such as in the East and a few western states. Where water is scarce, prior appropriation, granting water rights to the first users, generally prevails. Central to the doctrine of prior appropriation is the beneficial use of scarce water. Many western states have adopted legislation that provides for the allocation of water resources through a permit system. Some states in the east also control resources in this manner.

Mineral rights in the land have increased in importance as technology has developed. These rights may be acquired by deed, by reservation, by lease or by option.

Oil and gas rights differ from mineral rights in that these underground substances may migrate from one person's property to another. Just as water rights theory varies, so do these property theories vary from one state to another.

Air rights have also been affected by recent change in the laws regarding their use, by changes in building practices as population expands and by demands for more efficient transportation.

Review and Discussion Questions

1. Outline those arguments supporting individual ownership of land. Evaluate these arguments.

2. Compare the riparian doctrines of reasonable use and natural flow. What limitations exist upon reasonable use? From a public policy viewpoint, which doctrine is most valuable? Why?

3. (a) List the four methods of acquiring mineral rights. (b) What are the major legal differences among them?

Case Problems

1. Richards and Schneider owned adjoining land. Richards drilled several oil wells on his property very close to the boundary between the two parcels. When Richards began to pump substantial quantities of oil from these wells, Schneider sought an injunction. At the hearing Schneider's witnesses, all expert geologists, testified that most of the oil came from under Schneider's land. (a) In a state that had no correlative rights legislation, would Schneider's injunction be granted? (b) Would your answer differ if the state's oil and gas law were based upon ownership theory? Discuss.

2. Gilliam owned an airplane that he used for crop dusting. While he was flying over Shrock's property to reach a field that was to be sprayed, crop dust was released. Although it was not clear *how* this occurred, Gilliam clearly was not negligent. At the time the dust was released, Gilliam was flying at a safe altitude. Shrock sued for damages as the poison dust destroyed valuable nursery stock. Would Shrock be successful? Discuss.

3. In 1968 Coffin purchased land along St. Vrain Creek. He built a dam and used water from the creek to irrigate his farm. Several years prior to Coffin's purchase, the Left Hand Ditch Co. had constructed a ditch diverting water from St. Vrain Creek to James Creek and then to Left Hand Creek, where it irrigated land adjacent to that stream. None of this land was adjacent to St. Vrain Creek. When a drought struck, the Left Hand Ditch Co. tore out a portion of Coffin's dam, which was impeding the flow of water to land irrigated by Left Hand Creek. Coffin sought damages and an injunction. Although this was a prior appropriation jurisdiction, he argued that he had a better right to the water because his land was adjacent to St. Vrain's Creek. (a) Explain prior appropriation. (b) Discuss the validity of Coffin's argument. See *Coffin v. Left Hand Ditch Co., 6 Colo. 443 (1882).*

4. Rodney Pape owned a farm that had two major springs feeding into Racoon Creek. This creek was a major tributary of the Licking River. The river flowed through a state park near a second farm owned by Pape. This farm was not on the river. During a period of severe drought, Pape entered the state park and attempted to draw water from the river. When stopped, he argued that he had a right to do so, as his farm on Racoon Creek was in the watershed of the Licking River. Is he correct? Support your answer.

5. Nilsson and Latimer both owned land that bordered on the Little Cossatot River. In an exceptionally dry year, Latimer's irrigation pumps pumped dry two or three holes on the river. This action deprived Nilsson of occasional recreational fishing at these particular pools. Nilsson sued Latimer for damages based on Latimer's unreasonable use of the water. Would she be successful? Support your answer. *Nilsson v. Latimer 664 S.W.2d 447 (1984).*

6. Harris had title to 11 acres of vacant land. Unknown to her, the Wabash Coal Co. had recorded mineral rights in the land. A state statute provided that a person having apparent title or "a semblance of title" to vacant land who plays taxes on the land for seven successive years becomes the legal owner. When Harris discovered the existence of the mineral rights, she claimed title to them; she argued that the payment of taxes on the property constituted payment of taxes on the mineral rights that had been separated from it. The taxing authorities had not assessed separate taxes against the Wabash Coal Co. owner of the mineral rights. Would Harris be successful? Discuss.

3

Property and Related Concerns

Property

Legal rights that an individual possesses with respect to a thing; rights that are themselves of economic value.

In traditional legal usage, *property* generally refers to an aggregate or "bundle" of rights that people have in tangible items. People often refer to the items—the automobile, guitar or home—as their property; from a legal point of view, however, the items themselves are not significant. What is important are the rights the person has in these items. These rights include the right to use the item, sell it or even destroy it if the person wishes. In his famous *Commentaries on the Law of England*, Blackstone describes property as an "absolute right, inherent in every Englishman . . . which consists in the free use, enjoyment, and disposal of all his acquisitions, without any control or diminution, save only by the laws of the land." Today, the term *ownership* is often used as a synonym for *property*.

The concept of property is readily understood when related to something tangible like an automobile or land. A person can, however, own something that is related only indirectly to a tangible item. An example would be a lease. The tenant of a commercial building has a right to occupy space. This right is valuable because of the building's existence, but the right itself is intangible. Property also is used to refer to rights that people possess independent of anything tangible. Contracts, trademarks, copyrights and patents are examples. They are all property as they establish rights that the owner can enjoy, sell, give away or deny to others.

The protection of property rights is a function of the government. State and federal laws provide guarantees and protections creating and maintaining the "bundle of rights" that the legal system refers to as property. For example, in our society property exists in land because numerous laws allow individuals to do certain things with land such as sell it, dispose of it to one's heirs or exclude others from it. On the other hand, although one's right to vote is important, it is not property. The state provides no aggregate of rights related to a person's right to vote. All that the individual can do is vote or refrain from voting. Whether or not something is a property right has important constitutional implications because the Bill of Rights prohibits government from taking property without due process of law. Thus, in taking property government must follow legal procedures that safeguard the owner's rights, the property must be taken for public use, and the owner must be compensated adequately. (See Chapter 10)

Property is a dynamic concept that is continually being reshaped to meet new economic and social needs. In the United States today, appreciable legislation and case law are developing that modify traditional property rights, or at least reevaluate them, in relation to civil rights. Many good examples can be found in cases and legislation protecting fundamental interests of minorities.

Case Example

Shelly, an African-American man, purchased real estate from Fitzgerald. The sale violated a recorded restriction upon which former owners of this parcel and a number of other owners had agreed. This restriction prohibited occupancy by "any person not of the Caucasian race." Kramer and others who owned real property subject to the restriction sued to restrain Shelly from taking possession and to divest him of title. When the Missouri courts granted the relief requested, the United States Supreme Court reversed. The court held that state courts are prohibited by the equal protection clause of the Constitution from enforcing a private agreement denying a person because of his race the right to own real property. *Shelly v. Kramer, 334 U.S. 1 (1948).*

Although one clearly visible trend in the law is to limit property rights when weighed against civil rights, in other areas property rights have been expanded. In a number of cases, plaintiffs have contended that they have a property interest in their employment or in the facilities necessary to practice a chosen profession and even in their status and reputation. At present the movement of the law in this direction is slow, but the trend is discernible.

Real Property Rights

Ownership or proprietary rights in land and anything permanently affixed to land.

Legal institutions reflect dominant economic, political and social values. Laws and the legal system sustain the existing order and are used to attain objectives that society considers important. Throughout the history of England and the United States, land and law have been closely interwoven. In both countries, as well as in most other nations of the Western world, land has been an important form of wealth. In addition, for many hundreds of years in England not only was land the major source of wealth, but the possession of land, even particular tracts of land, determined an individual's social position. Possession or ownership of land also had important political connotations in both England and the United States. For many years in England and in most of the United States, only landowners were permitted to vote.

One result of the historic importance of land is a distinction in the law of English-speaking countries between it and other forms of wealth. Because of land's economic significance, the early common law provided extensive protection to landowners. A landowner ousted from possession could immediately bring an action to recover the land (called an *action in ejectment*). In contrast, the right of an owner of personal property against one who wrongfully took that property was limited to a lawsuit for money (called *damages*). Legal actions like ejectment that protect the rights of owners in their land were known as *real actions*, and that is the reason land is called *real property* or *real estate*. The lawsuit for money of a person who lost control of something of economic value other than land, usually a movable item, was known as a *personal action* because the items involved were personal property. In modern law, as will be discussed later, the distinction between real and personal property continues to be recognized in many areas.

Personal property generally is characterized as being movable. Historically, the items of personal property of importance were tangible things such as cattle, farm equipment and the tools of a person's trade. Today, many intangible forms of wealth exist. An example would be a franchise. These intangible rights are also personal property. Over the centuries these forms of personal property have expanded, and personal property has become more equivalent to real property as wealth. One result has been a narrowing of the legal distinctions between the two, but differences continue to exist and to influence American law.

Real and Personal Property: Legal Problems

The fact that real and personal property continue to be treated differently in the law of English-speaking countries causes many problems. For example, a deed, the written document transferring ownership of real estate, conveys only real property, separate from personal property. This sometimes results in confusion when a home or business is sold. The potential buyer of a home, an apartment for investment, a factory or a farm examines the premises from a functional, not a legal, viewpoint. If the real estate is a residence, the buyer is thinking about a place to live, not about the distinction between real and personal property. Items such as the stove, refrigerator, storm windows and perhaps a bar are functionally related to the reason for the purchase. The buyer understandably considers these items integral parts of the building. At the same time the seller, perhaps having purchased the items separately, often thinks of them as independent of the structure. If the law considers these articles part of the real estate, they pass to the buyer by deed unless specifically excluded by agreement. If the items are deemed personalty and hence not part of the real estate, they are not covered by the deed, and the buyer does not get them.

Case Example

David, by deed, conveyed land to Bessie. A hay barn was located on the land. The barn contained equipment for unloading hay. The equipment consisted of a track, hangers to support the track, a carrier, a hay harpoon, two pulleys and rope. The hangers were bolted to the rafters, and the track was attached to the hangers. David removed the equipment. Bessie demanded that he return it, claiming that it was real estate as it was a part of the barn. Although a court would find for Bessie if David refused to return the equipment, the problem could have been avoided if David and Bessie had agreed in the contract how the equipment was to be treated.

The distinction between real and personal property is also significant in real estate financing. A debt secured by a mortgage is secured only by the real estate. Personal property is not part of the security. For example, if a bank takes back a mortgage on a motel as security for a debt, the furniture that is integral to successful operation of the business is not covered. Of course, the furniture could also be used as security if designated as such by a separate security agreement.

Case Example

National Bank lent funds to a small manufacturing company and took back a mortgage on realty owned by the company. On the premises was a 2,000-gallon tank set on concrete blocks. The tank was used to store gas and was connected to a garage by lines that ran above ground. The bank was forced to foreclose because the debt was not paid. Both the bank and the company claimed the tank. If the court held the tank to be part of the real estate, the tank could be sold at the foreclosure sale.

Whether an item is real or personal property also raises important insurance, tax and inheritance questions. Sometimes state statutes help provide answers to these questions, but most continue to be settled by case law. Contracts and mortgages should make clear what property the parties intend to be personal property and what they intend to be real property.

Fixtures (Real Property)

Separately identifiable items that were once personal property but that have become real property generally through annexation to land or buildings.

Chandeliers, carpeting, electric hot water heaters and shrubbery are common examples of fixtures associated with residential real estate. All these items are personal property while part of the seller's inventory, but when annexed to land or buildings they are generally considered part of the real estate. On a farm, items such as cattle stanchions, water pumps and fencing would ordinarily be fixtures. Many items associated with industrial or commercial real estate are also classified as fixtures. How would you classify the mirror behind the bar in your favorite restaurant or the overhead track for moving heavy material in a factory? Both could be readily detached without harm to the building, and they appear movable as is personal property, but they, too, are probably fixtures.

The chief test in determining whether an item is a fixture is the intention of the party who attached it to the real estate. Intention will, however, be determined by the manner in which the one who affixed the item acted, not by his or her secret intention. In the case that follows, intention is clearly established by the evidence.

Federal Land Bank of Omaha v. Swanson
Supreme Court of Nebraska
231 Neb. 868 (1989)

Background: On April 8, 1983, Jerald E. and Pamela A. Swanson (codefendants) gave a note and mortgage on their farm to the Federal Land Bank of Omaha (plaintiff—appellant). In September 1983, the Swansons borrowed money from Arlington State Bank (defendant—appellee) to purchase two grain bins. The loan was evidenced by a properly executed promissory note and secured by a security agreement on the grain bins. A financing statement was thereafter filed. In 1986, the Swansons defaulted on their mortgage loan and voluntarily surrendered the real estate to the Federal Land Bank.

The Arlington State Bank initiated a procedure to obtain possession of the grain bins, so they could sell them at an auction. On November 5, 1986, the Federal Land Bank obtained a temporary restraining order prohibiting the sale. On July 27, 1987, the district court dissolved the temporary restraining order and awarded possession of the grain bins to the Arlington State Bank on grounds that the bins were the personal property of the Swansons. The Federal Land Bank appealed.

Decision: The Nebraska Supreme Court affirmed the judgment of the lower court.

Justice White

The appellant's claim to the grain bins and accessories necessarily arises from its interest in the Swansons' real estate pursuant to the April 1983 mortgage. The appellee bank contends the grain bins and accessories are personalty in which it has a valid security interest because of the promissory note and financing and security agreement. Hence the threshold question is whether the grain bins are, as the district court found, personalty.

In *Metropolitan Life Ins. Co. v. Reeves,* this court said:

> Three main factors determine whether an article, or combination of articles, is a fixture. They are (1) whether the article or articles are actually annexed to the realty, or something appurtenant thereto; (2) whether the article or articles have been appropriated to the use or purpose of that part of the realty with which it is or they are connected; and (3) whether the party making the annexation intended to make the article or articles a permanent accession to the freehold. . . .
>
> . . . [T]he third factor, the intention of the annexing party to make the article or articles a permanent accession to the realty, is the factor which is typically given the most weight.

In our de novo review of the record, we address each factor.

With respect to the first factor, the evidence shows that the disputed bins are utilized for drying and storing grain. One bin is a 30-foot-diameter eight-ring bin with a 14,000-bushel capacity, and the other is a 24-foot-diameter seven-ring bin with a 6,000-bushel capacity. The bins are provided with several accessories for drying and moving the grain, such as drying fans, heaters, and augers. Each bin sits on a concrete slab. On the bottom ring of each bin is an angle ring which lies flush on top of the concrete slab. Clips, which are not part of the bin structure, are placed over the lip of the angle ring and are attached to bolts protruding from the concrete slab around the outside of the bin. The clips are adjustable and can easily be slid off the lip of the angle ring, allowing removal of the bin. The contractor, Isadore Stoetzel, whose company erected the bins, testified that the bins were designed to sit on top of the concrete and that the purpose of the clip anchoring system was to prevent the bin from blowing away in the wind. Though Stoetzel has never moved this particular type of grain bin before, he has moved several bins similar to the ones in dispute. Stoetzel stated that on one occasion it took him only 4 hours to move two larger, 36-foot-diameter bins. On cross examination, the following testimony occurred:

Q. Did you ever discuss with [Jerald Swanson] whether [the bins] were ever going to be moved or not?

A. He asked me if they could be moved prior to signing the contract.

Q. And you told him—

A. I told him basically what I am telling you, that they can be moved.

The evidence also demonstrates that the accessories are items which are either attached to the grain bins or are readily movable. Accordingly, we find that the grain bins and accessories are not annexed to the real estate, and for the remainder of this opinion we treat the accessories as part of the grain bins.

The evidence going to the second factor, whether the grain bins have been appropriated to the use or purpose of that part of the realty with which they are connected, showed that Jerald Swanson used the bins to store crops raised on the surrounding land. However, on one occasion he did store some of his neighbor's grain for a short period of time.

Though finding that the evidence satisfied the second factor, as stated above, the third factor, regarding the intent of the annexing party, is given the most weight. We note that the evidence shows that Jerald Swanson purchased the grain bins in August of 1983, approximately 5 months after the the mortgage was executed. The loan from the appellee bank was used exclusively for the purchase and erection of the two bins. During a deposition, Jerald Swanson testified as follows:

Q. . . . [W]ere you giving something to the [appellee] bank when you signed [the financing statement and security agreement]?

A. Well, you were giving an agreement that you were going to pay them back, I guess, for the property that they had. I guess they had the right to it until you paid it off.

Q. And the property that you are referring to then would be what?

A. My personal property which, you know.

Q. Would that include the grain bins?

A. Right, yes.

. . . .

Q. So if you did not pay off the loan, it was your intention that the bank would be entitled to the grain bins?

A. Yes.

In addition, every year appellee bank required a property statement from Jerald Swanson. On the 1984 statement, Jerald Swanson listed the grain bins as farm equipment and noted that appellee bank held a lien on the bins. Based on the foregoing, it is clear that Jerald Swanson's intention was that the bins were his personal property subject to a lien held by the appellee bank. He never intended the grain bins to be fixtures. Thus, we find that the evidence clearly establishes that the grain bins were personal property and not fixtures. The appellant failed to establish by a preponderance of the evidence each factor to support its claim to relief.

Because of our finding, it is not necessary to address appellant's other assignments of error except to note, with regard to its third assignment of error, that appellant cannot claim a superior interest in the grain bins on the alleged weakness of appellee bank's failure to perfect its security interest.

Accordingly, the judgment of the district court for Cheyenne County is affirmed.

Affirmed.

Many problems arise in identifying fixtures because infinite variations in facts complicate legal analysis. For parties involved in a real estate transaction, the most effective way to prevent these problems is for them to agree in writing as to whether particular items are to be treated as personalty or real property (fixtures).

Trade Fixtures

Items annexed to land or buildings by a tenant to be used in the tenant's trade or business.

We have seen that items of personal property, annexed to realty with the intention that the item become part of the realty, are fixtures. *Fixtures are real estate* and usually may not be removed or treated separately unless the parties agree. It is clear, however, that a business firm leasing real estate would be seriously hampered if this rule applied to items needed to operate a plant or shop effectively. Therefore, the legal system differentiates between fixtures and trade fixtures, the latter being personalty attached to real estate in order to carry on a trade or business. A tenant may generally remove trade fixtures. Agricultural fixtures have been treated in a similar manner. In order to remove a trade or agricultural fixture, the tenant must restore the premise to its original condition and remove the trade fixture before the lease terminates.

Allowing tenants to remove trade fixtures has social benefits. It encourages both the use of land and efficiency in business. Tenants are more likely to invest in new and improved equipment if they can remove these items after they have been attached to the realty. Statutes in a number of states establish tenants' rights to remove trade fixtures.

Although the law allows tenants to remove trade fixtures at the end of a lease even if the lease doesn't mention this point, parties to a commercial lease should include provisions that express their agreement as to how trade fixtures will be treated when the lease ends. They might agree that the tenant shall not remove items that ordinarily would be trade fixtures. On the other hand, a lease provision stating the tenant's right to remove those items added to carry out the business or trade shows the intention of the parties and lessens possibilities for disagreement and litigation as to whether or not the items may be removed.

Growing Crops

Traditionally, courts classified growing crops in two categories. An annual crop that was the product of human effort was referred to as *fructus industriales*. This classification included crops such as wheat, corn, oats, cotton and rice. Crops that were produced on perennial roots such as trees, bushes and vines were categorized as *fructus naturales*. Fructus naturales were crops such as citrus fruits, apples, berries and grapes. As a general rule, fructus industriales were considered personal property and fructus naturales real property.

Today, in most states, for most purposes the classification of fructus industriales has been broadened considerably. In general, it includes any crop that owes its value to human care and labor. Thus, fruit and berry crops as well as crops like hay are classified as fructus industriales. In a limited number of states the courts consider the produce of perennial roots fructus industriales, although the trees, vines and bushes that produce the crop are fructus naturales.

Although these classifications continue to be of importance when a dispute arises involving growing crops, modern courts consider a number of other factors when determining whether a crop is realty or personalty.

One significant factor in some states is the maturity of the crop. The more mature the crop, the more likely courts are to consider it personal property. In addition to maturity, courts often consider factors such as the relationship of the parties, their intentions and the type of transaction. Many present-day legal problems involving growing crops are solved by statutes, which individual states have adopted because of the uncertainty of the case law.

One of the most significant of these statutes is the Uniform Commercial Code (UCC), which has been adopted by all states. Article 2 of the UCC deals with the sale of goods. "Goods" under the UCC are always personal property. Furthermore, the UCC defines growing crops as goods whether they are grown on annual or perennial roots. This definition eliminates the traditional legal distinction between fructus industriales and fructus naturales, at least for UCC purposes. The UCC also states that growing crops become goods if they can be removed without harm at the time buyer and seller contract for their sale even if they are part of the real estate at the time. Thus, Christmas trees and sod grown on the land become personal property before severance if they are identified as the subject of a contract.

Although statutes such as the UCC bring some certainty to the law, the real estate practitioner should realize that the most effective method of preventing controversy is to have the parties agree how the crops are to be treated. This agreement should then be included in the lease, deed, purchase offer or other written documentation that covers the transaction.

Secured Transactions

A transaction in which the parties agree that personal property or fixtures will secure a loan or the purchase of an item on credit.

Lenders use various types of personal property to secure repayment of loans. Sellers, too, often retain an interest in goods being sold on credit to ensure payment of the purchase price. Secured transactions of this nature are very important to the economy of the United States. They range from relatively minor purchases by consumers of appliances and television sets to extensive financing of inventory and equipment by business firms. These secured transactions frequently involve real estate, inasmuch as fixtures are often used as collateral, or security for the loan. Common examples would be air-conditioning equipment and industrial machinery. Even after these are installed in a building, the credit seller may retain a security interest until the purchase price is paid.

The law pertaining to secured transactions is found in Article 9 of the UCC. Article 9 applies to all personal property and fixture security interests created by agreement. For Article 9 to protect a creditor effectively, both attachment and perfection must occur.

Attachment

The process by which a secured party acquires a security interest in collateral.

A security interest is not effective between the parties until it has attached to the collateral. Three events must take place for a security interest to attach. Although these events usually occur in the following order, no particular order is required. The security interest attaches when the last event occurs.

1. The debtor and secured party (creditor) agree that a security interest attaches.

2. The secured party (creditor) gives value to the debtor.

3. The debtor has or acquires rights in the collateral.

In most secured transactions, the agreement must be in writing; however, if the secured party retains possession of the security, an oral agreement is sufficient. The written agreement is known as a *security agreement*. The UCC defines a security agreement as "an agreement which creates or provides for a security interest." In those situations in which the secured party retains possession of the security, the transaction is known as a *pledge*.

Ordinarily, a security agreement is initiated when the secured party supplies a standard form that is to be completed by the borrower or buyer. This form is usually labeled "Security Agreement," but other terms such as "Conditional Sales Contract" are also used. Whatever the form is called, if it includes the necessary information, a security agreement exists under the UCC.

Perfection

The process by which the secured party establishes priority in the collateral over claims of third parties.

The purpose of perfection is to notify third parties of the existence of a security agreement. Under general legal principles, when a third party knows of or has available information as to the existence of a security interest, the third party's rights are subordinate to that security interest. Two principal methods for perfecting a security interest under the UCC are (1) *public filing* of a notice, called a financing statement, that such an interest exists; and (2) *possession* of the collateral by the secured party. A good example of the latter is the security interest a pawnbroker has in articles of personal property taken as collateral for loans. (This is a pledge, as defined earlier.)

State law must be checked to determine the proper place for filing a financing statement for most items, but the UCC specifically states that to properly perfect a security interest in a fixture, the secured party must file in the office where real estate mortgages are recorded. This *fixture filing* must contain the name of the real property owner and the address of the property.

Sometimes there is a question as to whether an item is a fixture. In this event, the secured party should file twice. The second filing should be made as state law directs for items other than fixtures.

Fixture Filing

A section of the UCC that allows a security interest to persist in goods (personal property) that later become fixtures.

With few exceptions, a security agreement that has been perfected by filing a financing statement provides the secured creditor with priority over claims of third parties. This sometimes results in problems where fixtures are involved. For example, conflict can occur between a mortgage lender who has a security interest in the real property and a second party who has a security interest in a fixture located on the same real property.

Case Example

Fran's Pizza needed a new oven. One was purchased on credit from Only Oven, Inc., which had Fran sign a security agreement. The oven was installed in the pizza parlor, which was owned by Fran but heavily mortgaged to the Bank of Durango. Despite the new oven, Fran's business was unsuccessful, and she became bankrupt. Only Oven tried to remove the oven, but the bank argued that it was a fixture and should be sold as a part of the building.

In the past, the law relating to security interests in fixtures varied from state to state. Initial efforts through the UCC to deal with the problem created by conflicting interests between a real property lender and a person whose security is a fixture were not very successful. A number of states did not accept the UCC's provisions; in others, real estate lenders objected, since the UCC appeared to favor the fixture security interest. In the early 1970s, the UCC was amended to reduce these objections. By 1981 a majority of states had adopted the amendments.

Under the current provisions of the UCC, Only Oven would have priority over the Bank of Durango if it had properly perfected its security interest. Perfection requires filing of a financing statement covering the fixture described in the security agreement before the goods become fixtures or within ten days thereafter. The ten-day grace period given to the creditor applies only against prior recorded interests in the real estate. A fixture filing has priority against subsequent interests as of the date of filing. If the Bank of Durango had advanced funds after the manufacturer had installed the oven, (i.e., after it had become a fixture), Only Oven would not enjoy a priority unless its security interest were already perfected by a fixture filing.

Fixture security interests are subject to an exception when a construction mortgage is involved.

Case Example

Claude Real Estate is building an office on land that it owns. The construction is being financed by Central Bank, which has agreed to advance funds as the work progresses. The bank has recorded a construction mortgage. Claude purchases plumbing fixtures from Little John, which perfects a security interest by filing a financing statement. Soon after the building is completed, Claude fails, and Little John attempts to remove the fixtures. Central Bank objects, claiming a prior interest on the basis of its construction mortgage.

In this situation, Little John would not be able to remove the plumbing fixtures. The UCC expressly gives priority to a *construction* mortgage recorded before the filing of a fixture security interest. In addition, the UCC provides that no fixture security interest exists in ordinary building materials, such as bricks and lumber, once they are incorporated into a structure, for obvious reasons.

Mobile Homes: Real Property or Personal Property?

A transportable structure built on a chassis and designed for year-round living, usually set up on a permanent foundation and connected to utilities.

The UCC offers a solution to problems that arise when lenders use as security personal property that can readily become a fixture. However, in those areas dealing with property whose classification as real or personal is not clear, problems abound. One kind of property the courts find difficult to classify as real or personal is the mobile home.

A substantial percentage of housing in the United States consists of mobile homes. United States government figures for 1987 indicate that nearly six million mobile homes are used as dwellings. As the average number of occupants is two, about 12 million people live in dwellings of this type.

The unique quality of locomotion of mobile homes has made it difficult for courts to decide whether to classify them as real or personal property. This has caused legal controversy, especially regarding taxation. Owners argue that mobile homes are not real estate and thus cannot be taxed as real estate. On the other hand, taxing authorities contend that mobile homes use local services supported by real estate taxation and therefore should contribute to the cost of these services.

Summary

The term *property* generally refers to various rights a person has in a tangible item—a building, car or other possession—but it can also refer to something intangible, such as a lease or even the right to use a trademark. Possession of this "bundle of rights" depends on the laws a government creates and maintains for the benefit of citizens.

Historically, personal property in general is differentiated from real property—land and buildings a person owns—because of the economic significance attached to land. Personal property is characterized as being movable, although in today's usage some personal property, such as a franchise, is intangible. Real estate professionals need to be aware of the distinction between the two kinds of property so that contracts and other legal documents will be written properly.

The legal distinction becomes important when courts determine whether an item attached to land or buildings becomes real property. If so, the item (such as built-in shelving or certain kitchen appliances) is characterized as a *fixture* and must not be removed upon sale of the realty. A number of states have established tenants' rights to remove *trade fixtures* upon termination of a commercial lease. Even so, parties to a commercial lease should agree in writing on the terms at the outset in order to reduce possibilities of litigation.

Often a purchaser of business fixtures uses the fixtures themselves as collateral to secure a loan for their payment. The Uniform Commercial Code, Article 9, provides legal protection for both buyer and seller in this type of *secured transaction,* when the two legal requirements of *attachment* and *perfection* are met. In the attachment process, three events occur: both parties consent in writing to the arrangement, value must be given by the secured party and the debtor must have rights in the collateral. In perfection, the secured party establishes priority in the collateral over other debtors through an official recording of the transaction. The UCC requires that all documents be both written and filed, as a mortgage agreement would be.

In some areas the distinction between realty and personal property is not so clear. One example is *mobile homes,* which, although similar in many ways to realty, are still considered movable.

Review and Discussion Questions

1. Define trade fixture and explain how the law relating to trade fixtures differs from the law relating to fixtures generally.

2. What legal problems might arise because American law distinguishes between real and personal property?

3. Explain the difference between attachment and perfection of a security interest.

4. Discuss the factors courts consider when attempting to determine if an item is a fixture.

Case Problems

1. Stephens purchased a steel grain-drying bin from B. C. Manufacturing and executed a conditional sales contract and a financing statement. The financing statement was filed in the county clerk's office but not in the office of the registrar for deeds. The bin was placed on a concrete base on property owned by Newman Grove Grain Company. This property was later mortgaged to Battle Creek Bank. The mortgage was foreclosed, and Tillotson purchased the real estate at the foreclosure sale. B. C. Manufacturing sued for the value of the bin. Would B. C. Manufacturing be successful? Discuss. *Tillotson v. Stephens, 195 Neb. 104, 237 N.W.2d 108 (1975).*

2. Holsopple obtained a building permit for construction of a single-family dwelling. Zoning regulations prohibited use of mobile homes in the area. The structure in question consisted of three units. The main unit, about 12 by 70 feet, was mounted on a metal frame with three axles. Each axle had two wheels. The main unit was pulled by a truck to the site, where two smaller units were bolted to it. The entire structure was mounted on a concrete foundation. The wheels were removed and stored under the structure; the frames and axles remained attached. The basic assembly of the three units took two men working 19 hours each. Was the unit a mobile home or single-family dwelling? Discuss. *Bowman v. Holsopple, 155 Ind. App. 272, 292 N.E.2d 274 (Ct. App. 1973).*

3. Stanley King purchased an old Victorian residence from its owner, Helen Floyd. After King took possession of the home he discovered that Floyd had taken drapes that had been tailored to fit an odd-sized window, a window air conditioner and an antique bathtub. The tub had been replaced by a new tub of excellent quality. The contract of sale signed by both parties did not

mention any of these items. Is King entitled to recover damages? Support your answer.

4. Thatcher was interested in buying a business. She finally located a gift shop and agreed to buy it. The business was located in a building that Thatcher leased for three years. In order to increase the shop's business, she purchased several new display cases. These were attached to the floor. The business was successful; however, the landlord notified Thatcher that the lease would not be renewed. Does Thatcher have the right to remove the display cases? Support your answer.

5. Los Angeles County included in its real estate tax assessment of Allstate's regional office building the value of computer equipment located in it. The equipment was housed in a room that took up approximately three percent of the total building space. The room had been specially modified to house the equipment; however, the modifications were easily reversible. The computer weighed more than 16 tons, but it consisted of separate parts. Extensive heavy cables connected the components to their own 220-volt power source and to each other. The units were movable, but moving them was inconvenient and required extensive advance planning. Allstate protested the assessment arguing that the computer equipment was not a fixture. Is Allstate or Los Angeles County correct? Support your answer.

6. Agins purchased five acres of unimproved land in the city of Tiburon. Some time later, before any construction on the property, the city adopted two zoning ordinances. The ordinances permitted the construction of one-family homes in the area where the Agins property was located; however, the ordinances established density limitations. These limitations allowed construction of between one and five one-family homes on the five acres. This significantly reduced the value of the tract. Agins filed a suit against the city seeking two million dollars in damages. On what theory would Agins sue? Would he be successful? Support your answers. *Agins v. City of Tiburon, 447 U.S. 255 (1980).*

4

Estates in Land

Allodium

Land owned absolutely; the holder owes no obligation to a superior.

Interests in land existing in the United States today are the result of two different systems of ownership. For several centuries, both systems existed side by side in Europe. One of these systems was *feudalism*, in which everyone holding land except the sovereign owed rents or services to a superior. In the *allodial* system, on the other hand, all land was owned absolutely. The holder had no obligation to pay rents or services to another.

Absolute ownership was the basis of Roman real property law. After the collapse of the Roman Empire, feudalism gradually became dominant in most of Europe except in some sections where the Roman influence persisted. In many of these areas the Roman idea of absolute ownership continued as the basis for holding land. Land was held without obligation to superiors. The owner had an absolute title with few limitations or restrictions on rights to use or dispose of it.

Today, the allodial concept of ownership is the distinguishing feature of real property ownership in the United States. Private ownership of land is free and absolute, subject only to governmental and voluntary private restrictions. However, traces of the feudal system continue to influence English and American law.

Feudalism

The fundamental principal of feudalism was tenure; all land was held on the condition that certain duties and services be performed for a superior.

Tenure

In the tenurial system, land was not owned in the sense that we think of ownership today. A person holding land was spoken of as being "seised" of the land. As a tenant, the occupant owed certain services that arose because he had possession but the overlord also enjoyed rights arising out of the same parcel. In many instances this immediate overload owed duties and services to another based upon his rights in the land.

Tenure in the United States

In the eastern part of the United States, some of the early colonial grants were based upon tenure. The proprietor held his land directly from the king. The small monetary payment required as a token of this relationship was called a *quitrent*. When the proprietor of a colony granted smaller tracts to individual settlers, each owed a quitrent by an extension of the feudal theory. These quitrents were very often ignored because of the ready availability of land on the frontier. In Massachusetts, Rhode Island and Connecticut, the tenurial system never existed; land there was held allodially. After the Revolution quitrents were abolished, and the notion prevailed that a person who owned land had an absolute title limited only by the state.

Vestiges of feudalism and tenure are retained in American real property law. One example is the law of *escheat*, in which the state is paramount, with land reverting to it if a person dies without heirs. Probably more important is the English concept of estates in land, for our legal system continues to recognize the idea that separate divisible interests can exist simultaneously in the same piece of land.

Estates

The extent and character of a person's rights and interests in land; to be an estate, the person's interest must be one that is (or may become) possessory.

The feudal notion of tenure is the foundation of the doctrine of estates in land. This doctrine has substantially influenced the rights that individuals may have in real property. The term *estate*, as used in this context, has a restrictive and technical meaning. It should not be confused with more common usage—that is, as a synonym for all of a person's assets.

In the system of tenure as it developed in England, land was separated from interests that might exist in it. Because land was one thing and interests in it another, several people could possess interests or estates in the same piece of land. This idea continues to be a feature of the law of English-speaking countries. Although a complete estate in land may exist at the present moment, it can be divided into various slices in such a way that each slice is regarded as existing now.

Case Example
Lansing Thomas owns a large farm. He directs by will that, upon his death, the property pass to Beverly Lane, his only daughter, for life and then to her oldest son. When Lansing dies, two estates exist in the land simultaneously.

Lansing's daughter Beverly has a *life estate*. This is a possessory estate because she is entitled to the rents and profits from the farm for her life. Beverly's oldest son has a *future estate*. Upon his mother's death he is entitled to the farm, but he can claim nothing in possession until she dies.

Although the nature, quality and extent of their interests often differ, each holder of an estate invariably has a present or future right of possession. Sometimes this right may be deferred until a future time, or it might even be conditional, but it is currently recognized by the courts. During his mother's life, the son in the example above does not have a right to occupy the land or profit from it. He does, however, possess an interest or estate that would be recognized in American courts as it was in the English. Further, he has rights to prevent *waste* of the property by the life tenant.

As there are many possible interests in land, estates have numerous dimensions. Several classifications of estates have developed reflecting these differences. This chapter distinguishes between two types of estates characterized by the duration of the owner's right to possession: freehold and nonfreehold estates. Nonfreehold estates are discussed in full in Chapter 25. Defeasible estates, those concerned primarily with the quality of the owner's interest, and future estates are discussed in this chapter along with other types of freehold estates. A later chapter deals with estates from the viewpoint of the number and relationship of owners.

Freehold Estate

An estate of uncertain duration.

Numerous freehold interests exist in land. Although they all have in common uncertainty as to their termination, other rights of the owners differ. The holders of most freehold estates may pass their interests along to their heirs. These are generally called *freehold estates of inheritance*. The most usual is the *fee simple* or *fee simple absolute*. Life estates are also freehold estates since their duration is uncertain. Life estates, however, are not estates of inheritance because they terminate upon the owner's death.

Some estates are created for a fixed period of time. The principal estates of this nature are the estate or tenancy for years and the tenancy from period to period. At common law, these nonfreehold estates were distinguished from freehold estates. For many purposes, they were treated as personal, not real, property. The holder of a nonfreehold estate did not have the same status or legal rights as the holder of a freehold estate. Tenancies at will and tenancies at sufferance are other estates less than a freehold.

Fee Simple or Fee Simple Absolute

The most extensive interest in land that a holder might possess; one that is potentially indefinite in duration.

Most land in the United States is held in fee simple. A fee simple is a freehold and, in addition, the most extensive estate known to the law. The holder of a fee simple title possesses all rights commonly associated with property or ownership. Possession is one of these rights. Subject to limitations by the state, the owner may sell the estate or give it away during his or her lifetime; the owner may direct the disposition of the estate by will; if the owner dies without a will, the fee will be disposed of according to the laws of the jurisdiction in which the fee is located. Creditors may levy against the estate, or the owner may use it as security. The holder of a fee may voluntarily limit uses to which it may be put or carve out lesser estates from it. Use limitations will be recognized by the courts if they do not violate public policy. Although the term has its roots in feudal times, in most respects the holder of a *fee simple* has the rights of allodial ownership.

Except in cases of conveyances to institutions such as corporations or government, the common law required the grantor to use specific words to create a fee simple. The words *and his heirs* continue in common use today, although in most states any words that indicate an intention to create a fee simple are sufficient. Thus, the granting clause in a deed will generally state "to [grantee] and his heirs" or "to [grantee] and his heirs forever." In some parts of the country, this estate is referred to simply as a *fee*.

Defeasible Fee

A fee simple that terminates upon the happening of some future stated event.

The holder of a fee simple or lesser estate has the right to create other estates in the land, which may be limited in several ways. Although this factor has complicated property law of English-speaking countries, it has also provided variety in the uses to which real property may be put. A grantor, by using the defeasible fee, is often able to benefit society and, at the same time, protect interests he or she considers important. The two types of defeasible fees next discussed have been used for self-serving, narrow-minded purposes, but they also have been used for benevolent purposes in a manner benefiting the entire community. In this context, it is important to remember that, until a defeasible fee terminates because the stated condition has occurred, the interests of the owner are the same as those possessed by the owner of a fee simple absolute.

Case Example

Mrs. Zahn, who is an environmentalist, owns a large tract of land in Wisconsin on which she desires to establish a wildlife sanctuary. She proposes to do this by giving the land to the National Wildlife Society. Although the directors of the society have agreed to administer and maintain the sanctuary, Mrs. Zahn fears that, as time passes and the land becomes more valuable, her original intent might be forgotten.

The law provides a number of methods for Mrs. Zahn to accomplish her objective and ensure that her intentions are honored. One of these would be to limit the future use of the land by imposing conditions in the deed. This task can be accomplished in two ways.

Fee simple determinable   This is a fee simple that automatically terminates when a stated condition is fulfilled. If the granting clause in the deed to the wildlife society states, "to the National Wildlife Society and its successors and assigns so long as the property is used as a wildlife preserve," a fee simple determinable would be created. The estate thus created is also known as a *base* or *qualified fee*. The fee is indefinite in duration as it is a fee simple, but the grantee's interest terminates automatically and reverts back to the grantor if the condition is fulfilled.

Fee simple subject to condition subsequent   This is a fee simple that may be terminated by the grantor or the grantor's successor when a stated condition is fulfilled. This estate is very similar to a determinable fee. The major difference is that termination is not automatic. The estate continues when the stated condition is fulfilled unless the grantor or the grantor's successors take steps to terminate it. The grantor or successor is said to have a *power of termination*. The environmentalist might create an estate of this nature by stating in the deed: "to the National Wildlife Society and its successors and assigns forever on condition that the land is used as a wildlife preserve, but if the land is used for any other purposes, Mrs. Zahn and her heirs shall have a right of entry and repossession."

Future Estate (Future Interest)

An interest in land that may become possessory in the future.

The common law accepted the idea that several estates of different duration could exist in land at the same time. Our legal system continues to recognize this concept. Only one of these interests is possessory, but because of the estate concept the party in possession does not necessarily have all interests associated with ownership. If *A*, the holder of a fee simple, grants a life estate to *B*, *B*'s interest terminates with death and something obviously is left over. As *A* has a fee simple, *A*'s estate, from which the grant to *B* was carved, is infinite in duration. If *A*'s grant to *B* said nothing about what was left after *B*'s death, *A* and his heirs have a future interest. This is an interest that entitles them to possession at that time in the future when *B* dies. This particular type of future interest is called a *reversion*, as the residue reverts back to *A* or his heirs.

Suppose, however, that *A*'s deed is worded "to *B* for life remainder to *C* and her heirs"; then *C* has a future interest. Although *C* has no present right to possession, her future interest is probably more valuable than *B*'s life estate, for upon the death of *B*, *C* or her heirs acquire a fee simple absolute. *C*'s interest is called a *remainder*. As *C*'s interest is not subject to any condition except *B*'s death, the remainder is said to be *vested*.

In addition to the reversion and the remainder, other future interests also exist. An example is the previously mentioned fee simple determinable. In creating this estate, the holder does not make an absolute grant of his or her entire interest. When the condition limiting the grant is fulfilled, the interest of the party in possession automatically terminates. The grantor and his or her heirs thus have a possibility of regaining possession at some time in the future. This future interest is called a *possibility of reverter*.

The creation of a fee simple subject to a condition subsequent also creates a future interest. This future interest is referred to as a *right of reentry* or a *power of termination*. When the possessory estate terminates because the condition is fulfilled, the holder of the right of reentry may get the land by filing suit.

Current Status of the Future Interest

The acceptance of the concept of possessory estates in land followed by a future interest lends flexibility to the disposition of real property; in many instances, however, future interests exist because a grantor wishes to limit the free transferability of land. Often the creator of the estate wishes to control the use of the land not only during his or her lifetime but after death as well. Conditional and defeasible fees have been used in the past for this purpose and continue to be used today.

The right of reentry and the possibility of reverter cause especially serious problems. The fees that give rise to these interests are created to last forever and often do last for many years. As a result, the right of reentry and the possibility of reverter are merely expectant interests with almost no present economic value. Often the current possessors of these interests are remote descendants of the original creator. Frequently they are unaware that another interest exists. When a title search reveals the existence of these interests, a person attempting to clear the title is presented with a difficult, if not insoluble, problem arising from the fact that often it is impossible to contact many of the parties who might retain an interest in the land because of the future interest.

A small but growing number of states have attempted to solve this problem through legislation. This legislation often places limitations on the time a future interest can last. Another type of legislation places limitations on the time during which a future interest can be enforced. Other states have adopted legislation that ensures a person who has an unbroken chain of title extending over a given number of years a fee simple free of future interests.

Life Estate

An estate of limited duration measured by a life or lives.

Granting an estate to an individual for life has been a common practice in the United States. A life estate typically is measured by the life of the owner, but it may be measured by the life of some other person. If the holder of a fee simple absolute makes a grant "to A for life," A has an estate that terminates with his or her death. If the grant were "to A for the life of B," A's estate would terminate upon the death of *B*. This type of life estate is called an estate *pur autre vie*. In modern practice, estates *pur autre vie* are seldom created.

Rights and Duties of Life Tenants

The holder of a life estate, usually called the *life tenant*, has an ownership interest in the land. This interest can be sold, mortgaged or leased, but it is not very valuable. Any interest a buyer, mortgagee or lessee acquires ends with the death of the life tenant. Life tenants are entitled to rents and profits from the property while their tenancy lasts, but they may not use the property in a manner that will permanently reduce its market value. If they do so, the owner of the estate that follows may bring an action against them for *waste*.

Life tenants must make ordinary repairs to the property. They are responsible for annual property taxes, but for only a proportionate share of special assessments for sewers, sidewalks and other permanent improvements. As a general rule, the life tenant is required to pay the interest on a mortgage but not the principal. The life tenant's obligations generally are limited to the extent the property provides income or profits.

Life estates frequently cause legal problems. In many cases, these problems involve the relationship between the life tenant and the holders of the estate to be enjoyed upon the termination of the life estate.

Case Example

Bridges owned a life interest in realty upon which there was a building worth $10,000. She insured the building, using her own funds. The building was destroyed by a hurricane and the proceeds of the policy paid to Bridges. The court approved a petition by the owner of the remainder that Bridges be ordered to rebuild or hold the insurance proceeds for the remainderman with interest going to Bridges for life. *Crisp Lumber Co. v. Bridges, 187 Ga. 484, 200 S.E. 777 (1939).*

In modern practice, the use of the life estate in the disposition of real property is gradually being replaced by use of the trust. Lawyers have found that the trust provides a more effective and flexible method of disposing of wealth. A trustee can be given legal title to land to hold for the life of a beneficiary. Proceeds from the land are paid to the beneficiary. Upon the death of the beneficiary, the land or proceeds from the sale of the land are distributed as the creator of the trust has directed. The trustee can also be given additional authority such as power of sale, which would permit disposal of the property if a profitable opportunity arises. Trusts will be discussed in greater detail in a later chapter.

Despite the potential legal problems, the life estate concept has been used in some states to provide security for one spouse upon the death of another. The law grants the surviving spouse a life interest in the real property of the deceased. Life estates of this nature are called *legal life estates*.

Legal Life Estates

In common law, several types of life estates in land were created as a result of marriage. A primary objective of these estates was to provide support for the wife upon the death of her husband, but a husband also had a life interest in the wife's real property upon her death. In some states, features of these marital life estates continue as important elements of real property law. A considerable number of states, however, have abolished them and substituted a statutory plan to provide for the widow or widower. These plans provide that the surviving spouse be entitled to choose what is called an *elective share*.

Elective share   These statutory plans allow the surviving spouse a specified share of the decedent's net estate. The surviving spouse can elect to take this share if not provided for in the will or if the provisions of the will are deemed by the surviving spouse to be less beneficial than the elective share provided for by statute. The decedent's net estate consists of real and personal property minus funeral and administration expenses, family allowances and debts. Under the Uniform Probate Code, which has been adopted in 16 states, the elective share is one-third. Many other states also allow a right to elect one-third, and some states allow one-half. Statutes providing the spouse with a right to elect almost always contain provisions that prevent a married person from deliberately disposing of property during his or her life to defeat the right of the surviving spouse to the elective share.

Dower   *Life estate of a widow in one-third of any real property to which her husband had legal title during marriage.* For many generations, dower was an important right that a widow acquired in her husband's real property upon his death. This right minimally entitled her to a one-third interest in his lands for life. The widow was entitled to dower as well as any gifts made in the husband's will, unless the will clearly stated that the gifts were in lieu of dower. If it was clear that the bequests were in lieu of dower, the widow had to elect one or the other.

While the husband was alive, the wife's right, which did not materialize unless the husband died before she did, was protected against both the husband's acts and claims of his creditors arising after the marriage. The wife's interest, which was called i*nchoate dower,* was a potential estate. She acquired a legal estate only if she survived her husband.

Case Example

Mary and Ed were secretly married in 1974. At that time, Ed owned a large office building. In order to modernize the building, in 1976 Ed borrowed a substantial amount of money and gave a mortgage to secure the loan. As a result of depressed economic conditions, Ed could not meet payments on the loan, and the mortgage was foreclosed. Any purchaser at the foreclosure sale would be subject to Mary's inchoate right of dower.

In order for dower to be allowed, the parties must have been legally married at the time of the husband's death. Consequently, in most states the right to dower is terminated by divorce, although some states allow dower if divorce is the result of the husband's fault. A wife can ordinarily release her inchoate right of dower by joining in any conveyance of the husband's real property. In the event a husband mortgages his property, the wife will release her inchoate right of dower if she signs the mortgage, but dower is restored upon payment of the debt.

Curtesy   *A common law estate that provided a husband with a life interest in all his wife's real property as soon as a child was born of the marriage.* English common law provided a husband with extensive rights in his wife's real property. While both were alive, he was entitled to the rents and profits as well as the use and enjoyment of any real estate that she owned. In addition, upon birth of a living child, he acquired a life estate in her lands that survived her death. This was the legal life estate of curtesy.

Although common law curtesy and dower had some similarities, they also differed extensively. First, for the husband to acquire curtesy, a living child had to be born of the marriage. The wife's dower interest did not depend upon the birth of a child. Secondly, the life estate the husband acquired by curtesy was in all the real estate owned by the wife, not just in one-third, the interest the wife acquired by dower. Finally, unlike dower, curtesy was a present, not just a potential, estate. This meant that the husband could encumber or sell his interest.

The extensive control over the wife's property that the common law afforded to the husband is no longer law in either the United States or England, but variations of common law curtesy exist to a limited extent in a number of American jurisdictions. These are generally the states that continue to recognize dower. In states where a modified form of curtesy exists, the principal change has been to remove any distinction between it and dower. In the many jurisdictions that have abolished both dower and curtesy, protection for the surviving husband or wife is provided by statute. These statutes ordinarily allow the surviving spouse either to elect a share, generally a one-third interest for life, in both the decedent's real and personal property or to take the interest given by the will.

Homestead Exemption Laws

Laws that (1) exempt the family from a forced sale of its home by certain classes of creditors; (2) may prevent an owner from selling or mortgaging the home without consent of the spouse; and (3) allow the designated family homestead to be used for the family's benefit after the head of the family dies.

Homestead laws, which have been adopted in most states, provide for heads of families some exemptions from creditors' claims. A family is defined in various ways, but most courts take a very liberal approach. They consider that a family exists when two or more persons reside together with one having a legal or moral obligation to support the others. A common and certainly more restrictive definition used in some states limits the family to a currently married husband and wife or a widow or widower still living in the homestead. Some states have extended the exemption to single, unmarried persons.

In spite of the fact that the statutes grant exemptions in favor of the head of the family, they are intended primarily to protect dependents. The exemption rests upon an expression of public policy. A legislature adopting a homestead exemption statute indicates it believes that a person's obligation to support dependents is at least as important as payment of debts. The expressed objective of homestead statutes in most states is to secure a family home beyond the reach of financial misfortune.

In addition to requiring that the owner have a family, most state homestead laws require that the exempt real estate be the permanent residence of the family. Several states also require the owner to formally declare a particular piece of real estate as a homestead. In the case that follows, the court discusses the policy underlying its state's homestead statute.

In Re Grindal
U.S. Bankruptcy Ct.
30 B.R. 651 (1983)

Background: Grindal and his wife owned a home and operated a business in Charleston, Me. As the business was doing poorly, Mr. Grindal secured employment in East Millinocket, Me. In order to avoid commuting expenses and because they believed that they were going to lose their home through foreclosure, the Grindals moved to East Millinocket on November 20, 1982. On November 30, they filed a bankruptcy petition, claiming an exemption in the Charleston house under Maine's homestead statute. The trustee in bankruptcy asked the court to disallow the exemption.

Decision: The bankruptcy court held that the Grindals did not qualify for the exemption.

Bankruptcy Judge
James A. Goodman

The debtors claim their exemption under Me.Rev.Stat.Ann., which provides an exemption in real or personal property that the debtor (or his dependent) uses as a "residence." The critical time for determining the debtors' entitlement to the exemption is the date the bankruptcy petition is filed (here, ten days after the debtors moved

to East Millinocket). Thus, the issue to be decided is whether the Charleston property was the debtors' residence on November 30, 1982.

The concept of "residence" is a flexible one, and must be construed in light of the policies underlying the exemption statute. ("The words `permanent residence' may have a variety of meanings depending upon the context in which the term is used."). In general, the purpose of exemption statutes is to secure for the debtor the means to support himself and his family. In particular, homestead statutes promote the stability and welfare of the state by encouraging property ownership, and they secure to the householder a home for himself and his family. While the homestead exemption should be liberally construed in order to afford all the relief the legislature intended, it must not be so broadly construed as to ignore the Maine legislature's clearly expressed intention to favor homeowners over non-homeowners. The legislature chose to "opt out" of the federal exemption scheme, which provided non-homeowners an exemption in other property equal in amount to the homestead exemption, and in its place granted non-homeowners a limited exemption. Thus, it appears that the Maine homestead exemption is intended to help homeowners to maintain that status; but not to provide the debtor funds for other purposes. (the homestead exemption is "for the benefit of the family as a place of actual residence mot as a refuge from the law's exactions. . . . ").

Given the purposes of the homestead exemption, a finding that the debtors actually occupied the homestead on the filing date is neither necessary nor sufficient to qualify for the exemption. Occupancy may be constructive as well as actual. The primary factor is the debtor's intention on the filing date. A debtor who does not actually occupy the homestead on the filing date, but who intends to return when circumstances permit, may qualify for the exemption.[1] Conversly, a debtor who actually occupies the homestead on the filing date, but who intends to sell it and not purchase another home, may not qualify for the exemption.

In the case before the court, the debtors were not, on the filing date, actually occupying the Charleston property, having moved to East Millinocket ten days before. The facts show clearly that the debtors' move was meant to be permanent—they moved to be closer to Mr. Grindal's new place of employment while believing that the loss of the Charleston property was a certainty. Nothing before the court indicates that the debtors either intended to return to Charleston or that they have any intention of purchasing another home in East Millinocket. On the evidence before it, the court is compelled to conclude that on the date of filing the debtors had abandoned their Charleston property, and that they do not qualify for the homestead exemption. . . .

Enter order.

Exempt property usually includes a lot and improvements up to a stated dollar or acreage amount. Some states use a combination of acreage and dollars. The dollar amounts vary widely. They range from a few thousand dollars to much higher amounts. Five to ten thousand dollars is a common dollar limitation. In rural areas, exempt acreage is frequently 160 acres; urban area exemptions are one-third to one-half acre. As a general rule, if the value or extent of the homestead exceeds the exemptions, creditors may force a sale of part of the property. The debtor retains the amount of the exemption.

---

1. Similarly, it has been held in some jurisdictions that the homestead exemption extends to proceeds from the sale of the home when the debtor intends to use the proceeds within a reasonable time to purchase another home. See *Field v. Goat*, 70 Okl. 113, 173 P. 364 (1918); *Annot.*, 1 A.L.R. 483 (1919), supp. 46 A.L.R. 814 (1927). Such an interpretation would seem to be consistent with a liberal construction of the homestead exemption, as it would further the purpose of aiding homeowners in maintaining their *status* as homeowners. Debtors often must sell their homes, perhaps to purchase less expensive homes, perhaps to pursue distant employment opportunities. It seems unlikely that the Maine legislature intended to aid only those homeowners who never move, for such an interpetation would often deny the exemption to those who most need it in order to maintain their homeowner status.

Case Example

Richard Rainey owned and occupied a 250-acre farm. He incurred a number of debts that he was unable to pay. When his creditors obtained judgments against him and attempted to sell the farm, Rainey claimed his homestead exemption. State law limited the exemption to 160 acres, and the court ordered 90 acres sold and the proceeds applied to pay Rainey's debts. As was customary, the unsold portion included the residence.

Although the homestead exemption provides some protection to a debtor and his or her family, the exemption does not protect the debtor against all claims. The following claims are often given priority by state law:

- an existing mortgage or deed of trust;

- a mortgage or deed of trust given to secure purchase of a residence;

- real property taxes and assessments;

- mechanics' liens;

- debts incurred before the homestead was acquired.

The homestead exemption is probably an anachronism in today's economy. Most exemption statutes were enacted at a time when the American economy was primarily agricultural. The statutes protected the farmer and his family and helped to ensure that food would be available to the nation. Today, many families live in apartments or rented homes. Homestead exemptions provide them with limited protection. Although the amount of the exemption has been increased recently in some states, many of the homestead exemptions are set at such low levels that the debtor's equity often exceeds them. The result is a forced sale and loss of the home. The owner does get the amount of the exemption in cash, but usually this amount is small and not sufficient to purchase a new home.

Homestead Property Tax Exemption

A number of states also use the term *homestead exemption* for statutes that afford property tax relief to older people of limited income and to people with limited income who are permanently and totally disabled. These statutes provide for a reduction of the taxable value of a person's residence if the person has reached a certain age—usually 65—or if a person is totally disabled. In both instances, for a person to qualify for benefits that person's income must not exceed an amount specified by statute. This amount usually is quite low.

Summary

Two systems have shaped real property ownership in the United States: the *allodial system* and the *feudal system*. The primary feature of modern real estate practice, however, is the allodial concept that private ownership of realty is free and absolute, subject only to governmental and voluntary restrictions. The feudal system, on the other hand, granted only the right to occupy land owned by a superior.

The concept of *estates* in land has its roots in the feudal notion of tenure. Several types of ownership or estates in land exist. A *freehold estate* is an estate of uncertain duration. The *fee simple absolute* is the most extensive freehold estate. *Defeasible fees* are also freehold estates. They terminate on a stated future event. However, when that event might occur is uncertain. The *fee simple determinable* and the *fee subject to condition subsequent* are defeasible fees.

Future estates and many of the conditional forms of ownership have been used by the creators of estates to limit the free transferability of an estate. But they often make it impossible for a new owner to gain clear title. Some states have adopted legislation to remedy this problem.

Another form of ownership is the *life estate,* granted for the life of the owner or some other person. After death of the life tenant, the person(s) named as remainderman takes possession. Legal problems frequently result from this relationship.

The legal life estate is a form that has arisen from the desire to protect the surviving spouse in a marriage. Life interests related to marriage are dower, the wife's interest and curtesy, the surviving husband's interest. Both have roots in the British common law.

Modern law is changing in response to social changes. Most states have some form of *homestead exemption law* to provide some exemption from creditors' claims for heads of families where the property is a principal residence. Even the homestead exemption may be out of date, however, since many family residences are now rented and exemption amounts are small.

Review and Discussion Questions

1. (a) What is the chief characteristic of an *estate?* (b) Explain how the concept of estates has influenced the development of real estate law.

2. Distinguish between a freehold estate and a nonfreehold estate. Give an example of each.

3. Explain the difference between a *fee simple subject to condition subsequent* and a *fee simple determinable.*

4. Explain the difference between the *homestead exemption* and *dower.*

Case Problems

1. In 1904 John F. McElveen conveyed to the trustees of Central Common Free School a tract of one acre. The deed contained the following provision:

Provided, always nevertheless notwithstanding, that in case it should so happen at any time that a free common school shall not be maintained on the described premises for a period of three consecutive years, then the said premises shall be considered abandoned and revert back to John F. McElveen.

Describe the interest of John F. McElveen in the one-acre tract. Does he have a right to sell his interest? Discuss.

2. Ann Shelf was married to Brian Shelf in a state that recognized common law dower. During the marriage Brian leased land for 99 years for the purpose of erecting an office building. Brian also took title to a large farm, which he sold several years later. Neither of those transactions was known to Ann until Brian's death. Discuss her interest, if any, in the two properties.

3. Sterner, by his last will and testament, granted a life estate in his residence to Virginia Sullivan. Other than the residence, the estate had few assets. Sullivan paid the real estate taxes for 1980 and a special sewer assessment. She filed a claim against the estate for reimbursement. Is she entitled to recover? Support your answer.

4. In 1965 Maricopa County executed two quitclaim deeds to the City of Tempe. The deeds contained the following provision:

> Subject to the restriction that the . . . real property shall be operated and maintained solely for park, recreation, public accommodation, and convenience purposes.

No words creating a right of reentry or indicating a reversionary interest in the county were used.

The city leased the land to Baseball Facilities, Inc. (BFI). In 1973 BFI applied for a sales tax permit to conduct activities such as a music festival and evangelical meetings on the land. None of these uses was prohibited by the lease. The city, however, denied the permit on grounds that the use for these purposes would create a right in Maricopa County to recover the property. The city argued that the provision in the deeds created a defeasible fee. Was the city correct? Discuss. *City of Tempe v. Baseball Facilities, Inc., 23 Ariz. App. 557, 534 P.2d 1056 (Ct. App. 1975).*

5. Melody Davis purchased a farm from Boyd Bishop, who was very ill. After Melody and her son Don moved into the farmhouse, Don discovered an old deed that conveyed the farm to "Boyd Bishop and his heirs forever." As Bishop had several children, Don was concerned that the children might, as heirs, have a claim to the farm when Bishop died. Explain to Don what these words mean.

6. Ronald Guard was married to Loretta Guard in a state that had abolished dower and curtesy. The state had, however, adopted the Uniform Probate

Code. Loretta was a successful investor in real estate. She owned several multifamily buildings, appraised at $500,000. In addition, she held securities valued at $100,000. When Ronald and Loretta quarreled, she destroyed her will, under which he had been left her entire estate. What claim, if any, might Ronald have against Loretta's estate if she dies before he does?

5

Co-Ownership

Co-Ownership

A form of ownership in which two or more persons have undivided interests in the same property.

Rights and interests in real estate may be divided in various ways, and a number of different interests often exist simultaneously in the same parcel. A common division of interests is horizontal in relationship to space. Chapter 2 indicated that one person might own the surface while others owned the minerals below or the airspace above the surface. Rights and interests are sometimes divided over time. For example, a life estate might be followed by a remainder in fee. Both estates are valuable, but the owner of the life estate has a present possessory interest. Simultaneously, the owner of the remainder in fee has a present interest, but the right to possession will not materialize until the life estate terminates in the future. A third division of rights exists when several people own undivided interests in a parcel of land at the same time. Generally, in this type of ownership each person is entitled to a specific fraction of the parcel but also shares with the others a single right to possession and profits from the land. This is generally referred to as *concurrent ownership* or *co-ownership*.

Co-ownership was important to the common law, and the various concurrent estates that developed at common law remain important today. A number of legal problems are associated with these common law concurrent estates. Many of these problems are reduced or eliminated if multiple owners use a partnership, corporation or trust to hold title to the property. As a result these devices are becoming increasingly important in real estate holdings and to a degree are replacing the common law forms of multiple ownership. This chapter discusses the traditional concurrent estates: joint tenancy, tenancy in common, tenancy by the entirety and tenancy in partnership. State laws regarding community property are considered briefly. Some modern alternatives for multiple ownership of real estate are also presented.

Joint Tenancy with Right of Survivorship

A form of co-ownership significant in that the entire estate passes to the survivor upon the death of the other joint tenant or tenants.

The principal feature of the joint tenancy is the *right of survivorship*. Upon the death of one of the co-owners, that person's interest passes automatically to surviving joint owners.

Case Example

Tom Casicollo conveys Blackacre in fee simple to his wife Helen and son Tony "as joint tenants." Helen dies. Tony becomes the sole owner of the fee. As this is a joint tenancy, upon Helen's death her interest in Blackacre does not become part of her inheritance estate, but automatically becomes Tony's property.

Joint tenancy with the right of survivorship is an additional example of the manner in which law tends to reflect existing economic and social conditions. During the feudal period, when English property law was developing, owner-ship of an estate by a single individual facilitated the lord's collection of the dues and services to which he was entitled. As a result, when a deed or will created rights in co-owners, the common law courts presumed that a joint tenancy was intended unless some other form of co-ownership was clearly indicated. Thus, in an earlier time, if Tom had not stated that Helen and Tony were to hold as joint tenants, the law would have presumed that they held in this manner. The survivor possessed the entire fee. The estate was in the possession of one owner, and the overlord had only to deal with a single individual.

Additional forms of co-ownership developed during the feudal period, and, after feudalism ended, the joint tenancy with its right of survivorship continued to meet the needs of English society. Throughout the 17th and 18th centuries, the wealth and power of the English aristocracy was based upon large landholdings. Land was a principal source of political power, the chief source of wealth and the basis of social status. If the landholding became fragmented because of too much division of property among multiple owners or through inheritance, the power of the English upper class would have been diluted. Because joint tenancy helped to prevent this dilution of power, it continued to be the dominant form of co-ownership and the form assumed by the courts to have been selected when the grantor's intention was not clear.

Although joint tenancy played a role in colonial American real property law, it was never as important in this country as it was in England. The reason for this was the marked difference in social and economic conditions between the two countries.

As forms of wealth other than land have become important, joint tenancy gradually has been replaced by other types of co-ownership. Most of these developed because they were more readily adapted to modern society's need for the free transferability of property.

Rights of Joint Tenants

Each co-owner who holds as a joint tenant has an equal right to possession of the entire property. This is referred to as an *undivided interest*. Although a joint tenant may not exclude other joint tenants from possession, strangely enough the law considers occupancy by one as occupancy by all. In the above example, if Tony Casicollo occupied Blackacre as a residence without his mother's objection, he would not be responsible to her for a proportionate share of the rent; neither would he be required to share income with her if Blackacre were a farm or commercial real estate. Helen Casicollo, however, has the same rights; hence if each tenant is to benefit, all must agree to share the proceeds of the property. Where agreement cannot be reached, the tenancy must be terminated.

Severance of Joint Tenancy

A number of different methods exist to sever or terminate a joint tenancy. Traditionally, for a joint tenancy to be created or to continue, four "unities" are required. First, the *unity of possession* requires that each have an undivided right to possession. Second, the *unity of interest* requires that each receive a similar estate. For example, one joint tenant cannot hold as a life tenant while the other holds in fee simple. Finally, they have to take effect at the same time (*unity of time*) and from the same instrument (*unity of title*). If any of these unities terminates, the joint tenancy also ends. The new form of ownership is tenancy in common, a form in which the right of survivorship does not exist.

Tenancy in Common

A form of concurrent ownership in which each owner possesses an undivided right to the entire parcel of land, with each owner's rights similar to those possessed by a sole owner.

In the United States today, the tenancy in common is probably the most frequently occurring form of concurrent ownership. Although tenancy in common developed contemporaneously at common law with joint tenancy, the joint tenancy was for centuries the favored form of multiple ownership. This is no longer true. Many states have abolished the joint tenancy. In those that have retained it, a tenancy in common is implied unless a joint tenancy is clearly indicated by the instrument creating the concurrent estate.

Case Example

By a provision in his will, Patrick Cross gave all his property to his sons, Thomas and William, "share and share alike, or to the survivor of them." William died before Thomas, and Thomas's heirs claimed the property, arguing that their father was a joint tenant with the right of survivorship. The court held that

William and Thomas were tenants in common, not joint tenants; as a result, the share of each, upon death, became part of his separate estate. *Cross v. Cross, 324 Mass. 186, 85 N.E.2d 325 (1949).*

Rights of Tenants in Common

Like joint tenants, each tenant in common has an undivided right to possession of the entire parcel. Normally, a tenant in common will not be responsible to the co-owners for any benefits obtained through exclusive occupancy unless he or she excludes the others from participating. At the same time, no tenant in common is entitled to the exclusive use of any part of the land. The result is that problems arise when one cotenant wrongfully excludes the others or when it is practical for the property to be occupied by only a single tenant. Under the circumstances, in a number of states, the cotenants not in occupancy will be entitled to a fair compensation for the use of the property. Similar problems arise where a cotenant not in possession receives benefits from the property exceeding those of his or her co-owners. These types of problems can best be solved by agreement among the parties, as can problems involving liability of co-tenants for upkeep and improvements. When agreement cannot be reached, partition of property may be the only solution.

Partition

An action by which a co-owner obtains a division of property termi-nating any interest of other co-owners in the divided portion.

Partition is the historic method by which unwilling concurrent owners of real property may terminate the interests of fellow co-owners. Although courts traditionally ordered partition even when no statute authorized them to do so, today partition exists in some form by statute in every state. Many states make the remedy available to some holders of future interests. Under the law of almost all states, co-owners of personal property enjoy the right to partition to the same degree as co-owners of realty.

Partition may be voluntary or compulsory. Voluntary partitions are the result of agreement among the co-owners to end the relationship. They are usually carried out by deeds in which each co-owner is allocated a described portion of the realty by all the other part owners. It is also possible for all the co-owners to convey to a third party, the third party in turn conveying to each former co-owner his or her agreed-upon parcel. Although a few states recognize oral voluntary partitions, a written instrument is usually required, primarily to permit recording in the title history. Voluntary partition requires not only the consent of all the parties to the act but also agreement as to the division of the estate. Compulsory partition by judicial action is necessary when one or more of the multiple owners desire to terminate the relationship and agreement cannot be reached for dividing the property.

The right to partition appears to be absolute unless the parties themselves have agreed they will not use the remedy. A co-owner may demand partition without regard to the size of his or her share. The fact that the interest of a co-owner is subject to a mortgage or other lien, though it is a complicating factor, will not defeat the right. So extensive is the right to partition that state condominium statutes must specifically prohibit the right of condominium owners to seek partition of the condominium elements that are owned in common.

Partition is accomplished in one of three ways. The preferred method is by a physical division of the property. The court orders the property divided, allocating to each co-owner a share that is equivalent to his or her interest. Often, however, physical division is not practicable or desirable, and in these cases the property will be sold and the proceeds divided among the co-owners in relation to their interests. The third method involves physical division of the property into shares that are as nearly as possible equivalent in value to the interests of the individual owners. The court then orders monetary payment to those co-owners whose physical shares were not equivalent to their interest.

Tenancy by the Entirety

Co-ownership of property by husband and wife; upon the death of either, the survivor remains as sole owner.

Nearly half the states recognize tenancy by the entirety, a type of co-ownership existing only between husband and wife. This type of co-ownership is based upon an ancient legal fiction by which the common law regarded husband and wife as a single legal person. One result was that, if the two acquired equal interests in real estate by the same instrument, the property was considered owned as an indivisible legal unit. Upon the death of either, the survivor remained as the parcel's sole owner. This result has long been accepted by modern law. Today, a right of survivorship similar to that existing for the joint tenancy exists for the tenancy by entirety. In a small estate, this right benefits the surviving spouse as it avoids the necessity and cost of probate proceedings.

Case Example

Jim Seaver and his wife Helen purchased an apartment building and took title in both their names. Jim died without making a will, and children by a former marriage claimed that a part interest in the property vested in them. They argued that Jim and Helen were tenants in common. The court held that Helen was the absolute owner because, when a husband and wife take title in both their names, a tenancy by the entirety is created unless otherwise indicated.

The result would not be the same in all states that recognize a tenancy by the entirety. Some of the states that accept this type of tenancy do so only if it is expressly stated in the granting instrument.

Termination of the Tenancy by the Entirety

A tenancy by the entirety is a more stable type of co-ownership than the joint tenancy. Because the marital partners are considered a single unit, neither husband nor wife can sever the tenancy without the other's consent. Unlike the joint tenancy, a sale by either the husband or the wife does not terminate the tenancy or end the right of survivorship.

In many jurisdictions, a tenancy by the entirety cannot be terminated by the forced sale of the husband's or wife's interest. This means that if either spouse individually incurs debts and then refuses to pay them, the creditor cannot *execute upon*—that is, judicially seize—the property. This rule has been criticized because it permits the debtor to escape responsibility while owning an interest in a valuable asset. In a few states, creditors of the husband, but not the wife, may reach the income, profits and title of the property. Whatever interest these creditors acquire is lost if the wife survives. Other states permit the separate creditors of either spouse to levy upon and sell the share of the debtor, whether husband or wife. If the opposite spouse survives, the creditor is deprived of his or her interest. If the creditor holds a joint judgment against both spouses, resulting from an obligation both incurred, the creditor can attach the estate held by the entirety.

Tenancies by the entireties are terminated by divorce because the marital relationship is essential to this form of co-ownership. Upon divorce the parties become tenants in common.

The common law allowed the husband almost complete control of all of his wife's property. This included her individual share in a tenancy by the entirety. The husband, thus, was entitled to all the income from the estate, and he had sole discretion as to occupancy and use. In fact, the husband could even sell the real estate, although sale was subject to the wife's right of survivorship.

A husband's absolute power over his wife's property was terminated by the passage of a number of married women's acts during the past century. These statutes entitle the wife to control and benefit from her property. Today, in most states that recognize tenancy by the entireties, the wife has the same rights in the property as her husband.

Estate Tax Problems of Joint Interests

Co-ownership often is the source of complicated problems involving both estate and gift taxes. Most of these are beyond the scope of this book, but one common misconception needs clarification at this point. As we know, in both the joint tenancy and the tenancy by the entirety, the share of a deceased co-owner automatically passes to the survivor or survivors. Because of this, people sometimes assume that the estate of a deceased co-owner is not subject to federal estate tax on the jointly owned property.

It is true that for the tenancy by the entirety probate is unnecessary. State taxes on the decedent's estate may be avoided on the interest of the first spouse to die, but the estate is responsible for any federal estate tax.

The Internal Revenue Code requires the legal representative of the deceased spouse to include in the decedent's estate the entire value of any real property held as a co-owner with the right of survivorship. The estate may exclude any part of that value that it can show was purchased with funds supplied by the surviving co-owner(s).

Case Example

Martin and Harold Chang purchased a small building for $60,000. They took title as joint tenants with the right of survivorship. Each furnished 50 percent of the purchase price. Over several years, the building appreciated in value to $80,000. When Martin died, $40,000 would be included in his gross estate for federal estate tax purposes.

If Martin had contributed the entire purchase price, the entire $80,000 value of the property could be included in his gross estate. If the joint tenancy was a gift to the Changs, then only a share proportionate to the number of joint tenants would be included. Again, if Martin had contributed nothing, the entire price being paid by Harold, nothing would be included in Martin's taxable estate. Appropriate gift taxes would have to be paid on Martin's share.

The Internal Revenue Code treats joint tenants and tenants by the entirety in a similar manner. Some limited concessions are made if the joint tenants are husband and wife. If the joint owners are husband and wife and the tenancy was created after December 31, 1976, only one-half the value of the property need be included in the gross estate of the decedent's spouse, no matter which spouse furnished the consideration. But the donor must elect to treat the joint tenancy as a gift at the time of its creation. This limited right might be advantageous if the parties intend to terminate the tenancy prior to death. In this instance, a gift tax is paid on the purchase price, not on the appreciated value of the half interest given.

Tenancy in Partnership

A form of co-ownership in which each partner owns partnership property together with the other partners; each partner's share is treated as personal property; partnership property of a deceased partner passes to the surviving partners.

The common law did not recognize the partnership as a legal entity. As a result, property could not be held in the partnership name. This not only caused confusion but also frequently led to complex legal problems when a partner died or experienced financial difficulty. Creditors of an individual partner could then attach specific partnership assets; upon the death of a partner, his or her share in specific partnership property passed to that person's estate, and an individual partner could terminate the relationship by selling his or her interest in a particular property.

Case Example

Kane and Waldron entered into a partnership agreement to operate a creamery. Partnership funds were used to purchase real estate to operate the business. Title was taken in both Kane's and Waldron's names. A short time later, Kane died. At common law, his interest in the real estate would pass to his heirs, not to the surviving partner.

Most states have now adopted the Uniform Partnership Act, which creates the tenancy in partnership. Specifically, the Uniform Partnership Act permits the firm to buy, hold and sell real estate in the partnership name. Individual partners share ownership in particular property only as members of the firm. Spouses, heirs and creditors of individual partners have no rights in partnership property.

Individual partners may not assign partnership property unless the assignment involves the rights of all partners. Although an individual partner can transfer partnership real property, any such transfer is made only as an agent for other partners of the firm.

Upon the death of any partner, his or her share passes to the surviving partners. In the previous example, Waldron, as the surviving partner, acquires Kane's share. Waldron, however, possesses this property only for the purpose of liquidation inasmuch as Kane's death terminates the partnership. During liquidation, Waldron can operate the business without interference from Kane's legal representatives.

Kane and his heirs—in fact any partner—all have a valuable interest in the partnership. The interest stems from the individual's right to share in the profits and surplus of the firm. The interest is not in specific firm property. Under the Uniform Partnership Act, this interest is regarded as personalty, not real property. The partner's interest is unlike the interest of a joint tenant or a tenant in common. If the partner's interest is sold separately, the partnership is destroyed and the interest is not subject to partition.

Community Property

A form of co-ownership between husband and wife in which each has a one-half interest in property acquired through the labor of either during the marriage.

Several jurisdictions in the United States apply the doctrine of community property to real estate owned by a husband or wife. Generally, the community property states are those located in the Southwest; the law of these states was influenced by the laws of France and Spain, countries that have traditionally used the concept of community property in determining property rights of married persons. The states in which community property is an integral part of the legal system are Arizona, California, Idaho, Louisiana, Nevada, New Mexico, Texas and Washington. Other states have from time to time adopted some of the community property ideas. Since community property ownership is statutory, each state varies the characteristics of the system to fit its own needs. It is therefore difficult to generalize about a community property doctrine. When decisions are to be made, legal advice should be obtained in the particular state involved.

Community property is based upon the marital relationship. In community property jurisdictions, the husband and wife are regarded as partners. Each spouse becomes a co-owner with the other in all property acquired through the labor or skill of either or both while the two are married. This fact applies even if title to the property is held individually by the husband or wife.

Case Example

Tanya and Bob Kane, residents of California, were married in 1949. Tanya, following the traditional role of homemaker, managed the domestic establishment and cared for the family. Bob successfully practiced his profession as a doctor. From 1959 until 1977, Bob's practice prospered, and he earned a great deal of money. Some of this was invested in real estate, which was held in Bob's name. When Bob died in 1977, one-half of this real estate, which was community property, belonged to his wife; the other half would be in Bob's estate.

Community property is at odds with the law in other states, which recognize that property held in the name of one of the spouses is solely the property of that person, although the other spouse usually has some rights in relation to the property upon the death of the owner and in some instances upon the termination of the marriage by divorce.

Separate Property

Property owned by the husband or wife prior to marriage and property acquired during marriage by gift, inheritance or will.

Not all property owned by husband and wife in the community property states is community property. The parties retain separate title to property they owned separately before marriage and to property each acquired by gift or inheritance during marriage.

Case Example

The will of John Earles, who died in 1933, gave a one-third interest in a 1,600-acre ranch to his son Jesse. The remaining two-thirds was given to Helen Earles, John's wife. Jesse was married in 1940. In 1948 Helen Earles, retaining a life interest in her two-thirds share, transferred title to her portion of the ranch to Jesse. Upon Jesse's death the ranch would pass as a part of his separate estate, not as community property.

Real property purchased with the separate property of one spouse who takes title in his or her name remains separate property. In the example involving Tanya and Bob Kane, if Bob had inherited money from his mother and invested it in real estate, the real property acquired would be separate property. In some community property states, rents and profits from separate property are considered separate property. In others, rents and profits from separate property become community property.

Control of community property in most states has been given to the husband. The rationale appears to be the traditional view that the husband is the head of the family. Both the statutes that allocate this power to the husband and numerous judicial opinions require the husband to deal with the property in good faith. Recent statutory developments in several community property states have expanded protection of the wife against abuse of the husband's power to manage and control community property.

Investment Alternatives for Multiple Owners

Trust

A legal relationship in which a grantor transfers legal title to property to a trustee, who holds the property for the benefit of third parties, or beneficiaries.

The trust is a device that has been used in the United States and in England for several centuries. It has been an important instrument in law reform and the legal basis for some significant economic innovations.

Case Example

Elaine Morgan, a successful business executive, was married to Carl Morgan, a well-known musician. Carl had little interest in financial matters. In order to ensure that Carl had adequate income throughout his life, Elaine irrevocably transferred certain securities and real estate to Central Trust Company to be administered by the company with the income going to Carl for life. Upon Carl's death, the property was to go to the Juilliard School of Music.

Elaine has created a living, or inter *vivos*, trust. If she had made these provisions in a will, upon her death a *testamentary* trust would have been created. Today, trusts are used for many different purposes. They are used extensively in family estate planning of the type mentioned in the example, but they are also important in business. Trusts are frequently utilized to finance real estate ventures and to protect bondholder creditors of a corporation. Many large charities are organized as trusts; wealthy individuals convey assets to a trustee, who administers them for some designated public benefit.

The premise upon which the trust is based is the division of property interests among owners. In a trust, one person or an institution is given title to specific property that is managed for the benefit of others. The property may be real or personal. In the example, Central Trust Company legally owns the securities and real estate, but it must administer them for Carl Morgan's benefit.

With few exceptions, trusts involving real property must be in writing. Some states permit inter vivos trusts of personal property to be created orally. All testamentary trusts—whether the property is real or personal—must be in writing and executed in the same manner as required for an effective will. Testamentary trusts that are frequently part of an estate plan often supplement a will.

Fiduciary Duty

Every trust must have a trustee to hold and manage the property. The trustee has a *fiduciary duty*, the responsibility for the utmost good faith and undivided loyalty to the beneficiary in administering the trust.

The doctrine of fiduciary responsibility applies to numerous legal relationships. Because some of these—such as the attorney-client and broker-seller relationships—are very important to real estate transactions, a brief outline of the duties common to all fiduciaries is in order. A fiduciary (1) must act for the benefit of the other party in matters within the scope of the relationship, (2) must not profit at the other party's expense and (3) must make full disclosure of all information affecting transactions with the other party. In a case involving a trustee's fiduciary duties, Justice Benjamin Cardozo once said:

> Many forms of conduct permissible in a workaday world for those acting at arm's length are forbidden to those bound by fiduciary ties. A trustee is held to something stricter than the morals of the marketplace. Not honesty alone but the punctilio of an honor the most sensitive is then the standard of behavior. As to this there has developed a tradition that is unbending and inveterate. Uncompromising rigidity has been the attitude of courts of equity when petitioned to undermine the rule of undivided loyalty by the "disintegrating erosion" of particular exceptions. Only thus has the level of conduct for fiduciaries been kept at a level higher than that trodden by the crowd. It will not consciously be lowered by any judgment of this court. *Meinhard v. Salmon, 249 N.Y. 458, 464, 164 N.E. 545 (1928).*

Under the terms of most trusts, trustees are usually granted extensive powers. Sometimes these powers are statutory, but they are also included in most well-drawn trust instruments. A trustee's powers will usually include, but not be limited to, making new investments, managing real estate, carrying on a business, selling property, borrowing money, reviewing mortgages, settling litigation, voting stock, collecting income and making distributions.

The fiduciary responsibility of the trustee protects the trust beneficiary. As a result, trusts continue to be important in personal financial planning. Since World War II the trust has been one of several devices used by investors to organize real estate syndicates.

Real Estate Syndicate

A group of investors who combine funds and managerial resources to develop, manage or purchase real estate for a profit or as a tax shelter.

As a syndicate is not a form of ownership, the investors involved must organize in some legal form. To answer legal questions involving a real estate syndicate, a lawyer needs to know in what legal form the syndicate holds the realty. Probably the simplest form for the organization of a syndicate is the tenancy in common. More important forms of ownership today are the S corporation (formerly called *Subchapter S corporation*, general and limited partnerships, joint ventures and real estate investment trusts (REITs). Each of these forms will be discussed in the following pages. Chapter 27 provides additional discussion of REITs and other types of real estate investments.

Tenancy in Common

The tenancy in common has been used by real estate investors for years. This form of ownership has the advantage of allowing the investors appreciable tax flexibility. Each co-owner is free to select the most beneficial tax treatment of his or her share. When the syndicate is organized as a partnership or corporation, the participants are bound by the tax characterization of the entity.

As a vehicle for syndication, the tenancy in common suffers from several legal and practical disadvantages. Individual owners are personally liable for all obligations arising out of property ownership. If someone is injured on the property or large debts are incurred, the individual assets of the co-owner can be reached. This compares unfavorably with the liability of the owners of a corporation, in which liability of each shareholder is limited to the amount that the shareholder has invested. The second legal drawback is the potential problem of marketability of property owned as a tenancy in common. If one of the owners dies or becomes insolvent and the remaining owners wish to sell their property, they usually must establish that the title is marketable. Death or insolvency of a co-owner clouds the title, causing delay and expense in clearing it to make it marketable.

S Corporations

To remedy these problems, federal law authorizes syndicates to use a modification of the corporate form. The modification allows investors to escape double taxation—that is, taxation of earnings of both the corporation and each shareholder. The S corporation allows the syndicate to pass income through without its being taxed at the corporate level. Thus the owners are not subject to the double burden associated with the ordinary corporation. Unfortunately, S corporations are limited to 35 shareholders, and some limitations are placed upon the type of income allowed. Losses that a shareholder may take are also restricted. Because of these limitations and additional complex tax problems, S corporations are used only for relatively sophisticated syndications.

Partnership

An association of two or more persons to organize a business venture and divide the profits.

Many syndicates are organized either as general or limited partnerships. Both partnership forms also avoid double taxation—the nemesis of incorporation. A partnership is not taxed on its income; any income is taxed directly to the partners as individuals.

Investors who syndicate as a general partnership face three legal handicaps. Probably the most serious is the unlimited liability of the partners. Each partner is personally responsible for all partnership obligations, and his or her property, both real and personal, can be reached if partnership assets are not sufficient to satisfy claims against the unit. A second handicap is the power of individual partners to make agreements binding the firm. Under Section 9 of the Uniform Partnership Act, "[e]very partner is the agent of the partnership for the purpose of its business . . . and the act of every partner binds the partnership. . . . " Finally, death, withdrawal or bankruptcy of one of the partners automatically terminates the partnership. The syndicate must be re-created by a new agreement. In order to facilitate securing capital for business ventures, many states have legislation that allows the creation of partnerships in which some of the members have *limited liability*. Partnerships of this kind are called *limited* or *special partnerships*. They are a popular form of organization for real estate syndicates.

Limited partnership   State laws providing for the creation of limited partnerships are based either on the Uniform Limited Partnership Act (ULPA) or on a 1976 revision of that act, known as the Revised Uniform Limited Partnership Act (RULPA). By 1989, 42 states had adopted the revised act, though one commercially significant state, New York, had not done so.

Both acts define a limited partnership as a partnership having as members one or more general partners and one or more limited partners. Under most circumstances a limited partner's liability to creditors of the partnership is limited to that person's capital contribution. Under the provisions of both acts, to be considered a limited partner the individual must be designated as such in a certificate filed with a designated state official.

Case Example

Anna, Ben and Carla Lane formed a limited partnership to invest in real estate. Anna, the general partner, invested $10,000 and agreed to manage the property. Ben and Carla, as limited partners, contributed $25,000 each. The project failed after accumulating debts of $65, 000. Individual assets of Anna could be reached to cover any claims of creditors not satisfied on liquidation. Ben's and Carla's individual assets could not be reached by the syndicate's creditors beyond the amounts of their initial investment.

If limited partners participate in the "control of the business," they lose their defense against liability to creditors. However, the ULPA does not define what constitutes "taking part in control." This has been left to the courts. Generally they have interpreted "taking part in control" in a manner that significantly restricts the limited partner's ability to participate without forfeiting limited liability. In addition, under the ULPA, if the limited partner's name appears in the partnership name, the limited partner becomes liable as a general partner. This is intended to protect creditors who extend credit to the business on the basis of the financial resources of a person who is actually only a limited partner.

The RULPA specifically allows a limited partner to act in a number of situations for the business without forfeiting limited liability. For example, the revised act permits a limited partner to be a contractor for or an agent or employee of the limited partnership. A limited partner can also consult with and advise a general partner, act as a surety for the partnership and approve or disapprove an amendment to the partnership agreement. In addition, the act permits a limited partner to vote on the following matters:

- dissolution and winding up of the business;

- sale, exchange, lease, mortgage, pledge or other transfer of all or substantially all of the assets of the limited partnership;

- incurrence of indebtedness by the limited partnership other than in the ordinary course of business;

- change in the nature of the business;

- admission or removal of a general partner.

More importantly, under the RULPA, a limited partner is liable only to persons who transact business with the partnership with actual knowledge of the limited partner's participation in control. Additionally, to recover, a plaintiff must be misled into reasonably believing the limited partner is a general partner. If, however, the limited partner's participation is substantially the same as that of a general partner, the limited partner will be liable to any person who transacts business with the partnership.

Joint Venture
A business entity in which two or more persons have agreed to carry out a single undertaking for a profit.

A joint venture is a form of business organization very similar to the partnership. Most of the law that applies to partnerships also applies to the joint venture. Like a partnership, the joint venture is based upon agreement, and the members have a fiduciary relationship to each other. They share profits and losses; each enjoys the right to manage and direct the venture; and the venture is treated as a partnership for federal tax purposes.

The major difference between the partnership and the joint venture is that the latter is usually created to carry out a single transaction. Although some limited partnerships are created for a single purpose, most partnership operations are more extensive, carrying out a general business for a period of years. Other differences also exist between a partnership and a joint venture. In a joint venture, each participant has limited power to bind the others. However, the participants can agree that each will have this power. Death of a joint venturer does not automatically dissolve the joint venture. Finally, because a joint venture cannot be adjudicated as bankrupt, claims of creditors against the joint venture's real estate holdings are limited.

Real Estate Investment Trust (REIT)

An organization in which trustees own real estate or loans secured by real estate that they manage for beneficiaries who hold transferable shares representing their respective interests.

During the late 19th century the American economy was expanding rapidly. Large sums of money were needed for investment in many segments of the economy. Real estate was no exception. Unfortunately, the corporate form of business organization that was used to attract capital into most business activity could not be used in real estate because most of the states prohibited ownership of real property by corporations. The business trust, or Massachusetts trust, evolved to circumvent this prohibition. The trust had many advantages of the corporation, such as limited liability, ready transferability of shares and continuous existence. Because the trust was not a corporation, it was a permissible form of enterprise for real estate investment.

With the passage of time, state prohibitions against corporate ownership of property were abolished, but the business trust continued to be important. It provided investors with a major tax advantage over the corporation. For tax purposes the trust was treated as a conduit through which income passed. Income it earned was not taxable to it as long as the income was distributed to the trust beneficiaries. Corporate income is not treated in this favorable manner but is taxable to the corporation and also to the shareholder when distributed. The tax advantage enjoyed by the business trust was eliminated in 1935 by a number of court decisions that emphasized the corporate characteristics of the trust and held these sufficient to classify the trust as an association taxable as a corporation.

These rulings had little immediate impact because of the depressed economic conditions of the 1930s, and, later, the influence of World War II. The need for capital in the real estate market was limited. Conditions changed late in the 1940s as the postwar U.S. economic boom created a need for large sums of money to be invested in real estate. About this time, an effort was made to restore to the business trust the tax advantage that it had enjoyed until 1935. This effort was finally successful in 1960 when Congress approved legislation that allowed business trusts and investment trusts dealing in real estate under certain prescribed conditions, once again to serve as a conduit through which income passes without being taxed twice. REITs are discussed in more detail in Chapter 27.

Government Regulation of Syndicates

Many real estate syndicates are financed by the public sale of participation certificates, which are securities. The public sale of securities is regulated extensively by both state and federal law.

The term *security* is defined broadly by federal and state statute. An investment in which a person is induced to participate with others expecting to profit solely through the efforts of others is usually subject to regulation as a security. Many real estate syndications fit this description. In addition to real estate syndication, statutes regulating the sale of securities have been applied to transactions as diverse as the sale of lots in undeveloped land and the sale of resort condominiums that are to be rented with profits to be divided among condominium owners. During the past decade, enforcement of federal and state statutes regulating the marketing of investments to the public has intensified. People in the real estate industry should expect this trend to continue.

State "blue-sky" laws generally require those who sell securities to be registered in the state. Practically all states also require that the security sold be registered. Usually these state laws include standards against which the quality of the security can be measured. This permits state officials to refuse to register securities that do not qualify or are fraudulent.

Two important federal statutes also regulate the sale of most securities. They are the Securities Act of 1933 and the Securities Exchange Act of 1934. Both statutes are discussed in more detail in a later chapter as they apply to many real estate syndicates.

Summary

Several legal forms have evolved by which real property can be owned by more than one individual. *Joint tenancy with right of survivorship* is one of these forms. Upon the death of one of the co-owners, that person's interest passes automatically to the remaining joint owner.

Under this form, each co-owner has an equal right to possession, or an undivided interest. Joint tenancy is based on four "unities": unity of possession, of interest, of time and of title. Lacking any one of these unities, the *co-ownership* becomes a *tenancy in common*. Joint tenancy can also be terminated if the interest of one of the parties is sold as the unity of possession no longer exists. In some states joint tenancy is not permitted; in some the right of survivorship must be expressed in order for it to be upheld legally.

In the modern U.S. economy, the tenancy in common is a more usual form of co-ownership. Rights of tenants in common are similar in some respects to those of joint tenants. Each has an undivided right of possession, but none has the right of exclusive use. In a tenancy in common no right of survivorship exists.

Partition is the legal method used to sever the interests of co-owners so that they may take their separate shares. Partition would be the solution to a situation in which one co-owner wished to sell and the others do not. To be valid, an act of partition must be in writing and permanently recorded in the title history. Partition may be accomplished by physical division of the property or by sale of the property and division of the proceeds.

A third form of co-ownership, when co-owners are husband and wife, is *tenancy by the entirety*. In case of the death of one, the survivor becomes sole owner. It is a more stable form than joint tenancy because under the law the marital partners (owners) are considered a single unit. In some states the property is protected against attachment by a creditor of one of the owners.

Termination occurs mainly by divorce, upon which the parties become tenants in common.

Tenancy in partnership, a fourth form of co-ownership, is used primarily when co-owners have a business relationship to each other. Tenants who own in partnership are regulated by the Uniform Partnership Act, and the property is protected against the interests of spouses, heirs or creditors of individual co-owners. This form has become possible in recent times because of the recognition of the partnership as a legal entity.

Community property, like tenancy by the entirety, is a concept that applies only to persons married to each other. In those states where community property is recognized, any property acquired through labor or skill by either spouse during the marriage is owned equally by both. How the property is acquired is key here, because property acquired by one spouse through gift or inheritance is classed as *separate property* and belongs to that spouse alone.

Property may also be held and managed by another party in a *trust*—a legal device that has been the basis of significant economic innovations. Trusts are frequently used to finance real estate ventures and for estate planning. The person responsible for the property is known as the trustee; his or her relationship to the owner or beneficiary of the trust requires the utmost good faith and undivided loyalty. This is known as the fiduciary duty. The fiduciary relationship is pervasive in the real estate profession and its many transactions.

For business ventures in the real estate field, syndication is an important recent development. Through a *real estate syndicate*, investors of many types can pool their resources to purchase, develop or manage real estate. Syndicates take many forms, including tenancy in common, S corporations, *partnerships, joint ventures* and *real estate investment trusts (REITs)*. Knowledge of these developments and their legal requirements is essential to those engaged in commercial real estate sales, management or investment.

Federal and state governments exercise considerable control over the public's participation in real estate syndicates. Federal securities statutes enacted in the 1930s are particularly stringent regarding registration, sale and advertising of securities offerings.

Review and Discussion Questions

1. During the past 15 years, the S corporation and the limited partnership have been used extensively in real estate syndication. What factors account for this?

2. Under what circumstances will a court order the property owned by tenants in common to be partitioned?

3. Compare and contrast a *joint tenancy*, a *tenancy by the entirety* and a *tenancy in common*.

4. Outline some of the problems that real estate sales personnel face as a result of co-ownership of real property.

Case Problems

1. Lars Olsen is a general partner and Swen Nielson a limited partner in Olsen and Sons, a limited partnership engaged in the construction and sale of bowling alleys. Nielson had been in the construction business for many years but had retired because of ill health. Olsen has been in the construction business for a short time but had served as Nielson's accountant for a number of years. Although Olsen makes all business decisions, he frequently phones Nielson for advice. When asked for advice, Nielson usually replies, "Lars, I'm not telling you how to do it, but if I were doing it, I would do it this way." Olsen generally follows Nielson's advice. (a) If the venture fails, could Nielson be held liable as a general partner? Discuss. (b) Would the result be different if the business had been run by Nielson prior to his retirement? Explain.

2. Matilda Schomas owned a small apple orchard, which was operated by her son. Matilda did not wish to write a will, but she wanted her son to succeed to the property upon her death. Without the aid of counsel, she decided that she and her son should hold the orchard as joint tenants. Matilda then conveyed the orchard to herself and her son "as joint tenants, not as tenants in common." When she died, the son claimed the orchard by right of survivorship. Was a joint tenancy created? Explain why or why not.

3. Marie Rodesney and Fred Rowlett owned property as tenants in common. They had acquired the property for speculative purposes, each agreeing to use his or her best efforts to sell it at a profit. While they owned the property, Rowlett rented it to a Mr. Wood for a used car lot. Rentals under the agreement amounted to $5,230. Rowlett disbursed $3,511.52 for taxes and improvements, leaving a net balance of $1,718.48; however, the reasonable rental value of the property while it was owned by Rodesney and Rowlett was $15,900. Upon sale of the property, Rodesney contended that in addition to her share of the proceeds she was entitled to one-half of the reasonable rental value. Is her contention correct? Discuss. *Rodesney v. Hall, 307 P.2d 130 (Okla. 1957).*

4. Cranston and White decided to invest in some rental real estate. Cranston was a wealthy doctor. White was his son-in-law. White had recently graduated from business school and opened up a small business. Although White was an able person, the economy in the area was depressed, and the business was barely succeeding. What legal problems might Cranston face if the two took title to the rental property as tenants in common?

5. James Huff and Carol Burns owned a condominium as tenants in common. From February 1978 until September 1985, they lived in the condominium as a family with Burns's minor child. During this period, Huff paid the maintenance expenses on the condominium. In 1985, the two quarrelled and Burns changed the locks to the condominium, excluding Huff. Huff petitioned to partition the condominium and the property was sold. In addition

to his half share from the sale, Huff argued that he was entitled to half of the maintenance expenses and half of the rental value during the period that he was excluded from the property until the judicial sale. Is Huff correct? Discuss treating each claim separately.

6. Ellen and Jack Slaney lived in a community property state. Jack was employed as an accountant. Ellen managed the home. When Ellen became pregnant, they decided to build a home. They purchased land upon which to do so. After the baby was born, Jack changed his mind, as he preferred apartment living. Several years later, Ellen inherited money from an uncle. She used the inheritance for the construction of a home on the land. Is the land community property? What about the home? Support your answers.

6

Easements and Other Nonpossessory Rights

Easement

A nonpossessory interest in real property; the right to use another's real estate for a limited purpose.

Most of the ownership interests considered in prior chapters provide the holder with a current or future right of possession. In these forms of ownership, the owner enjoys or will enjoy in the future the right to proceeds from the property and the right to occupy it to the exclusion of all others.

Some people have interests in real estate that are limited to use, not possession. These are referred to as *nonpossessory rights*. One important nonpossessory right is the easement. Easements are used extensively in real estate. For example, they are essential to the operation of utilities. They also provide a legal basis for condominium ownership, scenic and open-space protection and preservation of historic buildings. Indeed, few land developments would be successful without the extensive use of easements. Although easements are interests in real estate, the person who has an easement is never entitled to possession of the land itself, either currently or in the future.

The holder of an easement has a right to use another's land or buildings for a specified purpose. That purpose might be as simple as crossing the land to reach a beach or as complicated as using a portion of a neighbor's building to support one's own. The person who owns an easement has neither title nor estate in the land burdened by it. The easement holder's limited interest is, however, protected against interference by third parties, and the easement cannot be terminated at the will of the owner of the land that it burdens.

Frequently, easements authorize a person to perform a particular act. An example would be a right to use a neighbor's driveway to reach the back portion of a lot. These authorizing easements are called *affirmative easements*. Others, called *negative easements,* prohibit the owner of the land from doing something that ordinarily an owner would be entitled to do. Easements of this nature are not as common. A negative easement might prohibit a landowner from constructing a building taller than a designated height in order to provide adjoining land with an unobstructed view; owners of lots in a development might be restricted from painting their houses a particular color.

Easements are also classified as appurtenant or in gross.

Easement Appurtenant

The right of an owner of a parcel of land to benefit from the use of another's land.

Case Example

Stump and Levit own adjoining parcels of land at Lake Feather. Stump's property borders the lakefront; Levit's does not. Stump has granted to Levit an easement, by deed delivered and accepted, across his lakefront property to the beach. Stump has created an easement appurtenant.

An easement appurtenant involves two parcels of land, usually but not necessarily adjoining. The easement allows the possessor of one parcel to benefit by using the other parcel of land. The parcel that benefits is referred to as the dominant estate or *dominant tenement.* The owner of such easement is also called the *dominant tenant.* The property that is subject to the easement is known as the *servient estate.* Stump's property in the example above is the servient estate; Levit's, the dominant. An easement appurtenant cannot exist without a dominant estate.

If an easement is appurtenant, any conveyance of the dominant estate automatically includes the easement even if the easement is not mentioned in the deed. The easement is said to *run with the land.* When Levit sells his Lake Feather property to Bach, for example, Bach automatically acquires the right to cross Stump's property to get to the beach.

While the easement is automatically transferred with the dominant estate, it cannot be separated and conveyed independently. In the above examples, Levit cannot simply sell or convey to some neighboring landowner the right to cross Stump's property.

Sometimes the dominant tenement or estate is divided into two or more parcels. In such cases, provided that there is not an unreasonable number of new parcels, the courts have held that the existing easement runs with all of the newly created parcels. If, instead of conveying his entire Lake Feather property, Levit had divided the parcel into two lots and sold one of them to Bach, both Bach's land and Levit's land would have the same easement appurtenant across Stump's property. Suppose, however, that Levit had substantially increased the burden on the servient estate by dividing the parcel into six or seven lots. In that case Stump could get a court order preventing the increased use. In some states courts have held that substantially increased use terminates an easement.

In addition to running with the land, an easement appurtenant is irrevocable. It cannot be canceled by the servient owner or terminated by a conveyance of the servient tenement. When the servient tenement is sold or otherwise conveyed, the property remains subject to the existing easement.

Party Wall

A single wall located on the boundary of neighboring properties; it simultaneously serves as a common support for buildings on each of the two parcels.

In many metropolitan areas, adjacent buildings often share a single wall in order to save space and expense. Walls of this type are referred to as *party walls*. Generally, a party wall is constructed on the boundary line between two parcels of real estate, with half of the wall on one side of the line and half on the other. In the United States, the courts uniformly have held that each landowner owns that portion of the wall on his or her land and holds an *easement appurtenant* for support in the other half. If the party wall is entirely on the property of one landowner, the wall belongs to him or her; the other landowner normally has an easement in the wall.

Party walls are commonly constructed as the result of agreement, with each party contributing half of the cost. Because party walls have created many legal problems, these agreements must be drawn carefully. Related problems often involve use of the wall for advertising or purposes other than support.

Case Example

Berk and Ershowsky owned adjoining buildings supported by a party wall. The building on Ershowsky's property was much taller than the building on Berk's, and Ershowsky painted a large advertising sign on that portion of the wall above the top of Berk's building. Berk sued to enjoin use of the wall for that purpose. The injunction was granted, and damages were awarded. The court stated that defendant's use of the wall was improper because it prevented plaintiff from using it for a similar purpose. *Berk-Fink Realty Co. v. Ershowsky, 116 N.Y.S.2d 529 (1952).*

Contributions for *repairs* to party walls can generally be compelled even if the agreement does not cover the issue. The cost of improvements, however, must be borne by the owner who authorizes them. Neither owner can ordinarily remove the wall, but each may remove the remainder of the building without liability if reasonable care is taken.

Easement in Gross

An easement that exists as a personal right apart from a dominant estate.

An easement in gross is not tied to another parcel of land as is the easement appurtenant. Thus an easement in gross exists without a dominant estate.

Although a servient estate does exist, the privileges given by the easement belong to an individual. Stump, for example, might give the telephone company an easement to bury its line along the road bordering his Lake Feather property.

In the past, the easement in gross granted to an individual for a noncommercial purpose was considered a personal right or privilege. Only the person to whom the easement was given could use it. The easement could not be sold, assigned or otherwise transferred, and it terminated upon the death of its holder. For this reason, if the parties wished to have the easement continue or to have any value, they had to tie it to a dominant estate. If this were done, it would be appurtenant and would run with the land.

Traditionally, the courts have treated easements in gross granted for commercial uses differently. Because of their importance to the public, they are considered freely transferable. For example, a utility easement can be sold or assigned by one utility company to another. Although transferable, an easement given for a specific purpose, such as a sewer, cannot be used for another purpose, such as an electric line.

Inasmuch as the easement in gross is not intended to benefit a parcel of land, it is considered a personal right in another's property. Because of this, it is frequently confused with a somewhat similar personal right—a license. Licenses are discussed later in this chapter.

Profit à Prendre

A nonpossessory interest in real property that permits the holder to remove part of the soil or produce of the land.

Most authorities consider the profit, correctly known as the *profit à prendre*, a type of easement. Others distinguish the profit from the easement, as the profit allows the holder to take specified resources from the land, such as soil, produce, wild animals, coal and timber. A person who has an easement does not have this right. Suppose, for example, that Stump grants the Cazenovia Lumber Company the right to take "any and all standing timber" from his property at Lake Feather. Although the lumber company does not have title to the timber, it has a right to remove it from the land. This is a profit.

Few differences exist between easements and profits. Like other types of easements, a profit is an interest in land, but it is nonpossessory and limited to a particular purpose. The holder of the profit has a right of reasonable ingress and egress in order to use the right advantageously. In most states, unless specifically limited by the agreement, the owner of land does not lose the right to use the resource that is the subject of the profit. Like easements, profits may be appurtenant or in gross. The usual profit is in gross. This makes it a personal right not related to a dominant estate. Unlike the noncommercial easement in gross however, the profit à predre is freely transferable.

Creation of Easements

An easement is generally created in one of three ways: by deed, by implication or by prescription.

Creation of an Easement by Deed (Conveyance)

The most common method of creating an easement is by deed. Among other things, a deed describes the land and, in the case of an easement, describes the location of the easement. Deeds are discussed in Chapter 8. Although most courts recognize that an easement can be created by implication or prescription, they have refused to accept the idea that an easement can be created orally. The reason is that an easement is an interest in real estate, and statutes in all states require that an interest in real estate—such as an easement—be created only by a written instrument.

Case Example

Paul Brangs owned a lot at Lake Feather next to his home. Paul wished to sell the lot but was having difficulty because it was narrow. Paul's driveway bordered the lot. To induce Nan Crampton, a prospective purchaser, to buy, Paul agreed to grant her an easement over his driveway to reach the back portion of the property. At the closing, Paul delivered a deed passing title to the lot and a separate deed conveying an easement over his driveway to Crampton.

The granting of an easement may be an independent transaction. Utility companies often seek easements when they need to run their lines over another's property. In many states the law gives these companies the right of eminent domain if the landowner refuses to grant the requested easement. Gas pipelines, sewers and roads are based upon easements from property owners.

Deeds creating easement may do so by express grant or express reservation.

Express Grant

An easement created by an owner expressly granting in a deed a specific right to another to use the property.

Case Example

Morgan owns two adjoining lots at Lake Feather. She sells one to Betterman. Morgan's lot includes a private alley, and Morgan's deed to Betterman *expressly grants* by deed to Betterman the use of this alley.

Express Reservation

The owner of property conveys title to another by deed while specifically reserving an easement for him or herself or a third party within the deed.

Case Example

Morgan sells Betterman the lot with the alley and keeps the other for herself. Morgan's deed includes a clause that *expressly reserves* her right to use the alley.

Provisions expressly reserving an easement are usually found in a deed; some easements are created by will, but easements may also be included in a mortgage or lease.

An easement may also be created by a *contract* between the parties. This is not a preferred method, but if the courts will enforce by specific performance or injunction an agreement in which one party promises to allow another to use land for a limited purpose, an easement has been created. A few courts have even enforced oral contracts that create a limited interest in land. Usually, these involve something like a common driveway or access road.

Creation of an Easement by Implication (Implied Easement)

Courts sometimes presume that the parties intend to create an easement because certain facts exist when real estate is conveyed. The easement supposedly reflects the intention of the parties and is called an *easement by implication*. Courts have traditionally assumed easements by implication in two situations. *In both, the easement results only if one or more parcels are severed from a larger tract under common ownership.*

In the first situation, the effective use of one parcel (the dominant estate) depends upon continuation of a use already being made of the other (the servient parcel). As a result, the easement is sometimes referred to as an *easement implied from prior use*. The other situation occurs if the severed portion is landlocked and cannot be used without passage across the other. This type is generally referred to as an *easement by necessity*. This second example is much less common than the first.

Support for the creation of easements by implication is found in the idea that a sale of real estate includes that which is necessary to use the property beneficially. If a property owner visibly and continuously has used one part of land for the benefit of another, and this use is reasonably necessary for the fair enjoyment of the other, an easement is actually created when either part is sold separately. This is true even when neither party expressly makes any commitment creating the easement. The case that follows involves creation of an easement implied from prior use.

Cash v. Craver
Court of Appeals of North Carolina
302 S.E.2d 819 (1983)

Background: Ted Cash (plaintiff) and Mary Craver (defendant) own adjoining tracts of land. Both tracts formerly had been wholly owned by W.J. Roberts. In 1917, the 170-acre Craver tract was severed from the whole by a deed. The 70-acre Cash tract was severed by deed in 1942. Roberts School Road ran across the Cash and Craver tracts prior to severance. The road had always been used by the plaintiff, the defendant and others as a schoolway and farm-to-market road, as well as a general means of ingress and egress to interior lands for farming and transfer to major highways abutting the tracts.

In 1981, Cash sued for a permanent injunction barring Mary Craver and others from using the portion of Roberts School Road that crosses Cash's property. The trial court refused to grant this injunction, ruling that the defendants owned an easement by implication. Cash appealed.

Decision: The appellate court affirmed.

Judge Hill

Relying on the trial court's findings, which are supported by competent evidence and thus are conclusive, we consider the facts on which the court's order was predicated. We conclude the trial court properly found an easement by implication in favor of defendants and affirm the judgment below.

The trial court found that, while rights to Roberts School Road were never granted defendant by deed, "the use of the roadway in question was and is reasonably necessary to and for the lands now owned by the defendants" for purposes of farming and transporting crops to market. The court concluded an implied easement over Roberts School Road exists in favor of defendants largely because, prior to severance, "the use, which gave way to said easement, had been so long continued, observed and manifest as to show that it was meant to be permanent one and that the easement was and is necessary to the defendant's beneficial enjoyment of the interior lands."

We hold, in affirming its order, that the trial court properly denied plaintiff's motion for a permanent injunction and found an easement by implication in favor of defendants; plaintiff's argument to the contrary is without merit.

It is apparent from Judge Friday's order that he found an easement implied from prior use. The elements of proof for easements implied from prior use are: (1) separation of title; (2) prior use "so long continued and so obvious or manifest as to show that it was meant to be permanent," and (3) that

the claimed easement was "necessary to the beneficial enjoyment of the land."

The plaintiff, who apparently concedes the existence of severance and prior use, contends in support of his first assignment of error that necessity has not been shown. While we need not discuss the sufficiency of the evidence in order to reach our conclusion, *id.*, we briefly consider the question to dispel any confusion regarding the degree of necessity required for an easement implied from prior use.

A showing of strict necessity is not required for an easement arising from prior use. It is sufficient to show such physical conditions and such use as would reasonably lead one to believe that grantor intended grantee should have the right to continue to use the road in the same manner and to the same extent which his grantor had used it, because such use was reasonably necessary to the "fair" . . . "full" . . . "convenient and comfortable" . . . enjoyment of his property.

The party must establish by the greater weight of the evidence that the easement is reasonably necessary to the beneficial enjoyment of the land. The presence of a second or alternate way onto the property is not conclusive proof that an implied easement arising from prior use is unnecessary. Indeed, perhaps of greater significance is evidence that supports the inference that the parties intended the use to continue after severance.

In the present case, the road had been used regularly for farm and travel purposes before severance. That the road has been regularly and similarly used by defendants, their predecessors in title, lessees and neighbors is certainly probative of their right to use the road. While there was evidence of another road on the Craver property by which access to a major abutting highway could be gained, there was also evidence that (1) the road would require major repairs to be passable; and (2) use of the road might necessitate defendants' crossing land belonging to others over which they have no enforceable right-of-way. In any event, the prior, regular and continuous nature of the use and the difficulties inherent in exploiting an alternate way, if one does exist, amply suppoet the findings.

We further hold that the findings of fact and evidence presented at hearing sufficiently identify the easement over plaintiff's land.

At trial, a county tax map of the premises on which witnesses marked location of the easement was used for illustrative purposes. The trial judge found that "the defendant has shown by the greater weight of the evidence an implied easement over the roadway

in question, and the same is hereby established, ordered, and decreed to so be."

The evidence reveals the roadway had been substantially in place for over sixty years. One witness indicated the course of the roadway on the map. Another testified in reference to the map, "The roadway still runs the same course as during the time I was using it. You can see the old roadbed all the way through there . . . . " This witness identified monuments along the right of way and stated that he had attended the Roberts School. It is apparent the Roberts School Road may be readily located on the parties' land, a fact of which the judge obviously took account. We conclude the description to be adequate and find plaintiff's contention to the contrary to be without merit.

Easement Implied from Necessity (Easement of Necessity)

An easement permitting the owner of a landlocked parcel to cross a portion of land of which the easement formerly was a part.

Most courts consider the easement by necessity a form of implied easement. They reason that the parties intended that the grantee of a landlocked parcel have a means of access to his or her land. Without a right to cross the lands of the grantor, the grantee would derive no benefit from the conveyed property. A few courts have taken the position that presumed intent is not necessary. These courts feel that sound public policy dictates that no land should be inaccessible. Whatever theory prevails, two factors *must* be established for an easement to be created by necessity:

1. Both parcels must at one time have been part of a single unit.

2. Necessity must exist—some states require absolute necessity; others only reasonable necessity.

Case Example

O'Mally purchased from Flynn a lot that was part of a larger parcel that abutted on Lake Feather. O'Mally did not think to get an easement to reach the lake across Flynn's remaining land. As a result, he had to drive more than five miles to use Lake Feather. If he sued to establish an easement by necessity, a court probably would reject his suit on the grounds that no real need existed.

Easements Implied from Plats and Maps

Courts sometimes refer to an easement that arises when a document such as a deed refers to a plat or map with designated streets or areas as an easement by implication.

Case Example

Keene purchased several acres on the north side of Lake Feather. He subdivided the property and had prepared a map designating streets, parks and a beach area. Several of the lots were sold and described by reference to the map. Controversy arose between Keene and a number of the lot owners. Keene, as a result, attempted to restrict their use of the beach.

Courts in most states would rule that the lot owners had acquired easements, even if no easements were mentioned in their deeds. When a person buys property described by lot number on a particular map, that person acquires the right to use all common areas designated on the map. A similar rule applies when a deed describes a tract as bounded by a particular street. The purchaser acquires an easement in the street. A majority of states extend the purchaser's interest to include easements in all streets reasonably necessary for access and reasonably beneficial to the lot owner. A few states limit the easement to abutting streets.

Dedication   The granting of real property such as a private street to a governmental unit for public use is known as *dedication*. Litigation involving public easements in streets and other parcels of land is often complicated. Complications arise because almost all states have laws dealing with dedication of land designated on plats and maps for public use. When a plat is recorded, land indicated as set aside for public use becomes public property. In many states the local government automatically acquires an easement in the land. In other states the government acquires title to the designated areas.

A completed dedication solves numerous problems for landowners because the street or area becomes public and open to all users. Complications arise when the property is abandoned by the state. Does it revert back to the former owner, or do those whose interests may be injured now have private easements in the designated parcel? A majority of courts take the position that interests for which the easement was created continue to have a right to use the street.

Creation of an Easement by Prescription

Prescription is the term used to describe the acquisition of an intangible property right such as an easement through wrongful use of another's land for a period of time. The period of time is usually specified by statute and differs markedly from state to state. Although a 20-year period exists in some states, in numerous other states prescriptive rights can be obtained in ten years or less. Several states apply a 15-year period. Basic to the creation of the *easement by prescription* is the idea that an owner who does not take some legal action against wrongful use of his or her property within a certain period of time is *estopped* or legally prohibited from asserting whatever rights he or she had. *Adverse possession*, a similar doctrine that allows actual acquisition of the real estate and all ownership rights, is discussed in Chapter 10.

At one time, the easement by prescription was justified on the presumption of a lost written document. Modern courts reject this presumption, but they continue to approve the prescriptive easement. Most courts apparently feel that land use will be stabilized and controversy reduced if the easement by prescription is recognized.

In addition to use for the designated period, two additional requirements must be met before a prescriptive easement is recognized. The use must be *adverse* to the owner's interest as well as *continuous and uninterrupted*. Over the years, both of these requirements have been the source of substantial litigation; the resulting interpretations have been both confusing and constantly changing.

A use that is adverse to the owner's interest must be open and notorious. It must be obvious enough that an owner reasonably concerned with protecting his or her property rights could readily discover it. A use is not adverse if the user has the owner's permission; no matter how long it continues, it will not ripen into an easement. If, however, the owner who has given permission revokes it, later use becomes adverse. Likewise, if the use made of the land differs from the permitted use, the use becomes adverse.

A difference of opinion exists as to the extent to which the use must be hostile to be considered adverse. In this case *hostile* refers not to ill will but to the wrongdoer's actually claiming the right to use another's property. Many courts take the position that whenever an easement has been used for the prescribed period, the user did so under a claim of right. Under these circumstances, adverse use will be presumed unless the owner introduces sufficient evidence to overcome the presumption. Adverse use has thus been found in cases where the user actually believed that he or she owned the property. A use under these circumstances is clearly hostile to the owner's interest.

In a number of situations, however, use longer than the prescribed time is not presumed to be adverse. These include use by a relative, use of land that is open and unfenced and use by many people, none of whom claim an exclusive right.

Creation of an easement by prescription also requires that the use by the person claiming the easement be *continuous and uninterrupted*.

Case Example

Dryer and Thurston owned adjoining summer properties near Lake Feather. For some time beyond the prescription period, Thurston had used a path across the Dryer property to reach the lake. In 1967, Dryer constructed a fence across his property, blocking the path. When Thurston claimed an easement, Dryer argued that, as the path was used only in the summer, its use was not continuous. The court rejected this argument.

Continuous use does not mean *constant use.* Use is continuous when a person uses the easement as the occasion may demand. A critical factor is that the person claiming the right does not recognize a superior claim or abandon the use during the prescriptive period. In addition, the use does not have to be a continuous use by the same person. Most states allow *tacking*—the process of adding together periods of prescriptive use by a latter user who has succeeded to the interest of earlier users.

Uninterrupted and *continuous* are not synonymous. *Uninterrupted* refers to the failure of the owner of the land to act. For a use to be uninterrupted, the owner must not succeed in causing a discontinuance of the use. The running of the prescriptive period is stopped when a discontinuance is effected.

Prescription and Easements for Light and Air

The energy crisis of the late 1970s has spurred interest in prescriptive easements. Owners considering installation of solar heating units in buildings need assurance of enough sunlight to operate the units effectively. Operation of these units could be hindered if the owner of the adjoining parcel were to build a structure that would block much of the incoming light. Easements for light and air over a neighbor's land are a means of dealing with this problem, but the vast majority of American jurisdictions do not recognize this type of easement except where the parties have entered into an express agreement creating it. English courts have recognized a doctrine of "ancient lights." This doctrine allows an easement for light after a prescriptive period of 27 years, but the "ancient lights" concept has been rejected consistently by American courts.

American courts have also refused to apply the concepts of implied easement or easement by necessity to create easements for light and air. The result is that the potential user of solar energy faces a substantial cost to ensure the required sunlight to operate his or her unit. The prospective user of solar energy must bargain with neighbors to prevent blocking of the necessary light. Few property owners are willing to enter into agreements restricting the height of buildings on their land because this might markedly decrease the land's value.

Termination of Easements

Although an easement is actually a nonpossessory interest, in many respects it resembles a possessory interest. Like an estate, an easement may be created for a specific period, for life or for a designated purpose. Stump, who you recall granted an easement across his property to reach Lake Feather, might have limited the easement to a designated number of years or until a road was constructed to the lake. When an easement is created for a period of time or a designated purpose, it terminates when either the time expires or the purpose is accomplished. Easements for life terminate when the measuring life ends. An easement created by necessity does not last once the necessity disappears. Most easements, however, do not expire automatically. Like the fee simple, they have the potential to last forever.

A number of methods exist for terminating easements that do not expire automatically, including release, merger, estoppel, abandonment, prescription, conveyance and eminent domain. Each of these methods is discussed below.

Release

The holder of an easement appurtenant or in gross may extinguish it by means of a written agreement to give up the right. This document is referred to as a *release*. An oral release alone is ineffective. Except for automatic termination of easements, extinguishing by release is probably the most common method.

Merger

An easement terminates by merger when the holder of either the dominant or servient estate acquires the other. An easement establishes a right to use land owned by someone else. As a result, a person cannot have an easement in his or her own land. The principle applies whether the easement is in gross or appurtenant. Either expires if ownership changes in this way.

Estoppel

A doctrine by which a person is not permitted to deny the consequences of facts that are inconsistent with his or her previous actions or statements.

Two factors must unite before the doctrine of estoppel is applied. First, a person must act in a manner that causes another to believe something. Second, the other person must rely upon the belief and stand to suffer some loss if reliance upon such belief should be barred or penalized.

An easement is extinguished by estoppel if the holder causes the servient estate owner to believe the easement will no longer be used and the servient owner relies upon this belief and suffers some damage as a result. The belief might be the result of a statement made by the easement holder or might be inferred from the person's conduct.

Case Example

Stump asked Bach to use another path a cross Stump's property to reach Lake Feather. Bach orally agreed to do so. Stump then built a tennis court that was partially on the original right-of-way. Bach found the new path inconvenient and demanded to be allowed to use the old recorded right-of-way. Bach's easement had been terminated by estoppel.

Nonuse of an easement for a substantial period of time is generally not a sufficient basis on which to terminate an easement by estoppel.

Abandonment

Although nonuse alone does not extinguish an easement, it may indicate an intention to abandon it. For an easement to terminate by abandonment, the holder's intention to give it up must be clearly established. This can be done if the holder discontinues use, states his or her intention to do so or acts in a manner consistent with discontinued use.

Case Example

Suppose Bach purchases additional land giving him frontage on Lake Feather. He builds a fence along his line abutting on Stump's land and clears a path across the newly acquired tract to Lake Feather. Bach has probably abandoned his easement across Stump's property.

Prescription

An easement may be extinguished after the owner of the servient estate acts in a manner adverse to the easement for the prescriptive period. This use must be open, notorious and uninterrupted. That is, the servient owner must act in a manner similar to that which occurs when an easement is created by prescription.

Case Example

Stump builds a garage on his property, blocking Levit's right-of-way to Lake Feather. Levit does nothing about the garage because he has no interest in reaching Lake Feather. The prescriptive period in the state is seven years. Levit's easement will terminate by prescription unless he asserts his right before the end of the period.

Conveyance

An easement is sometimes terminated when the servient estate is sold to a person who has no knowledge of the easement's existence. When a written easement is not recorded, or when the easement is not visible from indications on the property, the servient estate may become free of the easement. Easements created by necessity and by prescription, however, are not subject to this doctrine.

Eminent Domain

The right of the state to take private property for public use applies to easements. If the state takes the servient estate for a purpose that is not consistent with the continued use of the easement, the dominant tenant loses his or her right to continue this use. This is true even if the dominant estate itself is not taken. The owner of the dominant estate is entitled to compensation for the loss in value of his or her easement right. Similarly, condemnation of the dominant estate may terminate the easement. This occurs if the condemnation and the new use destroy the usefulness of the easement.

License

A personal privilege to enter another's property for a specific purpose.

Case Example

Able and Baker are neighbors. Baker is having work done on his driveway, and Able gives him permission to park in Able's driveway for two weeks. Baker has a license.

Purchasing tickets to attend the theatre or a sporting event and obtaining a camping permit at a state park are other examples of licenses. Although both easements and licenses are intangible, an easement is an interest in land; a license is not. It is a right that is personal to the licensee, the party to whom it was given. Without a license, if Baker had parked in Able's driveway, Baker would be a trespasser.

Licenses may be created orally or may be in writing. Because a license is personal, the licensor may revoke it at any time. If the license was created by a contract, the revocation is a breach of the contract. Nevertheless, although the licensee can collect damages, he or she cannot require the licensor to honor the agreement by specific performance because the licensee has no interest in the realty. If Baker had paid for permission to park in Able's driveway, Able could revoke the license. Although Able would be responsible for money damages because of the revocation, Baker could not get a court order requiring Able to make space available.

Because licenses are personal, they are usually invalidated by the licensee's death and may not be transferred. An exception exists when the individual's license is coupled with an interest in the real estate. Under these circumstances the license is irrevocable. Instead of merely giving Baker permission to park in the driveway, Able sells Baker timber on Able's property. Because of his interest in the timber, Baker has, in addition, an irrevocable privilege to enter and remove it. Baker's license to enter the land is irrevocable because of the interest in the timber. The license is said to be coupled with an interest.

Case Example

Durell had an oil and gas lease and was operating wells on property owned by Freese. A former owner had orally given Durell permission to place equipment on the land to aid in pumping oil. Freese removed this equipment on the grounds that all Durell had was a license that could be revoked at any time. Durell could get an injunction prohibiting Freese from removing the equipment because the license was irrevocable, as it was coupled with the oil and gas lease. *Durell v. Freese, 151 Okla. 150, 3 P.2d 175 (1931).*

Summary

Ownership interests described in previous chapters are those that provide owners with the right of possession—either current or future. Some interests in real estate, however, do not allow the holder the right to posess or occupy the land. An important example of one type that does not is the *easement*, which provides only a right to *use* the property in a limited way, such as for operation of utilities or to gain access to a roadway or beach area. This type of easement is called an affirmative easement. Another type—negative easement—prohibits an owner of land from doing something an owner would normally have the right to do.

Two other types of easements are *easements appurtenant* and *easements in gross*. The former is the right of one owner, the dominant estate, to benefit from use of the land of another, the servient estate. Characteristics of this type of easement are that it runs with the land and it is irrevocable; that is, it cannot be canceled or terminated by sale of the realty. The easement in gross is not attached to the land but is personal to the owner of the land. It cannot be sold or otherwise transferred. However, commercial easements in gross, such as those utility companies enjoy, have been treated by the courts as transferable.

Another nonpossessory interest, generally considered a type of easement, is the *profit à prendre*, which entitles the holder to remove something of value, such as a crop or harvest, from the land. The profit à prendre, like other easements, may be either appurtenant or in gross.

Easements may be created in three ways: by deed (express), by implication or by prescription. One type of easement best created by written agreement is the *party wall*—a wall shared by two neighboring buildings. Agreements relating to party walls ought to be carefully drawn by an attorney.

Easements by implication have traditionally been upheld by the courts in two kinds of situations. First, effective use of the dominant estate must depend on the continuation of the easement. In the second case, the land cannot be used at all without the easement, as, for example, in a landlocked parcel (*easement implied from necessity*). The existence of easements is a very important factor to check when selling or listing a property. Discovery of an easement would avoid complicated litigation resulting from the absence of written documents relating to the easement.

Easements may also be created by prescription over a period of time, usually specified by statute. This type of easement depends upon the continuous, open and adverse use of an easement, such as a roadway, without interruption by the owner of the servient estate.

Although easements have the potential to last forever, they may be terminated legally in a variety of ways.

A *license*, which grants permission only to enter another's land for a specific purpose, is sometimes confused with the profit à prendre. Licenses, which may be revoked by the grantor at any time, expire upon the grantor's death.

Review and Discussion Questions

1. Compare and contrast an *easement appurtenant* and an *easement in gross*.

2. Explain the factors that must exist for an easement to be created by prescription.

3. What is a license? How does it differ from an easement?

4. What is a profit? How does it differ from an easement? In what ways is it similar?

5. Is an easement an estate? Support your answer.

6. Is an easement property? Support your answer.

Case Problems

1. Hamilton and Tucker owned adjoining farms. For more than 40 years, Mrs. Tucker, her predecessors in title, her agents and her employees had reached her farm by a roadway across the Hamilton farm.

   At one time, the two farms had been a single unit, but it had been divided in 1884 by Mrs. Tucker's grandfather. He had given approximately 200 acres to each of his two sons. The Hamiltons had purchased their farm in 1972 from the widow of one of the sons.

   Upon purchasing the farm, the Hamiltons blocked the roadway to the Tucker place. Mrs. Tucker seeks an injunction to restrain this action. Will she succeed? Discuss. *McIlroy v. Hamilton, 539 S.W.2d 669 (Mo. Ct. App. 1976).*

2. Anderson owned and operated a small motel in a resort area. One of the area's principal attractions was a well-known golf course. Although it was difficult to reach the clubhouse by automobile from the motel, the clubhouse was within easy walking distance.

   In order to provide easy access to the clubhouse for his guests, Anderson acquired an easement over a neighbor's land "for use as a connecting walk by guests of the Anderson Motel." Three years later Anderson sold the motel to a national franchise, which doubled the room capacity. The neighbor attempted to stop motel guests from crossing the land, and the new owner sought an injunction prohibiting interference. Would the new owner be successful? Present arguments for both the neighbor and the new owner.

3. Soergel owned lot A. He granted Smith, who owned lot B directly to the west of lot A, a ten-foot-wide easement for installation of a sewer line. Smith sold lot B to Preston, who owned lot C directly to the west of lot B. Preston began to install a sewer line from his house on lot C across lots B and A. Soergel sought an injunction prohibiting Preston from constructing the sewer line. Was Soergel successful? Support your answer. *Soergel v. Preston, 367 N.W.2d 366 (Mich. Ct. App. 1985).*

4. Devlin leased a restaurant in a shopping center. The owner of the shopping center did not object when Devlin erected a sign in the parking lot advertising the restaurant. When the shopping center was sold, the new owner demanded that the sign be removed. (a) If Devlin refused to remove it, could the new owner do so legally? (b) Would the result be the same if Devlin had permission from the former owner to erect the sign? Discuss. *Devlin v. The Phoenix, Inc., 471 So.2d 93 (Fla Dist. Ct. App. 1985).*

5. Todd operated a business that provided laundry machines for use in apartments. In 1979, Todd entered into an agreement with Lake Feather

Realty giving him the exclusive right to install and maintain laundry equipment in an apartment owned by Lake Feather Realty. The contract was for a ten-year period and purported to be binding "on the heirs, successors and assigns" of the parties.

When the apartment was sold in 1981, the new owner demanded that Todd remove the machines. Todd sought a permanent injunction to prevent the removal of the machines, arguing that the contract gave him an easement to maintain them. What do you think was the result? Why?

6. Elaine Owens owned property in Lake Feather Village. For 25 to 30 years, during the summer, people had used the property as a short cut to reach the beach. In the spring and fall, the property was used by children as a baseball diamond or a football field.

    When Owens built a fence around the property, Fink, an abutting owner, sued to prevent the area from being blocked. Would Fink be successful? Support your answer.

7

Liens Against Title

Lien

A claim against another's property securing either payment of a debt or fulfillment of some other monetary charge or obligation.

Liens are important in all spheres of commercial law. They take many forms and are subject to extensive variations from state to state. Despite these differences, the underlying concept of all liens is much the same. The purpose is to provide security for a debt obligation or duty. A lien cannot exist in the absence of a financial claim against another person.

Case Example

Revisi, a contractor, obtained a long-term lease on land outside of Utica, New York, for construction of a small warehouse. Wilson Building Supply furnished all materials for the project. When Revisi did not pay his bills, amounting to $275,000, Wilson obtained a material supplier's lien (mechanic's lien) on the building.

Shortly thereafter, the state acquired Wilson's lumberyard as part of a slum clearance project. This left the company without facilities, and it demanded possession of Revisi's building on the basis of the lien.

Although courts sometimes refer to liens as property, a lien is not a property right in the thing itself. The lienholder has neither title nor the rights of a titleholder. His or her only right is to have a monetary obligation satisfied out of proceeds from the sale of the property. A lien thus differs from an estate, which is the right to possess realty, or an easement, which is the right to use realty. No court would award Wilson Building Supply possession of Revisi's warehouse on the basis of the material supplier's lien, even if the lien exceeded the value of the property, because a lien does not give the holder of the lien title or the right to possession or use.

Because the fundamental nature of a lien is security, interests in real estate are frequently the subject of liens. Land and buildings provide excellent security. They are valuable, their value is relatively stable and they are difficult, if not impossible, to move or conceal. Further, in the United States, land is subject to a system of recording that gives constructive notice of existence of any liens against a parcel of land to anyone who deals with that parcel. For example, Wilson Building Supply, in obtaining its lien, had to follow a procedure designed to notify other creditors of Revisi of its claim against the property by filing its mechanic's lien.

Types of Liens

Liens are either voluntary or involuntary. Voluntary liens are those the owner places against his or her land, usually to secure repayment of long-term debt. Funds are advanced to the property owner, who agrees to repay the debt and provide a lien on the property as security. In many states a real estate mortgage is regarded as a lien. Real estate mortgages are discussed extensively in Chapters 18, 19 and 20. A number of involuntary liens are also important to real estate practitioners. Involuntary liens, discussed in this chapter, are created by law to protect interests of persons who have valid monetary claims against the owner of real property. The claim might arise out of a judgment, sale or furnishing of a service of some kind. Involuntary liens are also created to aid government in the collection of taxes and special assessments.

Liens are also classified as *general* or *specific*. Specific liens apply to a specific parcel of realty only. The mechanic's lien, which is analyzed initially in this chapter, is an example. Other specific liens considered in the chapter are the vendor's lien and the property tax lien. A general lien, in a real estate context, is a lien against all the realty of a person in a given jurisdiction. Thus, a judgment against Jones in a lawsuit in Washington County imposes a lien against *all* of his realty in that county, not just against one or more specific parcels owned by him in Washington County. This type of general lien is known as a *judgment lien*. The federal tax lien, also discussed in the chapter, is a general lien.

Mechanic's Lien

The right of one who renders services or supplies materials in connection with the improvement of real property to seek a judicial sale of the realty to satisfy unpaid claims.

By statute in most states, contractors and suppliers who work on real estate or furnish material for such work are entitled to a lien if they are not paid. The lien provides them with a means of compelling payment because it allows the property to be sold to satisfy the claims. Generally, the lien attaches to both buildings and the land, and the work must have been done at the owner's request. The mechanic's lien, also known as a *material supplier's lien* or *contractor's lien*, is not the only action an unpaid supplier or contractor may take. By filing the lien, the supplier or contractor does not lose the right to recover on the contract.

Case Example

Eldon Horn and his wife purchased a lot. Shortly thereafter they contracted with Jamco Builders for the construction of a home on the lot. Jamco subcontracted some of the work to Mid-American Homes. Mid-American, as required by law, notified the Horns of its right to place a lien against the real estate. Jamco did not pay for the subcontracted work, and Mid-American filed a mechanic's lien against the property. This established its right to petition a court to have the property sold and the proceeds applied against the debt.

Valid reasons exist for granting contractors and suppliers a special lien against real property. In collecting for services and materials, they are at a disadvantage when compared with credit sellers of personal property. When not paid, the seller of personal property, who has a valid security agreement, can usually repossess the item. This remedy does not exist for suppliers whose materials have been incorporated into a structure. Similarly, a contractor or laborer cannot get back time and effort expended on the job. Except for the mechanic's lien, such claimants are limited to suing for the contract price. Litigation such as this is time-consuming and expensive, and the winning plaintiff may have difficulty collecting the judgment. The lien also has nuisance value in that, until the debt is paid, a purchaser takes title subject to the lien. The mechanic's lien laws thus aid many small entrepreneurs who might be reluctant or financially unable to take judicial action to collect an unpaid claim.

Mechanic's lien laws also encourage economic activity. Because a substantial amount of construction is done on credit, these laws increase security for the contractors, subcontractors and suppliers who have invested their capital. The additional security induces financial institutions to provide more credit for additional projects in the construction industry.

Mechanic's lien laws did not exist at common law. They are the result of 19th-century state legislation that was necessary to protect the contractors, laborers and suppliers who were crucial to the building of American cities.

Every state in the United States now has some type of mechanic's lien legislation. Since this legislation is often merely the ad hoc response to problems of a particular area and time, it is extremely varied and often complicated. In those jurisdictions that have a basic mechanic's lien statute, political pressures may lead to substantial amendments, which increase variability and add further complications. Any person in real estate working with transactions involving mechanic's lien laws must be particularly concerned with local statutes on the subject. These statutes are usually quite technical, and their requirements must be followed strictly for the lien to be valid.

Claimants

Mechanic's lien statutes generally include several categories of potential claimants. A typical statute might name mechanics, material suppliers, contractors, subcontractors, lessors of equipment, architects, engineers, surveyors and teamsters. In addition, a statute usually includes a catchall provision that allows anyone to claim a mechanic's lien who has performed labor upon or supplied materials to improve property. Courts, too, have interpreted such statutes in a manner that extends the classes of persons who may claim mechanic's liens for making improvements to realty.

Case Example

Reet Development was constructing a large office building. It hired Francis Trucking Company to deliver materials to the site and Payne to serve as watchman. When Francis and Payne were not paid, they filed mechanic's liens. Reet argued that they were not entitled to liens, as their labor did not improve the premises. Although courts in numerous states would disagree, it is reasonable to hold that the services improved the premises, as they were necessary for ultimate completion of the job. These services could thus be the basis for a mechanic's lien.

Ownership Interest

Mechanic's lien laws apply to various ownership interests in real property. Absolute ownership is not required, but the lien ordinarily attaches only to the interest of the party ordering the work. Usually when the term *owner* is used in a statute, that term has been defined broadly. In addition to persons having fee simple title, other owners include those who have life estates, persons with a remainder and tenants under lease. As the following case example illustrates, in some situations an owner's interest may be subject to a mechanic's lien even though the owner did not contract for the improvements.

Case Example

Balbo purchased property from Sanchez on a land installment contract. The contract was recorded. Balbo commenced to build on the property, serving as his own contractor. Balbo contracted with American Wallboard to put in the walls. American purchased the necessary wallboard from Tri-City Building. Although Balbo paid American, American did not pay Tri-City. When the wallboard was delivered, Tri-City notified Sanchez of delivery, although Sanchez had not ordered the material. Most courts would hold that this notice was sufficient to establish mechanic's lien rights against Sanchez inasmuch as Sanchez had ownership rights.

In a land installment contract (see Chapter 20), the buyer pays the purchase price on an installment basis. The owner/seller—Sanchez in the example above—retains title until the purchase price is paid.

In most states, statutes allow a noncontracting owner to block a lien against his or her interest by posting a *notice of nonresponsibility*. In general, these statutes require the owner to post a written notice indicating that he or she will not be responsible for the improvements. The notice must be in some conspicuous place on the land and be posted within a short time after the owner finds out about the work being done. Depending on the state, the time ranges from three to ten days.

Type of Work

The statutes that establish mechanic's liens use various general terms to describe the type of work for which a lien may be obtained. Frequently, the terms are defined in the statutes themselves. When they are not defined by statute, the courts as a rule have tended to interpret these general terms broadly.

A number of statutes use the term *improvement* or *improvements*. This term has been defined to include demolition, erection, alterations or repairs. Some courts have refused to allow mechanic's liens for tearing down a building unless the term *demolition* is included in the statutory definition or is necessary for improvement. Terms such as *building, structure* and *appurtenance* usually have also been defined broadly when included in mechanic's lien laws. Mechanic's lien laws in a number of states use *improvements* as a synonym for *building* or *structure*, not to indicate the type of work for which a lien may be granted.

Consent

In order for property to be subject to a mechanic's lien, most states require that improvements be made with the consent and knowledge or at the request of the owner. A contract is the basis for a mechanic's lien in most states, but a contract between an owner and a person seeking a lien is not required. As a result, numerous circumstances exist in which a lien can attach even when the owner has not personally entered into a contract with the lienor.

Consent of the owner may be express or implied. One example of implied consent is when a lease provision requires a tenant to make alterations or specific improvements. If a lease contains this type of provision, the lessor's interest is subject to a lien in most jurisdictions even if the modifications are made at the tenant's expense. On the other hand, a lease that contains the usual covenant that the tenant maintain or repair the premises and nothing more does not establish implied consent. In addition, except in states that have implied consent based on knowledge, mere knowledge by a lessor that improvements are being made is not sufficient to establish a lien against the lessor's interest.

Consent of the owner may be given by an agent. Some states have, by legislation, established classes of persons as statutory agents for the owner. These people have the implied authority to consent in the owner's behalf. The statutory agents are contractors, subcontractors, architects, builders and any others who are in charge of work. An artisan or material supplier dealing with one of these persons is entitled to a lien, although a supplier is ordinarily not considered an agent of the owner for the purpose of passing on lien rights.

Case Example
Manner Electric Company entered into a contract to supply all electrical equipment for a new building. Manner then contracted with Ace Wire to furnish the necessary wire. Ace delivered the wire as per the agreement. When Manner became bankrupt without paying Ace's bill, Ace filed for a material supplier's lien. In most states Ace would not be able to acquire a lien.

Permanency
The concept that work or materials to be lienable must result in a *permanent benefit* underlies most mechanic's lien laws. *Permanent* refers to material and labor that become part of the premises. Permanent labor and materials are distinguished from those that are part of the contractor's plant or equipment in the project, which are not lienable.

Case Example
ABC Plumbing had a contract to furnish plumbing fixtures to a developer. The contract required delivery of fixtures to the individual units. In order to protect its delivery truck and to store fixtures, the company built a small storage shed at the site. When the company was not paid, it filed a notice of lien that included $1,500, the cost of the structure. A court would probably hold that this amount did not become a lien against the premises since the benefit was not permanent.

Permanent is construed broadly to last as long as the item remains part of the premises. As a result, many improvements of short duration as well as items detached from the structure may be the basis for a mechanic's lien. This includes work done to protect a permanent installation or even a structure not intended to be permanent, but designed to be removed at a future time. Electrical signs, telephones and telephone equipment have been the basis for mechanic's liens. Items such as tables and benches have been considered permanent when necessary to the normal use of a structure and furnished for this use. Services such as mowing, trimming and spraying plants as well as weeding and raking lawns are not permanent improvements.

Perfection of Lien
The performance of those steps required by statute to sell real property under mechanic's lien laws.

The time periods and procedures involved in and required for perfecting a mechanic's lien vary appreciably from state to state. They also frequently vary within the same state for different categories of claimants as well as for different types of benefits conferred. For example, in a number of states the steps that a subcontractor must take to perfect a lien differ from those the prime contractor must follow. Material suppliers usually have to follow procedures different from those required of the artisan supplying labor. Despite these and other differences, two almost universal requirements for perfecting a mechanic's lien are notice to the owner and the filing of a mechanic's lien claim in the county or city land records.

Notice   Statutes generally require a lien claimant to notify the owner before filing a lien. In most states, a defective notice or failure to provide the owner with notice invalidates a lien. The purpose of this requirement is to warn the owner not to pay a contractor against whom outstanding claims exist in favor of laborers, subcontractors or material suppliers. Knowing of the existence of these claims, the owner may protect himself or herself against paying twice by retaining funds due to the contractor until the lien claimant is paid.

Notice to the owner ordinarily includes the following information: the name and address of the lienor, the name of the person with whom the lienor contracted if not the owner, the labor performed or material furnished, dates when the work was started and completed, the balance due and a description of the property and the owner's interest. Most states require the notice to be in writing; some require an affidavit as to the amounts due. Usually the statute gives the potential lienor a limited time period of 20, 30 or sometimes 60 days after the work is completed to notify the owner of the claim.

Some categories of claimants are excused by statute from giving a preliminary notice. An example would be a laborer working for a daily wage. The reason for this exception is to protect these people from losing the lien right because of a technicality of which they might not be aware. In a number of states, preliminary notice is necessary only if the lien claimant did not deal directly with the owner. In jurisdictions following this rule a prime contractor would not be required to give notice, but a subcontractor would. A few states permit notice to the owner after the lien has been filed.

Filing   A second critical point in perfecting a lien is filing for record. Doing the work or furnishing the materials merely gives the claimant a right to acquire a lien. In some states this right is referred to as an *inchoate lien*. Usually the statute requires that the claimant file a verified statement of the claim. This statement ordinarily includes a brief explanation of the contract, the balance due and a description of the property as well as the names and addresses of the parties.

A filed lien, like a recorded deed or mortgage, is part of the public record. The act of recording ensures that third parties dealing with the property will have knowledge of claims against it if they search the record. In a number of jurisdictions, filing is unnecessary if the mechanic sues for the sum owed. These states reason that the suit provides sufficient notice of claims against the property.

Most jurisdictions require that the verified statement, sometimes referred to as the *lien claim* or *affidavit*, be filed within a specified time after work is completed. This period varies, but 30, 60 and 90 days is common. In *Daniels v. Deseret Federal Savings and Loan*, a state court is asked to determine if a mechanic's lien was filed in a timely manner. Additionally, the court considers if the state's mechanic's lien statute applies to the interest the plaintiff is trying to protect.

Daniels v. Deseret Federal Savings and Loan
Court of Appeals of Utah
771 P.2d 1100 (1989)

Background: In 1980, Daniels (plaintiff) invested $28,000 in the development of a condominium in Park City, Utah. He was to receive $80,000 for his share in the profits from the sale of condominium units. Additionally, he was hired to serve as general contractor for the project at $15,000.

The condominium was completed in July 1981, and Daniels was paid the $15,000, but he did not receive the $80,000. As a result, Daniels decided to file a mechanic's lien, but at the request of the owners who were trying to refinance, he did not immediately do so. Consequently, he did not file within 100 days of completion as required by state law.

On December 1, 1981, several water pipes in the condominium froze and Daniels was called in to make repairs. On February 3, 1982, he filed a notice of lien against the project for his $80,000. He listed December 1, 1981, as the last day labor had been performed. Desert Federal Savings and Loan, the construction mortgagee, and CEN Corporation, an owner, moved for a summary judgment to declare Daniels' lien void. The trial court granted summary judgment and Daniels appealed.

Decision: The appellate court affirmed.

Judge Davidson

Daniels raised two issues on appeal: Did the trial court err when it found Daniels' work on December 1, 1981, did not extend the time limit for filing a notice to hold and claim a lien? Did the trial court err when it held Desert is not estopped from raising the affirmative defense that the mechanic's lien was not timely filed?

Time of Filing—Extension: A general contractor must record a mechanic's lien within 100 days after completion of the contract. Completion is marked by the end of a related series of tasks required for substantial completion of the contract. "Trivial or minor adjustments made casually or long after the main work is completed cannot be used to tie on to as the last labor done or materials furnished."

Well over 100 days after completion of the contract, Daniels spent a day inspecting the damage from the frozen water pipes and calling subcontractors in order to make repairs. Daniels contends that this extends the period for filing his mechanic's lien. However, the trial court found:

> The work the owners wanted done in December of 1981 was not a continuation of the earlier project, but merely repairs. If repairs to a completed project could be construed as extending the time in which a mechanic's lien could be filed, mechanic's [sic] liens could be filed many years after a project had been completed.

We agree with the trial court's findings. In order to extend the time for filing his mechanic's lien, the work Daniels did in December 1981 would have to substantially relate to the performance of the contract. "The work done or material furnished must be something substantial in connection with the performance of the contract and this is not satisfied be trivialities which may be used as a pretext to extend the lien period." . . . (T)he inspection and repairs undertaken by Daniels in December 1981 were not services used in the construction, alteration, or improvement of the building, nor did the services add directly to the value of the property. Therefore, the inspection cannot extend the time period for filing notice of a mechanic's lien.

Daniels contends that Park Avenue and subsequent owners are estopped from pleading untimely filing of the notice of the lien as an affirmative defense because he was induced by the project owners not to file a lien within the requisite 100 day filing period. Deseret contends that it had no knowledge of the agreement between Park Avenue and Daniels and that it was not in privity with Daniels. Therefore, Deseret argues, estoppel cannot be asserted against it.

Services and Materials Furnished: We do not need to reach the merits of the estoppel argument. Even if Daniels had filed a timely notice for the $80,000 owing to him for "profit and overhead," this amount was not owed to him for the value of the services he rendered or for materials furnished but from his ownership in Park Avenue as a limited partner. Utah Code provides that contractors, and laborers who furnish material,

provide services, or bestow labor for the construction, alteration, or improvement of a building or structure shall have a lien upon the property for the value of the services and material provided. The value of the services provided by Daniels in his performance as general contractor, was approximately $15,000 for which he was compensated.

The purpose of the mechanic's lien law "is to preclude landowners from having their lands improved by others, without becoming personally responsible for the reasonable value of materials and labor." In order to ascertain when an improvement has been made upon the land, for purposes of determining whether notice of a mechanic's lien can validly be filed, it is necessary that "there be an annexation to the land, or to some part of the realiy; or a fixture appurtenant to it, and this must have been done with the intention of making it a permanent part thereof.

Daniels' claim is for the profits he was entitled to as an investor and not for any services or materials that he provided as a contractor. The profits a person is entitled to as the result of an investment do not constitute improvements to the realty nor do they fall within the statutory meaning of services or materials as contemplated in the mechanic's lien law statutes. Accordingly, Daniels' notice to hold and claim a lien, for the profits allegedly owing to him is invalid. Therefore, the summary judgment in favor of Deseret is affirmed.

Some states attempt to solve the problem of determining when completion has occurred by allowing the owner to file a notice of completion. This notice is the equivalent of completion and begins the time period within which the lien claim must be filed.

When a premature notice of completion is filed, the time period for filing commences from the date of actual completion. If the parties disagree as to whether there was actually "substantial completion" when the notice of completion was filed, litigation similar to that in the previous case is the only means of settling the dispute.

Although proper filing of a lien is necessary for its validity, the lien is often effective from an earlier date. In many states the properly filed lien reverts back to the time construction began. In these states the lienholder's claim thus acquires priority over claims against the premises recorded or filed before the lien claim was filed but after the work was begun.

Case Example

Scarlet and Grey Construction Company contracted to build a stable for Perry. Work began on November 10. On December 5, before the job was completed, Perry executed a mortgage on the property in favor of Betz. The stable was finished on December 12, but a portion of the contract price was not paid. Scarlet and Grey filed a lien against the property on January 3. In many states this lien would have priority over Betz's mortgage because the lien reverts back to November 10, the day work began.

In a few states, the lien attaches as of the time the original contract was made. In others, the lien attaches from the date materials were first furnished at the site.

Termination

Mechanics' liens may be extinguished in numerous ways. Probably the most common is by payment of the obligation upon which the lien is based. Other procedures are also widely used.

Ordinarily, discharging a debt terminates existing liens securing the debt and precludes a future lien based on the same debt. In some jurisdictions, however, mechanic's lien rights of subcontractors and suppliers survive payment to a principal contractor. In these states, the subcontractors may obtain liens for the full value of their respective claims *even if the principal contractor has been paid*. This practice is known as the *Pennsylvania Rule*. In states following this rule, the subcontractor's lien is considered direct, not a right that derives from the general contractor. These jurisdictions consider the contractor the owner's agent; thus, through an agent, the subcontractor is deemed to have contracted directly with the owner. When a state has a mechanic's lien statute of this type, the owner may be required to pay twice.

Case Example

Randolph Estates contracted with the ABC Pool Company for construction of a $28,000 pool. The pool was to serve residents of an apartment complex being constructed by Randolph Estates. ABC subcontracted excavation and grading to Montefresco Company for $1,500. Upon completion of the pool, Randolph paid ABC as per the contract. When ABC went bankrupt, Montefresco filed a mechanic's lien against the premises. In states following the Pennsylvania Rule, Randolph would have to pay the $1,500 again, this time to Montefresco, in order to extinguish the lien.

Probably the majority of states follow what is called the *New York Rule*. In these jurisdictions, a subcontractor's lien is limited to the amount still owed the general contractor at the time the lien is filed. The owner is not compelled to pay more than the contract price, inasmuch as any subcontractor's lien derives from the principal contractor. The result is that the owner may pay the principal contractor as work progresses without fear of a subcontractor's lien for the same work.

Many jurisdictions permit the owner to release an existing lien not only by paying the claim it represents, but by giving a bond or paying cash into court to cover potential claims by contractors and/or subcontractors and artisans. If the claim is disputed, this process protects both the owner and the claimant. The owner is protected because the funds are controlled by the court; the claimant is protected because monies are available to pay any valid claim. This procedure is also valuable to the owner since the property is not tied up during litigation by being subject to a filed mechanic's lien.

Liens may also terminate by *waiver*. The waiver may be made before the improvement, as part of the contract, as a *"no-lien"* provision. This provision must be clear and unambiguous. Any doubts will be resolved against the waiver. Some state courts have held that a waiver by a principal contractor is also applicable to subcontractors claiming through him or her. In other states a subcontractor is bound by this type of provision only if he or she had actual knowledge of or expressly consented to the contractor's waiver.

Mechanics' liens are also extinguished by the lienor's *failure to foreclose* within a reasonable time. This period is often short. Six months and a year are common, although in some states a two-year limitation is applicable. A number of jurisdictions shorten the time further by permitting the owner to demand that the lienholder commence an action to foreclose the lien. Failure of the lienor to begin foreclosure proceedings within the allowed time results in forfeiture of the lien. The purpose of these statutory provisions is to eliminate the cloud on the title resulting from a properly filed mechanic's lien claim.

Judgment Lien

A lien that automatically attaches to real property of a defendant when a plaintiff wins a judgment in the jurisdiction in which the property is located.

Case Example

Justin Lane purchased a lot for $10,000. Lane was the defendant in a tort case, and a judgment was entered against him for $8,500. Lane refused to pay the judgment as he believed it to be unfair. When Lane attempted to sell the lot, the purchaser's attorney refused to certify that the title was marketable because of a judgment lien resulting from the tort case.

Collecting a money judgment in a civil case is often almost as difficult as winning it. In most instances the losing defendant does not rush up to the winning plaintiff with check in hand, but is very reluctant to pay. If the judicial process by which the money judgments are awarded is to be respected, the law must assist plaintiffs in collecting their judgment.

The ultimate method is the forced sale of enough of defendant's property, real and personal, to cover the judgment. Although some property may be exempt by statute, the nonexempt property of a defendant may be seized and sold to satisfy the judgment. This is known as an *execution* or a *levy of execution*. It is accomplished by a writ from the court rendering the judgment. The writ authorizes a court officer, usually the sheriff, to sell the property.

A judgment lien is an involuntary lien attaching to real property when a judgment is obtained against the owner. The lien establishes the claim of the *judgment creditor* against the defendant's real estate in the jurisdiction of the court that awarded the judgment and helps to ensure that the plaintiff will eventually collect the judgment. While the lien exists, a sale or mortgage of the property is subject to the judgment creditor's interest. As a result, the defendant often pays the judgment to free the property from the judgment creditor's lien. If the judgment is not paid, the real estate can be levied against and sold. Some states use a process similar to that used to foreclose a mortgage.

A judgment creditor can also obtain a lien against a defendant's personal property. Personal property, unlike real estate, must be levied against by a court order before being subject to a lien. This type of lien is generally referred to as an *execution lien*. In most states the execution lien and judgment lien are treated in a similar manner. Ordinarily, the personal property must be used to satisfy the judgment before the real property becomes available for that purpose.

Judgment liens did not exist at common law. They are created by statute, and their existence and operation depend upon the statutory provisions establishing them. Not all states have provided the judgment creditor with this method of enforcing his or her judgment. If no judgment lien statute exists in a state, a lien against real property, like one against personal property, arises only when proper execution and levy have occurred.

A judgment lien is a general lien. It applies to all real estate owned by the defendant in the county where the judgment was rendered. The lien may be made specific by levy of execution. Most states have a simple procedure for extending the lien to other real estate owned by the defendant within the state. This is done by filing a transcript of the judgment in other counties in which the judgment debtor has real property. Federal statutes provide that a judgment of a United States district court sitting in a state having a judgment lien statute is a lien to the same extent as the judgments of a state court of general jurisdiction.

Requirements

The time at which a judgment lien attaches depends upon state statute. This time is important because it determines the conflicting claims of creditors. In a few states the lien commences when the judgment is rendered; however, most state statutes require that the judgment be made part of the public record in some manner before the lien is created. This is a reasonable requirement. Official records should be available to third parties dealing with a judgment debtor so that they have a source whereby they can determine potential problems. A common requirement for establishing general notice of the judgment is that it must be filed, docketed (officially listed) and indexed before a lien based upon it is effective. Some states require only that the judgment be filed and docketed.

In a few states legislation provides that when a judgment is indexed the lien reverts to some earlier date. Sometimes this is the first day of the court term during which the judgment was rendered; more often it is the day the judgment was rendered. The *doctrine of relation back* means that the judgment lien might be superior to interests created before the lien became part of the public record.

Not all judgments rendered create liens. Of course, it is critical that the judgment be rendered validly by a court having jurisdiction. Another basic requirement is that the judgment be final. An interlocutory judgment or one that settles some intermediate plea or motion is not final and cannot give rise to a judgment lien. In addition, the judgment must be for a specific sum of money. In most states liens are based upon the judgments of any court of record. Frequently, however, state statutes require judgments of inferior courts to be filed with the statewide court of original jurisdiction before becoming a lien.

Legal Effect

As a general rule, liens and other interests in realty rank in the order in which they are created. This is the principle of "first in time, first in right." As a result of this principle, judgment liens have important consequences for two classes of people: buyers from a judgment debtor and other creditors of the judgment debtor.

If a judgment lien has been perfected before the execution of a contract for the sale of realty, the buyer takes the real property subject to the lien. Because the real property is subject to a judgment lien, the real property may be sold by the sheriff to satisfy the judgment debt. As the lien existed at the time the buyer obtained his or her interest, the buyer will lose the real property unless the debt is paid off. On the other hand, in the absence of fraud, if a buyer and seller have contracted for the sale of land and the contract has been recorded, the buyer's interest will not be defeated by a later judgment against the seller even if the contract has not been performed.

Creditors of a judgment debtor are also affected by a judgment lien. A valid judgment lien has priority over the claims of creditors who have not established a security interest in the debtor's real property prior to the judgment. The reason is that the judgment lien was created first. Prospective creditors also consider real property less valuable as security to the extent of judgment liens against it. If a loan is made and the debtor defaults, when the property is sold any judgment is satisfied out of the proceeds before the secured creditor's claim is paid.

Termination

In most instances, statutes creating the judgment lien also establish the lien's duration. Usually the period is short. Periods of three to five years are common. In only a few states are judgment liens enforceable for more than ten years from their commencement. A few states extend the life of a judgment lien if the plaintiff obtains a levy of execution based on the lien.

In many states the period of time in which a suit on a judgment may be initiated is longer than the period during which a judgment lien may be enforced. If this is the case, the judgment lien terminates but the judgment remains outstanding.

Both the common law and a number of states by statute provide for the revival or renewal of expired judgment liens. In order to revive a judgment lien, the judgment itself must still be enforceable. Any liens that attach during the period in which the judgment lien was dormant and before its revival take precedence over the revived lien.

Notice of Lis Pendens

A recorded document that gives constructive notice that an action has been filed that might affect the title or possession of a specified parcel of real estate.

At common law a general principle existed that all persons were bound to take notice of suits affecting title to property. This principle was known as the doctrine of *lis pendens*, or "suit pending." A person acquiring an interest in real estate that was the subject of litigation, such as a suit to foreclose a mortgage, enforce a lien or set aside a deed, took the interest subject to any judgment that might later be rendered in the lawsuit. This doctrine was harsh because it was often difficult to determine if the property was the subject of litigation.

Because of the harshness of the common law doctrine, most states by statute provide for the filing of a notice of lis pendens in the county in which the property that is the subject of litigation is located. If the plaintiff does not file this notice, a person acquiring an interest in the real estate who has no actual knowledge of the litigation will not be subject to any judgment that might be awarded as a result of the lawsuit.

A notice of lis pendens is not a lien, but in many ways it has the effect of a lien, for once such a notice has been filed, the title to the real estate is encumbered. As a result, the title is unmarketable until litigation is settled or the notice of lis pendens vacated.

Attachment

The act of seizing a defendant's property by legal process, to be held by the court to ensure satisfaction of any judgment that might be awarded.

In some cases, after winning a judgment, the plaintiff discovers that the defendant has disposed of all assets that might be used to satisfy the judgment debt. In order to prevent the defendant from doing this, statutes in many states allow a plaintiff to seize property of the defendant by judicial order at the commencement of litigation. The property is held in the custody of the court as security for any judgment that the plaintiff might win.

The circumstances under which a plaintiff is entitled to attach defendant's property are regulated in detail by the various state statutes. Requirements for obtaining an attachment order usually are strict. In general, the statutes allow attachment only if the plaintiff is seeking money damages. In a number of states the monetary amount of the plaintiff's claim must be fixed or undisputed and only its validity contested.

A minority of states have unlimited attachment statutes. In these states the plaintiff is permitted to attach defendant's property in actions for money damages without showing special circumstances. Most states, however, require the plaintiff to show that some special reason exists to attach defendant's property. Permissible reasons are indicated by the state statute establishing the attachment remedy.

Typical state statutes allow attachment of the property of nonresident defendants. They also allow attachment of property that might easily be concealed or where facts indicate that the defendant might leave the jurisdiction. Ordinary business or pleasure trips outside of the state, openly made, are not within the contemplation of the statute as grounds for attachment. In many jurisdictions the fact that a defendant cannot be found is sufficient for the issuance of a writ of attachment. In almost all cases a defendant may obtain the release of attached property by posting sufficient bond.

Vendor's Lien

In some states, a right of a seller to a lien against land conveyed for any unpaid or unsecured portion of the purchase price.

Case Example

Dwayne and Beulah Blankenship contracted to exchange their ranch in Bonner's Ferry, Idaho, for one owned by Roy C. Myers and his son Ron. In addition, Roy Myers agreed to pay them $105,000 in contracts and cash.

Myers delivered the contracts and cash to his agent, Patrick, who converted $50,000 of these assets to his own use. A short time later Myers conveyed his entire interest in the Bonner's Ferry ranch to his son. Both the senior Myers and Patrick became insolvent, and the Blankenships asserted a vendor's lien against the Bonner's Ferry property.

Although a lower court refused the lien on grounds that the Blankenships were not unpaid, the Idaho appellate court reversed. The appellate court stated, "if through no fault of the seller the seller never receives such consideration or collateral from the buyer, then the seller is unpaid and unsecured and has a vendor's lien." *Blankenship v. Myers, 97 Idaho 356, 544 P.2d 314 (1975).*

The term *vendor's lien* is used in several ways. In some situations, if the buyer does not pay the full purchase price, the seller reserves a lien in the deed. This is frequently referred to as an *express vendor's lien*. A lien of this type is very similar to a mortgage. It provides security for the unpaid seller just as a mortgage would. Like the mortgage, the express vendor's lien is the result of agreement between the parties. Although most of the states allow express vendor's liens, they are not in common use in this country. The probable reason is that a mortgage to the unpaid seller provides greater protection because the buyer also signs a note for the debt. In a few states, however, the vendor's lien is an important element in real estate sales when the seller is not fully paid at the closing.

In a number of states a vendor's lien arises by implication if the buyer does not pay the full price and the seller takes no other security. This is the type of lien involved in the Bonner's Ferry case. The implied vendor's lien exists without express agreement. It is based upon the principle that a person who has acquired another's property should not be allowed to keep it without paying for it. An unpaid seller should be allowed to satisfy the debt from the proceeds of a foreclosure sale of the property. Courts in some states also justify the vendor's lien on the theory of implied trust. These courts consider the buyer a trustee for the seller, holding legal title for the seller's benefit until the price is paid.

Courts and legislative bodies have often been critical of the implied vendor's lien. They consider the lien unfair because it is secret. They contend that third parties dealing with the buyer have no way of knowing of the lien's existence. Public records show that the buyer has legal title and no security interests exist against the property. As a result, a third party might be induced to buy the property or grant credit with the property as security. Although the public record is clear, a seller might have a lien that could be a cloud on the title or take priority over a mortgage. To eliminate this injustice, many states, by statute or judicial opinion, hold the vendor's lien unenforceable against encumbrances or purchasers in good faith who do not know of the lien's existence. For example, if Ron Myers had sold the Bonner's Ferry ranch to a bona fide purchaser prior to the Blankenships' efforts to assert a vendor's lien, the property would no longer be subject to the lien. Even so, a vendor's lien is not without value; it may be asserted against the seller, the seller's heirs or those who take from the seller knowing of the lien's existence.

Requirements

In those states in which it is recognized, the vendor's lien is created the moment the seller transfers legal title to the buyer. In order for the lien to exist, however, the seller must not have accepted some other type of security for the unpaid portion of the purchase price. For instance, if the seller takes back a mortgage, the lien is waived. Taking other land or personal property as security also waives the lien. In a number of states a seller who agrees to pass a title free of encumbrances is not entitled to a vendor's lien unless one has been expressly reserved in the deed. Retention of possession by the vendor after passing title also generally negates a vendor's lien. The vendor, however, does not waive the lien by instituting an action to recover the unpaid purchase money.

Priority

As has been noted, in many states the vendor's lien has no priority against the interest of a bona fide purchaser from the vendee or security rights in the property given to a creditor without notice. In most states the vendor's lien is also subject to a mechanic's lien for home construction, even if construction takes place after sale. The vendor's lien does have priority over the claims of unsecured creditors. These priority rules do not apply if an express vendor's lien is reserved in the deed and the deed is recorded. Under these conditions, third parties have a means of knowing that the lien exists.

In some sections of the United States the term *vendor's lien* has been applied to the interest of a person who sells real estate under a land contract. The vendor holds the legal title as security. If the vendee defaults, the vendor may foreclose the vendee's interest and apply the proceeds of the sale to the purchase price.

Tax Lien

A lien imposed against real property for payment of taxes.

The power of government to levy taxes is commonly coupled with the right to place liens on real and personal property to facilitate tax collection. Liens are encountered as part of the tax structure at all levels of government. In addition to federal and state governments, counties, cities, towns and villages as well as nonpolitical units such as school and irrigation districts are authorized to use liens as security when taxes are unpaid.

Many types of taxes, when unpaid, create liens upon property. These include both real and personal property taxes, income taxes and estate taxes, as well as local assessments for sidewalks, sewers, water distribution systems and so on. Less frequently, liens may be used to collect contributions to unemployment funds, wages that have been withheld and unpaid social security contributions.

Although tax liens may be placed against both real and personal property, liens on real property are generally more effective than those on personal property for several reasons. Personal property is easier to conceal than real property. Personal property can be moved from the taxing district or disguised with little difficulty. Real property's value is relatively stable, whereas many types of personal property deteriorate when used. As a result, personal property is often not of sufficient value to cover the defaulted tax.

Tax liens are not restricted to the property subject to taxation. In some jurisdictions taxes assessed on personal property may be the basis for a lien upon real property. A state may also collect taxes assessed against one parcel of real estate within its jurisdiction by proceeding against other parcels owned by the same person. A lien on property other than that against which the tax was assessed is limited to property owned when the taxes became collectible. Inasmuch as tax liens are statutory creations, the legislature has the authority to exempt certain types of property. Property exempt from tax liens varies considerably from state to state. Usually the statutory provision establishing lien exemption parallels statutes exempting property from taxation in general.

Priority

People who are unable to pay a particular tax generally have other financial problems. Often, many claims exist against their property. These claims may have been the basis for liens for other taxes, judgments or mortgages. The result is that litigation involving tax liens often concerns priority problems.

Legislative bodies have usually made tax liens superior to all other liens against the property, even those liens in existence before the tax lien. The rule of "first in time, first in right" does not ordinarily apply to tax liens.

Case Example

Graceland Savings and Loan held a mortgage on property owned by Ron Blue. The mortgage was recorded properly. Blue failed to pay his general property tax, and a lien was assessed against the property. The tax lien had priority over Graceland's mortgage.

State statutes ordinarily set forth any priorities existing between liens for different types of taxes. In the absence of a specific statute, the lien for general taxes is coequal with liens of other taxing units. Tax liens for general taxes are usually superior to liens for special assessments even if the special assessment lien was prior in time. The reason is that the claim for the necessary support of government is a higher obligation than the demand for the costs of a local improvement. Maintenance of civil government is the first and paramount necessity for social order, personal liberty and private property, and government cannot exist without revenue. Only upon specific legislative direction will the priority of the sovereign claims of the state be denied.

Foreclosure of Tax Liens

Sale of tax liens on real property is one method commonly used in the United States to collect delinquent taxes. When taxes that are a lien against real property are in default, tax collectors in most states are authorized to sell the lien. These sales are usually by public auction. The successful bidder acquires the right to receive the overdue taxes and interest as these are paid. If there are no bidders, the taxing unit acquires the tax lien.

A successful bidder at a tax sale of the lien does not get title to the property but a lien against it. This lien is evidenced by a tax certificate. If the delinquent taxes are not paid after a period of time, the holder of the tax certificate can foreclose against the property. Usually this period of time is two or three years. During this time the property owner can redeem the property by paying the delinquent taxes, interest and any penalties.

The purchaser at the foreclosure sale obtains title to the property. In most jurisdictions the foreclosure procedure is very similar to that for a mortgage. A few jurisdictions continue to allow certain taxing units to conduct an absolute sale of real property at public auction if taxes are delinquent. The highest bidder acquires immediate title to the property on payment of the bid and delivery of the deed.

Federal Tax Lien

The federal taxing authority uses liens against real property to aid in the collection of federal income, estate and gift taxes. Federal tax liens for income taxes are not valid against a mortgagee, pledgee, mechanic's lienor, purchaser or judgment creditor until a notice of lien is filed. Liens for federal estate taxes do not require recording or filing. They come into existence against all of a decedent's taxable assets automatically upon that person's death. Relatively simple procedures have been developed to release a decedent's real property from the tax lien. These are designed to facilitate sale of the property. They ordinarily require a bond by the estate or partial payment of the tax. Federal gift taxes also attach automatically upon all gifts made. If the tax is not paid, the donee can be personally liable up to the value of the gift.

Summary

A *lien* is a claim against property that either secures payment of a debt or binds a party to fulfill some other monetary obligation. Although a lien does not transfer title to the lienholder, it establishes the right to have an obligation met out of proceeds from sale of the property.

Because land and buildings provide excellent security for a debt, liens occur frequently in real estate practice. Liens are classed as voluntary—those the property owner enters willingly—and involuntary—those attached by legal process to satisfy creditors. The home mortgage is an example of a voluntary lien. Involuntary liens important to the real estate professional are the *mechanic's lien*, the *judgment lien*, the *vendor's lien* and the *tax lien*.

The mechanic's lien provides contractors or suppliers who furnish labor or materials to improve buildings or land the right to seek a sale of the property to satisfy unpaid claims. The value of the improved property acts as security for the labor and supplies furnished. Usually, building supplies are sold on credit, and the additional security induces financial institutions as well as suppliers of materials to provide more credit for the construction industry.

Perfection of lien is the term given to the legal steps necessary to establish an enforceable mechanic's lien. The steps and the time period required to perfect vary according to the type of lien. Basically, however, two steps are common to perfecting most liens: providing written notice of the claim to the owner and placing the lien in the public record. Payment of the full amount to the creditor is the principal method of terminating a lien.

Another common type of lien—the judgment lien—automatically attaches to real property when a claimant wins a money judgment in court. Forced sale of the defendant's property, usually by the sheriff, may be ordered by the court in a levy of execution to satisfy a judgment lien.

A third type is the vendor's lien. This lien establishes the right of a seller to levy against land conveyed to another for any portion of the purchase price not paid. In an express lien, this right is established in the deed. The implied vendor's lien, on the other hand, exists without express agreement. It may arise when the buyer does not pay the full price and the seller has not taken other security, such as a mortgage note or other property. The debt may then be satisfied from the proceeds of a foreclosure sale.

The tax lien is created by an owner's failure to pay taxes. It may be placed against real property by governments at all levels. Federal, state, county and municipal agencies and even school districts have this right. Generally, tax liens are superior to all other obligations, even those that are prior in time.

Review and Discussion Questions

1. When a contractor improves real property, the work is done on the basis of a contract with the owner. A contractor who is not paid can sue for breach of that agreement. Explain why a contractor should also be entitled to file a mechanic's lien against the property.

2. Mechanic's lien law differs appreciably from state to state. (a) Indicate at least five of these differences. (b) What public policy concerns might explain some of these variations?

3. Judgment lien law differs appreciably from state to state. (a) Indicate at least five of these differences. (b) What public policy concerns might explain some of these variations?

4. What is the chief criticism of the vendor's lien? Is this criticism justified?

Case Problems

1. Kile borrowed $15,000 from Chatfield, giving her a promissory note to cover the debt. The note was unsecured, but Chatfield knew that Kile owned substantial unmortgaged real property. A short time later, Hude won a judgment against Kile for $150,000. When Kile filed as a bankrupt, both Chatfield and Hude claimed priority in the real estate. Which of the two has the superior claim? Explain.

2. Wood owned several hundred acres of land in Texas. In 1952 he decided to explore for oil on the land and leased an oil-drilling rig from Cabot. Under the terms of the lease, Cabot was responsible for moving the rig to the Wood property. Cabot then hired White Heavy Haulers to transport the equipment. White Heavy Haulers was not paid and filed a mechanic's lien against Wood's property. (a) Is the lien valid? Discuss. (b) Would your answer differ if under the lease the expense of moving the rig was to be borne by Wood? Explain.

3. Dodd owned land that he platted into lots and blocks. The plat was recorded properly as the Woods Hills Subdivision. Dodd then hired Dix to blacktop the streets and roads in the subdivision. Upon completion of the work, Dix

was not fully paid; he filed a mechanic's lien against all the land, premises and improvements described in the recorded plat.

Gordon and Jenkins owned lots in the subdivision. These lots were not on streets that Dix had blacktopped, although Gordon and Jenkins sometimes used these streets to reach their lots. Would the properties of Gordon and Jenkins be subject to the mechanic's lien if one were granted? Should any of the properties be subject to a mechanic's lien? Support your answer.

4. Ransonne won a judgment against Sneed for $120,000. A certified copy of the judgment was filed in the office of the county recorder of Mesa County, a county in which Sneed owned real property with a market value of about $80,000. A short time later, Sneed contracted to sell this property for $82,000. Ransonne immediately sued to enjoin the sale upon the basis of her judgment lien. She contended that the property would appreciate in value over the next few years and could then be sold to satisfy the judgment. Discuss the validity of her contention.

5. Jethro Construction Co., Inc. (Jethro) was the general contractor on two separate construction projects. Lasater Electric Co. (Lasater) was the electrical subcontractor on both projects. Lasater purchased its materials for their projects as well as others from Mac's Electrical Supply (Mac's). Lasater maintained an open account with Mac's. Over several projects, payments by Lasater to Mac's had been increasingly slow, and Mac's was worried about Lasater's ability to pay. What steps should Mac's take to ensure mechanics' liens against the projects if Lasater fails to pay?

6. A state statute created a mechanic's lien in favor of all persons "bestowing skill or other necessary service on . . . the construction . . . either in whole or in part, of any building, structure, or other work of improvement . . . " In the course of supplying general engineering services to subdivide land into residential lots, Nolte located boundaries and set monuments in the ground to mark them. When Nolte was not paid, he filed a mechanic's lien. The owner argued that Nolte's lien was invalid because it was not related to any "building, structure, or other work of improvement," as the mechanic's lien statute required. Is the lien valid? Support your answer. *Nolte v. Smith, 189 Cal.App.2d 140, 11 Cal. Rptr. 261 (1961)*

7. Tabet Lumber Company supplied materials for a house being constructed for Richard and Jan Baughman. The Baughmans paid the contractor in full and moved into the house on October 25, 1985. On January 15, 1986, the contractor hung two mirrors in the bathrooms, installed handrails on the stairs and weather-stripped two basement doors. These items were included in the original agreement. The contractor did not pay for all of the materials, and on April 15, 1986, Tabet filed a lien claim for the unpaid portion. The Baughmans asked the court to dismiss, contending that this filing was invalid as the state's mechanic's lien statute required filing within 90 days of

completion. Their view was that substantial completion was sufficient and the 90-day period started running in October. Should the case be dismissed? Support your answer.

Part 2

Transferring Ownership Interests

8

Deeds

Deed

A legal instrument conveying title to real property upon delivery to, and acceptance by, the grantee.

The deed is the primary method of transferring title to real estate. Title is the totality of rights and obligations possessed by an owner. The term is also used in the sense of evidence of ownership. Therefore, the deed is one of the critical documents in the real estate transaction. Although problems involving deeds are ordinarily the concern of the attorney, the real estate professional needs to be familiar with the different types of deeds, the formal elements of a deed and the steps required for a deed to be executed properly.

The deed is a two-party instrument. One party, called the *grantor*, conveys real estate to the other party, the *grantee*. A deed does not have to follow any particular form to be valid. Any written document containing the few essential elements will be effective. Most states have adopted statutory forms for the different types of deeds. The statutory forms are almost always short, often a single page, and all the essentials are included. Although the statutory form is acceptable for all transactions, lawyers sometimes prepare a longer, more formal document.

States have adopted the statutory forms in order to cut the costs of recording and to preserve records of deeds and other instruments affecting title to real property. Considerable expense is saved by photocopying and storing a single sheet instead of four or five pages. In some areas of the United States, especially heavily populated areas, space has become so acute a problem that recording offices are turning to microfilm or microfiche storage or computerized systems to preserve the public records.

Several types of deeds are common in the United States. Ordinarily, in a real estate transaction, the type of deed that the seller uses is agreed upon in the contract of sale. This is one of several reasons why each party should consult an attorney before signing the agreement. A seller is bound to furnish the type of deed stipulated by the real estate sales contract, and this is what the buyer must accept, even though another type of deed might provide the buyer more protection.

Warranty Deed

A deed that conveys title and warrants that the title is good and free of liens and encumbrances.

Custom often influences what type of deed will be agreed upon in the contract. Real estate attorneys like to use the instrument in general use in a particular locality. In some areas, one type of deed is standard for residential sales, whereas a different type of deed is used to convey commercial property. Parties should remember, however, that the type of deed is subject to negotiation at the time of contracting.

Case Example

Olvic's contract with Ziebarth called for a general warranty deed. At the closing, Olvic offered another type of deed customarily used in the area. Nonetheless Ziebarth was entitled to a general warranty deed.

There are two types of warranty deeds—the general or full warranty deed and the special or limited warranty deed. More frequently used is the *general* or *full warranty deed*. A general warranty deed conveys the seller's title and contains covenants of title respecting the title. These covenants provide the buyer with some protection against claims that might interfere with ownership.

General Warranty Deed

The covenants in a general warranty deed vary from one locality to another, but five covenants are customary: covenant of seisin, covenant against encumbrances, covenant of quiet enjoyment, covenant of warranty and covenant of further assurances (see Figure 8.1). In some states, such as Illinois, the general warranty covenants are implied by statute by simply "warranting" the title. Other states require express reference to the warranties.

By *covenant of seisin* the seller guarantees his or her ownership of the property and the existence of a right to convey. The covenant has also been construed to mean that the seller has an estate of the quantity and quality purportedly conveyed. This covenant is sometimes referred to as the *covenant of right to convey*.

The *covenant against encumbrances* is the seller's assurance that, at the time of conveyance, the property is free of *encumbrances*. Typical encumbrances are easements, liens, mortgages and leases (discussed more fully in Chapters 6, 7, 18, 19, 25, 26). The covenant does not apply to those encumbrances specifically excepted in the deed, because the buyer has agreed to accept them. In many states

Figure 8.1: General Warranty Deed

This general warranty deed is made the seventeenth day of May, 1992, between Honus Grantor and Elsie Grantee.

Witness that Grantor, in consideration of $1.00 and other good and valuable consideration, paid by Grantee, does hereby grant and release to Grantee and assigns forever, the following described real estate, together with the appurtenances and all the estate and rights of Grantor in and to said premises:

[Insert description here]

And Grantor covenants as follows:

1. That Grantor is seised of said premises in fee simple, and has good right to convey the same.

2. That Grantee shall quietly enjoy the said premises.

3. That the said premises are free from encumbrances.

4. That the Grantor will execute or procure any further necessary assurance of the title to said premises.

5. That Grantor will forever warrant the title to said premises.

In witness hereof, Grantor has hereunto set his hand on the above date.

_____   _____
Witness   Grantor

_____
Witness

Acknowledged before me this 17th day of May, 1992.

_____
Notary Public

---

encumbrances that are open and visible and that benefit the land are also excluded from the covenant against encumbrances.

Case Example

Al Wilson purchased a lot from Bonnie McConnell. The lot and several others in the area were subject to certain building restrictions. At the time Wilson contracted he knew of these restrictions, but they were not mentioned in the contract. Wilson refused to accept a deed from McConnell on grounds that the restrictions violated the covenant against encumbrances. Because Wilson knew of the restrictions and they benefited the land, however, this argument would be unsuccessful.

The *covenant of quiet enjoyment* and the *covenant of warranty* are very much alike. The covenant of quiet enjoyment warrants that the buyer will not be evicted by someone with a superior title. This covenant is not breached unless the buyer is actually evicted by a third party who has a superior title. The covenant of warranty warrants that the warrantor will defend title on behalf of the purchaser against all lawful claimants.

In some states the general warranty deed also contains a *covenant of further assurances*. This covenant obligates the grantor to perform all acts necessary to confirm the grantee's title, including the execution of any additional conveyances or instruments that are needed.

The covenant of quiet enjoyment, the covenant of warranty and the covenant of further assurances protect future purchasers as well as the immediate purchaser. They are regarded as future covenants and are said to *run with the land.* As a result, their breach may be the basis for suit by a remote buyer against a previous seller who has given a warranty deed. This suit may occur many years after the particular defendant sold the property. The phrase *run with the land,* discussed more fully on page 142, is used because these covenants pass from one person to another as title is transferred.

Case Example

Several years after buying the property from Olvic, Ziebarth sold it to Lance Murphy. Ziebarth did not convey by a general warranty deed. Murphy's title was contested, and he was evicted from the property. Unable to sue Ziebarth, Murphy commenced an action against Olvic. Olvic defended on the grounds that he had not sold the property to Murphy. In this litigation, a court would find for Murphy on the grounds that the covenants of quiet enjoyment and warranty run with the land and extend to future owners.

Covenants in a warranty deed do not assure the buyer that the seller has title or guarantee any rights to the buyer. All they do is give the buyer a right to sue if a covenant is broken. Although they provide the buyer with some protection, that protection is limited by many factors. The seller who has given the covenants might become insolvent or leave the jurisdiction. In that case any judgment against the seller would be difficult to obtain or of little value. Many states limit the seller's liability to the original purchase price. In these states improvements or appreciation in value is not included as part of the buyer's losses. Not covered by the traditional covenants are invalid claims and threats of litigation. Because of the limited nature of the protection offered, a buyer should never rely only upon a warranty deed. Additional assurances, such as an attorney's opinion of title or title insurance, should be obtained.

Special Warranty Deed

A *special* or *limited warranty* deed restricts the extent of the seller's warranties. In this type of instrument, the seller guarantees only against acts that he or she has done that might affect title. Of course the deed conveys the seller's title to the property.

Case Example

Ziebarth's conveyance to Lance Murphy was by a limited warranty deed. When Murphy discovered that Ziebarth's title was defective because of an undischarged mortgage given by Olvic in 1977, Murphy brought suit against Ziebarth. Because the defect arose before Ziebarth had acquired title, the special warranty had not been breached. As we have seen, Murphy had a good cause of action against Olvic, who had conveyed by general warranty deed.

Bargain and Sale Deed

A deed that conveys title but gives no covenants.

In common use in a number of jurisdictions, the bargain and sale deed conveys title but contains no warranties. Sometimes the bargain and sale deed contains covenants against the seller's acts. When this is the case, the bargain and sale deed has the same effect as the limited or special warranty deed.

An important variation of the bargain and sale deed is the fiduciary deed. A *fiduciary* is a person who has been placed by law in a position of trust regarding property that is not his or her own—for example, the administrator or executor of a decedent's estate. The fiduciary might need to convey title to the decedent's real property but would not want to make guarantees or warranties concerning the title. In that case a special form of deed, similar to the bargain and sale deed, may be used. In it the fiduciary guarantees only that he or she has been properly appointed and authorized to sell and convey. The deed does not make any other warranties.

Quitclaim Deed

An instrument that conveys the grantor's interest only.

Unlike the warranty deed and the bargain and sale deed, the quitclaim deed does not purport to convey title; it merely releases whatever interest the grantor possesses. If the grantor has title, the quitclaim deed conveys that title as effectively as a warranty or bargain and sale deed. A grantee who takes title by a quitclaim deed does not acquire any of the covenants that are given to a grantee accepting a warranty deed. If the contract does not mention the type of deed to be used, many states permit the seller to give a quitclaim deed.

The quitclaim deed is commonly used to clear a *defective* title by having a third person who has a possible claim against the realty convey whatever rights he has back to the owner. The defect could be an outstanding lien, an easement or a potential dower right.

Case Example

Martin Russo contracted to sell property to Elmer Hunter. At the time, Russo was single, but before he signed and delivered the deed, he married. Unbeknownst to Hunter, only Russo signed the deed. In their state, Russo's wife has an inchoate right of dower. Upon discovering the marriage, the attorneys for both parties asked Mrs. Russo to execute a quitclaim deed releasing her inchoate right to Elmer Hunter. In executing and delivering this instrument, Mrs. Russo would surrender any interest she might have in the property.

Essential Elements of a Deed

A deed is a complicated instrument that should be drafted by an attorney. A properly drafted and executed deed is critical to any real estate sale. Errors in a deed can cause problems not only for the current owner but also for future generations of owners. Sale of the property, financing, and even occupancy, can be affected by errors that seem inconsequential. In order to help prevent these errors, the real estate salesperson needs some knowledge of the basic requirements of a valid deed. Since the deed should be drafted by an attorney, the salesperson's knowledge need not be extensive, but it should be sufficient to recognize potential problems. With this background the salesperson should be able to alert the drafter to issues that might lead to errors in the deed.

In order to be valid, a deed must include words of conveyance, a competent grantor and grantee properly identified, and a legal description. The instrument must be signed by the grantor, witnessed, and notarized, and a valid delivery and acceptance must occur.

Words of Conveyance

The heart of a deed is the granting clause. A deed must contain words of conveyance sufficient to transfer an estate from one party to another. No particular words are necessary, provided that those used express an intention to convey title. Words customarily used are *grant, convey* and *bargain*. A typical granting clause might read as follows: "Grantors . . . do by these presents grant, bargain, sell, and convey unto the said grantees forever. . . . " The word *quitclaim* or *release* is commonly found in quitclaim deeds.

A deed without words of conveyance does not transfer title; the courts have, however, been indulgent in interpreting words in order to a give a deed effect.

Case Example

Mary A. Searle conveyed land to her four children as tenants in common. Approximately seven years later, the four joined in the execution of an inartfully drawn instrument, which purported to change their rights as cotenants and to convey to others certain remainder interests.

The granting clause of this document stated, "Said premises are to be held so that as each of said parties shall die, the property shall vest in the survivors or survivor for their respective lives. . . . " Remainders were created using as granting words "to go," "to be his," and "shall go."

In an action to establish who had title, plaintiffs argued that the operative words of grant "are to be held" and the phrases used to grant the remainder interests were insufficient and that the instrument was not a valid deed.

The court did not agree, stating, "To be effective to transfer an interest in realty, a deed necessarily must contain words of present grant. . . . But no particular verbal formula is required under our rule of construction as previously given. The quoted words express an intention to create among the original cotenants new incidents of survivorship and power of sale, and to grant remainder interests to other persons subject to defeasance upon the exercise of the power of sale. The instrument was not ineffective as a deed for lack of a sufficient granting clause." *Dennen v. Searle, 149 Conn. 126, 176 A.2d 561 (1961).*

Competent Grantor

To be valid, a deed must have a competent grantor. Any natural person except a minor or a person who lacks mental capacity may convey real estate by deed. Corporations also have the capacity to convey real property.

Minors   Deeds made by minors or incompetents are not void, but they are *voidable*, which means that the minor or incompetent acquires the option of either ratifying or disaffirming the transfer.

The minor wishing to disaffirm his or her transfer by *deed* cannot ordinarily do so until reaching the age of majority, but a minor can avoid a *contract* to buy land at any time during minority and for a reasonable time after reaching majority. Today in many states the age of majority is 18. Once having reached majority, the minor must institute proceedings to disaffirm within a reasonable time. If this is not done, the right is lost.

Case Example

John Spencer and his sister inherited land from their father. At the time John was a minor. He attained majority five months later. John's sister was of full age at her father's death. Before John attained his majority, he and his sister sold the property to Alpheas MacLoon. Shortly thereafter, MacLoon conveyed part of the property to the Lyman Falls Power Company and the residue to William Hutchins. Three years later the power company commenced substantial improvements on the land. John Spencer attempted to disaffirm. The company's attorney pleaded that Spencer had a right to disaffirm when he reached majority, but the right had been lost because he failed to assert it within a reasonable time.

Mental capacity   To cancel a deed for lack of mental capacity, evidence of a grantor's incompetency must be clear and convincing. The test of mental capacity to make a deed is the grantor's ability to understand the nature and effect of the act at the time the deed is signed.

Case Example

Florence Woodward owned a 120-acre farm near Verna, Oklahoma. When she was nearly 80, she became ill and moved to a nursing home. While a resident at the home, she conveyed the farm to a nephew. After Woodward's death, a niece contested the validity of the deed on grounds that the grantor was incompetent.

Conflicting testimony was given at the trial concerning Florence Woodward's competency. Witnesses testified that prior to her hospitalization she was often confused and vague. Her concentration was described as poor. There was testimony that her home was untidy, and she often took care of her cattle at odd hours, such as midnight. A nurse from the nursing home testified that in her opinion Woodward would not have understood the effect of signing a deed, but she always recognized her nephews and would talk about her property. Other witnesses testified that Woodward was generally alert, competent and normal.

The court held the deed valid, stating that fragmentary evidence of isolated instances of failing memory or confusion is insufficient to overcome evidence that the grantor was competent. *Matter of Woodward, 549 P.2d 1207 (Okla. 1976).*

Corporate grantor   A number of special rules apply to transfers of real property by corporations. The corporate officer who executes a deed must be authorized to do so. This authorization is obtained from the board of directors, which adopts a written resolution permitting the officer to act. In most states, if the corporation sells real estate that is a substantial portion of the corporation's assets, statutes require the sale to be approved by a designated portion of the shareholders, usually two-thirds or more. Nonprofit corporations are often required by statute to obtain approval of a majority of members before selling real estate.

Grantor's marital status   A deed by a natural person should state that person's marital status. In most states a surviving spouse has either a vested or an inchoate (expectancy) interest in a deceased's property even when the property is held separately. The extent of this interest varies from state to state, but ordinarily it will be terminated if the spouse has also signed the deed. A number of states have homestead laws, which were discussed in Chapter 4. These laws prohibit a spouse from selling the family residence unless the other spouse agrees and signs the deed. The failure to state the grantor's marital status never invalidates the deed.

Identifiable Grantee

A deed does not convey title unless it names an existing identifiable grantee. Of course, few transactions exist in which the grantee does not legally exist. One example might be a deed that designated an unincorporated association as the grantee. A deed naming this group would be invalid. It would need to name the legal trustees of the association. However, as the next case illustrates, courts permit extrinsic evidence to determine the identity of the grantee.

Case Example

I. A. Garraway and Mrs. I. A. Garraway signed a general warranty deed conveying to "The Trustees of Oak Grove Consolidated High School and their Successors" a parcel of land. The deed was delivered and recorded. The trustees built a public school on the property and operated it for 28 years until the school was closed. The Perry County Board of Education succeeded to all rights of the former Trustees of the high school. The Garraways' heirs sought to have the warranty deed declared null and void on the legal theory that no legal person was named as trustee in the deed. The trial court rejected the theory and the Supreme Court of Mississippi affirmed the trial court. The court stated:

> "In the first place, the Trustees of the Oak Grove Consolidated High School were indeed a corporate body politic. . . . In any event, the conveyance is effective because all our law requires is that the grantee be described in such terms that by reference to objective evidence otherwise available, his identity may be ascertained with reasonable certainty. . . . There are minutes before the court reflecting that . . . the Trustees of the Oak Grove Consolidated High School were W. A. Hegwood, Forrest Cochran, Arthur Breland, H. I. Breland and Charlie Herring."

Garraway v. Yonce, 549 So. 2d 1341 (Miss. 1989).

Ordinarily, the determination of the proper designation of the grantee is a responsibility of the attorney or other person who drafts the deed. The real estate professional can aid this drafter by informing him or her of unusual circumstances regarding the name or marital status of the grantee. For example, during negotiations the real estate salesperson may learn of the grantee's use of another name or a variation in spelling.

Adequate Legal Description

Problems involving descriptions in deeds are, like those involving designation of the grantee, not primarily the concern of real estate personnel but of legal personnel. Sales personnel, however, are apt to be aware of boundary controversies, which may result from, or indicate, description problems. Legal description and controversies involving boundaries are discussed in Chapter 9.

The salesperson who is aware of a boundary or description issue should urge the seller to obtain a solution before placing property on the market. This will save time and embarrassment as well as prevent hard feelings that arise when these issues come up after agreement is reached.

Descriptions probably cause more litigation than any of the other formal requirements of the deed. Property to be conveyed must be described well enough in the deed to identify it with reasonable certainty. An imperfect description does not render a deed invalid, but the description must accurately depict the land in question. Presumably the grantor intended to convey *something;*

the deed will usually be upheld unless the description is so vague or contradictory that the particular land cannot be identified.

Most courts interpret words of description liberally in order to uphold a conveyance. The basic rule in construction of deeds is to ascertain and carry out the real intention of the parties. To accomplish this, courts first look to the document itself, but they will accept extrinsic evidence if the description furnished a guide to identifying the property conveyed.

Case Example

Plaintiff and defendant owned adjoining land. A former owner of plaintiff's property had conveyed a ten-foot strip of ground to the township to be used as a drainage ditch. The ditch drained defendant's land as well as that of other landowners. The description in the deed to the township indicated a point of beginning and described the ditch as "running due south for 2,200 feet." For several years defendant had maintained the ditch, which was at the time of suit six feet wide.

Plaintiff commenced a trespass action against defendant, asking for an injunction prohibiting defendant from maintaining and using the ditch. Plaintiff argued that the deed to the township was ineffective because the description contained no boundaries. The court rejected this argument on the grounds that logically the line described was intended as the center of the ditch. The description thus furnished the means by which the property could be identified. *Franz v. Nelson, 183 Neb. 122, 158 N.W.2d 606 (1968).*

Proper Execution

To be valid, a deed must be signed by the grantor; however, the grantee's signature is unnecessary. A few states require that a deed be signed at the end of the instrument. Otherwise the signature does not have to be in any particular place, but the signature must clearly apply to the entire instrument. Customarily, even when not required, a deed is signed at the end. Signature may be by the grantor's mark or by any writing the grantor intends as a signature. If a grantor signs by a mark, the name should appear near the mark, and the act should be witnessed.

Attestation is the act of witnessing the execution of an instrument and subscribing as a witness. In general, the law does not require witnesses to a grantor's signature to establish a deed as valid. Witnessing and attestation, however, are almost universal prerequisites to recording. The attesting witness subscribes the document for the purpose of verifying and identifying it. Usually two witnesses are required.

Acknowledgment is the act by which a grantor declares before a duly authorized official that a deed is genuine and executed voluntarily. Acknowledgment, like attestation, is in most states a prerequisite to recording rather than an essential requirement of a valid deed. The purpose of acknowledgment is to prevent forgery and fraud. The official witnessing the grantor's signature is charged with determining the grantor's identity. Each state by statute prescribes the officials before whom an acknowledgment must be made and the general form the acknowledgment must follow. Attestation and acknowledgment are discussed more fully in Chapter 17, which deals with recording.

Power of attorney   A power of attorney is a written instrument authorizing a person, the attorney-in-fact, to act as agent on behalf of another to the extent indicated in the instrument. (See Figure 8.2.)

A deed executed by an agent for the grantor, in the grantor's absence, is invalid unless the agent has a power of attorney. In a real estate transaction the parties should use a special limited power of attorney instead of the all-inclusive general power of attorney. Courts strictly construe the power of attorney, and thus the power must specifically authorize the attorney-in-fact to convey the real estate. A general power to sell does not grant the power to convey. In some states, *the equal dignities* rule requires that a power of attorney in a real estate conveyance be executed with the same formalities that are required to execute the deed properly. In some states, a deed executed by a person with a power of attorney cannot be recorded unless the power of attorney is also recorded.

Normally, a power of attorney may be revoked at any time. In most cases the death of either the principal or the attorney-in-fact also revokes the power of attorney. Therefore, the purchaser taking a deed signed by an attorney-in-fact should be extremely cautious. The power of attorney should not be old, and the purchaser should require evidence that the principal is living. The purchaser should also insist that the power of attorney be recorded. This provides some protection because an unrecorded revocation is ineffective against a recorded power of attorney.

Delivery and Acceptance

A deed does not transfer title until delivered by the grantor and accepted by the grantee. Although manual transfer of the instrument is the common method of delivering a deed, manual transfer alone is insufficient to pass title. The grantor must *intend to pass title* and *surrender control of the instrument.* Unless these two components exist, the fact that the grantor has given up physical possession of the deed is of no consequence.

Case Example

Beatrice Curtiss executed a quitclaim deed to herself and to her granddaughter, Marilyn Feriss, as joint tenants. Although the deed was recorded, Mrs. Curtiss continued to occupy the property and paid all maintenance and insurance expenses. Both Mrs. Curtiss and other members of the family stated and acted as if Mrs. Curtiss were the sole owner. Mrs. Feriss was regarded and spoken of as "the inheritor." Mrs. Feriss never occupied the property or stayed there longer than a single night.

In litigation involving the Feriss title, the appellate court stated that "the deed in question did not operate to pass an interest in the property . . . to Marilyn Feriss as the grantor did not intend for it to do so." *Curtiss v. Feriss, 168 Colo. 480, 452 P.2d 38 (1969).*

Figure 8.2: Special Power of Attorney

Power of Attorney

I, Eberly Furston, do hereby invest my attorney-in-fact, Leroy Stutz, with full power and authority to sign a deed in my name in my stead and on my behalf and to execute all other documents necessary to transfer title to my real estate located at 1100 Wilder Ave. N., Decatur, Illinois, to Francine Harbaugh for the purchase price of $125,000.

_____   _____
Witness   Eberly Furston

_____   Date: 11-8-92
Witness

Eberly Furston, known to me, did execute this Power of Attorney on November 8, 1992.

_____
Notary Public

My commission expires on April 1, 1995.

Conversely, even though physical transfer is the generally accepted procedure, delivery can be effective without it. Constructive or implied delivery, which is delivery without change of possession, is valid although rare. As with actual delivery, the essence of constructive delivery is the intention of the parties, not the manual act of transfer. If the grantor, by words or acts, manifests an intention to be divested of title and for it to vest in another, the law determines that delivery is sufficient, even if the instrument itself (but not control) remains in the hands of the grantor.

Case Example

On August 10, 1940, Frank and Elizabeth Agrelius, husband and wife, executed two warranty deeds, one deed conveying 80 acres of land to Clair T. Agrelius, the other deed conveying a nearby 80 acres to Paul Kenneth Agrelius. Neither deed was recorded during the lifetime of either grantor.

On July 27, 1944, a safety deposit box was leased . . . in the names of Mr. and Mrs. Agrelius, who signed the lease at that time. Clair was also named as lessee, although he did not sign the lease contract until 1962. The deeds were placed in the safety deposit box. At some later time in 1944 . . . Mr. Agrelius told Clair of the two deeds executed in 1940. . . . At this time Mr. Agrelius handed Clair a key to the safety deposit box and said this would constitute delivery of the deed to him. After the death of Mrs. Agrelius in 1967, Clair removed the two deeds from the box and had them recorded.

The trial court held that " . . . when Frank and Elizabeth Agrelius told Clair they had executed a deed conveying one 80-acre tract to him and another deed to the other 80-acre tract to Kenneth and placed the deeds in their lock box and then handed the key to the box to Clair, such actions constituted an effective constructive delivery of the deeds, and all the circumstances showed a purpose on the part of the grantors that there should be an immediate vesting of title in Clair and Kenneth, enjoyment only being postponed until the death of the grantors." *Agrelius v. Mohesky, 280 Kan. 790, 494 P.2d 1095 (1972).*

Delivery is ineffective unless the grantor parts with legal control of the instrument during his or her lifetime. The grantor may not retain the power to recall the deed from either the grantee or a third party. Once a valid delivery has occurred, the deed may, however, remain in the grantor's custody or be returned to the grantor for safekeeping.

A deed may be effective even if it contains a provision that it is not to become operative until the grantor's death. Delivery must take place during the grantor's lifetime. Delivery can be made directly to the grantee, who holds the deed until the grantor's death. Whatever the situation, the grantor must be effectively divested of control of the deed. This does not occur if the grantor places the deed with private papers or merely leaves the instrument in a mutually accessible trunk, as the next case illustrates.

Jones v. Jones
Supreme Court of Alabama
470 So. 2d 1207 (Ala. 1985)

Background: Sanford and Daisy Lee Jones had two children, Alfred and Arthur. On December 7, 1981 Sanford and Daisy executed a deed to certain lands to Alfred Jones and his wife Luverne. Daisy died on March 3, 1983, and Sanford Jones died on June 13, 1983. The deed from Sanford and Daisy to Alfred and Luverne was not recorded until July 29, 1983.

Arthur Jones filed suit questioning the validity of the deed, and the trial court judge held that the deed was void due to lack of a valid delivery. Alfred and Luverne appealed.

Decision: The Supreme Court of Alabama agreed with the trial court judge that the deed was void for lack of delivery.

Justice Adams

The single issue for our review is whether the trial court's judgment that the deed was void for lack of a valid delivery was supported by the evidence.

. . .

Alfred Jones testified at trial that he received two earlier deeds—one dated January 8, 1980, and the other dated May 7, 1980. He testified that he recorded the January 8 deed the following day, and the May 7 deed the same day it was executed and delivered to him. In fact, one of the two deeds executed on December 7, 1981, was recorded by Alfred Jones on December 8, 1981; yet the deed in question, executed on the same day, was not recorded until July 29, 1983, approximately six weeks after the death of Sanford Jones.

There was also testimony adduced at trial that on August 16, 1982, Alfred told Arthur that he had found the deed in their father's trunk. The trunk was located in the bedroom of their father's house, and was used by their father to store his valuable papers.

Alfred testified that Sanford Jones never divested himself of control over the title to the property and could have sold it at any time. Sanford Jones also retained all the incidents of ownership of the property, as he was the one who paid taxes, collected the rent, and paid for repairs to the property from December 7, 1981, until his death one and one-half years later.

Finally, Alfred testified that he went to an attorney's office on December 7, 1981, and left with one deed, which he read to his family and placed in a drawer with some other deeds. Later, he testified that he had two deeds, but only recorded one of them. He stated that the reason he did not record the deed in question was that his father was still collecting rent on the property.

The trial court had the chance to view the witnesses and observe their demeanor, and after considering all the relevant factors before it, found that there was no valid delivery of the deed. We simply cannot say that the court's finding is clearly erroneous or against the great weight of the evidence in this case. Therefore, the judgment of the trial court is affirmed.

A grantor may deposit a deed with a third party to satisfy the legal requirement of delivery. This is an effective delivery if the grantor has surrendered all control over the instrument and is powerless to recall it. A deed delivered to a third party is effective from that time even if the grantor dies or becomes insane before the grantee obtains possession of the instrument.

The estate created by the deed may be conditioned upon the performance of some act or occurrence of some event. Until the condition is fulfilled, the grantee's estate does not come into existence.

Case Example

M. A. Hinkson, while suffering from a paralytic stroke, called Hazen, an attorney, to his bedside. Acting upon Hazen's advice, Hinkson signed and acknowledged a deed naming his two daughters, Mrs. Young and Mrs. Bury, as grantees. This deed was given to Hazen with instructions not to record it but to deliver it to the grantees upon Hinkson's death. Hinkson recovered and attempted to secure possession of the deed from Hazen. Hazen refused to return it.

Later, Hinkson made a will leaving all his real property to Young. Upon Hinkson's death, Hazen turned the deed over to Bury. In litigation involving Young and Bury, the court held that the deed effectively conveyed title to the two daughters when delivered to Hazen. *Bury v. Young, 98 Cal. 446, 33 P. 338 (1893).*

Escrow   A means by which delivery may take place, escrow is a process by which money and/or documents are held by a third party until the terms and conditions of an escrow agreement are satisfied. Escrow is discussed in detail in

Chapter 16. In a number of localities, real estate transactions customarily close through a third party called an *escrow agent* or *holder*. This system is prevalent in some of the western states, including California. The escrow holder may be an attorney, a bank, a title insurance company or an independent escrow agent.

Buyer and seller in an escrow closing agree to submit the necessary documents and funds to the escrow holder. The escrow holder is responsible for seeing that the transaction closes upon the conditions agreed to by the parties. As stakeholder, the escrow holder retains the funds and mortgage documents submitted by the buyer. When the seller has delivered to the escrow holder a properly executed deed to the property, and the holder is assured the seller is passing good title, the funds and mortgage documents are turned over to the seller. Completion of an escrow transaction may depend upon other conditions. The escrow holder is responsible for seeing that these conditions are fulfilled before delivering the deed or disbursing the funds.

Consideration

A deed does not have to state a consideration to be valid. The owner of land has the right to convey it as a gift as well as to sell it. The primary function of a deed is to convey title.

Deeds generally do state a consideration. A deed without consideration is vulnerable against the grantor's creditors. If the deed states a consideration, it is more difficult for the grantor's creditors to assert claims against the property. If creditors can prove that the grantee gave no consideration, they may successfully levy against the property even though ownership has been transferred. Under the recording acts in all but a few states, the grantee must have given value in order to be protected. As will be seen in Chapter 17, most recording statutes provide protection only for bona fide purchasers for value.

Customarily, deeds will recite a nominal consideration such as "one dollar ($1.00) and other good and valuable consideration." This is done because buyers are often reluctant to have the actual purchase price shown in the public record. A recital of a nominal consideration is effective, for if the question of actual consideration arises, the courts allow the parties to prove by extrinsic evidence the actual purchase price.

Deed Restrictions

In addition to passing title, a deed may be used to regulate land use. This is accomplished through a condition in the instrument or a covenant. Conditions must be included in the deed; covenants usually are, but a valid covenant may be created by an ancillary document.

Chapter 4 discussed the use of conditions to limit the use of an estate. That chapter indicated that, when a condition in a deed is fulfilled, the owner's estate is subject to termination. In some instances, depending upon the wording of the condition, termination is automatic; in others, termination depends upon some action being taken by the person holding the reversionary interest.

Sometimes a purchaser of land will agree that it not be used in a particular manner. This type of commitment is called a *covenant*. Although both a covenant and a condition limit land use, the legal effects of the two differ. When a condition is fulfilled, the owner's interest terminates or is subject to termination. When a covenant is broken, the owner may be sued for damages or enjoined from breaking the contract, but the owner does not lose title to the property.

Restrictive Covenant

A provision in a deed limiting uses that may be made of the property.

Restrictive covenants are an important tool used by developers to ensure consistency in land use. They are also used by persons selling a portion of their land to protect themselves from undesirable uses that the buyer might make of the property. Restrictive covenants are in effect a private type of zoning regulation. By accepting delivery, the grantee is bound by restrictions in the deed.

Typical restrictive covenants limit property to residential use, provide minimum setback and acreage requirements, prohibit certain types of buildings, limit the number of structures or set a minimum cost for housing to be constructed. Because restrictive covenants limit land use, courts do not always favor them. Today, however, most restrictive covenants will be enforced if they do not violate public policy. An example of a covenant violating public policy would be one restricting ownership of the land to members of a particular racial or religious group.

Affirmative Covenant

Affirmative covenants are recognized in most states. Typical affirmative covenants involve agreements to build fences, maintain party walls, provide railroad crossings and join and pay dues or an annual assessment to a homeowners' association for maintenance of roads, parks or similar facilities. In a few states affirmative covenants are not recognized as valid because courts feel that they are too difficult to enforce.

The Concept of "Running with the Land"

If they are to have much value, covenants must apply not only to the original parties but to future owners of land as well. In general, American courts have accepted the proposition that both restrictive and affirmative covenants run with the land if three factors exist. First, this must have been the intention of those who made the agreement. Second, knowledge of the covenant must actually exist or be readily determinable from the public record. Third, the covenant must "touch and concern" the land. This means that the covenant must benefit or burden the land in question and not be merely a personal commitment for an individual's benefit.

Case Example

Mary A. Schaefers conveyed land to her daughter Rosemary. The deed contained a provision that required Rosemary to provide a home for her brother William, if he requested it. Rosemary Schaefers conveyed the land to Edward Apel. William brought an action to set aside the conveyance for violating the restriction. The lower court dismissed William's action, and the appellate court affirmed.

The appellate court stated, "The covenant is not enforceable against the Apels or any subsequent grantees . . . because it does not touch the land in question. The covenant is merely a personal obligation from Rosemary to William to provide him a permanent home in some location if he requests one." *Schaefers v. Apel, 328 So.2d 274 (Ala. 1976).*

Termination

Although many covenants are part of a planned pattern of land use, they also constitute a burden on the land. Frequently, buyers and sellers wish to terminate covenants because they interfere with more profitable uses of the property. A few states have passed legislation that provides for the elimination of stale restrictions after a fixed period of time or when the limitation no longer substantially benefits those for whom it was created. Most states, however, do not have legislation of this nature. In these states deed covenants often interfere with real estate development unless they can be eliminated.

Although several methods exist for eliminating covenants, each is either costly to accomplish or legally impractical. Covenants may be terminated by a release, by waiver or by abandonment, but these methods are usually impracticable since several people often have the right to enforce a single covenant. Other methods are by acquisition of the property subject to the covenant by the owner of the property benefiting or by litigation showing that changing conditions in the neighborhood have nullified the benefits of the covenant. Because of the difficulty of terminating covenants, a very desirable practice is to write the covenant initially to expire automatically after a period of time. Land use restrictions and covenants are discussed more fully in Chapters 21 and 22.

Summary

The *deed* is the legal instrument that conveys title when real property is bought and sold. As each sale occurs, the transfer is officially recorded, adding to the chain of title. The real estate professional needs to be familiar with state statutes concerning recording and with the various types of deeds. One type, the *warranty deed*, contains clauses known as covenants that provide the buyer with some protection against claims that might interfere with ownership. These covenants in general guarantee that the owner has the right to sell, that the property is free of liens or the claims of creditors and that the buyer will not be ousted by someone with superior title. If any of these covenants is broken, the buyer can recover damages from the seller. In practice, however, it is often difficult to collect such a judgment, so the buyer should seek title insurance for additional protection.

The *bargain and sale deed*, another type, does not ordinarily contain warranties. The *quitclaim deed* is another type of deed; it does not convey title as such, but merely relinquishes whatever interest the grantor has. It is often used when a defective or questionable title must be cleared.

The deed is such an important instrument legally that it should be drafted by an attorney. Errors in the written document can cause problems in the title for future generations. It is beneficial for real estate salespeople to know the elements necessary to create a valid deed. These requirements include words of conveyance that express the intention to convey title from one party (the grantor) to another (the grantee), a competent grantor and an identifiable grantee. The deed must contain a legal description of the property. It must be signed by the grantor or an authorized representative. Finally, delivery and acceptance must be demonstrated for a deed to be valid. One means for delivery to take place is by escrow; that is, the money payment and/or the document may be held by a third party until all conditions are met. Most deeds state a consideration, and a deed can be challenged in court by creditors if no consideration has been given.

On occasion a deed is also used to limit the use to which land will be put. These *restrictive covenants* usually appear in writing in the deed. If worded properly, these provisions run with the land and are difficult or impossible to terminate.

Review and Discussion Questions

1. Explain the difference between (a) *general warranty deed* and a special or *limited warranty deed* and (b) *bargain and sale deed* and a *quitclaim deed*.

2. What is the result of a purchaser's failure to record a deed upon (a) the purchaser's title and (b) a subsequent purchaser who relies upon the seller's recorded title?

3. Explain the assurances provided a grantee by (a) covenant of seisin (b) covenant of quiet enjoyment and (c) covenant of warranty.

4. Why is it important for a purchaser to acquire additional assurances, such as title insurance, when acquiring title by warranty deed?

5. Name the essential elements of a deed and give an example of each.

Case Problems

1. Dunlap owned a large farm, which he worked for many years with his son Sam. Dunlap had a daughter, Celeste, who lived in the city. Dunlap had often told Sam, Celeste and various relatives that Sam was to inherit the farm; nevertheless, nothing was ever done to ensure that it would happen. As

Dunlap aged, he became senile and difficult to live with, but in lucid moments he talked about Sam's inheriting the farm. Because Sam knew that his father had no will, Sam had a deed prepared conveying the property to himself. Dunlap signed the deed. The execution of the instrument was done properly, according to state law. Two years later Dunlap died and Sam had the deed recorded. Celeste has sued to have the deed declared invalid. What arguments should she make?

2. Everett Wine conveyed his property by deed to his son, Benjamin. He failed to read the deed before signing it. He was very old and suffered from lung disease, cirrhosis and chronic brain syndrome. Concerning his mental capacity, his doctor wrote: "Mr. Wine's mental state fluctuated from psychotic to perfectly appropriate. There were times when Mr. Wine understood fairly well what he was doing, and there were times he was out of touch with reality." What additional evidence would you like to pursue in order to determine whether Mr. Wine posessed the legal competency to sign a deed? See *Harper v. Rogers, 387 S.E. 2d 547 (W. Va. 1989)*.

3. Cossette Furr deeded land to Peidmont and Western Investment Corporation. At the time of the conveyance, Peidmont and Western Investment Corporation's charter had been dissolved by the Secretary of State for failure to file any report or return or to pay taxes or fees. Thereafter, the corporation was reinstated. Did the deed operate to convey title to the property? Explain. *Peidmont and Western Investment Corp. v. Carnes-Miller Gear Co., Inc., 384 S.E. 2d 687 (N.C. Ct. App. 1989)*.

4. Clarence and Helen Haines deeded property to Ray and Barbara Mensen described as follows:

> Part of the Northeast Quarter of the Northeast Quarter of Section 9 Township 16 North Range 13 East all in Douglas County Nebraska.

Comment on the adequacy of the description of the property. See *Haines v. Mensen, 446 N.W. 2d 716 (Neb. 1989)*.

5. Stephen Takacs and his son John purchased property as tenants in common. After sharing the costs of building a house, father, son and the son's wife lived together on the premises for two years. During this period Stephen paid $40 per month for his room and board.

   While the parties were living together in the home, the three went to the office of an attorney. The attorney, at Stephen's insistence, prepared a quitclaim deed conveying Stephen's interest to John Takacs and Mabel R. Takacs, John's wife.

   At the time there was an understanding that the deed would become effective on Stephen's death and would not be recorded during his lifetime.

The deed, however, was delivered to John. It was never in Stephen's possession, nor did Stephen reserve the right to recall it. Shortly thereafter, John died. Mabel Takacs recorded the conveyance and attempted to sell the property.

Stephen sued to set aside the deed. Will he be successful? Discuss. *Takacs v. Takacs, 26 N.W.2d 712 (Mich. 1947).*

6. Chris Stevens, a farmer, owned 40 acres of land that he did not use. He leased the land for three years to Orlando Baron. The lease was for farming purposes. Before the lease expired, Stevens conveyed the property by general warranty deed to Morgan Kettlewell. Kettlewell planned to subdivide the property. He had no knowledge of the lease and believed the crops on the land were Stevens's. What right, if any, does Kettlewell have against Stevens? How could Stevens have protected himself?

7. In 1937, Joseph A. Hanns executed, dated and acknowledged a deed to his home. The grantees were his son Santolli and his daughter Sylvania. The deed was discovered by another son, P. J., in his father's safe deposit box after the father's death. P. J. Hanns was appointed administrator of his father's estate.

For 18 years after their father's death, Santolli and Sylvania occupied the residence. P. J. recorded the deed in 1956. In 1962, the property was sold to Dunham Motors. A short time later P. J. died. Suit was then brought by P. J.'s son Frank, asking the court for a share in the proceeds of the sale. Frank claimed this interest on grounds that the deed from Joseph A. Hanns to Santolli and Sylvania had never been delivered. As a result, his father, P. J., was entitled to an intestate share of the property. What factors would a court have to consider to determine the validity of Frank's claim? *Hanns v. Hanns, 262 Or. 282, 423 P.2d 499 (1967).*

9

Land Descriptions

Legal Description

A description of a parcel of land that will be accepted by courts because it is complete enough to locate and identify the premises.

This chapter deals primarily with descriptions found in real estate instruments. Boundary disputes are also discussed, as an intricate relationship exists between descriptions and boundaries. A description in a real estate instrument sets forth the physical dimensions of what is being conveyed. Boundaries are based upon this description. They establish the property on the earth's surface. Often they are imaginary lines, but sometimes they are marked by an object.

With only a few exceptions, American law requires a written instrument to transfer an interest in real estate. To be enforceable in a court of law, the written instrument must contain a valid description of the property involved. The courts will not enforce the written instrument if the description is incorrect or ambiguous. A seller or lessor who has agreed to transfer an interest in real estate is in breach of contract if the instrument executed does not properly describe the property. Even if the physical boundaries of a property are clear, no interest will pass if the property is not described properly.

The chief purpose of the description is to furnish a means for identifying a particular parcel of land. In addition, the description must describe an area that is bounded completely. In other words, the boundaries indicated by the description must close the parcel.

For a deed or other conveyance to be enforceable in a court of law, the description must make possible positive identification of the land. Courts consider this accomplished if a surveyor or other person familiar with the area can locate the property and determine its boundaries using the description in the conveyance. Although a description by street and number is not advisable, it passes title if the property is located in a municipality that has established a standard system of numbering.

A technically accurate description that provides all the information necessary to locating land is preferable to one that needs clarification by other evidence. Courts, however, are exceedingly liberal in allowing outside evidence to clarify an ambiguous description. Testimony of the circumstances surrounding the transaction, the interpretation placed upon the description by the parties, statements of surveyors, neighbors and public officials as well as the physical elements of the area may be introduced. What the courts are searching for is the intent of the parties.

Case Example

Mr. Roger and his wife owned a large piece of land. The land included a lake in which there were several islands. Seventy acres of land jutted into the lake, forming a peninsula. When the tides were high and the wind right, this peninsula was separated from the mainland by a watercourse. Boats could traverse the watercourse at these times. At other times, only an inch or two of water was in the watercourse.

The Rogers deeded all their mainland holdings to Inches and the islands to Burgess. A dispute arose between Burgess and Inches over ownership of the 70 acres. Burgess contended that the jutting piece of land was an island and belonged to him. Inches argued that it was part of the mainland and he was the owner. A court eventually resolved this dispute in favor of Inches. In doing so, it considered the testimony of fishermen who sometimes traversed the watercourse, aerial photographs, the original government survey (which didn't show the watercourse), a motion picture of a boat navigating the watercourse and the testimony of surveyors. *Burgess v. Pine Island Corp., 215 So.2d 755 (Fla. 1968).*

The description in the deed in this transaction was general, not specific. Almost all courts will try to sustain a deed even though it contains a general description. They are reluctant to declare the instrument void. Judges reason that the parties must have intended to do something or they would not have been involved in the transaction.

One type of general description that courts have consistently upheld conveys all the grantor's land in a particular area. This is sometimes referred to as a "Mother Hubbard" description. Similarly, if a deed describes a particular plot in fairly general terms, but provides a clue to the land's location in a specific city, county or state, the description is effective if evidence indicates the grantor owned no other land in the designated area.

Although courts are liberal in accepting outside evidence, a deed conveying land will be invalid if the description does not identify the specific parcel or at least provide a key to identifying property to the exclusion of all other sites.

Case Example

The City of Atlanta owned land at the foot of Climax Place. Berchenko owned all the land on the north of Climax Place, a frontage of 1,035 feet. Berchenko also owned a tract on the south, which had a frontage of 195 feet. Climax Place was only 22 feet wide, and the city wished to widen it to 50 feet.

In order to accomplish this, the city obtained from Berchenko a deed to "a 28-foot strip along Climax Place." The city then demanded that Berchenko remove a building that encroached on the north of Climax Place. Berchenko refused, claiming the deed invalid because the description was uncertain and insufficient. Both the lower court and the appellate court agreed. The appellate court stated, "no surveyor, however expert, could take the description contained in the instrument just mentioned, and by the aid of any extrinsic evidence, locate the precise body of land." *See City of Atlanta v. Atlanta Trailer City Trailer Park, 213 Ga. 825, 102 S.E.2d 23 (1958).*

Reference to Other Documents

As illustrated by the *Burgess v. Pine Island Corp.* case, different kinds of outside evidence may be used to clarify a description. The most effective clarification is provided by a deed's reference to a survey, map, plat or some similar document that correctly describes the land. The details of this extrinsic document become part of the description and can be used to resolve ambiguities or to locate the parcel. In fact, many deeds describe a parcel of land by reference to a master survey, plat or map. This is a common practice that saves time and provides clarity.

Because of the complicated nature of boundaries and the economic importance of real property, the art of surveying has been in use since antiquity to establish and verify boundaries. The Babylonians, Assyrians, Egyptians, Hebrews, Greeks and Romans perfected the art. In the Americas the sedentary Indian peoples, such as the Incas and Mayans, were remarkable surveyors.

In the sophisticated technological world of today, surveys by trained professionals are an integral part of the real estate business. Although the basis of a real estate conveyance is what the parties agree to as the boundaries, agreement is seldom reached without the help of a survey. An agreed-upon boundary cannot be changed by a survey, but a survey is generally used to establish new boundaries. Only in rare instances would a tract be subdivided without a survey or would unplatted land be sold without being mapped. In these situations the surveyor's work is the basis for any description in a deed or other real estate instrument. Where title to land has been established either through an informal survey by the parties or by a prior professional survey, the surveyor's sole function is to help determine the boundaries of the grant. In litigation involving this type of boundary problem, the surveyor often testifies as an expert witness, giving an expert's opinion as to what the grantor's intention was. The surveyor's work is a critical factor in each of the three types of descriptions discussed in this chapter and commonly used in the United States: metes and bounds, the rectangular survey, and plats and maps.

Metes and Bounds

> *A method of describing land by specifying the exterior boundaries of the property using compass directions, monuments or landmarks*

where directions change and linear measurement of distances between these points.

As the eastern United States was settled and developed, probably the most common method of describing land was to name the parcel. For example, the property would be described as the Jacktown plantation or the Ebenezer Smith farm. Usually boundaries were indicated by naming the owners of adjoining property or by natural landmarks called *monuments.* An early 19th century deed in a trespass case described the property as follows:

> A certain tract or parcel of land, including the mill-seat and mill known as the "Jethro R. Franklin Mill," the said tract situated in the county of Gates, embracing as far as the highwater mark, and bounded as follows: on the north by the lands of Richard E. Parker, Reddick Brinkley, and others, on the east by the lands of Harrison Brinkley and others, south by the desert road, west by the lands of Josiah H. Reddick and others.

A description based primarily on *adjoiners* (names of owners of contiguous property, a road or something similar) and monuments is still used if the costs of a survey are out of proportion to the amount of money involved. Descriptions of this nature may cause problems if some impermanent monuments are selected.

Metes-and-bounds descriptions provide a more sophisticated method of describing real property. A metes-and-bounds description is based upon a survey that commences at a beginning point on the boundary of the tract and follows compass directions, called *courses,* and distances around the area to the point of beginning. Monuments are placed at the corners or at points where directions change. Monuments are visible objects, sometimes natural but often artificial. They can be posts, iron pipes, piles of stone, trees, streams or similar objects. By following the courses and distances, a person should be able to walk the boundaries of the property.

A typical metes-and-bounds description follows:

> Beginning at an iron pipe marked A and thence running South 8 degrees 15 minutes East 75 feet to a pipe marked B thence North 78 degrees 27 minutes East 34-3/10 feet to a pipe marked C thence North 11 degrees 28 minutes West 74-9/10 feet to a pipe marked D thence South 78 degrees 27 minutes West 30-2/10 feet to the place of beginning containing 2410.7 square feet, more or less.

In reading a metes-and-bounds description, one always says "north" or "south" first and then announces the number of degrees east or west of that north or south line. The number of degrees east or west of the north or south line cannot exceed 90. Thus, to say "North 95 degrees East" as a designation for Line A in Figure 9.1 is incorrect. The correct reading is "South 85 degrees East."

Figure 9.1: Metes and Bounds

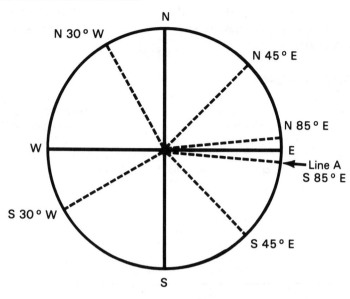

Metes-and-bounds descriptions based upon a survey provide a very accurate method of designating the physical dimensions of a particular tract of land. When the land itself is supplied with permanent markers at each corner or angle, the parcel can be readily located for a long period of time. This method of describing land continues to be used extensively in the eastern United States. Metes-and-bounds descriptions are also used extensively in other areas of the country in conjunction with the rectangular survey to designate small parcels.

Call

> *A term used to refer to the different monuments, courses and distances that make up a metes-and-bounds description.*

Metes-and-bounds descriptions are not always based upon a survey. Sometimes natural monuments used as calls are destroyed; in other instances, conflicting calls are the result of human error. To solve problems resulting from conflicting calls, courts have established a general order of preference to be given to calls when the intention of the parties is not clear. Natural monuments are preferred because they are considered more reliable than courses and distances. The general order of preference is as follows:

1. natural monuments,
2. artificial monuments,
3. courses,
4. distances, and
5. quantity of acreage.

Adjoining landowners (adjoiners) are also important elements in some descriptions and receive a high degree of priority. Unless the adjoiner is clearly a mistake, it ranks with monuments, prevailing over courses, distances and quantity of acreage.

Case Example

Jones and Morrison purchased contiguous parcels from a common grantor. The deed to Jones described the east line of his property as being from the center of Edison Street south to a bois d'arc tree, a distance of 79 feet. Morrison's deed described his property's east line as being from the center of College Street north to a bois d'arc tree, a distance of 210 feet. Actually, the distance from the center of Edison Street to the tree was 86 feet; from the center of College Street the distance was 207 feet, as shown on the map.

$\uparrow$
N

Edison St.

Jones	86 feet
X	Bois D'Arc Tree
Morrison	207 feet

College St.

Morrison constructed a building on the property that encroached upon what Jones believed was his land. Jones sued to require the removal of the encroaching portion of the building. In finding for Jones, the court stated, "[t]his makes the case a classic example . . . for application of the rule that courses and distances must yield to natural monuments . . . " *Morrison v. Jones, 58 Tenn. App. 333, 430 S.W.2d 668 (1968).*

Rectangular Survey System

System of land description that applies to most of the land in the United States.

After the Revolutionary War, the United States acquired a vast area of land west of Pennsylvania and north of the Ohio River. This area, known as the Northwest Territory, was acquired when states ceded their claims to the United States as a means of paying their war debts. Faced with pressures from land speculators and settlers as well as the need for revenue, Congress in 1785 passed legislation to prepare these lands for disposal.

An important element of this legislation was the establishment of a *rectangular survey system*. Although the government survey was criticized and attacked by the private land companies, it eventually became the foundation upon which vast areas of the West were surveyed and sold.

With the exception of Texas, land descriptions in all states west of the Mississippi, the five states formed from the Northwest Territory and most of Alabama, Florida and Mississippi are based upon this massive survey. Eventually, the survey covered more than two million square miles in the continental United States. It has been extended to Alaska, where hundreds of thousands of square miles remain unsurveyed. Although modified by legislation from time to time over the 200 years that the system has been used, the fundamentals of the rectangular survey have remained fairly consistent.

Initially, a large area is selected for survey and a starting point is chosen. This initial point is chosen by astronomical observation. A line called a *baseline* is run east and west through this point. A perpendicular line also runs north and south through the initial point. This is called the *principal meridian*. The survey for the entire district is based upon these two lines. Over the long history of the government survey, 32 baselines and 35 principal meridians have been established.

Principal meridians and baselines are designated in various ways. At first they were numbered, but later they were given names. The first principal meridian is the western boundary of Ohio. The 41st parallel is its accompanying baseline. All land descriptions in a particular area surveyed with reference to a principal meridian will refer to it. The basic unit of the survey is the *township*.

Township

An area of land approximately six miles square, containing as nearly as possible 23,040 acres and divided into 36 sections, each of one square mile.

Legislation guiding the surveyors required a township to be a square, as nearly as possible six miles on a side. Because the lines that run parallel to the principal meridian converge toward the north, townships in the north would be smaller than the required 36 square miles. To remedy this, correction lines are run parallel to a baseline at 24-mile intervals north and south. These lines are called

Figure 9.2: Starting Point for a Survey

standard parallels or correction lines. Lines called guide meridians are then surveyed east and west at 24-mile intervals with a standard parallel as a base. Although the townships in the North are slightly smaller than those in the South, the constant correction kept the difference at a minimum. Some early surveys established correction lines at intervals much greater than 24 miles, leading to substantial discrepancy in township size. Continuous establishment of guide meridians and standard parallels reduced the compounding effect of surveying errors.

Each guide meridian and standard parallel, as shown in Figure 9.3, is designated by numerical order and compass direction from the appropriate principal meridian and baseline. The intersections of guide meridians and standard parallels create square blocks or tracts 24 miles on each side. Townships are created by dividing these 24-mile tracts at six-mile intervals. The result is 16 township units approximately six miles square in each tract.

Although these 24-mile-square blocks are not a factor in describing real estate, townships are an integral part of a land description. Over an entire area surveyed, tiers of townships are numbered north and south from the baseline. They are also numbered consecutively east and west from the principal meridian. The east-west tiers are called ranges. Each township as a result has two numbers and two directions. These numbers and directions thus provide a specific designation for each. Since all townships and ranges are numbered in reference to a particular principal meridian and baseline, no two have the same designation.

The shaded unit in Figure 9.4 is 3 north, Range 3 west of a principal meridian. This would be indicated as T3N, R3W. Townships are not only important elements in many land descriptions, they also are often important political subdivisions.

Figure 9.3: U.S. Public Land—Rectangular System of Subdividing

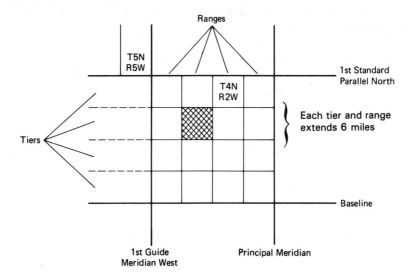

Division of Land into Tracts 24 miles square.

Figure 9.4: Township Designations

Figure 9.5: U.S. Public Land Survey—Typical Method of Numbering Sections

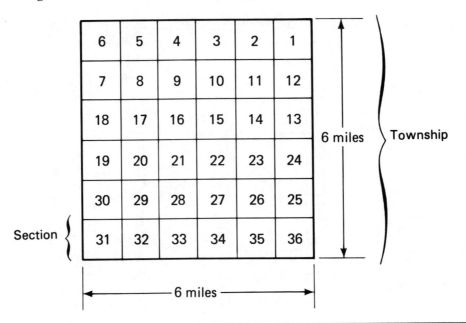

Section

An area of land approximately one mile square, containing as nearly as possible 640 acres.

Each township of approximately six miles square is further divided into sections. A township thus contains 36 sections. The sections in a township are numbered consecutively, beginning in the northeast corner with the number 1. Six sections are numbered westerly along the far north of the township. Section 7, just south of section 6, commences a row numbered in an easterly direction (see Figure 9.5). This pattern of alternating west-east numbering is followed, with section 36 being the southeast unit in the township.

Although a different numbering system was used in some of the early surveys, most of the land surveyed has sections designated in this manner. As a result, the number of the section is also a key element in describing a particular parcel of land.

Commercial realities of land disposal often resulted in a need to divide each section further. Half sections, quarter sections, and even smaller units were needed. This division is readily accomplished by surveying and designating smaller units by their geographic location within the section.

A half section may be described as the north one-half of section 15 and a quarter section as the northwest one-quarter of section 15. As each section consisted of 640 acres, the number of acres in each of these smaller units is easy to determine. A half section is 320 acres; a quarter section is 160. Figure 9.6 indicates additional divisions of a section that are commonly used. As each township has a numerical designation in relation to a particular baseline and

Figure 9.6: Divisions of a Section

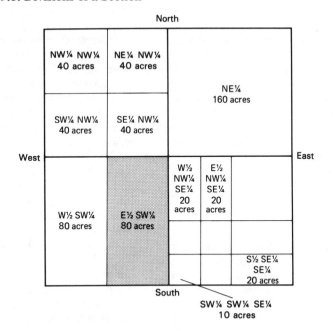

each section a number, any of these smaller plots is precisely located within the square mile of which it is a part.

The section designation of a description using the rectangular survey system might read as "the east 1/2 of the SW1/4." This would be the shaded portion of Figure 9.6. If the tract conveyed were in two quarters, the quarter section designations would be joined by "and." For example, the description might be worded as "the east 1/2 of the northwest 1/4 and the east 1/2 of the southwest 1/4."

Governmental surveys were not made under ideal conditions. Errors often resulted because of weather, harsh terrain, hostile Indians, primitive equipment and plain ineptitude. The prevailing legal rule, however, has consistently been that, once land has been conveyed on the basis of a government survey, the conveyance will not be disturbed even if error is found in the survey. This is indicated in the case that follows.

Bishop v. Johnson
District Court of Appeals of Florida
100 So. 2d 817 (1958)

Background: Ralph and Francis Johnson (plaintiff, appellees) obtained title to a peninsula extending into Water Pen Lake. Their title was based on an official government survey and plat made in 1894. In 1949, a private survey of the lake showed a second peninsula just south of the first. This peninsula and adjacent land were conveyed to Wilbur Bishop (defendant, appellant).

Later it became clear that the official survey was erroneous. There was no peninsula as indicated on the official plat. The only peninsula was that indicated by the private survey. Both Bishop and the Johnsons claimed the peninsula and the Johnsons brought a suit to quiet title to the area. Their title was affirmed by the trial court and Bishop appealed.

Decision: The decree quieting title in the Johnsons was affirmed.

Judge Wigginton
Suit was brought by plaintiffs, the appellees here, to quiet title to portions of a certain peninsula of land which extends westerly from the eastern shore of and into the navigable waters of Water Pen Lake, commonly known as Cow Pen Lake, in Putnam County.

Appellees, as plaintiffs at trial, claimed title by mesne conveyances out of the United States Government. Appellants claimed record title under deed from the Trustees of the Internal Improvement Fund, and as owners of the mainland to which the peninsula is physically attached. On motion for summary decree the Chancellor entered a decree finding record titled in the appellees.

A copy of the map showing the contended location of the disputed lands is here inserted for convenience and clarity of explanation:

During the last quarter of the year 1849 an official federal government survey was made of lands now constituting Sections 20, 21, 22, 27, 28 and 29 of Township 10S, Range 23 East. From this survey, and the field notes compiled as an incident thereto, an official township plat was constructed, approved and recorded.

This peninsula as it is identified by the government survey plat is depicted above by the letter "P", and consists of Lot 9 of Section 21, containing 12.10 acres, and Lot 3 of Section 22 containing 40.13 acres.

By patent dated November 18, 1903, the United States conveyed Lot 9 of Section 21 and Lot 3 of Section 22, both lying in Township 10 S, Range 12 E, to the State of Florida. Thereafter, on September 16, 1927, the Trustees of the Internal Improvement Fund conveyed both lots to one Phillip Bersch, who, on August 8, 1953, conveyed them to the appellees. It is under title thus dereigned that appellees based their claim.

Late in 1949 a private survey was conducted from which it was concluded that the peninsula, designated as Lots 9 and 3, was actually situated south and west of the point shown on the official plat. According to this private survey, the peninsula is appended to the mainland at the Northwest corner of Lot 1, in Section 27, as shown by the letter "E" on the above map. In reliance upon this private survey, and under the mistaken belief that there existed a second peninsula, the Trustees of the Internal Improvement Fund issued to appellants as grantees a deed which purported to convey, by metes and bounds, the peninsula described in the aforementioned private survey. Some time after July 6, 1950, the date of the last mentioned deed, appellants acquired title to the northern portion of Lot 1, Section 27. Appellants rely upon the deed of July 6, 1950, and the subsequent deed to Lot 1 in asserting their title to the disputed peninsula.

It is admitted by the parties hereto that there is, in fact only one peninsula extending westwardly from the east shore of the lake and into the waters thereof.

It is to be noted at the outset that the government survey of 1849 did not merely ascertain or identify the disputed lands, but created Lots 9 and 3, in Sections 21 and 22 respectively, being that peninsula lying in Township 10 S, Range 23 East. The mere fact that a subsequent private survey shows an error by the United States Deputy Surveyor in locating the peninsula on the official plat is immaterial, since the latter survey is not admissible in evidence to affect or change the lines or location of land sold in accordance with an official government survey and plat.

It is well settled that the description of land and plats from field notes of an original survey filed in the General Land Office are conclusive, and section lines and corners as laid down therein are binding upon the General Government and all parties concerned. When lands described in a deed are by reference to or in accordance with a plat or survey, the courses, distances and *other particulars* appearing on the plat are to be as much regarded as if expressly set forth in the deed itself. The plaintiff and his predecessors in title acquired the land in question with reference to the official government plat which showed the property purchased to be a peninsula of land designated as lying in Sections 21 and 22, and extending from the eastern shoreline westward into the lake. The defendants are charged with knowledge, either actual or constructive, that the peninsula in question had been surveyed, platted and conveyed by the sovereign with reference to and in accordance with the official plat and that title thereto had become vested in the plaintiffs long before the defendants sought to acquire the lands by reference to a private resurvey. A resurvey that purports to change lines or distances or to otherwise correct inaccuracies and mistakes in an old plat is not competent evidence of the true line fixed by the original plat. Accordingly, it must be concluded that, as between the parties hereto, the government survey is paramount.

Further, there being but one peninsula, appellants' contention that title thereto vests in them as owners of the mainland to which it is attached on the theory that it is an unsurveyed finger of land cut off by meander lines is untenable. According to the undisputed facts, the only existing peninsula was actually surveyed and platted by the United States Government while the land was a part of the public domain; and title thereto was subsequently vested in appellees. Such facts cannot be overcome by an attack upon alleged inaccuracies in the government survey attempted to be shown by an inadmissible private survey. Appellants being thus without evidence to overcome appellees' established record title, it must be concluded that a summary decree for appellees was proper.

Therefore, we are of the opinion that the Chancellor properly entered a summary decree finding title to the disputed peninsula to be vested in appellees. Accordingly, the decree appealed from must be and is hereby affirmed.

In most cases a survey does not create boundaries. Boundaries are created by the agreement of parties. The official government survey of the public land does, however, create boundaries. An original government survey, whether correct or erroneous, controls the boundaries of a section and parcels of land surveyed and platted from it. Courts feel that the parties who purchase property based upon a plat from an official survey have a right to rely on it. If the survey is confirmed by the proper officials of the Department of the Interior, attack in the courts is no longer permitted when the property is sold.

Plat

A map showing items such as natural and artificial monuments, lots, blocks and streets in a town or subdivision; generally drawn from a survey.

A third method of describing land is by reference to a recorded plat or map. This method is used frequently in metropolitan areas. Usually it is used in conjunction with the rectangular survey or a metes-and-bounds description of a larger tract that is being divided. The property to be divided is surveyed and laid out in lots that are numbered in sequence. These lots are platted and when sold are described by their designated numbers. A description of this kind might read as follows:

All of lot 8 in block 41 in Taylors Astoria, an addition within the corporate limits of the City of Astoria, Clatsop County, State of Oregon, as said addition was laid out and recorded by the Peninsular Land & Trust Company.

Although the deed does not contain the description of the entire survey, the United States Supreme Court in an early case supported this system. The court stated:

> . . . when lands are granted according to an official plat of the survey
> . . . , the plat itself along with all its notes, lines, descriptions, and
> landmarks becomes as much a part of the grant or deed . . . as if such
> descriptive features were written out upon the face of the deed . . .
> *Cragin v. Powell, 128 U.S. 696 (1888).*

The use of maps and plats of surveys has become an important means of describing land in the United States. Plats are readily available because almost all states and many localities require a developer, when subdividing property, to have the property surveyed and a plat of it made by a competent surveyor. A typical plat is shown in Figure 9.7.

Although requirements vary, the plat generally shows the proposed streets, blocks and lots of the subdivision. The plat will also show such items as easements, rights of way and topographical details, such as elevations, as well as other physical features. School sites and recreational areas are indicated on plats for larger developments. Blocks and lots are designated in some manner, usually by number but sometimes by letter.

In most areas subdivision plats must be approved by some governmental body before land is sold. Usually this is a local planning commission or a designated official such as the county engineer. The approved plat is then recorded in a *plat book* as part of the public land records. The property in the subdivision is thus accurately described by reference to this record. In addition, recording of the plat serves to dedicate to public use land indicated on the plat as streets, parks and school and church sites.

In preparing land for a subdivision, the surveyor must carefully mark with permanent monuments physical boundaries of the parcels involved. The survey actually fixes the boundaries of the property, and these are reflected in the plat. If the plat and the boundaries fixed by the survey differ, the boundary as established by the physical monuments prevails.

Boundary Disputes

Courts have adopted several rules in efforts to solve boundary disputes equitably. A fundamental principle is that the intention of the parties establishing a boundary should prevail. Although the plain meaning of the words used in a description is the best indication of intention, conflicting and ambiguous designations of boundaries must often be resolved by other rules. An example is the doctrine of "agreed boundaries."

For the doctrine of "agreed boundaries" to apply, the owners of adjoining property must be uncertain as to the true boundary. They must then agree as to what the true boundary is. This agreement does not have to be in writing. A minority of states require that there be some visible evidence of the boundary to be established. In any case, the boundary agreed upon must be definite and certain. In a few states the parties must continue to agree for a period equal to that required in cases of adverse possession. In most states acquiescence for a shorter period is sufficient; however, the period varies greatly from state to state.

Figure 9.7: Plat Adapted from *Davis v. DeVore, 16 Ill. App. 334, 306 N.E.2d 72 (1974)*

MAP OF BROOKVIEW
SCALE 1″ = 200   JUNE 22, 1945
FRITZ LEROV WASHBURN SR.
SURVEYOR

NOTE
*INDICATES IRON DIN

Case Example

Rouse owned a quarter section of land. In 1932 he sold the west portion to Cooper. In 1944 Rouse sold the east portion to Huggans. At the time of the sale to Cooper, the parties did not determine the exact boundary between the two properties but described the property using an old fence as one line. When Rouse conveyed the east parcel to Huggans in 1944, the description in the deed referred to the west boundary of the Huggans tract as the Cooper fence.

Huggans used the land up to the fence from 1944 until 1978. In 1978 the Cooper property was acquired by Weer. A survey at that time established the true property line 60 feet east of the fence. Upon acquiring the information, Weer attempted to remove the Cooper fence and Huggans petitioned the court for a temporary restraining order.

Huggans claimed that he had title to the 60-foot strip up to the fence, based upon adverse possession and the doctrine of agreed boundaries. This claim was rejected by the court because he had not met statutory requirements for adverse possession and proof of an agreed boundary was not clear and convincing. *Huggans v. Weer, 615 P.2d 922 (Mont. 1980).*

Intention in many situations is determined by what courts presume or infer the parties probably desire to occur. An example is found in the common solution to the substantial litigation involving title to a public thoroughfare. When land abutting on a public road or street is conveyed, the grantee takes title to the centerline unless the description specifically excludes this area. This rule applies even if the description designates the tract as "bounded by" or "bordering on" the particular public way. The reason is that courts consider it unlikely that a grantor conveying land on a public way had any intention of retaining title to the area dedicated to public use. Since the grantor has conveyed the abutting property, the small strip of land is of little value to him or her. It is, however, important to the grantee, who now owns the adjacent land. On the other hand, if the conveyance specifically reserves the narrow strip for the grantor, the intention of the parties will be honored as this intention is the most significant factor.

Sales Personnel and Property Description

Property description is an important element of almost every real estate transaction. Although it is ordinarily the concern of the real estate lawyer, all real estate sales personnel should be aware of its important legal aspects. If problems involving descriptions are discovered early in the proceedings, before the deed or other document involving the property is prepared, time can be saved and trouble averted.

Sometimes real estate personnel obtain information about boundary problems when listing property or drawing up a contract. These should be carefully noted and an effort made to have the owner resolve the problems before entering serious negotiations with prospective buyers. Because boundary disputes may indicate description problems, a sales associate who becomes aware of a boundary controversy when negotiating a sale of real estate should alert the seller's attorney so that the description can be verified.

Summary

In order to be enforceable, a real estate instrument must contain a *legal description* of the property. The description must be complete enough to locate and identify the premises. The physical boundaries are integral to this description because they locate the property on the earth's surface. The boundaries in a legal description must be complete; they must enclose the parcel. In cases where boundary disputes exist, courts hear testimony of the parties to the dispute, surveyors, neighbors and others to determine what property the parties intended to convey.

The work of a surveyor in measuring the actual parcel and translating it to a map is an integral part of real estate business. The surveyor's work is critical to the three types of land description commonly used in the United States today: *metes and bounds*, the *rectangular survey*, and *plats* and maps.

The first type, metes and bounds, specifies the exterior boundaries of the property, based on a survey that commences at a beginning point on the boundary and follows courses (compass directions) and distances around the area. By following the description and observing any *call* or monument (a tree, stream or post, for example) noted in the wording, a person should be able to walk the boundaries of the property. Over time monuments may be destroyed or obliterated. In the case of conflict courts have established an order of priority, with natural monuments taking precedence over artificial ones as well as over courses and distances. Established boundaries of other owners (adjoiners) rank along with natural monuments.

The rectangular survey is a system established by the government over 200 years ago to map a large portion of U.S. land. Based on a grid of baselines (east-west) and principal meridians (north-south), the survey for each district refers to these lines, which are either named or numbered. The basic unit, the *township*, is six miles square. This area is divided into 36 *sections*. A section is a square one mile on each side. The sections in a township are numbered consecutively. These parcels can be further divided by survey for purchase as individual lots.

Maps that are platted from official surveys are the third method of land description. They are used frequently in metropolitan areas. In most areas of the country subdivision plats, prepared by the developer from official maps and by the developer's own surveyors, must be approved by an official agency, usually the county engineer. When approved, the map is recorded in the plat book as part of the public record.

Boundary disputes in the past have led the courts to adopt several rules or guidelines for their solution. Principal among them is that the intention of the parties should prevail. To reduce the incidence of disputes, however, real estate professionals should be aware of the need for a clearly written description as part of the legal conveyance.

Review and Discussion Questions

1. Sketch an imaginary principal meridian and baseline and indicate the location of (a) Township 3 North, Range 3 East and (b) Township 1 South, Range 3 West.

2. Define the following terms and indicate their relationship to the rectangular survey system: (a) principal meridian, (b) baseline, (c) township and (d) section.

3. The sketch below represents a section. Indicate the correct rectangular survey designation for the shaded protions labeled A and B.

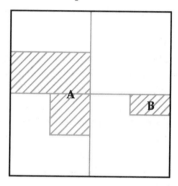

4. Locate the following tracts of land in a section and indicate the acreage of each.

(a) E1/2 SE1/4

(b) NW1/4 NW1/4 NW1/4

Case Problems

1. A contract for sale of real estate described the property as follows:

> Property of Greene D. Spillman located at Spillman, La., in Sections 48 and 49, T1S, R2W, West Feliciana Parish, La., and improvements. Bounded on the North by lands of Merrick on the South by lands of Thoms and heirs of C. H. Bickham on the East by Hwy. 967 and on the West by Mills Creek. The grounds measuring about 275 acres as per title for the sum of Sixty Thousand, Five Hundred Dollars.

Engquist signed a contract to purchase this property. A survey indicated that the farm contained only 223.64 acres. When Engquist refused to perform, the owner sued for breach of contract. (a) Would the owner be successful? Support your answer. (b) What is the meaning of the terms T1S, R2W? *Adams v. Spillman, 290 So.2d 726 (La. 1974).*

2. Sketch the following parcel.

    Beginning at a point 447.18 feet East of the N.W. corner of SE1/4 SE1/4, said Sec. 21; thence North 88 degrees 57'30" East 402.00 feet; thence South 987.68 feet; thence North 89 degrees 56' West 401.93 feet; thence North 979.48 feet to the point of beginning. *LeBaron v. Crimson, 412 P.2d 705 (Ariz. 1966).*

3. Brasker, a real estate broker, claimed an interest in one and one-half acres in Lot 4 on the north end of Sapelo Island. Brasker supported his claim with a deed that included the following description: "All of that certain lot, tract or parcel of land situate, lying and being in the 1312 District, G.M., McIntosh County Georgia, at Raccoon Bluff on Sapelo Island, containing Twenty-One (21) acres, more or less and being Lot (4) Four of the Raccoon Bluff Subdivision of William Hillary. Said property being bounded Northerly by Lot 3; Easterly by Blackbeard Island River; Southerly by Lot 5; and Westerly by the lot line of Raccoon Bluff Tract. This being that same property conveyed to Ben Brown by deed and plat from William Hillary dated July, 1882 and recorded in Deed Book `U' at Page 298 and 299, to which said deed and plat reference is hereby made for all intents and purposes."

    A plat showed one-acre and four-acre tracts out of Lot 4 established by a surveyor in 1882. The defendant argued that the deed was ineffective. Who is correct? Support your answer. [Adapted from *Brasker v. Tanner, 356 S.E. 2d 478 (Ga. 1987)*]

4. Brasker also claimed an interest an interest in a three-acre tract on Sapelo Island. The three acres had conveyed from a larger lot in a 1907 deed to Jack Handy. The defendants argued that the deed was ineffective because the tract's boundaries were not clear. The legal description from the warranty deed from Jack Handy's heirs was as follows: "that certain tract of land in McIntosh County on Sapelo Island, three (3) acres, more or less, and being in the 1312 District, and bounded on the North by Toni Handy and brothers, on the East by public Road, South by John Bailey and West by Sam Roberts."

    Is the description adequate? What is the key factor in determining the description's adequacy?

10

Involuntary Transfers

The conveyance of real property by deed, sometimes called *voluntary alienation*, was discussed in Chapter 8. A conveyance by deed is generally the result of a mutual agreement set forth in a real estate sales contract. There are, however, several circumstances under which title to real property is transferred involuntarily. These include involuntary alienations and transfers of property upon death, which are discussed in this chapter.

Involuntary Alienation

The transfer of title to land against the owner's wishes.

Involuntary alienation includes forced sales resulting from liens, foreclosures, condemnation or adverse possession and transfer by natural forces such as accretion. Various ways in which title to real estate may be transferred against the owner's wishes are discussed below. Forced sales resulting from liens are treated in Chapters 18 and 19.

Adverse Possession

Acquisition of title to real property by means of wrongful occupancy for a period of time established by statute.

Adverse possession is based upon the statute of limitations. As a general rule, a person in possession of realty has good title against everyone but the true owner. The true owner has a right to bring legal action to gain possession if the occupant wrongfully withholds it. The statute of limitations requires that this cause of action be brought within a certain time. The time varies from state to state but is usually 12, 15, 20 or 21 years. If the owner does not sue within the statutory term, the adverse possessor, upon meeting certain conditions, acquires title to the land.

Although the adverse possessor actually acquires title to the property, litigation is usually necessary to establish clear title before it can be sold. The reason is that the public records of land ownership shows someone other than the adverse possessor as the owner.

The Elements of Adverse Possession

A number of conditions must be met for a person to acquire title to land by adverse possession. Both case law and statutes establish requirements, although they differ from state to state and even from case to case. Some common qualifications are that such possession must be open, hostile, continuous and exclusive. Other adjectives sometimes used are *adverse, notorious, under claim of title* and *under color of title*. These requirements express a judicial and legislative intention that possession must be sufficiently evident to give the owner notice of what is happening, that possession be without the owner's permission, and that possession be exclusive and for the full term set by the statute.

Case Example

Marengo Cave Company owned land upon which the only entrance to a large cave was located. The cave was occupied exclusively by the company for the statutory term and was used as a tourist attraction. When Ross, an adjoining landowner, discovered through a survey that a portion of the cave extended under his land, he brought a quiet title suit. The court found that, even though the company's possession was widely publicized in connection with the tourist business, it was still not "open and notorious" because an ordinary observer on the land could not have readily seen that the owner's rights were being invaded. Hence, Marengo Cave Company did not gain title by adverse possession. *Marengo Cave Co. v. Ross, 212 Ind. 624, 10 N.E.2d 917 (1937).*

The courts also require that possession be *exclusive and continuous* for the entire statutory period. This means that, if the land is abandoned or the true owner reenters either in the absence of the adverse possessor or simultaneously, the statutory term is interrupted and must start over again. A brief absence, such as a vacation, by the adverse possessor is probably not enough to defeat this requirement, however. With nonresidential property, what constitutes continual and exclusive possession may be difficult to resolve.

A related issue arises when there is a succession of adverse possessors. Most jurisdictions allow the "tacking" of one possessor's term to that of another if one acquired directly from the other, as with a sale or conveyance by will.

Case Example

Martin was the owner of a lot, but Boyer was in possession for five years from 1940 to 1945. Then Boyer purported to sell the lot to Lucas, who possessed it for eight years and devised it to Tenton in 1953. Tenton, however, did not enter the land. When Tenton died in 1956, his heirs took possession. They sued to quiet title in 1969.

The heirs would lose this suit in a jurisdiction with a 20-year statute, because even tacking Boyer's term to Lucas's would bring the total to only 13 years. During the three years the lot was empty (1953 to 1956), possession reverted to Martin, the true owner. Adverse possession was not exclusive and continuous for the requisite 20 years. The heirs would win in a state with a 12-year statute, however, since their own entry and possession in 1956 would start the running of the statutory term.

When Adverse Possession Does Not Apply

In addition to these elements of adverse possession, statutes and case law also often provide that in some situations statutes of limitations are prolonged or do not run at all. For example, adverse possession cannot be applied against the state or against one whose interest is not yet a possessory right, such as a holder of a future interest. It cannot be applied against those who have certain disabilities, such as infants, the mentally incompetent and the insane. For a disability to prevent the running of the statute, however, it must exist at the time a right to sue accrues, usually when the adverse possessor enters the land. An intervening disability does not bar the running of the statute. In addition, the disability is personal to the owner and cannot pass to his or her successors.

The Purpose of Adverse Possession

To many, adverse possession seems like a legal way of acquiring land without compensating the owner, and some question whether, with modern legislation like model title acts, recording acts and the like, society needs this ancient doctrine. Nevertheless, public policy has historically supported the doctrine. Those who defend adverse possession argue that the state has certain duties to citizens:

- It should eliminate stale claims since evidence and witnesses may be unavailable.

- It should discourage *laches*—that is, delayed enforcement of one's rights.

- It should encourage full and efficient use of land.

- It should facilitate land transfer by providing a means to remove old title problems and thus quiet titles.

It seems likely that adverse possession will continue to be an aspect of property law for the foreseeable future. The prudent owner of vacant land held for development or investment will make periodic inspections of the property to check for adverse possessors. The mere posting of "no trespassing" signs is probably not sufficient to protect the owner's interest.

Eminent Domain

The power of government to take private property for public use; state and federal constitutions require just compensation to the property owner.

The power of eminent domain is one of the major attributes of sovereignty. In the United States, both federal and state governments are sovereign and may exercise this power. No specific constitutional grant is necessary for government to have the right to take private property for public use, although several state constitutions do contain provisions allocating the power of eminent domain to the state.

Eminent domain is a power that government may delegate. The result is that eminent domain is often exercised by villages, cities and counties as well as public bodies such as school boards and sanitation districts. The power can also be delegated to private corporations such as railroads, power companies and other public utilities. Upon a proper delegation, eminent domain may be exercised by individuals and partnerships. In any case, the status of the party exercising the power is not the critical factor. For a delegation to be proper, the property must be devoted to a public use.

Public Use
A use that benefits the community.

The Fifth Amendment to the U.S. Constitution and the constitutions of the individual states require that property acquired through eminent domain be used to benefit the public and that just compensation be paid to the owners. Historically, in the United States, eminent domain has been used mostly to acquire land for public transportation systems and to satisfy government's need for space to conduct its business. As government has become increasingly involved in many aspects of life, the use of eminent domain has likewise increased. Today, government may use the power to acquire interest in land for diverse purposes such as parking lots to relieve congestion and traffic hazards, scenic beauty along highways and public recreation.

Case Example

Before 1967 most of the land in Hawaii that was not owned by the state or federal government was owned in fee simple by 72 private landowners. These landowners, who had acquired their titles through the descendants of Polynesian chiefs, refused to sell land. They would only lease it on long-term leases. At the termination of a lease that was not renewed, the land and improvements reverted to the landowners.

In 1967 the Hawaiian legislature, using its power of eminent domain, enacted a Land Reform Act designed to extend the fee simple ownership of Hawaiian land. The act created a mechanism for condemning residential tracts and transferring ownership to existing lessees, while affording the landowners just compensation.

The owners of the fee simple estates challenged the constitutionality of the legislative action. They argued that their property was not taken for a public use or purpose because the government itself never possessed or used the land but transferred it to individuals. The United States Supreme Court determined that the statute was constitutional. The court stated that correcting inequities in the housing market satisfied the constitutional requirement that land be taken for a public use or purpose. *Hawaii Housing Authority v. Midkeff, 467 U.S. 229 (1984).*

Although land taken by eminent domain must be used for a public purpose, different interpretations exist as to what this means. A number of jurisdictions require that the property actually be used by the public. Even in these jurisdictions, the facility does not have to be open to the public, as long as some arm of government actually supervises the operation. Thus, public use is satisfied if a utility acquires property by eminent domain even though the general public cannot use the facility. A public utility commission supervises the overall business of the company and ensures that the property is used in the public interest.

In most jurisdictions, the public use requirement is met if some benefit to the public results from the acquisition of the property. The benefit does not have to be direct, nor does all of the public have to receive some advantage. Courts have allowed the state to transfer lands acquired by condemnation to a private firm to build a plant that would increase employment in the area and to a developer to eliminate a slum. And, as the next case indicates, a physical invasion of the land is not necessary in order for eminent domain to occur.

United States v. Causby
Supreme Court of the United States
328 U.S. 256 (1946)

Background: Appellant, the United States, repeatedly operated aircraft passing 83 feet over the respondents' (the Causbys) farm property. The aircraft passed 63 feet above their barn and 18 feet above the highest tree. Respondents claimed this amounted to a taking of their property and that they were entitled to just compensation. They sued and the U.S. Court of Claims agreed, awarding them $2,000. The government appealed to the United States Supreme Court.

Decision: The United States Supreme Court agreed with the Court of Claims that a taking occurred, but remanded the case to that court to make specific what property was taken and its value.

Mr. Justice Douglas

This is a case of first impression. The problem presented is whether respondents' property was taken, within the meaning of the Fifth Amendment, by frequent and regular flights of army and navy aircraft over respondents' land at low altitudes.

Respondents own 2.8 acres near an airport outside of Greensboro, North Carolina. It has on it a dwelling house, and also various outbuildings which were mainly used for raising chickens. The end of the airport's northwest-southeast runway is 2,220 feet from respondents' barn and 2,275 feet from their house. The path of glide to this runway passes directly over the property—which is 100 feet wide and 1,200 feet long. Since the United States began operations in May, 1942, its four-motored heavy bombers, other planes of the heavier type, and its fighter planes have frequently passed over respondents' land and buildings in considerable numbers and rather close together. They come close enough at times to appear barely to miss the tops of the trees and at times so close to the tops of the trees as to blow the old leaves off. The noise is startling. And at night the glare from the planes brightly lights up the place. As a result of the noise, respondents had to give up their chicken business. As many as six to ten of their chickens were killed in one day by flying into the walls from fright. The total chickens lost in that manner was about 150. Production also fell off. The result was the destruction of the use of the property as a commercial chicken farm. Respondents are frequently deprived of their sleep and the family has become nervous and frightened. . . . The air is a public highway, as Congress has declared. Were that not true, every transcontinental flight would subject the operator to countless trespass suits. Common sense revolts at the idea. To recognize such private claims to the airspace would clog these highways, seriously interfere with their control and development in the public interest, and transfer into private ownership that to which only the public has a just claim.

But that general principle does not control the present case. For the United States conceded on oral argument that if the flights over respondents' property rendered it uninhabitable, there would be a taking compensable under the Fifth Amendment. . . . If, by reason of the frequency and altitude of the flights, respondents could not use their land for any purpose, their loss would be complete. It would be complete as if the United States had entered upon the surface of the land and taken exclusive possession of it.

. . .

There is no material difference between the supposed case and the present one, except that here enjoyment and use of the land are not completely destroyed. But that does not seem to us to be controlling. The path of glide for airplanes might reduce a valuable factory site to grazing land, an orchard to a vegetable patch, a residential section to a wheat field. Some value would remain. But the use of the air-space immediately above the land would limit the utility of the land and cause a diminution in its value.

. . .

As we have said, the flight of airplanes, which skim the surface but do not touch it, is as much an appropriation of the use of the land as a more conventional entry upon it. . . . While the owner does not in any physical manner occupy that stratum of airspace or make use of it in the conventional sense, he does use it in somewhat the same sense that space left between buildings for the purpose of light and air is used. The superadjacent airspace at this low altitude is so close to the land that continuous invasions of it affect the use of the surface of the land itself. We think that the landowner, as an incident to his ownership, has a claim to it and that invasions of it are in the same category as invasions of the surface.

The airplane is part of the modern environment of life, and inconveniences which it causes are normally not compensable under the Fifth Amendment. The airspace, apart from the immediate reaches above the land, is part of the public domain. We need not determine at this time what those precise limits are. Flights over private land are not a taking, unless they are so low and so frequent as to be a direct and immediate interference with the enjoyment and use of the land. We need not speculate on that phase of the present case. For the findings of the Court of Claims plainly establish that there was a diminution in value of the property and that the frequent, low-level flights were the direct and immediate cause. We agree with the Court of Claims that a servitude has been imposed upon the land.

· · ·

Since on this record it is not clear whether the easement taken is a permanent or a temporary one, it would be premature for us to consider whether the amount of the award made by the Court of Claims was proper.

The judgment is reversed and the cause is remanded to the Court of Claims so that it may make the necessary findings in conformity with this opinion.

Reversed.

Just Compensation

The award the owner is entitled to when property is taken by the government under its power of eminent domain, measured by the property's fair market value.

The government and the landowner often dispute what constitutes proper compensation to the owner for taking his or her land. State constitutions and the U.S. Constitution require that such compensation be "just" or "reasonable." In each case, just or reasonable compensation must be determined by balancing the interests of the taxpaying public against those of the property owner to arrive at a result fair to both parties.

Compensation should not be more extensive than the owner's loss. The principal measure of the owner's loss is the fair market value of the property at the time. The U.S. Supreme Court has held that market value and just compensation are synonymous. Market value is normally determined by what a willing buyer would pay in cash to a willing seller in an arm's length transaction. The seller is entitled to have the property valued at its highest and most profitable use, even if the property is not currently being used in that manner.

Case Example

The state of Maryland condemned Kamin's property for a highway improvement project. The property was zoned as Rural-Agricultural (R-A). Based upon the present use and zoning of the property, experts appraised the Kamins' property at about $136,000. Kamins produced evidence at the condemnation hearing that if the condemnation did not take place, the property could be rezoned to EIA, an Employment and Institutional use Area. A planning supervisor for the Maryland Planning Commission testified that had a application for a zoning upgrade to EIA been made, it would have been granted. Because the court concluded that there was a reasonable probability of rezoning of the property to EIA within a reasonable period of time, it assigned a value commensurate with that higher use, $500,000. *State Roads v. Kamins, 572, A. 2d 1132 (Md. App. 1990).*

The most common method of determining value is to compare the property being taken with similar land recently sold. This information is generally presented to the courts through the testimony of expert witnesses. Real estate sales personnel are often expert witnesses in condemnation cases because they are familiar with the selling price of land. A good expert witness must be well prepared. He or she must be very familiar with the parcel of land involved as well as the selling price of comparable property.

Condemnation

Legal proceeding by which the government exercises the right of eminent domain, acquiring private land for a public use.

The Fourteenth Amendment to the U.S. Constitution prohibits state government from taking private property without due process of law and the Fifth Amendment imposes like restraints on the Federal government. As a result, some type of notice and some type of legal proceeding are required when a landowner is unwilling to convey to a condemning authority for the price offered. Due process does not ensure any particular manner of proceeding, and federal and state law vary extensively as to the method and procedures that will be used. For example, many states use juries extensively in condemnation cases. However, as long as the state legislature has provided a fair method of evaluation of eminent domain "takings," by providing the parties ample opportunity to be heard and to present evidence, due process is satisfied.

The Federal Rules of Civil Procedure provide that in federal cases either party may have a trial by jury on the issue of compensation unless Congress by statute establishes some other method.

Even within a state, condemnation procedures may vary. A number of states have established a general procedure by statute, but this procedure may be ignored or modified by the legislature for particular situations. Constitutional protections are not violated so long as the special procedure affords the property owner reasonable notice of the proceeding and a reasonable opportunity to establish just compensation.

Several states require the condemning authority to attempt to negotiate a voluntary settlement before commencing a condemnation action. Even when not a statutory requirement, this practice is followed in almost all cases. If the condemnor's offer is rejected, the most common procedure is to condemn by judicial proceeding. This action requires filing a petition in court, giving notice to the owners and others having an interest in the land. Ordinarily, the condemning authority has the burden of establishing the right to acquire the property. Once this right is established, the owner must prove the value of the property taken and any additional damages to which he or she is entitled. Upon the court's making the condemnation award, the interest necessary for the condemnor's purpose passes to the governmental authority involved. This interest may be an estate for years, an easement, or a fee simple absolute, but it may not exceed what is necessary to accomplish the public purpose for which the property was taken.

Accession

The bundle of rights and principles the law uses to deal with changes in the size and shape of land due to natural causes, usually the actions of bodies of water.

Accretion refers specifically to a gradual increase in riparian or littoral property as a result of deposits of sediment made by a body of water so as to create dry land where there once was only water. *Alluvion* is the term used for the land so created. *Reliction* is the word applied when water recedes and creates dry land without depositing more material. *Erosion* is simply the decrease in size of a piece of property as the result of water washing away material from the shore. Finally, *avulsion* is an abrupt and perceptible change in the size and shape of a tract as a result of unexpected events, such as a change in the course of a stream.

The general rule is that when accretion or reliction occurs the riparian or littoral landowner's boundary line and land area are extended to take in the alluvion, but when avulsion occurs it effects no change in boundary or title. One reason often given for the doctrine of accretion is that the landowner, who is subject to a diminution in the size of his or her tract through erosion, should have the corresponding benefit when the land is enlarged by natural processes. Another rationale for the rule is that the riparian or littoral owner is usually the only one in a position to use the land efficiently. A third explanation is the desirability of preserving the riparian owner's access to the water. The exclusion of avulsion from the general title-by-accretion rule is intended to mitigate the hardship that would result to abutting landowners when a river or stream abruptly changes course.

Case Example

Cummings owned shoreline property on the Arkansas River. Surveys from the late 1800s showed the existence of Beaver Dam Island near his property. Cummings contends that Beaver Dam Island was completely washed away in the flood of 1927, that subsequently a sandbar gradually built out into the river from his property and that by slow accretion the land now constituting Beaver Dam Island resulted. The court held against Cummings, saying: "When the formation begins with a bar or an island detached and away from the shore and by gradual filling in by deposit or by gradual recession of the water, the space between bar or island and mainland is joined together, it is not an accretion to the mainland in a legal sense and does not thereby become property of the owner of the mainland." *Cummings v. Boyles, 242 Ark. 38, 411 S.W.2d 665 (1967).*

Because of these underlying policies, one necessary element of accretion, reliction or erosion is that it be a gradual and imperceptible change. Another frequently stated requirement is that of *contiguity;* that is, that there be no separation between the riparian owner's original tract and the alluvion. It is not generally required that the alluvion be the result of natural causes alone. For example, if an upstream owner builds a breakwater that affects water flow so as to increase accretion, the downstream riparian owner can still acquire title. An owner, however, cannot use the doctrine to enlarge property boundaries through his or her own acts.

Much of the case law in this area has to do with how to draw the boundaries once accretion, reliction or erosion has altered the shape of the land. Arising most often in suits for damages, declaratory judgment actions, quiet title cases or actions for ejectment, this issue is usually resolved by reliance on two general principles: (1) that the share of each party should be proportionate in size and quality to the prior holding and (2) that each party should have a fair share of the access to the water. The actual method of line drawing necessarily varies greatly depending on the topography in each case. The courts will strive for an equitable solution and favor compromise settlements by the parties. The law varies somewhat from state to state, and the applicable rule is that of the jurisdiction in which the accretion occurred.

Transfer of Property upon Death

When a person dies, title to that person's property can be transferred in one of two ways. If the decedent has made a valid "last will and testament," title to the decedent's property is transferred to the beneficiaries named in the will, subject to limitations imposed by the state. The person who has made a valid will is called a *testator* and is said to have died *testate*. A person who dies without making a valid will is said to have died *intestate*. State statutes direct to whom an intestate's property is transferred.

Intestate Succession

Distribution of property of a person who dies without leaving a will or whose will is invalid.

The general philosophy underlying the laws of intestate succession is that property should descend to those persons the intestate individual probably would want to own it. If the decedent expressed no preference by executing a will, society assumes that he or she would want the property to go to those closely related by blood or marriage. Society also benefits from this assumption because it keeps property within the family and tends to strengthen that important institution.

Laws of intestate succession are statutory. No one has a constitutional or natural right to a decedent's property. People inherit because the legislature says that they can. The law might direct that all property of an intestate decedent revert to the state, as it did in England immediately following the Norman Conquest. This system was opposed by powerful tenants of the king, however, and the English rulers were soon forced to recognize the principle of inheritance by members of the tenant's family.

In modern U.S. real estate law the concept of inheritance by family members is integral to the succession to property upon death. The idea that the state should acquire the property of an intestate is offensive to the sense of justice of almost all Americans. The state acquires title to the property only when the decedent has no relatives. Later in this section we will discuss this alternative (escheat) in greater detail.

Historical Background

The origin of state statutes of intestate succession is found in English law. Primarily because of the importance of land to the political and social structure of England, English law treated the transfer of real property upon the owner's death very differently from the transfer of personal property.

Until 1926 in England, when an owner died intestate, title to that person's real property passed directly to the heirs according to statutes of descent. Title to personal property went initially to an administrator. After the administrator had paid the claims against the estate, the personal property passed according to the Statute of Distribution.

Currently, in England and a majority of jurisdictions in the United States, the laws of intestate succession no longer distinguish between real and personal property. Statutes, commonly referred to as *statutes of descent and distribution*, treat the two types of property in the same manner.

Statutes of Descent and Distribution
   Statutes that provide for the distribution of the property of a person who dies without a valid will.

Today in the United States the distribution of the estate of an intestate is modeled, in a general way, upon the English Statute of Distribution. Both current American and English statutes provide for distribution of the entire estate—not just personal property. American law also focuses primarily upon provision for the surviving spouse and children.

A surviving husband or wife ordinarily is entitled to a half or a third share of the decedent's property. Many states increase this portion if the couple had no children. Some states give the surviving spouse a specific dollar amount and a fraction of the net estate exceeding that amount. Community property states normally differentiate between intestate distribution of separate property and that of community property.

In every state a surviving spouse and children share all of the intestate's estate. The children take whatever remains after the spouse's share. If there is no surviving spouse, the entire estate passes to the children, who divide the assets equally.

Per stirpes   Distribution of intestate property to persons who take the share is allocated to a deceased ancestor by representing that person is called *per stirpes distribution*, also referred to as *distribution by the stocks*.

A difficult question of fundamental fairness arises when a child who has children dies before a parent. When the grandparent dies, should the surviving grandchildren share equally with their aunts and uncles, or are they entitled only to the share of the deceased parent?

Case Example

Trent Hightower died intestate. His wife had predeceased him by many years. They had three children: Stephanie, Joseph and Douglas. Stephanie and Joseph survived their father, but Douglas died before him. Douglas, however, left three children of his own: Trent, Jr., Eliza and Anne. Trent Hightower's estate was divided into thirds, with one-third going to Stephanie, one-third to

Joseph, and one-third to the children of Douglas. This allocation is *per stirpes* distribution.

In some states, when the only distributees are grandchildren, distribution is by modified per stirpes. In these states each grandchild takes in his or her own right as in *per capita* distribution. The decedent's estate is divided by the *number* of grandchildren.

Per capita   Distribution of intestate property to persons who take equal shares as members of a class, not as representatives of an ancestor, is called *per capita distribution*.

Case Example

Jennie E. Martin died intestate, leaving as distributees three grandchildren: Alice E. Martin, Bourke Martin and Ned Martin. Alice E. was the daughter of Earl Martin; Bourke and Ned were the sons of Charles Martin. Both Earl and Charles had died before their mother died. The court divided Jennie Martin's estate into three parts, giving one to each grandchild. Alice E. Martin argued that the distribution should have been per stirpes and that she should have received one-half.

The appellate court affirmed the lower court's action. The court stated, "those who take as a class take equally. . . . We hold that it was the intention of the legislature that grandchildren, who alone survive the ancestor, should take equally. . . . " In other words, they should take as heirs, not by representation. *In re Martin's Estate, 96 Vt. 455, 120 A. 862 (1923).*

Order of distribution   In the absence of children, American distribution statutes generally distribute the intestate's property to parents, subject to the share of a surviving spouse. In a few states, brothers and sisters share with parents. Issue of deceased brothers and sisters take their parents' share. In a number of states, the amount of the estate determines the relative shares of parents, brothers and sisters.

Statutes provide for the property to go to the "next of kin" if no specific relatives survive and in some states, if there are no relatives or next of kin, to stepchildren. Most states by statute provide a method for determining next of kin. Usually the method is based upon that used in England to determine kinship under the Statute of Distribution. Other than the surviving spouse, relatives by marriage ordinarily are not entitled to the intestate's property. (See Figure 10.1)

Escheat
   Reversion of property to the state when a person dies intestate with no heirs or when property is abandoned.

Case Example

Gene DiMond, who inherited property in St. Augustine from his only brother Henri, had no immediate surviving relatives. His parents were dead, and Gene had never married. Although he had one aunt, she had died many years before, leaving no children. Upon Gene's death, the state claimed the St. Augustine property because Gene had died without leaving a will and without heirs.

Figure 10.1: A Statute of Intestate Succession

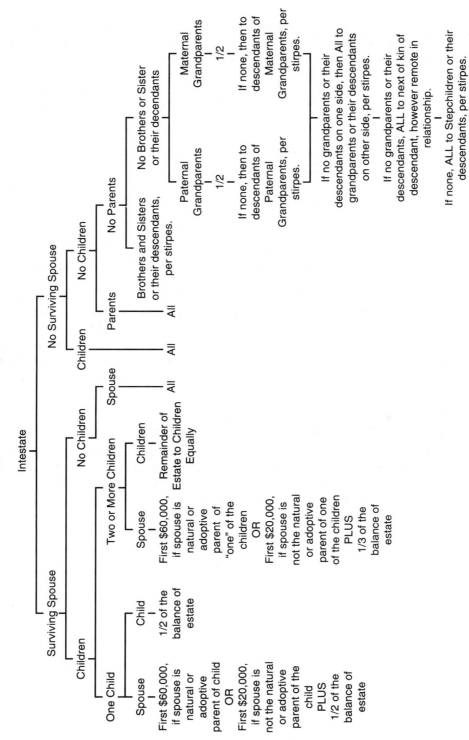

As we have seen, statutes in each of the states indicate the categories of relationship of those who are a decedent's heirs. Generally, these statutes are narrowly drawn, restricting the term *heirs* to the spouse and those closely related to the decedent by blood. If the decedent dies intestate without heirs, decedent's property escheats to the state. Because most decedents have heirs or make a will, escheat is not a common method by which a state acquires title.

Escheat is an incident of state sovereignty. Because the people possess the ultimate property in land, land should revert to the state for the people's benefit when no heirs exist. State constitutions in some instances contain provisions for escheat. Ordinarily, rules governing the details of escheat are statutory, and in a number of states the only mention of escheat is in the statute.

Some type of judicial proceeding is necessary to establish the state's right to the property. In a number of jurisdictions, title vests immediately in the state when a landowner dies intestate without ascertainable heirs. In these states the judicial proceeding will be in the probate court and similar to proceedings to establish heirship. Other states require a more extensive action; in these states title to escheated property does not vest in the state until a court so orders. Escheat statutes are not favored by the courts and, as a result, are strictly construed.

Although historically the term *escheat* was applied only to real property, today the term is also applied to personal property. Many types of personal property escheat to the state when they have been unclaimed for a period of time, including bank deposits, parimutuel winnings, insurance proceeds and corporate dividends. Most legal problems that involve escheat are the result of state statutes that attempt to deal with unclaimed personal property.

Testate Succession

Transfer of property when a person dies leaving a will.

The right of an owner of property to direct to whom it should go upon death has always been subject to significant limitations. Initially the right to will one's property applied only to personal property. This right evolved in England shortly after the Norman Conquest in 1066.

Historical Background

It was not until the enactment of the Statute of Wills in 1540 that English law granted real property owners a limited right to transfer it by will. This right was curtailed substantially by dower and curtesy, discussed in Chapter 4, as well as the customs and traditions of the English landed aristocracy. Many restrictions on the disposition of real property by will also existed in the United States. During the late 19th and 20th centuries these restrictions lessened. As land became less important as a source of wealth in relation to personal property, statutes in both England and the United States provided owners with comparable rights to dispose of both real and personal property by will. Today, in both countries, a person can dispose freely of both types of property by will, subject to limitations imposed by the state to protect the family and to ensure that the debts of the decedent's estate are paid.

Will

A written instrument that permits distribution of an owner's property after death and must contain certain elements to be legally enforceable.

Our English legal heritage has had an extensive influence on requirements for making a valid will. As a result, similar requirements exist throughout the United States, although individual states deviate significantly from the common pattern. In most American jurisdictions, formality is a general characteristic of the procedure involved in executing a will. Formality is predicated upon a legislative desire to prevent fraud, undue influence, coercion or a testator's impetuousness. Legislatures apparently believe that ceremony helps to prevent rash actions. In addition, formality helps to memorialize the transaction. To be legal and valid, a will must be in writing, signed by the testator, *witnessed* and *attested*. (See Figure 10.2)

Written All states require a will to be in writing, but a limited number of states do permit oral wills of personal property under limited circumstances. Generally, oral wills are valid if made by military personnel in actual service or under certain conditions by a person suffering a terminal illness. A will written entirely in the testator's own hand, known as a *holographic* will, is considered valid in a number of states, even though it was not witnessed.

Signed American courts are liberal in their interpretation of what constitutes a signature. A mark or an initial is sufficient if intended as a signature. Usually, the testator must sign personally, but someone else may if directed to do so by the testator. Usually, this must be done in the testator's presence. Generally, a signature any place on the document is sufficient if the intention is to validate the will. Some states require the signature to be at the end of the instrument. In those states, the entire document is invalid if the signature is in some other place.

Witnessed Most state laws require only two witnesses for a will to be valid. Any competent adult may ordinarily act as a witness. In some states a beneficiary under a will should not be a witness; that person's testimony is sufficient to sustain the will in court, but he or she is not entitled to take under the will.

The common practice is for the testator to sign first in the presence of the witnesses. In many states the actual signing does not have to be viewed by the witness if the testator later acknowledges the signature.

Attested Attestation is a requirement in all jurisdictions for most wills. Attestation means that the person must intend to act as a witness and must sign for the purpose of validating the will. In a very few states the witness need not sign the instrument, but attestation is necessary even in those states. In order to validate the will, witnesses must be able to testify at a later date that the testator signed or acknowledged the signature in their presence.

In the vast majority of cases, a will includes an attestation clause. This clause appears at the end of the will following the testator's signature. Each witness signs the attestation clause, which recites the witness's observation of the formalities necessary for the proper execution of the will.

Rights of the Family

Prevailing public policy in the United States is to encourage provisions for spouse and children out of a decedent's estate. As noted earlier, if a person dies intestate, inheritance statutes in all states provide first for the decedent's immediate family. State laws also furnish some protection for the spouse, and to a lesser degree the children, of a person who fails to provide for them by will. Historically, many of these laws applied specifically to real estate. Dower, curtesy and homestead rights discussed in Chapter 4 are examples. Today, protection for a decedent's spouse in most states is accomplished by giving the spouse a right to elect a share against the will. The right of election is charged against the entire estate, both real and personal.

Elective Share

A share of a deceased spouse's estate that a surviving spouse may claim if the other by will did not provide at least this amount.

Dower and curtesy have been replaced in many states by the right of a surviving spouse to elect a share against the decedent's will. The right of election is based on statute, and the share varies from state to state. Inasmuch as the right of election is a relatively recent trend in the law, state legislation usually reflects modern developments for this purpose, such as the elimination of distinctions between real and personal property, and similar treatment of husband and wife.

The right of election is also influenced by past laws and customs. Many state legislatures regard it as a substitute for dower. Thus the survivor's elective share is often set at a fractional amount, such as one-third of the decedent's estate. In a number of states the share is less if the couple has children. However, children may be disinherited by their parents, and no state has a law that provides children an elective share.

Case Example

Royce and Helen Hurley were married for many years. Early in their marriage Royce made a will leaving Helen $100,000. At the time, this was the bulk of Royce's estate. Over the years Royce prospered, but he did not change his will. When Royce died in 1975, his net estate was more than $500,000. State statute gave Helen a right to take under the will or to elect to take a one-half share against the will. She elected to take one-half share ($250,000) instead of the $100,000 legacy.

One of the objections to dower was that in small estates the surviving spouse was provided for inadequately if reliance upon dower was necessary. Although a right of election ordinarily provides more for a surviving spouse because it includes personal property, the fractional share in some estates is insufficient to support the survivor adequately. In most cases this problem never arises because the decedent provides adequately for the surviving spouse in the first place.

Administration of Estates

A general term used to describe the management and settlement of a decedent's estate by a person appointed by the courts.

Many of the procedures for settling the estate of a decedent are similar for both testate and intestate decedents. A very important initial step is the appointment of a personal representative to act for the estate. The person charged with administration of the estate of an intestate decedent is called an *administrator;* the person who is appointed to administer the estate of a decedent who dies testate is an *executor*. Sometimes the person nominated in a will as an executor is unable or unwilling to serve. Under these conditions, the court appoints an administrator with the will attached.

The administration of a decedent's estate is ordinarily supervised by a special court, frequently referred to as a *probate* or *surrogate's court*. The appointment of a personal representative is an important element in administering a decedent's estate. In the will, the testator almost always nominates a personal representative. The personal representative may be either a person or an institution, such as a trust company. The decedent's nominee is usually appointed by the court, unless that person is not qualified or refuses to serve.

Probate

Proof that an instrument is genuine and the last will and testament of the maker.

In the vast majority of cases, probate is a straightforward procedure. Ordinarily, the person nominated in the will as personal representative files a written application or petition for probate. In many jurisdictions, the probate court supplies the proper forms for this procedure. The petition alleges the testator's death and domicile at the time of death. The will is usually attached to the petition unless it has been filed previously with the court. Usually the names, relationships and residences of the heirs at law, as well as those receiving gifts under the will, must be included because they will be notified of the proceeding. Some states permit probate without notice to interested parties. Although the practice is legal, it can adversely affect land titles in case someone with a claim presents it later.

If a petition is unopposed, the court may order probate on the documents filed. Usually, a limited hearing is conducted in which the court takes testimony on the validity of the will. A number of states have developed less formal probate procedures for small estates, especially when no real property is involved.

Figure 10.2: Last Will and Testament

Last Will and Testament
of
Will B. Done
1775 College Road
Columbus, Ohio 43210

I, Will B. Done, over the age of twenty-one years, a legal resident of the county of Franklin, State of Ohio, and being of sound mind and memory and not acting under menace, duress, fraud or undue influence, do make, publish and declare this to be my Last Will and Testament, hereby revoking all other Wills and testamentary writings heretofore made by me.

Item I. I direct my executor to pay out of my estate all of my just debts and funeral expenses as soon as reasonably practical after death.

Item II. I hereby devise and bequeath all property of whatsoever kind, real and personal, wheresoever situate to my wife, Ima, if she shall survive me.

Item III. In the event that my wife, Ima, does not survive me, I give, devise, and bequeath all the residue and remainder of my estate, real and personal, of whatsoever kind and wheresoever situate, absolutely and in fee simple to the children of our marriage, share and share alike, or to the survivor, per stirpes.

Item IV. In the event my wife, Ima, does not survive me then I appoint Harold Greene and Sally Greene or the survivor as guardians over the person and property of said children under the age of twenty-one (21). Said guardians shall hold the money in trust for each minor until said child attains the age of twenty-one (21) and use such money until then for the support and education of the minor child. When each child attains the age of twenty-one (21), the guardians shall transfer the remaining funds held in trust for that child to said child and the guardianship of that child shall terminate.

Item V. I hereby appoint my wife, Ima, as executor of my Last Will and Testament if she survives me and is otherwise qualified; otherwise I nominate, constitute and appoint Rhesa Andrews, Columbus, Ohio. I hereby authorize and grant my executor full power without order of the Court to settle claims in favor of or against my estate, to sell at public or private sale for cash or credit, to mortgage, lease or convey all or any part of my estate, real or personal, of whatsoever kind wheresoever situate, without application to or confirmation by any court or government agency.

Item VI. In the event that my wife and children do not survive me then I give, devise and bequeath all the residue and remainder of my estate, real and personal, of whatsoever kind, wheresoever situate, absolutely and in fee simple to my brother, Lance, my sister Elgin and my brother-in-law, Peter, share and share alike. I have intentionally not included by brother Conley because I know that adequate provision has been made for him.

In testimony whereof, I have hereunto set my hand at Columbus, Ohio this 15th day of August, 1992.

Will B. Done

Signed and witnessed in the presence of the testator and in the presence of each other.

Witness   Witness

Probate establishes that the will is valid and genuine. After the petition for probate is granted, the will can no longer be attacked on the ground of forgery, improper execution or revocation except in a proceeding to set aside probate. Probate does not establish the validity or meaning of particular provisions of the will. If the court is satisfied that the nominated personal representative is qualified to serve, this person will be furnished with *letters testamentary* as evidence of authority to settle the estate.

State statutes prescribe the persons eligible for appointment as administrator and the order in which they must be considered. The order, based upon relationship to the decedent, parallels the order of intestate inheritance in most states. Preference is given to the surviving husband or wife. If there is no husband or wife, the relative next entitled to distribution is selected as administrator. The court selects from among those who stand in equal right the person best qualified to manage the estate. Usually, preference is given to residents of the jurisdiction, and in many states the representative must reside in the county where the estate is probated. The court grants *letters of administration* to the person appointed to administer the intestate's estate.

The personal representative, whether an executor or administrator, is authorized by the court to settle the decedent's estate. He or she is responsible for ensuring that assets are distributed in an orderly manner to those who are entitled to them. Although the personal representative has a wide variety of miscellaneous chores, four basic steps comprise the settlement of the estate:

1. collection of estate assets,

2. processing and payment of claims against the estate,

3. management of estate assets, and

4. accounting and distribution of estate assets.

Proof of Death

It is axiomatic that neither a will nor an inheritance statute is operative until a property owner dies. Ordinarily, the occurrence and time of death are easy to determine, but problems arise in at least two instances. One instance is a disaster in which several closely related people die at approximately the same time; another is a situation in which a property owner has been missing for an extensive period.

Many wills solve the problem of determining who has died first in a common disaster by including a provision in the instrument.

Case Example

Lance Beck and his wife, Hilda, were killed in a common disaster. Because of the nature of the accident, determining which one had died first was impossible. Lance's will left all his property to his wife if she survived him. If she did not, his estate was to go to his parents and to charity.

Lance's will contained the following provision: "In the event my wife and I shall die under such circumstances that there is insufficient evidence to determine the survivor, it shall be conclusively presumed that I survived her." As a result of this provision, the estate went to Lance's parents and the charities that he had named, not into his wife's estate.

Most states by statute make special provisions for applying distribution rules when close relatives are killed under circumstances that make it impossible to determine the survivor. Almost all states have adopted the Uniform Simultaneous Death Act. In general, this act provides that in a common disaster each decedent's property shall be disposed of as if that decedent had survived.

States also solve by statute the problem caused by a missing owner. Generally, these statutes provide that a person whose absence is unexplained for seven years is presumed dead. The presumption, however, may be rebutted.

Summary

Real property is usually conveyed voluntarily by deed; however, some transfers of land are involuntary. One procedure by which title passes involuntarily is *adverse possession*. The person who takes title in this way acquires it by wrongful use or possession for a period of time prescribed by statute. This possession must be open and notorious, hostile, continuous and exclusive. Owners who are holding vacant land for resale or for future development should make periodic inspections to guard against adverse possession.

Land may also be taken from a rightful owner by certain government bodies exercising the power of *eminent domain*. The right of eminent domain is exercised through the legal process of *condemnation*. Methods and procedures for exercising this power vary markedly from one area to another. Nevertheless, the U.S. Constitution prohibits the taking of private property without *just compensation*, as do most state constitutions. When an owner does not wish to give up the land for the terms offered, some type of legal proceeding is required to determine just compensation. Just compensation is based upon the fair market value of the property.

Property is also transferred upon the death of the owner. *Intestate succession* is the term given to the transfer of real and personal property when a person dies without a will. Property then passes according to state statutes governing inheritance, usually referred to as *statutes of descent and distribution*. These laws differ to a degree from one state to another but generally follow similar patterns: the spouse and children have the primary right to the estate. When a person dies without a will, has no discernible heirs, or property is abandoned, the state acquires title by *escheat*.

When the deceased has made a valid *will*, both real and personal property pass as the decedent directs. All states have laws that prevent the decedent from totally disinheriting his or her spouse.

Laws in each state dictate the proper form for executing a will. To be valid, a will must be in writing, signed, witnessed and attested. Generally, a will also names a personal representative charged with carrying out the distribution according to the decedent's wishes. This person is usually supervised by the state's *probate* court. Probate establishes that a will is valid and genuine and protects it from attacks by claimants.

Review and Discussion Questions

1. What are the major arguments for allowing a person to acquire title by adverse possession?

2. Explain the difference between per stirpes and per capita distribution.

3. Briefly indicate some of the limitations that exist upon the transfer of real property by will.

4. Discuss the major duties of a person appointed to settle a decedent's estate.

Case Problems

1. Kittrell owned four house trailers that were parked on the edge of his property. Unknown to Kittrell, the trailers extended a few feet over his neighbor's property. This condition was discovered by a survey after the trailers had been there several years. At the time, Kittrell offered to buy the strip of land upon which the trailers encroached. The owner refused to sell but, because permanent plumbing had been installed, did not order the trailers to be moved. Several years later the property was sold and the new owner demanded that Kittrell remove the trailers. Kittrell claimed ownership of the strip by adverse possession because the trailers had encroached on the land for more than ten years, the statutory period in the state. Discuss the validity of Kittrell's claim. *Kittrell v. Scarborough, 287 Ala. 177, 249 So.2d 814 (1971).*

2. Fran, an adult, owned a tract that had been adversely possessed for 18 of the 20 years set by the statute when she died and the tract passed under the statute of descent and distribution to her infant son Jamie. Jamie possesses the property adversely for two years. What is the result? Explain.

3. The Nollans purchased a beachfront lot in Ventura County, California. The lot contained a small bungalow which was in disrepair. They desired to demolish the bungalow and replace it. They sought a permit to do so from the California Coastal Commission. The Commission granted the permit subject to the condition that the Nollans allow the public an easement to pass across a portion of their property to make it easier to get to a nearby county park. The Commission reasoned that the new bungalow would increase blockage of the view of the ocean and thus would prevent the public "psychologically" from realizing the benefit of a stretch of coastline. Is the condition constitutional? Explain. *Nollan v. California Costal Comm'n, 483 U.S. 825 (1987).*

4. Berman owned a department store on property in a District of Columbia slum. The property was well maintained, and no building violations existed. Using the power of eminent domain, the District of Columbia Redevelopment Agency acquired Berman's property, along with that of others in the area. The purpose of the acquisition was for "the development of blighted territory." Berman argued that the taking was unconstitutional as his property was not substandard and, after redevelopment, was to be managed privately. Discuss the validity of Berman's contention. *Berman v. Parker, 348 U.S. 26 (1954).*

5. The statute of descent and distribution of the State of Y is as follows:

    If a person dies intestate, his or her real and personal property, if any, shall pass:

    (a) If there is no surviving spouse, to the children of the intestate or their lineal descendants, *per stirpes.*

    (b) If there is a spouse and one or more children or their lineal descendants surviving, the first $60,000 to the spouse, plus one-half of the remainder to the spouse and the balance to the children equally or to their lineal descendants, *per stirpes.*

    (c) If there are no children or their lineal descendants, the whole to the surviving spouse.

    (d) If there is no spouse and no children or their lineal descendants surviving, to the parents of the intestate equally or to the surviving parent.

    (e) If there is no spouse, no children or their lineal descendants and no parent surviving, to the brothers and sisters equally or their lineal descendants, *per stirpes.*

(f) If there is no spouse, no children or their lineal descendants, no parents and no siblings surviving, to the next of kin.

(g) If there is no next of kin, escheat to the state.

Answer the following hypothetical questions based on this statute.

(1) Graham dies, leaving a valid will that bequeaths his entire estate to his sister-in-law, Ruth. He is survived by Ruth and by his mother, his grandson and his brother. What is the result under the statute?

Ruth, has will

(2) Willis died intestate and is survived by his wealthy wife, Angela; his poverty-stricken mother, Rose; and his deserving second cousin, Ned. How will the estate be distributed?

all to Angela

(3) Susan died intestate, <u>survived by her son, Jack,</u> and by three grandsons, Dennis, Randy and Rob. Dennis and Randy are the sons of Susan's <u>deceased oldest son, David,</u> and Rob is the only child of Susan's <u>deceased daughter, Cheryl.</u> How will the estate be divided?

Jack ⅓
Dennis ⅙ Randy ⅙
Rob ⅓

(4) Rebecca died intestate, survived by her husband, Gus; her father, Bruce; her daughter, Nancy; and her grandchildren, Chuck and Jill, the children of her deceased son, Rick. The net probate estate is $50,000. How will it be divided?

(b)
all $50,000 to Gus

6. Martha had two children, Peter and Mary. Upon Martha's death, neither Peter nor Mary were living. Mary left three children and Peter left two children. Assuming all of Martha's property was left to Peter and Mary, how much will each grandchild get if the property devolved per stirpes? How much if it devolved per capita?

7. John and Larue Morgan were married in 1960. In 1965 Larue disappeared. Although extensive efforts were made to locate her, she was never found. In 1973 John brought a legal action to have Larue declared dead. At the hearing, Larue's brother attempted to introduce as evidence a Christmas card that he had received from her in 1967. The judge refused to accept this evidence and declared Larue dead because she had been missing for more than seven years. Was the judge correct? Discuss.

Part 3

Sales of Ownership Interest

11

Agency and Brokerage

Agency

A legal relationship in which one party, called the **principal,** *authorizes another, called the* **agent,** *to act in the principal's behalf in dealing with third parties.*

Agency is a useful legal relationship in business and personal transactions. A substantial amount of business in the United States is done through agents, both by corporations and partnerships that are unable to act for themselves and by individuals, who find acting through agents convenient and efficient in their business and private affairs.

Agency and Real Estate Transactions

The agency relationship is used extensively in many phases of the real estate business. It is especially prevalent in selling and leasing residential and commercial property. Owners of these types of properties often retain agents to help them find buyers or tenants, as agents usually have extensive knowledge of the market as well as contacts with potential occupants.

Agencies created to bring about the sale or lease of real estate differ in two significant ways from agencies in many other businesses. One difference is that in all states an agent appointed to sell or buy real estate must be licensed. License requirements for real estate agents will be discussed later in the chapter.

A second difference between the real estate agent and other agents is the extent to which the real estate agent has the power to contract on behalf of the principal. In many, if not most business agencies, the agent has this power. For example, if the president of a corporation that is developing land for a shopping mall signs a contract to have the land cleared, the contract is binding on the corporation. However, in most transactions that involve the sale of lease of real estate, the agent does not have the power to contract for the principal. If the owner wishes the agent to have this authority, the owner must execute a written document called a *power of attorney*. The power of attorney grants the agent, usually referred to as an *attorney-in-fact*, the authority to contract for the owner.

Creation of Agency

The usual method of creating an agency is by agreement. The principal authorizes the agent to act in the principal's behalf, and the agent agrees to do so. As a general rule, no particular formality is required to create an agency; the agreement may be oral or in writing. This rule ordinarily does not apply to transactions involving the sale or lease of real estate. To be valid, a power of attorney must be in writing. In addition, almost half the states by statute require that the appointment of an agent to procure a buyer or tenant for real estate be in writing.

Broker

> *An agent who for a commission or fee brings parties together to negotiate or conducts negotiations to complete a transaction, usually involving the sale or exchange of property or the acquisition of contract rights.*

A broker is an intermediary or go-between whose primary function is to facilitate a transaction. In many fields brokers play important roles in bringing business dealings to fruition. Although stockbrokers and real estate brokers are common examples, the long list of brokers includes those who arrange the sale of yachts, produce, hides and furs and, in some societies, even marriage. What brokers do and the authority they enjoy differ from one business to another, but brokers almost always represent buyers or sellers in some capacity.

Most states have statutory provisions that define real estate brokers and sales personnel for the purpose of licensing and regulation. These statutes frequently designate brokers in terms of activities relative to real estate transactions. When people engage in these activities for others and for a commission or fee, they are brokers or salespersons for regulatory purposes and must be licensed.

The statutes contain words such as *appraises, auctions, sells, offers for sale, buys, solicits prospective sellers or buyers, negotiates the sale* and *exchanges*. Similar broad terminology is used to describe activities relative to rental of real property. In some statutes, activities such as finding borrowers or lenders, negotiating or collecting loans and arranging investments secured by real estate also are included in the statutory definition of *broker*.

A corporation or a partnership may be a real estate broker. Members of the firm who actively engage in the brokerage business must be licensed. A few states require that anyone actively engaged in management be licensed as well. In some states one member of the firm may be designated on the license as a broker and others as associate brokers or sales personnel. License requirements will be discussed more fully later in this chapter.

The legal responsibility of a person who hires someone else to act for him or her depends upon the relationship between them. As a general rule, the more extensively the person for whom the job is being done *controls* the manner in which it is accomplished, the greater that person's responsibility. For example, an employer has appreciable control over how an employee does the job. Thus, if the employee is acting within the scope of his or her employment, the employer is legally liable for any harm the employee causes. For example, if a driver of a department store delivery van goes through a red light and injures a pedestrian while making a delivery, the department store is liable. This is known as the doctrine of *respondeat superior, i.e.,* "let the superior respond." The rationale for this doctrine is that one who carries out business activities through another whose actions he or she directs should be liable for that person's negligence in doing the job. In most real estate brokerage agreements, the seller who "hires" a broker does not direct or control the manner in which the broker performs the task. The relationship between the seller and broker is not one of employer and employee. The broker is said to be an *independent contractor.*

Independent Contractor

> *A person who is retained to do a job and uses his or her own judgment as to how the work will be done.*

The broker is in a technical sense retained by the seller as an agent. Nevertheless, the agency agreement establishes only the broker's authority to act, not the manner in which the broker is to accomplish the result. The broker controls the hours, methods and details of the job. As the broker's actions are not controlled by the seller, the seller is not liable for negligent harm caused by the broker unless the act causing harm was authorized or within the broker's inherent powers. In addition, as the broker is not an employee but an independent contractor, the seller does not have to withhold federal or state income taxes or make contributions to social security or unemployment compensation funds in the broker's behalf.

Listing

> *A contract between a seller of real estate and a broker authorizing the broker to secure a buyer for the property upon specified terms in return for a fee if the broker is successful.*

The listing creates the agency relationship between the seller and the broker. A number of states by statute require a listing to be in writing. In these states, if there is no written listing, the broker is not entitled to a fee. In the absence of statute requiring a writing, an oral listing is enforceable. This question should not come up, however, since both the prudent seller and the broker would insist upon a written contract clearly spelling out the rights and obligations of the parties. An appreciable portion of the litigation that centers around suits for brokers' commissions could be prevented by carefully drawn brokerage agreements. This problem as well as some others that can be alleviated by a writing will be discussed later.

In those states that recognize the oral listing, a broker may establish employment by implications arising from a property owner's actions.

Case Example

Frewert owned a home that he had been trying to sell. Carlson, a real estate salesperson, obtained permission to show the home to the Coopers. Carlson obtained an offer, which she presented to Frewert. In discussing the transaction, she told Frewert that she was representing him. Frewert then quoted a minimum net price that he wanted for the property and discussed possession with her. Carlson obtained a second offer from the Coopers that was slightly less than Frewert's minimum net price. Frewert rejected this offer. Two days later, he signed a contract directly with the Coopers and refused to pay a commission.

In a successful suit against Frewert for a commission, the court stated, "[W]hile a contract of employment is necessary to create an agency relationship . . . no particular form is required. Ordinarily, all that is necessary is that the broker act with consent of his principal either by written instrument, orally, or by implication from the conduct of the parties." *Dickerson Realtors, Inc. v. Frewert, 16 Ill. App. 2d 1060, 307 N.E.2d 445 (1974).*

The listing agreement should contain all the important elements of any contract: the amount of compensation, duration of the listing, when the commission is earned and the like. The contract should also outline defects and encumbrances to which the title is subject, terms upon which the owner will sell and details as to possession. The listing should also indicate whether it is a nonexclusive, or open, listing or an exclusive one.

Exclusive Agency

A listing in which the seller gives one broker authority to procure a buyer for property but retains the right to procure a buyer for the property himself or herself.

The exclusive agency is one of the two types of exclusive listings common in the United States. In this type of exclusive listing, if the seller procures the buyer the broker is not entitled to a commission.

Exclusive Right to Sell

A listing in which the seller gives one broker authority to procure a buyer for property. The broker is entitled to a commission even if the buyer is procured by the seller.

The *exclusive right to sell* differs from the *exclusive agency* in that the exclusive right to sell entitles the broker to a commission even if the seller procures the buyer without the broker's assistance. Courts in most states require unequivocal language in a listing before accepting it as an exclusive right to sell. These courts reason that the ordinary seller should be clearly informed that even if he or she makes the sale alone, the commission must be paid.

Both types of exclusive listings protect the broker against appointment by the seller of any other broker. Brokers prefer these types of listings because they provide added assurance that time and money spent procuring a buyer will be rewarded. The broker does not have to fear loss of a commission if another broker arranges a prior sale of the property.

Most exclusive listings are given for a specified period of time. They terminate automatically at the end of that period unless renewed. For a broker to take an exclusive listing for an indefinite period is generally considered poor practice. In many states an indefinite exclusive listing is illegal. This protects sellers who, unaware that the exclusive listing is still in effect, list with another broker and thus find themselves liable for two commissions. If an exclusive listing is open-ended, it is subject to cancellation upon notice. A few states allow the broker a reasonable period of time to arrange the desired transaction. In any case, most courts agree that a seller may not terminate a listing where the only objective is to sell to a buyer with whom the broker has been negotiating.

Open Listing
A listing that entitles the broker to compensation only if his or her activities bring about the desired result.

The open or nonexclusive listing is common in the United States. Unless the agreement clearly indicates otherwise, courts presume that a listing is open. A seller who enters into an open listing agreement may list the property with any number of brokers. The broker who brings about the sale is entitled to the commission. Authority of all of the brokers is automatically revoked without notice if and when the seller enters into a contract to sell the property.

In an open listing the seller retains the right to negotiate a sale on his or her own. If the sale is effected by the seller without the aid of a broker, no commissions are due and all listings are automatically terminated. Ordinarily, an open seller listing has no time limit and the seller can withdraw at any time. The seller has no commitment until the broker has procured a buyer ready, willing and able to buy. In order to escape paying a commission, a dishonest seller, suspecting that a broker is about to submit an offer, might revoke the broker's authority and attempt to deal directly with the potential buyer. A seller who revokes in bad faith under these circumstances is subject to liability if the property is sold to a buyer located by the broker. Some open listings contain provisions entitling the broker to a commission after the expiration of the listing if the property is purchased by one to whom it has been shown by the broker.

Multiple Listing Service
An organization in which brokers have contracted with each other to share their exclusive listing contracts.

Multiple listing is a marketing strategy that brokers have developed among themselves to increase their effectiveness in brokering real estate. Brokers participating in the service have agreed to pool their exclusive listings and to divide the commission received for negotiating a sale. Multiple listing services are common in most areas of the United States.

In a transaction involving broker members of a multiple listing service, the selling broker is considered to be a subagent of the listing broker. Each of the brokers involved receives a percentage of the commission that had been negotiated by the listing broker with the seller. The percentage that each receives is determined by the rules of the multiple listing service. The division of the commission differs from one multiple-listing service to another. Some multiple-listing services allow their members to withhold certain real estate from multiple listing; others require that all listings be submitted. Multiple-listing services also generally allow the listing broker a period of time to attempt to sell the property before registering it with the organization. Since brokers have limited rights to delegate their authority, the members of a multiple-listing service should be sure that their contracts with the owners permit them to submit property to multiple listing.

Authority

Term used in the law of agency denoting the agent's power to perform acts authorized by the principal.

The broker is a special agent with limited authority, usually restricted to a single transaction. In addition, although many people in real estate—and often the courts—refer to a broker's authority to sell, most listings merely authorize the broker to find a buyer, not to enter into a contract on behalf of the principal.

Case Example

Vance entered into an exclusive-listing agreement for three months with Management Clearing, Inc. His wife did not sign the listing, although community property was involved. Management Clearing, Inc., obtained an offer on terms identical to the listing, but Vance rejected it. Management Clearing, Inc., sued for its commission.

Vance defended on grounds that in a community property state, a husband alone cannot authorize the sale of community real estate. The court refused to accept this defense. The court stated, "[A] brokerage contract places only the duty on the broker of finding a buyer . . . It does not authorize the broker to sell the property." *Management Clearing, Inc., v. Vance, 11 Ariz. App. 386, 464 P.2d 977 (1970).*

The broker does not bargain as to terms but assists the parties in arranging terms upon which agreement can be reached. Although the seller may give the broker authority to execute a contract of sale, this authority must be clearly spelled out in the listing. Because brokers usually do not have the power to contract for a seller, a buyer should demand evidence of the broker's authority to do so if the broker signs on the seller's behalf. Brokers who are employed as property managers or rental agents often have the authority to contract for their principal.

Express Authority

Authority a principal confers upon an agent explicitly and distinctly; may be conferred orally or in writing.

An agency authorization in the listing "contract" between the broker/agent and the owner/principal is the foundation upon which the broker's authority rests. Such authorization establishes certain tasks the broker is given the power to accomplish.

Implied Authority

An agent's authority to do those things necessary and proper to accomplish the express terms of the agency.

Implied authority includes activities such as advertising, showing the property and transmitting from buyer and seller proposals relating to the sale. The broker has the implied authority to do these things as they are necessary to achieve the result sought by his or her express authority, that is, to find a ready, willing and able buyer.

The broker also has the implied authority to make certain representations about the property. A real estate broker, however, is a special agent. This means that the broker's implied authority is confined strictly to the terms of the agency, and the broker is bound by his or her obligation as an agent to obey the directions of the principal.

Case Example

Mustafa Ali owned a profitable bakery that he desired to sell. He listed the business and property with Dave Gould Realty, Inc., for $150,000.

Gould obtained an offer for the property, which Ali accepted; a $1,500 deposit to be held by Gould accompanied the offer. The contract provided that the *deposit* on the purchase price would be paid *to the seller* if the buyer defaulted. The buyer refused to close the sale because of alleged defects in the title. Without contacting Ali, Gould returned the $1,500. Because the contract did not close as scheduled, Ali sold the property to another. If Gould sued for a commission, the court would rule against him because he had no implied authority to modify the contract by returning the deposit to the buyer.

The extent of the broker's authority is a critical issue in determining the seller's responsibility for representations made by the broker about the property. In a majority of jurisdictions, these statements are binding upon the seller. If the statement is material and untrue, the buyer may rescind the contract and in some cases collect damages. These results follow even if the broker thought the statement was true or if the seller was unaware that the statement was being made. As a general rule, courts consider statements made by a broker within the scope of the broker's implied authority. Any loss occasioned by these statements should be borne by the seller, who selected the broker, and not by the buyer, who was misled by the false statement.

Brokers, like agents, generally are chosen for their knowledge, skill and judgment. The relationship between the broker and employer is personal, and the broker has no authority to delegate to another the tasks that he or she has been hired to perform. This rule applies, however, only to broker's actions that are discretionary, such as determining the terms of the sale.

A broker may delegate to another authority to perform acts that are ministerial or mechanical in nature. Thus the broker may assign to a salesperson the task of showing the property or finding a buyer, inasmuch as these acts do not involve the broker's discretion. When a ministerial task is accomplished by a broker through a subagent, the broker is entitled to collect a commission even if the subagent's relationship to the broker was unknown to the seller.

Case Example

Dave Gould Realty, Inc., was authorized to sell property that belonged to Mrs. Philbrick. Gould mentioned this to Arthur Clairmont, a fellow broker. Several days later, Clairmont obtained Gould's permission to show the property to one of Clairmont's customers. Clairmont described the property and terms to this buyer. The buyer on his own examined the property and entered into an agreement with Mrs. Philbrick, who refused to pay Gould a promised commission. Mrs. Philbrick argued that she had not authorized Clairmont to procure a buyer.

Courts would ordinarily find for Gould in this situation, as Clairmont's verbal description and transmittal of terms represented a mechanical act.

Broker's Duties to Seller

A real estate broker owes his or her principal essentially the same duties that any agent owes to a principal. Like other agents, the broker is a *fiduciary*. A fiduciary is a person who acts primarily for the benefit of another in a relationship founded on trust and confidence. In selecting the broker as agent, the principal has relied upon the broker's integrity, fidelity and ability. This relationship of confidence and trust requires high standards of conduct, and the broker must exercise good faith and loyalty in all matters relating to the agency.

Good Faith and Loyalty

Good faith and loyalty require the broker to advance the principal's interest even at the expense of his or her own. A broker may not purchase the principal's property unless the principal has complete knowledge of all the facts and freely consents to the sale. This prohibition applies even if the broker can show that the transaction was beneficial to the principal and the principal was not injured in any way.

The duty of good faith and loyalty controls situations in which the broker can represent both parties. If a broker has the authority to enter into a contract for either buyer or seller, the broker violates the fiduciary duty if he or she accepts compensation from both. Courts reason that it is impossible for a broker under these circumstances to satisfy the diametrically opposed interest of both parties.

In the common brokerage agreement, however, the broker is employed merely to bring the parties together. In this situation the broker may act for both and receive a commission from each as long as this dual capacity has been fully disclosed and permitted by both buyer and seller. In the effort to bring the parties together, the broker who is to receive compensation from buyer and seller must be certain to act impartially.

Abstract terms such as *trust*, *good faith* and *loyalty* indicate the general scope of the broker's responsibility to his or her employer. In reality a broker must take at least three positive actions to meet these general requirements:

1. The broker must fully disclose to the principal all matters relating to the agency.

2. The broker must obey the principal's lawful instructions.

3. The broker must account to the principal for any proceeds of the agency coming in to his or her hands.

Full disclosure requires that the principal be informed of all offers, the identity of purchasers, commission-splitting arrangements with other brokers, relationships between buyer and broker, financial limitations of the purchaser and the selling price of comparable property.

Case Example

Neibert listed property with Alfred C. Moore, a broker. One of Moore's salespeople obtained a purchase offer for the property. The offer acknowledged receipt of $3,000 from the buyer and provided that the deposit should be "forfeited as liquidated damages" if buyer failed to close.

Unknown to Moore, the deposit was in the form of a promissory note, not cash. Moore discovered this later but failed to inform Neibert, since the buyer assured Moore that the note would be honored. When the sale did not close, Neibert demanded the deposit to cover losses incurred. The buyer refused to pay the note.

In an action affirming the real estate commission's 60-day suspension of Moore's license, the court recognized that the temptation to withhold information is "especially strong when it is only a matter of disclosing bad news which may improve." The court added that "it is an agent's duty to give his principal timely notice of every fact or circumstance which may make it necessary for him to take measures for his security." *Moore v. State Real Estate Commission, 9 Pa. Commw. Ct. 506, 309 A.2d 77 (1973).*

Skill and Care

In addition to meeting the high standards of conduct of a fiduciary, the broker must not be negligent in carrying out the duties of the agency. A broker is negligent if he or she acts in an unreasonable or careless manner and this action is the proximate cause of loss to the principal.

Case Example

Ponia Towski, who could neither read nor write English, owned a house in Camden, New Jersey. There was a vacant lot on each side of the house. Between the lot on the east and the house was an alley. Towski's house was on the boundary of the west lot. Because of this, Towski wished to purchase that lot and erect a dwelling, using his west wall as a party wall.

All of this was explained to Joshua Griffiths, a real estate broker. Through Griffiths, Towski purchased what he thought was the lot on the west and built an adjoining structure with a party wall. Unfortunately, Griffiths had negotiated a sale with the owner of the eastern lot. Because Towski did not own the property on which the adjoining building was located, his tenants were forced to vacate the premises. Towski then brought a successful damage action against Griffiths. *Towski v. Griffiths, 91 N.J.L. 663, 103 A. 192 (1918).*

Although the facts of this case are unusual, in finding for Ponia Towski the court applied a test that is relatively common. It held the defendant liable because he had not used the degree of care and skill ordinarily employed by people engaged in the brokerage business.

Liability for negligence depends upon factors that vary from one case to another. As a result, it is impossible to say that a broker is negligent because of acting in a particular manner. A slight variation in the circumstances might cause a court or jury to consider a particular act careless in one instance and not in another. There are, however, a number of relatively common situations in which principals have brought successful negligence actions against their brokers or have used the broker's conduct as a defense in an action brought for commissions. Cases exist in which brokers have been found negligent because they did not use ordinary care and skill in securing an adequate purchase price, investigating encumbrances, preparing papers relative to the sale, collecting payments due the principal and filing discharges for mortgages and liens.

It has been held that a broker who fails to make a determined effort to sell, especially a broker with an exclusive agency, is liable to the principal. Other cases have held that a broker charged with renting property is liable for failure to properly investigate prospective tenants who later damage the property.

Numerous remedies are available to the principal when the broker violates these duties. The principal may:

- sue for breach of contract;

- bring a tort action for negligence;

- require the broker to defend a suit against the principal;

- discharge the broker without compensation;

- force the broker to account; or

- recover for loss and misuse of the principal's property.

In many cases principals use the broker's violation of duty as a defense when sued for the commission.

Broker's Duty to Buyer

Business relationships between buyers and brokers arise in one of two ways. In the typical real estate sale the seller lists his or her property with the broker. The listing authorizes the broker to act as the seller's agent in procuring a buyer for the property. The buyer is a third party. In negotiations with third parties (buyers), the broker is acting in the seller's behalf and, like the seller, deals at arm's length with the buyer. In an arm's-length transaction each party acts in his or her own interest. In the past, courts have applied the principle of *caveat emptor*, that is, "let the buyer beware," to the relationship between the seller's broker and the buyer.

Seller's brokers are liable to buyers in some situations. Traditionally, to recover against a broker representing the seller, the buyer needed to rely on some tort theory, not on any duty the broker owed to the buyer arising out of the relationship between them. Sellers' brokers are liable to buyers for misrepresentation of material facts about the property. If the misrepresentation is intentional, the broker is liable for fraud; if the misrepresentation is made innocently, the broker is liable, but the buyer's remedies may be limited. Fraud and misrepresentation are discussed in Chapter 14.

The liability of the seller's broker to the buyer for fraud or misrepresentation has been expanded in a number of states during the last 20 years. Courts in states as far apart as Alaska, Florida, Kansas, Ohio, Illinois, California and Washington have held sellers' brokers liable to buyers for failing to disclose material facts about the property. For example, buyers have recovered against sellers' brokers who have not disclosed a termite problem, a defective sewer, a leaky basement or personal interest in the property.

Courts holding that sellers' brokers have a duty to disclose material facts to buyers justify this stance in several ways. Some have applied a theory of negligence or negligent misrepresentation. To establish a claim of negligence, the buyer must show that the broker owed the buyer a duty to conform to a certain standard. In a number of cases, to establish this standard, courts have referred to standards in ethical codes promulgated by state real estate commissions and/or the Code of Ethics of the NATIONAL ASSOCIATION OF REALTORS®. These codes impose upon the broker a duty to treat all parties fairly. In other cases courts have held sellers' brokers to a high standard of care in relations with buyers on grounds that state legislation licensing real estate brokers must be interpreted in the light of its obvious purpose of protecting the public. A broker does not stand in the same shoes as a seller. Brokers owe the buyer the same duties of integrity owed the public at large. They must be answerable at law for breaches of statutory duty to the public. In addition, courts have stated that the broker's license is a privilege conferred by the state in return for which the broker must act in the public interest.

Case Example

Hagar was the holder of a long-term lease granted by the Wyoming Recreation Commission. The property covered by the lease was a trailer park operated by Hagar on 18 acres of state land. In 1978 he decided to sell the business and listed the property with United Farm Agency of Wyoming (United). Hagar represented to United that the lease expired in 45 years and contained an option to renew for 25 years. In fact, the lease expired in five years and had an option to renew for 30 more years. Hagar was aware of this.

United's sales associate Milton wrote to Mobley, a prospective buyer, about the business. In her letter Milton repeated the information about the lease that Hagar had provided. At that time she had not seen the lease. Later, when a copy of the lease was obtained from the Wyoming Recreation Commission, she read it briefly and told Mobley that she didn't understand it and that it was almost illegible anyway.

After inspecting the property, Mobley contracted to purchase the business. When he discovered that the lease was not as represented, he sued Hagar, United and sales agent Milton. The trial court dismissed the case against United and Milton on grounds that all Milton did was to repeat representations made by Hagar. The court stated that Milton had no independent duty to inquire into the truthfulness or accuracy of these representations. Mobley appealed.

The appellate court reversed. It concluded that the liability of United and Milton attached on the grounds of negligence. According to the court, to someone who had placed herself before the public as knowledgeable in the field, the lease was clear enough to show that the number of years remaining did not add up the way Hagar claimed. The court went on to say that a real estate broker has a statutory duty to the public to be honest, ethical and competent. This includes a duty to disclose material facts that may affect a customer's decision to purchase. *Hagar v. Mobley, 638 P.2d 127 (Wyo. 1981).*

In most states that recognize a duty on the part of the seller's broker to disclose all material facts to the buyer, the duty is limited to facts the broker actually knew or should have known. In addition, most of these states hold the broker liable only if the buyer has no reasonable opportunity to discover the information himself or herself. One intermediate appellate court in California, however, has held in a case involving residential property that the broker has not only a duty to disclose material facts but also an affirmative duty to conduct a reasonable inspection to discover all facts materially affecting the value or desirability of the property.

Buyer's Broker
A broker who has contracted to locate real estate for a buyer.

In most real estate transactions, the seller hires a broker to procure a buyer for the property. However, in some transactions the agency relationship is created by a buyer who authorizes a broker to negotiate for the purchase of real estate suitable for the buyer's needs. In these transactions the broker's fiduciary duties are owed to the buyer.

Until the 1980s the buyer-broker relationship was not common in residential transactions. On the other hand, buyers often hired brokers to locate commercial property. In commercial transactions the buyer usually compensated the broker. As buyer brokerage became popular in residential transactions, the broker often received compensation from the seller. If the buyer's broker receives compensation from the seller, the buyer must be informed and consent or the broker will have violated his or her fiduciary duty. Additionally, at an early stage in the negotiations the broker must inform the seller of the existence of the agency relationship with the buyer.

Multiple listing poses additional problems for the broker members who are representing buyers. A presumption exists that a broker member of a multiple listing service attempting to negotiate a sale is a subagent of the listing broker. If the broker is representing the buyer, the broker must reject the offer of subagency by notifying the listing broker at the initial contact between them. If the buyer broker does not do so, a dual agency has been created. This can have serious consequences for the broker. These range from loss of a commission from either party to revocation of the broker's license.

Dual Agency
A transaction in which an agent represents both principals.

In a real estate transaction, a dual agency would exist if a broker were to represent both buyer and seller or owner and tenant. Dual agency is neither a wise business practice nor ethical. Additionally, dual agency is generally considered to be illegal. Courts reason that an agent cannot adequately fulfill his or her fiduciary duty of loyalty to both principals. If representing the seller, the broker is obligated to obtain the best price for the seller's property. If representing the buyer, the broker's obligation is to obtain the property for the lowest possible price.

There are limited conditions under which dual agency is permissible. The key seems to be for the broker to obtain the consent of both parties. The two principals must clearly understand that the agent is representing both of them and the broker should contain their consent in writing. If the broker is to collect a fee from both principals, this should be clearly expressed in writing. In some states it is illegal for the broker to collect a fee from both principals even though both have agreed.

As an agency may be created by implication, in some cases brokers who have an express agency with the seller have unintentionally, by words or actions, created an agency relationship with a buyer. An unintentional dual agency of this kind can have unpleasant consequences for a broker as the following case indicates.

Cashion v. Ahmadi et al.
Supreme Court of Alabama
345 So.2d 268 (1977)

Background: Phillip and Donna Cashion (plaintiffs, appellants) purchased a home from Timothy and Nettie Ahmadi (defendants, appellees) through the realty firms of Pope and Quint (defendants, appellees) and Vergos Realty Company (defendant, appellee). After the purchase, the Cashions discovered a serious water seepage problem in the basement. They tried, unsuccessfully, to have this stopped, and then moved out. The Cashions then sued the former owners and the realty companies. The defendants moved for summary judgment. The trial court dismissed the case and plaintiffs appealed. Additional facts are in the opinion.

Decision: The appellate court affirmed in part; reversed in part; and remanded.

Justice Almon

Marge Mills, realtor for Pope and Quint, was initially contacted by Mrs. Cashion because of a newspaper advertisement either about the house in question or another house. The house in question had been previously listed by Pope and Quint, but at the time Marge showed it to Mrs. Cashion, it was listed under an exclusive contract with Vergos Realty and Bauer Realty (not a party to this suit). At no time did the Cashions converse directly with Gus Vergos or the Ahmadis.

The Cashions sued the appellees alleging a confidential relationship existed between themselves and the Ahmadis, Pope and Quint, and/or Vergos Realty, and because of the confidential relationship, anyone or all of the appellees had a duty to disclose that the house had a water problem which the appellees knew about. The complaint also contained allegations of misrepresentation; however, the parties stipulated that no affirmative misrepresentation occurred. The trial judge dismissed the counts based on confidential relationship, apparently on the basis that the facts alleged did not show such a relationship.

By amendment, the Cashions alleged further (1) that they employed Pope and Quint to find them a residence to purchase, that they reposed trust and confidence in Pope and Quint, that Pope and Quint knew about the water problem, and that Pope and Quint breached their obligation arising out of their confidential relationship in failing to inform the Cashions about it, and (2) that Vergos Realty, as agent for the Ahmadis negligently failed to disclose the water problem.

The Cashions contend they should have been allowed to prove that Pope and Quint was their agent, or, alternatively, that a confidential relationship existed because of the "particular circumstances" associated with this case. The Cashions also argue that they should be allowed to prove that the appellees committed certain acts of concealment designed to fraudulently mislead; however, we see nothing in the pleadings or the record to indicate that the issue of fraudulent concealment was raised in the trial court, and we will consequently not consider it on appeal.

A real estate broker may be hired to find a buyer or to find a seller. In either case the broker owes a duty of faithfulness to his principal.

> "A broker is a fiduciary and holds a position of trust and confidence. He is required to exercise fidelity and good faith toward his principal in all matters within the scope of

his employment, and to account for all funds or property rightfully belonging to his principal. He cannot put himself in a position antagonistic to his principal's interest, by fraudulent conduct, acting adversely to his client's interests, or by failing to communicate information he may possess or acquire which is or may be material to his employer's advantage, or otherwise."

The more common situation appears to be where the broker is hired by the seller to find a buyer for a percentage of the sale price, to be paid by the seller. From there, the house may be placed on a multiple listing, whereupon any number of realty firms may partake in the commission by finding a buyer.

In the instant case the house was listed under an exclusive contract with Vergos and Bauer Realties. However, Pope and Quint was allowed 50% of the commission for finding a buyer. In essence, the sale was treated as if it were a multiple listing.

The question raised by the Cashions is where did Pope and Quint's duty of faithfulness lie in this sale, with the sellers, the Ahmadis, or the buyers, the Cashions. Interestingly, Marge Mills, Frank Hicks (ex-broker for Pope and Quint), and Gus Vergos all acknowledged that if they were aware of a material defect in a residence they were selling, they should and would inform the buyer of the defect. (The question of whether there is a scintilla of evidence that any of the appellees knew about the water problem is addressed later.)

The Cashions contend that Pope and Quint was their agent and that it violated its duty of faithfulness to them in not disclosing the water problem. A broker, as well as any agent, may be an agent for both parties in a sale transaction; however, he opens himself to possible liability when he does so without full disclosure to both parties. As Judge De Graffenreid stated in *Minto v. Moore,* this is merely an expression of the ancient principle that "a servant cannot serve two masters." Any broker, though especially a broker working with a multiple listing in which he has to work through another broker who deals directly with the seller, often finds himself in the precarious situation of seeking the trust and confidence of the prospective buyer while still claiming faithfulness to the seller. He cannot have it both ways.

In the case before us the Cashions claim that Marge Mills suggested to them that the asking price of the house was too high, and that they should submit a lower bid. While Mills denies the allegation, even she admits in her deposition that she suggested to Gus Vergos that the price was too high. Furthermore, while she contends that the Cashions were her customers and that the Ahmadis were her clients, she queried to the attorney deposing her, "Who represented Dr. Ahmadi if he [Gus Vergos] didn't?" in response to the question of whether Gus Vergos would normally attend the closing.

Whether one is an agent of another is normally a question of fact to be determined by a jury. We believe that whether the total circumstances of this case require the conclusion that Pope and Quint, via their agent, Marge Mills, was an agent of Cashions, regardless of whether it may have been also an agent of the sellers, the Ahmadis, is a question for the jury under our scintilla evidence rule.

As to the question of whether Pope and Quint knew about the water problem, we note that while Marge Mills, Frank Hicks (ex-real estate agent for Pope and Quint) and Arthur Pope deny such knowledge, Dr. Ahmadi was sure that he had informed Hicks about the problem, though what seepage problem existed while he owned the house had been remedied several years prior to the sale to the Cashions. Dr Ahmadi also stated that dampness in the basement was the reason the price of the house was reduced, though such is denied by the realtors. Again, the scintilla evidence rule makes disposal of the case based on this question premature.

The judgment in this cause is affirmed as to the Ahmadis and Vergos Realty Company and reversed as to Pope and Quint, Inc.

Affirmed in part; reversed in part; and remanded.

During the 1980's the unintentional dual agency problem was of major concern to the real estate agency. Many consumer protection groups and regulatory agencies sought a solution to it that would protect both buyers and the reputation of the real estate industry. As a result a number of state legislatures and administrative agencies charged with regulating real estate sales personnel mandated that the agency relationship be disclosed in every transaction in which a broker is involved.

The rules and regulations that evolved require the broker to disclose to the parties the party he or she represents. The disclosure must be in writing usually on a standard form that has been prescribed by the state's real estate regulatory body. (See Figure 11.1.) Additionally, disclosure must occur before the submission of an offer to purchase. Dual agency is not prohibited as long as the parties agree and proper disclosure is made.

The Broker's Commission

Disputes sometimes arise between broker and seller over whether or not the broker has earned a commission. One reason may be that terms of the parties' agreement are vague, without clear provisions as to matters that later become subjects of disputes. In addition, legal misunderstandings may arise. The seller makes the agreement believing that no commission is due until the property has been paid for and plans to pay the commission out of the purchase price. On the other hand, the broker expects compensation for finding a purchaser whose offer is accepted even if title never passes. Potential problems involving payment also occur because payment is not a primary concern of the parties when the broker is hired.

When there is a problem concerning the commission, some brokers as a matter of policy refuse to litigate. They believe that a lawsuit can damage their reputation. They reason that adverse community reaction to litigation outweighs any monetary gain resulting from a successful suit. It is true that litigation is unpleasant and should be avoided, but civil suits are not publicized extensively. In fact, the word-of-mouth injury to the broker's reputation caused by a quarrel over commissions with a dissatisfied seller probably occurs even if the broker does not sue. A broker should not avoid litigation to collect a commission that has been earned, although all other solutions to the problem should be exhausted first.

Commission disputes generally involve two questions. Although they are frequently interrelated, either question may be the subject of the dispute. One common question is: Has the broker done the job he or she was hired to do? The other is: When has the broker's job been accomplished so as to entitle him or her to a commission?

In one typical scenario, the broker locates a buyer willing to purchase the property on terms agreeable to the seller. When presented with an offer, the seller refuses to accept for one reason or another, although he or she previously indicated that the terms were acceptable. In another common situation, the broker negotiates a contract between buyer and seller, but the seller cannot perform because the title is defective. Or, perhaps the owner just decides not to sell and refuses to honor the agreement. The broker cannot compel performance of the contract, and the buyer, reluctant to sue, looks for property elsewhere. The broker, feeling that he or she has performed, now seeks to recover a commission.

For the broker to be entitled to a commission, a number of threads must come together. Initially, the court needs to determine what the broker was hired to do. The broker may have been hired to sell or lease property on specific and detailed terms. If so, the broker's sole responsibility is to find a ready, willing and able buyer on these terms. Once this has been accomplished, the broker is entitled to the fee even if the parties never enter into a contract. When there is a variance between the terms authorized by the seller in the listing agreement and those tendered by the prospective buyer, the broker is not entitled to a commission if the seller refuses to contract.

Case Example

Corbin listed property with Rucker, a real estate broker. The listing described the property as 120 acres more or less and specified a price of $3,500 an acre. Rucker brought Corbin an offer which was for $3,500 per acre. Corbin rejected the offer because of two provisions in the proposal. The first read "exact acreage to be determined by current survey which is to be provided by the purchaser at time of closing." The other stipulated that "(t)he rights of purchaser hereunder may be assigned without consent of the seller." Rucker sued for a commission. The lower court dismissed and the appellate court affirmed. The appellate court stated that the two terms constituted variances from the listing. As a result, Rucker was not entitled to recover. *Rucker v. Corbin, 372 S.E.2d 512 (Ga. App. 1988).*

In a few states sellers have successfully avoided paying commissions by overpricing the property when listing it, rejecting initial offers below that price and negotiating a subsequent sale at less than the listing price. When the broker demands a commission, the seller defends upon grounds that the offer

Figure 11.1: Notice to Prospective Real Estate Purchasers/Tenants

In Ohio, real estate licensees are required to disclose which party they represent in a real esate transaction. Under Ohio law, a real estate licensee is considered to be an agent of the owner of real estate unless there is an agreement to the contrary and that agreement is disclosed to all parties.

Some duties of the licensee, as the agent of the owner, are to:

- Treat all parties to a transaction honestly
- Offer the property without regard to race, color, religion, sex, ancestry, national origin or handicap
- Promote the best interest of the owner
- Obtain the best price for the owner
- Fully disclose to the owner all facts which might affect or influence a decision
- Present all offers to the owner

As a buyer, if you choose to have a real estate broker represent you as your agent, you should enter into a written contract that clearly establishes the obligations of both you and your agent and specifies how your agent will be compensated.

Under Ohio law, the disclosure statement below must be submitted to the prospective purchaser/tenant in each transaction. This form has been approved by the Ohio Real Estate Commission for use by Ohio real estate licensees. Please sign below.

AGENCY DISCLOSURE STATEMENT

The listing broker and all agents associated with the listing broker represent the owner. The _____ (Selling Broker) and _____ (Selling Agent) represent (please check one): the purchaser/tenant _____; the owner _____.

If a broker/agent is representing both the purchaser/tenant and the owner as a dual agent, he/she must attach a copy of the agreement signed by the purchaser/tenant and owner acknowledging their agreement to this arrangement.

By signing below, the parties confirm that they have received, read and understood the information in this Agency Disclosure Form and that this form was provided to them before signing a contract to purchase/lease real estate.

_____   _____
Purchaser/Tenant   Date   *Owner   Date*

_____   _____
Purchaser/Tenant   Date   *Owner   Date*

Any questions regarding the role or responsibilities of real estate brokers or agents in Ohio can be directed to an attorney or to:

State of Ohio
Department of Commerce
Division of Real Estate
Telephone: In Ohio 1-800-344-4100 or in Columbus 614/466-4100

---

submitted did not meet the terms specified. If a seller accepts an offer lower than the asking price from a purchaser found by the broker, most courts protect the broker by holding that he or she is entitled to a commission. The broker, however, must remain active in the negotiations unless deliberately excluded by the seller.

In some listing agreements, the broker is merely informed of general terms that the seller would like to get for the property. Although a price is usually mentioned, specific terms are left for future determination. In this type of contract, the broker is not entitled to a commission until the buyer and the seller execute a binding contract.

Procuring Cause

A broker must be the procuring cause in bringing about a "meeting of the minds" between buyer and seller. A broker is the procuring cause of a sale if he or she initiates a series of continuous events that result in a sale upon the seller's terms. Merely introducing buyer and seller will be enough if the seller takes over the negotiations and completes the transaction. If the broker is unable to obtain an offer and abandons his or her efforts, the seller is not liable for a commission if the sale is completed without the broker's aid.

Sometimes two brokers contribute to the sale. Problems may arise if the seller pays the full commission to one of the brokers, knowing that broker is under a duty to share the commission with the other. The seller would be liable for the half of the commission unpaid to the broker if the broker who has been paid the full commission refuses to share.

The best solution to this problem is to have the brokers agree as to the manner in which the commission will be divided. If no agreement is reached or if the seller does not realize that two brokers were involved, some courts insist that the full commission go to the broker who was the "primary, proximate and procuring cause of the sale." Which broker fits this definition is determined in court on the basis of whose efforts tipped the scale and induced sellers and purchasers to come to terms.

Ready, Willing and Able
Capable of present performance.

To be entitled to a commission, the broker must procure a buyer "ready, willing and able" to complete the transaction. The test of whether the buyer is ready and willing is his or her intention at the time the contract is made. Intent at the time the contract is to be consummated (closed) is not material. Most courts infer readiness and willingness if the buyer submits an offer on terms stipulated by the owner.

A buyer is said to be able if he or she has the financial ability to complete the transaction.

Case Example

Chester Winkelman, a real estate broker, brought suit against J. R. Allen to recover a commission. The basis of Winkelman's action was that he had procured a ready, willing and able buyer. The evidence indicated that Allen had listed his ranch with Winkelman at $350,000. The listing was open. Winkelman showed the ranch to Russell Bird and his father, Randall. Randall Bird was a prosperous rancher. Russell, age 22, had appreciable ranching experience but little capital.

The Birds and Allen discussed the sale on several occasions. On one of these, Allen was informed that only Russell, the son, was to sign the contract. After apparent agreement was reached on terms satisfactory to Allen, a written offer signed by Russell and a $1,000 deposit were submitted. Allen held the offer for several days and then sold the property to another.

After a lower court found in Winkelman's favor, an appellate court reversed and ordered judgment for Allen. The court stated, "[W]here the only available source from which the money is to come is . . . admittedly in the possession of a third person . . . who is in no way bound . . . such a purchaser cannot be considered able to buy . . . " *Winkelman v. Allen, 214 Kan. 22, 519 P.2d 1377 (1974).*

In the *Winkelman* case the broker did not produce a ready, willing and *able* buyer. No commission was due. A buyer is considered financially ready and able to buy under any of three conditions:

1. The buyer has cash on hand to complete the sale.

2. The buyer has sufficient personal assets and a strong credit rating that ensures with reasonable certainty that he or she can complete the sale.

3. The buyer has a binding commitment for a loan with which to finance the sale.

When Commission is Earned

In most states, the broker has procured a buyer when the broker submits a binding, enforceable offer from a buyer on the seller's terms. The result is that, as long as the buyer is financially able, the broker has earned the commission at that time. The broker and seller may, and frequently do, agree that the commission will be earned on conditions other than submission of a binding offer. Their contract may state that the commission is due on closing of title or out of the proceeds of the sale. If this is the case, the broker's commission has not been earned until that condition is met. As a general rule, if the broker procures a counteroffer that deviates in price or otherwise from the specified terms, the seller may accept or decline. If the seller accepts, the commission is due the broker for services rendered.

Recent case law in some states modifies the traditional general rule as to when the commission is earned. Courts in these states hold that the broker is not entitled to a commission if the buyer defaults on the contract. As a result, the broker does not earn the commission until the transaction closes.

Several reasons exist for this change. For one, most sellers listing property with a broker anticipate paying the broker's commission out of the proceeds of the sale. If the sale fails to close through no fault of theirs, sellers feel that they should not be responsible for a commission. A second reason is that the rule obligating the seller to pay a commission upon contracting places upon seller the burden of determining the buyer's financial ability. But the seller is the wrong person to make this decision. Determining the prospect's financial status and willingness should rest with the broker, for ordinarily that person has had closer contacts with the buyer and is better able to measure financial capacity and willingness. From the point of view of paying a commission, the time when financial ability and willingness are important is not when the agreement is signed, but at the time of closing. If the buyer refuses or is unable financially to perform at that time, the broker has not really done the job. If, however, failure to complete the transaction results from the seller's wrongful act or refusal, the broker has a valid claim for the commission.

Traditionally, the broker's compensation has been based upon a percentage of the selling price. Most brokers in the same market customarily charge a similar commission, although even informal agreement among brokers to do so is illegal. In the late 1970s and early 1980s, as competition in the real estate industry increased, some brokers adopted alternative methods for determining fees. An obvious competitive strategy was to reduce the percentage charged to below that being charged by other brokers in the market. Another approach was to charge a flat fee instead of a percentage of the selling price. A third approach was to separate or "unbundle" the services provided a client and charge for each on an individual basis. For example, a broker might determine a separate fee for appraising the property and suggesting a selling price, advertising and showing the home, conducting negotiations or assisting at the closing. Clients could select the services desired and be billed only for these. Although discounting, flat fees and unbundling have been resisted in the industry, they probably will be used more frequently as real estate brokerage becomes more competitive.

Termination of Agency

The agency relationship may be terminated in numerous ways. Probably most agencies terminate upon accomplishment of the purpose for which the agency was created or upon expiration of the time agreed upon for performance. The latter is important in real estate as many exclusive listings contain a date upon which the listing will end. In fact, regulations in many states require that a listing include a specific termination date. Of course, the agency will continue if the parties renew the agency at that time.

By Acts of the Parties

As agency is a consensual relationship, either party has the *power* to end it at any time. However, the fact that one has the power to terminate the agency does not necessarily mean that he or she has *the right* to do so. For example, if a seller gives a broker an exclusive-right-to-sell listing for 90 days, the seller has the power to revoke the broker's authority before 90 days have passed, but if the seller revokes without justification, the broker can sue for damages.

Case Example

Hague owned 240 acres of farmland. He listed 80 acres with Hilgendorf, a licensed broker. Before the listing expired, Hague terminated it as he had encountered financial problems and decided to sell the entire farm. The farm was not listed with Hilgendorf.

Hilgendorf found a ready, willing and able buyer for the 80 acres. When Hague refused to accept the buyer's offer, Hilgendorf sued for his commission. Hague argued that Hilgendorf's duty of loyalty required him to give up the listing. Both the trial and appellate courts rejected this argument. The appellate court stated that "[i]n performing agency functions an agent does indeed occupy a fiduciary position, and his duty requires him to place the principal's interests first. But in the contract of agency . . . neither of the parties is acting for the other; each is acting for himself."

On this basis the appellate court rejected Hague's argument and awarded damages to Hilgendorf. The court stated that, although the principal has the power to terminate an unexpired agency, the principal subjects himself to damages for doing so. *Hilgendorf v. Hague, 293 N.W.2d 272 (Iowa 1980).*

By Operation of Law

In addition to termination by the acts of the parties, the agency relationship terminates automatically by operation of law if any of the following events occur:

- death, incompetency or bankruptcy of principal or agent,
- destruction of the subject matter,
- change in law making the agent's duties illegal,
- loss of license required by either principal or agent, or
- conflict of interest.

Although termination for any of the above reasons is easy to understand, a difficult termination problem arises when an unusual change in conditions related to the agency takes place. For example, if a broker is authorized to sell land at a specified price and the value of the land suddenly increases substantially, has the original authority terminated? Most courts would say so.

Agency Coupled with an Interest
An agency that cannot be revoked by the principal.

Although ordinarily an agency can be terminated at the will of either party, an agency coupled with an interest is irrevocable. In this type of agency the principal has given the agent certain powers and coupled these with a financial or security interest in the subject matter of the agency. As a result the principal does not have the right to revoke the agent's power. In addition, when an agent has authority coupled with an interest, the death, incompetency or bankruptcy of the principal does not terminate the agency.

One common example of the agency coupled with an interest is a mortgage in which the borrower gives the lender the power to have the security sold if the mortgage debt is in default (see Chapter 18 and discussion of power of sale foreclosure). A less common example would be a business arrangement in which a broker advances funds to a contractor to complete a home on speculation. In addition to agreeing to repay the loan, the contractor gives the broker an exclusive right to sell the property when the home is completed.

Real Estate Sales Associate
A person employed by a real estate broker who, under the broker's direction, lists and sells real estate.

In many real estate transactions much of the work is done by sales personnel who are not licensed brokers. Although many state licensing statutes use the designation *salesman* for both male and female sales personnel, the term *associate* is becoming more common. That word will be used in this chapter.

All states require real estate sales associates to be licensed. The procedures that are followed to license sales associates are similar to those for licensing brokers; however, the requirements for obtaining a sales associate's license are less demanding. For example, to obtain a broker's license a person is usually required to have experience in selling real estate, but experience is not necessary to obtain a sales associate's license. If a competency examination is required to obtain a sales associate's license, it is almost always less comprehensive than the licensing examination for brokers.

In large firms, sales associates do much of the legwork for the business. A sales associate prospects for buyers and sellers, assists the seller in determining price and completes listings and sales contract. Sometimes the sales associate helps to arrange financing and may provide assistance to lenders and attorneys with regard to title evidence and documents necessary to complete the sale of real property.

A sales associate is required by law to be associated with a broker. The broker holds the sales associate's license and directs and supervises his or her work. Commissions on each sale are collected by the broker. The sales associate receives as compensation a previously agreed-upon percentage of the commission. There is some judicial disagreement as to the relationship between broker and sales associate. A majority of courts conclude that the sales associate is an independent contractor, not an employee. Under this view the broker is not responsible for workers' compensation, unemployment insurance premiums or withholding taxes. Some recent cases, however, tend to view the relationship between broker and sales associate as that of employer-employee. Where this view is taken, the broker has the same legal responsibility to the sales associate that all employers have to their employees. Actually, whether an employer-employee or independent contractor relationship exists depends upon the facts of the particular relationship.

Case Example

McGinnis worked exclusively for Berens on a commission basis. He was hired to obtain listings of property suitable for sale to commercial developers. McGinnis was required (a) to clear all listings with Berens, (b) to attend sales meetings, (c) to report all transactions before they were finalized and (d) to comply with requirements, standards and methods of doing business established by Berens. Berens also provided office support, advances on expenses, hospitalization and life insurance.

McGinnis was injured because of the negligence of another Berens sales associate who was driving the two in a company car to inspect real property listed by Berens. When McGinnis sued to collect damages for the injury, Berens argued that he was not liable as McGinnis was an independent contractor, not an employee. The court disagreed. It held McGinnis an employee because Berens exercised "control" over the manner in which McGinnis did his job. As the injury was caused by the negligence of another Berens employee, Berens was liable. *McGinnis v. Frederick W. Berens Sales, Inc., 308 A.2d 765 (D.C. 1973).*

Other cases have also held the real estate sales associate an employee, even though the parties themselves have agreed that the sales associate was an independent contractor. These courts looked beyond the parties' understanding of their relationship to the degree of control exercised by the broker. A sales associate can work only for a single broker who holds his or her license; state regulatory statutes require the broker to exercise supervision of the sales associate's activity; therefore, control is usually relatively simple to establish.

Licensing Laws

State laws that require a person to obtain a license in order to act as a real estate broker or sales associate and regulate the conduct of those who act as brokers or sales associates in real estate transactions.

Real estate licensing laws are an exercise of the police power by the state. Based upon this power, each state as sovereign may legislate to protect the general welfare of its citizens. In 1917, California became the first state to adopt a comprehensive, statewide licensing statute. Since then, all states have passed some type of legislation regulating the activities of real estate brokers and sales associates. The core of this legislation is a licensing requirement. A major goal of these laws is to ensure that only people who are honest and competent operate as brokers and sales personnel.

Most state statutes define *broker* broadly, using as a basis typical activities involved in the sale and rental of real estate. Usually these statutes exempt lawyers and others acting in special relationships under court supervision. These would include administrators, executors, trustees and receivers. All states allow an individual owner to sell his or her own property without a real estate license, although some questions arise when the owner is a corporation. The general rule appears to be that a corporation selling its own land is not required to be licensed if it operates through regular employees who have actual authority to exercise the general powers of the corporation. Ordinarily, the board of directors and corporate officers such as the president and secretary have this power. However, when a corporation hires sales personnel solely to attempt to sell corporate land, these people must be licensed.

A number of sanctions exist for engaging in brokerage activity without a license. Most states merely deny the unlicensed broker the right to collect a commission or other fee. In a few states, acting as a broker or sales associate without a license is a misdemeanor, punishable by fine and/or imprisonment. Some states allow any person who suffers a monetary loss because of the acts of an unlicensed broker or sales associate to sue for damages.

Although the license laws of the states have many differences, some relatively common elements do exist. One reason for this is that many state laws are based on a pattern of law recommended by the NATIONAL ASSOCIATION OF REALTORS®.

Licensing statutes are usually administered by an appointed real estate commission. The commissioners are usually highly regarded people active in the real estate business. The commission has the power to make rules and regulations of its own to carry out the directives of the legislature. In addition to the commission, a full-time executive director is hired by the state to perform the administrative duties of the commission. Although the primary function of the commission is to administer licensing laws, most real estate commissions have other responsibilities. These commonly include the establishment and promulgation of educational and ethical standards.

In most states the competency of applicants for brokers' and sales associates' licenses is established by written examination. Many states have added minimal educational requirements, which must be met before a person is eligible to take a broker's or sales associate's license examination. Usually, to be eligible for the broker's examination, an individual must have had some experience as a sales associate or met certain educational criteria. The examination for a broker's license is ordinarily more comprehensive than that for a license to sell. A number of states have adopted legislation requiring continuing education for brokers and sales associates. In Ohio, for example, they must complete 30 classroom hours of real estate education every three years in order to retain their licenses.

The principal sanction available against a broker or sales associate is the revocation of his or her license. Numerous actions serve as the basis for revocation or suspension. Frequently these actions are indicated by statute, but in some states the real estate commission has authority to promulgate its own rules and regulations. Misconduct punishable under statute by suspension or revocation need not involve real estate transactions or dealings with the licensee as a broker, and a broker may be punished for misconduct even when no one actually suffers a monetary loss.

Unauthorized Practice of Law

In attempting to bring buyer and seller together to complete a sale, one of the perennial problems faced by brokers is the extent to which they can give legal advice, draft legal instruments or fill in blanks on printed forms without practicing law illegally. Little agreement exists in the United States as to what the broker can do with out being involved in the unauthorized practice of law. Some states allow conduct clearly prohibited in others. Nevertheless, two principles do seem commonly accepted. First, permitted activities must be incidental to a transaction in which the broker is involved. A number of states, for example, allow brokers to fill in blanks on printed forms drafted by lawyers. In any state, however, a broker who did this for someone not a client or a prospective purchaser of real estate listed with the broker would be guilty of unauthorized practice of law. Second, a broker is not entitled to charge a separate fee for any legal work that is permitted.

Some states have attempted to clarify by statute what constitutes unauthorized practice. These statutes generally prohibit someone who is not a lawyer from giving legal advice and from drafting legal instruments. A few of these states exempt real estate brokers and title insurance companies from prosecution for drafting certain types of legal instruments related to real estate. At least one state, Arizona, by a constitutional amendment adopted in 1970, specifically gives real estate brokers the right to prepare legal documents incident to their trade.

In a majority of states, by judicial decision interpreting unauthorized practice statutes, it is clear that a broker may neither give legal advice nor draft instruments relating to real estate. For the broker to do so constitutes the unauthorized practice of law. This is true even if the broker does these things only for his or her own clients, only occasionally and receives no compensation for such work. A few states do permit a broker to draft simple deeds or other real estate instruments if this is done on isolated occasions and without compensation.

Brokers in most states are permitted to fill in blanks on certain printed forms that have been prepared by attorneys. In a majority of states the forms are restricted to the contract, offer and acceptance. The rationale for this position is that these are the only forms that are incidental to the broker's business. Other states allow the broker to complete blanks on lawyer-approved instruments such as a deed or mortgage.

An additional complicating factor in a number of states is that the information that the broker is permitted to fill in must be clerical in nature. Clerical information would include items such as date, price, names, addresses, property location, date of possession and duration of offer. This position can result in confusion for brokers as it is often unclear just what information courts consider clerical.

Penalties for practicing law without a license are harsh. In most states the unauthorized practice of law is a crime. The person convicted is subject to both a fine and imprisonment. A real estate broker who engages in unauthorized legal practice can have his or her license suspended or revoked. In addition, a person who suffers a monetary loss because of a broker's erroneous legal advice can collect from the broker in a suit for malpractice.

New Home Construction and Sales

The examples given in this chapter have dealt with the broker's role in the sale of homes or other structures, generally with an individual owner as the principal, selling to another individual who will reside in the home or use the structure as a business.

The broker also often has a role in the sale of new homes. Frequently a broker may be engaged by a builder or developer to sell one home or many, even before the homes are completed. Because of the importance of the legal relationships of the many parties involved in such a venture—subdivider, developer, architect subcontractor—the balance of this chapter will discuss their legal and ethical responsibilities.

Like so many other areas, home construction is something done by a specialist, or more likely a group of specialists, acting in a legal relationship for the individual or group that wishes to build one home or many.

One of the most common ways to have a home constructed today is to purchase one from a subdivider. The *subdivider* may be merely a developer who divides up a parcel of land into lots and sells the lot. The subdivider or developer prepares the site for housing by dividing the acreage into lots, installing the *infrastructure*—the roads and utilities—and doing preliminary grading. When the developer has finished, the lots are ready for construction of the houses; final site grading is done as houses are completed.

The developer and the builder or contractor may be the same person, although the site is often developed by one person, and the houses are constructed by another or several others. The method chosen is of little consequence to the buyer (the individual or group) seeking to have the house built. Each has responsibilities for work performed and can be held accountable by the buyer under the contractual arrangement that is entered.

All new housing is not the product of subdividing. A person can purchase a lot and hire a general contractor to construct a house to certain specifications. Or the person can hire an architect to draw up the plans and specifications for the house and to supervise the work of a contractor, who does the actual construction. Or a well-informed person may undertake to hire and supervise construction of a house drawn to his or her specifications.

Regardless of the approach taken, there is a cast of characters with whom the owner may have to deal. The following material discusses the roles played by these people and the legal rights and duties that arise as a result of those roles.

Developer

The person or firm that subdivides a parcel of land and otherwise prepares the site for the construction of housing.

Generally, the developer takes raw land and develops it to the point where it is ready for construction of the house. Initially, the developer must acquire the land. The acquisition may be as simple as an outright purchase in fee simple from the landowner. In other instances the developer and landowner enter a joint venture arrangement, sharing in some fashion the risks, costs and profits of the development project. For example, the developer may purchase the land, with the landowner taking back a mortgage for all or a portion of the purchase price. As the developer sells each developed lot, the landowner is paid an agreed-upon percentage of the mortgage.

The developer must be reasonably careful to select land that is appropriate for the proposed construction.

Case Example

Several purchasers bought condominium units constructed by Salishan Properties, Inc., in a resort area in Oregon. Due to erosion from the ocean, their lots were severely damaged. The owners sued the developer/builder, contending that it had held itself out as an expert in resort-type construction and was, therefore, negligent in selecting an appropriate site for construction of their condominium units. Salishan countered that it had no liability since it was powerless to control the erosion problem.

The court held that the developer could not be held liable for latent defects. It could, however, be held liable for negligence in site selection. Since the developer held itself out as an expert in resort construction, it was required to take reasonable precautions to assure that the lots were suitable for residential construction. *Beri, Inc. v. Salishan Properties, Inc., 282 Or. 259, 580 P.2d 173 (1978).*

Once the land is acquired, the developer undertakes to install the infrastructure for the development. The roads, sewer and water lines, power and telephone wires, gutters and sidewalks and site grading must be completed. Most of these items are installed to specifications established by federal, state, county or municipal governments.

When the infrastructure is in place, the developer, when not also the builder, undertakes to market the lots to one or more homebuilders. The lot or lots may be sold outright to the builder. When a poor market exists for housing, the developer may agree to postpone full payment for the improved lot until the house is sold by the builder.

The Developer and Government Agencies

It is the developer's responsibility to obtain governmental approval for the site and for the individual installations. The land must be zoned properly for the type of housing that will be constructed. If it is zoned inappropriately, the developer seeks to have the zone changed to dovetail with the planned development.

Once the zoning is correct, the developer must obtain subdivision approval from the municipal planning board. The board will check to see whether the developer's plans comply with its regulations. For instance, the roads must be adequate in width and depth of roadbed, sewer lines must be adequate for anticipated flow and drainage layout must prevent flooding or ponding problems.

The most extensive cost in many subdivisions is that of installing utilities (using that term to encompass the full range of items that go into site preparation). These costs may be handled in a variety of ways. Some municipalities will bond for the full cost of the utilities, recouping their money for bond retirement from the increased taxes obtained from the new homeowners in the subdivision. In other cases the locality will bond for only a fixed amount for utilities, generally on a per-lot basis. If costs exceed that amount, the developer bears the financial obligation to pay the difference between the cost and the municipal bonding limit. In still other municipalities the developer must pay the full cost of utilities without the assistance of public bonding. In the case of power and telephone lines the utilities themselves may bear the cost of installation up to a fixed maximum.

The developer is legally responsible for the construction to specification of any utility installed by it. Many times the municipality will demand that the developer provide a performance bond to guarantee that the utilities will be properly installed. The bond will be released in stages as portions of the utility installation are constructed and found to conform to public regulations.

The legal relationship lies between the municipality and the developer. The actual builder contracts for the purchase of lots with the developer, but the developer remains primarily responsible for compliance with local laws. One area where this lack of legal connection between the municipality and the builder causes trouble is final site grading. The developer grades the site pursuant to municipal specifications. Final grading on each lot, however, is usually the responsibility of the builder upon completion of construction of the house. It is the builder's contractual obligation with the developer to grade the site properly, but it is the developer that will be held accountable by the municipality.

There are various other approvals that the developer must obtain, depending on local laws. Sewer installations may need state or county health department approval. An environmental impact statement or other environmental permits may be mandated. In all of these, generally the developer has primary responsibility for compliance.

Architect

A professional person hired to prepare the plans and specifications for the construction of a house.

The subdivider or contractor uses the architect to design the model home plans that he or she will sell to buyers. Also, the architect may lay out the design or configuration of the subdivision, locating the roads, the home lots and the drainage flow. The architect may, in addition, be employed to oversee construction. For an individual home, supervision may be confined to spot-checking materials that come onto the site and labor that is being performed. In larger projects, the architect may be hired to be on the site continuously to oversee the quality of work.

In any event, the architect who is hired by the buyer, owner or subdivider in one or more of these capacities has certain authority to act and certain rights and duties that arise from that authority.

The Authority of the Architect

The architect and buyer enter a personal service contract. Selection is based on the architect's skill as well as his or her reputation for honesty and fairness in business dealings. Although the basis of the authority granted is spelled out specifically in that contract, some generalizations can be made.

When the architect is hired to design a subdivision or an individual residential unit, an *employer-employee relationship* arises between the hiring party (the buyer) and the architect. This relationship requires the architect to follow the general instructions of the buyer in drafting the design. No architect is required to comply with instructions that would make the structure unsafe or would violate the regulatory ordinances of the community.

Since the architect is hired because of particular skills and characteristics, the contract is not assignable to another architect without the hirer's consent. If a firm of architects is hired, then any architect within that firm can do the design work unless otherwise stipulated in the contract.

When the architect is hired to supervise the construction, a *principal-agent* relationship arises between the architect and the buyer.

Case Example

Forty-O-Four Grand Corp. hired the architectural firm of Roland A. Wilson and Associates to supervise construction of a luxury apartment building in Des Moines. A dispute arose over the performance of the architect, and the owner withheld the architect's fee.

In an action by the architect for the remainder of his fee, the court described the parties' legal relationship. When one employs an architect to supervise construction, the architect is the agent of the one who employs him or her. The architect is bound to use reasonable care to see that the work is done properly with the proper materials. *Roland A. Wilson & Assoc. v. Forty-O-Four Grand Corp., 246 N.W.2d 922 (Iowa 1976).*

The architect has no general authority to bind the buyer but has the authority to do what is reasonably necessary to complete the job according to the plans and specifications provided.

Although the extent of the architect/agent's authority is specified in the contract, certain implied authority exists unless prohibited. The architect is implicitly authorized to make minor changes in the plans needed to correct errors made but does not have the authority to alter the plan *materially* without the buyer's approval. In addition, the architect has the implied authority to inspect materials that come onto the site to assure that they are of the requisite quality.

The architect has a third type of authority that does not neatly fall into a traditional legal category. When supervising construction, the architect has the implied authority, if not otherwise expressed, to settle disputes that arise between the buyer and the contractor. Though hired by the buyer and primarily responsible to that buyer, the architect is under a duty to resolve these disputes impartially. The architect must apply notions of equity to the dispute resolution and lay aside any duties owed to the buyer, which may put the architect in an uncomfortable position at times.

The Architect's Rights and Duties

The architect who designs a subdivision or residential unit has a duty to perform in a workmanlike manner. Design work must be completed on time, or within a reasonable time if a date is not stipulated in the contract. An architect who fails to perform in a timely fashion will be liable in damages for that tardiness.

When the architect is the construction supervisor and therefore an agent, the fiduciary relationship demands the duty to act in good faith and with loyalty. The architect is prohibited from having a financial interest in the contract or in any way benefiting personally from the contract unless there is full disclosure and consent by the buyer.

The architect does not warrant a perfect job but does assure that the contract will be supervised with reasonable care. Failure to use reasonable care or to be loyal will make the architect susceptible to a suit for money damages by the buyer and to the withholding of the fee for failure to perform adequately. In the case cited above, the court stated that "this obligation does not make the architect a guarantor of the contractor's work. Instead, it requires the architect to exercise reasonable care in supervision and inspection of the work to protect the owner against payment of money to the contractor for work not performed or materials not delivered." *Roland A. Wilson & Assoc. v. Forty-O-Four Grand Corp., 246 N.W.2d 922 (Iowa 1976).*

If the buyer fails to pay the architect for services performed, the architect has a mechanic's lien on the property. The architect can compel judicial sale of the structure if the lien is not satisfied. Lien rights are discussed in more detail in Chapter 7.

Contractor (Builder)

The person or firm that undertakes to construct a house at a given price.

The term *contractor* or *builder* can mean several different things, depending on the building arrangement that is made by the buyer. Generally, the buyer hires a general contractor to construct the building to certain plans and specifications. The general contractor is obligated to provide the materials and labor necessary to construct the planned house. Much of the work is performed by subcontractors, whom the general contractor will hire and be solely responsible for. The general contractor is neither an employer nor an agent of the buyer, like the architect, but is classified legally as an independent contractor. The independent contractor agrees to provide a house to specifications, but the buyer has no direct control while the contractor is performing the services contracted for.

The general contractor may be constructing homes in a subdivision in compliance with the model home selected by the buyer or may be hired to construct an individually designed house on a lot owned by the buyer. Also, the general contractor may be building homes on speculation, hoping to sell them during or after construction. Although these are the most common arrangements, others exist as well. The buyer may choose to act as his or her own general contractor, hiring and coordinating the subcontractors or unit contractors.

The contractor may be selected personally by the buyer or may be obtained through a bidding process. If a bidding process is used, the potential contractors will be requested to bid on plans and specifications for a specific house. The bid entered by the contractor is an *offer*, and the buyer is free to select from among the various offers unless he or she has previously agreed to accept the *lowest bid without reservation*. There is no contract until the bid is accepted by the buyer. Any attempt to alter the bid materially by the buyer will be treated as a rejection of that bid.

The contract to build entered into by the contractor and the buyer will be governed by the usual rules of contract discussed in Chapter 12. The contractor's authority is simply to provide a final product, a house that complies with the plans and specifications provided by the buyer or the architect.

The chapter on contracts provides a thorough discussion of the various legal problems surrounding contracts. Satisfactory performance, delays in performance, mutual or unilateral mistake, modification of the contract and various actions for damages are discussed there. These general contract principles apply as well to the contracts entered into by the parties discussed in this chapter and will not be covered here.

The requirement of a *building permit* from a municipal official prior to beginning construction of a house is nearly universal. Failure to obtain a building permit allows the municipality to halt construction at any time and order compliance. Prior to issuing a building permit, the municipal official examines the plans for the house to ensure that no municipal code violations will occur.

If the building permit is issued and the contractor carelessly or willfully violates the municipal code, the contractor will be required to allow a reduction of the contract price equal to the cost of remedying the defects. If payment has already been made, a suit for money damages by the buyer is the appropriate remedy.

Rights and Duties of the Contractor

One of the chief responsibilities of the contractor is to coordinate the work of the subcontractors. If the general contractor fails to coordinate the work reasonably and that failure causes injury to the buyer or to a subcontractor, the general contractor will be liable in a suit for damages.

The contractor has the duty to inspect the materials brought onto the construction site. If such materials have defects that are reasonably discoverable upon an inspection and the contractor fails to inspect them or inspects but does not reject the defective materials, the contractor will be liable for injury caused by those materials. Injury includes the final product being a less valuable house, and the contractor will be liable for money damages for the difference between the value of the house contracted for and the one actually built.

The contractor, and any commercial home seller, implicitly warrants that the house he or she constructed is habitable. If the house proves not to be habitable or otherwise does not conform to any express warranty given by the contractor, the contractor will be liable in damages for the injury caused the owner.

Case Example

David and Patricia Elmore purchased a new home from a builder, Robert Blume. The Elmores told Blume that they planned on carpeting and making a recreation room in the basement. Blume assured them that the basement, which contained standing water upon inspection, would be dry when the gutters and windows were in place. After the Elmores took possession of the home, it continued to have a wet basement, and they sued for the cost of drain tiles.

The court stated that the contractor/vendor gives an implied warranty of habitability to the vendee in the contract for the sale of a house. Water damage caused by faulty construction would breach that warranty. *Elmore v. Blume, 31 Ill. App. 2d 643, 334 N.E.2d 431 (1975).*

If the house is destroyed by fire, flood or other natural disaster during the period of construction and the contract does not address this contingency, the contractor continues to be liable to provide a house completed to specifications. Once the building is finished, the contractor's responsibility to replace the house in case of destruction not due to the contractor's negligence terminates. If the buyer tells the contractor what lot to build on and supplies the builder with plans, the contractor is not legally responsible for soil characteristics that make the area unsuitable for construction nor for structural weaknesses in the house.

In general, the contractor agrees to perform in a workmanlike manner commensurate with accepted community norms. In exchange, the buyer agrees to make payments without unreasonable delay as they come due. If there is unreasonable delay in payment, the contractor may be justified in abandoning the job.

Summary

An *agency* exists when one person, called a principal, authorizes another, called an agent, to act for him or her. Real estate *brokers* usually act as agents for sellers. Sometimes, but less often, they act as agents for buyers. An agency is created between a seller and a broker when the broker acquires a *listing*. The listing authorizes the broker to negotiate a sale of the seller's real estate. To prevent later conflict, the listing should be written, should specify the rights and duties of the parties and should indicate whether it is open or exclusive.

An *open listing* entitles the broker to compensation only if his or her efforts bring about the desired result. The seller may list with any number of brokers, but only that broker directly responsible for the sale is entitled to the fee. A second listing, the *exclusive agency*, allows the seller to sell without paying the fee. Another type, the *exclusive right to sell*, entitles the broker to a commission even when the seller finds a buyer independently. By prior agreement, when a broker who is a member of the multiple listing service secures a buyer, he or she is entitled to share the commission with the listing broker.

The scope of the broker's *authority* as an agent is limited to the terms of the agreement. In fact, the broker is not normally authorized to sell, but merely to locate a qualified buyer. A broker's authority may be either express or implied. *Express authority* refers to the terms stated in the agreement; *implied authority* relates to activities necessary to carry out this authority.

Laws of agency define the duties of the agent to the principal as fiduciary. A fiduciary relationship requires high standards of conduct, good faith and loyalty. Specifically, at least three positive duties are involved: full disclosure to the principal of all matters relating to the agency, adherence to the principal's lawful instructions and full accounting for all money exchanges relating to the agency.

In most real estate transactions, the broker is the seller's agent. When a broker contracts to locate real estate for a buyer, the broker is referred to as a *buyer's broker*. A *dual agency* exists if the broker represents both parties. This practice should be avoided but is permissible if both buyer and seller agree.

Although the broker is usually not the buyer's agent, the broker has a duty to treat the buyer fairly. In general, this means that the broker cannot misrepresent the property. In several states, courts have held that the broker has a duty to disclose all material facts about the property known to him or her that a buyer could not readily discover.

Payment of commission is sometimes disputed. Litigation generally involves one of two questions: Has the broker done the specified job? Has the job been accomplished so as to earn the commission? In most listings the broker's sole duty is to locate a qualified buyer or tenant who is *"ready, willing and able"* to buy or rent. The job is complete when the two parties are brought together. In most states the commission is earned at the time the broker submits a binding, enforceable offer from a buyer on the owner's terms, unless the listing agreement specifically states otherwise. In some states, unless the transaction closes, the broker is not entitled to a commission.

The law requires that each *real estate sales associate* be associated with a licensed broker who holds that person's license and supervises performance of the work. Licensing of sales associates and brokers is regulated by state laws. These laws most often require acceptable performance on a written test and adherence to certain standards of conduct. Some states require continuing education to retain the license. The *licensing laws* are administered by state real estate commissions. The commission is empowered to revoke a license if a sales associate or broker is found guilty of misconduct.

One problem brokers face is the charge of unauthorized practice of law. The states vary widely in their rulings as to what is unauthorized practice. In most states, however, it is clear that the broker is not permitted to give legal advice to clients or to draft legal instruments such as contracts or deeds. They are normally permitted to fill in the blanks when such forms are prepared by an attorney.

In the sale of new homes, the duties of *subdivider*, *developer*, *architect* and *builder* (*contractor*) are varied and entail certain legal responsibilities. Often the duties of the parties overlap, as when an architect owns a development company to carry out his or her own designs.

Review and Discussion Questions

1. Define *independent contractor* and indicate why a real estate broker ordinarily acts in this capacity.

2. What are the two types of exclusive listings? Explain how they differ.

3. Compare and contrast *express authority* and *implied authority*. Provide some examples of implied authority.

4. Although appreciable differences exist in the United States as to what constitutes unauthorized practice, two principles are commonly accepted. State these principles.

5. Define *procuring cause*.

6. Explain how the authority of an architect supervising construction differs from the authority agents generally enjoy.

Case Problems

1. Ed Kelly gave Dave Gould Realty an exclusive listing on property owned by Kelly. Gould showed the property to Nadine McNicols, a real estate developer. McNicols had numerous questions relating to zoning, and Gould referred her to Kelly's attorney, who answered her questions and supplied her with additional information.

   When McNicols learned that Gould was showing the property to other prospective buyers, she made an offer directly to Kelly. Kelly accepted the offer but refused to pay Gould a commission. (a) What argument could be made for Kelly? (b) For Gould? (c) Who would win if Gould sued? Why?

2. Sam Guidi, a real estate broker, learned from a friend that Arro, Inc., was interested in buying vacant land for a warehouse. Knowing that Byron Lane owned land that he was trying to sell, Guidi phoned Lane, who quoted him a price of $35,000 for the parcel. Lane knew that Guidi was a broker, but no commission or other arrangements were discussed. Guidi obtained an offer of $28,000 from Arro, which Lane rejected. Shortly thereafter Lane contacted Arro directly and entered into a contract at $33,000. In a suit by Guidi against Lane for a commission, what resulted? Why?

3. Caldwell listed property with Burnette, a broker, at $3,000 per acre. The listing was open. Burnette showed the property to Donaldson, who stated that the price was too high. He requested Burnette to persuade Caldwell to reduce it. Burnette submitted an offer of $2,750 to Caldwell, but Caldwell would not accept the lower price.

    Several months later, Caldwell listed the property with Crutchfield at $2,500. Crutchfield showed the property to several prospective purchasers, including Donaldson. Donaldson offered $2,750 and the property was sold to him at that price. When Burnette heard of this, he demanded a commission. When Caldwell refused, Burnette sued. Would Burnette be successful? Support your answer. *Leon Realty, Inc. v. Hough, 310 So.2d 767 (Fla. Dist. Ct. 1973).*

4. Lewis, a licensed real estate sales associate, listed residential property owned by Flavin. Flavin informed Lewis that the property was in the South West School District. Actually the property was in the Columbus School District. Flavin, however, did not know this because he had no children and had frequently received mailings from the South West schools. In addition, children who lived next door attended schools in the South West District.

    Katz and his wife were looking for a home, but they did not want to buy property in the Columbus district because children were bused substantial distances to achieve racial balance. The Katz family was interested in Flavin's home and agreed to buy it after Lewis assured them that it was in the South West District. Would the erroneous statement made by Lewis be a basis for revocation or suspension of his real estate license? Discuss.

5. Klos purchased a home constructed by Gockel. A mud slide wrecked the patio of the house, although the house itself received only minor injury. Klos sued Gockel for breach of warranty of habitability. What was the result? *Klos v. Gockel, 554 P.2d 1349 (1976).*

6. Sierra Pacific commissioned Carter, a licensed broker, to sell real estate for an asking price of $85,000. Sierra Pacific was to receive $80,000 and Carter $5,000. The $85,000 figure was arrived at by Sierra Pacific upon the advice of Carter, who was familiar with property in the area. At the trial the parties agreed that it represented fair market value. Carter received several offers of less than $85,000, but all were rejected by the seller. Finally, Carter sold the property to his daughter and son-in-law for $85,000. Carter retained the $5,000 without informing Sierra Pacific of his relationship to the buyers. Upon discovering it, Sierra Pacific initiated suit against Carter for the $5,000. Will it be successful? Support your answer. *Sierra Pacific Industries v. Carter, 163 Cal. Rptr. 764 (1980).*

12

Basic Contract Law

Contract

A promise or an agreement between two or more parties that the law will enforce.

Citizens are obliged to obey laws the government imposes upon them. No one likes to pay taxes, but failure to do so results in penalties. The obligation to pay taxes arises from a legislative act. Obligations may also arise by individual agreement. Two or more persons may come together in agreement to be bound by their own "private legislation." The law will enforce that agreement through the courts if certain ingredients are present. Such an agreement is called a *contract*.

Contracts are the essential fabric of commercial transactions. Most people enter into contracts on a daily basis, by asking for fuel at a gas station, ordering a sandwich to carry out or purchasing a paper from a newsstand. Real estate listing and purchase agreements, leasehold agreements, options and mortgages are more complex forms of contracts. Each of these agreements is governed by contract law. Every state has its own body of contract law, derived from the common law and from statutes. The general body of contract law applies to all commercial agreements, including real estate agreements.

Not every agreement entered into between parties is enforceable. The law enforces agreements arising in a commercial context, assuming that certain other ingredients discussed in this chapter are present. The law will not, however, enforce a purely social arrangement.

Case Example

Sam promises to buy his friend, Rhena, a steak if she agrees to meet him for dinner after work. Rhena agrees. Sam shows up, but Rhena does not. Since this is merely a social arrangement, Rhena has incurred no liability as a result of her failure to show. *See Balfour v. Balfour, 2 K.B. 571 (1919).*

Social arrangements normally do not evince the type of expectation and reliance that commercial agreements do. Generally, the economic harm that could result from breaking a social promise is comparatively small. The law deems that this type of transaction is best left to the conscience of the individual.

A contract entitles each party to certain rights, as well as imposing certain duties upon them. When a legally binding contract exists, each party is assured that, should the other party or parties not perform in accordance with the terms, the court will offer a remedy to the aggrieved party. The remedy may be in the form of money damages or a court order for *specific performance*—that is, that the party perform according to the terms of the contract. A contract thus provides an incentive for each party to perform.

Preliminary negotiations normally precede an agreement. Obviously, each party desires the best possible bargain. But when negotiations ripen into an agreement, the law ensures its enforceability. The real estate purchase or sale is the largest single transaction into which many people will enter. The parties expend substantial time and expense in preparing for the closing of the real estate transaction. If the parties were not legally committed to each other by a binding contract, either the seller or the purchaser could walk away from the transaction, leaving the other party without remedy. A contract is the best legal protection against such behavior.

This chapter is designed to provide a basic introduction to Chapter 13 "Real Estate Purchase Contracts." In the following pages the general principles of contract law are examined. First, each of the elements essential to the formation of a contract—offer, acceptance, capacity, consideration and lawful purpose—is discussed. Next, the chapter covers contract interpretation, the assignment (transfer) of contracts, breach of contract and remedies available to the parties in the event one party breaks the contractual agreement. Finally, this chapter discusses the circumstances under which parties are released from their contractual obligations.

Elements of Contracts

Certain essential ingredients must be present in any contract, including real estate contracts, in order for it to be enforceable. Basic to the agreement are the *offer* and *acceptance.* There also must be a genuine assent to the terms of the agreement. In addition, the parties must possess the requisite *capacity*, or state of mind, to contract. *Consideration* must be present, and the subject matter of the contract must be *legal*. These and other elements of contracts are covered in the following sections.

Offer

A proposal intended to create a contract upon acceptance by the person to whom it is made.

The offer is made by an *offeror*—one who communicates a proposal. The offer is made to an *offeree*—one to whom an offer is communicated. If Mary offers to sell her house to Martin for $70,000, Mary is the offeror and Martin is the offeree. If Martin offers to buy Mary's house for $70,000, Martin is the offeror and Mary is the offeree.

The offer must state with *specificity* what the offeror is willing to do and what is expected in return. Terms of an offer must be certain enough to be interpreted by a court. The names of the parties and a clear identification of the subject matter of the contract are essential inclusions within the offer. Indefinite or vague language such as "a price between $80,000 and $100,000 is not sufficiently definite to constitute a valid offer. However, omission of the date or place of closing or even the price does not necessarily invalidate the offer. The courts may infer a reasonable place, date and price and, when necessary, look to the usage and customs within the real estate industry to give effect to the intent of the parties.

Case Example

Mr. and Mrs. Beadle desired to purchase three lots in San Rafael, California, and to build homes on those lots for resale. They contacted Vera Rivers, a California real estate broker. Rivers agreed to represent the Beadles regarding the purchase, without compensation, in return for which the Beadles agreed to build a speculative home on each of the three lots, place the lots on the market for sale as soon as the homes were complete and give Vera Rivers the exclusive right to sell said houses and pay her a three percent commission on the selling price.

After the transaction the Beadles refused to build homes on the lots and maintained that the agreement was too vague. The court, in awarding $1,800 commission to Ms. Rivers, held that, within the context of the real estate industry, "the term speculative *home* means a home built with expectation of selling it for a profit . . . and that in relation to the area of said lots and the type of homes in said area, the homes, if constructed by the defendants, would have been homes that would sell for approximately $20,000." Hence, in arriving at an $1,800 damage award, the court computed three percent of $20,000 for commissions for each of the three houses. *Rivers v. Beadle, 183 Cal. App. 2d. 691, 7 Cal. Rptr. 170 (1960).*

An offer must be *communicated* in order to be effective. Communication may be actual or constructive. *Actual* communication occurs when an offeree receives and then reads or hears the offer. *Constructive* communication occurs when a reasonably prudent offeree, under the circumstances, should have read the contents of the offer, regardless of whether an actual reading occurred.

An offeror has the power to control the terms of a contract. The offeror may make a reasonable offer or an unreasonable offer. If it is to ripen into a contract, the offeree must accept the terms of the offer. Before acceptance, certain events may occur that will cause the offer to terminate.

If unaccepted, an offer may terminate in several ways, including revocation, rejection, lapse of a reasonable time, destruction of the subject matter, death of the offeror, insanity of the offeror or illegality of the subject matter of the offer.

Revocation

An offeror may withdraw an offer any time before the offeree's acceptance. The revocation becomes effective upon actual communication to the offeree. If the offeree receives a revocation prior to acceptance, the offer is terminated. Any purported acceptance after receipt of a revocation merely operates as a new offer (counteroffer), which the original offeror may accept or reject. The revocation need not in every instance be communicated by the offeror to the offeree in order to be effective.

Case Example

Behee made a written offer to the Smiths to purchase their real estate for $42,500 plus $250 for a dinner bell and flower pots. The offer was mailed on March 3. On March 4 the Smiths signed the proposed agreement. Before Behee was notified of the acceptance, he withdrew the offer by notifying the Smiths' real estate agent.

The Missouri Court of Appeals held that the withdrawal was an effective revocation of his offer, because "an offeror may withdraw his offer at any time before acceptance and communication of that fact to him. . . . Notice to the agent, within the scope of the agent's authority, is notice to the principal. . . ." *Hendricks v. Behee, 786 S.W. 2d 610 (Mo. Ct. App. 1990).*

Sometimes a revocation is implied. An implied revocation occurs when the offeree learns from a reliable source that the offeror has acted in a manner incompatible with the outstanding offer.

Case Example

Frank makes a valid offer in writing to Dale to sell his residence to Dale. Before Dale accepts, Dale learns from Jackie, Frank's agent, that Perry purchased Frank's property. The communication of such information to Dale results in an implied revocation of Frank's offer. See *Dickinson v. Dodds, 2 Ch. D. 463 (1876).*

Rejection

An offeree may simply reject an offer by communicating to the offeror a refusal to accept the offer. If the offeree makes a counteroffer, an implied rejection of the offer results. An offeree, who communicates a rejection of an offer and then decides to accept the offer, has actually rejected the offer. The purported acceptance merely results in a counteroffer, which the original offeror is free to accept or reject.

Case Example

Mr. and Mrs. Leavey owned the Hereford Ranch in Wyoming. They desired to sell the ranch. Edward Murray, a real estate broker, learned the ranch was for sale and actively looked for buyers. Verne Woods and A. Trautwein were interested in purchasing the property for $2,300,000. After negotiations, the Leaveys made an offer that was communicated by Murray to Woods and

Trautwein. Woods and Trautwein signed the agreement but attached three material amendments to the instrument. The Leaveys refused to accept the agreement with the amendments because "they changed the whole deal." After learning of the Leaveys' refusal to accept the amendments, Trautwein advised Mr. Leavey that the amendments were removed and the original offer acceptable. The Leaveys refused to sell the property to Woods and Trautwein, who sued for breach of contract. The court held that the Woods-Trautwein amendments constituted a rejection of the Leaveys' offer, which terminated the offer. Consequently, the subsequent assent to remove the amendments did not result in a contract. *Trautwein v. Leavey, 472 P.2d 776 (Wyo. 1970).*

Lapse of Reasonable Time

An offeror may specify an expiration date for an offer. A purported acceptance after the specified date is ineffective. If no date is specified, then the offer lapses after a reasonable period of time. What is considered reasonable varies from case to case, depending upon the circumstances. In general, however, an offer to purchase realty will not expire as rapidly as, for example, an offer to purchase shares of stock because the price of stock normally fluctuates more rapidly than that of realty.

Destruction of the Subject Matter

Destruction of the subject matter of the offer, before acceptance, results in a termination of the offer. If a seller offers to sell land and the house on it to a prospective purchaser, the offer will automatically terminate, before acceptance, upon the destruction of the house. This would be true even if the prospective purchaser was unaware of the destruction. Nevertheless, a *contract* does not necessarily terminate because of the destruction of the subject matter. Obviously, one who willfully destroys the subject matter of the contract will not be excused from performance, but will be liable for damages. Normally, the contract specifies who bears the loss in the event the property is destroyed by accident.

Death of the Offeror

Death of the offeror results in a termination of the offer whether the offeree knows of the death or not. If the offeree accepts the offer and then the offeror dies, a contract exists. However, death will normally not excuse performance of one's contractual obligation unless the performance involves personal services. If a seller who was bound under a purchase contract to sell realty dies, the seller's representative, pursuant to probate law, may execute a good deed conveying the property to the buyer. If the buyer dies, the purchase price may be paid out of the proceeds of his or her estate, and the seller may convey the deed directly to the buyer's estate, heirs or next of kin, as the law provides.

Insanity of the Offeror

An offer terminates before acceptance in the event the offeror becomes insane. Otherwise, the offeror would be at a disadvantage because an insane person does not normally possess the faculties necessary to decide to revoke an offer. A contract for the sale of realty, however, is not affected should a party become insane after entering the contract; the guardian or other representative of the insane person is required to perform.

Illegality of the Subject Matter

A change in the law may cause an offer that was legal when made to become illegal. Such a change causes an offer to terminate. Assume, for example, that a domestic corporation offers to purchase five platypuses from an Australian zoo. Thereafter, a law is passed that prohibits the importation of platypuses. The offer would automatically terminate due to illegality. Similarly, a valid contract that later becomes illegal due to a change in law is generally unenforceable.

Acceptance

Assent to the terms of an offer.

Acceptance is the second component of the agreement. The offeree has the power to create a contract merely by communicating an acceptance. The offeree does not have the authority to modify the terms of a proposal. As mentioned earlier, should the offeree change the terms of the offer, the variation creates a *counteroffer*, which actually constitutes a rejection of the original offer. The original offeror may then reject or accept the counteroffer.

At times an offeree appears to add terms to an offer when in fact the new terms were implied within the original offer. In such a case the purported terms will not defeat the acceptance.

Case Example

Allen offers to sell Solid Rock to Baldoro for $70,000. Baldoro responds by saying, "I accept, provided the title is good." Since the law implies in Allen's offer that Allen will tender good title, Baldoro has added no new terms and the acceptance is valid.

The offer and the acceptance constitute the agreement. It may not always be feasible or possible to determine which party made the offer and which party accepted. In many instances, after final negotiations, the entire agreement is reduced to writing. Both parties then sign the agreement. It is only academic in such a case to break the agreement down to the offer and acceptance components. However, the party who signed first could be considered the offeror and the second signer the offeree. In reality this is not always true, since a contract may have resulted prior to the signing of the agreement. In such a case the signing is merely the evidence of the oral agreement.

Manifest Intent

Courts often articulate that no agreement exists without a "meeting of the minds." This subjective test requires an examination of the psyche of each of the parties, which is, of course, impractical and usually impossible. The more acceptable approach is the *objective test,* one that is designed to determine whether the parties manifested an *intent* to be bound. Regardless of the mind of the offeror, if a reasonable offeree believes an offer to have been communicated seriously, then an acceptance of the offer ripens into a contract. This is true even when the offer was made in excitement, or jest, as contended in the following case.

Lucy v. Zehmer
196 Va. 493, 84 S.E. 2d 516 (1954)

Background: Mr. Lucy sought to purchase the Ferguson Farm from its owners, the Zehmers. He made contact with them at a restaurant Mr. Zehmer operated. Lucy said, "I bet you wouldn't take $50,000.00 for [the farm]." Zehmer replied, "Yes, I would too; you wouldn't give fifty." Lucy asked Zehmer to write up the agreement. On the back of a restaurant check Zehmer wrote, "We do hereby agree to sell to W. O. Lucy the Ferguson Farm for $50,000 complete." It was signed by Mr. and Mrs. Zehmer. Both Lucy and Zehmer had been drinking.

The Zehmers attempted to back out of the transaction contending that the agreement was signed in jest. W. O. Lucy and J. C. Lucy, husband and wife, sued A. H. Zehmer and Ida S. Zehmer for specific performance of the contract.

Decision: The trial court found in favor of the defendants, the Zehmers. The court of appeals reversed and remanded the case to the trial court, ordering specific performance of the contract in favor of the plaintiffs, the Lucys.

Justice Buchanan
In his testimony Zehmer claimed that he "was high as a Georgia pine," and that the transaction "was just a bunch of two doggoned drunks bluffing to see who could talk the biggest and say the most.". . . [This] is contradicted by other evidence as to the condition of both parties, and rendered of no weight by the testimony of his wife that when Lucy left the restaurant she suggested that Zehmer drive him home. The record is convincing that Zehmer was not intoxicated to the extent of being unable to comprehend the nature and consequences of the instrument he executed, and hence that instrument is not to be invalidated on that ground. . . .

. . .

The appearance of the contract, the fact that it was under discussion for forty minutes or more before it was signed; Lucy's objection to the first draft because it was written in the singular, and he wanted Mrs. Zehmer to sign it also; the rewriting to meet that objection and the signing by Mrs. Zehmer; the discussion of what was to be included in the sale, the provision for the examination of the title, the completeness of the instrument that was executed, the taking posession of it by Lucy with no request or suggestion by either of the defendants that he give it back, are facts which furnish persuasive evidence that the execution of the contract was a serious business transaction rather than a casual, jesting matter as defendants now contend.

. . .

If it be assumed, contrary to what we think the evidence shows, that Zehmer was jesting about selling his farm to Lucy and that the transaction was intended by him to be a joke, nevertheless the evidence shows that Lucy did not so understand it but considered it to be a serious business transaction and the contract to be binding on the Zehmers as well as on himself. The very next day he arranged with his brother to put up half the money and take a half interest in the land. The day after that he employed an attorney to examine the title. The next night . . . he was back at Zehmer's place and there Zehmer told him for the first time, Lucy said, that he wasn't going to sell and he told Zehmer, "You know you sold that place fair and square."

. . .

In the field of contracts, as generally elsewhere, "We must look to the outward expression of a person as manifesting his intention rather than to his secret and unexpressed intention. `The law imputes to a person an intention corresponding to the reasonable meaning of his words and acts.' "

At no time prior to the execution of the contract had Zehmer indicated to Lucy by word or act that he was not in earnest about selling the farm. They had argued about it and discussed its terms, as Zehmer admitted, for a long time. . . . In any event there had been what appeared to be a good faith offer and a good faith acceptance, followed by the execution and the apparent delivery of a written contract. Both said that Lucy put the writing in his pocket and then offered Zehmer $5 to seal the bargin. Not until then, even under the defendant's evidence, was anything done or said to indicate that the manner was a joke. Both of the Zehmers testified that when Zehmer asked his wife to sign he whispered that it was a joke so Lucy wouldn't hear and that it was not intended that he should hear.

. . .

An agreement or mutual assent is of course essential to a valid contract but the law imputes to a person an intention corresponding to the reasonable meaning of his words and acts. If his words and acts, judged by a reasonable standard, manifest an intention to agree, it is immaterial what may be the real but unexpressed state of his mind.

So a person cannot set up that he was merely jesting when his conduct and words would warrant a reasonable person in believing that he intended a real agreement.

[The case was reversed and remanded back to the trial court for specific performance under the contract.]

Transmittal of Acceptances and Revocations

An acceptance is effective upon actual communication to the offeror or the offeror's agent. The offeror may expressly name an agent, or one may be implied. The law deems that an offeror impliedly invites acceptance from the offeree by the same mode of communication the offeror used to communicate the offer. This is known as the *implied agency rule.* If an offeror communicates an offer by mail, then the mailboxes would be the offeror's implied agents. Under that circumstance the deposit of an acceptance in the mail results in a valid acceptance at the time of deposit. The offeror assumes the risk of nondelivery of the acceptance in such a case, so that even if the offeror never receives the acceptance, it is nonetheless effective at the moment of delivery to the mailbox. Of course, the offeror may eliminate this risk by expressly stating as a term of the offer that acceptance is effective only upon actual receipt by the offeror. Many jurisdictions have expanded the implied agency rule to apply to any reasonable mode of communication.

An offer may be revoked anytime before it is deemed accepted. Revocation is effective upon actual receipt by the offeree. The implied agency rule does not operate in the area of revocation.

Case Example

Jan. 3   A offers by mail to sell Landacre to *B* for $2,000 an acre.
Jan. 4   B mails an acceptance.
Jan. 5   A mails a letter to *B* revoking her previous offer.
Jan. 6   B receives the letter of revocation.
Jan. 7   A receives the telegraphic acceptance.

A contract exists on January 4 since an effective acceptance was delivered to *A's* implied agent prior to actual receipt by *B* of *A's* letter of revocation.

The law of transmittal of acceptances and revocations is based upon fairness and establishes firm rules that a businessperson may rely upon in decision making.

Reality of Assent

There must be reality of assent to an agreement between the parties; the *appearance* of assent is not sufficient. Any nonassenting party may avoid the contract. Causes that may intervene to negate a party's assent include fraud, innocent misrepresentation, mistake, undue influence and duress.

Fraud is an intentional misrepresentation of a material fact that induces justifiable reliance to the detriment of a party. Fraud is examined in detail in Chapter 14. The defrauded party not only may seek cancellation (rescission) of the contract but also may have an action in tort to recover damages against the defrauder. *Innocent misrepresentation* is an unintentional misrepresentation of a material fact that induces justifiable reliance to the detriment of a party. Because the misrepresenter does not do so intentionally most courts permit the party relying on the material fact to rescind the contract but deny recovery for damages.

Mistake is an unintentional error. When both parties enter into a contract under a mistaken belief as to a material matter related to the contract, either party may rescind the contract. If, for example, a seller and buyer of Redacre enter into a real estate sales contract under the misimpression that the property is an historical landmark when in fact it is not, rescission is available to either party. If only one party is mistaken concerning a material fact, rescission is not generally an available remedy.

Undue influence is the exertion of dominion over another person that destroys that person's ability to exercise independent judgment. Undue influence cases giving rise to a right of rescission involve situations where one party has developed a total trust or dependency upon another. An elderly aunt may be so mentally overpowered by a nephew that she conveys her land to him at his insistence. Or a sick patient may develop such a trust in a nurse that he loses his power to resist the nurse's plea to convey his property to her. *Duress* is coercion that overcomes a party's will. Duress results when one is coerced to enter into an agreement by force or threat of force. The threat must be of such a nature as to place a reasonable person in fear, such as the threat of bodily harm.

Capacity

The legal ability to enter into a contract.

For a legally binding agreement to exist, both parties must have *capacity* to enter into the contract. Some persons have no capacity to contract; their contracts are designated as *void*. Other persons possess limited capacity to enter into contracts; their contracts are classified as *voidable*. Examples of both categories are discussed below.

Insane Persons

An insane person, under the law, is one who lacks the requisite reason to comprehend the nature and consequences of transactions. Any contract entered into by a person who has been determined to be insane by a court—that is, one who has been *adjudicated insane*—is automatically void. Since such information is a matter of public record, all are deemed to be on notice that the person cannot enter into a valid contract and may not be held liable because the court has determined him or her to be insane. A person who is *actually insane,* but has not been adjudicated insane by a court, is deemed to possess limited capacity to enter into contracts. His or her contracts are classified as voidable. A *voidable contract* is one that may be voided or validated at the option of the party who possesses limited capacity. During the course of the insanity, up to a reasonable time after being restored to sanity, a person who is actually insane may elect to *disavow* the contract and treat it as void. In such a case the insane person must tender back the property received and is then entitled to a return of the property he or she previously conveyed. Or, after being restored to sanity, that person may *ratify* the contract and treat it as valid.

Minors

The law seeks to protect the immature as well as the insane. For that reason the law discourages adults from contracting with them. In some states those under the age of 21 are considered minors, but in most, minors are those under 18. Generally, a contract entered into with a minor is voidable by the minor. That means that the minor may choose to disaffirm the contract anytime during minority and up to a reasonable time after attaining majority. If the contract is *executory* (unperformed), then that disaffirmance releases the minor from the obligation to perform the contract. If the contract is *executed* (performed), then the disaffirming minor need only give back to the adult that which remains of what he or she received from the adult. Then the minor would be entitled to a full return of the money or property originally conveyed to the adult. In most states, however, when the transaction involves a completed sale of the minor's realty, the minor is obliged to await the age of majority before disaffirming the transaction. In these states the minor must disaffirm within a reasonable period of time after attaining majority.

Case Example

Clifford Spencer and his sister owned land. Clifford was a minor and did not attain majority until April 5, 1919. On November 30, 1918, MacCloon purchased the property from Clifford and his sister. MacCloon later conveyed the property to Lyman Falls Power Company and Hutchins. Thereafter Lyman Falls conveyed its interest in the property to the Public Service Company of New Hampshire. On September 8, 1936, Clifford sued to disaffirm the contract and sought to have the property reconveyed to him. The court held that, although Clifford could disaffirm upon attaining majority, "a delay of 17 years and 5 months after the plaintiff attained his majority until the bringing of this suit . . . was unreasonable." Consequently, Clifford's attempt to disaffirm was unsuccessful. *Spencer v. Lyman Falls Power Co., 109 Vt. 294, 196 A. 276 (1938).*

Minors are obligated to pay for the necessities of life for which they contract and receive. Although minors may still disaffirm contracts for necessities, they will nonetheless be required to pay the reasonable value of the property or services received. Normally, real estate that provides housing is not deemed to be a necessity for a minor since the minor can live with his or her parents.

Drugged Persons

Contracts entered into by a person who is intoxicated or under the influence of drugs are voidable if the drug renders such a person unable to appreciate the nature and consequences of his or her acts. Most courts are less sympathetic to this classification of persons than to minors and will permit disaffirmance of a completed contract only if the person contracting with the drugged person can be restored to the original position without suffering loss.

Consideration

> *A promise, act or forbearance bargained for and given in exchange for a promise, act or forbearance.*

Consideration is a necessary element of a contract. Generally, if a defendant's promise is not supported by consideration, then it is unenforceable. In order for a promise to be supported by consideration, it must result in a benefit to the promisor (the one who makes a promise) or in a detriment to the promisee (the one to whom a promise is made). The benefit or detriment may be in the form of a return promise, an act or a forbearance.

A return promise to do something that one was not otherwise obligated to do is sufficient consideration. Most real estate contracts take the form of a promise for a promise. This type of contract is designated as *bilateral*.

Case Example

Burnside promises to pay Yerkes $25,000 for Needleacre, and Yerkes promises to sell Needleacre to Burnside for $25,000. All the details of the contract are reduced to writing. Since there is a promise for a promise, a bilateral contract exists. Each promise is supported by consideration supplied by the other's promise.

An *act* may constitute good consideration for a promise. If the promisor is bargaining for the act, the performance of the act usually constitutes a legal benefit to the promisor as well as a legal detriment to the promisee. Such a contract is termed *unilateral* because there is only one promise.

Case Example

Burnside promises to convey Needleacre to Johannes if Johannes cares for Burnside's mother for her life. Johannes cares for Burnside's mother for her life. Since there is a promise for an act, the contract is unilateral. The act is sufficient consideration to support Burnside's promise since it was bargained for and results in a detriment to Johannes.

Consideration also may take the form of a *forbearance*. Such a contract is also unilateral, since there is only one promise.

Case Example

Burnside promises to convey Needleacre to Lasser if Lasser refrains from smoking for ten years. Lasser refrains. Since there is a promise for a forbearance, the contract is unilateral. The forbearance is sufficient consideration to support the promise since it was bargained for and results in a detriment to Lasser. *See Hamer v. Sidway, 124 N.Y. 538, 27 N.E. 256 (1891).*

In a unilateral contract, the act or forbearance constitutes both the consideration and the acceptance. If the promisor is looking for a promise and receives an act, then the act does not constitute sufficient consideration since it was not "bargained for and given in exchange." Similarly, in the event the promisor is looking for an act, a return promise is insufficient consideration.

Promissory Estoppel

Promissory estoppel is a doctrine that prevents a party from denying that a promise is supported by consideration. The doctrine of promissory estoppel is applicable when no consideration exists but it is necessary to enforce a promise in order to prevent an injustice. The following elements must also be present: (1) a promise calculated to induce reliance, (2) actual justified reliance by the promisee and (3) injury.

Case Example

Montrasor is in arrears on her mortgage payments and requests additional time from the mortgagee to permit her to pay the arrearage. The mortgagee extends the time by 90 days. There is no consideration to support the promise to extend.

Thirty days thereafter Montrasor makes substantial improvements to the property in reliance on the mortgagee's promise. The mortgagee files an action in foreclosure prior to the expiration of the 90 days. Since the ingredients of promissory estoppel are present, the mortgagee's promise not to foreclose for 90 days is enforceable.

Lawful Purpose

A contract must have a legal purpose. For example, a number of state landlord-tenant statutes forbid the inclusion of certain clauses within the lease contract. Such prohibitions include entering the tenant's premises without notice and removal of the tenant without court process. Any contract that runs afoul of a statute or public policy is illegal and hence void.

A party to an illegal bargain will not normally be assisted by the courts. Simply, the courts will leave the parties in the same position as they are found. There are, however, some exceptions to this rule.

Sometimes the parties to the contract are not deemed to be *in pari delicto*—that is, not at equal fault. A landlord who lets property to a tenant who uses the property to traffic drugs may be innocent of the illegal purpose for which the property was intended. In that instance the courts aid the innocent party in the collection of the rents. An elderly man who is tricked out of his real estate or other property will be protected in many jurisdictions regardless of the fact that he was a willing participant in an unscrupulous scheme.

When a contract involves an illegal provision, the courts may excise that portion and enforce the remainder of the contract. However, if the illegal provision is so interconnected with the whole as to render it nonseverable, the entire contract will be rendered void.

Contract Interpretation

All the essential terms of an agreement must be definite and certain in order for an enforceable contract to exist. Courts will not normally construct terms or fill in gaps where the instrument is deficient. It is the duty of the courts to interpret language within a contract and to give effect to the intent of the parties. If the language is ambiguous and the court cannot arrive at the intent of the parties, then it will not enforce the instrument. In a real estate purchase contract the parties and property must be identified. Essential terms left open for future negotiation may invalidate the contract.

Courts use various rules for interpreting contractual provisions, each designed to ascertain the intent of the parties. Words are assigned their plain meaning and are read in context of the entire contract. Technical language often pervades real estate contracts. Terms such as *escrow, balloon payment, wraparound mortgage, land contract* and others must be interpreted. Courts are prone to look to the real estate industry to assign meaning to these technical terms.

Sometimes there is a conflict between provisions in the contract. To resolve the conflict, specific provisions will control over general provisions. In addition, handwritten provisions will take precedence over typewritten provisions, and typewritten provisions will prevail over printed-form provisions. Once again, these rules are intended to effectuate the intent of the parties.

Assignment

The present transfer of a property right from one person (the assignor) to another (the assignee).

The purchaser, as a party to an executory (unperformed) contract, is the equitable owner of the property; the purchaser has a right to receive title to the property from the seller in accordance with the terms of the contract. This right may be transferred to a third party. A party who transfers this right is called an *assignor*. The third party who receives the right to title is called an *assignee*. An assignee succeeds to the rights that were previously invested in the assignor. The assignee of a right to receive a deed may enforce that right against the seller.

Case Example

Walter and Thelma Terry entered into a contract to sell real property to William and Shirley Born, husband and wife. The Borns agreed to pay the purchase price in monthly installments over a specified period of years. A provision within the contract stated that the contract was "not assignable nor [could] the buyer convey the property without the seller's written consent." The Borns subsequently contracted to assign the contract to Rollins without the Terrys' consent. The Terrys commenced an action against the Borns seeking forfeiture of the contract. The appellate court held that the provisions prohibiting assignment were unreasonable restraints on trade unless necessary to protect the sellers' security. The case was returned to the trial court to determine whether the Terrys' security would be impaired by the Borns' conveyance to Rollins. *Terry v. Born, 24 Wash. App. 652, 604 P.2d 504 (1979).*

An assignee is bound to perform the obligations the assignor promised the seller, including payment of the purchase price. Failure to perform on the part of the assignee constitutes a breach of the agreement and results in liability for damages. An assignment does not relieve the assignor from obligations under the contract. In the event that the assignee does not perform, the seller may hold the original purchaser (assignor) responsible to perform in accordance with the agreement.

The seller, as a party to an executory contract, has an equitable interest in the purchase price; the seller has a right to receive the purchase price in accordance with the terms of the contract. The seller may assign the right to receive this purchase price. The same rules that apply to the assignment of a purchaser's rights apply to the assignment of a seller's rights.

Breach of Contract

The unexcused failure to perform an obligation under a contract.

The failure of a purchaser to tender the purchase price for the property at the appointed time is one example of a breach of contract. Another example is the seller's failure to tender title to the purchaser at the appointed time. Any nonperformance of a term within the contract may give rise to a breach of that contract. The law provides remedies in the event of breach. This serves as an incentive to both parties to live up to the terms of the agreement.

Anticipatory Breach

A breach of contract that occurs as a result of repudiating a contract before the due date for performance.

It is not always necessary to await the day designated for performance to determine that a party is in breach. Sometimes an anticipatory breach occurs. In order to constitute an anticipatory breach, the nonperforming party must communicate to the other party an intention not to perform. Or, an intention not to perform may be determined from a party's behavior.

Case Example

R. Brower, a contractor, agreed to paint John Dooley's home for $2,500. Pursuant to the contract, the work was to begin August 1. Thereafter Brower informed Dooley that he was going out of business and asked him to find someone else to do the work. On July 15 Dooley learned from a reliable source that Brower went out of business, sold all of his equipment and had dishonored all of his existing contracts. Under such a circumstance, Dooley may treat Brower as in anticipatory breach of contract and immediately sue for damages.

Substantial Performance

The amount of compliance under the terms of a contract that discharges a party from further obligation where a party has failed to perform totally under the contract.

The law recognizes that humans, frail as they are, cannot always perform their contracts according to the exact specifications. Consequently, if the closing date is set for April 5 and the purchaser desires it to be moved to April 7, the two-day delay does not amount to a material breach, barring a provision in the contract to the contrary or exceptional circumstances. In the area of building contracts, a contractor who builds a home and incurs minor deviations from the specifications may nonetheless have substantially complied with the contractual provisions. In such a case, the contractor will be entitled to the contract price less the cost to remedy the deviations to the property. If, for example, a contractor complies with all the specifications under a $60,000 building contract but fails to paint three out of 14 window panels, the contractor is entitled to $60,000 less the cost of having the window panels painted.

Case Example

Thomas Haverty Company entered into a contract with Jones whereby Haverty agreed to build and install plumbing, heating and ventilation equipment in Jones's building for $27,332. The total cost of the building was $186,000. After completion Jones refused to pay a balance of $10,123 to Haverty Company. Jones maintained that Haverty's performance was defective. The company sued Jones for the balance. The trial court held that Haverty's performance deviated from the contract specifications in 12 respects, that nine could be resolved at a cost of $99, that the remaining three defects could not be remedied without a greater expenditure than was justified and that the damage to the building as a result of the three deviations amounted to $2,180. The court found that the deviations were made as a result of mistakes and misinterpretations. Finding that the contract had been substantially performed, the court awarded $7,844 ($10,123 minus $99 and $2,180) to Haverty Company. The appellate court affirmed the decision. *Thomas Haverty Co. v. Jones, 185 Cal. 285, 197 P. 105 (1921).*

There is no substantial performance if the utility of the property or its purpose is significantly affected by the contractor's deviation. If the specifications in the contract called for gas heating and the contractor installed oil heating instead, the deviation would amount to a breach, and the contractor would not be entitled to any compensation. Some courts do, however, permit the contractor to recover the reasonable value of the services rendered and goods supplied where a substantial deviation is not willful.

Remedies for Breach of Contract

Before a party is entitled to a remedy, he or she must show a readiness, willingness and ability to perform the obligations under the contract. A seller must tender (offer) the deed, and a buyer must tender the purchase price, unless it is clear from the circumstances that the tender would be rejected. The common remedies enjoyed by each party in the event the other breaches the contract are specific performance, rescission, damages and foreclosure.

Specific Performance
A court decree mandating a party to perform according to the contract.

The remedy specific performance is ordinarily applicable to contracts involving real estate. The buyer is entitled to the deed after completion of the requirements under the contract. Should the seller refuse performance, a court may award specific performance requiring the seller to execute a deed in favor of the buyer. Refusal by the seller to comply with the decree may result in contempt of court and punishment. The court may also execute a deed in the buyer's favor, or, in the event of the seller's refusal to perform in accordance with the decree, the very court decree may be deemed to pass title to the buyer. In many jurisdictions specific performance is also available to a seller against a defaulting buyer. A decree of specific performance in such a case compels the purchaser to pay the purchase price and accept title to the property.

A court will grant specific performance only if the party seeking it has "clean hands." If one of the parties has taken advantage of the other's unsound condition, for example, or has been guilty of fraud, the court will deny this equitable relief.

Rescission

Cancellation of a contract that results in the parties being restored to the position they were in before the contract was made.

A buyer, upon a seller's default, may elect to *rescind* the contract. Under such a remedy, the seller must return to the buyer all payments received. The remedy is especially desirable for the buyer when the real estate has depreciated in value below the contract price. In the event the buyer is in breach of the contract, the seller may elect the remedy of rescission, thus restoring the parties to their original position.

Either party may seek rescission on grounds of fraud, innocent misrepresentation, mistake, duress or undue influence. In addition, a contract may be rescinded by mutual consent of the parties.

Damages

Money recoverable by one suffering a loss or injury due to breach of the contract.

A buyer may, for example, incur actual damages when the seller breaches the obligation to tender the deed. The damages may be in the nature of the loss of the bargain. Translated into monetary terms, loss of the bargain is the difference between the market value of the property at the date set for closing and the contract price. That difference represents the value of damages to which the purchaser is entitled, assuming that the market value of the property at the time of breach is greater than the contract price. In addition, damages may include the deposit made by the purchaser and actual costs incurred incidental to the contract. Incidental expenses include attorney fees for handling the purchase transaction as well as the expense related to a title search.

Case Example

Joe Deal, seller, refused to tender his deed to John Tiehl, purchaser, on March 13, the date set for closing. Tiehl had previously paid Deal $5,000 to be applied to the purchase price of $85,000. Tiehl additionally expended $500 for a title search of the property. The market value of the property was $90,000 on March 13. In an action by Tiehl against Deal for damages, Tiehl will be entitled to $5,500, computed as follows: $90,000 (market value) − $85,000 (contract price) = $5,000 + $500 (title search). Tiehl will also be entitled to a return of the $5,000 deposit.

When the buyer breaches the contract, the seller is entitled to retain any deposit the buyer made and to keep the real property. In the event the market value of the property falls in an amount greater than the deposit forfeited, the seller may also sue for damages. Damages in such a case are computed by deducting the market price from the purchase price minus any earnest money payment forfeited to the seller.

A court judgment for damages becomes a general lien on all real property a party owns until the judgment is satisfied. As a judgment creditor, a party may foreclose on the real property to satisfy the judgment. Other means of satisfying a judgment can include the attachment and sale of the debtor's personal property and garnishment of his or her wages.

Foreclosure

A legal process where a nonbreaching party can obtain possession of the real property and sell it in order to recover an amount due.

The buyer of real property has *equitable* title to the property—the right to obtain ownership upon payment of the purchase price. This right gives the buyer an equitable lien on the property securing the amount of money paid. Consequently, the buyer may foreclose on the property to recover the purchase payments in the event the seller breaches the contract.

The seller possesses a lien for the unpaid purchase price on property that has passed to the buyer. The seller may foreclose on the property to satisfy this lien in the event the buyer fails to make timely payment.

Discharge

The release of contractual obligations.

Parties who complete their obligations under a contract are discharged from any further performance. Normally, total performance is required before discharge occurs. Discharge may occur, however, after substantial performance (discussed earlier in this chapter). In addition, under certain circumstances parties may be discharged from their obligation to perform by operation of the parties or by operation of law.

Operation of the Parties

Parties to a contract may mutually agree to cancel a contract. Such an agreement results in a discharge. Or, the parties may agree to substitute another person's obligation to perform. This agreement to substitute indebtedness is called a *novation.*

Case Example

Cary is indebted to Ponce in the amount of $5,000. Ponce is indebted to Darin in the amount of $5,000. Cary, Ponce and Darin may agree that Ponce will release Cary of the debt, Darin will release Ponce and Cary will pay $5,000 directly to Darin.

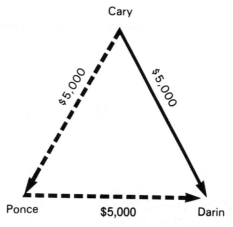

Finally, parties may agree to substitute a kind of performance that is different from that originally required under the contract. This agreement is called an *accord,* and the performance of the agreement is referred to as a *satisfaction.* An accord and satisfaction discharges a party from his or her original obligation.

Case Example

Castor Andora was indebted to Andrea Hammer, a former employer, in the amount of $2,000. Hammer made a demand for the amount. Andora was out of work and did not have the money. He offered, however, to paint Hammer's house in lieu of the $2,000. Hammer agreed, and Andora, pursuant to the agreement, painted Hammer's house. This constitutes an accord and satisfaction. Andora is discharged of any further obligation to pay Hammer $2,000.

Operation of Law

Circumstances may occur that make it impossible or impractical for a party to fulfill his or her obligation under a contract. Under these circumstances the law will excuse the party from performance. Assume, for example, that Dante and Raymond enter into an agreement whereby Dante is to purchase Hellacre. Before closing, the house on Hellacre burns down. In most jurisdictions, in absence of a provision in the contract covering this event, the parties would be excused from performance because the subject has been destroyed.

Death of a party is not ordinarily an excuse for nonperformance of a contract. In the event a party dies, the representative of the estate will be required to complete performance. However, if the contract involves personal services, the rule is different. Assume, for example, that a carpenter agrees to build a tree house. Death of the carpenter will result in a discharge of obligations under the contract because of the personal nature of carpentry services. The same rule holds regarding insanity of a party. A party to a contract who is unable to complete a personal service contract due to insanity is excused from performance.

When a contract that was legal when entered into becomes illegal, the parties are discharged from performance. Suppose, for example, that a contractor enters into a contract with a shipper to transport specified building materials from a foreign country. Should the U.S. government issue an embargo forbidding the transport of goods from that foreign country, the parties will be discharged from their contractual obligations.

Finally, the law has evolved to recognize that certain contracts cannot be performed because it is commercially impracticable to do so. Some courts have discharged parties from their obligations in these types of cases. The impetus for this rule emanates from Section 2-615 of the Uniform Commercial Code, which reads in part:

> Delay in delivery or non-delivery in whole or in part by a seller . . . is not a breach of his duty under a contract for sale if performance as agreed has been made impracticable by the occurrence of a contingency the non-occurrence of which was a basic assumption on which the contract was made. . . .

Courts have not limited this doctrine to sale of goods cases but have extended it to other cases as well.

Case Example

Northern Corporation entered into a contract with Chugach Electric Association. Under the contract, Northern was to install protective riprap on a dam located on Cooper Lake, Alaska, owned by Chugach. The work required Northern to transport rock and install it on the face of the dam.

The contract was silent as to the method for transporting the rock to the dam site. Apparently the parties contemplated that it would be transported across the frozen lake during the coming winter.

Attempts to haul the rock across the ice were frustrated by the unsafe condition of the ice. On one occasion two trucks broke through the ice, resulting in the drivers' deaths.

Northern ceased performance and sought a ruling discharging it from any further obligations under the contract. Chugach countersued, seeking damages for breach of contract. In upholding the trial court's ruling in favor of Northern, the Supreme Court of Alaska said:

> Under [the doctrine of commercial impracticality], a party is discharged from his contractual obligations, even if it is technically possible to perform them, if the cost of performance would be so disproportionate to that reasonably contemplated by the parties as to make the contract totally impractical in a commercial sense. . . .
>
> [The concept of commercial impracticality]—which finds expression both in case law and in other authorities—is predicated upon the assumption that in legal contemplation something is impractical when it can only be done at an excessive and unreasonable cost. . . .

> There is ample evidence to support [the findings that] "the ice haul method of transporting riprap was within the contemplation of the parties and was part of the basis of the agreement which ultimately resulted in the contract amendment," and that that method was not commercially feasible within the financial parameters of the contract. . . .

Northern Corporation v. Chugach Electric Association, 518 P.2d 76 (Alaska 1974).

Summary

A *contract* is a promise or an agreement that is enforceable by law. Laws in each state govern contracts in general and real estate contracts in particular. Contracts entitle the parties to certain rights but also entail obligations. Basic to any contract are an *offer*, an *acceptance* and *consideration*. Additionally, both parties must possess the *capacity* to contract, and the subject matter of the contract must be *legal*.

In a real estate transaction an offer is a proposal to sell or purchase real property. The offer may be terminated at any time before acceptance, and in such a case no contract exists. An acceptance involves an assent to the terms of an offer. Even after acceptance, however, the contract may be voided because of fraud, misrepresentation or other conditions such as duress. Consideration involves a benefit to the promisor or a detriment to the promisee, bargained for and given up in exchange for a promise or an act. Capacity requires that both parties be sane and of legal age to contract. Finally, persons may not contract for an unlawful purpose.

Failure of either party to perform as promised constitutes a *breach of contract*. Remedies under the law vary from state to state and include *specific performance, rescission, damages* and *foreclosure*. Parties may be released from their contractual obligations to perform by agreement or by operation of law.

Review and Discussion Questions

1. (a) Which agreements will a court enforce? (b) Which agreements will a court not enforce? (c) Why?

2. Name five elements of a contract and define each.

3. Explain the rationale behind the objective test of contract formation.

4. Give an example of when the doctrine of promissory estoppel will be applied.

5. When does a breach of contract occur? What is the consequence of a breach of contract?

6. (a) Explain the remedies available to a buyer when the seller breaches the contract for the sale of real property. (b) Explain the remedies available to the seller in the event of the buyer's breach.

7. Name ways in which parties to a contract may be discharged from their obligation to perform by operation of law.

Case Problems

1. Burns and Pugmire entered into a contract for the sale and purchase of real estate. The contract stated that the purchase price was $79,500, to be paid in installments of $675.00 per month, including taxes and insurance for the contract "period remaining, or until buyer elects to refinance." The contract was silent as to the closing date, which party was to pay closing costs and when transfer of title and delivery of a deed would take place. Is this agreement sufficiently definite and certain? Explain. *Burns v. Pugmire, 194 Ga. App. 898, 392 S.E. 2d 62 (1990).*

2. The Bakers made a written offer to purchase Nelson's home. Nelson was unhappy with the down payment provision and formulated an addendum which was added to the Bakers' original offer and returned to them. The Bakers signed it. Nelson then purported to accept the Bakers' offer by sending a mail-gram to the Bakers which included financing terms that varied from those found in the original offer and also introduced additional terms relating to the fixtures and appliances. After receipt, the Bakers withdrew from the transaction in writing. Nelson maintains that there is a contract. Do you agree? Explain. *Nelson v. Baker, 776 S.W. 2d 52 (Mo. Ct. App. 1990).*

3. On November 27, 1937, Morrison, seeking to purchase a tract of land from Thoelke, executed and mailed Thoelke a contract for the sale of the property. On the same day, Thoelke signed the contract and placed it in the mails, addressed to Morrison's agent. After mailing the contract, but before Morrison's agent received it, Thoelke called the agent and repudiated the contract for the sale of the land. (a) Was Thoelke's call an effective rejection of Morrison's offer? See *Morrison v. Thoelke, 155 So.2d 889 (Fla. Dist. Ct. App. 1963).* (b) What would be the result if Thoelke died after mailing his acceptance and his executor (representative of the estate) refused to honor the agreement? (c) What if Morrison died after mailing the offer and Thoelke accepted the offer before learning of Morrison's death?

4. Hazel Miller listed her real estate for sale with a local real estate agent. Michael Normile and Wawie Kurniawan signed a written offer to purchase the property. The offer stated that "this offer must be accepted on or before 5:00 P.M. August 5, 1980." Miller signed and returned the offer with several changes, including an increase in the deposit from $100 to $500 and an

increase in the down payment from $875 to $1,000. Normile and Kurniawan neither accepted nor rejected the new terms. At 12:30 A.M. on August 5 Segal signed an offer to purchase the property, which was accepted the same day at 2:00 P.M. The agent then informed Normile that Miller had revoked her counteroffer. Before 5:00 P.M. on the same day, Normile and Kurniawan accepted the counteroffer. Who owns the property and why? *Normile v. Miller, 326 S.E.2d 11 (N.C. 1985).*

5. Miss Roland, owner of a parcel of land, leased it to Mr. Kent for a term of five years. A second agreement between the parties granted Kent an option to extend the lease for another four years if Kent undertook to make about $10,000 of improvements to the property. Kent engaged and paid an architect to study the property and suggest possible improvements. Roland died after the architect completed his sketches but before the construction of any of the contemplated improvements. Roland's executor sought to set aside the option contract on the grounds that it is a mere offer unsupported by consideration and is therefore revoked by the death of Roland. (a) Does the payment of the architect's fee qualify as good consideration? Discuss. See *Bard v. Kent, 19 Cal. 2d 449, 122 P.2d 8 (1942).* (b) Assuming that there is no consideration, what doctrine may aid Kent? Explain.

6. Plaintiff entered into an agreement with defendant whereby plaintiff agreed to construct a country house for defendant, who in return agreed to pay plaintiff for his work. A proviso of the agreement stated that Reading pipe was to be used in the plumbing system of the house. Plaintiff completed the house, yet through inattention installed Cohoes pipe, a different brand of pipe though one of substantially similar quality to Reading pipe. Defendant now refuses to pay plaintiff the balance of the contract price unless he replaces all the Cohoes pipe in the house with Reading. Defendant's demand would involve the demolition and reconstruction of a major portion of the house. (a) What doctrine, if any, can plaintiff rely on to force defendant to pay for the work "as is"? (b) Would the result be different if Reading pipe was found to be of significantly higher quality than the Cohoes pipe? Explain. See *Jacob & Youngs, Inc. v. Kent, 230 N.Y. 239, 129 N.E.889 (1921).*

7. Carmen Ruggerio contracted to sell 10.24 acres of industrial land for $38,912 to Tanners Realty. The sale was conditioned on Tanners' ability to obtain financing. The agreement provided that Ruggerio would convey good marketable title to said premises, except for utility easements. In addition to utility easements, a search of the title revealed a railroad easement on the property. (a) What remedies are available to Tanners Realty? (b) What would it have to prove in order to prevail? *Tanners Realty Corporation v. Ruggerio, 490 N.Y.S.2d 73 (App. Div. 1985).*

8. Taylor and Caldwell entered into an agreement whereby Taylor was to receive the use of Caldwell's concert hall for four days. Before Taylor had an

opportunity to use the hall, it was completely destroyed by fire, rendering its use impossible. (a) Can Taylor recover against Caldwell for damages sustained as a result of being deprived of the use of the concert hall? Explain. See *Taylor v. Caldwell, 122 Eng. Rep. 309 (1863).* (b) Would the result be different if Caldwell owned two halls and only one was destroyed? Explain.

13

Real Estate
Purchase Contracts

The previous chapter on basic contract law provided the background necessary for a specific look at real estate purchase contracts. The purchase contract is the instrument that legally "obligates" the buyer and seller to perform. Normally, the total understanding of the parties is contained within that agreement. Consequently, the conduct of the parties will be largely dictated by its terms. For that reason careful attention to the form and substance of the real estate contract is important. This chapter details the prerequisites for a valid real estate purchase contract and the provisions customarily contained in that contract. It also examines the real estate option contract.

Real Estate Purchase Contract

An agreement whereby a seller promises to sell an interest in realty by conveying a deed to the designated estate for which a buyer promises to pay a specified purchase price.

Generally, contracts need not be in writing in order to be enforceable. Real estate purchase contracts, however, fall within a unique class of contracts that necessitate a writing. They are governed by the Statute of Frauds.

Statute of Frauds

A statute that necessitates that certain contracts, in order to be enforceable, must be supported by a written memorandum and signed by the party against whom enforcement is sought.

The British Parliament enacted the Statute of Frauds in 1677. This statute modified the common law that enforced oral contracts for the sale of real estate. The Statute of Frauds was intended to protect against fraud and perjury. Prior to the Statute of Frauds, it was not uncommon for a person to pay witnesses to fabricate testimony to support a nonexistent oral contract for the sale of realty. Section 4 of the statute required a contract for the sale of an interest in land to be in writing, or supported by a written memorandum, and signed by the party to be charged. Nearly every state has modeled its version of a statute of frauds after the English statute. The Ohio statute, for example, reads in part:

> No lease, estate, or interest, either of freehold or term of years, in lands . . . shall be assigned or granted except by deed, or note in writing, signed by the party assigning or granting it, or his agent thereto lawfully authorized. . . .

Case Example
Wayne Gibbens and Mark Hardin entered into a joint effort to purchase three parcels of real estate. A purchase offer of $2.4 million for the property was accepted. Gibbens claimed that he had an oral agreement with Hardin that Hardin would make a 3.075 acre boundary adjustment to the property in favor of Gibbens. Gibbens would receive the two houses located on Parcel #3 and an easement of access to one of the houses. Hardin denied this. The Supreme Court of Virginia found "[t]he alleged oral boundary agreement . . . unenforceable because it fails to comply with Virginia's statute of frauds." *Gibbens v. Hardin, 389 S.E. 2d 478 (Va. 1990).*

Memorandum
   A writing that contains essential terms in satisfaction of the Statute of Frauds.

Normally, the entire agreement of the parties—the real estate purchase contract—is reduced to writing. This writing will, of course, satisfy the memorandum requirement of the Statute of Frauds. The entire agreement of the parties need not be in writing, however, to satisfy the Statute of Frauds. The statute only requires a written memorandum, which may be the "skeleton" of the contract. A memorandum must ordinarily contain:

- the names of the parties to the contract,

- a description of the property,

- the purchase price,

- other essential terms and conditions of the sale, and

- the signature of the party against whom enforcement is sought (a few states also require the signature of the party seeking to enforce the transaction).

The memorandum need not be contained within one instrument. It may be gleaned from a series of related writings, such as letters and telegrams. The memorandum may be prepared anytime before suit on the contract is commenced. Loss or destruction of the memorandum does not render the contract unenforceable. In such a case, the existence of the memorandum may be proved by witnesses or other documents. In most jurisdictions the Statute of Frauds is deemed waived unless it is pleaded as a defense in court.

Party Against Whom Enforcement Is Sought

In many jurisdictions a contract for the sale of real estate may be enforced only against the party who signed the memorandum. Consequently, it is very possible that a purchaser of a parcel of real estate may not be legally able to enforce the contract against the seller, while the seller may be legally able to enforce the contract against the purchaser. The reverse is also true.

Case Example

Bill Barley, seller, contracts with John Harley, buyer, for the sale of Lodgeacre, with complete details of the sale contained in a writing. Barley signs the writing, but Harley neglects to sign. The contract is enforceable against Barley but not against Harley, because Harley failed to sign the writing.

The best way to ensure compliance with the Statute of Frauds is to require that all parties sign the real estate purchase contract. Although the entire agreement of the parties need not be reduced to writing, as a practical matter it is best to do so. This prevents uncertainty and provides a controlling document to resolve disputes.

Part Performance

There are certain exceptions to compliance with the Statute of Frauds. The most notable exception is the doctrine of *part performance*. There are various views as to what constitutes an act of part performance sufficient to remove a contract from the Statute of Frauds so that a writing will not be required. Some courts take the position that part performance is satisfied if a purchaser takes possession pursuant to an oral contract. Other courts require both possession and payment of the purchase price to prevent the seller from raising the defense of the statute. Still others require that possession be accompanied by a substantial improvement to the property. Finally, other jurisdictions limit the scope of the doctrine of part performance by requiring payment of the purchase price, the purchaser's possession and a change of position in reliance on the contract that would result in irreparable harm unless the contract were enforced.

Case Example

Brown entered into an oral contract to purchase a farm from Burnside. Brown took possession of the farm, made several improvements, tore down an old farmhouse, paid taxes and made payments on the purchase price. Burnside thereafter refused to deed the farm to Brown. Brown sought specific performance of the contract. The court held for Brown on the theory that the Statute of Frauds does not apply when there has been partial or complete performance, as under these circumstances. *Brown v. Burnside, 94 Idaho 363, 487 P.2d 957 (1972).*

Parol Evidence

Oral or other evidence extraneous to the written instrument.

Parol evidence is not admissible for the purpose of varying or contradicting the terms of a contract. The rule, however, does not exclude parol evidence consistent with the writings of the parties. Nor does the rule exclude parol evidence for the purpose of clarifying ambiguous terms in the contract or proving that the writing was induced by fraud, illegality, duress, undue influence or mistake. Neither does the parol evidence rule exclude evidence of a subsequent agreement that alters the previous writings.

Case Example

Jim Hutchins and Jerry Bolen enter into a real estate contract for the sale of Hutchins's property. Afterward they enter into a contract canceling the prior real estate contract. The introduction into evidence of the new contract containing the cancellation does not violate the parol evidence rule, since it was entered into after the purchase contract.

Brokers' Authority

Many localities use preprinted purchase contract forms that have been approved by the local attorney bar association and the board of realtors. The provisions within these form contracts are designed to reflect the practices within the locality. Normally, the broker assists the parties in filling in the blanks in such a contract, including the names of the parties, a description of the property, the price and such. A standard real estate purchase contract is shown in Figure 13.1. Sometimes it is necessary to delete certain inapplicable provisions from the form. Often lengthy additions are necessitated by the particular nature of the transaction. To what extent a broker may prepare a purchase contract without engaging in the offense of unauthorized practice of law differs from state to state. Some states prevent a broker from drafting a purchase contract because that act constitutes the practice of law. Other states permit such brokerage activity on the theory that it is normally incident to the practice of a broker's profession. Although most states permit brokers to fill in the blanks, there is often a thin line between filling in the blanks and drafting.

Cultum v. Heritage House Realtors, Inc.
694 P. 2d 630 (Wash. 1985)

Background: Yvonne Ramey, a real estate agent for Heritage House Realtors, Inc. (Heritage), prepared a real estate purchase contract (earnest money agreement), setting forth Cultum's offer to purchase Smith's home. The agreement was prepared on standard forms drafted by attorneys. Ramey filled in the blanks and also prepared an addendum which stated: "This offer is contingent on a Satisfactory Structural Inspection, to be completed by Aug. 20. . . . " The Smiths accepted the offer. Based upon the inspection report Cultum found the condition of the house unsatisfactory. He demanded return of a $3,000 deposit. Heritage refunded the money and Cultum sued Heritage for loss of use of the money during the period Heritage held it, and sought a permanent injunction restraining Heritage from engaging in the practice of law.

Decision: The trial court found in favor of Cultum, holding that Heritage engaged in the unauthorized practice of law and it granted damages and permanently enjoined Heritage from "completing, filling in the blanks, or otherwise preparing any clause with respect to any real estate purchase or sale agreement. . . . " The Supreme Court of Washington affirmed the damage award but found that Heritage was not engaged in unauthorized practice of law.

Justice Pearson
At issue in this appeal is whether the completion by a real estate salesperson of a form earnest money agreement containing a contingency clause constitutes the unauthorized practice of law. . . .

. . .

[A]lthough the completion of form earnest money agreements might be commonly understood as the practice of law, we believe it is in the public interest to permit licensed real estate brokers and salespersons to complete such lawyer prepared standard form agreements; provided, that in doing so they comply with the standard of care demanded of an attorney.

For a long time suppression of the practice of law by nonlawyers has been proclaimed to be in the public interest,

a necessary protection against incompetence, divided loyalties, and other evils. It is now clear, however, as several other courts have concluded, that there are other important interests involved. These interests include:

(1)   The ready availability of legal services.

(2)   Using the full range of services that other professions and businesses can provide.

(3)   Limiting costs.

(4)   Public convenience.

(5)   Allowing licensed brokers and salespersons to participate in an activity in which they have special training and expertise.

(6)   The interest of brokers and salespersons in drafting form earnest money agreements which are incidental and necessary to the main business of brokers and salespersons.

We no longer believe that the supposed beliefs to the public from the lawyers' monopoly on performing legal services justifies limiting the public's freedom of choice. The public has the right to use the full range of services that brokers and salespersons can provide. The fact that brokers will complete these forms at no extra charge, whereas attorneys would charge an additional fee, weighs heavily toward allowing this choice.

Another important consideration is the fact that the drafting of form earnest money agreements is incidental to the main business of real estate brokers and salespersons. These individuals are specially trained to provide buyers and sellers with competent and efficient assistance in purchasing or selling a home. Because the selection and filling in of standard simple forms by brokers and salespersons is an

Figure 13.1: Real Estate Purchase Contract

Real Estate Purchase Contract
Adopted by The Columbus Board of Realtors
and by The Columbus Bar Association

It is recommended that all parties
be represented by legal counsel

REALTOR®

_____, 19____

The undersigned Buyer agrees to buy and the undersigned Seller agrees to sell, through you as Broker, upon the terms hereinafter set forth, the following real estate located in the State of Ohio, County of _____

On the following terms:

1.

2. **Possession:**

3. **Evidence of Title:** Seller shall furnish and pay for an owner's title insurance commitment and policy [ALTA Form B (1970 REV. 10-17-70 & REV. 10-17-84)] in the amount of the purchase price, with copy of subdivision or condominium plat. The title evidence shall be certified to within 30 days prior to closing with endorsement as of 8:00 A.M. on the business day prior to the date of closing, all in accordance with the standards of the Columbus Bar Association, and shall show in Seller marketable title in fee simple free and clear of all liens and encumbrances except: (a) those created by or assumed by Buyer; (b) those specifically set forth in this contract; (c) zoning ordinances; (d) legal highways; and (e) covenants, restrictions, conditions and easements of record which do not unreasonably interfere with present lawful use. Buyer shall pay any additional costs incurred in connection with mortgagee insurance issued for the protection of Buyer's lender. If Buyer desires a survey, Buyer shall pay the cost thereof.

If title to all or part of the real estate is unmarketable, as determined by Ohio law with reference to the Ohio State Bar Association's Standards of Title Examination, or is subject to liens, encumbrances, easements, conditions, restrictions or encroachments other than those excepted in this contract, Seller shall within thirty (30) days after written notice thereof, remedy or remove any such defect, lien, encumbrance, easement, condition, restriction or encroachment or obtain title insurance without exception therefor. At closing Seller shall sign an affidavit with respect to off-record title matters in accordance with the community custom.

4. **Deed:** Seller shall convey to Buyer marketable title in fee simple by transferable and recordable general warranty deed, with release of dower, if any, or fiduciary deed, as appropriate, free and clear of all liens and encumbrances not excepted by this contract, and excepting the following:

5. **Taxes and Assessments:** At closing, Seller shall pay or credit on purchase price all delinquent taxes, including penalty and interest, all assessments which are a lien on the date of contract and all agricultural use tax recoupments for years prior to the year of closing. At closing, Seller shall also pay or credit on the purchase price all other unpaid real estate taxes which are a lien for years prior to closing and a portion of such taxes and agricultural use tax recoupments for year of closing prorated through date of closing and based on 365 day year and, if undetermined, on most recent available tax rate and valuation, giving effect to applicable exemptions, recently voted millage, change in valuation, etc., whether or not certified.

Seller warrants that no improvements or services (site or area) have been installed or furnished, or notification received from public authority or owners' association of future improvements of which any part of the costs may be assessed against the real estate, except the following: _____ (None, if nothing inserted.)

6. **Rentals, Interest, Condominium Charges, Insurance, Utilities and Security Deposits:** Adjustments shall be made through date of closing for: (a) rentals; (b) interest on any mortgage assumed by Buyer; (c) condominium or other association periodic charges; and (d) transferable insurance policies, if Buyer so elects. Seller shall pay, through date of possession, all accrued utility charges and any other charges that are or may become a lien. Security deposits shall be transferred to Buyer.

7. **Damage or Destruction of Property:** Risk of loss to the real estate and appurtenances shall be borne by Seller until closing provided that if any property covered by this contract shall be substantially damaged or destroyed before this transaction is closed, Buyer may (a) proceed with the transaction and be entitled to all insurance money, if any, payable to Seller under all policies covering the property, or (b) rescind the contract, and thereby release all parties from liability hereunder, by giving written notice to Seller and Broker within ten (10) days after Buyer has written notice of such damage or destruction. Failure by Buyer to so notify Seller and Broker shall constitute an election to proceed with the transaction.

Figure 13.1: Real Estate Purchase Contract (continued)

8. **Fixtures and Equipment:** The consideration shall include any fixtures, including but not limited to: built-in appliances; heating, central air conditioning, and humidifying equipment and their control apparatus; stationary tubs; pumps; water softening equipment (unless leased); roof antennae; attached wall-to-wall carpeting and attached floor coverings; curtain rods and window coverings excluding draperies and curtains; attached mirrors; light, bathroom and lavatory fixtures; storm and screen doors and windows, awnings, blinds, and window air conditioners, whether now in or on the premises or in storage; garage door openers and controls; attached fireplace equipment; security systems and controls (unless leased); smoke alarms; satellite TV reception system and components; all exterior plants and trees; and the following:

The following shall be excluded: _____

9. **Inspections:** Before closing, Seller shall furnish and pay for: (a) a report on FHA/VA approved form, by an Ohio Certified Pest (Termite) Control Applicator stating whether based upon an inspection of the areas visible or accessible, the inspector discovered any evidence of infestation or damage by termites. Infestation and resulting damage by termites or other wood destroying insects shall be treated and repaired at Seller's expense, provided that if the cost of repair exceeds 1% of the purchase price, Seller may terminate this contract unless Buyer agrees to pay the cost of such repair in excess of 1% of the purchase price; (b) a written guaranty from a gas line repair company or a licensed plumber, guaranteeing the non-existence of gas leaks at the time of transfer of gas service to Buyer, including all repairs and alterations to gas lines, valves, meters not owned by the local natural gas distribution company, vents, connected gas appliances sold with the premises, and restoration of premises (excluding grass, shrubs & trees) necessary to accomplish the transfer; and (c) a written health department report showing in essence that the water from the primary water supply, other than that provided by a municipality or water supply utility or company, is bacterially safe and that any individual sewage disposal system is in operating condition. Seller warrants that at time of closing, water is available in sufficient quantities for ordinary household purposes.

10. **Property Inspection:** (Not applicable if number of days not inserted.) Buyer, at Buyer's expense, shall have _____ days after the acceptance hereof to have the property and all improvements, fixtures and equipment inspected. Seller shall cooperate in making the property reasonably available for such inspection(s). If Buyer is not, in good faith, satisfied with the condition of the property as disclosed by such inspection(s), Buyer may terminate this contract by delivering written notice of such termination to Seller, along with a written copy of such inspection report(s), within the time period specified above, which notice and report(s), shall specify the unsatisfactory conditions. Failure of Buyer to so deliver written notice and copy of the inspection report(s) within such time period shall constitute a waiver of Buyer's right to terminate pursuant to this provision.

11. **Home Maintenance Plan:** Seller, at Seller's expense, shall provide _____ (Not applicable if plan name not inserted.)

12. **Deposit:** Buyer has deposited with Broker the sum receipted for below, which shall be returned to Buyer, upon Buyer's request, if no contract shall have been entered into. Upon acceptance of this contract by both parties, Broker shall deposit such amount in its trust account to be disbursed, subject to collection by Broker's depository, as follows: (a) if Seller fails or refuses to perform, or any contingency is not satisfied or waived, the deposit shall be returned; (b) deposit shall be applied on purchase price or returned to Buyer when transaction is closed; (c) if Buyer fails or refuses to perform, this deposit shall be paid to Seller, which payment, or the acceptance thereof, shall not in any way prejudice the rights of Seller or Broker(s) in any action for damages or specific performance.

In the event of a dispute over the disposition of the deposit, Broker shall retain the deposit until (i) Buyer and Seller have settled the dispute; (ii) disposition has been ordered by a final court order; or (iii) Broker deposits said amount with a court pursuant to applicable court procedures.

13. **Miscellaneous:** Buyer has examined all property involved and, in making this offer, is relying solely upon such examination with reference to the condition, character and size of land and improvements and fixtures, if any. This contract constitutes the entire agreement and there are no representations, oral or written, which have not been incorporated herein. Time is of the essence of all provisions of this contract. All provisions of this contract shall survive the closing. In compliance with fair housing laws, no party shall in any manner discriminate against any purchaser or purchasers because of race, creed, sex or national origin.

14. **Duration of Offer and Closing:** This offer shall be open for acceptance to midnight _____, 19____, unless the parties agree in writing to an extension. This contract shall be performed and this transaction closed within _____ days after acceptance hereof, unless the parties agree in writing to an extension.

Buyer acknowledges receipt of a copy of this contract.

The undersigned agrees to and accepts the foregoing offer.

Seller shall pay a brokerage fee of _____ of the purchase price in connection with this transaction.

Seller acknowledges receipt of a copy of this contract.

_____ (Buyer)

Address _____ Phone _____

Deed to _____

Name of Buyer's Attorney _____

_____ (Seller)

Address _____ Phone _____

Signed this _____ day of _____, 19____

Name of Seller's Attorney _____

©CBR and CBA 1989

EQUAL HOUSING OPPORTUNITY

Broker acknowledges receipt of the sum of $ _____ by cash/check which shall be held, deposited and disbursed pursuant to paragraph 12, above.

By _____

incidental service, it normally must be rendered before such individuals can receive their commissions. Clearly the advantages, if any, to be derived by enjoining brokers and salespersons from completing earnest money agreements are outweighed by the fact that such conveyances are part of the everyday business of the realtor and necessary to the effective completion of such business.

The interest of protecting the public must also be balanced against the inconveniences caused by enjoining licensed brokers and salespersons from completing form earnest money agreements. Although lawyers are also competent to handle these transactions, lawyers may not always be available at the odd hours that these transactions tend to take place. . . .

In a few instances earnest money agreements may be complicated and one or both parties may realize the need for a lawyer to prepare the contract rather than use a standardized form. In fact, if a broker or salesperson believes there may be complicated legal issues involved, he or she should persuade the parties to seek legal advice. More often, however, these transactions are simple enough so that standardized forms will suffice and the parties will wish to avoid further delay or expense by using them.

It should be emphasized that the holding in this case is limited in scope. Our decision provides that a real estate broker or salesperson is permitted to complete simple printed standardized real estate forms, . . . approved by a lawyer. . . . These forms shall not be used for other than simple real estate transactions actually handled by such broker . . . or salesperson and then without charge for the simple service of completing the forms.

The trial court awarded Cultum damages . . . representing the interest lost during the time that Heritage retained her earnest money. If a real estate broker fails to exercise reasonable care and skill, the real estate broker is liable to the client for damages resulting from such failure. Based on this rule and our conclusion that Ramey failed to exercise the reasonable care and skill of a practicing attorney, we affirm the trial court's award of damages. . . .

A broker should exercise caution when rendering advice to a party or giving detailed explanation of the terms of the contract; these activities may be deemed the unauthorized practice of law.

Provisions of the Real Estate Purchase Contract

Some of the provisions included within the real estate purchase agreement are there to satisfy the Statute of Frauds. Others are present to clarify the details of the agreement. Common real estate contract provisions include the date, the names of parties and other elements presented on the following pages.

Date

A contract comes into being when the purchase offer is accepted. The contract should be dated. The date may appear at the beginning or the end of the contract or in both places. Failure to include the date does not render the contract unenforceable. However, the question of the date of the signing may arise in several situations. The contract may contain provisions that require the happening of events by reference to the date the contract came into existence. For example, a clause within a contract might read, "Buyer shall obtain financing within 45 days of the signing of this contract." In some instances the statute of limitations may begin to run on the date the contract was signed. The statute of limitations is the time period within which one must sue or be barred from recovery. Also, certain legal ramifications attach on the date the contract comes into being. For example, the buyer becomes the equitable owner of the property. As equitable owner, the buyer may enforce the contract by specific performance in the event the seller fails to perform.

Parties

In order to satisfy the Statute of Frauds, the names of the parties must be included within the writing. Care should be taken to ensure that the names of the buyer and seller are accurate. An attorney who later draws up the deed may derive the names to insert in the deed from the contract. Accurate spelling prevents problems at a later date when a title search may otherwise uncover discrepancies.

The marital status of the seller should be included; if the seller is married, then the spouse should be named as well. A seller's spouse possesses certain legal rights, including dower, that must be relinquished by signature in order for the buyer to be assured of a good title. For this reason, the spouse must sign the contract.

There may be more than one seller or buyer. All parties should be named. If there are multiple buyers, it is essential to include a statement of the type and fraction of ownership interest each will receive.

Sometimes a party to the sale (seller or buyer) designates an agent to negotiate and/or sign the contract. This practice should be reserved for extreme cases where it is not feasible for the actual party to act. When a party designates an agent, such appointment should be evidenced by a written power of attorney. A copy of the power of attorney should be attached to the contract and, in some states, recorded. Even here problems may occur because no one can be absolutely sure that the power of attorney has not been revoked by subsequent act or event.

Case Example

Howard Moore, owner of a tract of land that is for sale, is planning a visit to Australia. To prevent his absence from the country from impeding the sale, he executes a power of attorney, giving his real estate broker power to negotiate, contract and sign the deed of conveyance. Hugh Fine, a farmer, enters into a contract for the sale of Moore's land. The broker appears at the closing and executes a deed in behalf of Moore. Fine takes possession and learns later that before the date of closing Moore was killed in Australia in a hunting accident. Since death revokes a power of attorney, Fine's title is seriously impaired.

Property Description

Property descriptions contained in the contract must sufficiently identify the property. Courts are rather liberal in upholding descriptions of real property contained within the contract. Consequently, a contract for the purchase of "all my lands" has been held sufficient to identify the subject of the sale and to comply with the Statute of Frauds. Even where the quantity of the lands to be sold is not accurate, it is enough if the terms within the description are sufficient to identify the subject property accurately.

Case Example

Vander Graff contracted to sell "all my lands lying on the Miami River, in the State of Ohio, 1,533 1/3 acres . . . in my name." Should the actual quantity be greater than the acreage mentioned, the sale would include the excess of the quantity stated in the contract.

Parol evidence is admissible to clarify specific lands. However, parol evidence will not be admitted to reform a description to include lands not specifically referred to by the description.

Case Example

"December 13, 1950, received of P. H. Pilgreen ten dollars ($10.00) as binder on 20 acres of land and timber; price to be $200.00 for land and timber. Deed to be made later." Parol evidence will not be admitted in this particular case because the description as written does not allude to a definite parcel of property.

It is best to include in the real estate purchase contract a complete and accurate legal description of the property so that there is no room for any alternative interpretations. In many jurisdictions, however, it is customary to include only the street address for sales of residential property.

Price

In order to satisfy the Statute of Frauds, the amount of the purchase price must be clearly ascertainable. See the following example.

The total purchase price shall be $60,000 payable as follows:

- $500 upon the signing of the contract,

- $5,500 in cash or the equivalent to be paid at closing upon delivery of the deed, and

- The balance to be paid by assuming the existing mortgage on said property in the amount of $54,000 held by Citizens Saving & Loan Company.

In the event the purchase price is not specified, then it must be subject to ascertainment by computation. For example:

The acreage of the property is to be determined by survey, and the price is to be computed by multiplying the number of acres and any fraction thereof by $5,000.

The usual and safest form of payment is certified check or bank draft. These forms of payment prevent the buyer from stopping payment after tender, which could occur if a personal check were issued.

Contingency Clause

A provision within a contract that makes performance under the contract conditional upon the occurrence of a stated event.

A contingency clause may be inserted within a contract to benefit a purchaser or a seller. A common contingency within a purchase contract conditions performance upon the buyer's obtaining financing. The details of the acceptable financing are normally specified, for example, "The within obligations of the buyer are conditional upon buyer obtaining a 25-year loan from a financial institution in the amount of 80 percent of the purchase price at 10 percent interest; otherwise this contract to become null and void." This contingency is for the benefit of the purchaser. In the event that the purchaser can not obtain terms as favorable, he or she could elect to waive the contingency and proceed with the purchase. Other contingencies that benefit a buyer may be contained within a purchase contract—for example, making the contract conditional upon the sale of buyer's house or upon the change of a zoning regulation.

Contingencies may also be included within a contract for the seller's benefit. The seller may desire to make performance under the contract conditional upon confirmation of a job transfer by a present employer. Or perhaps other circumstances make it desirable for the seller to include other contingencies within the contract.

Case Example

Pete Perry owns a home in Tulsa, Oklahoma, and he is interested in selling that home and moving to Seattle, Washington. Perry enters into a valid purchase contract with Sam Sells whereby Perry is to buy Sells's residence for a stated sum. After signing the contract, Perry is not able to sell his residence in Tulsa and consequently is unable to accumulate the funds necessary to close on the Seattle property. Nonetheless, Perry is obligated to perform. A contingency clause as follows would have adequately protected Perry against such a misfortune: "The purchase of Sells's residence is contingent upon Perry selling his residence in Tulsa at market price within at least 30 days prior to the date set for closing."

Contingency clauses are often cunningly drafted in an attempt to permit a party to be relieved of obligations at the party's whim. Courts will often construe such clauses in such a way as to require good faith and honesty on the part of the party the contingency benefits.

Case Example

Brenda Rodgers enters into a purchase contract to buy Hedgeacre. A contingency clause within the contract reads, "Said contract contingent upon buyer obtaining a ten percent loan for 80 percent of the sales price." Brenda had a change of mind about Hedgeacre and refused to attempt to obtain financing. Brenda's refusal would be considered a lack of good faith and would constitute a breach of contract.

Possession

The date the seller is required to surrender possession to the buyer is usually negotiable. In many contracts the date the purchaser is entitled to possession coincides with the closing. Ordinarily, in absence of a possession provision, the buyer is entitled to possession upon payment in full. This usually occurs at the closing. The parties can always agree to a different date of possession. It is not uncommon for the parties to agree for the buyer to take possession upon the signing of the contract, especially when the property is vacant. Sometimes a purchaser is impliedly entitled to immediate possession; for example, when the contract requires the purchaser to maintain the premises from the date the contract is signed.

There are dangers to the seller associated with the purchaser's possession before payment. The purchaser in possession may commit waste to the property and then fail to make payment to the seller pursuant to the contract. Or the purchaser might remain on the property and refuse to close the transaction. If this occurs, the seller may have to engage in a lengthy suit before possession is legally returned to the seller or some other favorable remedy is achieved. From the seller's viewpoint, it would be much better for the buyer who takes possession before payment of the purchase price to be characterized as a tenant until payment. In this event the seller would be in a position to evict the purchaser/tenant, an action that would normally result in a quick return of possession to the seller.

Sometimes in residential sales the contract allows the seller to maintain possession rent free, for a period of time after closing, such as 30 or 60 days. In such a case a danger exists that the seller will holdover or commit waste to the premises. For protection against this possibility, the purchaser may require a security deposit, returnable to the seller if the premises are vacated in the condition they were in at the time of contract, reasonable wear and tear excepted.

Evidence of Title

A document such as an abstract or title insurance verifying ownership of property.

The seller is not under any affirmative obligation to prove that title to the realty is *marketable*—that is, free of liens or other encumbrances. If a general warranty deed is used, the seller personally warrants that the property is free and clear of encumbrances other than those specifically excluded and that the seller will warrant and defend the title against the lawful claims and demands of all persons. A purchaser may maintain an action for damages against the seller under the general warranty in the event of a breach of the warranty against encumbrances. However, the warranty is only as good as the seller's net worth. When making an investment in realty, the purchaser should take extreme precaution. Toward that end, the purchaser may hire an attorney to effect a title search and render an opinion as to the marketability of the title. Or the purchaser may purchase title insurance from a reputable company. (Title search and title insurance are discussed in Chapter 17.) Still better, the purchaser may insist on a clause in the contract that the seller provide evidence of title in the form of an abstract of title or an owner's title insurance policy. The prevailing custom within the real estate industry in many localities is for the seller to provide such proof of title. The standardized real estate purchase contract within the locality normally reflects the common and approved practice within that area.

Form of Deed

The type of deed to be conveyed by the seller may be controlled by the terms of the contract. It is most desirable for the contract to specify the type of deed, whether it be a general warranty deed, bargain and sale deed, quitclaim deed or some other type. In the absence of agreement, the law within the jurisdiction governs the type of deed the seller is required to convey. Under this circumstance some jurisdictions obligate the seller to convey a general warranty deed, whereas other jurisdictions require only a quitclaim deed.

Proration

Certain expenses or income associated with the realty at the time of closing may be due but unpaid. Other expenses or income may have been prepaid. Because these expenses and income are related to the use of the premises, in part by the seller and in part by the buyer, apportionment is necessary. A clause within the contract may read:

> Taxes, insurance, utilities, assessments, and rental income shall be apportioned *pro rata* as the interests of the parties may appear at closing.

Taxes on real property, for example, may be payable annually, semiannually or otherwise. The fiscal year may not correspond to the calendar year; the tax assessment period may be, for example, July 1 to June 30. To complicate matters, some local jurisdictions run six months to a year behind in their billing so that the owner is always paying taxes due in the past. Fairness demands that an adjustment be made so that the seller is charged with accrued but unpaid taxes.

Case Example

Olivieri pays $260 a year for real estate property taxes on her home. The fiscal period for tax purposes is July 1 to June 30. Olivieri is billed $130 twice a year, in December and June. Each installment of $130 covers the previous six months. On March 31, 1993, Olivieri appears at a closing on her house. The contract provides for apportionment of taxes as of the date of closing. Olivieri is current in her payments of taxes and presents a paid receipt for the December installment. Olivieri will owe $65 for accrued and unpaid taxes for the period January 1 to March 31, which amount will be credited to the buyer against the selling price.

Hazard insurance policies may be transferred from the seller to the buyer. However, the transfer may necessitate an apportionment. Insurance is often payable in advance, and the unaccrued portion that was paid by the seller for a period during which the purchaser has the use of the premises must be reflected in the apportionment.

Sometimes it is possible to notify the insurance carrier to refund the un-accrued portion to the seller and bill the purchaser for the applicable amount. Another method is for the seller to cancel the insurance policy and receive a rebate for the unused premium and for the buyer to purchase another policy.

Other expenses, such as fuel, electricity, water and other assessments, are often prorated. Usage of these utilities is not always the subject of exact computation. The parties can notify the respective companies to read the utility meters as of the date of closing and divide the bill accordingly.

Income from rentals is often apportioned as of the date of closing. Normally, rentals are paid in advance. If the closing occurs in the midst of a rental payment period, then an adjustment is required, because the seller in such an event receives from the tenant a rental payment covering a portion of the time after ownership has passed to the buyer.

Case Example

Jerry Rogers, seller, and Ronald Dodge, buyer, are to close July 15 on commercial property owned by Rogers. A tenant is under a leasehold agreement for such property and pays $350 per month on the first of each month. A clause within the real estate purchase contract requires apportionment of rentals as of the date of closing. On July 15 the buyer would be entitled to $175, which represents the unused portion of the rental.

Prorations are also covered in Chapter 15.

Property Inspection

The condition of the property may be the subject of dispute at closing or thereafter. To reduce the possibility of such a dispute, the contract may contain an inspection clause. The normal inspection clause requires the seller to have the property inspected and to produce a certificate by the inspector stating the results of the inspection. Types of inspection include termite, gas line, electrical, structural and plumbing.

In the event that the inspection shows a defect, the contract governs as to the responsibilities of the parties. The following is an example of a contractual provision:

> Seller shall make all repairs to the property not to exceed 5% of the purchase price. In the event Seller fails to make said repairs Buyer may make the repairs and deduct the amount from the purchase price at closing. In the event the cost of repairs exceeds 5% of the purchase price and Seller agrees to make the repairs, the Buyer may (1) close the sale with the completed repairs or (2) terminate the contract.

Under such a provision, assume that the purchase price of a home is $200,000.00. A termite inspection reveals termite infestation and structural damage. The cost of repair is $8,000.00. The Seller must make the necessary repairs. If, however, the cost of repairs is over $10,000.00 (over 5%) the Seller does not have to make the repairs. In such a case the contract is rescinded. In the event that the Seller agrees to make the repairs, the Buyer may accept the repairs or refuse the repairs and terminate the contract.

Home Maintenance Plan

Many contracts contain protection for the buyer through home maintenance plans. Various private companies, for a fee, will contract to repair major systems and appliances for a period of time, normally one year. The cost may range from $250–500, depending upon the location and terms of the plan. In the event that a home maintenance provision is not included within the purchase contract, the option is usually open for the Buyer to pay for and obtain coverage.

Earnest Money

A real estate purchase contract normally calls for the purchaser to deposit earnest money. Contrary to popular belief, this deposit is not necessary to validate the contract. Sufficient consideration exists in the form of mutual promises contained within the agreement.

Earnest money may be a nominal sum, such as $100, or it may be as substantial as ten percent of the purchase price or more. Normally, the real estate broker holds the deposit in an escrow account pending closing. At closing the earnest money may be returned to the purchaser or credited against the amount due to the seller.

Signing

A contract for the sale of real estate should be signed (executed) by both parties. A writing not executed by all parties is arguably not the agreement of any party who has failed to sign.

An agent acting in behalf of a party to the contract may bind a principal by signing the contract. Authority of the agent in some states may be oral; nevertheless, even in those states written authority is preferable. If an agent lacks proper authority, then only the agent is bound. An unauthorized act of an agent may be subsequently ratified (approved) by a principal.

Only a few states require that a contract for the sale of realty also contain a *seal*. A vestigial remnant of the seal can be seen in some form contracts that have a mark, *L. S.* (for *locus siligis*), the Latin initials meaning "place of the seal."

Attestation and Acknowledgment

In most jurisdictions a contract for the sale of realty need not be witnessed (attested). The parties who sign the writing need not acknowledge their signatures as genuine before a notary public. However, some jurisdictions do not permit recording of a contract that is not witnessed and so acknowledged. A contract, however, does not have to be recorded in order to be considered binding between the parties. (Some jurisdictions require that the land installment contract, discussed in Chapter 20, be recorded.) Recording a contract would provide protection for the buyer; anyone considering purchasing the property under contract would have notice of the buyer's ownership interest in that property. The seller may, however, for good reason, object to recording because of potential problems it may cause. In the event the buyer defaults on the contract it may be costly and burdensome to remove the encumbrance that the recorded contract presents.

Closing

The contract normally states the date and place of closing. The closing is discussed in detail in Chapter 15. At closing the buyer makes payment to the seller and the seller passes title by signing and conveying the deed in accordance with the terms of the contract. In the event that the time and place of closing are not specified within the contract, the law presumes that the parties intended that the closing take place within a reasonable time at a reasonable location.

Normally, time is not of the essence in real estate closings. Hence, even if a date is specified, failure to close on that date is not considered critical as long as the noncomplying party has acted in good faith and is able to close within a reasonable time thereafter. The parties, of course, may agree within the contract that time is of the essence, and under such a clause even a day's delay on the part of a party would be deemed a breach of contract.

Under certain circumstances, time is of the essence even in absence of express language in the contract to that effect. Time is of the essence in an option contract. An option terminates after the expiration of the time provided in the option contract for exercise of the option. Also time is of the essence when parties are dealing in highly speculative land transactions that are subject to rapid fluctuations in value. In addition, when one party is made aware of particular circumstances that make the timing of the closing date critical (such as the necessity for the buyer to vacate an apartment the day of closing), time is deemed as an essential element to the contract.

When one party fails to appear at the closing, the other party must make a tender in order to declare the nonappearing party in default. A *tender* is an offer of money or property as required by the contract.

A buyer who appears at the closing unattended by the seller must be ready, willing and able to perform. The buyer must tender the purchase price by depositing it in escrow or through a show of the money to witnesses in attendance. Conversely, a seller makes tender by showing a readiness, willingness and an ability to deliver marketable title to the buyer.

Unconscionable Contract

The Uniform Commercial Code (UCC), which has been enacted into law at least in part by all states, applies to the sale of goods but not to the sale of real property. Nevertheless, trends in the law of real property may be derived from an examination of certain provisions within the UCC; courts often reason by analogy from this code in reaching results in non-code-governed cases. Section 2—302(1) of the UCC recognizes that some contracts or provisions within contracts may be unconscionable:

> If the court as a matter of law finds the contract or any clause of the contract to have been unconscionable at the time it was made the court may refuse to enforce the contract, or it may enforce the remainder of the contract without the unconscionable clause, or it may so limit the application of any unconscionable clause as to avoid any unconscionable result.

In a seller's market the seller can dictate provisions on a take-it-or-leave-it basis. A buyer may be compelled to sign a contract including the provision "Buyer represents that he has examined the entirety of the property and asserts that he has not relied upon any representation made by the seller." The effect of such a clause may be to prevent the buyer from raising the defense of fraud or misrepresentation should their existence be revealed later. Some courts may relieve a buyer of this helpless position by striking the clause as unconscionable, thus treating it in a way similar to the way the UCC does when dealing with transactions involving the sale of goods.

Option Contracts

An agreement between an owner of property (optionor) and another (optionee) whereby the optionee has a right to purchase property within a specified time for a designated price.

Under an option agreement the optionor agrees not to revoke an offer to sell for a period of time. Unlike a buyer, the optionee is not under an obligation to purchase the property but may elect to do so within the time specified in the option agreement. The option confers upon the optionee the right to buy, whereas a buyer under a purchase contract or land installment contract is under an obligation to buy.

Unless there is consideration to support the optionor's promise to keep the offer open, the optionor may revoke at any time prior to acceptance. Consideration sufficient to support an optionor's promise to keep an offer open may be in the form of a payment of a sum of money. The law of consideration is discussed more fully in Chapter 12.

Case Example

On July 1 Jack Kelvin made an offer to Harry Hilton to sell specified property for $25,000. Kelvin agreed to keep the offer open for 30 days. On July 15 Sally Hammond offered Kelvin $30,000 for the property. On July 21 Kelvin accepted Hammond's offer. On July 23 Kelvin revoked his original offer to Hilton. On July 25 Hilton accepted Kelvin's original offer. Since there was no consideration to support Kelvin's offer to Hilton, Kelvin's revocation on July 23 was effective. See *Echols v. Bloom, 485 S.W.2d 798 (Tex. Civ. App. 1972)*.

Other clauses contained within the option agreement pertaining to the sale of the property are those normally found within a purchase contract. The precise manner of exercising the option should be detailed, including the time and place of delivery of the notice to exercise the option. The following is an example of a notice specification:

Notice of exercise of this within option to purchase Cornacre shall be delivered in writing to the optionor at (his) (her) place of business at [address] on or before midnight [date].

When the optionee elects to exercise the option, the optionee becomes a buyer and both parties are bound by the terms of the sale included within the option agreement. The terms should be specific; otherwise, the agreement may be unenforceable because it is indefinite. The purchase price should be designated with provision as to whether the price paid for the option is to be applied to reduce the purchase price. The price of the option may have been as nominal as $1 or may be very substantial in the case of highly speculative property. Options are desirable from the optionee's viewpoint under several circumstances.

Case Example

A land developer may desire ten parcels of land. The developer wants all or none. Instead of purchasing the parcels one by one, the developer may choose to attempt to purchase options on all the parcels from the various owners. If successful, the developer, upon exercise of each, acquires all the desired parcels. If the developer cannot secure options on all the parcels, then only the price paid for the options is lost.

Case Example

A charitable organization desires to build a physical structure to house its operations. It locates the land but does not have the cash or the financing to purchase the land. By purchasing an option to buy the land, it may be in a better position to solicit sufficient funds from contributors to permit the exercise of the option. If the organization's efforts fail to raise the funds, then only the option price is lost.

Case Example

A parcel of land is located in an area that may be developed in the future and hence causes the value of the land to increase substantially. An investor may desire a long-term option to buy the land. If the area is developed and the value of the land rises, the investor may make a substantial profit by exercising or assigning the option. On the other hand, in the event the area is not developed and the value of the land is less than the price stated in the option, the investor will not exercise the option and has lost only the price paid for the option.

An option is assignable by the optionee unless assignment is prohibited expressly within the agreement. The optionee's assignee has the same rights under the option as the optionee. Upon exercise of the option by the prescribed manner, the assignee is entitled to the property subject to the terms of the option agreement.

The optionor has a right to sell the property that is under option in absence of a prohibition against sale within the option agreement. In such a case, if the sale occurs, the optionor's buyer takes subject to the option, if on notice of the option. Notice need not be actual. If the option has been recorded, then any buyer would be deemed on constructive notice.

Summary

The *real estate purchase contract* is the instrument that legally obligates the buyer and seller to perform terms contained within it. Real estate purchase contracts are governed in all states by the *Statute of Frauds*. Therefore, to be enforceable the contract must be supported by a writing.

In practice, brokers normally use legal contract forms approved by local professionals. In most cases brokers or salespeople are permitted by law to assist the client by filling in the blanks of a form contract. They are not permitted to draft legal forms.

The real estate purchase contract governs the conduct of the parties. It customarily includes various provisions such as the purchase price, the type of *evidence of title* and deed the seller is required to tender, the various charges to be apportioned and the date the closing is to take place.

Finally, some real estate contracts are deemed unconscionable because their terms are grossly unfair. Reasoning by analogy to the Uniform Commercial Code, courts are apt to refuse to enforce the contract or modify it to prevent an unconscionable result.

An *option contract* is a kind of contract that enables a buyer to purchase property at some future time for an agreed-upon price. Options should be drawn so that they are very specific not only with regard to price and terms but also as to the time and place of delivery of notice to exercise the option.

Review and Discussion Questions

1. What are the elements necessary to satisfy the Statute of Frauds?

2. (a) Why does the Statute of Frauds apply to sales of interests in real estate? (b) Give an example of a case involving a real estate transfer that is excepted from the Statute of Frauds.

3. What is the purpose of the parol evidence rule?

4. What limitation may a broker confront when preparing real estate purchase contracts?

5. Describe five major provisions contained within the real estate purchase contract.

6. (a) What is a contingency clause? (b) What purpose does it serve? (c) Whom does it benefit?

7. When does the closing occur? Explain.

8. Explain how the Uniform Commercial Code influences real estate transactions.

9. Under what circumstances would it be desirable for an owner of real property to extend an option to buy the property to a prospective buyer?

Case Problems

1. A trustee of real property held a public auction to sell the property. Charles McCabe was the highest bidder. There was no written contract or memorandum of sale. The next day, when the trustee of the property submitted a deed for delivery, McCabe refused to pay the price. The trustee sued for specific performance. Who wins and why? *Watson v. McCabe, 527 F. 2d 286 (6th Cir. 1975).*

2. Shaughnessy, by oral agreement, leased a house and lot from Eidsmo for a term of one year. The agreement also gave Shaughnessy an option to purchase the property at the end of the one-year period. Shaughnessy entered into possession of the property and continued in possession throughout the one-year term, making all required rental payments. At the end of the year he informed Eidsmo of his desire to exercise his option. Shaughnessy continued in possession of the property after the expiration of the lease period and made payments toward the purchase price of the

property. Eidsmo refused to honor the option, claiming that there was a failure to comply with the Statute of Frauds. (a) What is Shaughnessy's rebuttal to Eidsmo's claim? See *Shaughnessy v. Eidsmo, 222 Minn. 141, 23 N.W.2d 362 (1946)*. (b) Would your answer be different if Shaughnessy, in accordance with his agreement with Eidsmo, added a new room to the dwelling?

3. The Roths entered into a contract to purchase real property from Loye Ashton and his co-owners. There was no writing evidencing the sale. The Roths paid most of the purchase price for the property and constructed a building on the property in which they were operating a business. Is it possible for Ashton to rescind the agreement? Explain. See *Williston Co-op Credit Union v. Fossum, 459 N.W. 2d 548 (N.D. 1990)*.

4. The Whites entered into an agreement with the Rehns to purchase "all land west of road running south to the Rehn farmstead containing 960 acres." Nothing within the description pinpointed exactly which 960 acres was to be transferred. Immediately before the purchase agreement was to be signed, the extent of the specific parcel was explained orally to Mr. White. (a) Should the Rehns desire to back out of the sale, what argument could they make? (b) How should the Whites respond? *White v. Rehn, 103 Idaho 1, 644 P.2d 323 (1982)*.

5. River Birch Associates, a developer, entered into a plan to develop a 144-unit town home project on 19.6 acres. River Birch agreed to convey fee simple title to the "common area" to the Homeowner's Association of the project. The specific identity of the common area was not designated in the contract. Can the Homeowner's Association resort to extrinsic evidence to clarify the quantity and the specific identity of the common areas? Explain. What extrinsic evidence may be helpful? *River Birch Associates v. City of Raleigh, 326 N.C. 100, 388 S.E. 2d 538 (1990)*.

6. A contract of sale required the Laddons, the buyers, to pay, as part of the purchase price, a $1,000 deposit to be held by Rhett Realty, the broker, "in escrow on behalf of seller until settlement." The contract further provided that the deposit would be forfeited to the sellers in the event the Laddons breached the contract. In such a case, under the terms of the contract, Rhett Realty would be entitled to 50 percent of the amount forfeited. The contract was contingent upon the buyers obtaining financing, which they were unable to do. Who is entitled to the earnest money? Explain. *Laddon v. Rhett Realty, Inc., 63 Md. App. 562, 493 A.2d 379 (1985)*.

7. 805 Third Avenue Co. (Third Avenue) and M.W. Realty Associates entered into a contract whereby Third Avenue was to purchase M.W. Realty's air rights. Third Avenue needed the air rights to construct an office building. Third Avenue obtained a city permit authorizing it to commence construction, and it began to excavate and enter into contracts for the erection of the

structure. M.W. Realty refused to complete its obligations under the purchase contract, insisting upon a modification of the contract on terms less favorable to Third Avenue. Knowing that any delay would result in serious injury, Third Avenue agreed to the unfavorable terms. (a) What remedy is now available to Third Avenue? (b) What is the legal justification for the remedy? *805 Third Avenue Co. v. M.W. Realty Assoc., 58 N.Y.2d 447, 461 N.Y.S.2d 778 (1983).*

14

Fraud and Deceit

Fraud

A deceptive act or statement deliberately made by one person in an attempt to gain an unfair advantage over another.

No evidence exists that misrepresentation and fraud are more prevalent in real estate than they are in other sectors of the economy. However, deceptive acts that occur in real estate transactions probably have a greater impact than they do in other areas for several reasons. First, most real estate transactions involve large sums of money; as a result, people who feel deceived are more apt to complain or take legal action to assert their rights. A second reason is that licensing laws in every state have placed substantial supervisory responsibility upon brokers for the conduct of sales associates, as was seen in Chapter 11. Unauthorized and even unintentional deception by the sales associate can subject the broker to liability, including the loss of license. Finally, in many transactions little direct contact takes place between buyer and seller. Inasmuch as information is often transmitted through a third party, misunderstanding and error can result in the buyer, seller or both feeling that they have been deceived.

Many definitions exist for fraud; however, fraud can be classified into two major categories, based upon the intent of the one who practices it. *Actual fraud*, or misrepresentation, is based upon intentional deception and is usually accomplished by misstating or concealing a material fact. Actual fraud is often called *deceit*, and the two terms are used synonymously in this chapter. *Constructive fraud*, on the other hand, is not based upon *intentional* deception. Constructive fraud often consists of a breach of duty arising out of the fiduciary relationship discussed in previous chapters.

Liability for constructive fraud may be based upon a negligent or even an innocent misrepresentation. The law reads fraud into the actor's conduct because of its tendency to deceive another or to injure the public interest.

Those who enter into an agreement because they have been deceived by a misrepresentation are entitled to some form of remedy for any injury suffered as a result. The remedy available often depends upon the extent to which the person making the misrepresentation intended to deceive. Remedies will be discussed more fully later in the chapter.

Actual Fraud

Almost any of the parties involved in a real estate transaction is potentially liable for fraud or deceit: buyer, seller, broker or sales associate. The party may be found guilty if it can be established that a statement made by that party was an intentional misstatement of a material fact that is justifiably relied on and results in damages. Although it is relatively simple to list these elements, their application in practice is much more difficult.

Intentional

An intentional, conscious misrepresentation is an essential element of actionable frauds. Courts usually refer to this as an intention to deceive. The technical term *scienter* is also used. *Scienter* exists if a person knowingly makes a false statement or asserts that something is true or false without actual knowledge of whether or not this is the case. An evil intention is not necessary, nor is it required that the speaker intend to injure the other party.

Early cases found the requisite intent only in those situations in which the speaker had actual knowledge of the falsity of the representation; the courts equated intent to deceive with knowledge of falsity. This restrictive interpretation did not long survive. Today all American jurisdictions find scienter not only when the speaker knew the representation to be false but also when the representation was made either without belief in the statement's truth or with reckless disregard of its truth or falsity. Included are statements made by a person who realizes that he or she does not have sufficient basis or information to justify them.

Case Example

Gertrude Hall contracted to exchange her home for one being built by Haskins. The agreement was conditioned upon rezoning her property from residential to commercial use. After the property was rezoned, Haskins asked her to sign a blank deed. Mrs. Hall questioned this and inquired of Wright, her attorney, about the title to the Haskin property. Although Wright had never examined the title, he told her to sign the deed and that he would see that she got an abstract showing clear title.

Hall moved into the Haskins property. Some time later, Wright discovered that it was heavily mortgaged. Hall refused to make the mortgage payments, and she was ousted from possession. She then sued Wright for fraud. Wright defended on the grounds that he had not intended to deceive her. This defense was unacceptable to the court on the grounds that Wright spoke without knowledge. *Hall v. Wright, 261 Iowa 758, 156 N.W.2d 661 (1968).*

A majority of courts in the United States will not award damages for fraud if the speaker honestly believes, upon the basis of creditable evidence, that the representation is true. A substantial and growing minority do not accept this limitation when the innocent misrepresentation is made in a transaction involving the sale, rental or exchange of real estate. In these transactions the courts allow damages but limit them to the difference in value between what the listener has parted with and the value of what has been received and retained.

Case Example

Glenn, a father of two preschool children, leased a house from Takio on a five-year term. The rental was $400 per month. Takio had innocently represented to Glenn that a new school was to be built in the neighborhood. Takio did not know that plans had been canceled. When Glenn discovered the cancellation, he sued Takio for damages, claiming deceit. Glenn was able to prove that the rental value of the property without the new school was $350. The court awarded damages to compensate him for the reduced value of the property.

In all jurisdictions, even an honest misrepresentation of fact supplies the plaintiff with grounds to *rescind* the agreement. *Rescission* is the disaffirmation or cancellation of a transaction.

Misstatement of a Past or Present Material Fact

Case Example

Elfrieda A. Scantlin contracted to purchase a house being constructed by Superior Homes (Superior). In the course of the negotiations leading to the sale, an agent for Manning Real Estate, the builder's broker, stated that Superior was "a good builder and constructed excellent homes." After Scantlin took title, she found several things wrong with the building. When Superior did not repair these defects satisfactorily, she sued both Superior and Manning Real Estate. Scantlin claimed that the statement made by the agent was fraudulent. Scantlin's case against Manning was dismissed as the court held the agent's statement was merely his opinion. *Scantlin v. Superior Homes, 627 P.2d 825 (Kan. Ct. App. 1981)*.

An important premise of American contract law is that adults are competent and have the ability to make rational decisions. As a result, courts do not aid those who rely upon statements not worthy of belief. Judges reason that the rational person discounts statements that are not factual.

Although the rule that only factual statements that are misrepresented can be the basis for fraud is clear, often it is difficult to determine what statements are factual. A fact is something that is knowable, a physical object that actually exists or existed or an event that is underway or has taken place. Understanding what the law means by a statement of fact is often clarified by considering statements generally considered by courts as not factual. These include opinions and estimates (as illustrated by the previous case), predictions, guesses and promises.

Promises require a special word of caution. As discussed in the chapter on contracts (see Chapter 12), a person who makes a promise that later is broken is subject to a suit for breach of contract. Fraud is not the basis for the injured party's action. This makes a difference in the damages that the injured party can recover. For example, in a contract action the successful plaintiff is entitled to compensatory damages only. If successful in a suit based upon fraud, however, the plaintiff can collect punishment damages as well.

Puffing   Sellers have a natural tendency to commend the item they are selling. Such expressions as "I built it with the best," "It's the best building in town" and "You have nothing to worry about; it's a good well" are examples. Statements of opinion like this, made by a seller to induce the purchaser to buy, are often referred to as "puffing" or "dealer's talk." Such statements are not actionable as fraud, even when false, since courts treat them as expressions of opinion. A leading American jurist, Judge Learned Hand, explained why in the following language.

> There are some kinds of talk which no sensible man takes seriously, and if he does he suffers from his credulity. If we were all scrupulously honest, it would not be so; but as it is, neither party usually believes what the seller says about his opinions, and each knows it. Such statements, like the claims of campaign managers before election, are rather designed to allay the suspicion which would attend their absence than to be understood as having any relation to objective truth. *Vulcan Metals Co. v. Simmons Mfg. Co., 248 F. 853 (2nd Cir. 1918).*

Although generally the law does not protect the credulous buyer who relies upon the seller's opinion, a number of situations exist in which courts allow recovery for fraud based upon nonfactual statements. Opinions expressed (1) by a person who enjoys a relationship of trust and confidence or has superior knowledge, (2) by an expert hired to give advice or (3) by a person who actually does not have this opinion are all actionable.

In the following examples, assertions that ordinarily would have been treated as opinion became the basis for fraud. In each case the court determined that the other party had a right to rely upon the representation. Courts often rule this way when there has been a pattern of deceptive conduct or the speaker has concealed something that fairness dictated should be revealed.

Case Example

Mel Erickson, a licensed real estate broker, specialized in investment properties. Tillitz, a wealthy rancher, wished to invest in a multifamily dwelling. Erickson showed Tillitz several properties. After inspecting one large unit, Erickson stated, "That's a fine building, and the return on your investment would be substantial." At the time, Erickson had never inspected the records and was unaware of some major problems with the heating units.

Tillitz purchased the building, lost money and sued Erickson for fraud. Because of Erickson's superior knowledge, many courts would consider the statement as the basis for fraud.

In the case that follows, a statement is clearly opinion, but the speaker is asserting an opinion that she doesn't actually have.

Case Example

Grover and his wife owned a house on a bluff overlooking Lake Michigan. For a number of years, the Grovers and their neighbors had been concerned with erosion along the shore and the safety of their homes. In fact, a group of people from the area, including the Grovers, had met with the Army Corps of Engineers to work out a solution to the erosion problem.

A prospective buyer of the Grover property expressed concern as to the safety of the house. Mrs. Grover responded, "The house is perfectly safe. We are living here, aren't we?" In an action to rescind the contract of sale, the Grovers defended upon the grounds that the statement was merely an expression of her opinion. This defense would not be successful, inasmuch as the Grovers did not actually have this opinion. *See Groening v. Opsota, 67 Mich. 244, 34 N.W.2d 560 (1948).*

During the past 50 or 60 years the trend has been to expand the type of statement that can serve as the basis for fraud. Courts look beyond the form of the statement and consider the circumstances in which it was made when attempting to determine whether there was deceit. One example is the manner in which most state courts treat statements of law made by a layperson. Courts traditionally considered these statements of opinion. They arbitrarily reasoned that all laypeople had comparable knowledge of the law; as a result, the person to whom that statement was made had no right to rely upon it. Today, the law in most states differs. Courts generally examine the context in which such statements are made. In many instances, they conclude that the circumstances are such that a reasonable person has the right to rely upon what the layperson says the law is.

Both buyers and sellers of real estate have been successful in actions for fraud, even when specific words concerning particular facts were never spoken. Most actions for fraud are based upon oral or written statements, but numerous other methods are used to deceive. Actions, failure to act, concealment and silence can all be employed to mislead another.

Case Example

Lawson purchased land in a development called Vanderbilt Hills. He had a house constructed upon this property. After a few months, the house began to sink. Upon investigation, Lawson discovered that the developer had filled a large gully with logs, stumps and other types of debris and covered this with clay. The land apparently was level, and enough clay had been dumped into the gully so that excavation for the foundation did not disclose the fill. Lawson was successful in a suit against the developer for fraud, inasmuch as the court held that the seller had a duty to disclose what he had done because the purchaser could not discover this through a reasonable inspection. *Lawson v. Citizens So. Nat'l Bank of South Carolina, 259 S.C. 477, 193 S.E.2d 124 (1972).*

The most difficult legal questions arise in cases in which a buyer has suffered a loss because of the seller's failure to speak. In some instances the seller simply fails to disclose an element important in the transaction. In others the seller employs some trick or scheme to conceal a condition or fact that is material to the transaction.

The cases that involve concealment are much easier to decide than those that merely involve silence. Active effort to hide something usually overcomes any reluctance courts have to refuse relief on the grounds of caveat emptor.

As a general rule, a party's silence—even silence concerning a critical factor—is not actionable as a misrepresentation. American contract law does not ordinarily require an individual to disclose facts detrimental to the agreement. In a few instances, however, there is a positive obligation to disclose known facts. Courts call this a *duty to speak.* In the following situations, courts in most states have ruled with consistency that a person must speak out about relevant circumstances and facts known to him or her:

- A hidden defect exists that is likely to result in personal harm to persons using the property.

- A hidden defect exists that is likely to limit a use the seller knows the buyer intends to make of the property.

- The seller enjoys a confidential relationship with the buyer.

- The buyer has asked a question that the seller has answered truthfully, but the situation changes and the answer is now false.

Another troublesome problem exists where the seller has made an oral or written representation that is only partially true. Like silence and concealment, the "half-truth" is a misrepresentation actionable as fraud. In many cases a half-truth is more misleading than a statement that is completely false. The half-truth can more easily lull the listener into accepting other representations that are made.

Case Example

Franks owned property on the outskirts of town. Although sewer lines had been constructed to the area, Franks's property was not yet connected. A prospective buyer asked Franks if the property was connected to a sewer. Franks replied, "The sewer line is across the street." Later, the buyer discovered that sewage from the house was being piped to the back end of the property. She sued

Franks for the cost of having the property hooked to the sewer. Franks argued that his statement was true, but the court awarded damages to the buyer. *McWilliams v. Barnes, 172 Kan. 701, 242 P.2d 1063 (1952).*

Reliance

To be successful in an action for fraud, the injured party must prove that (1) he or she acted in reliance upon the false information and (2) the reliance was justified. A person cannot have relied upon false information if the information was acquired after the person acted, nor may a person rely upon statements that investigation indicates are false.

Case Example

Grace Kiner was interested in purchasing a music store from Helen Little. Kiner's marketing strategy required a large volume of potential customers. Little informed Kiner that on the average 250 people came in daily. Little knew that this was false.

Upon several occasions, Kiner visited the store, remaining for appreciable periods of time. After Kiner purchased the store, it became apparent that Little's statement was false. As a result, Kiner sued to rescind. Rescission would be denied if the jury determined that Kiner had relied upon her own inspection, not Little's statement.

In spite of the previous example, the fact that a purchaser makes an independent investigation does not in itself show reliance only upon his or her own judgment. In these situations the courts must weigh the circumstances of the particular case to determine whether continued reliance upon the misrepresentation after investigation is justifiable. Critical factors are such elements as (1) the background of the person investigating, (2) the amount of time available to investigate, (3) the sources of information available and (4) the techniques needed to secure correct information.

Courts use different criteria to determine whether reliance is justifiable. Some states measure the plaintiff's conduct against that of a reasonably prudent person. If a jury decides that a reasonably prudent person, one who uses ordinary care under the circumstances, would not have relied upon the statement, the plaintiff's reliance was not justified. Most states have rejected this standard. The test that is applied is tailored to the particular individual to whom the misrepresentation has been made. Courts in these states take the position that the law should not protect positive, intentional fraud practiced upon the simpleminded or unwary. At the same time, a person who has special knowledge and competence is not justified in relying upon statements that the ordinary person might believe. Similarly, a person whose background and information are those that a normal person might have is not barred from recovery because he or she carelessly accepts a misrepresentation; but if the alleged fact is preposterous, reliance is not justified, and recovery for fraud will be denied.

Material

Not only must the misrepresentation be relied upon; it must also be material. A person is not justified in acting upon a false statement that is trivial in relation to the entire transaction. Inconsequential information of this nature is not material and thus not grounds for suit. On the other hand, some false statements that in themselves seem to be of no significance are important in particular situations. Consider the following examples, in both of which representations are false.

Case Example

Rex Todor is purchasing a house in Memphis, Tennessee. The sales associate states, "Elvis Presley's uncle once lived here."

Case Example

Rex Todor is purchasing an inn in Memphis, Tennessee. The sales associate states, "Elvis Presley often stayed here."

In the first example, the misrepresentation would not be material. A reasonable person would not consider this a significant factor. If, however, the speaker knew that this was important to the buyer, the result would be different. Courts ordinarily will not allow a person knowingly to practice a deception, even though the supposed fact might be unimportant to most people. In the second example, the misrepresentation is material. The fact that Elvis Presley had often stayed at a particular inn would increase the property's value as an attraction for tourists.

Materiality also has a second dimension, which causes some legal problems. Frequently, a false statement is only one of several reasons that causes the person to act. A difficult factual question exists when the plaintiff has numerous bits of valid information upon which a decision could logically be reached but, in addition, has been given some information that is false. It is the view of most courts that for the false information to be material, it must have contributed substantially to the plaintiff's decision to act. If without this information the injured party would not have contracted, the false information may be the basis of an action for deceit. Whether the information is material is a question for the jury. As noted in Chapter 1, the parties may waive a jury trial. If they do so, the judge is the trier of the facts.

Remedies Available to the Injured Party

A majority of courts in the United States have taken the position that a party deceived by an innocent misrepresentation is entitled to rescind the contract but not to collect damages. A few courts have held that even an innocent misrepresentation may justify an award of both rescission and damages.

If the misrepresentation is intentional, the injured party may proceed in a number of ways. He or she may:

- Refuse to perform, using the deceit as a defense if sued for breach of contract,

- Affirm the contract and sue for damages, or

- Ask a court for a decree rescinding the contract.

In a number of states, courts will not allow the party who rescinds to collect damages except for the return of any consideration that has been given up. Courts in these states reason that rescission is based upon a theory that no contract ever existed. Thus rescission is inconsistent with an award of damages for breach of contract. The trend in most states is to allow the deceived party who rescinds to collect damages notwithstanding the rescission.

Case Example

Mrs. Slade sold her house to Garrity. At the time that Garrity inspected the property, Slade informed him that the heating unit was new. Actually, the unit had been installed several years earlier.

In a suit for fraud based upon the deceit, Garrity would be entitled to damages. These would be related to the cost of installing a new unit. He could also, if he desired, rescind the contract and recover the expenses involved in replacing the old unit.

Although American courts generally have been solicitous of people injured by deceit, they recognize the potential harm to the defendant who is charged unjustly. Allowing recovery against a person for fraud or deceit can affect many aspects of that individual's life. His or her ability to earn a livelihood and to purchase a home or other items on credit are sorely jeopardized. As a result, the law has been reluctant to find against a defendant in a fraud action unless the plaintiff's case is sound and evidence clearly establishes all the necessary elements.

Damages

In an action for fraud and deceit, a plaintiff is not entitled to recover damages unless actual monetary loss can be proved. Ordinarily, this requirement is met easily because usually the relationship between the misrepresentation and monetary injury is clear. Few people would sue for misrepresentation unless they believed the deception caused them to lose money. The costs and trauma of litigation make it an expensive way to prove a person a liar if the plaintiff lost nothing.

Generally, the more acute legal problem involves the amount of the damages, not their existence. The following case, *Kramer v. Chabot*, discusses different theories of damages in cases involving fraud and negligent misrepresentation.

Kramer v. Chabot
Supreme Court of Vermont
564 A.2d (1989)

Background: Marilyn Kramer (plaintiff, appellant) sued Lee Chabot (defendant, appellee) for breach of professional duty and misrepresentation in his inspection of a house on her behalf. The trial court awarded her $50 in damages. Plaintiff appealed from the determination of damages. Additional facts are included in the opinion.

Decision: The appellate court vacated and remanded for further proceedings.

Justice Gibson

In June of 1979, plaintiff decided to buy a house in Manchester, Vermont for $42,500. Prior to the purchase, she signed an agreement with the seller stating, inter alia, that the purchase was contingent upon plaintiff's obtaining a favorable inspection report on the property. Plaintiff hired defendant, a builder, to carry out this inspection.

Defendant gave plaintiff a one-page report which stated that the house (including the foundation, structural timbers, plumbing, electrical wiring, and roof) was in good condition. Plaintiff, relying on the report, then completed the purchase.

Despite the representations made in defendant's inspection report, plaintiff discovered, after the sale, numerous defects in the house which required substantial repairs. In the course of the next few years, she spent over $25,000 to put the house into shape, and then sued the defendant to recover the sums she had expended, alleging that he had a duty to perform the inspection in a professional manner, and that his breach of that duty was the proximate cause of damage to plaintiff. In addition, plaintiff claimed that defendant either negligently or intentionally misrepresented certain facts about the property, and that she relied on his representations in deciding to purchase it.

Defendant did not appear personally for trial, although his attorney was present, and the trial court entered a default judgment against him on the issue of liability. The court then proceeded to take evidence on the issues of damages. Plaintiff claimed damages totaling $25,214.10, the amount she had spent on repairs after buying the house.

Acknowledging that the "sole question" before it was the amount of damages to be awarded, the court concluded that compensating plaintiff for all her reasonable expenses in bringing the house into line with the inspection report would produce "an eminently unfair result," since evidence showed that the value of the property at the time of trial, some seven and one-half years after the purchase, was in excess of the $67,714.10 she had ultimately spent on it (purchase price plus repairs):

> If this [c]ourt were to grant her the reasonable cost of her repairs, it would be giving her a reward rather than award. . . . Our purpose is not to put an injured plaintiff in a better position than he or she would have otherwise occupied. Such would be the result if the plaintiff received the damages she seeks. . . .

Instead—and noting it was only "small consolation"—the court awarded plaintiff a judgment for $50, representing the fee she had paid defendant for the inspection report in 1979.

In a tort action, compensation is provided so as to restore the person damaged, as nearly as possible, to the position he or she would have occupied had no wrong been committed. In such cases, the tortfeasor is liable for damages which directly or proximately result from the wrong committed. In actions involving misrepresentation, this Court has reiterated the compensatory nature of the damages to be awarded:

> [A] party seeking damages for fraud is entitled to "recover such damages . . . as will compensate him for the loss or injury actually sustained and place him in the same position that he would have occupied had he not been defrauded."

Generally speaking, there are two theories of damages in cases involving fraudulent or negligent misrepresentation in property sales cases. Some jurisdictions rely on the "out-of-pocket" rule, which permits recovery of the difference between the price paid for the property and the actual value of the property acquired, necessarily calculated as of the time of the transaction. Other courts allow damages based on a "benefit-of-the-bargain" rule, which awards the difference between the price paid and the value of the property had the representations been true.

Some jurisdictions apparently use both rules depending on the facts of the particular case before them. For example, in *Corea v. Maggiore,* the New Jersey appellate court recognized both rules, but subordinated them to the basic objective of making the injured party whole. In that case, which involved fraud in the deliberate concealment of material defects in the sale of property, the court that the diminution of value caused by the deceit, rather than the cost of repairs, was the proper measure of damages where the latter approach would far exceed what was necessary to make the purchaser whole. See also *Harman v. Masoneilan International, Inc.* ("The damages available for deceit or fraudulent misrepresentation are generally limited to those which are the direct and proximate result of the false representation and which represent the 'loss-of-the-bargain' or actual 'out-of-pocket' loss.")

The Court, while using the phrase "benefit of the bargain," has similarly adopted a flexible, rather than a dogmatic, approach to calculating damages in fraud cases. In *Cushman v. Kirby,* noting that compensation was the goal, we stated: "The precise measure of damages that will provide the defrauded party with the benefit of his bargain, however, depends on 'the facts and circumstances surrounding the fraud, and the nature and extent of the injury suffered by the defrauded party.' " Relying on *Bean v. Sears, Roebuck & Co.,* we held that if the harm could be cured by restoration, the reasonable cost of repair might provide adequate and fair compensation; if, however, the damages were found to be permanent and beyond repair, then the "value of the property before and after the injury often affords the better guide to a just reward. It all depends upon the character of the property and the nature and extent of the injury."

Within those general guidelines, this approach leaves to the trial court's discretion the determination of the best measure of damages to make the injured party whole again.

To deny plaintiff any recovery because the property as a whole appreciated in value over the seven-year period between purchase and trial would be clearly inequitable, since this is not a case where the repair price substantially exceeds the original contract price or current market value of the house, and since this would deprive plaintiff of any means of compensation for the injury she sustained at the time the misrepresentation was made and relied on by her.

Instead, in calculating damages here, the trial court should have looked first to the nature and extent of the injury to plaintiff in determining what would make her whole again. Plaintiff bargained for a house in good condition, and did everything within her power to assure herself that that was what she obtained. Due to defendant's misrepresentation—negligent at the very least—she obtained a house in less than good condition, but which could be repaired so that it would be as represented in the inspection report. On remand, the trial court must determine what it will take to give plaintiff the benefit of her bargain, considering all of the surrounding facts and circumstances. (Benefit-of-the-bargain damages may be either the cost of repair to make property conform to the condition as represented, or difference between the value of the property conform to the condition as represented, or difference between the value of property at time of sale with defects and the value it would have had if defects did not exist.) This might be the cost of all repairs made by plaintiff; it might instead entail calculating her benefit-of-the-bargain loss

by ascertaining the difference between the value of the premises as represented and the price actually paid by plaintiff, although we realize that this approach may be difficult of proof given the lapse of time since the misrepresentation and resultant injury in 1979.

We note that it is unclear from the trial court's findings whether all of the $25,214.10 expended by plaintiff arose out of repairing the items represented by defendant to be in good condition in his report, or whether some portions of those expenses were general improvements to the property over and above the necessary repairs. While any general appreciation of the property cannot relieve defendant of his monetary liability, he should not be held liable for expenses incurred by plaintiff which were not directly related to the state of affairs represented in his erroneous inspection report. Thus, on remand, if the trial court determines that the cost of repairs is the appropriate measure of damages required to give plaintiff the benefit of her bargain, it should ascertain what repairs would have been necessary to put the house into the condition represented in defendant's report at the time of the purchase.

The damages portion of the judgment is vacated, and the cause is remanded for further proceedings consistent with this opinion.

Punitive damages   Punitive damages are those awarded in addition to those actually incurred by the injured party as a punishment to the wrongdoer. To recover punitive damages for the tort of fraud and deceit, plaintiff must have suffered actual damages. In most states punitive damages will not be awarded unless the action is gross, oppressive and committed with ill will. Thus a person whose misrepresentation was the result of negligence would not be responsible for punitive damages.

The purpose of punitive damages is to deter others from committing similar acts. The award of punitive damages is discretionary with the jury. Punitive damages usually include an amount sufficient to cover the injured party's attorney's fee and an amount the trier of fact considers appropriate to dissuade others. Punitive damages must have some fair relationship to the compensatory damages that have been proved. Punitive damages awards that shock the conscience of the court will not be permitted.

Negligent Misrepresentation

The rules of negligence apply to a false representation made carelessly in a business transaction. The person supplying false information because he or she failed to exercise reasonable care in obtaining or communicating it is responsible for actual loss suffered by the listener. Because there was no intent to deceive, the speaker's liability is more limited than in a case of intentional misrepresentation. In addition, the defendant may assert defenses, such as plaintiff's contributory negligence, that are not available in an action for deceit.

Waiver

Intentional surrender of a known right or privilege.

Under certain circumstances, one who has been induced to enter a contract because of fraud or deceit waives the available remedies. Generally, waiver occurs when a person discovers the fraud and then does nothing about it. American courts have generally taken the position that, once a person learns that he or she has been deceived, ordinarily he must take some action, or the contract based upon the deception will be confirmed.

In a majority of American jurisdictions, if the contract is wholly *executory*—that is, neither party has performed—the defrauded party upon discovery of the fraud must rescind. Often courts in these jurisdictions do not allow the injured party to recover damages when an executory contract is rescinded. This rule is open to criticism because it denies the injured party the benefit of any bargain that has been made.

If a contract has been substantially performed, the injured party may elect to rescind or affirm the contract and sue for damages. Some action, however, must be taken, and the position of the person defrauded must be made clear to the perpetrator of the fraud. Waiver occurs if, after discovery of the fraud, the injured party merely continues to perform. This is not to say that he need proceed with the contract. Completion of the contract and a subsequent suit for damages is an available option, but the injured party's position must be established, and within a reasonable period of time.

Real estate contracts sometimes contain provisions stating that the purchaser has not relied upon any representations made by the owner or broker. A modification of this is a statement that the purchaser has personally examined the property and enters the contract relying solely upon his own inspection. A typical example is a clause such as "buyers agree that they have entered into this contract relying upon their own knowledge and not upon any representations made by the seller or any other person." Clauses of this type do not waive the injured party's rights to sue for fraudulent representations made by an owner or a broker. The courts reason that to accept such clauses as defenses would provide the seller and the seller's agent with a license to commit fraud. Most buyers would neither recognize the significance of the language nor consider that it applied to outright deception. To allow its enforcement would violate the clear public policy of protecting people who act on the basis of deceptive statements.

Summary

Fraud is a deceptive act or statement made in an attempt to gain an unfair advantage. It is separated into two categories based upon intent. Actual fraud, also called deceit, usually involves an intentional misstatement or concealment of material fact. Constructive fraud, the other type, stems from an act that violates another's trust or confidence. Intent to deceive is not required. Remedies available to defrauded parties vary, depending on the offender's intention and the extent of damages.

To establish fraud, the plaintiff must prove an intentional misrepresentation of a material fact. In addition, he or she must establish that the misrepresentation was justifiably relied upon and that it resulted in damages. Fraud may also exist if a person conceals a material fact, such as a hidden defect, or deliberately makes a statement that is only partially true.

When accusations of fraud are established in court, rescission is the normal remedy. If the injured party can show a monetary loss, damages may also be awarded. Damages are measured by two different rules. Under the benefit-of-the-bargain rule, damages are measured by the difference between what the injured party actually received and what he or she would have received if the deceitful statement had been true. Under the out-of-pocket rule, damages are measured by the amount the injured party actually gave up in relation to value received.

The right to prosecute for fraud may be lost, or waived, by the victim under certain circumstances. One example is the person who enters into a contract to buy and then finds evidence of fraud. This buyer may not be entitled to damages if he or she does not take action before accepting title. Rescission may be the only available remedy in this case.

The injured party also loses the right to sue for fraud if, knowing of the fraud, he or she enters into a new contract for the property, perhaps on new terms. In this case, the party also loses the right to rescind and must perform under the new contract.

Finally, one cannot use as a legal defense against fraud a provision in the contract stating that the "buyer has not relied on any representation made by the seller...." To honor such a clause would amount to the court's giving the seller a license to defraud the public.

Review and Discussion Questions

1. Explain the difference between actual and constructive fraud.

2. What is the meaning of *scienter?*

3. A limited number of situations exist in which silence can be the basis for a successful action based upon fraud. Discuss these situations.

4. (a) How does the benefit-of-the-bargain rule for measuring damages differ from the out-of-pocket rule? (b) Which is more beneficial to the injured party?

5. Under what circumstances might a court award punitive damages in a case involving fraud?

6. Many courts refuse to award damages for fraud if a contract is wholly executory. Critically evaluate this rule.

Case Problems

1. Able hired a contractor to repair several cracks in the walls of his home. The cracks were the result of settling, but the contractor never mentioned this fact to Able. Somehow Able got the impression that the cracks were caused by green lumber. When Able later tells Baker, a prospective purchaser, about the cracks, he explains the cause as green lumber. Baker purchases the property. When additional cracks appear and Baker discovers their true cause, he sues Able for fraud. Is Able liable? Discuss.

2. J. B. Williams was an experienced businessman. In 1977, he entered into a written contract to buy realty from Threlkeld and Murray for $1 million. During the negotiations, Van Hersh, who represented the sellers, stated that New York Life had made a commitment to loan $6 million to develop the property. The terms of this loan were never discussed, nor did the parties ever talk about interest rates or any possible conditions. Williams did not check with New York Life.

   When Williams discovered that the life insurance company had not made a commitment, he attempted to rescind the contract on the grounds of fraud. Would he be successful? Discuss. *Williams v. Van Hersh, 578 S.W.2d 373 (Tenn. 1978).*

3. Kaye was interested in buying a large piece of land from Katzenberry, who lived nearby. Katzenberry did not want to sell the land to a buyer who would use it for commercial purposes; he asked Kaye what he planned to do with the property. Kaye told Katzenberry that he was going to build a house on part of it and probably would use the rest for a garden. This was true, but before the closing Kaye changed his mind and made plans to build a hamburger stand next to his house. Katzenberry learned of this and refused to convey the property. Kaye sued for breach of contract; the defense claimed fraud. Would Kaye be successful? Discuss.

4. Fifty Associates (Fifty) is a firm that has been engaged in the real estate business for many years. In 1959 Fifty and the Prudential Insurance Company (Prudential) joined to finance construction of an office building on land

owned by Fifty but leased to Mayer-Central Building Company. Prudential advanced $2.5 million to Mayer-Central to construct the building. Fifty's financing commitment was conditioned upon the value of the property upon completion. As a result, Fifty refused to sign necessary documents without an appraisal.

In order to overcome this obstacle, Oaks, Prudential's officer in charge, wrote two letters to Fifty. One contained the following statement: "It is not possible for us to disclose a precise valuation of a property. We can state that upon disbursement of $3 million now and $400,000 later, the loan amount will be approximately 70 percent of valuation." Fifty knew that this statement was based upon Prudential's appraisal of the property.

When the project failed, Fifty suffered a financial loss and sued Prudential for fraud based upon this statement. (a) What defense, if any, is available to Prudential? (b) How might Fifty argue to overcome this defense? (c) Who would win? *Fifty Associates v. Prudential Insurance Co. of America, 450 F.2d 1007 (9th Cir. 1971).*

5.   Scott successfully bid $227,065 to clear land for construction. He subcontracted some of the work to Hollis for $98,000. Hollis needed financing to begin the job, and he applied to the Farmers State Bank for a line of credit. The bank extended credit after a meeting with Hollis and Scott. One reason for granting the credit was a representation made by Scott that Hollis could expect $20,000 profit on the subcontract and $20,000 on sale of timber from the site. Hollis was unable to complete the work, defaulted on repayment of funds advanced by the bank and filed as a bankrupt. The bank then sued Scott for fraud on the basis of the statements made at the meeting. Would the bank be successful? Discuss. *Scott v. Farmers State Bank, 410 S.W.2d 717 (Ky. 1967).*

6.   Hattie Griffin agreed to give a lot to Charles Spence, a self-educated itinerant preacher, and his wife. Mrs. Griffin had befriended the Spences and they had provided her with spiritual comfort upon the death of her son. The transfer was conditioned upon the Spences building a church on the lot and allowing Mrs. Griffin the right to use the church parking facilities as a parking lot for her restaurant on an adjoining lot. The parties had also agreed that the lot was to revert to Mrs. Griffin if it wasn't used for a church.

At the closing, which was hastily arranged, Mrs. Griffin read the deed, but not carefully. Both Spence and his attorney assured her that it was "drawn up like you asked." However, the deed did not contain wording that restored the property to Mrs. Griffin if it was not used for a church. At the trial the attorney testified that he had tried to explain the contents of the deed to Mrs. Griffin, but he felt she didn't understand it.

When problems arose concerning the use of the parking facilities by Mrs. Griffin's customers and financing a building on the lot, Mrs. Griffin sued for rescission on grounds of fraud. Would she be successful? Discuss.

7. Reilley owned a small ranch that he planned to sell. The ranch was in a rural area, and the exact boundaries were not clear. Although a survey of the ranch existed, Reilley felt that it was incorrect. As a result he hired Gavin, a licensed surveyor, to resurvey the ranch. Reilley placed stakes in the ground at what he believed to be one of the corners, and Gavin surveyed with that as the starting point.

When Reilley placed the property on the market, he used Gavin's survey as the basis for the description of the property. Herman contracted to purchase the ranch on the basis of the Gavin survey. During the negotiations, Herman and Reilley walked what Reilley informed Herman were the boundaries. Reilley did not inform Herman of the questionable boundaries or the existence of the first survey.

After Herman took the title, he discovered that boundaries were questionable and that another survey existed. This survey indicated that the ranch was smaller than the Gavin survey indicated. Herman sued to rescind, arguing fraud in that Reilley had not informed him of the questionable boundaries and the discrepancy between the two surveys. Would Herman be successful? Support your answer.

15

Closing the Real Estate Transaction

Closing or Settlement

The final stage of the real estate purchase transaction, when the deed and the purchase money are exchanged.

After the buyer and the seller sign a real estate purchase contract, they need time to prepare for the closing. The buyer ordinarily must search for financing, while the seller needs time to prepare evidence of title. Other documents need preparation as directed by the purchase contract, laws and local customs. There is a deed to be drawn, inspection certificates to be obtained, expenses and income to be apportioned, and other preparatory matters to be completed. The interval between the signing and the closing date is intended to provide the necessary time to accomplish these matters.

The date of closing is normally specified in the contract. The date may be as early as two weeks from the date of the contract or as long as two months and occasionally even longer. One difficulty with a long interval is that lending institutions normally do not extend a loan commitment for more than 30–60 days without some additional cost to the borrower.

A postponement of the closing date does not result in a breach of the purchase contract as long as the adjournment is reasonable. On the other hand, if the contract specifies that "time is of the essence," even a one-day postponement could be considered a breach for which the law would afford a remedy to the innocent party.

When the contract does not provide for a closing date, a reasonable time is implied. Since the purpose of the interval is to provide the necessary time to accomplish certain aims, a reasonable time would be a period within which these aims could reasonably be accomplished.

The rights and obligations of the parties are defined by the contract. To a large extent the contract governs the closing format. Local custom, to the extent that it does not contradict contractual provisions, also shapes the closing. Some localities, for example, customarily use the *escrow closing,* wherein the deed and purchase price are delivered to a third party, who is directed to close the transaction outside the presence of the parties. The escrow closing is the subject of the next chapter. In other jurisdictions the parties meet each other face to face at the closing. This conference type of closing is the subject of this chapter.

The object of the closing is to complete the transaction so that the purchaser is vested with title to the realty and the seller receives the purchase price. Various persons who may be responsible for the closing proceedings (other than the buyer and seller) include the real estate broker, attorney and settlement clerk.

Broker

The broker has an economic interest in the closing; at this stage the real estate commission is paid by the broker's principal, who is normally the seller. For that reason the broker usually participates in the closing preparation and is present at the closing. State law varies concerning the broker's permissible role in the closing. Some states permit the broker actually to draw up legal documents, whereas other states relegate the broker to a more passive role. Often the broker facilitates the closing by communicating with the lending institution, the purchaser, seller and/or their representatives on last-minute details. The broker may hand-deliver closing documents to the parties or their legal representatives to minimize the risk of a breakdown in the critical last hours before closing. The broker may be responsible for reminding the parties what documents they need to bring to the closing. To the extent permitted by local law, the broker may even assist in the computation of prorations and the preparation of closing statements. In absence of an attorney representing the seller, the broker will explain to the seller the closing process as it unravels, thus reducing anxiety and confusion at the closing.

Attorney

The attorney's role at the closing varies, depending upon state law, the type of closing and local custom. Although not every real estate closing involves attorney representation, when it does occur, purchasers are more apt to be represented than sellers. Perhaps this is because it is legally more difficult to ascertain whether a purchaser has received good marketable title to the real estate than whether the seller has received the full purchase price prescribed by the contract. In other words, the lay seller is in a better position to ensure receipt of the full purchase price than the lay buyer is to ensure receipt of marketable title to the real estate.

At the ordinary closing the attorney's role is routine, being confined to explaining the various documents to the client. Most of the attorney's preparation for the closing—examination of documents such as the deed, abstract or title insurance policy, mortgage, mortgage note and closing statements—occurs in advance. If the attorney has properly prepared in advance, the routine closing is normally smooth and may seem anticlimactic. An attorney has a more important role, however, in the rare closing where a difficult legal problem arises. Since no one can determine beforehand whether the closing will present an extraordinary problem, it is best for all parties to be represented by counsel. When parties are represented by attorneys, closings are likely to be smoother and less confusing because each party generally has confidence in his or her legal representative.

The seller is responsible for delivering a deed in conformity with the contract. For this reason the seller must hire an attorney for the preparation of the deed or permit the lending institution's attorney to prepare it, in which event the fee will be charged to the seller. The purchaser's attorney will examine the deed to ensure that the description of the property is accurate and that compliance with the necessary formalities for execution of the deed has occurred. The seller may be responsible, pursuant to the terms of the contract, for producing an abstract showing the history of the transactions that relate to the title of the property. An abstract may be prepared by the seller's attorney; in some jurisdictions professional abstractors who are not attorneys may perform this service. Based upon the abstract, the buyer's attorney may be called upon to provide a certificate or letter of opinion regarding the marketability of the title. An attorney who negligently renders a wrong opinion to the buyer will be liable for damages.

Settlement Clerk

> *The person who is designated to coordinate the exchange of documents at the closing.*

The settlement clerk is responsible for ensuring that all documents are properly signed and delivered to the appropriate party. The settlement clerk may be an attorney, real estate broker, employee of the lending institution or title insurance company or any other designated person. A few states require the settlement clerk to be licensed. The deed and other documents may require acknowledgment before a notary. Hence, it is advisable that the settlement clerk be a notary public. Otherwise, a notary public should be present.

At the closing, a lot of paper changes hands. The closing is routine for the settlement clerk, who has undoubtedly performed numerous closings; for the buyers and sellers, however, it may be bewildering. Unless the settlement clerk is sensitive to that fact, the closing may be less than successful. Each document and transaction should be explained to the parties, either by the clerk or by the attorney representing the client. Most problems that emerge at the closing can be remedied by thoughtfulness and a calm spirit.

Preparation for Closing

Preparation is the key to a successful real estate closing. Both the buyer and the seller need to take care of certain items preliminary to the closing. Failure to do so may result in a breakdown at the closing. The laws and customs that govern the buyer's and seller's conduct in preparation for closing do not vary greatly from state to state.

Buyer's Preparation

The buyer's preparation involves obtaining financing, examining the title, securing hazard insurance, calculating the amount needed at closing, inspecting the premises and securing corporate documentation, when necessary.

Obtaining Financing

The buyer ordinarily lacks the available cash to pay for the property and must therefore search for a loan. The prudent purchaser selects a lending institution on the basis of the best buy available, comparing interest rates and other charges. A difference of one half of one percent in the interest rate may be very substantial over the life of the loan. The real estate contract is usually contingent upon the buyer obtaining a loan. If, after exercising good faith, the buyer is unable to obtain the necessary financing, then the parties are discharged from any further obligations under the contract. A lending institution requires an application, a credit check and an appraisal before it will approve a loan. Various federal laws related to the loan, discussed later in this chapter, place certain obligations upon the lender.

The lending institution that loans money to the buyer will require the buyer to sign a note promising repayment, plus a mortgage of the property, which secures repayment by giving the lender an interest in the property. At the closing, the lending institution will make sure that these instruments are signed by the buyer before disbursing the proceeds from the loan.

Examining Title

The contract usually calls for the seller to provide evidence of title in the form of an abstract, certificate of title or title insurance. The buyer should insist on the evidence of title prior to closing so that an attorney can scrutinize the documents to ensure their reliability. An abstract should be up to date and contain no gaps in the chain of title. A certificate of title should be signed by a reputable attorney. Title insurance policies should be checked to ascertain what encumbrances, if any, are excluded from protection. These exclusions may draw attention to title problems.

The purchaser is entitled to a marketable title in absence of a provision in the contract to the contrary. Marketable title is one for which a reasonable, prudent purchaser would be willing to accept and pay fair value. A marketable title is free from objections or encumbrances that would significantly interrupt the owner's peaceful enjoyment and control of the land or impair its economic value. In order to be marketable, it is not necessary that the title be free from every possible encumbrance or suspicion of encumbrance. It need only be free of a reasonable possibility of contentious litigation. Nobody wants to purchase a lawsuit, and, indeed, the law will not require a person to do so.

A defect that renders a title unmarketable may be in the chain of title (see Chapter 17). It may be discovered, for example, in tracing the title of a parcel of land, that the spouse of a grantor failed to sign the deed releasing dower. Or probate records may reveal that a previous grantor was incompetent at the time of transfer. A break in the chain of title may result from an inability to find a record of a previous owner ever having conveyed the property to a grantee.

The title may be rendered unmarketable because of an encumbrance on the property. An encumbrance is a charge upon realty that impairs the use of the land, depreciates its value or impedes its transfer. Liens, mortgages, easements, leases, tenancies, covenants, significant encroachments and building restrictions are examples of encumbrances. Slight encumbrances that do not interfere with the use and enjoyment of the premises do not render a title unmarketable. A two-inch encroachment over a setback line is an example of a slight encroachment. Zoning and building code regulations do not render a title unmarketable. Nevertheless, a *violation* of either is deemed an encumbrance that renders the title unmarketable.

When the evidence of title is examined by the purchaser before closing, objections may be raised with the seller to be remedied before closing. If no time limitation is stated within the contract, then the seller is entitled to a reasonable time to cure any defect. In some contracts the buyer possesses the specific right to cure the title and charge the cost to the seller. Under such a provision the buyer may cure a defect out of the proceeds of the purchase price. If the defects cannot be remedied, or are not remedied, the purchaser may refuse title and sue the seller for breach of the contract.

Purchase contracts commonly require the seller to convey a title free of all encumbrances except "deed restrictions and easements of record." The purchaser should not sign such a contract until he or she knows what restrictions and easements, if any, are of record and is satisfied that they are immaterial. Otherwise the purchaser may find out too late that the encumbrances excepted are of such a nature as to render the property valueless.

If the contract does not require the seller to provide evidence of title, the purchaser will undoubtedly desire to obtain such evidence. Obtaining that assurance before the closing is always better than winding up in a costly suit because of title defects discovered later.

The contract may provide that the purchaser takes the property subject to tenants' rights: tenants are living on the premises, and the purchaser is required to honor their leases. Of course, the purchaser should examine the leases prior to signing the contract or require that the details of the leases be specified in the contract.

The purchaser should make sure that the seller prepares an assignment of the leases in the purchaser's favor and a letter notifying the tenants of the new ownership. At closing the seller can sign the assignment and the tenants' letter, which can be delivered to the tenants along with a notice of where to send future rental payments.

Securing Hazard Insurance

It is important for the purchaser to secure hazard coverage on the property to take effect on the day of closing. In fact, the mortgagee requires proof of coverage at the closing and will specify what type of evidence of coverage the purchaser needs to supply. Some mortgagees desire a copy of the policy; others require only a letter or binder evidencing coverage. Most mortgage instruments include a clause requiring the mortgagor to keep the premises insured at an amount at least equal to the balance due on the mortgage. Failure to do so constitutes a default. This failure is usually discovered when the insurance carrier notifies the mortgagee of a discontinuance of insurance coverage.

Calculating Amount Needed at Closing

The seller is entitled to the purchase price at closing, plus or minus any appropriate adjustments for apportionment of taxes, insurance and other apportionable expenses. The purchaser usually pays closing costs, which include the loan origination fee, appraisal charges, the credit report fee and other charges connected with the loan. Other miscellaneous fees for surveys, preparation of documents, conveyance taxes and recording costs may be payable by the purchaser at closing. In addition, the lending institution may require the purchaser to deposit an amount for taxes and insurance into an escrow account. Normally, the lending institution collects one check from the purchaser and then writes its own checks for payments to the seller, seller's mortgagee, seller's broker and any other parties entitled to funds. Determining the amount that the purchaser needs to bring to the closing necessitates a calculation that takes all these factors into consideration. The lender should determine the amount in advance and communicate it to the purchaser so he or she may have time to obtain the money needed. If a lending institution is not involved, either the real estate agent or the attorney for the purchaser can calculate the amount. In any event, the purchaser needs to review the amounts and calculations and be satisfied that they are accurate.

The purchaser needs to know what type of payment is acceptable; cashier's check, certified check or money order is the customary form of payment. When the purchaser is a trusted customer of the financial institution handling the closing, the institution will often accept a personal check drawn on that institution and then issue its own check to the seller.

Inspecting Premises

The real estate contract may afford the purchaser the right to inspect the premises prior to the closing. If so, the purchaser should arrange for an inspection to ensure that the condition of the premises is as stated in the contract and that the seller has made all repairs agreed upon. In addition, the premises should be searched for zoning and building code violations, potential mechanic's liens or any other encumbrances. Most buyers prefer the inspection to be near the closing date. If an inspection that is too near the closing date reveals objectionable defects, however, there may not be sufficient time before closing for the seller to remedy the problems. In absence of specific language in the contract granting the buyer the right to inspect, the buyer enjoys no such right. However, as a practical matter, the seller would not normally deny the buyer a preclosing inspection.

The purchaser may desire a survey, or the contract may call for it. A surveyor or an engineer must be contracted to perform the task. Sometimes surveys raise questions concerning encumbrances.

Securing Corporate Documentation

Corporations that purchase real estate must obtain authority to purchase from their board of directors or shareholders, depending on state law and the corporation's charter. At the closing the corporate purchaser should be prepared to present the corporate charter and the proper minutes or resolution authorizing the purchase. In addition, if the corporation is borrowing money to make the purchase, the mortgagee requires similar evidence of authorization to extend the loan.

Seller's Preparation

The seller's preparation involves obtaining evidence of title, preparing the deed, removing encumbrances, gathering utility bills and tax receipts, bringing sundry certificates and securing corporate documentation, when necessary.

Obtaining Evidence of Title

The contract may require the seller to supply the buyer with the evidence of title in the form of an abstract or title insurance. The seller may have received an abstract on the property from the previous seller. In such an event the seller must call upon an attorney or abstractor to update it. If the contract calls for title insurance, then the seller must select a title insurance company from which to purchase a policy.

Preparing Deed

In most states the preparation of the deed is the seller's obligation. Even if the seller is not represented by an attorney at the closing, the seller must hire an attorney or authorize someone else to employ an attorney to draw the deed. The basic content of the deed is prescribed by the purchase contract, state law and local custom. Normally, the deed is signed at the closing. In the event the seller or anyone else who must sign the deed cannot be present at the closing, it must be properly executed beforehand.

Removing Encumbrances

The title search or inspection of the premises may reveal objectionable liens or other encumbrances not excepted in the contract, such as unrecorded easements, encroachments or building code violations. Unless these encumbrances are removed, the closing is in danger of breaking down. The seller will have an opportunity to remove any encumbrances brought to his or her attention. In the event the seller removes an encumbrance prior to closing, evidence of this removal should be produced at closing. The seller should obtain satisfaction of judgments, affidavits evidencing payment to laborers, or any other appropriate documents evidencing removal of the encumbrance. Sometimes the encumbrance is removed at closing when the seller deposits an amount of money necessary to discharge the encumbrance or authorizes a deduction for that purpose from the proceeds of the sale.

Case Example

Lone Star Development Corporation entered into a contract with Michael Miller and David Cross to sell certain realty in Pueblo County, Colorado, for $588,000. One thousand dollars was paid at the time of the agreement, and the remaining amount was to be paid at the closing on September 16, at which time Lone Star was to deliver a warranty deed and furnish a marketable title. There was an unpaid lien on the property in the amount of $479,756.71, of which all parties were aware. Lone Star intended to satisfy the lien out of the proceeds of the purchase price. Miller and Cross refused to tender the purchase price, maintaining that the unsatisfied lien rendered the title to the property unmarketable. Lone Star sued Miller and Cross for damages for breach of contract. The court held in favor of Lone Star and said that "a lien on real property which is going to be paid off from the proceeds of the sale of the property is not to be regarded as failure or inability to furnish a marketable title." *Lone Star Development Corp. v. Miller, 564 F.2d 921 (10th Cir. 1977).*

The property may be encumbered by an existing mortgage, a fact which will be revealed by a search of the title. The exact amount due on the mortgage as of the date of closing must be ascertained so that it can be satisfied out of the purchase price at closing. The seller should secure a statement from the mortgagee listing the outstanding balance due as of that date and the daily interest, in the event the payment is received later than the closing date. The lending institution handling the closing often takes care of securing this statement. The statement is produced at closing; the appropriate amount is deducted from the purchase price and sent to the seller's mortgagee.

Sometimes objections to title may be cured by the use of a quitclaim deed. A quitclaim deed has the effect of conveying to the grantee any interest the grantor has in the property. For example, a title search may reveal that a prior conveyance in the seller's chain of title was the subject of an incorrect legal description, which created a title defect. The defect can be cured by the previous grantor signing a quitclaim deed in favor of the seller with the correct description.

A purchaser may question the seller's competency to deliver a deed at closing on the basis of age or mental capacity. Sometimes the purchaser desires additional assurance that the seller is not married or that no work has been performed or supplies have been furnished on the property that might become the subject of a mechanic's lien. Sworn statements verifying facts that satisfy the objections, as in the affidavit shown in Figure 15.1, are normally sufficient.

Gathering Utility Bills

The seller should gather and bring to the closing if requested, unpaid water, sewage and other utility bills and receipts. Water and sewage charges are usually minimal, but they often cause the biggest problem and concern. Water companies read the water meter at intervals, and the exact amount owing at date of closing may be difficult to ascertain. Some homeowners elect to pay a standard monthly charge that is adjusted at the end of the year, making it difficult to determine the accrued charges or credits.

Some jurisdictions permit the imposition of a lien upon property for unpaid water or sewer charges. Others treat them as a personal debt that does not run with the property, in which case judgment against the debtor would not encumber the property. Nonetheless, water companies do have the power to cut off one of life's necessities, and no new homeowner wants to litigate this issue.

Normally, the water companies are cooperative, and the seller can arrange for a meter reading at or near closing. Based upon an experience factor, the parties may agree to an amount at closing. In such a case the seller should produce prior bills so that an experience factor may be derived. If all else fails, a sufficient amount to cover the seller's water bill for the interval may be escrowed at closing. The same principles hold for gas, electric and phone service. The seller should coordinate the turnoff date for the utilities.

Providing Real Estate Tax Receipts

The contract usually calls for an apportionment of taxes as of the date of the closing. Some real property taxes are due twice a year. If the closing occurs on any date other than the dates taxes are payable, or if tax payments are for previous time periods, it is necessary to compute the portions of the tax chargeable to the seller and to the buyer. The seller should be prepared at the closing to produce receipts evidencing payment of taxes.

Bringing Sundry Certificates

The real estate purchase contract may require the seller to produce at closing a termite inspection certificate signed by a termite control inspector certifying that the premises are free from wood-destroying insects and damage from those insects. The contract may additionally call for a certificate from a gas company stating that the gas lines are free from leakage. Heating, plumbing, electrical, sewage or any other system may be the subject of required certificates showing the systems to be in good working order and free from defects. The seller should be prepared to produce the appropriate certificates at closing.

Securing Corporate Documentation

The requirements of a corporate seller are similar to those imposed upon a corporate purchaser. The corporate seller may be required to show proof of authority to sell the property. This may necessitate producing the corporate charter, bylaws, minutes or appropriate resolutions.

Action at the Closing

The place of the closing is controlled by local custom. Commonly, the closing is conducted at the office of the lending institution where the purchaser has obtained financing to purchase the property. Other possible places of closing include an attorney's office or the office of the real estate broker, title insurance company or seller's mortgagee.

Both seller and buyer have responsibilities at the closing. These are discussed below.

Seller's Actions

At the closing the seller tenders the deed, provides evidence of title, if required, and delivers any necessary assignment of leases.

Tendering the Deed

The seller is obligated to tender the deed to the buyer or to the settlement clerk for delivery to the buyer. The buyer should carefully check the deed to make sure its specifications are in accord with the contract. The deed should be of the type the grantor agreed to give. Any encumbrances that are excepted in the deed should be compared to the contract to ascertain whether they are found there. The description should be double-checked against the description contained in the prior deed of conveyance or another reliable source. The names of the grantor(s) and grantee(s) should be checked for accuracy. Even a minor misspelling of a name may cause future problems that will take time and money to remedy. Particular attention should be directed to the form of the execution to ensure conformity with state law. If, for example, the state law requires that the grantor subscribe the deed by signing an alphabetical signature, then a mark of the grantor should not be accepted. If the state law requires that two witnesses sign in the presence of each other, a deed otherwise witnessed is unacceptable. If the state law requires acknowledgment before a notary, the notary seal and notary commission expiration date should be examined for authenticity.

Evidencing Title

The seller may be required to provide evidence of title in the form of an abstract or attorney's opinion, sometimes called a *certificate of title.* Judgments or other encumbrances can intervene between the date of the abstract or attorney's opinion and the date of closing. For that reason, it is most advisable for the purchaser to make a final search of the title down to the moment of closing. Such a search is not always practical. One way to protect the buyer who is unable to conduct the final search is to close in escrow, which is the subject of the next chapter. Under this closing procedure, the settlement clerk or other escrow agent holds the executed deed and the purchase price pending a final check of the title. Upon notification by the buyer or buyer's attorney that the title is in order, the deed is transferred to the buyer and the purchase price to the seller. Sometimes the seller will be required to give the buyer an affidavit of title (as shown in Figure 15.1), which covers objections that might not appear in the title search.

Assigning Leases

In the event the property is sold subject to a lease, the seller should deliver a proper assignment of the lease to the buyer. In addition, the seller should deliver

Figure 15.1: Affidavit of Title

State of Ohio
County of Hamilton
Rod Ross, being first duly sworn, on May 1, 1987, deposes and says that:

1. He resides at 6415 Stover Avenue, in the City of Cincinnati, County of Hamilton, State of Ohio, and has resided at such place for approximately 10 years; he is a citizen of the United States, over the age of 18 years; he is the seller named in the contract of sale dated March 10, 1993, with Bert Haas as purchaser, and is the owner of the real property therein described.

2. He has been such owner since on or about July, 1983, having acquired the same from Harry Blythe by deed; ever since his acquisition affiant has been in peaceful and undisturbed possession of such real property and neither his possession nor his title thereto has been disputed or denied by anyone.

3. Affiant's predecessor in interest was in peaceful and undisturbed ownership and possession of the same real property for approximately eight years prior to conveyance to affiant.

4. No use, tenancy exchange or occupancy of such real property or any part thereof has been such as to give rise to any claim of title or interest by adverse possession.

5. All taxes and assessments levied against the property have been paid when due, and such property is free and clear of any tax lien except for current taxes not yet due or delinquent.

6. The real property is free of any encumbrance by mortgage, deed of trust, or otherwise except restrictive covenants specified in the deed.

7. Plaintiff has not suffered any judgment or decree in any court and no judgment lien has ever attached against such property during affiant's ownership thereof, or during the ownership of affiant's predecessor in interest, to the best of affiant's knowledge and belief.

8. No lien for unpaid income taxes has been filed or is outstanding against the property.

9. No laborer has worked on the premises, nor has anyone supplied materials used on the premises who remains unpaid.

10. Affiant is not married.

11. In acquiring title to the real property described in the contract of sale, and in all subsequent transactions relating to the property, affiant has been designated and described only by the name subscribed hereto.

12. The reason for making this affidavit is to induce the purchaser named in the contract of sale to accept title to the real property therein described and pay the agreed purchase price therefor; the affidavit is

made with the intent and understanding that each statement contained herein shall be relied upon.

_____   _____

Witness   Rod Ross, Seller

_____

Witness

               Affirmed to before me this 1st day of May, 1993

               _____

               Notary Public

---

to the buyer any security deposited by the tenants along with letters to tenants notifying them of the sale and advising them to pay future rentals to the purchaser.

Purchaser's Actions

The buyer's responsibilities at the closing include tendering the purchase price and closing the loan extended by the lender.

Tendering Purchase Price

The purchaser is obligated to tender the purchase price to the seller. Normally, in absence of an excusal by the seller, the purchase price must be produced and offered to the seller. It is normally not a sufficient tender for the purchaser to appear at the closing and maintain that he or she has access to the purchase money elsewhere. The purchaser must actually make a show of the money with the intent to deliver it to the seller. Of course, this is not necessary if the tender would be futile—for example, should the seller not appear at the closing.

Payment is usually made by some form of check—usually a cashier's or certified check. However, whatever medium the contract calls for must be honored.

Case Example

Benjamin Chertok entered into a contract to purchase realty from Aroosiag Kassabian. Chertok made a deposit and agreed to pay the remainder in cash at the closing. At closing Chertok tendered a third person's certified check to Kassabian. Kassabian requested that he cash the check, and Chertok refused. After Kassabian refused to tender the deed, Chertok sought a return of his deposit. The court held that Chertok's tender was not the equivalent of payment in cash, and consequently he was in breach and not entitled to a return of his deposit. _Chertok v. Kassabian, 255 Mass. 265, 151 N.E. 108 (1926)._

Customarily, the seller gives the buyer a receipt for the purchase money. Even if the payment is in the form of a check (which ordinarily serves as a receipt upon cancellation), it is nonetheless a good practice for the buyer to be extra cautious by requiring a written receipt from the seller at the time the purchase price is tendered.

Mortgaging the Property

Lending institutions charge closing costs, normally computed as a percentage of the amount borrowed. Closing costs are charged by the lending institution to cover the cost of services performed in connection with the loan and for servicing the loan. Closing costs vary among lending institutions.

If the buyer is financing the purchase through a new loan, the lender supplies a mortgage and a note for the borrower to sign at closing. Any existing mortgage on the property will be satisfied out of the purchase price, and a satisfaction of mortgage signed by the seller's lender will be given to the settlement clerk for recording.

In reality, most closings involve two distinct but related transactions. First, the sale of the property is closed between the seller and the buyer, with the seller receiving the purchase price and the buyer the deed. Second, the loan extended by the lending institution is closed between the lender and the borrower (buyer), with the borrower receiving the proceeds of the loan (which are used to pay the seller) and the lender receiving a note and mortgage from the borrower securing repayment of the loan. After the closing the seller pays off the old mortgage and the seller's lending institution cancels the old mortgage. These transactions are illustrated in Figure 15.2.

Real Estate Settlement Procedures Act (RESPA)

> *A federal law that requires lending institutions to disclose certain information to purchasers of residential real estate and prohibits those institutions from engaging in specified activities.*

A borrower who seeks a mortgage loan needs full information from lending institutions in order to select a lender prudently. RESPA requires the lending institution to make certain disclosures designed to help the borrower make informed judgments. Generally, RESPA is applicable to first mortgage loans made for the purchase of residential real estate. Residential real estate includes one-family to four-family properties. Cooperatives, condominiums and mobile home lots can qualify as residential real estate. The act applies only to purchases where a lender (other than the seller) takes a purchase money mortgage to secure the loan. A purchase money mortgage in which the seller takes a mortgage back to secure the unpaid purchase price is not covered by RESPA. The requirements of RESPA are applicable only to lenders involved in a "federally related mortgage loan." The definition of *federally related* is very broad and includes any lending institution whose deposits are federally insured or regulated.

Settlement Costs Booklet

RESPA is administered by the Department of Housing and Urban Development (HUD). HUD has prepared a settlement costs booklet. Every lender is required

Figure 15.2: Transactions Involved in a Real Estate Closing

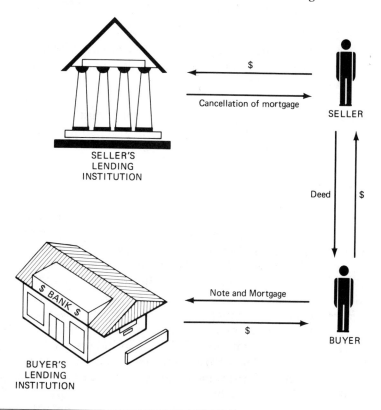

to provide an applicant for a mortgage loan with the contents of this booklet on the day of the loan application or, failing that, to deposit it in the mail to the applicant within three business days of the application. The booklet contains information about the real estate purchase process, including negotiating a sales contract and home loan financing. Under the heading "Selecting the Lender," the booklet suggests certain inquiries a borrower should make in order to compare lenders. For example:

- Am I required to carry life or disability insurance? Must I obtain it from a particular company?

- Is there a late payment charge? How much? How late may the payment be before the charge is imposed?

- If I wish to pay off the loan in advance of maturity, must I pay a prepayment penalty? How much? If so, for how long a period will it apply?

- Will the lender release me from personal liability if my loan is assumed by someone else when I sell my house?

- If I sell the house and the buyer assumes the loan, will the lender have the right to charge an assumption fee, raise the rate of interest or require payment in full of the mortgage?

- Will I be required to pay monies into a special reserve account to cover taxes or insurance? If so, how large a deposit will be required at the closing of the sale?

In addition, the booklet contains information regarding home buyers' rights and obligations, settlement services and escrow accounts, as well as a sample work sheet to calculate the settlement costs.

Good-Faith Estimate

Another RESPA requirement is that the lender must provide the borrower with a good-faith estimate of settlement charges at the time of the application. These charges may be expressed as a range. A lender who fails to provide the required information on the date must deposit the information in the mail within three business days of the application. The good-faith estimates include the breakdown of the costs of settlement charges rendered by the mortgagee—for example, loan origination fee, credit report fee, appraiser's fees, title search charges, attorney fees, surveys and document preparation. The complete schedule of all settlement charges is contained in Section L of the Uniform Settlement Statement (see Figure 15.3). The good-faith estimate does not have to include prepaid hazard insurance premiums or reserves deposited with the lender such as escrow for taxes and insurance since this information is not usually available to lenders at the application stage. Although the estimates must be made in good faith, they are subject to change as the market alters the costs of the various settlement charges.

Inspection of Uniform Settlement Statement

A closing or settlement statement is normally prepared by the settlement clerk handling the closing. The settlement statement consists of a summary of the buyer's (borrower's) and the seller's transactions, broken down into various categories. For some items it may be necessary to apportion income and expenses between the parties. For example, assume that the seller has paid the real estate taxes for six months in advance. Credit should be given to the seller for the portion paid that covers any period after closing. Apportionment of the taxes ensures that each person bears the expense only for the months that person had use of the premises. Other expenses often apportioned include water and sewer assessments, fuel and insurance. Rental income may also be adjusted for unearned rentals received by the seller in advance.

RESPA requires that a lender permit the borrower a right to inspect the Uniform Settlement Statement (USS) one day before closing. The USS is a form settlement statement that contains a summary of the borrower's and seller's transactions and an itemization of the settlement charges as allocated to the borrower and seller. In the event that this information is unavailable the day before closing, the lender is relieved of the responsibility. In this case the completed statement must be given to the buyer no later than the closing. This requirement may be waived by the buyer, but in the event of such waiver the USS must be mailed at the earliest practical date. Where there is a closing without an appearance of the buyer or the buyer's agent, the lender need only mail the statement to the buyer as soon as practical after the closing. The lender need not provide a USS to the buyer when there are no settlement charges to the buyer or when the settlement charges are a fixed amount communicated to the borrower at the time of the loan application. However, here the lender must provide the borrower with an itemized list of services provided within three days after closing.

In all transactions covered by RESPA, the USS must be used. Otherwise, a statement resembling that form is normally used.

Abusive Practices

One reason Congress passed RESPA was because certain abusive practices inflated closing costs. "Kickbacks" are one such practice expressly prohibited by RESPA. Kickbacks occur, for example, when a person or an entity gives a fee to another for business referrals.

Case Example

ABC Savings and Loan has an agreement with Alfred Hillman, attorney, whereby for every person ABC refers to Hillman for legal services in connection with real estate transactions, Hillman pays ABC ten percent of the fees generated. This is an illegal kickback under RESPA. In addition, Hillman would be violating the attorney's code of ethics and would be subject to disciplinary measures.

There are similar prohibitions against the payment of a "phantom" charge, a fee that is given where no service has been performed. Both kickbacks and phantom fees may result in a violation for which criminal penalties may attach. Also, an aggrieved party may sue to recover three times the amount of the kickback or the phantom fee. As the next case illustrates, not every service in connection with a real estate transaction is covered by the "anti-kickback— phantom fee" provisions of RESPA.

Eisenberg v. Comfed Mortgage Co., Inc.
629 F. Supp. 1157 (D. Mass. 1986)

Background: The Eisenbergs sought a $164,000 loan from Comfed in order to finance the purchase of a home being built for them. The loan was to be secured by a mortgage on the new home, and then it was to be assigned to Comfed's parent, the Bank. One provision required the Eisenbergs to pay two and one-half percent of the face value of the loan as a "mortgage origination fee." One-half percent of that amount was to be paid to Comfed as a commission and the remainder to the Comfed branch manager and to Comfed's overhead.

The Eisenbergs sued Comfed and its parent, the Bank, contending that the provisions allocating percentages were

Figure 15.3: HUD Settlement Statement

A. Settlement Statement

U.S. Department of Housing and Urban Development

OMB Approval No. 2502-0265

B. Type of Loan

1. ☐ FHA   2. ☐ FmHA   3. ☐ Conv. Unins.
4. ☐ VA   5. ☐ Conv. Ins.

6. File Number

7. Loan Number

8. Mortgage Insurance Case Number

C. Note: This form is furnished to give you a statement of actual settlement costs. Amounts paid to and by the settlement agent are shown. Items marked "(p.o.c.)" were paid outside the closing; they are shown here for informational purposes and are not included in the totals.

D. Name and Address of Borrower

E. Name and Address of Seller

F. Name and Address of Lender

G. Property Location

H. Settlement Agent

Place of Settlement

I. Settlement Date

J. Summary of Borrower's Transaction	
100. Gross Amount Due From Borrower	
101. Contract sales price	
102. Personal property	
103. Settlement charges to borrower (line 1400)	
104.	
105.	
Adjustments for items paid by seller in advance	
106. City/town taxes to	
107. County taxes to	
108. Assessments to	
109.	
110.	
111.	
112.	
120. Gross Amount Due From Borrower	

K. Summary of Seller's Transaction	
400. Gross Amount Due To Seller	
401. Contract sales price	
402. Personal property	
403.	
404.	
405.	
Adjustments for items paid by seller in advance	
406. City/town taxes to	
407. County taxes to	
408. Assessments to	
409.	
410.	
411.	
412.	
420. Gross Amount Due To Seller	

Figure 15.3: HUD Settlement Statement (continued)

200. Amounts Paid By Or In Behalf Of Borrower	
201. Deposit or earnest money	
202. Principal amount of new loan(s)	
203. Existing loan(s) taken subject to	
204.	
205.	
206.	
207.	
208.	
209.	
Adjustments for items unpaid by seller	
210. City/town taxes to	
211. County taxes to	
212. Assessments to	
213.	
214.	
215.	
216.	
217.	
218.	
219.	
220. Total Paid By/For Borrower	
300. Cash At Settlement From/To Borrower	
301. Gross Amount due from borrower (line 120)	
302. Less amounts paid by/for borrower (line 220)	( )
303. Cash ☐ From ☐ To Borrower	

500. Reductions In Amount Due To Seller	
501. Excess deposit (see instructions)	
502. Settlement charges to seller (line 1400)	
503. Existing loan(s) taken subject to	
504. Payoff of first mortgage loan	
505. Payoff of second mortgage loan	
506.	
507.	
508.	
509.	
Adjustments for items unpaid by seller	
510. City/town taxes to	
511. County taxes to	
512. Assessments to	
513.	
514.	
515.	
516.	
517.	
518.	
519.	
520. Total Reduction Amount Due Seller	
600. Cash At Settlement To/From Seller	
601. Gross amount due to seller (line 420)	
602. Less reductions in amt. due seller (line 520)	( )
603. Cash ☐ To ☐ From Seller	

HUD-1 (3-86)
RESPA, HB 4305.2

Figure 15.3: HUD Settlement Statement (continued)

L. Settlement Charges

			Paid From Borrowers Funds at Settlement	Paid From Seller's Funds at Settlement
700. Total Sales/Broker's Commission based on price $	@	% =		
Division of Commission (line 700) as follows:				
701. $	to			
702. $	to			
703. Commission paid at Settlement				
704.				
800. Items Payable In Connection With Loan				
801. Loan Origination Fee	%			
802. Loan Discount	%			
803. Appraisal Fee	to			
804. Credit Report	to			
805. Lender's Inspection Fee				
806. Mortgage Insurance Application Fee to				
807. Assumption Fee				
808.				
809.				
810.				
811.				
900. Items Required By Lender To Be Paid In Advance				
901. Interest from to @$ /day				
902. Mortgage Insurance Premium for months to				
903. Hazard Insurance Premium for years to				
904. years to				
905.				
1000. Reserves Deposited With Lender				
1001. Hazard insurance months@$ per month				
1002. Mortgage insurance months@$ per month				
1003. City property taxes months@$ per month				
1004. County property taxes months@$ per month				
1005. Annual assessments months@$ per month				
1006. months@$ per month				
1007. months@$ per month				
1008. months@$ per month				
1100. Title Charges				
1101. Settlement or closing fee to				
1102. Abstract or title search to				
1103. Title examination to				
1104. Title insurance binder to				
1105. Document preparation to				

Figure 15.3: HUD Settlement Statement (continued)

1106. Notary fees	to
1107. Attorney's fees	to
(includes above items numbers:	
1108. Title insurance	to
(includes above items numbers:	
1109. Lender's coverage	$
1110. Owner's coverage	$
1111.	
1112.	
1113.	

1200. Government Recording and Transfer Charges

1201. Recording fees: Deed $	; Mortgage $; Releases $
1202. City/county tax/stamps: Deed $	; Mortgage $
1203. State tax/stamps: Deed $	; Mortgage $
1204.	
1205.	

1300. Additional Settlement Charges

1301. Survey	to
1302. Pest inspection to	
1303.	
1304.	
1305.	

1400. Total Settlement Charges (enter on lines 103, Section J and 502, Section K)

Public Reporting Burden for this collection of information is estimated to average 0.25 hours per response, including the time for reviewing instructions, searching existing data sources, gathering and maintaining the data needed, and completing and reviewing the collection of information. Send comments regarding this burden estimate or any other aspect of this collection of information, including suggestions for reducing this burden, to the Reports Management Officer, Office of Information Policies and Systems, U.S. Department of Housing and Urban Development, Washington, D.C. 20410-3600; and to the Office of Management and Budget, Paperwork Reduction Project (2502-0265), Washington, D.C. 20503 in violation of the anti-kickback provision of the Real Estate Settlement Procedures Act.

Decision: The Federal District Court dismissed plaintiff's suit and found in favor of the defendants on the basis that the allocation of the percentages was not an illegal kickback for services rendered in violation of RESPA.

Judge Young

The Eisenbergs contend that one point of their two and one-half point mortgage origination fee constituted the "payment of a thing of value" bearing no reasonable relationship to the value of services received by them from Comfed. The percentage fee charged by Comfed was, they argued, "received for the rendering of a real estate settlement service in connection with a transaction involving a federally related mortgage" and bore no relation to "services actually performed."

The Eisenbergs support this contention by pointing to the fact that Comfed has admitted that the one point commission and overhead fee was arrived at, if not arbitrarily, at least with considerations in mind other than the actual cost of processing the Eisenberg loan. They further point out that, "although the same routine, mechanical services are provided for each borrower and in each loan transaction, the dollar amount equivalent to the points paid, determined solely on a percentage basis, varies dramatically from mortgage to mortgage." Thus the Eisenbergs paid much more for their comparatively large loan than would a mortgagor with a smaller loan, even though Comfed provided for each substantially the same services.

Even accepting . . . the Eisenberg's description of Comfed's point system of calculating mortgage origination fees, this Court refuses to stretch the words of the Act to cover that system. First, there has not been any "referral" shown.

Comfed did not receive a fee in return for a referral of business to its owner, the Bank. It received a commission for the origination of the loan, and fully assigned its rights in the mortgage to the Bank; it was not a referral of business but a transfer of . . . interests.

More important, however, this Court rules that the making of a mortgage loan is not a "settlement service" within the meaning of the Act. [The Act] defines the term "settlement services" as follows:

> The term "settlement services" includes any service provided in connection with a real estate settlement including, but not limited to, the following: title searches, title examinations, the provision of title certificates, title insurance, services rendered by an attorney, the preparation of documents, property surveys, the rendering of credit reports or appraisals, pest and fungus inspections, services rendered by a real estate agent or broker, and the handling of the processing, and closing or settlement. . . .

Clearly, the making of mortgage loans is not included in the list. Moreover, although the list is not meant to be complete, the Sixth Circuit in *United States v. Graham Mortgage Corp.* concluded that each of the "settlement services" in the illustrative list was "an ancillary or peripheral service that, unlike the making of a mortgage loan, is not directly related to the closing of a real estate sale" covered by the Act. . . . The *Graham* court concluded that "Congress's failure to specify the making of a mortgage loan in listing settlement services seems inexplicable unless the omission was intended."

This Court finds logic of the *Graham* decision compelling. The system of charging mortgage origination fees based on percentages of loan amounts is industry-wide. In the absence of a more unambiguous statement of Congressional intent, this Court refuses to disturb that practice by construing the words of the Act to cover a type of transaction not specifically mentioned in it.

. . .

. . . Judgment shall enter for the defendants.

Postclosing Procedures

After the closing, the purchaser is the titleholder of the property as evidenced by the deed. The deed must now be recorded to give constructive notice to the world of the new ownership and thus protect the buyer against rival claimants. The purchaser, purchaser's attorney or, in some instances, the mortgagee presents the deed for recording in the proper office in the county courthouse. After receiving the appropriate fees the clerk photocopies and records the deed and then returns the original deed to the purchaser. Satisfaction (cancellation) of the preexisting mortgage must also be recorded. The new mortgage instrument that secures repayment of the loan is recorded by the mortgagee, the institution extending the loan to the purchaser. After recording, the title insurer issues the title insurance policy in the name of the new owner and the mortgagee, if title insurance was purchased. In the event an abstract is given as evidence of title, the search of the title should be updated or brought down to the moment of recording.

At the closing, a problem may have been remedied by setting up an escrow and charging an escrow agent with the obligation of holding a portion of the purchase price necessary to assure the resolution of the problem.

Case Example

At closing, Fred Thomas, seller, is unable to produce any paid receipts for water bills for the last year. Frank Hander, purchaser, is wary of closing without an assurance that any unpaid bills will be borne by the seller. An escrow account is set up with $150 funded from the purchase price, an amount everyone agrees would be more than enough to pay any unpaid water bills for a year. After closing, the contact with the water company reveals an unpaid water bill of $31. The escrow agent will pay the amount out of the escrow funds and send the remaining $119 to the seller.

In the event the property was sold subject to an existing lease, the purchaser should secure a "tenants' letter" from the seller notifying the tenants of the sale and directing them to pay rent to the purchaser in the future. After closing, the purchaser should deliver that letter to the tenants.

Summary

The *closing*, also called the *settlement*, is the final stage of a real estate purchase transaction. At the closing the deed and the purchase money are exchanged by the seller and buyer according to the terms of the contract.

In most cases the broker may participate in the preparation for the closing by helping the buyer arrange financing, assisting in the preparation of the closing statement and coordinating various other details that will facilitate closing. Both buyer and seller may also be represented by an attorney at the closing. The date of the closing is normally specified in the contract. All preliminary work should be completed in advance.

Between the signing of the contract and the settlement date, the buyer must normally obtain financing, secure hazard insurance and should inspect the premises, examine the title and any existing leases on the property. The seller also needs this interval to prepare by obtaining evidence of title, preparing a deed and satisfying any liens or other encumbrances.

The closing may take place at the lending institution that has supplied financing or at the office of an attorney, a real estate broker or the seller's mortgagee. A *settlement officer*, usually an employee of the "host" office, is responsible for coordinating the paperwork. To aid in following the flow of funds at the closing, a settlement statement is prepared. The statement includes breakdowns for taxes, utilities, rents and any other payments that must be prorated. The settlement procedures are regulated by contract, local custom, state law and a federal statute known as *RESPA* (*Real Estate Settlement Procedures Act*).

After closing, the deed should be recorded to protect the purchaser. The old mortgage should be canceled and any new mortgage recorded.

Review and Discussion Questions

1. What is the role of a broker in a real estate closing?

2. What is the purpose for the interval between the signing of the real estate contract and the closing?

3. (a) What is the role of the settlement clerk at closing? (b) Who should act as a settlement clerk?

4. (a) Name four things the buyer normally must accomplish in anticipation of the closing and describe why each is important. (b) Name four things that the seller normally must accomplish in anticipation of the closing and describe why each is important.

5. What is the purpose of an affidavit of title?

6. List three documents that are normally signed at the closing and describe each.

7. (a) Upon whom does RESPA impose requirements? (b) What are those requirements?

8. Why is it important for the deed to be recorded after the closing?

Case Problems

1. Grace Zeigler and Harriet Milton entered into a contract for the sale of a parcel of land owned by Zeigler. The terms of the contract were established through negotiations between the parties. The contract did not make any provision for Zeigler to deliver an abstract of title. Zeigler neglected to furnish an abstract at the closing. Milton refused to pay the purchase price at the closing because Zeigler did not supply an abstract. (a) Is Milton's position sound? (b) Where should Milton look to determine whether Zeigler is bound to provide an abstract? (c) What can Milton do to ensure that she receives a clear title? See *Applebaum v. Zeigler, 246 Ala. 281, 20 So.2d 510 (1945).*

2. The Maple Ridge Construction Company and Kasten entered into an agreement for the purchase of lots in a subdivision owned by Kasten. Maple Ridge encountered problems in obtaining financing and requested postponement of the settlement date. Kasten agreed to an extension of four months. Maple Ridge continued to try to obtain a suitable financing arrangement without success. Repeated requests for additional extensions were turned down by Kasten. The settlement date passed with neither party performing or demanding performance from the other. Five days after the expiration of the settlement date Maple Ridge informed Kasten that it was ready to perform. Kasten refused Maple Ridge's tender, claiming that the contract had expired. Maple Ridge commenced an action in specific performance against Kasten in an attempt to force Kasten to comply with the terms of their contract. Who wins? Discuss. See *Kasten Construction Co. Inc. v. Maple Ridge Construction Co. Inc., 245 Md. 373, 226 A.2d 341 (Ct. App. 1976).*

3. Carolista Fletcher, purchaser, and Burton Jones, seller, entered into a contract for the sale of certain real property for $45,000. The contract provided for a closing date of January 9, 1981, and contained a clause stating: "Contract is subject to seller obtaining absolute divorce from present spouse." The condition was not met prior to the date set for closing. On January 29 the parties agreed in writing to extend the closing to March 19, 1981. The condition was not met by that date. However, on August 4, 1981, Jones's attorney informed Fletcher's attorney that the divorce was final and that he was ready to close. (a) Is Fletcher obligated to close? Explain. (b) What if Jones sells the property to someone else? Can Fletcher successfully sue Jones for breach of contract? Explain. *Fletcher v. Jones, 333 S.E.2d 731 (N.C. 1985).*

4. Vega applied for and received a conventional mortgage loan from First Federal to finance the purchase of his residence. First Federal's deposits are insured by the Federal Savings and Loan Insurance Corporation (FSLIC). (a) Which federal statute should First Federal pay close attention to before completing its loan agreement with Vega? What obligations are imposed upon First Federal by this statute? See *Vega v. First Federal Savings and Loan Association, 433 F.Supp. 624 (D. Mich. 1977).* (b) How would First Federal's

obligations be affected if Vega sought to borrow money for the purchase of a commercial lot?

5. Mr. LaFond negotiated a contract with Ms. Frame whereby Ms. Frame agreed to sell to Mr. LaFond a parcel of land free from all encumbrances. The date for the conveyance of the deed and the possession of the land was set for one year from the date the contract was signed. The contract was silent regarding the payment of taxes on the property during the pendency of the contract. On the date set for conveyance, taxes assessed for the prior year were unpaid. (a) Who has the duty to pay these taxes? Why? (b) How could the parties have eliminated any uncertainty on this point? See *LaFond v. Frame, 327 Mss. 364, 99 N.E.2d 51 (1951).*

6. Jim Darrow has obtained an 11 percent 30-year loan commitment from the Poplar Savings and Loan for $80,000 to purchase Liz Nodler's home at 1836 Cedarwillow, Columbus, Ohio. The sales price, pursuant to the contract previously entered into by the parties, is $100,000. The closing is to take place at the offices of the Poplar Savings and Loan on May 15. In addition to the purchase price of the house, Darrow has arranged to purchase the curtains for $300. County taxes on the property are $1,200 per year, payable semi-annually. The county is six months behind on billing and collecting taxes; Liz's last payment was made January 15, 1991. The seller prepaid $200 on January 1 for hazard insurance, which covers the calendar year. The house is heated by oil; 50 gallons of home heating oil costing $1.50 per gallon remain in the tank on the day of closing. Seller's tenant has paid $400 advance rent for the month of May.

   Darrow is paying $20,000 as a down payment, which will be paid at the closing. The payoff by the seller of the first mortgage on the home, as of the date of closing, is $37,120.

   Water and sewer assessments are payable quarterly at an even billing of $45 per quarter at the end of March, June, September and December. Nodler made the March 31 payment. Every six months a reading is taken to determine the actual usage for the six-month period, and adjustments are made at the end of the year. Average adjustments for the last five years have resulted in an additional assessment of $40 at the end of the year.

   A listing agreement with Decade Today Realtors requires the seller to pay 6 1/2 percent commission. The loan origination fee was two percent. Seller, pursuant to the terms of the contract, was to pay two mortgage discount points (two percent). The appraisal fee of $100 and $15 for a credit report was paid by Darrow at the time of the loan application. The survey fee of $150 to Survey Plat, Inc., is payable by the buyer at closing.

   Assume that simple interest based on a 360-day calendar year is to be paid at closing for the 17-day period encompassing May 15 to May 31. Darrow will be required to deposit two months' taxes at closing into escrow. Attorney fees for preparation of the deed to be borne by the seller are $35. The buyer's attorney fees for services connected with the closing are $350, payable to Lincoln, Todd and Harrison Law Firm at closing. The seller obtained a joint title insurance policy, as required per contract, to fully cover the lender and the owner. The cost to the seller, to be disbursed at closing to ABC Title, Inc., is $650. The Buyer's charge for recording fees for the deed and the mortgage amounts to $5 for each document. The seller must pay the recording fee for the release of the existing mortgage.

Additionally, a 0.1 percent county transfer conveyance fee is assessed against the seller. Seller, pursuant to the contract, agreed to pay for termite and gas line inspection costs. She employed Exterm Pest Control to do the termite inspection; the charge was $40 for the inspection and $210 for repair work. The seller employed the city to do the gas line inspection at a cost of $75. Using the HUD forms on pages 308 and 311 prepare the closing statement.

16

Escrow

Real Estate Escrow

A deed delivered by a grantor to an escrow agent, who is directed to deliver the deed to a grantee when a specified condition occurs.

In the previous chapter we examined a conventional closing, where buyer and seller come face to face to exchange the deed for the purchase price. The real estate escrow closing is a modification of this procedure that is practiced in some localities. Instead of the buyer and seller coming face to face, a third party acts as an intermediary. The third party, commonly called an *escrow agent*, is charged with certain responsibilities designed ultimately to invest the seller with the full purchase price and the buyer with a good deed to the property.

The subject of the escrow transaction is a written instrument. The written instrument in the normal real estate escrow transaction involves a deed. Technically, the term *escrow* characterizes the instrument—the deed itself—while it is held by the third party. This strict terminology has been relaxed, however, and it is common to refer to "depositing a deed into escrow." In this regard the escrow is the receptacle of the instrument rather than the instrument itself. Courts refer to escrows in both senses, and either reference is acceptable.

Escrow Closing Distinguished

The escrow closing should not be confused with the escrow account. Many mortgages include a clause requiring the mortgagee to set up an escrow account to be used to disburse payments for real estate taxes and/or hazard insurance. The particulars of this escrow account vary from jurisdiction to jurisdiction. Generally, the mortgagor pays into the escrow account monthly an amount equal to one-twelfth of the amount of the yearly property tax and hazard insurance. This constitutes an additional amount above the normal mortgage payment. The mortgagee then makes payments directly from the escrow account as the taxes and insurance become due. This type of escrow procedure is required for FHA-insured loans and for most conventional loans; it is suggested for DVA-guaranteed loans.

The escrowed funds are normally placed in non-interest-bearing accounts; depositors are not paid for the use of the funds. There is, however, a trend in recent years for buyers, particularly in commercial transactions, to require the escrowed money to be deposited in an interest-bearing account in favor of the buyer.

The Escrow Transaction

In the most elementary real estate escrow transaction a seller and a buyer enter into a contract for the purchase of specified real property. They agree to close the transaction in escrow, and they appoint a bank or other escrow agent to be responsible for handling the closing. As part of the agreement between the parties, the seller then deposits a fully executed deed with the escrow agent. The escrow agent is instructed to deliver the deed to the purchaser after receipt of the purchase price. When the purchase price is deposited by the purchaser, the escrow agent delivers the deed to the purchaser and the purchase price to the seller. At this point the escrow closing is complete (see Figure 16.1).

Another typical example of the real estate escrow transaction involves conditions relating to title. In this arrangement the seller deposits the deed, and the purchaser deposits the purchase price with the escrow agent. When the purchaser's attorney approves the title to the property, the escrow agent is bound by the purchase contract or other agreement to deliver the deed to the purchaser and money to the seller. The escrow agent may be instructed to record the deed in favor of the purchaser as soon as the purchaser deposits the money, even before the title to the property is approved. Then, in the event the title cannot be approved, the purchaser is entitled to a return of the purchase money upon reconveying the deed to the seller. A variation of this procedure requires the purchaser to execute a quitclaim deed in favor of the seller and deposit it with the escrow agent at the time the purchase money is deposited and the deed is recorded in favor of the purchaser. In the event that title cannot be approved, the escrow agent is required to record the quitclaim deed and return the purchase money to the purchaser, thus returning the parties to their previous position.

The real estate escrow device is not confined to money transactions but may also be used when the seller and purchaser are merely interested in exchanging deeds to real estate.

Case Example

Rocky Hayes owns a five-acre tract of land in Florida and is interested in selling his land and moving to Colorado. Johnny Ruskin owns a five-acre tract of land in Colorado and is interested in moving to Florida. A real estate broker brings the two together, and an even exchange of property is agreed upon. Hayes

Figure 16.1: Escrow Transactions

deposits his deed to the Florida property with Jerry Bloom, a third party, on condition that the Florida deed be delivered to Ruskin upon receipt of the deed to the Colorado property. When Ruskin deposits the deed to the Colorado property, Bloom will deliver it to Hayes and deliver the deed to the Florida property to Ruskin, thus completing the escrow transaction. *See Morris v. Davis, 334 Mo. 411, 66 S.W.2d 883 (1933).*

Advantages of Escrow

The objective of the escrow transaction is to ensure that the buyer is invested with clear title to the property and the seller receives the purchase price. The use of the escrow device in closing sales of real estate enjoys the advantages of convenience and protection against a party's change of mind.

Convenience

Sometimes it is simply inconvenient for parties to be present at a closing. The escrow method of closing enjoys the advantage of facilitating interstate transactions or other closings where it is not feasible for the parties to appear at the closing.

Case Example

Junior Wells, a resident of California, owns farmland in Kentucky that he desires to sell. Senior Johnson, a resident of Kentucky, desires to buy the farmland. The cost of Junior Wells's appearance at a closing in Kentucky is prohibitive. The parties enter into a purchase contract for the sale of the farmland and agree to close in escrow. Wells mails a fully executed deed for his Kentucky farm to Kentucky Loan & Trust Co., which is instructed to deliver the deed to Johnson upon receipt of the purchase price. When Johnson delivers the purchase price, Kentucky Loan & Trust, as previously instructed, delivers the deed to Johnson.

Protection Against a Party's Change of Mind

With the use of the escrow device the closing is less likely to fail because an independent third party is charged with carrying out mechanical details of the transaction. Both buyer and seller are to some extent protected from the other's change of mind. For example, in a conventional closing a seller who has "second thoughts" may refuse to appear at the closing and sign the deed. In an escrow closing, however, even if the seller desires to back out of the transaction, the escrow agent, who is in control of the deed previously deposited, is instruction-bound to deliver it to the purchaser upon the happening of a specified condition. This course may not be altered at the seller's whim.

The escrow device, while avoiding face-to-face contact between parties, also often avoids a confrontation of conflicting interests and personalities. The sale and the purchase of a home in most cases is an emotionally charged transaction. As such it may create a volatile atmosphere for the parties. The slightest innuendo can often trigger a dispute and present unnecessary problems. Since the escrow closing avoids a face-to-face encounter, it prevents this potential problem from arising.

Requirements of an Escrow

In order for a valid real estate escrow to exist, the following ingredients are necessary: valid deed, enforceable contract, delivery, escrow agent, escrow agreement and condition.

Valid Deed

A deed that is the subject of an escrow must be executed properly in accordance with the state law that is applicable to the transaction. A deed lacking the essentials of valid execution cannot be the subject of a valid escrow transaction, and the escrow agent holding such a deed is under an obligation to surrender it to the grantor upon request.

Case Example

John Hines signs a deed and delivers it into escrow. The deed is not witnessed at the time of delivery. State law requires the grantor to "acknowledge the signing of a deed to be his or her voluntary act before two witnesses." The deposit of the deed will not operate as an escrow because it lacks the appropriate attestation. The deed is subject to recall by Hines. *See Collins v. Kares, 52 S.D. 143, 216 N.W. 880 (1927).*

Omission of the grantee's name in the deed does not invalidate the escrow as long as the grantor authorizes the escrow agent to insert the grantee's name. Likewise, failure to include a legal description of the real estate within the deed does not invalidate the escrow if the grantor authorizes the depositary to insert the designated description.

Enforceable Contract

In order for an instrument to operate as a real estate escrow, there must be an enforceable contract between the parties concerning the property. In absence of a valid purchase contract, the deposit of a deed with an escrow agent cannot be the subject of a valid escrow. Consequently, the deed is subject to recall at the grantor's request. This is true even if the deed is signed properly and is in conformity with all the requirements of execution. Since a contract for the sale of real estate is within the Statute of Frauds, there must be a written memorandum to support the contract. An oral contract to sell real estate cannot be the basis of an escrow.

Case Example

Anna Skibosh entered into a land contract with Auto Acceptance for the sale of her premises. Two days later Auto Acceptance assigned its interest in the land contract to Interstate. Interstate then executed a quitclaim deed in favor of Joseph Sorce and delivered it to Auto Acceptance with an attached letter stating that the deed would be held in trust by Auto Acceptance until Sorce paid off certain debts owed to Auto Acceptance.

The land contract was fulfilled, and Skibosh conveyed the property to Auto Acceptance, which conveyed it to Interstate. Sorce's creditors claimed that Sorce was the owner of the property. The court disagreed, and stated as part of its rationale that the escrow of a deed to real estate must be accompanied by an agreement that satisfies the Statute of Frauds and that the letter attached to the deed was insufficient for that purpose. *West Federal Savings & Loan Association v. Interstate Investment, Inc., 57 Wis.2d 690, 205 N.W.2d 361 (1973).*

The deed itself does not ordinarily satisfy the Statute of Frauds, because the essential terms of sale such as price are not normally included in the deed. To insert the required terms in the deed would be a cumbersome departure from acceptable deed drafting. The most common practice is for the seller and the buyer to execute a writing that, independent of the deed itself, satisfies the Statute of Frauds. This is usually the purchase contract.

Delivery

Surrender of possession and control of a document to the third party depositary.

The deed must be delivered to the escrow agent by the grantor or grantor's agent with the intent to surrender possession of the instrument. This surrender is known as the *first delivery*. The grantor must absolutely relinquish control over the deed. In the event the deed is subject to recall by the grantor, delivery has not been accomplished. Accordingly, delivery does not occur until the instrument is beyond the legal power of the grantor to retrieve.

Case Example

Kevin Armstrong, who is afflicted with a serious kidney disorder, deposits a deed with an escrow agent before entering the hospital for surgery. Kevin instructs the depositary to deliver the deed to his sister "in the event I do not survive the operation; otherwise I will pick it up after I am released from the hospital." Since Kevin did not relinquish total control over the document, there was no legal delivery to the escrow agent. *See Gilmer v. Anderson, 34 Mich. App. 6, 190 N.W.2d 708 (1971).*

Escrow Agent

The third party who is the depositary in an escrow transaction.

The deed is delivered to an escrow agent. The escrow agent, designated as an escrowee or escrow holder, represents the interests of both the buyer and the seller. In that sense the escrowee is a double agent who owes a duty to both to act in good faith. The escrow agent has no authority other than that derived by agreement of the parties and is strictly confined to acting in accordance with that agreement. The escrow agent is a conduit bound by the terms of the escrow agreement.

Generally, neither the buyer nor seller should act in the capacity of an escrow agent since the objectivity of either is suspect. Moreover, an escrow held by the grantor violates the principle that control over the instrument must be surrendered. Delivery of an escrow to the grantee raises the question of whether delivery is absolute. As a rule, however, the intention of the grantor governs. If the grantor delivers a deed intended as an escrow to the grantee for purposes of transporting it to a third-party depositary, the grantee is deemed the grantor's special agent for that purpose and delivery to the grantee is incomplete. Nevertheless, most authorities agree that a deed fully executed and delivered as an escrow to the grantee immediately invests title absolutely in the grantee regardless of any stated preconditions.

The traditional rule is that attorneys or agents of either party can not act as an escrow agent because to do so could create a conflict of interest. Some states do, however permit agents of the parties or their attorneys to be escrow agents as long as their capacity as such is not antagonistic to their principal's interest. Although some states expressly permit a real estate broker or salesperson to be an escrow agent, customarily real estate agents avoid this potentially conflicting office.

The escrow agent may not act contrary to the escrow instructions. Deviation from the instructions constitutes a breach of the relationship of trust. In such a case the escrow agent would be liable for any resulting damages.

Case Example

Lon Luebel, escrow agent, delivers a deed to Mike Lerman, grantee, prior to the deposit of the purchase price, a precondition of the instructed delivery. The purchase price is $70,000. Lon is liable to Kim Sipe, the grantor, for damages because he acted contrary to the escrow instructions. *See Allen v. Allen Title Co., 77 N. M. 796, 427 P.2d 673 (1967).*

Sometimes an escrow agent is charged with delivering the deed to the grantee and the purchase price to the grantor when a title check proves that the title is free and unencumbered. If a title check shows that the title is not free and clear, the escrow agent must return the deed and purchase money to the respective parties. If the escrow agent instead tenders the purchase money to the grantor, the escrow agent will be liable to the grantee for the purchase price. However, a deviation that results in no damages does not result in escrow agent liability.

Case Example

The purchaser failed to provide evidence of fire insurance prior to an escrow closing contrary to the terms of the escrow agreement. Nonetheless, the escrow agent closed the transaction, delivering the deed to the buyer and the money to the seller. The lender objected to the closing and sought damages. The property did not burn. The California Court of Appeals, finding for the defendant, affirmed language of the trial court, which said "The court . . . cannot find that the failure to comply with the written instructions concerning the beneficiary settlement, [resulted in any] . . . [damages]." See *Claussen v. First American Title Guaranty Co., 186 Cal. App. 3d 429, 230 Cal. Rptr 749 (Cal App. 1986).*

In an escrow transaction property comes into the hands of an escrow agent who is in a relationship of trust to the parties involved in the sale. If the escrow agent unauthorizedly converts the property to personal use, by most state standards the escrow agent is guilty of a crime.

An escrow agent should open up an escrow account to receive funds related to the escrow transaction. Commingling of escrow funds with personal funds of the escrow agent may result in liability. However, sometimes an escrow agent is authorized to maintain the delivered funds in a personal bank account. In that case it is extremely important for the escrow agent to keep an account balance at least equal to the amount of the escrow funds. Otherwise the escrow agent is deemed to have converted the monies to personal use and is guilty of a crime.

When an escrow agent embezzles escrow funds, either the buyer or the seller bears the loss. The rule of law is that the party who was entitled to the funds at the moment of conversion is the one who must bear the loss. If the condition under which the purchase money was to be held in escrow was performed, then the loss falls upon the seller since the seller was entitled to the money. Until the happening of the condition, the loss falls upon the buyer since the legal right to receive the funds has not passed to the seller. The next case illustrates these principles.

Asher v. Herman
49 Misc. 2d 475, 267 N.Y.S. 2d 932
(Sup. Ct. App. Div. 1966)

Background: Pursuant to the terms of a real estate purchase contract, the purchaser left a deposit with Irvin Dickman, the escrow agent and the seller's attorney. Dickman embezzled the funds. The buyer sought the deposit from the sellers.

Decision: The Appellate Division of the Supreme Court of New York entered judgment in favor of the defendants.

Justice Shapiro

The question posed for decision in this case is who, as between the plaintiffs (vendees) and the defendants (vendors) must suffer the loss of moneys deposited by the vendees under real estate contract with an escrowee who has converted the funds to his own use.

. . .

The contract of purchase sale provided that "The seller shall give and the purchaser shall accept a title such as the Security Title and Guaranty Company will approve and insure."

It is undisputed that at the time of the closing the vendors were unable to deliver to the plaintiffs a good and marketable title by reason of the fact that a New York Estate Tax against a party in the chain of title had not been fixed and paid nor had an order of exemption been obtained.

The Security Title and Guaranty Company refused to approve and insure title to the premises by reason of the outstanding estate tax except that it would insure against collection out of the premises up to a sum not exceeding $797. This was unacceptable to the vendees. An offer by the vendors to deposit a specific sum of money as security for the payment of the estate tax was likewise rejected by the vendees. In refusing to accept such an arrangement, the vendees were within their rights, since no one could foretell whether the deposit would be ample. In any event, the vendors could not deliver a title which the Security Title and Guaranty Company would "approve and insure" and, since no request was made by the vendors for an adjustment to perfect their title, the plaintiffs were entitled to receive back the moneys deposited by them under the contract.

The vendees contend that since the escrowee was the attorney for the vendors it is they, the vendors, who must suffer the loss. . . .

Where in light of the general principles above set forth, should the result of the escrowee's dereliction fall? . . .

. . .

The rule . . . seems to be well settled and generally applied that if property is embezzled or lost by an escrow holder, the loss, as between seller and buyer, falls on the one who owned the property at that time. In this case the vendors were never entitled to receive the moneys deposited in escrow because they never had a title which the plaintiff's were obligated to accept. Under the circumstances, the escrow moneys at all times remained the property of the plaintiffs-vendees. When they were embezzled, it was the property of the plaintiffs that was embezzled and they are the ones that must suffer the loss.

. . .

The plaintiffs . . . contend that the clause in the contract which provides that,

"In the event that the seller is unable to convey title in accordance with the terms of this contract, the sole liability of the seller will be to refund to the purchaser the amount paid on account of the purchase price and to pay the net cost of examining the title, which cost is not to exceed the charges fixed by

the Security Title and Guaranty Company, and upon such refund and payment being made, this contract shall be considered canceled.",

specifically imposes upon the defendants "the liability to refund the down payment to the plaintiffs" and that by agreeing to this clause, the defendants became a guarantor of the escrow agent, who was also their attorney.

The clause in question is the stock clause found in a contract for the sale of real estate. It is applicable where the vendor receives the down payment under the contract and is, therefore, obligated upon his default "to refund" it. Such a clause cannot be deemed applicable to a situation where the vendor has nothing "to refund to the purchaser" because he has obtained nothing from the purchaser. It is also obvious that the escrow clause was intended to be solely applicable to the fact situation at bar.

. . .

Judgment is, therefore, directed for the defendants-vendors, dismissing the plaintiffs' complaint on the merits. . . .

Of course an escrow agent who embezzles or otherwise misappropriates funds is liable to the person upon whom the loss falls. As a practical matter, however, it is very difficult to collect against an absconding or incarcerated escrow agent.

Escrow Agreement

An agreement that directs the escrow agent regarding terms and conditions under which the deed or other instruments are to be delivered to the parties and the disposition of the deed or other instruments on default.

The escrow agreement need not be reduced to writing. Even so, in retrospect many buyers and sellers regret their failure to do so. Some lawyers who draft escrow agreements include the terms of the escrow agreement in the purchase contract; others include them in an entirely separate instrument. The escrow agreement should be sufficiently detailed in writing to express the intent of the parties and to cover various contingencies. Some of the terms commonly included within an escrow agreement are:

- Names and addresses of seller, buyer and escrow agent;
- Description of the property that is the subject of the escrow;
- Obligations of buyer and seller regarding the deposit of instruments and money into escrow;
- Directions to escrow agent regarding the recording of the deed and disbursement of the purchase money;
- The specific condition upon which title is to pass;
- Directions to the escrow agent regarding procedure in the event the condition is not met;
- Payment of escrow brokerage and attorney fees, recording charges and other costs; and
- Signatures of the seller, buyer and escrow agent.

The escrow agent is bound by the terms of the escrow agreement and may not deviate from it in any respect. Where a conflict exists between the terms of the purchase contract and the escrow agreement, the agent is bound to follow the instructions contained in the escrow agreement. The escrow agent may not follow oral instructions that contradict the terms of the written agreement. A typical escrow agreement is shown in Figure 16.2.

When the condition upon which title is to pass occurs, the escrow agent must deliver the deed to the grantee. If the condition does not occur, under the terms of the agreement the escrow agent is normally charged with returning the purchase money to the purchaser and redelivering the deed to the grantor.

An escrow agreement is a contract; it is not revocable by any party without the consent of all the parties to the agreement. In the event that one of the parties attempts to revoke and demands the return of the deposit, the escrow agent must ignore the demand. When conflict or doubt as to interpretation of the agreement arises, a judicial declaration should be sought.

Under the Federal Rules of Civil Procedure as well as many state laws whose civil rules are patterned after the federal rules, an escrow agent who is faced with conflicting claims of liability or ownership may secure a judicial declaration by *interpleading* the claimants. The practical result of this procedure is to force the parties to litigate their rival claims in one court action. The escrow agent becomes a stakeholder who holds the contested property pending the outcome of the lawsuit. The interpleader device is not available to an escrow agent who is guilty of misconduct in the escrow transaction.

Figure 16.2: Escrow Agreement

This agreement is entered into between Rocky Sylvester [hereafter referred to as Seller] and Andora Klimer [hereafter referred to as Buyer]. Whereas the Seller and Buyer have entered into a contract dated May 20, 1993, of which a true copy is attached, for the sale of premises described in Plat Book No. 13, Page 33, Parcel 17 of Wilona Township.

Now, therefore, it is mutually agreed:

That Henry Earnest is hereby appointed escrow agent and empowered to carry said contract and this agreement into effect;

That the Seller will deposit with said escrow agent a deed fo said premises to the Buyer with general warranty that the title is good and unencumbered except use restrictions and easements of record, if any, and taxes and assessments for the year 1993 and thereafter;

That the buyer will deposit with said escrow agent the sum of $125,000, being the balance of the purchase price of $137,500;

That said escrow agent is directed to file said deed for record and make disbursements when the terms of said contract can be complied with, and provided he can furnish to the Buyer a certificate of title showing record title to said premises to be good and unencumbered;

That the escrow agent shall return any deposit if all deposits and requirements necessary to closing are not made within 45 days from this date;

That Seller shall pay for the preparation of deed, the cost of obtaining a certificate of title, and one-half of the costs of the escrow charges;

That Buyer will pay the fees for filing the deed and one-half of the cost of the escrow charges;

That taxes and assessments, prepaid insurance premiums and rents will be prorated as of the date of closing, and no adjustments are to be made by the escrow agent for water or other utilities.

Dated this 20th day of May, 1993.

_____   _____
Seller   Buyer

_____
Escrow Agent

Condition

Before an instrument can be considered an escrow, its deposit with the escrow agent must be coupled with the depositor's intention that it not take effect until the happening of a specified condition. This condition is essential in order to suspend passage of the instrument to the buyer. If there is no specified condition, then delivery of a fully executed deed to the escrow agent immediately vests title in the purchaser.

The escrow may be used to require any number of conditions to attach before the deed and purchase money pass to the respective parties. Buyers' conditions may include, for example, conditioning the passage of title on the buyer's obtaining financing, making payment of the purchase price, selling a house or securing a zoning change. Sellers' conditions may include, for example, providing evidence of title, proof that the property is free from wood-destroying insect infestation or proof that the electrical system in the house is free from defects. Before the grantee is entitled to delivery of the deed, the specified condition must occur. Until such occurrence, the legal title to the deed remains with the seller. In the event the depositary delivers the deed over to a grantee prior to the happening of the condition, no title actually passes since the delivery is unauthorized.

Title Passage

In a completed escrow transaction there are two deliveries. The first delivery is accomplished when the grantor surrenders control over the deed and delivers it to the escrow agent. The second delivery occurs when the escrow agent surrenders the deed to the purchaser after the occurrence of the condition. As soon as the condition occurs upon which the escrow is predicated, the grantee is entitled to delivery of the escrow. The trend in authority is that title actually passes to the grantee when, pursuant to the escrow agreement, the grantee is entitled to the delivery.

Relation Back

A legal doctrine whereby the title acquired by a deed relates back to the moment of the first delivery to an escrow agent.

In some instances the *second delivery* of the deed is accounted as taking effect as of the time of the first delivery to the agent. This doctrine of relation back is applied when an event that would otherwise thwart the intent of the parties or cause a manifest injustice intervenes between the first and second deliveries.

Death and Disability

The doctrine of relation back avoids complications that might normally arise where death or insanity of the grantor intervenes between the first and second deliveries. The death of the grantor whose deed is held in escrow does not invalidate the escrow. Upon the happening of the escrow condition the grantee is entitled to delivery. The delivery relates back in time to the original moment of transfer to the escrow agent. Under this doctrine of relation back, title passage is deemed to have occurred while the grantor was living. Similarly, if after the delivery of a deed in escrow the grantee dies, the grantee's representative will be entitled to delivery upon the happening of the condition. Under the doctrine of relation back, the passage of title is deemed to have occurred at the time of the first delivery, during the life of the grantee.

Case Example

Birdie H. Fuqua executed a contract for the sale of a 50-acre tract of property to Selected Lands Corporation (SLC). Shortly thereafter she signed a deed and placed it in escrow. Under the terms of the agreement the escrow agent was to deliver the deed to SLC when SLC's attorney approved the closing papers. Before the approval Birdie died. Thereafter the attorney approved the papers. The court held that the death of the grantor did not invalidate the instrument and that upon the occurrence of the condition the grantee was entitled to the deed. Under the doctrine of relation back, title would be deemed to pass as of the date of the first delivery. *Fuqua v. Fuqua, 528 S.W.2d 896 (Tex. Civ. App. 1975).*

The doctrine of relation back is similarly applicable to a case where the grantor becomes insane or otherwise incompetent to effect a transfer after delivering the deed to the escrow agent but before delivery to the purchaser. Under the doctrine, upon the happening of the condition, the grantee is entitled to passage of title, which is deemed to have occurred on the date of the first delivery, thus avoiding frustration of the intent of the parties.

Dower

The doctrine of relation back may protect the purchaser from dower claims in the seller's wife where the wife of a deceased seller had no dower expectancy at the time the deed was deposited into escrow. This may occur as a result of a marriage by the seller after delivery of the deed into escrow but before the second delivery to the purchaser. In such a case, upon the happening of the condition the title passage relates back to the date of the first delivery; consequently, the seller's wife has no dower interest.

Case Example

Seth Nathan, unmarried, executes a deed and deposits it in escrow. The escrow agent is directed to deliver the deed to the buyer when the buyer secures financing and deposits the purchase price. Before the deposit of the purchase price Seth marries; thereafter, the buyer deposits the purchase price. Seth's wife refuses to release dower interests in the property. Regardless, the escrow agent is charged with conveying the deed to the grantee, who takes possession free of spousal interests pursuant to the doctrine of relation back.

Intervening Liens

Application of the doctrine of relation back may avoid problems caused by liens, encumbrances and judgments that attach between the time of the first and second deliveries. When a seller conveys title by deed to a third party who has knowledge that the deed is the subject of an escrow, the doctrine of relation back normally protects the original purchaser. Under this doctrine the purchaser is deemed to have taken title at the first delivery; consequently, the seller was without power to convey good title to the third party. If the third party is a bona fide purchaser for value without notice that the instrument is the subject of an escrow, however, the courts are less likely to apply the doctrine to defeat the third party's title. The same rules apply where the grantor creates an encumbrance on the property during escrow. If the lienholder is without knowledge of the escrow, the lienholder has priority. Otherwise the doctrine of relation back will protect the grantee since the grantor's title is deemed cut off at the time of the first delivery.

Other Uses of Escrow

Two other uses of escrow are notable. They are the long-term escrow and the mortgage escrow.

Long-term Escrow

The long-term escrow is a tool for financing a real estate transaction. A long-term escrow may range in duration from a year to 30 or more years. It is actually a combination of the land installment contract and the escrow.

A buyer may not be in a position to borrow funds. Nonetheless, a seller may desire to sell the land to such a purchaser by requiring installment payments. To secure the payment of the purchase price, the seller may withhold the deed from the buyer until the final installment is paid. Under such an arrangement the seller delivers into escrow a fully executed deed with instructions to the escrow agent to deliver the deed to the buyer upon full payment of the purchase price.

Case Example

Jake Rubin owns 50 acres of farmland that has been on the market for two years, listed at $100,000. Lance Lane desires to buy the land but is unable to obtain financing from a lending institution. Rubin and Lane enter into a land installment contract whereby Lane pays $10,000 down and agrees to pay the remaining $90,000 over nine years at 15 1/4 percent interest. Rubin executes the deed in favor of Lane and deposits it with Fidelity Trust Co., an escrow agent that is directed by the terms of the escrow agreement to deliver the deed to Lane upon receiving receipts evidencing that the purchase price has been paid in full. Rubin does not have control over the deed as long as Lane does not default on the terms of the installment contract. After nine years of timely payments, Lane is entitled to the deed. *See Beren Corp. v. Spader, 198 Neb. 677, 255 N.W.2d 247 (1977).*

If a purchaser fails to make the timely payments, the escrow agent is normally charged with returning the deed to the seller pursuant to the escrow agreement.

One major disadvantage of the long-term escrow is risk; the buyer takes a chance that the seller will convey the property by deed to another or mortgage the land in an amount that would interfere with the buyer's equity in the property. Since the seller remains the titleholder of record, a bona fide purchaser for value without notice of the contract may take from the seller and defeat the buyer's interest. However, if the installment buyer is in possession, then the purchaser has constructive notice of the buyer's interest and would not take good title. The installment buyer may also be protected by recording the land installment contract. This would be sufficient to give notice to subsequent grantees or mortgagees and thus protect the contract buyer. In fact, many states require a land installment contract to be recorded.

Mortgage Escrow

A mortgagee may desire to set up an escrow in order to be protected. In this event the money to be lent to the mortgagor is deposited in escrow, awaiting proof that there are no outstanding liens on the property. Upon such assurance the mortgage can be recorded and the funds released to the mortgagor as directed; the mortgagee is secure as a first lienor. The surrender of the money into escrow is deemed to be the creation of a debt, which is necessary for a mortgage to be a valid lien on property.

Summary

The escrow is a deed delivered by a third party, or escrow agent, when a specified condition is met. *Real estate escrows* are alternative means for transferring title to property. In an escrow transaction the buyer and seller do not meet face to face at the closing. The escrow closing is distinguished from the escrow account, also common in real estate practice, in which the mortgagor pays a monthly amount to the mortgagee to cover property taxes.

Escrow may be chosen as a transfer device for reasons of convenience or to assure that neither party backs out of a transaction. Six ingredients must be present for a valid escrow to exist: a valid deed, an enforceable contract, *delivery,* an *escrow agent,* an *escrow agreement* and one or more conditions. The escrow agent has a fiduciary duty to the buyer and seller and must not act contrary to specific instructions. For example, an agent who converts funds or property to his or her own use without authorization is guilty of embezzlement. It is very difficult to collect against an agent who has absconded even when embezzlement can be proven. For this reason the attorney or other party who is to act as escrow agent must be chosen with care. Further, it is good practice to express an escrow agreement in writing, with all terms and conditions clearly stated.

The legal doctrine of *relation back* applies in real estate escrow transactions. It states that the title acquired by a deed relates back to the moment of the first delivery to an escrow agent. Therefore, the death of the seller before the purchase price is paid by the buyer does not invalidate the deed. The doctrine also applies if the seller becomes insane or otherwise loses legal capacity to contract.

Another use of the escrow device is the long-term escrow, which resembles a land installment contract; the deed is held by an escrow agent until the final installment is paid. Finally, the mortgage escrow, another variation, may be used to protect the mortgagee.

Review and Discussion Questions

1. Name the parties to an escrow transaction and describe the flow of documents.

2. What are the advantages of an escrow transaction?

3. Name the six requirements of an escrow and briefly describe each.

4. What are the responsibilities of an escrow agent?

5. Name some conditions upon which an escrow may be predicated.

6. When does the loss due to embezzlement of funds held by an escrow agent fall upon the seller?

7. Describe the doctrine of relation back and give some examples as to how it affects the buyer.

8. What is a long-term escrow and when is it used?

Case Problems

1. Mary Jackson executed a deed in the name of her son Clarence. She placed the deed in escrow and instructed the escrow agent to deliver the deed to Clarence after the latter paid a specified sum to each of his siblings. Mary died, and Clarence tried to make the specified payments. His siblings refused to accept payment and claimed that the deed was ineffectual since the escrow condition was not met before Mary's death. (a) Why do you think that Clarence's siblings refused to accept the payment? (b) What doctrine can Clarence rely upon in his attempt to establish the existence of a valid contract? (c) What is the theory behind this doctrine and how will it help Clarence? *See Jackson v. Jackson, 67 Or. 44, 135 P. 201 (1913).*

2. Tillie Ganser entered into a contract with her four children whereby Tillie agreed to convey a specified tract of land to each child upon the payment by each child of a specified sum. It was agreed that an escrow would be used to handle the transaction. Tillie deposited four valid deeds with the escrow agent, but before any of the children paid the agent the amount due under the contract, Tillie died. Tillie's executor seeks to set aside the land sales as mere offers revoked by Tillie's death. (a) Will the executor be able to set aside the contracts for the sale of the land? Explain. *See Ganser v. Zimmerman, 80 N.W.2d 828 (N.D. 1956).* (b) Would the following fact pattern present a different result? Tillie deposited four valid deeds, executed in the names of each of her four children, with her attorney, accompanied by instructions to convey the deeds to her children when all contracts for the sale of the property were negotiated. Before any contracts could be negotiated, Tillie died. *See Merry v. County Bd. of Educ., 264 Ala. 411, 87 So.2d 821 (1956).*

3. Ellen Love deposits a fully executed deed in escrow. Pursuant to a purchase contract and escrow instructions, the deed is to be delivered to Sarah Gibson when the zoning of the property is changed from residential to commercial.

After the zoning change occurs, but before the escrow agent delivers the deed to Gibson, a judgment creditor of Gibson seeks to levy on the property. Will the judgment creditor be successful? Explain. *See Sturgill v. Industrial Painting Corp., 82 Nev. 61, 410 P.2d 759 (1966).*

4. Robert O'Neal agreed to sell to Thomas Ryan a parcel of land. The parties agreed to handle the transfer through an escrow agent. According to the escrow agreement, O'Neal was to deposit a valid deed executed in Ryan's name with the escrow agent. The agent was to deliver the deed to Ryan when Ryan deposited $12,000 with the escrow agent. Before Ryan or O'Neal performed his obligations under the agreement, O'Neal informed the escrow agent that the property was worth much more than $12,000 and that O'Neal would not deliver the deed unless Ryan paid $13,000. (a) Since neither party has performed his contractual duties, can O'Neal alter the terms of the escrow agreement? Why or why not? (b) What if Ryan agrees to the additional amount? Does that change the result? *See Gelber v. Cappeller, 161 Cal. App. 2d. 113, 326 P.2d 521 (1958).*

5. The Caulfields entered into a contract to purchase property owned by the Freddie Thomas Foundation, Inc., with a condition that the contract was subject to "the necessary Supreme Court approval authorizing this conveyance." The deed and closing papers were held in escrow, pending the Court's approval. The Caulfields took possession of the property on October 1. On October 4, the premises were partially destroyed by fire. Court authorization for the sale was obtained on October 29. Under the purchase agreement the risk of loss was to remain with the seller until the "closing." Whose insurer (the buyer's or the seller's) is responsible for the loss? Explain. *Caulfield v. Improved Risk Mutuals, Inc. 486 N.Y.S. 2d 531 (Sup. Ct. App. Div. 1985).*

6. Maxum and Nelson reached a tentative agreement for the exchange of a parcel of land owned by Nelson for a parcel owned by Maxum. Maxum had not seen the Nelson property, located in a distant state, and so planned to visit the site before consummating the deal. Before leaving, Maxum deposited a valid deed to his property with Wallace. Maxum instructed Wallace that if he found the property suitable he would write to Wallace and direct him to deliver the deed to Nelson. The delivery of Maxum's deed was contingent on Nelson delivering the deed to his land to Wallace. Nelson delivered his deed to Wallace. Maxum, after examining the property, found it unsatisfactory and promptly wrote to Wallace, instructing him not to deliver the deed to Nelson. Nelson objected to Maxum's action. Nelson claims that a valid escrow agreement was formed and, upon the tender of his deed to Wallace, Wallace was bound to deliver the Maxum deed to Nelson. Is Nelson correct? Discuss. *See Nelson v. Davis, 102 Wash. 313, 172 P. 1178 (1918).*

7. Mr. Konopka and Mr. Zaremba negotiated a contract for the sale of Konopka's residence to Zaremba. The parties agreed to establish an escrow account

with Ms. Wourms, Konopka's real estate agent. The escrow agreement required that Zaremba immediately deposit a down payment of $2,500 with Wourms, which he did. The ultimate sale of the residence was contingent on Zaremba's obtaining a mortgage loan of $20,500. Zaremba obtained the loan, at which time Konopka requested delivery of the down payment from Wourms. Wourms admitted that she was unable to deliver the money because she had used the money to pay her business creditors. Konopka refused to close the deal until Zaremba paid the contract price to him. Zaremba contended that he owed the contract price less the $2,500 he had already paid to Wourms. (a) Who was right? Upon whom did the loss of the money fall? Why? (b) Was it relevant that Wourms was employed by Konopka to act as his real estate agent? Explain. *See Zaremba v. Konopka, 91 N.J. Super. 300, 228 A.2d 91 (1967).*

17

Recording

Recording Statutes

Laws that require the entry into books of public record the written instruments affecting the title to real property.

Under common law, deeds and other instruments affecting the title to real property were not *recorded,* or officially entered into the public records. Problems arose for the owners when they lost or misplaced these deeds and other documents. Even more important, third parties had no way of knowing that a prior transaction had taken place. The person making a conveyance to an innocent third party may have previously conveyed to another and therefore had nothing to give to this subsequent party. These difficulties gave rise to the need for recording statutes. *The primary intent of these statutes is to protect third persons by giving them notice that a prior transaction has occurred.*

The recording statutes have been adopted by all states and provide a means for notifying third parties as to the ownership or other interests existing in a given parcel of land. The recording takes place when a deed, mortgage, easement or other legal instrument affecting the title to land is copied into the public record so that interested persons can discover the status of the title to the land. All entries regarding that title comprise the title history, also known as the *chain of title.*

Many centuries ago land could be transferred by a symbolic gesture, such as the giving of a handful of soil or a wild rose branch. Since England enacted the Statute of Frauds in 1677, however, a transfer of an interest in land must be in writing to attain legal recognition. The written document serves as proof of the transfer between the parties to the transaction—the buyer and the seller—and to anyone else who is aware of the writing. However, a prospective buyer unfamiliar with this transfer would have only the word of the seller as assurance that it did not take place. The buyer or the buyer's attorney can gain certainty about this transfer by referring to the public records to find the recording of the transaction. If the transaction is duly recorded, one can rely on it with relative safety. (Limitations on reliance upon the recording will be discussed later.) If the public records do not reveal the transaction, the prospective buyer would normally choose not to buy the parcel. The risk is that the seller is not telling the truth or that some other interest is outstanding in the land. To take a conveyance under these circumstances is to invite a lawsuit; under normal conditions it is too great a risk to the buyer. Thus the purpose of the recording act is to give to the prospective buyer and to the public *legal notice* of the status of a particular property.

Legal Notice

A knowledge of another's interest in real property sufficient to make the adverse interest legally binding to the prospective purchaser or any other party acquiring interest in the property.

The public recording gives legal notice to third persons as to the existence of a transaction. Under the principle of *caveat emptor,* a prospective buyer or lender is charged with the responsibility of determining whether or not the seller holds title to the property and whether or not there are any encumbrances that would adversely affect the title. If an individual has legal notice of a defect or an encumbrance before acquiring an interest, he or she takes *title subject to those prior rights.* Legal notice may take the form of actual notice, implied notice or constructive notice.

Actual Notice

Title information that is acquired personally by the interest holder.

A prospective purchaser may gain information from the seller or from other parties and from firsthand observation of the property.

Case Example

McCredy is negotiating an agreement to purchase Nagy's summer home. When McCredy inspects the premises, he finds several neighbors have been using a well on the property. If the neighbors have acquired and recorded an easement, that fact will appear on the record. If no easement is on the record, the users may have a prescriptive easement; that is, one imposed by law based on the extended use of his neighbors. If so, McCredy has actual notice of their easement.

An agreement between two parties gives *actual notice* to these two parties even if it is not recorded. However, unless a third party has actual notice of the parties' interests, an unrecorded deed gives no legal notice to the third party. Likewise, when a prospective purchaser is shown a house that is being occupied by someone other than the seller, the purchaser is put on notice that the occupant may have some kind of interest. The purchaser is thus obligated, under the theory of actual notice, to ascertain the status of this third party.

Implied Notice

Legal notice that is imposed by the law when conditions exist that would lead a reasonable person to inquire further into the condition of the title.

If a prospective interest holder has implied notice of a possible claim, he or she is said to have legal notice of any interest that would be discovered during the course of a reasonable inquiry into the condition of the title. *Failure to pursue such an investigation does not exempt the interest holder from notice.*

Implied notice occurs in some states when the conveyance of property by quitclaim deed is a release of rights rather than a conveyance. In such states, *use of a quitclaim deed is considered to give the purchaser implied notice that there may be defects in the title.* In states where a quitclaim deed is considered a conveyance, no legal notice of adverse claims is implied merely by the existence of that type of deed.

Constructive Notice

The knowledge of certain facts that might be discovered through a careful inspection of public records, provided that such information is within the history of title, or discovered through an inspection of the premises.

Under the concept of constructive notice, a prospective interest holder is considered to have legal notice of any information recorded within the history or chain of title, *whether or not that individual has actual notice of the existence of the document.*

Constructive notice also charges the prospective interest holder with any information contained within recorded documents. In addition, a person has constructive notice of all facts that would be revealed by an inspection of the property. For instance, constructive notice of an easement exists for a plainly visible drainage ditch that crosses the property. Notice occurs even if the person never visits the property or examines the public records, which may or may not reveal the existence of the easement.

Case Example

Sebastian leased land to Conley, who recorded the lease. The lease was for oil and gas exploration. Although the description in the lease was inaccurate, it did designate the land. Later Sebastian leased what he thought was adjoining land to Loeb. Part of the land leased to Loeb was the Conley parcel. Claiming that the record provided constructive notice of his interest, Conley sued to prevent Loeb from using the land. Both the lower court and an appellate court agreed that Loeb had constructive notice of Conley's interest and ordered Loeb to allow Conley access to the tract.

The appellate court stated as follows:

> The constructive notice furnished by a recorded instrument, insofar as the boundary of the land and every other material fact recited therein is concerned, is equally as conclusive as would be actual notice acquired by a personal examination of the recorded instrument, or actual notice acquired by or through other means. Every person must take notice of its contents to the same extent as if he had personal knowledge of every fact that it recites. This is the very purpose of our recording law. *Loeb v. Conley, 160 Ky. 91, 169 S.W. 575 (1912).*

In addition to notice of all items contained in the public records, prospective interest holders are also considered to have constructive notice of all taxes that attach to the property.

Types of Recording Statutes

The recording statutes vary markedly from state to state, although all have a similar purpose. They are designed to give notice to parties who are considering acquiring an interest in land. Reliance upon a warranty given in the deed is inadequate. The warranty gives the buyer the right to a lawsuit for damages, but not to the land in which he or she is primarily interested. The two general types of recording statutes are race-notice and notice.

Race-Notice Statutes

Statutes that provide that a subsequent buyer will prevail only if he or she has no notice of the prior transaction at the time of conveyance and he or she records first.

Under these statutes the subsequent taker must get to the recorder's office before the predecessor does.

Case Example

Nagy conveys Laneacre to McCredy. Later, to acquire funds for his permanent relocation to South America, Nagy conveys Laneacre to Brennan. Brennan knows of the prior conveyance to McCredy, but a check of the record indicates that McCredy has not recorded his deed. Brennan decides to take the proffered conveyance and beat McCredy to the recorder's office.

Brennan would prevail if he recorded before McCredy and if he had no idea that Nagy had previously conveyed Laneacre to McCredy.

Notice Statutes

Statutes that provide that the subsequent buyer prevails over all interested parties who have not recorded their interest at the time the buyer accepts the conveyance and pays consideration for the land without notice of the preexisting conveyance.

There is no *race* under these statutes. So long as the subsequent buyer takes without notice of the previous conveyance, he or she prevails over the previous conveyance. It is irrelevant that the first deed holder records thereafter or the subsequent buyer never records.

Case Example

On May 9, 1860, Dignowitz executed a deed to McMillan for land in San Antonio. The deed was signed by Dignowitz's wife, who testified that she did not know whether it was delivered to McMillan, but she assumed that it was. This deed was not recorded until 1889.

In 1875, several years after the death of her husband, Mrs. Dignowitz conveyed the land to the City of San Antonio. Shortly thereafter the city conveyed the parcel to the United States, to be a part of a military reservation. At the time, the mayor of San Antonio orally mentioned a possible outstanding claim; but after an exhaustive search of the record, the attorney for the United States approved the title.

In a claim against the United States for trespass brought in 1889, the U.S. Supreme Court stated, "The inevitable conclusion as a matter of law is that the United States acquired a good and valid title, as innocent purchasers for valuable consideration, and without notice of a previous conveyance to McMillan." The Supreme Court did not consider the oral mention by the mayor of an outstanding claim as actual notice of the preexisting conveyance. *Stanley v. Schwalby, 162 U.S. 255 (1896).*

It may seem unfair for the law to permit Dignowitz to make multiple conveyances of the same property. Theoretically, she no longer owns the property after the initial conveyance to McMillan and should be powerless to convey anything to San Antonio. This would be the case under the common law. Nevertheless, the impact of the recording statutes is to pry that title loose from McMillan and other nonrecording takers and to vest it in subsequent takers like the City of San Antonio.

The recording statutes are chiefly geared to protect good-faith purchasers for value. Consequently, these statutes do not afford protection to persons who acquire the land through gift or inheritance. To attain the protection of the statutes, the purchaser must give consideration, that is, a value of some sort. The value need not be equal to the fair market value of the premises, but neither can it be nominal or merely recited in the deed without actual payment. It must be a real value.

The Recording Process

Although the name of the specific office and official will differ, deeds are recorded at a county office created for that purpose. The recorder will be authorized under state law to record deeds, mortgages, easements, contracts for sale and, in some states, leases and any other transactions affecting the title to land. In addition, the recorder or some other county official will record notices of judgments, secured transactions, pending litigation, inheritance taxes and other dealings that may also encumber the free transfer of land. Each document either conveys a part of the owner's property rights or creates an encumbrance or lien on the parcel.

Case Example

George sells the western half of Laneacre to Herman. In the deed of conveyance George grants an easement to Herman to use George's driveway to get to and from the garage. To purchase the land, Herman borrows money from the bank and executes a mortgage for the western half of Laneacre to the bank in order to secure the loan. The deed conveys title to half of Laneacre and conveys an easement to Herman to use a part of the other half, and the mortgage to the bank is a lien on Herman's portion of Laneacre. Each of these documents is recorded to secure the rights of the party receiving an interest thereunder.

The early recordings under the recording statutes were handwritten, verbatim accounts of the deed or other instrument. Later these recordings were typed, and today they are in large measure photocopies of the original documents. The document presented for recording must be the original.

The recording process begins with the presentation of the instrument to the recorder, usually by the party seeking protection (for example, the buyer in a sales transaction). Upon payment of a recording fee, the recorder stamps the instrument, showing the precise time it was filed with that office. The instrument is later photocopied and entered into the deed books. These numbered books contain exact copies of all deeds ever filed in that county. Simultaneously, the names of the grantor and grantee are indexed in separate grantor and grantee index books, with a reference to the deed book number and page where a copy of the deed can be found. A similar procedure would be followed if the instrument were a mortgage, easement or other document transferring an interest in the land.

Approximately ten states use a tract index that simplifies the title searching process. In addition to the grantor and grantee indexes, the tract index lists in a single place all the transactions that have occurred affecting the parcel concerning the searcher. Once the correct page is located, all deeds, mortgages and other transactions are listed for the searcher's convenience. The title searcher can rely upon this page (or pages) as containing all the relevant transactions affecting the concerned piece of property.

The act of recording in no way legitimizes an instrument. If a deed is forged or was never delivered, recording will not remove this impediment to its validity.

Chain of Title

The recorded history of events that affect the title to a specific parcel of land, usually beginning with the original patent or grant.

Documents filed at the recorder's office are within the chain of title if they concern the parcel and are recorded during the period in which each grantee has title to the parcel of land. If the title searcher were to begin the search anew today, the chain of title would begin with the present owner's deed (who is also the last grantee of record). That deed would contain a recital stating from whom the present grantee's seller got the parcel. Continuing the example above, the last recorded deed would have as grantor, Herman, to grantee, Isaac, and something like the following: "being all of the same premises conveyed on June 16, 1968, by George to Herman and being contained in Deed Book 202 at page 1121." Normally each deed in the chain of title contains a recital of this nature so that the searcher can trace the title back to the original patent or grant.

The attorney or other agent doing an original title search examines the grantor index from the day the present grantee got the parcel until the day the search is being done, in order to ascertain whether or not the present grantee conveyed any interest in the land to another. He or she follows the same procedure for each preceding grantee, for the period of that grantee's ownership as recited. Any conveyance in the grantor index during this time period must be checked to see whether it affects the concerned parcel. Similarly, the mortgagor index is examined to assure that no mortgage is outstanding against the parcel. The county records must also be examined to determine whether there are any unsatisfied judgments, pending litigation, mechanic's liens or secured transactions against the grantee. Each of these is an encumbrance on the land and normally must be satisfied prior to a buyer's acceptance of the deed.

If every transfer of property involved a title search going back to the original deed, title searches would be cumbersome and expensive. In many states the title is merely reviewed for transactions that have taken place since the last conveyance, inasmuch as the seller will supply his or her search for the previous title history.

Any transaction that is found within the chain of title is deemed to be constructively known by the buyer. Constructive notice is as valid a notice of the status of the parcel as that of which the buyer has personal knowledge. If a recorded transaction does not appear within the chain of title, however, the buyer is not charged with constructive notice of the facts contained therein.

Case Example

In 1984 George conveys to Herman, who does not record the deed. In 1985 George conveys the same parcel to Isaac, who records the deed. In 1986 Herman finally records his deed. Later that year, Isaac enters an agreement to sell the parcel to Jeremy. When Jeremy has a title search done, the deed from George to Herman is not in the chain of title. The title searcher does not examine the records for possible conveyances by George after 1985, when Isaac became the new owner. Since Jeremy is not charged with constructive notice of the deed to Herman, he takes the parcel free and clear of the prior deed to Herman. Herman has the right to sue George for damages but not for title to the land.

Some encumbrances on real estate do not appear in the chain of title, yet the buyer is charged with knowledge of them. These encumbrances include zoning laws, building restrictions, property taxes for the year of sale and subsequent years, and special assessments or taxes.

If the reconstruction of the chain of title reveals a gap or a flaw in the title, then the buyer is excused from the purchase agreement because the seller cannot deliver *marketable* or *unencumbered title* for which the purchaser contracted. A *gap* occurs when the recorded documents do not indicate who owned the parcel during a given period. An example of a *flaw* in the title occurs when the buyer, in the purchase agreement, has been promised an unencumbered fee simple interest and a life estate is found outstanding in the title to the parcel. In either of these situations it is said that there is a *cloud on the title*. A cloud on the title is created whenever doubt is created as to the validity of the grantor's title. The property is unmarketable so long as a cloud on the title exists. If the seller is willing, a *quiet title action* may be brought in order to get a judicial (court) ruling that the title is marketable. The seller joins as defendants all those parties who have a potential interest in the land. The plaintiff-seller requests that the court declare his or her title valid, thereby "quieting title" to the land. The buyer can then rely on the judicial assurances of good title and consummate the deal.

Acknowledgment

A formal declaration by the person who executes an instrument that he or she is freely signing it; this signing is attested to by a public official, usually a notary public.

The recorder does not pass judgment upon the legitimacy of the instrument upon recording it, nor does the fact of recording add any degree of validity to a document that is otherwise defective or void. Most states have, however, established some prerequisites that must be satisfied before a document is acceptable for recording. The chief requirement is that the deed or other instrument be *acknowledged*.

For instance, when preparing the deed, the seller of land may sign the deed and a separate acknowledgment before a notary public. The notary public then indicates in the acknowledgment that he or she has witnessed the seller's affirmation or signature. The witnessing of the signature by a disinterested public official gives reasonable assurance that the signature on the deed is that of the seller and not an impostor. Under the statutes the deed is then acceptable for recording.

It should be noted that in most states the failure to have the deed acknowledged or to meet any other prerequisite for recording prevents the deed from serving as constructive notice to anyone. The rule seems to be overly technical and may be unfair since the subsequent purchaser has notice of the conveyance and yet because of the mistake can ignore it. As a result, some states have passed statutes to the effect that an unacknowledged or mistakenly acknowledged instrument will be notice to subsequent purchasers and to creditors.

The chief importance of the acknowledgment lies in recording, not in conveyancing itself. A deed need not be acknowledged to effectuate a conveyance because title will pass to the grantee upon delivery and acceptance of the deed, whether it is acknowledged or not.

Mistakes in Recording

Errors made by the recorder.

The rule in most states is that a person who has properly presented an instrument for recording has satisfied his or her duty; the instrument will be constructive notice to a subsequent taker. The result is that a mistake made by the recorder initially falls upon the future taker, even though that taker could not have discovered the instrument because of the mistake.

Case Example

Brownstein purchased a parcel of land from Peterson in 1951. In 1962 Brownstein conveyed a 20-foot drainage easement to the city. The city official presented the written easement for recording, but the recorder failed to enter Brownstein's name in the grantor index. In 1986 Brownstein conveyed the parcel to Jackson. Brownstein's conveyance to the city does not appear in the chain of title for the parcel. Jackson has no legal recourse against Brownstein or the city but would be able to recover against the recorder on that official's security bond.

A mistake by the recorder is a difficult dilemma for courts to resolve because neither the party presenting the instrument for recording nor the subsequent taker is at fault. A minority of courts, recognizing that the primary concern of the recording statutes is with good-faith purchasers for value, hold that the subsequent taker does have recourse against the grantor.

Case Example

Brownstein purchased a parcel of land from Peterson and presented the deed for recording. The recorder misplaced the deed and it was never recorded. Brownstein later enters a purchase agreement with Jackson in which he agrees to convey "good and marketable title" to him. When doing the title search, Jackson discovers that the deed by which Brownstein took title is missing. In some states Jackson would have a legal claim against Brownstein for breach of contract.

Regardless of which rule is adopted, the injured party has recourse against the recorder on his or her security bond.

Mistakes in the Instrument

Errors made in the preparation of the instrument to be recorded.

A mistake in the instrument recorded may affect the validity of the notice given. If the mistake is minor, it will not deter the instrument from being legal notice. For example, the grantor's name listed as Franc*is* Brown rather than Franc*es* Brown in a deed would be adequate notice to a third party. However, if the nature of the mistake is such that the instrument would no longer put the third party searcher on notice to inquire further, the instrument will not be constructive notice. Thus, if the grantor's name is George Thomas but is typed in the deed

Thomas George, it will be listed in the grantor index under *G* for George and not *T* for Thomas. This deed will not be notice to a subsequent purchaser.

The following case illustrates a situation in which a failure of the grantees to record their deed did not cause them, or their successors in title, to lose their property interest. Why not? The case raises the issue of notice discussed earlier in the chapter.

Graham v. Lyons
Superior Court of Pennsylvania
546 A.2d 1129 (1988)

Background: In 1952, Paul and Helen Lyons delivered a deed conveying a parcel of land to Mr. and Mrs. Mitchell in exchange for $100. The deed was lost by the Mitchells and never recorded. In 1971, the Mitchells sold the land to Thomas and Laura Graham, who promptly recorded their deed. In 1968, before the Mitchells' conveyance to Grahams, the Lyons reconveyed the same parcel to their four sons. Many years later, the Grahams entered an agreement to sell the parcel, but during the course of the title search, the unrecorded deed was discovered. The Grahams sued the Lyons and their sons in a quiet title action to obtain a declaration from the court that their title was valid so that they could consummate the sale. The trial court decided in favor of the Grahams, and the Lyons appealed.

Decision: The Pennsylvania Superior Court affirmed the trial court judgment.

Judge Del Sole
Appellants (Lyons) who claim to be the rightful owners of the property in question, contend that the trial court erred when it failed to take into account the fact that Mr. and Mrs. Lyons had conveyed the subject property to William H. Lyons, Paul G. Lyons II, Lynn C. Lyons, and Samuel H. Lyons on October 28, 1968, the deed to which was recorded the next day. Appellants maintain that the Pennsylvania Re-

cording Act protects their title since the conveyance was set down in writing and was recorded prior to the transfer of the property to appellees. (Grahams)

The argument advanced by Lyons must be dismissed since it is based on the faulty premise that the subject property was transferred in the 1968 conveyance. The deed conveying property from Mr. and Mrs. Lyons to their sons contains the following reservation:

> ALSO, EXCEPTING AND RE-SERVING five (5) campsites sold by Paul C. Lyons and Helen M. Lyons, his wife, to third parties totalling approximately eight (8) acres, more or less.

A title abstractor who testified at trial performed a title search and indicated that during his examination he discovered four recorded deeds transferring four different campsites. None of the four deeds consisted of a transferred campsite from Mr. and Mrs Lyons to Mr. and Mrs. Mitchell. The trial court concluded that the unrecorded "lost" deed executed in 1952 to Mr. and Mrs. Mitchell was the fifth campsite which was "excepted and reserved" in the conveyance from Mr. and Mrs Lyons to their sons. Although this conveyance was not recorded, the recording of a deed is not essential to its validity or to the transaction of title. The title to real estate may be passed by delivery of a deed without undertaking a recording since the recording is essential only to protect by constructive notice any subsequent purchasers, mortgagees and new judgment creditors. The question of whether Appellants had constructive notice that the property at issue was conveyed to the Mitchells is not at issue since Appellants' deed contains an exception which excludes this property from the description of the land transferred by the Lyons to their sons.

Since the property in question passed by means of a valid conveyance to Mr. and Mrs. Mitchell, who in turn transferred the property to Appellees (Grahams), and since the deed executed in 1968 from the Lyons to their sons excludes from its description the property at issue, the trial court properly ruled in favor of Appellees in this quiet title action.

Order Affirmed.

Assurance of Title

The average real estate buyer is not competent to determine on his or her own the status of the title to the parcel in question. Depending on the state, or often the local or county practice, the attorney hired by the buyer will have to provide evidence of the marketability of the title. This evidence of title may be provided by the lawyer's own research relating to the title. It is more often the case, however, that attorneys retain a title search firm or title insurance company to provide the necessary information. Specifically, evidence of title will be provided by abstract, by title insurance or by certificate.

Abstract of Title

A summary of all the recorded transactions, including deeds, mortgages, judgments and the like, that affect the title to a specific parcel of land.

The title searcher or abstractor will examine the chain of title, making a descriptive notation of all recorded transactions affecting the concerned parcel. Depending on local practice, the abstractor may be required to examine the title back to the original grant or only back to the preceding conveyance. The abstractor prepares for the party employing him or her a document—*an abstract*—that contains a description of the concerned parcel and a brief description in chronological order of all the instruments affecting the land that fall within the chain of title.

Case Example

The abstractor will examine the grantor index for the name George Lang for conveyances between the years 1975 and 1985, the period during which George was the record owner of Laneacre. Having noted the deed book pages of all such conveyances, the abstractor will look at the deeds to see whether they affect Laneacre in any way.

The abstractor similarly examines the mortgagor index and mortgage books for outstanding mortgages. He or she examines other books in search of easements, leases, judgments, mechanic's liens, secured transactions, tax liens and pending litigation. A summary of each of these transactions is provided to the buyer or the buyer's attorney.

Attorney's Opinion

Based on professional judgment, the attorney states his or her opinion as to the condition of the title based on the facts revealed in the abstract. The abstractor makes no assertions as to the quality of the title but merely presents in the abstract the recorded events affecting the parcel. The attorney then examines the abstract and renders a professional judgment as to his or her opinion of title. The attorney does certify that all instruments pertinent to the parcel of land are included in the abstract. In large measure the buyer can be expected to rely on this attorney's opinion of title. However, forged deeds or other errors in recording may well be undetected by the abstractor or attorney, and such imperfections may leave the buyer legally unprotected. Of course, if the abstractor or the attorney is negligent, the buyer would have a right to sue either or both for damages. A judgment for damages, however, is only as good as the ability of the judgment debtor to pay. If the attorney (judgment debtor) is financially sound, the buyer may recover the financial loss resulting from the attorney's professional error. If the attorney is not solvent, however, the money judgment may be uncollectible, and the buyer will not obtain financial satisfaction.

Case Example

Rite hired Pierson, an attorney, to represent him when he purchased Hilltop Acres from Jack Haney. Pierson had performed the title search and provided Rite with an attorney's opinion assuring him that title was transferred to Rite. Mary Haney, Jack's sister, returned to town and asserted an ownership interest in Hilltop Acres. The facts showed that their father left Hilltop Acres "to his children" and that Jack and Mary were his two children. Pierson had negligently failed to determine that Jack Haney, Rite's grantor, was not the only child. Rite may have to buy Mary's interest to get clear title but can then sue Pierson for damages because of his negligence in performing his professional duties. Recovery on the judgment by Rite will depend upon the financial capacity of Pierson to pay.

Title Insurance

A comprehensive indemnity contract that insures the titleholder against title defects and encumbrances that may exist at the time the policy is issued.

To overcome the limitations arising from the methods just discussed, the practice of obtaining title insurance has arisen in many areas of the country. Title insurance has the advantage of insuring against loss caused by forged deeds and other undiscovered errors on the record. In the case of negligence it may also provide more financial security to the grantee-insured than would an individual attorney's opinion on the title. The title insurer pledges itself to defend—in court if necessary—the title of the grantee-insured and will pay for losses up to the maximum amount stated in the policy.

The title policy usually covers forged instruments, undisclosed heirs, misfiled documents, incorrect marital status, confusion over similarity of names, and mistaken legal interpretation of wills. Any of these defects will be defended by the title company.

Though title insurance does alleviate some of the shortcomings of the previous method, it is not a panacea. The title insurance company obtains an abstract of title for its review, and it excepts from its coverage all those defects discovered by the abstractor. In addition to discovered defects, the title policy usually excludes from coverage the rights of parties in possession, taxes and assessments not yet due or payable, zoning and other public regulations and facts that would be revealed by a survey of the parcel.

Case Example

Bloom purchased a title insurance policy when he obtained his parcel of land from Cedeno. Bloom can feel confident that, if a deed in his chain of title described the grantor as single but his wife has suddenly been discovered, the insurer will pay off the wife up to the maximum policy amount. However, if the description of the parcel contained in the deed is unclear as to where the property line lies or the right of a neighbor to use a "common" driveway, his title policy will exclude these discovered defects from its coverage. Prior to the conveyance of the parcel, Bloom will have to decide whether or not he can live with these discovered defects.

The single-payment title policy will benefit the titleholder and his or her heirs or devisees. Coverage will continue until the titleholder or those heirs or devisees convey the property to another party. In short, courts have held that the title insurance coverage does not run with the land but ends when the interest of the insured terminates. Thus, a seller cannot transfer title insurance to a buyer.

Torrens Certificate

A document issued under the Torrens system, a type of land title registration.

In states where the Torrens system exists, it is not compulsory and exists along with the recording system previously described. The advantage of the system is that it eliminates the need for a title search, and the Torrens certificate shows the status of the title at any time.

The Torrens system can be used when a landowner applies in writing to the county court to have a title registered. A current title search is made and provided to the court, which holds a type of *quiet title action*. In this action all parties who may have an interest in the parcel are notified and given a chance to be heard by the court. The purpose of the notice and hearing is to obtain assurance that all encumbrances to the title are known prior to issuance of a Torrens certificate. When the court is satisfied that the landowner is the titleholder and that all liens and encumbrances to that title have been revealed, it orders the certificate of title to the parcel to be registered.

Henceforth, the certificate of title will depict the exact state of the title. The original is filed with the recorder, and a copy goes to the owner. A party alleging to have an interest arising prior to the registration of the Torrens certificate will be precluded from attacking the present owner's or any subsequent owner's title unless his or her interest was recorded on the original certificate. To assure that the Torrens certificate is always up to date, any conveyance, mortgage, lien or other encumbrance upon the parcel will not be valid until it is entered on the original certificate. Further, title does not pass until the registration takes place. If there is a defect of title, suit is usually against the state for the loss. A limited state fund is provided for such lawsuits.

As with the normal recording system, under the Torrens system it is usually necessary to go beyond the recorder's office (or the certificate) to determine whether there are unpaid taxes or special assessments, zoning and building restrictions or federal court judgments that may affect the parcel.

For reasons not completely clear, the Torrens system has not been widely used. Perhaps the title searching apparatus already in place has successfully resisted the abolition of the title search. There is also the initial expense of having the title registered and the fact that the system is voluntary, both of which militate against its wide adoption. The Torrens system has been adopted to some degree by 15 states, but it does not seem to be spreading rapidly and is not likely to replace the present recording system in the foreseeable future.

Summary

Recording statutes that govern the recording of transfers of real estate have been adopted by all the states. Their primary intent is to protect buyers of real estate by informing them of the status of a title to the land in question. Each successive act of recording serves as *legal notice* to the public of a transaction that changes the status of ownership.

Legal notice falls into three categories. When information is acquired personally by the interested party, it is called *actual notice*. *Implied notice*, a second type, is imposed by the law when conditions exist that would cause a reasonable person to inquire further. Finally, *constructive notice* occurs when information on record could have been uncovered in a reasonable search.

Statutes governing recording are established and enforced by the states. They can be classed in two types that relate to the priority of ownership of any claimant to the property. The first type, *race-notice statutes*, provide that a subsequent buyer can claim ownership by recording first, but only if he or she had no notice of the prior transaction. *Notice statutes*, the second type, provide that a subsequent buyer takes precedence over an earlier one if the prior transaction was not on record at the time of sale.

Deeds are recorded in numbered books at an office designated for that purpose in the county in which the property lies. Also recorded are liens, judgments or other dealings that prevent free transfer of the land. The attorney or other agent attempting to learn whether a title is marketable refers to the book in which the *chain of title* is recorded. If information is missing from the record or is contradictory, there is said to be a cloud on the title, and title is not marketable. A buyer finding this situation may choose to bring legal action to "quiet" the title.

The average buyer of real estate is not competent to judge the marketability of a title and should employ an attorney or perhaps a title search firm to provide evidence of title—that is, proof of ownership of the parcel. This agent may then provide an *abstract of title*, a summary of all the recorded transactions affecting the title. The buyer's attorney, after examining the abstract, gives an opinion as to whether the title appears to be marketable or whether it contains a flaw or gap. This opinion does not guarantee that the abstract is complete or accurate. To overcome this limitation, the practice of obtaining *title insurance* has gained popularity. This type of policy insures against losses caused by forgeries, undisclosed heirs, misfiled documents, incorrect marital status, confusion caused by similar names and mistaken legal interpretation of wills.

A final type of land registration is the Torrens system, under which the *Torrens certificate* of title status is available. When the certificate is issued and registered, it shows that a court is satisfied with the validity and marketability of the title. Although the Torrens system has been adopted in 15 states, its use is voluntary, and it does not seem likely to replace the present county recording system.

Review and Discussion Questions

1. (a) Explain the purpose of recording statutes. (b) What must a plaintiff establish to be protected by this type of legislation?

2. Define *constructive notice* and explain how it might affect a person who purchases real estate.

3. What is the difference between a race-notice and a notice recording statute?

4. What is a tract index? How does it facilitate the title searching process?

5. Describe the title searching process.

6. What are the prerequisites that must be met for an instrument to be recorded?

7. Explain why title insurance is often advisable even when the grantee receives a warranty deed.

8. What are the limitations in relying upon title insurance for protection?

Case Problems

1. Russell Ulrich claimed ownership to 38 acres of land through a chain of title dating back to a conveyance from the Loefler family to Ulrich's family in

1888. The Loeflers' claim to the land dates to an unrecorded deed prior to 1888. The Pennsylvania Game Commission (Commission) claims ownership to the same parcel through a conveyance from Handwerk. The origin of the problem is due apparently to a change in how land surveyors do surveys. The Commission argues that because the basis of Ulrich's claim is an unrecorded deed, his title is invalid. Does the Commission have a legitimate defense? *Commonwealth v. Ulrich, 565 A. 2d 858 (1989).*

2. In an agreement dated March 9, 1964, Jaynes granted Lawing an option to purchase real property. The option was open for two calendar years. Before the option expired, Lawing took it up, but Jaynes refused to transfer the property. In April 1966, Lawing sued. Lawing's action was awaiting trial in March 1971 when Jaynes conveyed the property to McLean. When Lawing instituted his litigation in 1966, he filed a notice of his claim in the county registrar's office. The notice had been indexed improperly. In a suit by Lawing to have the deed from Jaynes to McLean declared void, what must McLean establish for a successful defense? *Lawing v. Jaynes, 206 S.E.2d 162 (N.C. 1974).*

3. Dowse sold land to Pender by warranty deed dated April 1, 1984. The deed was recorded on June 3, 1984. On May 29, 1984, Dowse fraudulently sold the same land to Petez. Petez recorded his deed on June 4, 1984. Petez had no actual knowledge of the deed to Pender. Between Pender and Petez, who has the superior claim in (a) race-notice jurisdiction (b) notice jurisdiction? Explain.

4. Gagner purchased a parcel of land in 1969 after his attorney provided him with a certificate of title stating that the land was marketable and unencumbered by easements. In fact, a water district had previously been deeded a water pipe easement across the land, but the easement was not recorded until 1973. Although the easement was not in Gagner's chain of title, there were references in the chain indicating that the water district had certain rights in a larger parcel that included Gagner's land. The attorney relied on oral assurances from the seller, Crena, that these references did not affect the Gagner parcel. (a) Is the easement valid as to Gagner? (b) If it is valid, does Gagner have a remedy against the attorney? *See Gagner v. Kittery Water District, 385 A.2d 206 (Me. 1978).*

5. McDaniel discovered the existence of a utility easement along the eastern edge of his property that was not mentioned in his deed or noted in his title insurance policy. Since the title insurance policy purported to guarantee McDaniel fee simple ownership, he sued the title insurance company for the reduction in the fair market value of his land caused by the easement. The utility easement is recorded. Will McDaniel succeed? *McDaniel v. Lawyer's Title Guaranty Fund, 328 So.2d 852 (Fla. 1976).*

6. Nancy McGalin delivered a deed for a parcel of land she owned to her daughter, Annie Drake. Drake recorded the deed; however, the

acknowledgment on the deed was not valid under Texas law. Upon McGalin's death her other children challenged the validity of the conveyance to Drake. They contended that the faulty acknowledgment made Drake's title to the land invalid. Are they correct? *Drake v. McGalin, 626 S.W. 2d 786 (1981).*

Part 4

Financing
the
Transaction

18

Introduction to Mortgage Law

Mortgage

A written instrument that uses real property to secure payment of a debt.

A mortgage is one of the two principal instruments used in a loan transaction in which real estate is the security. The other instrument, the note, is also discussed in this chapter. The purpose of the mortgage is to provide security for payment of the debt. Without the existence of a debt, a mortgage has no effect.

Case Example

Anders Plumbing Company, Inc., owned a valuable building. The company needed money and sold stock to Lance and Jean Billingham. In order to induce the Billinghams to purchase the stock, they were given a mortgage on the property.

Lee Sickles, a contractor, made improvements on the property. When he was not paid, Sickles attempted to enforce a mechanic's lien. The Billinghams argued that their mortgage had priority over the lien. In a suit by Sickles, the court would hold the mortgage invalid because it was not given as security for a debt.

Secured and Unsecured Debts

From the purchase of a family's modest first home to the million-dollar commercial sale, financing is the key to almost every successful real estate transaction. People and institutions lend money because lending is profitable; much of the profitability stems from the risk entailed. A lender's risk is reduced when its loan is secured by property—an automobile, real estate, a firm's inventory or some other kind of valuable asset. When a loan is secured, the lender has a right to sell

355

the security and apply the proceeds against the debt if the borrower fails to pay or violates some other term of the loan agreement. As security, real estate has several advantages over personal property. Mortgages, therefore, increase the attractiveness of lending to individuals and firms having funds available for financing.

Not all loans are secured. Sometimes a lender will advance funds on the basis of the borrower's character and reputation. If the borrower *defaults*—that is, fails to pay according to the terms of the agreement—and the creditor wins a judgment, the creditor has a right to attach the borrower's assets. Claims of a secured creditor take priority over this type of judgment, however.

The true nature of a mortgage, no matter what its form, is to establish a security right against a debtor's interest in real property. Most often the debtor's interest will be fee simple ownership, but legally mortgages may cover almost any interest in real estate that may be sold or assigned. Mortgages may be applied to rental income, life estates, estates for years, remainders and reversions, as well as other valuable property rights. Most of these interests in real estate are seldom the subject of mortgage loans, however, since they are often of limited duration or conditioned upon something that cannot be controlled.

Mortgages are also used sometimes to secure obligations that are quite unrelated to the property mortgaged.

Case Example

Ray Adams wished to go into business for himself as a plumbing and heating contractor. He planned to hire one or two employees and open up a small showroom from which to sell plumbing fixtures. Although Ray had saved enough money to get started, he was advised by some of the manufacturers whose lines he wished to carry that he should have a line of credit with a local bank. Ray's bank was willing to give him a $45,000 line of credit; as security the bank asked for a mortgage against rental property that he owned.

Mortgage, Mortgagor and Mortgagee

Many common terms are not used with the precision they deserve, and the term *mortgage* is one of these. It is often confused with the underlying debt. Each month many people speak about paying "the mortgage," but what they pay is not the mortgage. They pay a debt so that a creditor will not have to turn to the mortgage, which secures the debt.

Many people, even some actually involved in real estate, are troubled by the terms *mortgagor* and *mortgagee*. This confusion arises because they ignore the true nature of the mortgage. They think of the funds the lender is advancing as the mortgage. Naturally then they have a tendency to refer to the lender as the mortgagor, but the funds are not the mortgage. The mortgage is the instrument the borrower gives to create a security right in the lender. The borrower thus is the mortgagor, just as the person who sells a home and gives a deed is the grantor. The mortgagee is the person or firm to whom the mortgage is given. Like the grantee of a deed, the mortgagee is the recipient of an interest in real estate.

Note

A written instrument signed by a borrower containing the provisions of a loan and a promise to repay according to the terms of the agreement between borrower and lender.

In addition to security aspects, mortgage transactions often involve the borrower's personal liability to pay the debt. Usually the borrower makes the commitment by signing a note promising to pay the debt. In some states the borrower signs a bond. The note or bond serves as evidence of the debt for which the mortgage is the security. The typical note contains the amount of the loan, the interest rate and the time and method of repayment as well as the borrower's obligation to pay. This instrument is sometimes referred to as a *promissory note* or *mortgage note*.

The existence of the note provides the lender with two remedies if the debt is not paid: (1) to sue on the note and to obtain a personal judgment against the debtor or (2) to have the real estate sold and the proceeds applied against the debt. If the lender wins a personal judgment on the note, the judgment may be collected by attaching other property of the debtor or by garnishing the debtor's wages. In addition, if the property when sold does not bring enough to pay the debt, a personal action can be brought on the note. A few states require the lender to choose one of the two methods, either to sell the collateral to pay the debt or to sue on the note.

Both note and mortgage are essential to the mortgage transaction. If the mortgage is transferred, the transferee has a right to the note. If the mortgage is invalid, however, the creditor may sue on the note (or bond), since it is a promise to repay the debt.

Title and Lien Theory

The historical theory that the mortgage conveys title to the mortgagee continues to be used in some states, referred to as *title theory* states. Even in these states, however, although the mortgagee acquires title, the mortgagee does not acquire the right of possession unless the mortgagor defaults.

Most states recognize that in reality a mortgage is a lien. It is a device used by debtors and creditors to secure a debt. The mortgagee is interested primarily in having the security sold and the proceeds applied to the debt if the mortgagor fails to pay or violates some other mortgage provision. States taking this position are called *lien theory* states.

In some states that consider the mortgage a lien, the mortgagee of real property has more rights than most other lienholders. Sometimes these rights are very similar to those a title holder would have. For example, in several states by statute the mortgagee is entitled to oust a defaulting mortgagor from possession. Most other types of liens permit the holder only to have the security sold and proceeds applied to the debt. Since vestiges of title theory appear in the law of lien theory states and lien theory remains in some title theory jurisdictions, few states can be classified rigidly. Writers who analyze real estate law have developed a third classification, *intermediate theory* jurisdictions. A more fruitful approach for the real estate practitioner is to recognize that, no matter what form the mortgage takes, the solution to most legal problems of mortgage law is recognition that the mortgage is a security instrument.

Forms and Content of Mortgage

Currently the mortgage most commonly used in the United States is a two-party instrument. By its terms one of the parties, the mortgagor, creates a security interest in property for the other, the mortgagee. Because historically the mortgage was a conveyance, the mortgage often has many provisions similar to those of a deed. In some states it is called a *mortgage deed*. Legislative bodies in a few states have adopted statutory mortgage forms. Although they contain all elements essential to a valid mortgage, use of the statutory form is not required.

In general, for an instrument to be effective as a mortgage, it should include at least the following information:

- names of the parties,

- legal description of the premises,

- language indicating that the instrument is given as security for a debt,

- statement of the debt secured, and

- terms for repaying the debt.

Additionally, the mortgage must be signed by the mortgagor and executed according to the laws of the state in which the property is located. At least between the original parties, the law treats many instruments as mortgages even without such information being contained. If the instrument is not in the proper form, however, the mortgagee often cannot assert it against other creditors, and it may not be recorded.

Most mortgages contain substantially more information than minimal requirements. Because the parties insert many provisions designed to protect their rights, mortgage instruments tend to be lengthy. The recording process is expensive and requires a great amount of storage space. A number of states have adopted statutes that allow mortgagees to record a *master mortgage* containing the desired covenants and clauses. This practice permits execution and recording of a mortgage that incorporates by reference the provisions of the master mortgage. Stated are the recording date, file number, volume and page of the master mortgage.

Default

Nonperformance of a duty or obligation accepted by either party as part of the mortgage transaction.

The mortgagee cannot institute a foreclosure action until the mortgagor defaults. The most commonly recognized default is the failure to pay the interest or principal. Obligations other than the payment of principal and interest found in most mortgages include payment of taxes, assessments and insurance. Often these commitments are worded in such a manner that failure to carry them out constitutes a default. Some mortgage instruments merely give the mortgagee the right to make the payment if the mortgagor fails to do so. The mortgagee can then add the amount to the mortgage debt, but the mortgagee cannot foreclose since there has not been a default.

Many mortgages are worded so that the mortgagor's failure to comply with statutes, ordinances and governmental requirements affecting the premises constitutes default. Other relatively common provisions that can result in default are related to bankruptcy or the mortgagor's failure to keep the property repaired. Some mortgages provide that a mortgagor who files a voluntary petition in bankruptcy or makes an assignment for benefit of creditors is in default. Permitting waste or allowing anything to be done on the premises that weakens the security are additional prohibitions often included in mortgages. If the covenant not to permit waste is breached, the mortgagor is in default.

A critical legal question when default has occurred is the mortgagee's right to collect the entire debt. This problem arises when the mortgagor breaches a covenant that is not related to payment or when the debt is to be repaid periodically and a payment is missed. What can the mortgagee do under these circumstances to protect its investment? The solution to this problem is a clause making the entire debt payable in event of default. This called an *acceleration clause*.

Waiver

The giving up or relinquishing of a known legal right.

Case Example

Brown owed Hewitt $8,500. The debt was evidenced by a note and mortgage containing an acceleration clause and a ten percent penalty for collection fees. Partial payments of $90 were due on the tenth of each month. Over a period of 14 consecutive months Hewitt had accepted overdue payments. In September Brown and Hewitt quarreled. When the October payment was late, Hewitt immediately accelerated the debt, demanding full payment plus the collection fee. Since Brown could not pay the entire debt, Hewitt commenced foreclosure proceedings. Brown's suit to enjoin these proceedings was successful. The court held that Hewitt could not accelerate without notifying Brown of Hewitt's intention to depart from the usual method of dealing between the parties. *Brown v. Hewitt, 143 S.W.2d 223 (Tex. 1940).*

Ordinarily an extension of time given to a defaulting mortgagor to correct the default is not a waiver of the mortgagee's right to accelerate the debt. Similarly, a mortgagee who fails to accelerate because of one default is not precluded from accelerating upon a later default. When the mortgagee continuously accepts late payments, some courts have held acceleration is precluded if the mortgagor makes a late payment in reliance upon the previous course of conduct.

Case Example

Andrew J. Evans and Mary, his wife, executed a $65,626 promissory note secured by a mortgage in favor of C & B Development Company. Interest on the note was payable in installments of $3,281.32. When the Evanses missed an installment, they were given an oral extension of 30 days. The note contained an acceleration clause. When the interest was not paid after 30 days, C & B exercised its option to accelerate. The Evanses argued that, as C & B had not stated that there would be an acceleration should the interest not be paid in the allotted time, the right to accelerate had been waived. Both the trial court and the appellate court rejected this argument. *Evans v. Scottsdale Plumbing Co., 10 Ariz. App. 184, 457 P. 2d 724 (1969).*

Generally, the mortgagee's acceptance of late payments is not a waiver of the right to accelerate for defaults other than those involving the late payment. A mortgagee accepting late payments may stipulate that this action shall not negate rights arising as a result of the default. When there has been a default, a mortgagee who intends to accelerate must immediately notify the mortgagor. This initial step normally must be taken before commencing a foreclosure action.

Equity of Redemption

The right of the mortgagor or another person with an interest in the property to reclaim it after default but before foreclosure.

In both title and lien theory states, the mortgagor has a right to redeem the property after default. Redemption can be accomplished by paying the full amount of the debt, interest and costs. To be effective, the right of redemption must be asserted prior to foreclosure. The purpose of foreclosure is to terminate the equitable right of redemption. Once the foreclosure sale has been confirmed, the mortgagor can no longer redeem the property, except in several states in which statutes provide an additional period. This statutory right of redemption is discussed later in the chapter.

In addition to the mortgagor, other parties having an interest in the property may redeem. Junior mortgagees, tenants under a lease, judgment creditors and grantees who have acquired through the mortgagor have this right. The junior mortgagee who redeems acquires the rights of the senior mortgagee, not title to the premises. A mortgagor redeeming has a superior right. Since the debt has been paid, he or she acquires the unencumbered fee.

The right of redemption is based upon equity's recognition of the mortgage as a security instrument. Although at common law the mortgagee acquired title, equity recognized the true nature of the transaction. It was clear to the courts that the mortgagee was not purchasing the premises but securing a debt. As a result, the mortgagor is entitled to reclaim the title even after default if the debt is paid in full.

Statutory Right of Redemption

The right of a debtor to redeem the property after a foreclosure sale.

Legislatures in more than half the states have provided the mortgagor with a right to redeem after foreclosure. The creation of a statutory right of redemption is generally the result of political pressure by debtors during periods of economic distress. Although the first such statute was enacted in New York, most of the legislation exists in the western states. Agricultural interests have often been behind efforts to establish this right.

The period in which the former mortgagor may redeem varies from state to state. Generally, the period is six months or a year. Laws in some states also give some classes of persons a longer period of time to redeem than others. In a number of states, instead of granting the mortgagor a right to redeem after the foreclosure sale, state laws postpone the sale to provide a longer period of time to pay a debt that is in default. Except in a few states, any attempt by the lender to have the mortgagor waive redemption rights violates public policy and is unenforceable.

Foreclosure of Mortgage

The legal procedure by which a lender has advanced funds with real property as security recovers in the event of default.

In the United States mortgage foreclosure is accomplished in several ways. The two most common methods are judicial foreclosure and power of sale foreclosure. Strict foreclosure, a method important historically, is permissible in a few states.

Judicial Foreclosure

A legal procedure in which a court orders real estate sold to enforce the mortgagee's rights under the mortgage.

Of the several methods of foreclosure, foreclosure by judicial action and sale is the most common. In a few states it is the only method allowed. Judicial foreclosure is favored because a court supervises the entire procedure. As a result the property is usually sold for close to its market value; in addition, chances for a defective foreclosure are reduced because the sale is based upon a court order. On the other hand, this type of foreclosure is expensive and time-consuming.

Most jurisdictions regulate many aspects of the foreclosure procedure by statute. These regulations, which vary from state to state, must be followed closely or the sale will be invalid. Usually an action to foreclose must be brought in the county where the mortgaged property is located. If a single mortgage covers property in several counties, the suit may be brought in any of the counties in which the property is located.

Procedural Requirements
Due process The requirements of due process that exist for litigation generally apply to mortgage foreclosures. Mortgagors and other interested parties are entitled to notice of the action and an opportunity to defend before an impartial tribunal having jurisdiction.

Notice If the mortgagor is within the jurisdiction, generally he or she will be served personally. Personal service is, however, unnecessary because the fore-closure action is *in rem*—that is, "against the property"—and, as such, service by publication is sufficient. Requirements for a valid service by publication vary from state to state, but generally they involve mailing a copy of the summons to the defendant and advertising the action in a general-circulation newspaper.

Parties Few legal questions arise as to the proper party or parties to initiate a foreclosure action. Ordinarily, it would be the mortgagee or one to whom the mortgage has been transferred. If there are joint mortgagees, they must join in the litigation. Any mortgagee who refuses to join should be made a defendant. If the security instrument is a deed of trust, the trustee brings the action.

The plaintiff should join as defendants any other parties with an interest in the property. This includes anyone with a junior mortgage. In most states, if this is not done, the junior mortgagee's interest is not terminated by the foreclosure sale. This means that the junior mortgagee has the right to foreclose its mortgage or to redeem the property.

Sound legal practice also dictates that a tenant under a lease executed after the mortgage be made a party to the foreclosure action. Although the tenant's rights are terminated by foreclosure, no later question can arise if the tenant is joined in the foreclosure suit. If the tenant's lease was executed prior to the mortgage, the lessee need not be joined as his or her rights are superior to the mortgagee's.

Foreclosure Sale
The chief purpose of a foreclosure action is to obtain a court order directing a public sale of the security. This sale terminates the right to redeem of all parties having interests in the property subject to the mortgage. The proceeds of the sale are allocated to pay expenses and the mortgage debt.

Various state laws regulate the method of conducting the sale. Usually it is carried out by the sheriff. In some states a court-appointed master or referee conducts the sale. In any case, it will be supervised closely by the court.

Most states have some type of law attempting to ensure an adequate *sale price*. One common method is to require an appraisal by a group of disinterested persons before the property is auctioned. The sale must bring at least a portion—

perhaps 60 to 75 percent of the appraised value. Unless the final bid is at least that amount, the sale is not consummated. A few states allow bidding in advance. Bids made at the sale must be at least as high as the highest advance bid. If they are not, the property goes to the highest advance bidder. Finally, a court can use its equity power to refuse to confirm a sale if the amount bid is grossly inadequate. Ordinarily, however, a properly conducted sale will not be set aside merely because of an inadequate price.

Deficiency Judgment

Money judgment awarded to the mortgagee when funds obtained as a result of a foreclosure sale are insufficient to pay the debt.

Case Example

Oscar Fong defaulted on a loan from Portland Trust. The loan was secured by a mortgage on real estate owned by Fong. At the time of default the outstanding indebtedness was $75,000. The mortgage was foreclosed and the property ordered sold. The selling price at the foreclosure sale was $70,000. After this amount was credited, the bank commenced a personal action against Fong to collect the additional $5,000 plus all expenses.

Most states allow the mortgagee to collect any deficiency remaining after foreclosure. Usually the right to sue for a deficiency is provided in the court decree ordering foreclosure. The theory underlying the deficiency judgment is that the creditor has a right based upon the bond or note to collect the entire amount owed. This right exists independently of the right to foreclose.

Deficiency judgments in residential foreclosures are rare, for reasons both legal and economic. Economically, situations in which sale of the property is insufficient to pay off the debt occur infrequently. Most residential loans are amortized on a monthly basis; the amount of the debt is constantly decreasing. Coupled with inflation and generally increasing property values, only in unusual cases will funds from the sale fail to cover the debt.

The law in a few states prohibits deficiency judgments. If a mortgagee elects to foreclose, that is the only remedy allowed. The reason is that the mortgagee often purchases at the foreclosure sale. If the purchase price is less than the debt, the mortgagee can thus acquire the security as well as collect the entire amount owed. This can be very unjust to the mortgagor because frequently the mortgagee acquires the property for less than its actual value. A mortgagee has an advantage as a bidder for the amount owed to it is credited against its bid. The result is that it must come up with less cash than other bidders. Other bidders are thus frozen out, and the property sells for less than its value.

Power-of-Sale Foreclosure

Foreclosure based upon terms in a mortgage, giving a mortgagee or third party the power to sell mortgaged property upon default without resorting to judicial foreclosures.

Legal complications, expense and delay associated with judicial foreclosure have encouraged alternate methods of applying the security to the debt. Many mortgages contain provisions granting a mortgagee or third party the power to sell the real estate at a public sale if the mortgagor defaults. Generally, the sale is authorized without court intervention, but a few states require judicial confirmation, and many have statutes that prescribe procedures that must be followed.

Some states by specific legislation require foreclosure by judicial action. Statutes of this type effectively prohibit the use of a power of sale. Most states, however, do allow the power-of-sale foreclosure, and it is the prevailing practice in several states.

At one time the power-of-sale foreclosure was touted as the solution to many of the problems of judicial foreclosure, but this expectation was not fulfilled. Lawyers representing potential purchasers are wary of the process because the title acquired is not based upon a judicial proceeding that establishes regularity. In addition, the purchaser's title is subject to attack because the sale does not have the official sanction of a court order. This attack can be made not only by the mortgagor but also by others who have an interest in the property.

Advocates of debtors' interests also object to extrajudicial foreclosure based upon a power of sale. In many states the terms of the power are the principal source for determining how the sale will be conducted. Because the mortgagor's bargaining position is generally weak, provisions of the power detrimental to the mortgagor's interest are often included. This is illustrated in a comparison of English and American law. English law absolutely prohibits the mortgagee from purchasing at a power-of-sale foreclosure. Generally, in the United States the rule is also that a mortgagee cannot be the purchaser when a power of sale is used, but in most states this rule can be avoided by a provision in the power allowing the mortgagee to buy. Many states also permit a deficiency judgment after a sale based upon a power. This, too, can be harmful to the mortgagor because there is no direct judicial supervision of the adequacy of the selling price.

Statutes in many states and case law in others provide some protection for the mortgagor whose real property is subject to a power of sale. These statutes generally require notice, usually by advertisement, and a sale that is conducted fairly in order to produce a good price. A sale will not be valid if factors exist that tend to stifle competition among the bidders. In conducting the sale the mortgagee is representing the mortgagor's interest as well as its own.

Case Example

Union Market National Bank held a $9,800 mortgage on property owned by Missak Derderian. The mortgage was in default, and the bank advertised a sale under a power included in the mortgage. The advertisement stated, in addition to a $500 cash down payment at the time of sale, "other terms to be announced at the sale."

At the sale the auctioneer announced that a $500 deposit would be required of anyone prior to that person's bid being accepted. This was a very unusual condition, and Derderian's brother, who was planning to bid, refused to comply. The auctioneer as a result refused to accept his high bid of more than $10,000 and sold the property to the mortgagee for $8,500. All parties at the sale knew that Derderian's brother was financially responsible.

When Derderian challenged the sale as improperly conducted, an appellate court agreed with him. The court stated that "[a] mortgagee with the power to select the methods of sale must act as a reasonably prudent man would to obtain a fair price . . . If the conditions announced at the sale . . . operate to prevent free bidding, it is the mortgagee's duty to change them." *Union National Bank v. Derderian, 318 Mass. 578, 62 N.E.2d 661 (1945).*

Strict Foreclosure

A judicial procedure that, by terminating the mortgagor's equity of redemption, gives the mortgagee absolute title to mortgaged real estate without a sale of the property.

Foreclosures by judicial action and by power of sale are identified with the lien theory of mortgages, which establishes a mortgagee's right to have the property sold following default. The proceeds of the sale are used to pay the debt and expenses of the sale. If a balance remains, it is turned over to the mortgagor. The mortgagee does not acquire title to the property unless the mortgagee is the purchaser at the foreclosure sale.

At common law the mortgagee had a more extensive right. The mortgage gave the mortgagee a conditional or defeasible title to the security. If the debt was paid when due, the mortgagor reacquired title; if the debt was not paid, the mortgagee acquired absolute title. Even at this point, however, the mortgagee's title was not quite absolute. The mortgagor retained an equitable right of redemption—the right to redeem the property by paying the debt.

The mortgagee had difficulty selling or leasing the property while the right of redemption existed because the property could be reacquired by the mortgagor merely by paying the outstanding debt. In order to perfect the title so that he or she could make good use of the property, the mortgagee had to eliminate the equitable right of redemption. This was done by asking the court to foreclose the mortgagor's right to redeem in an action known as *strict foreclosure*.

Strict foreclosure is no longer common in the United States except in two or three states; a majority of states prohibit its use. A few states expressly prohibit it by statute; others accomplish the prohibition by requiring that the security be sold to compensate the creditor. The principal reason for this decline is that often strict foreclosure severely penalizes the mortgagor. At the same time, the mortgagee has the potential for windfall profit, as indicated by the following example.

Case Example

Jason Bolder executed a mortgage in favor of Marcia Letski on property with a market value of $55,000. The mortgage was to secure Letski's advance of $25,000, which Bolder used to finance a travel agency. The agency prospered at first, and the debt was reduced to $22,000.

When a general recession occurred, Bolder's business suffered, and he defaulted on the debt. Were strict foreclosure available, Letski could obtain title to the property. Assuming the market value was still $55,000, she would now have property worth $33,000 more than the debt.

Deed of Trust

A written instrument that transfers title to real property to a trustee as security for a debt owed by the borrower to the lender, who is the beneficiary of the trust.

In a number of states the typical real estate security instrument involves three parties and is based upon the law of trusts. Instead of executing a mortgage in favor of a lender, the borrower transfers title to a trustee through a deed of trust. Although we have seen that in a few states the mortgage, at least in theory, passes title, even in the title theory states the mortgage is a lein in nature. The important difference between the mortgage and the deed of trust is that in a deed of trust legal title passes to the trustee. The trustee holds this title for the benefit of both the borrower and the lender. When the debt secured by the deed of trust is repaid, the trustee must reconvey title to the borrower.

The law of trusts, which has developed over hundreds of years, requires trustees to act in utmost good faith and fairness. Like the real estate broker, the trustee is a fiduciary. In addition to this fiduciary duty, the trustee has specific obligations and powers stated in the deed or trust. A trustee who fails to meet these obligations is personally accountable.

Importantly, the trustee has the power to sell the property if the borrower fails to maintain payments on the debt or breaches some other condition of the loan agreement by failing to keep the buildings insured, by selling the property or by committing waste. The power-of-sale provision makes judicial foreclosure procedure unnecessary, although the trustee usually can elect such procedure. Because judicial foreclosure can be avoided, collection from the security is more rapid and economical than through the court procedure.

Lawyers in states where the deed of trust is common argue that the ability to sell the security efficiently is the deed of trust's major advantage over the mortgage. This advantage does not exist in all states as in some states legislation requires that the trustee proceed through a judicial forecloure. Another advantage of the deed of trust is that in a number of states it avoids the borrower's right of redemption because a purchaser from the trustee acquires that party's legal title to the property. In addition, the borrower must also surrender possession to the purchaser of the trustee's legal title. There are several other reasons why lenders in many states prefer to make residential property loans under a deed of trust. For one, the statute of limitations may bar action on the note in some mortgage transactions, but not with a deed-of-trust power of sale in which the trustee has legal title. In addition, a deed of trust can be used to secure several notes. Finally, the lender may remain anonymous in a deed of trust.

Compared with the mortgage, a distinct disadvantage of the deed of trust lies in discharging the instrument. In most states a mortgage is discharged when the mortgagee executes a simple document called a *satisfaction of mortgage* or a *release of mortgage*. The deed of trust requires a reconveyance by the trustee. The trustee will refuse to reconvey the property without assurance that the underlying obligation has been paid. Otherwise the trustee would be personally liable to the lender for any amount still due. If the trustee is an individual, the problem of reconveyance can become especially acute because the person might be difficult to locate. For this reason the preferred practice is to name a corporate trustee.

Deed in Lieu of Foreclosure

A procedure in which the mortgagor conveys the mortgaged real estate to the mortgagee, who promises in return not to foreclose or sue on the underlying debt.

Case Example

As security for a $50,000 loan, Naomi Tilson executed a mortgage to the Pike County National Bank. After making two payments on the loan, she defaulted. At the time of her default the market value of the property was slightly in excess of $50,000. Because Naomi and her family were valued customers, the bank offered to accept a deed to the property instead of foreclosing. After discussing the consequences of this action with her attorney, Naomi agreed to convey the property to the bank.

The use of a deed in lieu of foreclosure is a common practice in the United States. In conveying to the mortgagee, the mortgagor surrenders any rights to a foreclosure sale and to redeem the property. In return, the mortgagee cancels the underlying debt and becomes the owner of the real estate.

Potentially, the transaction can benefit the mortgagor in a number of ways. For example, Naomi Tilson's credit rating would be protected. The conveyance would be carried out in the same manner as any sale, and adverse publicity that might accompany foreclosure would not exist. Economically, she could anticipate three important benefits. First, any obligation for taxes and assessments would terminate. Foreclosure costs would also be saved. Probably most important of all, she would not be responsible for any deficiency.

The deed in lieu of foreclosure is also advantageous to the mortgagee. Long delays usually associated with foreclosure by judicial sale are avoided. In addition, the mortgagee escapes the poor public relations that are often the result of resorting to a judicial sale. On the other hand, the mortgagee faces the problem of disposing of the security. Until the property is sold, the mortgagee has to maintain it, and expenses of the sale must be borne by the mortgagee because it now owns the real estate.

A number of legal problems associated with the practice are of special concern to the mortgagee. First, the mortgagee must completely cancel the debt. If it does not, the courts treat the deed in lieu of foreclosure as a substitute for the original mortgage. The mortgagor under these conditions retains any redemption rights that exist. On the other hand, once the debt is canceled, the mortgagee loses the right to a deficiency judgment. If the market value of the property in the previous example were to be less than $50,000, the mortgagee would suffer the loss.

A second important legal consideration involves junior liens on the property. The purchaser at a foreclosure sale takes title free of such liens, but a mortgagee who acquires title to real estate by deed in lieu of foreclosure is subject to these interests. If Naomi Tilson had not paid for improvements on the property and a mechanic's lien existed, the Pike County National Bank's deed would be subject to that lien. A deed in lieu of foreclosure is also subject to attack under the Bankruptcy Act. Were Naomi to file for bankruptcy within a period of, say, 90 days after delivery of the deed to the bank, the bank could be treated as a preferred creditor. The deed would be set aside as a preferential transfer.

Another legal problem exists in some states where the courts have regarded the deed in lieu of foreclosure with suspicion. As a consequence, courts have had a tendency to consider the deed not as a conveyance but as additional security unless the transaction is clearly free from coercion. In other states the courts require proof of the absence of fraud when the value of the property exceeds the debt.

Successful legal challenges sometimes have been launched against a mortgagee on grounds that it supplied no consideration for the mortgagor's conveyance of its redemption right. The rationale underlying this claim is that the mortgagee taking a deed in lieu of foreclosure supplies nothing additional to the mortgagor. The question of consideration, however, is probably not a major concern to the mortgagee as long as no gross disparity exists between the amount of the debt and the value of the security. If the debt is small and the property valuable, the mortgagee's action might be challenged as unfair.

Types of Mortgages

Many different types of mortgages exist. The principal reasons for this is that mortgage lenders, in order to be compeditive, in fact often to survive, have to adapt the mortgage loan to reflect prevailing economic conditions and needs.

The experiences of the past twenty-five years provide an example of the influence that economic developments have on mortgage lending. Many of these developments created problems of mortgage financing. During this period interest rates often rose rapidly and sometimes fluctuated widely. Additionally, inflation made financing decisions difficult for both borrowers and lenders. To cope with these other problems, new types of mortgage loans evolved.

The new types of mortgage loans often conflicted with state and federal regulations monitoring mortgage lending. As interest rates increased they often came into conflict with usury laws limiting the amount of interest that a lender could charge. At the same time state statutes that required fixed interest rates during the term of the loan conflicted with lenders' attempts to develop loans with flexible rates. Although legislative bodies, the courts and regulatory agencies gradually developed regulations to accommodate variations of the traditional mortgage loan, the process was often slow and not without strain.

The evolution of the flexible-rate mortgage during the 1970s is an example of adjustments made between governmental regulations and economic pressure. During the late 1960s and the early 1970s financial institutions, especially savings and loans which traditionaally carried between 35 and 40 percent of residential mortgage debt, experienced major problems because of interest rate increases. The result was that thrift institutions frequently found themselves caught in a credit squeeze. They had extended for long terms at fixed rates, depending upon additional deposits to meet reserve requirements and new commitments. When they experienced difficulty in attracting and retaining deposits because competing investments offered higher interest yields, they were often forced to liquidate existing mortgages at a loss to maintain reserves and meet new commitments. Mortgage funds thus dried up, and as new home purchases and construction slowed, the entire economy felt the pinch. The flexible-rate mortgage was an attempt to lessen the strain of "interest rate risk" on lending institutions.

The first mortgages with flexible rates appeared in the late '70s. They were known as variable rate mortgages (VRMs). In 1979 the Federal Home Loan Bank Board (FHLBB) authorized federally chartered savings and loans to make this type of loan. State and federal action authorizing lenders to make VRMs contained provisions to protect borrowers. Regulations limited the amount that interest could be increased over the life of the loan or at any single period, as well as the dollar amount that a periodic payment could increase. These limits are referred to as *caps*. In 1982 the FHLBB authorized lenders to make adjustable-rate mortgages.

Adjustable-rate Mortgage (ARM)

A mortgage that contains a provision permitting the mortgage to adjust the interest rate based on an index contained in the mortgage.

ARMs tie the interest rate to an index that reflects short-term money market conditions. The index should be outside the control of the lending institution, and it should be readily verifiable by the owner. Indexes that have been used include the Federal Reserve rediscount rate, the Treasury bill rate and national mortgage loan rates compiled by the FHLBB or the Federal Housing Administration. Although adjustable-rate mortgages are not inherently illegal, until the 1970s they were prohibited by statute in a number of states.

Although one difference between the ARM and the VRM is that the ARM can be written with or without caps, most ARMs are written with caps. Some ARMs limit the amount that the interest rate can be adjusted at any one payment period and the amount the periodic payment can increase. As a result of these provisions, *negative amortization* is a possibility in some situations.

Negative amortization occurs when a periodic payment is not sufficient to cover all of the accrued interest on a loan. The amount of unpaid interest must be added to the principal balance that is due. The borrower pays this additional interest when the monthly payments can be increased to exceed the amount necessary to amortize the debt. Regulations limit the amount of negative amortization to 25 percent of the original principal.

Case Example

The Intrepid Savings and Loan granted John Bell a loan to buy a home. The loan was to be repaid over 15 years and was secured by an ARM. Monthly payments were $620. The interest rate adjustment period on the mortgage was every six months; however, the payment adjustments were made every three years. When the interest rate was increased at the end of the first year, the $620 payment did not cover all the interest that was due. The difference was added to the principal to be repaid by the increased payments beginning at the end of the third year.

The VRM and ARM are responses made by lenders to some unusual economic conditions that existed in the United States during the 1970s and the 1980s. Other types of mortgage loans that real estate personnel should be familiar with are often also the result of lenders' efforts to deal with economic problems. These mortgages—purchase money mortgage, construction mortgage, open-end mortgage, wraparound mortgage, package mortgage and rollover mortgage—will be examined in the balance of this section.

Purchase Money Mortgage

A written instrument given by a buyer to secure part of the purchase price and delivered contemporaneously with the transfer of title to the buyer.

Case Example

Martin Sankovich purchased a small dairy farm from his uncle for $250,000. He paid $40,000 down and assumed an existing mortgage of $110,000. His uncle agreed to take back a purchase money second mortgage for $100,000. At the closing, Martin executed a mortgage and note in favor of his uncle, who in turn conveyed title to him.

The purchase money mortgage provides some protection for a seller who takes back a mortgage for part of the purchase price. The principal benefit to the mortgagee is that the purchase money mortgage takes priority, or preference, over liens against the buyer that might immediately attach to the property. Suppose, for example, that Martin at the time of closing had an outstanding judgment against him for $8,000. A judgment lien would usually attach immediately to his interest in the dairy and would be superior to his uncle's mortgage. However, the law assumes that the delivery of the deed and the purchase money loan are one transaction. The result is that there is no time for an intervening lien to attach. The judgment, though prior in time, is inferior in right to the seller's mortgage. In states that recognize dower and homestead rights, the purchase money mortgage takes priority over them. If the dairy were in a state that recognized dower, Martin's wife would have an immediate inchoate right of dower when Martin acquired title to the property. Even if she did not sign the mortgage, her right would be inferior to that of the purchase money lender.

In a few states only a seller who takes back a mortgage is afforded the limited benefits of a purchase money mortgagee. Most jurisdictions, however, have extended purchase money safeguards to any lender who advances funds that are applied to the purchase price. If Martin had borrowed $210,000 from a bank to purchase the dairy, the bank would have purchase money status if the funds were advanced simultaneously with the transfer of title to Martin.

Construction Mortgage

A mortgage given to secure funds advanced to construct or improve a building.

Construction loan is a term frequently used in the real estate industry. Like many common terms, it has a variety of meanings. Sometimes people use it in a general sense when discussing sources of funds to remodel or make relatively minor improvements. More specifically, the term refers to a number of industry practices that provide substantial funding for construction or renovation. A common characteristic of these practices is that the lender agrees to advance a total sum but supplies the funds over a period of time as work progresses. The loan is secured by a construction mortgage.

For some lenders the construction mortgage does not differ materially from a regular mortgage except that funds are advanced periodically, not in a lump sum. Upon completion of the work, the lender carries the mortgage as a permanent investment or assigns it to another lender. Some financial institutions will not make short-term construction loans, either based on internal decisions or because they are prohibited from making these loans by law. If financing through one of these institutions, the property owner first must obtain a short-term loan from an interim lender. When construction is completed, permanent financing is arranged. Usually this is based upon a prior agreement made by the permanent mortgagee to provide long-term financing.

A number of states have specific statutes regulating construction lending. Generally they prohibit certain financial institutions from making construction loans and direct the manner by which others must pay out construction loan funds. The purpose of these statutes is to facilitate construction lending by providing protection for the mortgagee as well as for artisans working on the project.

Both the construction mortgagee and the mechanic's lien look to the property as security. The periodic advances made by the lender are secured by the increased value of the property stemming from the completed work. At the same time, if those working on the structure are not paid, they have a right to a lien against the real estate. The time when the mechanic's lien attaches is critical to the rights of the parties. For example, in a number of states a mechanic's lien dates back to the start of construction. If a construction mortgage is not recorded until work commences, the mechanic's lien is superior even if perfected later. A number of states separate buildings from the land when attempting to adjust the interest of the construction mortgagee and the mechanic's lienholder. In these states the mechanic's lien has superior rights in the building even if a construction mortgage has been recorded against the property. Other states have different rules relating to time of attachment.

In order to establish the priority right of the construction mortgagee and to ensure that workers will be paid, state statutes provide the lender with a preferred position in the security if provisions for disbursing funds are followed. The construction mortgagee must be certain to follow these provisions exactly. Usually they involve two steps: obtaining detailed statements from contractors and subcontractors of the work that has been done and, when funds are disbursed, obtaining proper waivers from the parties to whom payments have been made. Not all states have statutes regulating construction loans. In those that do not, the construction mortgagee must develop procedures to ensure that the mortgage rights will be superior to the mechanics' liens.

Open-End Mortgage

A mortgage that permits the mortgagor to borrow additional funds, usually up to the original amount of the debt.

The open-end mortgage is a modern application of an old concept. In the years immediately following World War II, a number of financial institutions in the United States revitalized and expanded the mortgage to secure future advances. Probably the principal reason was to improve their competitive position, but the instrument that they developed had advantages for borrowers as well as lenders.

Traditionally, in most American jurisdictions, a mortgage to secure future advances provides the lender with priority over liens intervening between the recording of the mortgage and the future advance. This principle is especially well established when the future advance is obligatory.

Case Example

Midge and Tony McLaughlin, a young married couple, executed a $25,000 mortgage to United National Bank for funds advanced to purchase a small house. Midge and Tony planned to have a family and knew that additions would have to be made to the house. When they explained this to the loan officer, he suggested an open-end mortgage. A provision was included in the mortgage requiring the bank to lend them additional funds up to the original amount of the loan.

Several years later Midge and Tony requested those additional funds. During the intervening years, a judgment had been entered against Midge as a result of an automobile accident. Despite this judgment, United National advanced the money; the original mortgage provided security for the additional funds.

In most open-end mortgages the mortgagee is not required to advance the additional funds. If the mortgagee has this option, the priority of the lien over an intervening encumbrance in most states depends upon notice of the intervening claim. If the mortgagee has actual notice of an intervening lien and elects to advance the funds, any lien that results is inferior to that of the intervening claimant. In the previous example, if the mortgage was nonobligatory and United National had knowledge of the judgment against Midge, a lien resulting from any later advance would be inferior to the judgment lien.

Although the law generally agrees that actual notice of the intervening claim limits the priority of the open-end mortgage, the states are divided as to whether a recorded lien provides notice. A majority hold that the mortgagee does not have notice merely because a subsequent lien is recorded. In other states the mortgagee is charged with notice of any subsequently recorded interest. In these states the mortgagee whose instrument is nonobligatory must reexamine the record before advancing additional funds.

Benefits of the Open-End Mortgage

Open-end mortgages benefit both the borrowers and the lenders. The lender benefits because the device enables the lender to retain the business of valued customers. When a mortgagor needs additional funds, he or she will use the open-end privilege instead of going to a competitor. The general belief is that open-end mortgages also reduce the number of foreclosures. One reason for this is that borrowers can obtain needed funds without turning to short-term credit at high interest rates. The additional business is also more profitable to the lender because the costs of the loan are spread over a larger amount.

Benefits to the borrower are even more obvious. The funds are provided at the low interest rates afforded first mortgages on real estate, as compared with other more costly financing. Payments are spread over a longer period of time, and extra costs of refinancing or additional borrowing are eliminated.

Despite these advantages, the open-end mortgage has not been used extensively during recent years, primarily because of rising interest rates and inflation. Lending institutions are reluctant to lock themselves into loans that commit them to make additional funds available at the lower rates. Borrowers find the open-end privilege less attractive because of inflation. Ordinarily, they are entitled to borrow the difference between the original loan and the reduced principal. That privilege is of little value to the property owner if the difference is small compared to the cost of the item for which the loan is made.

Legal Requirements

Legal requirements for a valid open-end mortgage differ from state to state. Several states have enacted specific legislation to deal with these mortgages. The most common general requirement is that the instrument indicate clearly that it contemplates future advances. In addition, the instrument must describe the debt with enough accuracy to make identification certain. The other requirements that exist in a number of states are limits on time during which a future advance position is effective and limits on the amount that can be secured. Statutes in some states require that the instrument indicate at the beginning that it is an open-end mortgage.

Wraparound Mortgage

A second mortgage covering an existing debt that the lender agrees to service as well as providing the borrower with additional funds.

Wraparound financing is used in a variety of real estate transactions. This type of financing is another example of the manner in which legal and financial institutions react to economic conditions. The increase in wraparound financing during the past decade has been the result of relatively high rates of interest and tight money conditions that have prevailed during the period.

Case Example

Al Borne owned property appraised at $250,000. The property was encumbered by a $125,000 first mortgage at nine percent interest with 12 years until maturity. Al wished to expand his plumbing business, but he needed additional funds. A friend agreed to lend him $100,000. As security Al was to give his friend a $225,000 second mortgage on the property. Al was to pay interest on this mortgage at 13 percent. The friend agreed to service the first mortgage interest of nine percent out of the interest Al paid. Al's friend has a wraparound mortgage.

Typically, a wraparound mortgage has a higher rate of interest than the rate on the existing debt that it covers. The wraparound mortgagee collects interest exceeding that on the first mortgage, which the lender has agreed to service. This differential makes the loan attractive to the wraparound mortgagee, whose effective rate of return is increased. For example, Al's friend has advanced only $100,000, but he collects interest on $225,000. After paying the nine percent interest on the first mortgage, the friend retains the four percent difference on $125,000 as well as the 13 percent on the $100,000.

Advantages and Problems

Potentially, several factors exist that make this type of financing advantageous to Al. First, he is able to retain a substantial portion of his debt at nine percent. This is one of the reasons for the increasing popularity of wraparound financing in a market where interest rates have been increasing rapidly. Second, a good possibility exists that he will be financing at somewhat less than the market rate as the effective rate of return to the lender is increased by the wraparound. Third, the wraparound mortgage may be a potential tax-saving device because it permits installment reporting of capital gains.

Another common use of the wraparound mortgage is in selling real estate. Assume that, instead of refinancing, Al wishes to sell his property and a broker finds a prospective client who has $50,000. In order to facilitate the sale, Al might agree to accept the cash and a second mortgage for $200,000 at 14 percent. Al would be responsible for servicing the first mortgage out of the payments made by the mortgagor on the $200,000 second mortgage. Al's second mortgage has wrapped around the existing first mortgage.

Wraparound mortgages create a number of legal problems. Probably the most serious is that second mortgage loans are prohibited to many financial institutions, sometimes because of internal policy and other times because of legal prohibitions. Usury is also a question in some states; the actual rate of interest being collected might exceed the maximum rate, even though the instrument shows something less. Other problems might be caused by prohibitions in the existing first mortgage. Many first mortgages today contain clauses that limit the mortgagor's right to sell the property. Some mortgages prohibit additional financing using the same property as security. Both of these provisions would effectively limit the use of a wraparound mortgage.

Package Mortgage

A mortgage secured by both personal and real property.

Package mortgages are used today primarily in financing residential real estate, although they can also be used to finance commercial and industrial ventures. The mortgage covers not only the real property but also personal property essential to the operation of a home or business. In residential financing, a package mortgage lien attaches to real estate and to equipment needed to make the home livable. This might include a stove, refrigerator, dishwasher or freezer. In a commercial transaction the package mortgage would include items necessary to operate the business. In a mortgage covering a motel, for example, most lenders would require a lien on the furniture and other items necessary to operate the business. In the event of a foreclosure, the security would be much more valuable if it included equipment necessary for operation. Unless these items were included in the mortgage, the purchaser would have to buy them separately because the owner would have a right to remove them.

Benefits

For several reasons the package mortgage might be beneficial to the buyer/ mortgagor. First, the mortgagor is able to finance appliances at the same low rate of interest provided in the real estate mortgage. This rate is considerably lower than the rate for consumer loans. Second, the purchase price of these appliances can be spread over the entire term of the mortgage, thereby reducing monthly payments. Finally, some lenders contend that a package mortgage reduces the potential for default, especially for families buying their first home. Usually these people have to purchase all their appliances in addition to the realty. With a package mortgage, they are not saddled with additional payments for appliances simultaneously with initial payments on real estate debt. The cost of all items is included in the mortgage payment. The chief argument against the package mortgage is that the buyer, in paying for the appliances over the term of the real estate mortgage, is paying for them long after their useful life has expired.

Rollover Mortgage

A mortgage that must be refinanced every few years in order to adjust the interest rate up or down in response to prevailing money market conditions.

Rising interest rates create a substantial problem for financial institutions that make long-term loans. In recent years this problem has been especially acute for savings and loan institutions, which, in order to compete for funds, have to pay savers short-term rates. As interest rates increase, the return on mortgage money, invested at fixed rates often up to 30 years, lags well behind rapidly increasing short-term rates. The variable-rate mortgage (VRM) was one effort to solve this problem. The rollover, or renegotiated-rate, mortgage is another.

A rollover mortgage is written for a short term, generally three, four or five years. At the end of that period the loan is renegotiated to reflect prevailing interest rates. To protect borrowers, a maximum increase is sometimes established. In 1980, for federally chartered savings and loans this maximum was one-half percentage point per year and five percentage points over the life of the mortgage. This ceiling has since been lifted by the Federal Home Loan Bank Board. Other protections for the mortgagor include a requirement that the lender renew, formal foreclosure if the lender wants to terminate the loan and the right to pay off the loan in full with no penalty after 90 days. Many mortgagors object to rollover mortgages because they could lead to substantially higher costs if interest rates climb. On the other hand, if interest rates drop, the mortgagor will benefit when the loan has to be renegotiated.

Mortgage Insurance

Insurance provided by certain government agencies or private corporations protecting mortgage lenders against loss caused by a borrower's default.

Mortgage insurance has increased in importance since the 1940s and is today an integral part of the real estate industry. Authorities estimate that more than 25 percent of real estate mortgage loans are covered by some type of mortgage insurance. This type of insurance has numerous social benefits. Probably the most important is *liquidity*—the ease with which an asset can be converted to cash. Insured mortgage loans are much more liquid than those that are not insured. Liquidity is greater because firms initiating insured loans must follow established standards and procedures. These procedures include an approved appraisal of the structure as well as approval of the creditworthiness of the borrower. When a loan is insured, not only the lender but also the insurer must be convinced that the property value covers the loan and the borrower has the ability to repay.

Another benefit of mortgage insurance is a reduction in the number of foreclosures. When an insured loan is in default, the insurer pays the debt and takes over the property. The insurer then attempts to sell the property to cover its losses. During the 30 years following World War II, the most common type of mortgage insurance was provided by two federally supported agencies. Today, however, several private firms are gaining a substantial share of the mortgage insurance business.

FHA Insurance

Insurance provided lenders under Title II of the National Housing Act of 1934.

The National Housing Act is administered by the Department of Housing and Urban Development (HUD); the Federal Housing Administration (FHA) is an organizational unit of HUD. The FHA administers several programs providing insurance to lenders financing real estate transactions. Loans can be insured for the purchase, construction, repair and improvement of housing. Rental housing, cooperatives, condominiums, low-cost and moderate-income housing, housing for the elderly and nursing homes are among the many types of dwellings covered by FHA programs. Mortgages insured by the FHA are known as *FHA mortgages.*

The mortgage loan insurance program that resulted from Section 203 of the National Housing Act is the most important to have arisen over the years. This section authorizes insurance for loans to finance the purchase of one- to four-unit dwellings. Four common provisions of FHA insured mortgage loans are:

1. long term for repayment,

2. full amortization over the term,

3. low down payment, and

4. interest rates below market.

Since a major portion of the loan is guaranteed, usually the interest rates are lower than those on conventional loans.

Applications for mortgage insurance on one- to four-family dwellings have two requirements: approval of the property based upon an appraisal and approval of the purchaser's credit. Borrowers pay a one-time premium of 3.8 percent of the amount borrowed. From these premiums and fees, the FHA accumulates reserves to cover expenses and losses on properties acquired because of borrower default.

Department of Veterans Affairs Loan Guarantees

Guarantees provided by the Department of Veterans Affairs to lenders that finance housing construction and purchases by eligible veterans.

The loan guarantee program of the Department of Veterans Affairs provides protection to private lenders financing homes for veterans. As a result of the guarantee, veterans have been able to buy or build homes on long-term loans with no down payment. Loans may be guaranteed on one- to four-unit structures; the veteran must occupy one of the units. Most DVA-guaranteed loans are for the purchase of single-family homes, mobile homes and units in condominium projects.

Although the loan may be for any amount, the guarantee covers only 60 percent of the loan or a maximum of $36,000, whichever is less. The amount of the loan that the DVA guarantees is called an *entitlement*. As in the FHA insurance program, the DVA guarantees a loan only upon an approved appraisal of the property. In addition, before the loan is guaranteed the Department of Veterans Affairs must be convinced that the veteran is a satisfactory credit risk.

DVA-guaranteed loans have several advantages for the veteran. No down payment is required, and the loan may be paid in part or in full at any time with no penalty. If the veteran has financial problems, the FVA will arrange for a modification of terms. The loan may be assumed by any buyer, veteran or nonveteran, who is an acceptable credit risk. In addition, the veteran has the benefit of DVA appraisal, construction supervision and oversight of the lender's activities.

Summary

The *mortgage* is one of two legal instruments used when real property is utilized as security for a debt. Its purpose is to reduce the risk inherent in lending by providing the lender with collateral in case the borrower defaults. The other instrument is the *note*, a written promise to repay a loan according to specific terms and conditions. If the borrower defaults, the lender may collect the debt by foreclosing against the property. As an alternative remedy, the lender may bring a personal action against the borrower on the note.

A buyer who fails to pay according to the terms of the mortgage agreement or who fails to pay taxes or live up to other obligations of the agreement is said to be in *default*. In addition, a popular provision of recent mortgages is the due-on-sale clause, a clause making the sale of the mortgaged premises by the mortgagor a default.

Foreclosure of mortgage is the legal means by which a lender recovers property when a borrower defaults on a mortgage loan. The most commonly used form is *judicial foreclosure*, ordered by the court. Another type is the *power-of-sale foreclosure* granted in the mortgage. *Strict foreclosure* is the third type.

In judicial foreclosure the court orders real estate sold to enforce the mortgagee's contractual rights. It is the most common type of foreclosure. One reason that judicial foreclosure is common it that the procedure is closely regulated by the court. Because the requirements of due process apply to foreclosures, all perties must be notified and must have an opportunity to defend. In the event that the sale price is too low to cover the mortgage debt, most states allow the mortgagee to collect the balance due from the mortgagor by a *deficiency judgment*.

Some states allow foreclosures based on a power of sale granted in the mortgage document. In this form the mortgagor has the right to sell the property without resorting to judicial foreclosure. The practice is common in only about one-third of the states. Because it is not court supervised, it is not as acceptable to many people as judicial foreclosure. Nevertheless, statutes in some states do protect the mortgagor's interest by requiring that adequate notice be given and by providing remedies in case of an obviously low sale price.

Mortgage laws and procedures are influenced by economic conditions. As a result of the relative scarcity of funds during the 1970s and 1980s, new types of mortgage financing have developed. One example is the *adjustable-rate mortgage*. A clause in the mortgage permits the lender to adjust interest rates in response to changes in the money market. Several other types of mortgages exist. They include the *purchase money mortgage*, the *construction mortgage*, the *open-end mortgage* and the *rollover mortgage*. The appropriateness of each type varies according to economic conditions and the financial situations of both borrower and lender.

One of the basic aspects of real estate law reflected in this chapter is the idea of priority or preference between interests in real estate. Often more than one interest exists in the same property. The multiple interests might be those of owners, tenants, mortgagees or other types of lienholders. Sometimes the parties agree which of these interests is superior, but more often that decision is made by the law. Although the fundamental rule of priorities is "first in time, first in right," in numerous instances public policy considerations have led to modifications of this rule. In the chapter that follows, public policy is considered in its relationship to this and other aspects of mortgage lending.

Review and Discussion Questions

1. (a) Explain the differences between a mortgage and a deed of trust. (b) Compare their advantages and disadvantages as financing instruments.

2. Discuss the difference between the lien and title theories of mortgages.

3. What is foreclosure by power-of-sale? How does it differ from judicial foreclosure?

4. Define the following as they are related to Adjustable-rate Mortgages: (a) caps (b) negative amortization.

5. Indicate some of the advantages and problems of wraparound financing.

6. What is a package mortgage? Why have some consumer groups objected to its use?

7. Explain how the legal rights given to a mortgagee by a mortgage differ from those given by a note.

Case Problems

1. Hemmerle borrowed money to build houses on several lots that he owned. To guarantee payment of a loan, he signed several notes and executed mortgages on each lot in favor of First Federal Savings. The mortgages required First Federal to advance funds as construction progressed.

   Before the homes were completed and all funds advanced, Hemmerle defaulted. First Federal brought an action to foreclose. The court ordered a foreclosure sale with Hemmerle's debt being the full amount of the notes. Hemmerle argued that the judgment against him should be only for the amount disbursed. Is he correct Support your answer. *Hemmerle v. First Federal Savings, 338 So.2d (Fla 1976)*.

2. Alonzo Lane purchased a $60,000 home in a newly developed area. To finance the purchase, he executed a $50,000 note and mortgage to the Upland Bank. Shortly after Alonzo moved in, a newspaper article disclosed that much of the development was on land that had been partially filled with chemical waste. Real estate values in the area fell sharply. At about this time Alonzo accepted a job in another state, where he purchased a condominium. Unable to sell his home or keep up payments, Alonzo defaulted. The Upland Bank foreclosed. Discuss Alonzo's potential liability if the home sells at the foreclosure sale for $38,000.

3. Tom Hildebrant purchased a four-unit rental property for $175,000. River National Bank lent him $155,000 to complete the purchase. The loan was secured by a mortgage on the property. Because of a severe recession in the area caused by closing of several steel mills, Hildebrant was unable consistently to rent all of the units, and he defaulted on the debt. As a result the bank foreclosed. At the foreclosure sale, the property sold for $145,000. Does Tom have any liability on the unpaid portion of the debt? Discuss.

4. McCorriston purchased rental real estate in a lien theory state. The purchase was secured by a mortgage loan from the First Bank of Crooksville. When McCorriston defaulted, the bank attempted to collect the rents from the property to be applied against the loan. The mortgage did not contain a provision allowing them to do so. However, the bank argued that as McCorriston had defaulted, it was entitled to the rents. Was the bank correct? Support your answer.

5. Able, Baker and Charlie purchased a farm for investment. They took title as tenants in common. Part of the purchase price was secured by a purchase money mortgage on the property. The mortgage and note were signed by Able and Baker but not Charlie. When the parties defaulted, the seller joined the three in a foreclosure action. Charlie defended on grounds that she has

not signed the mortgage and note. Would she be successful? Support your answer.

6. Topper and Kim owned real estate that was mortgaged to the Gary Bank. The loan was in default, and the bank sued to foreclose. Notice of the foreclosure was publicized as required by state law and Topper was personally served. The bank's attorney could not locate Kim. Will the foreclosure sale be valid if Kim can not be personally served? Discuss.

19

Mortgage Lending and Public Policy

Loan Application and Commitment

Not too many years ago, a person who wanted to borrow on a mortgage from a bank, savings and loan or other financial institution was asked to appear before a loan committee for interrogation. Today most mortgage loans start with an application made on a printed form supplied by the lender. The information needed to complete the application is ordinarily given to a loan officer, and the form is signed by the party requesting the loan.

The application serves two purposes: it supplies the lender with information necessary to decide whether the loan should be granted and it serves as the borrower's *offer* to enter into a contract. If the lender approves the loan, it notifies the borrower and furnishes a formal commitment, often called a *loan approval*. The commitment, if it does not modify the terms in the application, is an *acceptance* of the offer. The parties have entered into a contract to make a loan with real property as security. Ordinarily, the commitment contains a clause terminating the contract if the borrower does not take advantage of the loan within a specified time.

Sometimes the lender modifies the terms in the application, in effect making a *counteroffer*. The counteroffer becomes a contract only if the borrower accepts these new terms. In practice, especially for construction lending and financing commercial real estate, the *commitment* is more important than the application. For these types of financing, the terms of the loan the lender is willing to make generally differ from those of the loan for which the borrower applied. The commitment becomes the basis for the contract; the parties are obligated by its terms if the counteroffer is accepted by the borrower.

Because the commitment is the basis of a contract between borrower and seller, all of the major loan provisions should be clearly and precisely indicated.

If the contract is breached, litigation may ensue. Since neither the lender nor the borrower is entitled to specific performance, each has only damages as a remedy.

When the lender refuses to honor the contract, the borrower's damages are relatively easy to calculate. They are the increased cost of obtaining the loan from some other source. Ordinarily, the bulk of this cost would be the difference between the interest rates charged on the two loans. If the borrower does not use the funds, damages to the lender are very difficult to measure. In a number of cases the courts have held that the lender is entitled only to nominal damages. Because of problems associated with measuring the damages, many commitments for major loans contain provisions for a nonrefundable commitment fee paid by the borrower. When the fee involved is reasonable, the forfeiture of this amount has generally been accepted by courts as valid liquidated damages.

Regulations Affecting Mortgage Loans

Both state and federal regulations influence mortgage lending. Usually these regulations favor borrowers as legislators recognize that the borrower's bargaining position is weaker than the lender's. Usury statutes, the "Truth-in-Lending Act" and the Equal Credit Opportunity Act are examples of regulations with which lenders must contend.

Usury

The practice of charging interest on a loan in excess of a rate allowed by law.

Religious disapproval of interest resulting in usury laws has influenced relationships between borrowers and lenders for centuries. The importance of usury laws depends to a large extent upon economic conditions. When money is scarce, lenders are able to charge higher rates for loans, and usury becomes a factor that they must consider. Almost every state has laws prohibiting lenders from charging excessive interest. These statutes vary appreciably from state to state. Not only do the permissible rates differ, but major differences exist in the transactions that are covered and the penalties levied against the usurious lender. This section looks at numerous aspects of usury laws, including requirements, exemptions, penalties and criticisms. Recent state and federal modifications of usury statutes are also discussed.

Requirements

In order for a debtor to take advantage of the protection afforded by a usury statute, all three of the following elements must exist: the transaction must involve the lending of money or its equivalent, an unqualified promise by the debtor to repay and a higher rate of interest than permitted by state law. Some states also require the debtor to prove that the creditor intended to violate the law, but intent is usually presumed if the rate exceeds that permitted by statute.

Borrowing money presupposes an obligation to repay. As a result, sales on credit and leases in most states do not come within the prohibitions of usury statutes, because the buyer or lessee has no obligation to repay. Transactions in which the borrower's obligation to repay is conditional upon making a profit would also not be usurious, as the obligation is not absolute.

Exemptions

Numerous defenses and exemptions to usury statutes exist. In many states corporate borrowers are not entitled to usury protection. The justification for this is that corporations deal on equal footing with financial institutions and are not likely to need the safeguards of usury statutes. In a few states the corporation exemption does not apply when a lender requires an individual to incorporate in order to obtain a mortgage loan.

Some states exclude loans over a fixed amount from usury protection. These amounts are substantial, usually $50,000 or more. The rationale underlying this exemption is that a person borrowing a large sum is capable of protecting himself or herself from excessive interest charges. In other states all loans for business purposes are exempt. The justification for this exemption, like that for borrower of large sums, is that the business person is a sophisticated borrower without the need of statutory protection.

Most states have special statutes governing interest rates on small loans. Licensed small-loan lenders are permitted to charge higher rates than other lenders, but their operations are closely regulated and restricted by statute. Since small-loan companies generally cannot lend more than $5,000, their business is not pertinent to real estate financing. In a number of states, banks, savings and loan institutions and insurance companies are exempted from usury statutes. Some states also exempt FHA-insured loans. Both of these exemptions are based upon the philosophy that these loans are supervised by responsible state and federal agencies.

Penalties

In some states usury is a criminal offense if an excessively high rate is charged. Civil penalties ordinarily fit into one of three categories:

1. forfeiture of all interest and the entire principal,

2. forfeiture of interest, or

3. forfeiture of interest exceeding the statutory rate.

Some state laws require the lender to forfeit all the interest and also allow the borrower to recover a multiple of the interest paid.

Although usury laws exist in all states but two, they have been criticized severely during last two decades. Usury laws have been criticized for ignoring the fact that market conditions determine interest rates, for having too many exemptions, for failing to protect those who actually need protection and for being difficult to enforce because of ineffective penalties.

Changes

During the 1970s and early 1980s, rapidly increasing interest rates caused serious economic problems in the United States. When market rates exceeded the interest that usury ceilings permitted lenders to charge, lenders stopped making loans to individuals. This decreased residential real estate sales, and the decrease was one of the causes for a severe recession. In order to stimulate real estate sales, a number of states adopted legislation to lessen the effects of usury statutes.

Some states simply raised the rate that could be charged. Other states adopted a floating rate as a determinant of the maximum allowable interest. Floating rates vary in relation to an economic indicator that is used as the index. A common index is the 90-day rate on commercial paper. Other indicators used are the monthly index of long-term United States bonds. Short-term money market indicators such as the Federal Reserve discount rate and the commercial bank prime rate are also used. The indicator serves as a base upon which the lender is allowed to add a fixed percentage. Depending upon the state and the index selected, the amount that can be added ranges from two to five percent.

In 1980, to provide additional stimulus to residential sales, Congress adopted legislation limiting state usury laws in some situations. The federal legislation called the Depository Institution Deregulation and Monetary Control Act (DIDMC) eliminated state interest ceilings on first mortgage loans made by financial institutions and secured by residential real estate. Individuals financing the sale of their own homes were also exempted. The DIDMC permitted states to override the federal law if they did so prior to April 1, 1983. Fourteen states elected to do so. In these states usury statutes continue to apply to residential mortgage loans as they have traditionally.

Truth-in-Lending

The popular name given to part of the Consumer Credit Protection Act of 1968, the federal statute that requires lenders to disclose the cost of consumer credit so that users can better compare terms available from different sources.

The purpose of the "Truth-in-Lending" Act is to foster the informed use of consumer credit, that is, credit extended to an individual to be used primarily for personal, family or household purposes. This legislation in no way fixes maximum or minimum charges for credit.

Real estate credit is only one of many types of credit covered by the act. To come within the scope of the act, real estate credit must be extended to a natural person and be granted to finance acquisition or initial construction of the borrower's principal dwelling. Thus, mortgage loans to corporations and to individuals for business purposes are excluded. Credit extended to the owner of a dwelling containing more than four units is also exempt.

The key to understanding "Truth-in-Lending" is *meaningful disclosure.* Provisions of both this act and of Regulation Z, the Federal Reserve Board's interpretations of the act, require that borrowers be furnished with the facts they need to make intelligent decisions on the use of credit. To accomplish this, information must be presented using terminology specified in the act and Regulation Z. This information must be clear, conspicuous and in writing. Generally, the information must cover all costs of credit, including in most cases the finance charge and the annual percentage rate.

Finance Charge
Dollar-and-cents total of all charges a borrower must pay, directly or indirectly, for obtaining credit.

Prior to "Truth-in-Lending," some lenders presented credit to borrowers in a manner that concealed or even misrepresented costs. Although institutions furnishing real estate credit were not generally as flagrant in this practice as other suppliers of consumer credit, some confusing practices did exist in the mortgage lending market. A relatively common practice was to charge a borrower for extras, loan fees, service charges or points that were not quoted with the interest rate. The 1968 act requires lenders to disclose the dollar total of *all costs* of credit. Extra charges cannot be tallied separately if they are a cost of credit but must be included in the finance charge.

Costs that a buyer would pay regardless of whether or not credit is extended need not be included in the finance charge. Items such as title examination fees, title insurance premiums, survey costs and legal fees fit into this category. These costs must be itemized and disclosed to the borrower separately if included in the total financed. One exception is a first purchase money mortgage on residential property, for which the mortgage is not required to state the total dollar finance charge.

Annual Percentage Rate
The relationship between the total finance charge and the amount to be financed in annual percentage terms.

Disclosure of the annual percentage rate (APR) allows consumers to compare finance charges on a comparable basis, making the cost of credit more understandable. Based on a time period of a year, the APR is similar to simple annual interest, a concept with which many consumers are expected to be familiar.

Credit Advertising
Regulation Z defines *credit advertising* broadly. The definition covers commercial messages that either directly or indirectly promote a credit transaction. Thus, developers or real estate brokers are subject to the act if their advertisement includes terms to be granted by a creditor. Although the definition of *advertising* includes oral as well as written communication, it does not encompass a broker or developer responding to a buyer's questions about available credit.

Of the several advertising provisions of "Truth-in-Lending," two are generally applicable to real estate transactions. A fundamental principle is that no advertisement shall contain terms that are not regularly granted by the creditor. For example, an advertisement offering new homes at "$1,000 down" violates the act if the seller does not customarily accept this amount as a down payment. A second advertising limitation that applies to real estate transactions is referred to as *triggering*. When an advertisement provides certain credit information in the message, Regulation Z mandates that additional information be supplied as well. The triggering terms are as follows:

- amount or percentage of any down payment,

- number of payments or period or repayment,

- amount of any payment,

- amount of any finance charge.

If the advertiser supplies any of the triggering information, the following additional information must also be given.

- amount or percentage of any down payment,

- terms of repayment,

- annual percentage rate.

Case Example

Cullen Builders advertised the sale of homes stating that "90 percent financing was available." As this is a triggering statement, Cullen's advertisement also was required to show the down payment required, the terms of repayment and the annual percentage rate.

Equal Credit Opportunity Act

Federal statute making it unlawful for any creditor to discriminate against an applicant regarding any aspect of a credit transaction on the basis of race, color, religion, national origin, sex, marital status, age or receipt of public assistance.

The Equal Credit Opportunity Act (ECOA) prohibits a lender from refusing credit to an individual on the basis of sex, marital status or other classification protected by the act. The act also limits the type of information that can be asked on credit applications and requires the creditor to notify the applicant within 30 days of action that has been taken. If credit is refused, the creditor must furnish the reason if requested to do so by the applicant.

The purpose of ECOA is to ensure that a person who applies for credit will be considered on the basis of ability to pay. Although the act applies primarily to consumer credit, business credit when not excluded by action of the Federal Reserve Board is also covered.

Under ECOA, creditors may ask questions about a person's spouse, marital status or age, but use of this information is permitted only for the purpose of determining creditworthiness. For example, a borrower applying for a joint account might be asked about his or her marital status if the spouse is to be permitted to use the account or the borrower is relying upon alimony, child support or separate maintenance payments to repay the credit. Information about age may be used to evaluate a borrower's length of employment or length of residence.

Creditors may not ask questions about a person's sex, race, color, religion or national origin, except in the case of a home mortgage; creditors are allowed to collect this information to show that they are complying with the law. The borrower does not have to supply answers, and failure to do so will not affect the credit application. Although a borrower can be asked to select a title such as *Ms., Miss, Mr.,* or *Mrs.,* the application must first indicate that this is optional.

An individual who is denied credit and can establish that the creditor has violated the Equal Credit Opportunity Act may recover his or her actual damages plus punitive damages up to $10,000. The plaintiff who brings a successful action under ECOA is also entitled to reimbursement for court costs and reasonable attorney fees.

Rights and Obligations of Parties

A substantial amount of mortgage litigation involves disputes concerning the rights and obligations of the mortgagor and mortgagee. The well-drafted mortgage will reduce the possibilities of litigation by incorporating provisions that clearly indicate each party's rights and obligations.

Often a mortgage instrument will be used that does not cover a problem arising between the parties. When this is the case, public policy—reflected in legislation or case law—determines what each can do. Inasmuch as questions involving possession, disposition of rents and profits and protection of the security are common, numerous rules exist to solve these problems.

Possession

The right to occupy and control real estate to the exclusion of all others.

The right to possession of mortgaged premises depends upon the theory of mortgages followed in a particular state. In title theory states the mortgagee has an immediate right to possession, but most mortgages in these states contain a provision in which the mortgagee surrenders this right. The common provision in title theory states allows the mortgagor to remain in possession and enjoy the benefits of ownership until default. Several title theory states have statutes prohibiting the mortgagee from taking possession until default.

In lien theory states, the mortgagee has no right to possession. This principle, however, is frequently modified by a provision in the mortgage allowing the mortgagee to take possession upon default. A number of lien theory states have reached a similar result by statute. Title and lien theory were discussed in Chapter 18.

As a general practice, either by statute or by mortgage terms, most mortgagors have the right to remain in possession of mortgaged premises until default. Realistically, no other result makes sense for residential real estate. For commercial property a mortgagee may find possession advantageous, especially if the property has been mismanaged. Profits from the property can be applied to the debt, and perhaps foreclosure can be prevented, an advantage to all parties. One other modification of general principles needs to be noted. In a few states with statutory right-of-redemption laws, the mortgagor is allowed to remain in possession even after a foreclosure sale. This right to possession exists until the redemption period terminates unless limited by a provision in the mortgage.

The status of a mortgagor in possession differs from that of a mortgagee. Generally, the mortgagor in possession is entitled to all of the rights of ownership as long as the value of the security remains unimpaired. A mortgagee who takes possession has special, but limited, rights that revolve around protecting the security and applying proceeds to pay the debt.

Case Example

Kansas and Missouri Bridge Company (Bridge Co.) executed a mortgage to the American Bridge Company (American) to secure payment on bonds issued by the mortgagor. The mortgage permitted American to take possession, manage the property and collect the rents upon default in payment of interest on the bonds. When Bridge Co. defaulted, American did not take possession. Later American obtained a judgment and asked that certain monies collected after default be applied to the debt. The United States Supreme Court refused this request. The court stated that "[u]pon the default which occurred, the mortgagees had the option to take personal possession of the mortgaged premises, or to file a bill, have a receiver appointed, and possession delivered to him. In either case, the income would thereafter have been theirs. Until one or the other was done, the mortgagor, as Lord Mansfield said in *Chinnery v. Black,* . . . was 'owner to all the world, and entitled to all the profit made.' "*American Bridge Co. v. Heidelbach, 94 U.S. 798 (1896).*

Rents and Profits

Possession is an important factor in determining who has a right to rents and profits from the property. The well-established general rule is that a mortgagor who remains in possession is entitled to these earnings. In the previous example, Bridge Co. retained the profits from the bridge even though the mortgagee had a right to possession after default—a right that it did not assert.

Case Example

Teal executed several mortgages to Walker on farmland and property in Portland, Oregon. The mortgages contained provisions allowing Teal to retain possession of the land but permitting Walker to take possession upon default.

When Teal defaulted, Walker demanded possession of the properties. Teal refused to yield possession, collecting earnings from the property until ousted from possession by a foreclosure sale. As the proceeds of the sale fell far short of paying the debt, Walker sued for the rents collected after Teal's refusal to surrender possession. The United States Supreme Court . . . determined that the mortgagee was entitled to rents and profits only if actually in possession. *Teal v. Walker, 111 U.S. 242 (1884).*

A mortgagee who takes possession has a right to earnings from the property, but they must be applied to extinguish the debt. Amounts collected that exceed expenses are first applied to interest and then to principal.

Most mortgages that cover commercial property contain provisions in which the parties allocate rents, profits and earnings. One approach is for the mortgagor to assign the rents and profits as additional security from the date of the mortgage. A more common provision allows the mortgagee to collect the rents upon default. Until that time, rents go to the mortgagor. In both lien and title theory states, the mortgagee has a right to appoint a receiver to collect the rents and manage the property when there is a default. This right is based upon either statute or the right to protect the value of the security.

Protecting the Security

A mortgagee has a right to protect the value of the security. This right is similar to the common law action for waste, although the mortgagee in most states has a right to sue for waste only if permitted to do so by the mortgage. But even without this right it has a right to protect the security. Actions that have been held to impair the value of the security include cutting, removing and selling timber; removing machinery; removing a dwelling; failing to pay liens and failing to keep the property repaired. The mortgagee's right to protect the value of the security may be asserted against third parties as well as against the mortgagor.

Generally, the courts have held that the mortgagee's security is not impaired unless the mortgagor's actions reduce the value of the security to an extent that it will no longer cover the debt. In some title theory states, however, courts reason that the mortgagee has title and as an incident of title may sue a mortgagor in possession for waste. Whenever the parties contemplate changes in the property such as rebuilding or extensive remodeling, the mortgage should contain clauses regarding the parties' rights and duties. A mortgagee who takes possession of the property must exercise the same care and supervision over the property that prudent persons exercise over their own. Failure to do so entitles the mortgagor to collect damages or obtain an injunction.

Insurance

Although the right to maintain the value of the security is important to the mortgagee, insurance is the best protection against many risks. The law is clear that both mortgagor and mortgagee have an insurable interest in the property.

With a few exceptions, the law is equally clear that neither is required to insure for the other's benefit in the absence of an agreement to do so. Commonly, in the United States, a mortgagor agrees to insure for the benefit of the mortgagee. The typical proviso not only commits the mortgagor to insure but also authorizes the mortgagee to obtain insurance if the mortgagor fails to procure it and add the premium to the debt. The mortgagee may, of course, agree to maintain insurance on the premises.

In addition to allocating responsibility for obtaining insurance, a well-drafted mortgage should contain a provision covering the application of insurance proceeds. A standard approach is a requirement that the mortgagor obtain a policy, making loss payable to himself or herself and the mortgagee "as interest may appear." The New York standard mortgage policy used extensively in the United States today also provides that the mortgagee's rights under this policy are not "invalidated by any act of neglect of the mortgagor."

When no agreement exists, each party may insure for its own benefit. In the event of loss the insured may use the proceeds as it wishes. This means that neither the mortgagor nor the mortgagee need apply the proceeds to reduce the debt. Because this rule is inherently unfair to mortgagors, courts have a tendency to find circumstances indicating that the mortgagee has insured for the mortgagor's benefit. Based upon such a determination, the mortgagee must apply the proceeds to reduce the mortgage debt.

Taxes and Assessments

Taxes and assessments are the responsibility of the mortgagor. Mortgages frequently authorize the mortgagee to pay taxes if the mortgagor does not. The mortgagee can then add these payments to the debt. Even without this provision, the mortgagee probably has the right to pay the taxes and add them to the debt. The reason is that the mortgagee has a right to protect the value of the security. A tax lien takes precedence over a mortgage. In the event of foreclosure, the mortgagee recovers only after taxes have been paid.

In the housing boom that followed World War II, numerous financial institutions adopted the practice of requiring mortgagors to pay a portion of taxes and insurance premiums each month, usually 1/12 of the estimated yearly total. These funds are held (in escrow) by the mortgagee, usually without interest. In recent years a number of consumer protection groups challenged the right of institutions to hold these funds without interest, arguing that the contract provision should be held unconscionable and thus unenforceable. On the whole, this litigation has been unsuccessful, as have been several legislative attempts to require lenders to pay interest on their tax and insurance escrow accounts.

Priorities

The general principles governing priorities and recording explained in previous chapters apply to mortgages. Priority rights of purchase money and construction mortgages were discussed in Chapter 18. The balance of this section will examine priority relationships between mortgages and leases, mortgages and mechanics' liens and mortgages and tax liens.

Mortgage priority problems generally occur when a debt is in default or probability of a default exists. Under these circumstances each secured creditor attempts to ensure that its lien has first claim to the proceeds if the security must be sold. Sometimes the rank of a creditor will be determined by a provision in the security document. At other times the creditor's position is established by case law or, more often, by some statute such as the recording acts.

The fundamental principle determining priority is "first in time, first in right," but modifications of this rule affect the mortgagee's position. Remember that as a result of the recording statutes, the first in time priority generally belongs to the first party to deliver his or her instrument for recording. In a majority of states this priority is not accorded if the person recording has actual knowledge of a prior unrecorded claim. Some states do have "race to the record" statutory provisions that apply to mortgages as described in Chapter 17. Under these statutes, the first mortgage on the record has a superior right even if the mortgagee knows of a prior unrecorded mortgage.

Mortgages and Leases

In general, the "first in time" rule applies to the priority relationship between mortgages and leases. If a lease is executed before a mortgage, the lease has priority. In a foreclosure sale, the purchaser takes subject to the lease. A lease entered into after a mortgage is subordinate to the mortgage if the mortgage has been recorded. In the event of a foreclosure sale, the purchaser of the property takes it free of the lease.

In practice, most mortgages on commercial property contain agreements by the mortgagee authorizing the mortgagor to lease the premises. Under these circumstances, a lease made by the mortgagor is not subject to the mortgage lien. Unless a lease contains unfavorable terms, a mortgagee entitled to possession will often recognize a lease made after the mortgage. Although the mortgagee has a right to eject the tenant, the mortgagee will be more interested in continued rental income, which can be applied against the debt.

Mechanics' Liens and Mortgages

Litigation as to priority between mechanics' lienholders and mortgagees is widespread. Its outcome varies appreciably from state to state, even when the facts are similar. Although all state courts apply the fundamental rule of "first in time," state law differs as to when the mechanic's lien attaches, and it is time of attachment that establishes the first position. At least three different approaches are taken in the United States as to when the mechanic's lien becomes effective against other claims:

1. The lien, when properly filed, reverts back to commencement of construction, no matter when the work was done or materials furnished.

2. The lien, when properly filed, reverts back to the time the claimant began work or furnished materials.

3. The lien attaches when the claimant files his or her claim.

Case Example

On April 12, 1978, Unity Bank advanced funds to Le Grand Corporation in order for the corporation to remodel facilities at its amusement park. The bank was given a mortgage as security. This mortgage was recorded on April 13. Prior to April 12, Valley Lumber Company had delivered material to the site. On April 20, Big Dig Company started excavation for an addition to the administration building. Several weeks later, when neither Big Dig nor Valley had been paid, both filed notices of mechanic's liens. When the property was sold at a foreclosure sale, questions of priority arose between Unity's mortgage and the mechanic's liens of Valley and Big Dig.

In most of the states that follow the rule that the mechanic's lien reverts back to the beginning of construction, both Valley's and Big Dig's liens would have priority. The general rule in these states is that construction begins whenever materials are delivered to the site. The result is that mechanic's liens of both Valley and Big Dig were prior in time to the bank's mortgage. In these states it is very important for a mortgagee to be sure nothing is at the site until its mortgage is recorded. If the rule in the state is that the lien attached when work or materials were furnished, Valley would have a priority over Unity's mortgage, but Big Dig would not because it began work after the mortgage was recorded. Neither Valley nor Big Dig would have a priority in states where the lien attaches when the firm files notice of its claim.

Mortgages and Tax Liens

One type of lien to which the "first in time, first in right" principle does not generally apply is the tax lien. As a general rule, liens for unpaid real estate taxes or assessments displace prior mortgages. Although this might seem unfair, it has become acceptable as one of the risks of lending. In a number of states liens for unpaid personal property taxes also become liens against the delinquent taxpayer's real estate. Mortgages, however, do have priority over federal tax liens for nonpayment of income taxes.

Subordination Agreement

An agreement that alters priorities between parties with interests in or liens upon real property.

Subordination agreements have become increasingly important in recent years to facilitate financing of many types of real estate transaction. A common use is the situation in which a purchase money mortgagee subordinates its lien to the later lien of a construction mortgagee.

Case Example

Randolph Enterprises wished to purchase and develop a 200-acre parcel of land near Frederick, Maryland. The property was purchased for $400,000 from Judson Boone. Randolph Enterprises paid Boone $150,000 in cash, and Boone took back a purchase money mortgage for the balance. Both parties knew that Randolph Enterprises would have to obtain additional financing for construction. As a result, Boone agreed to a provision in his purchase money mortgage subordinating it to a subsequent mortgage to be given by Randolph Enterprises to secure funds borrowed for development of the land.

A seller such as Judson Boone is often willing to accept a junior position for a purchase money mortgage because subordination enables the seller to obtain a higher price for the property. Sellers also know that the additional funds, if used properly, will increase the property's value. The loan, though now secured by a second mortgage, continues to be well protected. Because many state and federal regulations require loans of institutional lenders to be secured by first mortgages, the subordination agreement is frequently the key to selling undeveloped property.

Subordination agreements are used in a number of other transactions involving real estate. A tenant may agree that his or her lease will be junior to a mortgage or deed of trust subsequently executed by the landlord. On the other hand, it is also relatively common for a mortgagee to subordinate an existing interest to an interest arising out of a long-term lease that is created later.

Case Example

On August 24, 1928, Santa Monica Amusement Company (Santa Monica) leased space on a wharf to La Monica Dance Hall, Inc. (La Monica). Four years later Santa Monica mortgaged the property to Security Bank. At the time of the mortgage, La Monica executed a written agreement subordinating its lease to Security Bank's lien. When Santa Monica became bankrupt, the court found that the rights of the purchaser at the foreclosure sale were subject to the La Monica lease. This finding was reversed upon appeal. *Security National Bank v. Marxen, 28 Cal. 2d 446, 82 P.2d 727 (1938).*

The use of subordination agreements can create legal problems. Some subordination agreements are automatic, coming into existence when the interest or lien is created. Judson Boone's purchase money mortgage might be an example. The provision in Boone's mortgage could be worded to subordinate his lien as soon as Randolph Enterprises obtained its additional financing. Other types of agreements are not automatic. Such a provision might be worded to require Boone to give a subordination agreement when particular conditions are met. Enforcement of this type of subordination presents potential difficulties.

If a lender refuses to subordinate as promised, the buyer can bring an action for specific performance. In order to be successful, the buyer must prove that all conditions precedent to the lender's promise to subordinate have been met. This necessitates that the provision upon which subordination is based be clearly written. Courts will not grant specific performance unless the standard against which performance is measured is clear.

Terms of a subordination provision are sometimes critical in foreclosure litigation involving the subordinated and subordinating lenders. The subordinated lender will not lose its "first in time" priority if the subordinating lender advances funds upon conditions that differ from the subordination provision. In one case a seller who had taken back a mortgage agreed to subordinate to a "construction loan for the purpose of constructing on each lot a dwelling house with usual appurtenances." Partly on the basis of this provision, a construction mortgagee advanced the builder more than $2 million, but not all of the funds were used for construction. In litigation between the two lenders, the court refused the priority to the construction mortgagee because it knew the terms of subordination.

The question of priorities between different interests often raises problems for the mortgagee. Another type of security problem may occur if the mortgagor sells the premises. Although the lien of the mortgage is not affected by the sale, the mortgagee's position is weakened if the loan was approved primarily on the basis of the mortgagor's financial resources and credit reputation.

Sale of Mortgaged Real Estate

Case Example

Hal Zenick owned a home encumbered with an $85,000 mortgage at nine percent interest. The mortgage was held by the Harper Hill Savings and Loan Association (Harper Hill). Hal, who had purchased the property for $98,000, had lived there for about a year when he was transferred and forced to sell. During the year interest rates had risen considerably in Hal's area, and the broker with whom he listed the property suggested that Hal might sell his home more quickly and for a better price if the mortgage were retained. The buyer would not have to finance at the higher interest rates and might save in other ways.

Whether Hal lives in a title or a lien theory state, he has an interest in the property that he can sell. He cannot, however, escape personal liability for the mortgage debt unless Harper Hill, the mortgagee, releases him. In addition, the property remains subject to Harper Hill's lien. Nothing that Hal can do short of paying the underlying debt can eliminate the lien so long as the mortgage is recorded properly. Hal's right to sell his interest without discharging the mortgage may be restricted by a provision in the mortgage instrument. This is a common clause in many residential mortgages.

Due-on-Sale Clause

> *A provision found in some mortgages requiring the mortgagor to pay off the mortgage debt if the property is sold.*

A due-on-sale clause limits the mortgagor's right to convey the real property without discharging the mortgage. The clause treats the sale of mortgaged premises as a default; since almost all mortgages also contain a clause making the entire debt due upon default, the mortgagee may call the loan when the mortgagor sells the property. Of course a mortgagee such as Harper Hill can negotiate a modification of the debt with the mortgagor and the grantee and not call the mortgage. In Hal's case, Harper Hill might do this if the grantee were willing to pay interest at a rate that was closer to that the association was obtaining on new loans.

Although some mortgagees had included due-on-sale clauses in their mortgages for years, enforcement of these clauses was uncommon until the 1970s. In the 1970s, as interest rates increased, financial institutions wanted to eliminate from their portfolios low-interest loans that had been made in the past. One method of doing this was to enforce due-on-sale clauses, accelerating repayment of these loans when the property was sold.

The use of the due-on-sale clause to accelerate repayment was soon challenged by sellers in a number of states. Sellers argued that enforcement of the due-on-sale clause restricted their ability to sell and thus was a violation of public policy. A number of state courts, led by those in California, accepted this argument and refused to let mortgagees enforce these clauses. Some states, however, held that the clauses were legal.

In 1976 the Federal Home Loan Bank Board adopted a rule allowing federally chartered savings and loan associations to include due-on-sale clauses in their mortgages. The board's action was a direct response to state curbs on the use of these clauses. The board contended that restrictions on a savings and loan's ability to accelerate repayment upon transfer of the security would adversely affect the financial stability of these institutions. In addition, the board argued that the elimination of the due-on-sale clause would impair the ability of federal associations to sell home loans in the secondary market. This would reduce the flow of new funds for residential borrowing.

The board's action precipitated a conflict between state laws and federal regulation. The board's position was that its regulation totally controlled the actions of federal savings and loan associations. It contended that Congress had given it the power to regulate the federal associations and as a result state law was preempted. The states argued that their law controlled as local real estate was involved and Congress had neither expressed an intent to preempt state law nor fully occupied the field of federal savings and loan regulation. The conflict between the board and the states ended in 1982, when the United States Supreme Court, in *Fidelity Federal Savings & Loan Ass'n. v. DeLaCuesta, 458 U.S. 141 (1982),* supported the board's position and held that the board's regulation preempted state law.

Controversy involving the due-on-sale clause is interesting as an example of a classic conflict between two basic legal principles. The law of English-speaking countries has always encouraged the free transfer or alienation of property. People like Hal should be encouraged to sell property rights for their true market value. At the same time, our law encourages freedom of contract. If Hal, as a competent adult, enters into an agreement limiting a right that he owns, the courts should enforce what he has done. At present, at least in this area of the law, the freedom-of-contract principle appears to dominate.

If Hal's mortgage does not contain a due-on-sale clause, two major approaches exist to the manner in which he may sell the property without discharging the mortgage. The property may be sold with the grantee agreeing to "assume and pay" the mortgage, or the property may be sold "subject to" the mortgage.

Assumption

A contract between a grantor-mortgagor and a grantee in which the grantee agrees to assume responsibility for the mortgage debt.

Hal's broker found a buyer who was willing to pay $100,000 for Hal's residence. The buyer had $15,000 in cash and was anxious to assume the mortgage. The purchase offer that the buyer submitted to Hal contained the following provision: "Buyer assumes and agrees to pay the obligation secured by mortgage to Harper Hill Savings and Loan Association recorded in . . . according to the terms of the mortgage and the note accompanying it." When Hal accepted this purchase offer, a contract was created, one provision of which was the buyer's promise to pay the mortgage debt. This is a typical assumption agreement. Ordinarily, agreements of this nature originate in the contract of sale, but they may be made in a separate instrument. In some states an oral assumption, if provable, is binding, although certainly oral assumptions are not a preferred practice, and several states by specific statute require assumption to be in writing. In many cases the deed also contains an assumption clause. This binds the grantee upon acceptance of the deed even when only the grantor signs the instrument.

The assumption agreement does not relieve the mortgagor/grantor of personal liability for the debt. Hal continues to be responsible to Harper Hill, but he has acquired the right to sue the buyer if the debt is not paid. This right is based upon the contract between them in which the buyer has assumed the debt. As the buyer is assuming to pay the mortgage loan, if the buyer and Harper Hill Savings modify the terms of the loan, Hal is released from liability for the debt.

Implicit in the assumption agreement is the buyer's commitment that the seller may look to the land for reimbursement if forced to pay the debt. For Hal, additional monetary responsibility exists only if the land becomes less valuable than the debt.

The land, however, remains subject to the mortgage, and if the debt is not paid, the mortgage may foreclose. In addition, the mortgagee without foreclosing may sue the buyer on the assumption. The mortgagee's right exists in spite of the fact that it was not a party to the assumption agreement. Its right is based upon one of two theories: third-party beneficiary or subrogation. A *third party benefi-ciary* is one who is allowed to enforce a contract although not a party to the agreement. The third-party beneficiary's right is based upon the theory that the contract was made for its benefit. A diagram on page 402 illustrates the relation-ship among Hal, Harper Hill and the buyer. Although the contract with as-sumption provision is between Hal and his buyer, Harper Hill, the third-party beneficiary can sue the buyer if there is a breach.

In some states the mortgagee's right to sue the assuming buyer is based on *subrogation.* In these states the courts reason that the mortgagor/seller is a surety. He or she in effect guarantees the buyer's promise to pay the debt. The mortgagee, like any creditor, derivatively enjoys all the rights of the surety who guarantees payment. One of the mortgagee's rights is to sue the buyer if the mortgagor has to make good on its guarantee. Although the theories differ, the end result is the same. In each instance the mortgagee may enforce the buyer's promise to assume the debt.

In the case that follows, the original mortgagor argues that the mortgagee has agreed to an assumption by accepting payments from the firm that purchased the mortgaged real estate.

Hazifotis v. Citizens Federal Savings and Loan Association
Court of Appeals of Indiana
505 N.E.2d 445 (1987)

Background: Pete Hazifotis (defen-dant, appellant) borrowed $48,000 from Gary Federal Savings and Loan, se-curing the loan by a real estate mortgage on property that was to be used for a snow blower and lawn mower business. The note that the mortgage secured allowed Gary Federal to accelerate payments due if the loan was in default. Hazifotis sold the business to World Wide, Inc., whose operations were supervised by Thureanous.

At the time of the sale, Hazifotis, Thureanous and Dominic Cefali, presi-dent of Gary Federal, discussed World Wide's possible assumption of the mortgage; however, no paperwork was prepared to effect an assumption nor was Gary Federal's permission sought. Following the sale, World Wide, through Thureanous, made payments on the

loan for several months. Eventually World Wide missed a number of pay-ments and Hazifotis was sent a delin-quency notice. During this period, Gary Federal was acquired by Citizens Federal (plaintiff, appellee), which in-stituted a successful foreclosure pro-ceeding against Hazifotis. Hazifotis appealed from this judgment.

Decision: The judgment of the trial court was affirmed.

Judge Young
Pete Hazifotis appeals a judgment of foreclosure in favor of Citizens Federal Savings and Loan Association. He ar-gues that:

1) Citizens failed to notify him of its intent to accelerate the maturity of the mortgage debt;
2) The transfer of the business

property by Hazifotis to World Wide, Inc. terminated Hazifotis' obligation under the mortgage; and

3) The bank's acceptance of payments from World Wide, Inc. and Thureanos indicated that the bank had acquiesced in the assumption of the mortgage and therefore Hazifotis was no longer personally liable for the debt.

Hazifotis first argues that Citizens failed to clearly and unequivocally notify him of its intent to accelerate the maturity of the mortgage debt. Citing *First Federal Sav. & Loan Ass'n v. Stone.* His reliance upon that case is misplaced. In *Stone,* the debtor, pursuant to the bank's request, made tender offers for the amount due. These offers were rejected by the bank. The offers were held to have prevented the acceleration of the debt and foreclosure by the bank because the bank's intent to accelerate was not clear and unequivocal since the bank had solicited Stone's offer of payment. Contrary to Hazifotis' contentions, the *Stone* decision merely states that a mortgagee may not declare the entire amount of a debt due after the debtor has tendered an offer to pay the full amount due. In *Stone,* such an offer was solicited by the bank and made by the debtor. In the present case, Hazifotis tendered no offer to pay the full amount of the arrearage. Rather, Thureanos made some of the past due payments. but the loan was never brought current. Thus the *Stone* case is inapposite.

In addition, Hazifotis agreed to pay the purchase money loan according to certain terms and upon default repay the accelerated remaining balance without "notice of non-payment and protest...." Further, he agreed that the "[m]ortgagee is hereby authorized and empowered, at its option and without affecting the lien . . . to declare without notice, all sums secured . . . immedi-

ately due and payable . . ." and he agreed that "the mortgagee may deal with such successor or successors in interest . . . and . . . may extend time for payment . . . without in any way affecting the liability of the mortgagor." Promises of this variety in the mortgage agreement operate to discharge any need for the type of notice of acceleration claimed here, because the lender is by operation of the agreement requiring strict compliance even if payments are accepted late and can give notice by his foreclosure action. Thus by agreement, notice prior to commencement of the legal action is not required.

> [S]ince a security agreement is to be enforced to its terms, an agreement containing a non-waiver and non-modification clause gives the secured party the right to take possession of the collateral without notice upon default.

The principle is operative in a mortgage context in "preventing acceptance of late payments from operating as a waiver of a subsequent default." Thus, the argument that Gary Federal fortified its right to accelerate the mortgage by accepting some late payments is without merit. Similarly, the argument that Hazifotis was no longer obligated under the mortgage because of the transfer of the land to World Wide, Inc. must fail.

The conveyance by a mortgagor of the mortgaged premises to another does not exonerate him from personal liability for the debt secured.

> In our view, it is the law of Indiana that a conveyance of real estate subject to an encumbrance such as a mortgage, which is the personal obligation of the grantor, without any assumption by the grantee to discharge the encumbrance, does not operate to re-

lieve the grantor of his obligation to the mortgagee or to transfer such obligation to the grantee.

Thus Hazifotis remained obligated under the mortgage.

Hazifotis next argues that he was not personally liable for the mortgage note because Citizens by accepting payments from World Wide, Inc. and Thureanos somehow acquiesced to its assumption—not so. Citizens' acceptance of payments from World Wide, Inc. did not release Hazifotis from his liability. There was no assumption of the original mortgage by World Wide, Inc. and there was no modification of the original mortgage terms or alteration of the personal liability originally imposed. In fact, no written documents were prepared that would provide for an assumption by World Wide, Inc. Thureanos understood that in the absence of an appropriate written agreement there was no assumption. Likewise, Hazifotis admitted in his discussion with Thureanos that he was still liable on the mortgage and that he had not been able to complete the transfer of his obligation to World Wide, Inc. Moreover, Gary Federal had standing policy that it would not allow the release of the primary obligor and it evidenced nothing to indicate that it had. It never changed the rate of interest, waived the lateness of a payment, or withheld its efforts to bring the loan current. Rather, all of the evidence indicates that the parties recognized that any assumption would require refinancing at a different interest rate and the payment of additional points. This was specifically considered and rejected by Thureanos, and Hazifotis understood that without a new agreement based "a change in the interest rates and new points" all he could rely upon was Gary Federal's awareness of the sale. This is insufficient. That Gary Federal may have been aware of the transaction

does not release Hazifotis. Indeed the trial court found *inter alia:*

25. That Cefali discouraged HAZIFOTIS and Thureanos from pursuing and completing said assumption immediately, in the expectation that interest rates would drop in the near future.

26. That all three men knew, understood and expected that formal paperwork and renegotiation of the terms of said mortgage were required to complete a valid assumption of the mortgage and to discharge HAZIFOTIS' liability on said debt.

27. That said formal paperwork was never completed.

28. That all said parties were aware that said paperwork was not done.

29. That PETE HAZIFOTIS has been a licensed real estate broker since 1965, active in the real estate business since 1963, and is aware of the documents required to effect a valid mortgage assumption.

30. That George Thureanos has been a licensed real estate salesman since approximately 1956, and manages several businesses.

31. That neither Thureanos nor World Wide, Inc. assumed said mortgage and note, and Defendant PETE HAZIFOTIS remains personally liable on said debt.

Moreover, even if there were a proper assumption, this standing alone, does not release the obligation of the original mortgagor unless there was also some change in his rights relative to repayment of the debt. While it is true that when a mortgage is assumed a relationship between grantor and grantee may become as that of principal and surety, the relationship of the original borrower does not change as to the lender in the absence of an express agreement on the part of the mortgagee to look first to the grantee.

If the purchaser assumes the mortgage, he becomes as to the mortgagor the principal debtor, and the mortgagor the surety, but the mortgagee, unless he has assented to such an arrangement may treat both as principal debtors, and may take a personal judgment against each of them in addition to his decree of foreclosure.

Accordingly, Hazifotis' claims that he is released because Gary Federal ac-

cepted payments from World Wide, Inc. or because Thureanos responded to Jody Edinger's letter are incorrect. Absent dealings between World Wide, Inc. and Gary Federal or Citizen's Federal which would operate "in such a manner would jeopardize or alter the surety-principal relationship," there is no legal basis for allowing the release of Hazifotis on his obligation. Hazifotis is personally liable according to the terms of his original promise.

Affirmed.

Novation

> *A mutual agreement in which a creditor agrees to discharge an existing debt and to substitute a new obligation and a new debtor in its place.*

A novation differs from an assumption to which the mortgagee has consented. In the assumption, the original mortgagor has a secondary liability even after the property is sold. In a novation, the original mortgagor is discharged and the old debt is extinguished. Few mortgagees will consent to a novation during periods of increasing interest rates unless the new debtor agrees to pay interest at the prevailing rate.

"Subject To"

> *Refers to a sale in which buyer agrees to purchase property subject to the lien of the mortgage.*

Perhaps the buyer found by Hal's broker would not be willing to assume the mortgage debt. Under these circumstances, the buyer would pay Hal for his equity in the property. Any interest acquired by the buyer is "subject to" the lien of the mortgage. If there is a default, the property will be foreclosed, but the buyer has not agreed to become personally liable.

As noted, if a buyer takes property "subject to" the mortgage, he or she has no personal obligation. Both the mortgagee and the seller/mortgagor must look to the land to collect the debt in the event of default. If proceeds from a foreclosure are not sufficient, the deficiency is the seller/mortgagor's responsibility. A number of states have, however, extended the buyer's responsibility with the doctrine of *implied assumption*. In these states, the buyer is personally liable even when no promise to assume exists, when the amount of an existing mortgage is deducted from the purchase price and the buyer pays the difference.

Case Example

Metcalf contracted to sell property to Lay for $29,000. The property was encumbered with a $20,000 mortgage. The contract did not mention the

ASSUMPTION

NOVATION

existing mortgage because Lay anticipated financing without it. This financing did not materialize, and the salesperson for the seller suggested that Lay merely purchase the equity. Lay agreed. Lay never talked with the seller, and no express assumption was discussed. At the closing the price of the property was clearly shown as $29,000 with a $20,000 credit for the mortgage. The deed to Lay excepted the existing mortgage. When the debt was not paid, the mortgagee foreclosed. Not realizing enough from the sale to pay the debt, the mortgagee sued Metcalf, who in turn sued Lay. Lay would be held personally responsible although he had not assumed the mortgage if the court applied the doctrine of *implied assumption*.

The doctrine of implied assumption has been criticized frequently. This criticism is based upon the belief that a buyer should not be exposed to the risk of personal liability unless he or she clearly and explicitly has accepted this responsibility.

Assignment and Discharge

For a number of reasons, the mortgagee may wish to transfer ownership of the mortgage and note. The real estate professional should be familiar with the manner in which this is done. Additionally, the real estate professional should be familiar with the documents evidencing the discharge of the mortgage lien.

Assignment

> *The present transfer of a property right from one person (the assignor) to another (the assignee).*

One of the chief incidents of ownership is the right to assign, or to transfer to another, that which is owned. This principle applies to intangible as well as tangible property.

Case Example

South Central Savings financed the purchase of a residence for Marlene Jefferson. As a part of the transaction, Jefferson executed the customary note and mortgage in favor of South Central. South Central wished to obtain additional funds for lending and assigned the mortgage and note as part of a package to the Britan Insurance Company. The company discounted the notes and paid funds to South Central. Jefferson would be obligated to pay the insurance company because it now owned her obligation to South Central Savings.

The example illustrates a common situation in which mortgages and notes are assigned. South Central is the *assignor,* and Britan Insurance Company is the *assignee*. The mortgagor, Marlene Jefferson, is referred to as the *obligor*.

In addition to mortgages and notes, rights created by contracts, leases and options also may be assigned. Sometimes, however, the document that creates the right may limit assignment unless the obligor agrees. This is unusual in a mortgage but more frequent in a contract for the sale of land. The seller might be concerned with the identity of the buyer. A mortgagor usually is not concerned with the identity of the person to whom the debt must be paid.

Understanding the mechanics of mortgage assignment is complicated by the dual nature of the mortgage transaction. Remember that a mortgage loan includes both a note, which is the borrower's personal promise to pay, and the mortgage, which is security for the debt. An assignment that is properly drafted transfers ownership of both the note and the mortgage. The assignee becomes the owner of both the obligation and the security.

Sometimes an assignment will refer only to the note or the mortgage. In these situations most courts have taken the position that the debt is of primary importance and the mortgage merely an incident of the debt. If an assignment transfers only the mortgage, courts rule that the assignee also acquires the obligation, because a mortgage without a debt is meaningless. Conversely, courts have generally ruled that any transfer of the obligation also includes the mortgage, although the mortgage is not mentioned.

Estoppel Certificate

A statement by the mortgagor that recites that the mortgagor has no defenses against paying the note or enforcing the mortgage and indicates the amount still due on the debt.

A mortgagor who executes an estoppel certificate represents that he or she has no defenses against payment. Thereafter the signer is estopped from raising any defense except one that arises after the execution of the estoppel certificate. Most mortgages will contain a clause requiring the mortgagor to complete an estoppel certificate. In some areas a statement of this nature is known as a *waiver of defenses* or *certificate of no defense.*

Another problem that sometimes arises involves situations in which the mortgagor pays the original mortgagee instead of the assignee. If the note is nonnegotiable, part payment to the original mortgagee reduces the debt, and the mortgagor is not required to pay the assignee. Because of this rule, an assignee should immediately notify the mortgagor of an assignment. Once this has been done, the mortgagor can no longer pay the original mortgagee.

When the note secured by the mortgage is negotiable, the mortgagor is not released by a payment to anyone except the holder of the note. To be discharged if payment is in full, the mortgagor must obtain possession of the instrument. If payment is partial, the mortgagor should demand that the instrument be produced and payment endorsed upon it.

Discharge

A statement releasing property from the lien of the mortgage.

Mortgages are commonly discharged by one of four methods: merger, release, running of the statute of limitations or payment of the mortgage debt.

Merger is a combination of the interest of the mortgagor and the mortgagee in the same person. It ordinarily occurs when for some reason or other the mortgagor conveys title to the mortgaged land to the mortgagee. Although a mortgage usually formally releases the land when the debt is paid, a mortgage may be released either in whole or in part under other circumstances.

A blanket mortgage often contains a partial *release* provision. A provision of this nature is necessary when a mortgage covers a large tract of land that is to be divided and developed. In order to obtain financing to build or sell residences on the smaller tracts, the developer must be able to release them from the lien of the blanket mortgage.

Statutes of limitations that apply to enforcement of mortgage liens vary widely from state to state. The application of the statute of limitations to bar foreclosure actions is further complicated by the dual nature of the mortgage transaction. In general, states have adopted shorter limitation periods for debts evidenced by a note than they have for enforcement of a mortgage. This creates a problem when collection of the note is barred by a statute of limitations but the statutory period for a foreclosure action has not yet expired.

Case Example

On July 29, 1959, Carl Lundberg executed a promissory note payable upon demand to M. E. Tegels. The note, which was secured by a second mortgage, was for $9,100, with interest at six percent. Lundberg never paid any amount on the principal or the interest. No action was taken on the note, and by the time of Tegels's death payment was barred by the statute of limitations.

In 1971, Northwestern National Bank, trustees under Tegels's will, attempted to foreclose on the property. At this time Lundberg contended that the running of the statute of limitations on the note was a bar to the foreclosure action. Both the lower court and the Supreme Court of Minnesota disagreed. *Lundberg v. Northwestern National Bank, 299 Minn. 46, 216 N. W.2d 121 (1974).*

Although this case represents only one point of view, it is probably the majority position. Courts in a number of states have ruled that, if collection of a debt is barred by the statute of limitations, the mortgage can no longer be foreclosed.

The period established by statutes of limitations is effectively extended by various actions taken by the mortgagor or mortgagee. A mortgagor's part payment of the debt or new promise to pay starts the statute anew. His or her absence from the jurisdiction discontinues or, in legal terms, *tolls* the statute for the duration of the absence. The mortgagee may also toll the statute through a promise to extend the time for payment. As a result, the fact that a mortgage is old is not a reliable guide to its enforceability. Because of this, several states have adopted statutes that void a mortgage a specified period of time after maturity, usually 20 years. In addition, marketable title acts discussed earlier provide for the elimination of stale mortgages unless some notice of claim is filed.

Payment of the mortgage debt is the usual method of discharging a mortgage. Payment of the debt, however, does not clear the public record; this must be done by entering in the record an instrument releasing the mortgage. Various names are given to this instrument. In some places it is known as a *satisfaction piece* or *satisfaction*. In other areas it is called a *discharge* or a *release*. At one time it was a common practice merely to endorse on the margin of the recorded mortgage that it had been satisfied. A number of jurisdictions continue to follow this practice. Most states have statutes that provide for a monetary penalty if a mortgagee refuses to execute a release.

In those jurisdictions where the deed of trust is the popular form of financing instrument, the trustee who holds legal title will execute a release deed or deed of reconveyance when presented with the canceled notes indicating that the debt has been paid. Obtaining a deed of reconveyance or a satisfaction is important to the debtor. Unless these actions are taken, questions as to marketability of title may be raised.

Summary

The mortgage loan starts with an application, which constitutes the borrower's offer to enter into a contract to borrow money. If the loan is approved, the lender issues a commitment which constitutes acceptance, and a contract exists. In financing commercial real estate, a lender often proposes terms that differ from the loan for which the borrower applied. The commitment thus becomes a counteroffer. No contract exists unless the borrower accepts the new terms.

Both state and federal statutes regulate the terms and conditions of the mortgage loan. Historically, each state has established a maximum interest rate that lenders can charge. Interest rates in excess of this figure are termed *usurious* and are illegal. In recent years, because of economic conditions, most states have increased the maximum rate. In addition, recent federal legislation eliminates state usury ceilings for certain mortgage loans.

Mortgage transactions are also affected by other federal statutes. For example, the Consumer Credit Protection Act (1968) provides for *truth-in-lending*, requiring lenders to disclose fully the cost of consumer credit. Another federal statute, the *Equal Credit Opportunity Act*, prohibits many kinds of discrimination by lending institutions.

When mortgaged property is sold, different methods of treating the loan are available to the parties. Frequently, the loan will be paid off out of the proceeds of the sale because the parties wish to do so or because of a requirement of a *due-on-sale clause*. Without such a clause, a potential buyer may be able to assume the existing mortgage and continue to pay according to the same terms. Or, the owner may sell the property *"subject to"* the existing mortgage. In either of these cases, the mortgage continues as a lien on the property; the responsibilities of the buyer and seller differ, depending on whether the buyer *"assumes"* or purchases *"subject to"* the mortgage.

Mortgage lenders, when faced with the need to raise additional funds, often *assign* some of their mortgage loans to another institution. Payments on the loan so assigned must still be made according to the original terms. The new holder of the mortgage—the assignee—generally requires the borrower to sign a statement that confirms the debt. This statement is known as an *estoppel certificate.*

The usual method of discharging a mortgage—that is, releasing property from the lien—is by payment of the debt. Upon payment, a notice of satisfaction is placed in the public record. Other methods of termination include merger, which is combining the interests of the mortgagor and mortgagee in the same person, release and running of the statute of limitations.

Review and Discussion Questions

1. The terms *finance charge* and *annual percentage rate (APR)* are important in truth-in-lending legislation. Explain what each means.

2. Under the Equal Credit Opportunity Act a lender may ask questions about marital status and age under certain conditions. What are these conditions?

3. Outline the rights and privileges of a mortgagee who takes possession of a mortgaged premises upon the mortgagor's default.

4. (a) List the three different approaches taken in the United States as to when a mechanic's lien becomes effective. (b) In your opinion which of these is the most equitable? Why?

5. (a) What is a subordination agreement? (b) Under what conditions might a mortgagee be willing to subordinate its lien?

6. What is a due-on-sale clause? Explain why this clause has become increasingly important in recent years.

7. Compare and contrast the rights and obligations of the grantor/mortgagor with those of a grantee assuming responsibility for the mortgage debt.

8. Explain the doctrine of "implied assumption."

9. What is an estoppel certificate? Explain its importance when a mortgage is assigned.

Case Problems

1. Oellerich and his wife sold real estate that they owned. The purchasers assumed the mortgage. The assumption agreement provided that the Oellerichs were not released from liability on the original debt if the purchasers defaulted on the note. Shortly thereafter the lender and purchasers executed a modification agreement that increased the interest on the note. The Oellerichs were not parties to this agreement. Did the modification agreement affect the rights of the parties? Explain how and why. *Oellerich v. First Fed. Sav. & Loan Assn., 552 F.2d 1109 (5th Cir. 1977).*

2. Albert owns real property worth $35,000. He borrows $28,000 from Martin and executes a mortgage on the property in Martin's favor. The term of the mortgage is 15 years. Seven years later, Albert sells the property to Bobb for a cash amount with the mortgage remaining on the property. What difference, if any, will it make to Bobb if the deed from Albert states "subject to a mortgage indebtedness of _____" or "subject to a mortgage indebtedness of _____, which said indebtedness the grantee assumes and agrees to pay"?

3. Larson owned a commercial building that he had inherited from his mother. The original mortgage on the building had been satisfied. In January 1974, Larson leased a portion of the building to Hutchins for a five-year term. The lease was immediately recorded. In March 1975, Larson borrowed $75,000 from the Belville Bank, giving it a mortgage on the property. The mortgage was for a term of ten years. It was recorded on April 11, 1975. The $75,000 was used to renovate the property. In 1977, because the debt was not paid, the bank foreclosed.

    (a) Kane, the purchaser at the foreclosure sale, wished to use the entire building and brought an action to eject Hutchins. Would Kane be successful? Discuss.

    (b) Assume that, on March 27, Anderson began electrical work that was part of the renovation. The work was not completed until June. When Anderson was not paid, he filed a mechanic's lien. What are Anderson's rights vis-à-vis the Belville Bank? Discuss.

4. Smith agreed to purchase property from Layton. As part of the contract, Smith assumed and agreed to pay the existing mortgage. Smith immediately contracted to sell the property to Young. Layton agreed to convey directly to Young, who assumed the mortgage in the deed to him. Smith never had title to the property. The mortgage was not paid, and the foreclosure took place. There was a deficiency, and the mortgagee sued Smith. Would the mortgagee be successful? Discuss.

5. Lon Gabele is the president of Gabele Builders as well as its chief salesperson. Fredericktown Savings agrees to finance homes built by Gabele at a rate of 10 1/2 percent if the buyer makes a $2,500 down payment. Gabele places an advertisement in the local paper indicating that homes can be purchased at $2,500 down. The only other information in the advertisement is the offering price, Gabele's name and the location of the development.

    Prior to the advertisement's appearance, a number of buyers had visited the homes that Gabele had for sale. When asked about financing, Gabele informs them that it is available at 10 1/2 percent. He provides no additional information but refers them to Fredericktown Savings. Has Gabele violated the credit advertising provisions of the "Truth-in-Lending" Act? Support your answer.

6. Pearle conveyed property that she owned to her son Estrel. Dime Savings held a mortgage on the property. An escrow provision in the mortgage

required the mortgagor to pay monthly sums to cover insurance and taxes. Estrel fell into arrears on the mortgage payments. When the insurance policy became due, there was a negative balance in the escrow account. As a result, the bank didn't renew the policy, and it was canceled. The property suffered severe fire damage, and Estrel sued the bank for failing to renew. Is the bank liable?

20

Land Installment Contracts

Land Installment Contract

A legally enforceable agreement between buyer and seller whereby the buyer promises to make periodic installment payments to the seller toward the purchase price of real property and the seller promises to convey title to the property upon receipt of the last installment.

Chapter 13 considered the real estate purchase agreement, the ordinary contract for the sale of real estate. This agreement defines the rights and duties of the seller and buyer in preparation for the closing of the transaction, which is discussed fully in Chapter 15. Between the signing of the purchase contract and the closing there is a short interval ranging from about one to three months. During this interval the seller is expected to prepare an abstract or secure other evidence of title and the buyer attempts to obtain financing, typically through a lending institution.

Sometimes the buyer is unable to obtain financing from a lending institution. Lacking the necessary cash, the buyer may be forced to defer purchase until his or her financial situation improves. Several alternatives are open, however, that may enable the buyer to purchase the property. If the seller is willing to extend financing to the buyer for the purchase price, one alternative is the purchase money mortgage, which is discussed in Chapter 18. Under that method the seller transfers the deed to the property to the buyer and the buyer signs a mortgage in the seller's favor. The mortgage secures the remaining unpaid purchase price owed to the seller. The land installment contract, also known as a *land contract* or *contract for deed*, is another method of seller financing.

For the buyer, the land installment contract is a method of financing a real estate transaction through the seller; for the seller, it secures the payment of a debt. The rules that attach to ordinary contracts also apply to land installment contracts. The agreement must be supported by consideration and entered into by parties who possess the requisite capacity. Nevertheless, some obvious distinctions separate the land installment contract from the ordinary real estate purchase contract. In a real estate purchase contract the buyer's right to possession is deferred until closing or thereafter. Under a land installment contract possession is normally immediate and does not await final payment. In addition, the relationship between the parties to a real estate purchase agreement is of rather short duration, usually ceasing at the closing, when title is conveyed. The legal relationship of the parties to a land contract lasts longer. Such a contract may endure for as long as the seller is willing to extend the financing, perhaps 20 years or more, although shorter periods are more common. Often the seller extends a payment schedule based upon a 20- to 30-year payback period but requires the entire balance to be paid in full after a shorter period, for example, three to five years. The final payment is known as a *balloon payment* and normally requires the buyer to find outside financing to meet the payment. Before final payment the seller holds legal title, whereas the purchaser is normally in possession of the property and enjoys *equitable title*.

Title Problems

Upon completion of all terms of the contract, including payment of the last installment, legal title passes to the buyer and the deed can be recorded in the buyer's name. Until the last installment is paid, the property remains in the seller's name. During this interval the seller may encumber the property with mortgages or other liens. Unless the buyer is protected, he or she may pay the entire purchase price and find the property totally encumbered. By recording the land installment contract, however, the buyer can secure protection against most future encumbrances. Recording places all prospective mortgagees and lienors on notice of the buyer's interest in the property, and title problems are less likely to arise.

If the contract is unrecorded and the seller encumbers or sells the property, the installment contract buyer may be without remedy. A claim against the seller for damages will not necessarily help the buyer should the seller be insolvent. Sellers often discourage or impede the recording, since it is easier to resell the property upon the buyer's default if the contract is not recorded. However, some states by statute, require a land installment contract to be recorded.

Liens that attach before the creation of the installment contract may go unnoticed if the buyer fails to investigate the title beforehand. Title insurance protects the buyer's interest in the property. Normally this form of assurance is required when a third-party lender is involved. In land installment contracts, however, there is no third-party stimulus because the seller finances the transaction. The uneducated buyer may fail to have the title examined. The prudent buyer should require proof of title in the seller as a condition of entering into the contract, should be sure the contract is immediately recorded, and should require a clause within the contract clarifying that the seller agrees to tender a deed to the property free of all liens and other encumbrances.

After Acquired Title

In some cases the seller does not have title at the time of entering into the contract but subsequently acquires it. In this event the buyer is entitled to "after acquired title" when the time comes for the deed to be transferred to the buyer.

Case Example

Jim Ferguson, seller, enters into a land installment contract with Bill Hodd, buyer, whereby Ferguson is to tender a free and unencumbered deed to 20 acres of farmland designated as the Hill property, upon Hodd's completion of 60 monthly payments of $300 each. At the time the contract was entered into Ferguson possessed only a leasehold interest. Thereafter, however, he acquired the property in fee simple absolute from the lessor. Upon completing the last installment payment, Hodd is entitled to the fee under the doctrine of after acquired title. See *Bull v. Goldman, 30 Md. App. 665, 353 A.2d 661 (1976)*.

Should the buyer learn, after signing the contract, that the seller does not possess marketable title, in some jurisdictions the buyer may rescind the contract and seek return of the installment payments previously paid.

Contract Terms

Basic rules of real estate purchase contracts treated in Chapter 13 also govern land installment contracts. Since a land contract involves an interest in land, it must comply with the Statute of Frauds, which requires that the contract be supported by a written memorandum. Normally, the land installment contract must be properly executed before it can be recorded. State statutes vary and should be consulted to ascertain the particular requirements for proper execution.

The parties are free to agree on the terms of the contract, and the courts will enforce those terms to the extent that they do not offend public policy. Over the years certain typical terms have emerged. Generally, the specifics of the terms reflect the relative bargaining strength of the buyer and seller. It appears that the seller has traditionally possessed the upper hand.

Price

Normally the buyer pays a modest down payment and periodic installments. The installment payments include principal and interest. The installments may be payable monthly, quarterly, annually or at any other agreed-upon interval. Unless otherwise stated, taxes and insurance are the seller's responsibility, because the seller is the legal owner of the property until the entire purchase price is paid. Neither statute nor custom prevents an allocation of taxes and insurance to the parties on the basis of their respective interests in the property. In most cases, however, the bargaining position of the seller is strong enough to require the buyer to assume the whole burden of these charges. This is not an unreasonable burden considering that the buyer receives the present beneficial use of the property and expects full ownership in the future.

Waste, Removal and Inspection

The buyer is normally in possession of the premises in an installment contract. Consequently, the installment buyer is in the best position to maintain the premises and keep it in good repair. Customarily, the parties include a clause in the contract that makes the buyer responsible for the maintenance. Similarly, the installment contract may include a clause prohibiting committing waste or removal of fixtures or improvements without the consent of the seller. Failure of a buyer to comply with these clauses is a breach of the contract that gives rise to various remedies discussed later in this chapter.

The seller needs the right to inspect the premises in order to police these provisions. For that reason a clause similar to the following is often included: "Seller shall have the right to enter on and inspect the property and the buildings and improvements thereon after giving reasonable notice to do so."

Indemnification

The act of compensating another in the event of loss.

In the event that the buyer fails to keep the property in repair or causes waste, damages may result from either loss of property value or consequent injury to occupiers of the property. Mechanics' liens (discussed in Chapter 7) may also encumber the property if the purchaser fails to pay the workers or suppliers for renovations, repairs, improvements or other authorized work. An indemnification clause such as the following may be included for the seller's protection:

> Buyer shall hold seller free and harmless from any and all demands, loss, or liability resulting from the injury to or death of any person because of the negligence of the buyer or the condition of the property at any time after the date possession is delivered to the buyer. Buyer shall further indemnify seller for the amount of any and all mechanics' liens or other expenses or damages resulting from any renovations, alterations, building repairs, or other work ordered by the buyer.

Should the buyer fail to pay the tax assessments or insurance as agreed upon, the seller's security is jeopardized. The government, deprived of its taxes or assessments, may place a lien on the property and even foreclose for failure to pay. The seller's security would also be jeopardized should the property be destroyed by fire unless hazard insurance is maintained. If there is a mortgage on the property, the mortgagee may foreclose in the event taxes, assessments and/or insurance payments are in arrears. To protect the seller against these risks, a clause such as the following may be included within the installment contract:

> Should buyer fail to pay any amount pursuant to this contract for taxes, assessments, or insurance within ten (10) days before that amount becomes delinquent, the seller may pay the amount and buyer agrees to repay to seller the amount paid by the seller together with interest at the rate of ten (10) percent per annum.

Assignment

In the absence of a provision in the contract prohibiting assignment, the buyer is free to transfer his or her interest in the land contract. Assignment does not, however, relieve the installment buyer of the obligation to continue making installment payments to the seller. The seller may desire to limit the buyer's right of assignment, being concerned that the assignee (one to whom the property is transferred) may be more likely to jeopardize the seller's interest in the property than the installment buyer. For this reason the installment contract normally includes a provision prohibiting assignment without the seller's written consent. In absence of such a clause, the buyer may asign the contract, and the seller must respect that assignment.

Case Example

Wayne and Lucille Hickox entered into a written agreement for the sale and purchase of 864 acres of real estate with Barbara and Billy Bell. The purchase price was $700,000, payable $50,000 as a down payment and the remainder in installments, with the first five years interest payments only. Under the contract the purchasers had the option as payments were made, to have the sellers sign a warranty deed in favor of buyers to such land as paid for based upon $815.00 per acre. The Bells faithfully made payments the first four years and then assigned the contract to the Hesses, who made payments thereafter. The Bells requested that the Hickoxes execute a warranty deed conveying 83.67 acres based on the amount of principal paid to date. The Hickoxes refused to credit any amount of the payments made by the Hesses because it was not paid by the Bells.

Finding in favor of the Bells, the Illinois Appellate court said:

> "[W]hen a valid assignment is executed, the assignee (1) acquires all of the interest of the assignor in the property that is transferred and (2) stands in the shoes of the assignor.". . . [W]e find that the money paid by the Hesses under the contract is to be credited to the Bells as payment under the contract.

See *Hickox v. Bell, 195 Ill. App. 3d 976, 552 N.E. 2d 1133 (1990).*

At any time before title passes, the seller is free to transfer the property to someone other than the installment buyer. Installment payments are then directed to the new owner. The sale is subject to the rights of the installment buyer, who still remains entitled to the property upon fulfillment of the terms of the installment contract. The seller's power to assign may be limited by agreement, but normally is not because of the purchaser's weaker bargaining position.

Mortgage

Mortgages are discussed in detail in Chapters 18 and 19. A typical clause regarding the seller's right to mortgage the property, pending the full payment of the purchase price, is often included within the land contract. A clause similar to the following is not uncommon: "The seller may mortgage the property, but in no event may such mortgage exceed the amount of the balance due on the contract."

Case Example

Norma Livingston sells real property to Howard Kessler on a land installment contract for $120,000, payable $20,000 down and $5,000 annually thereafter at ten percent interest for 20 years. After five years Livingston desires to borrow money and gives a mortgage in the property to the Second National Bank as security for the loan. Livingston may mortgage the property up to $75,000, the balance due on the installment contract.

In addition, the buyer may be contractually safeguarded against the consequences of a seller defaulting on a mortgage by inclusion of a clause similar to the following:

> The seller shall keep any mortgage on the property in good standing, and if the seller defaults on any mortgage, seller agrees that the buyer may pay the delinquency and receive credit toward payment due under the terms of the contract.

An installment buyer who desires to borrow money from a bank or other lending institution can use as collateral the realty that is the subject of the land contract. Unless the contract expressly states otherwise, the buyer is entitled to mortgage the property to the extent that its value exceeds the amount owed on the land installment contract. A provision in the contract prohibiting assignment does not prevent the installment buyer from mortgaging his or her interest.

Case Example

Jaurel and Edna Fincher entered into a land contract whereby Lester Stacey and his wife agreed to purchase a one-half acre tract of land from the Finchers. The purchase price was $1,200, payable $200 down with the remainder payable in installments of $47.50 per month. Paragraph seven of the contract provided that the "Buyers may not assign their rights hereunder in whole or in part." Later the Staceys entered into an agreement with Miles Homes to purchase a precut home for erection on the tract for $6,378. The Staceys made a down payment and signed a promissory note for the balance due. The note was secured by a mortgage on the tract of land purchased. Miles Homes delivered the materials to the site in accord with the contract. The Staceys made payments to the Finchers but defaulted after the death of Mrs. Stacey. Similarly, the Staceys defaulted on their obligation to pay Miles Homes. The Finchers canceled the contract (with the consent of Mr. Stacey), reacquired possession of the land and sought a judicial order determining that the Miles Home lien was invalid. The court concluded that the prohibition against assignment did not prohibit the Staceys from entering into a valid mortgage and that the Finchers owned the property subject to the Miles Homes' lien. *Fincher v. Miles Homes, 549 S.W.2d 848 (Mo. 1977).*

If the buyer mortgages the property and then defaults on obligations under the land installment contract, a serious question arises concerning the mortgagee's rights. The seller must notify the mortgagee of the default before taking any action regarding the property. In some jurisdictions the mortgagee is entitled to acquire title to the property by paying the seller the amount due under the installment contract. In this circumstance the mortgagee may receive more value than the balance due on the mortgage loan. Other jurisdictions limit the mortgagee's recovery to the amount of the mortgagor's indebtedness due by requiring the mortgagee to invoke foreclosure, as discussed in Chapter 18. Under such an action the property is sold. The land installment seller is paid first from the proceeds an amount necessary to satisfy the amount due on the land contract. The remaining proceeds are used to satisfy the mortgagee's indebtedness, and the installment buyer receives the balance of any remaining monies. In a few states the mortgagee is obligated to pay the balance of the indebtedness owed to the seller before the foreclosure sale.

Conveyance

The buyer's ultimate objective is to receive good title to the property. Upon performance of the contractual obligations, including payment of the last installment, the seller is obligated to give a good title to the property by conveying the deed to the buyer. This requirement is normally reflected in a clause that reads as follows:

> When the buyer has paid the full purchase price with interest due and in the manner required by the terms and conditions of this contract; and, if the buyer performs all other provisions required of the buyer by the terms and conditions of this contract, seller agrees to convey the above described property to the buyer by deed of general warranty, with release of dower, if any.

Advantages to the Buyer

Most purchasers are not financially able to raise the entire purchase price in one lump sum; consequently, they must obtain financing in order to purchase the realty. A buyer, however, may not be able to secure financing from a lending institution because of an inability to meet down payment requirements or because of an unsatisfactory credit rating. Or the lender may refuse to extend credit because of the marginal value of the property.

The principal advantage that the installment contract offers to buyers is the ability to purchase the property. For little or no down payment, buyers are able to gain an interest in, and derive the benefit of, the property. The land installment contract increased in popularity as a financing tool in the early 1980s, when high interest rates decreased the borrowing power of many people. Its widespread usage continued even in face of declining interest rates.

Advantages to the Seller

The land installment contract may also benefit the seller. Such benefits may include attraction of buyers, tax advantages and continued incidents of legal ownership.

Attract Buyers

The main advantage to sellers is that the land installment contract provides a means for increasing the demand for property by attracting buyers who could otherwise not purchase the property because of an inability to secure outside financing. The ability to set the schedule of repayment so that it is affordable to the buyer often places the seller in a position to increase the purchase price above the market level and/or charge higher interest than the seller is paying on the mortgage. Normally, however, the property is priced in accordance with the market. The attractive terms often permit the sale of otherwise unattractive property.

Tax Break

Under an installment contract, the seller does not receive the entire purchase price in one lump sum. Payments are extended over a period of years. Under an Internal Revenue Code section, a seller may elect to partially defer tax treatment for gains in an installment sale transaction. A taxpayer who elects the installment method of reporting need only report as income, in a given year, the proportion of the installment payments that the gross profit bears to the total contract price. Consequently, income is spread over a period of time. As a result, the seller may defer taxable income to a future time when overall income may be less. The seller consequently receives a welcome tax break.

Case Example

Barry Martin sells property to Sheila Cable for $40,000, payable $10,000 down with the remainder to be paid over six years at $5,000 a year. Martin had previously purchased the property for $30,000. His gross profit is $10,000 ($40,000 contract price – $30,000 original purchase price). Cable pays the $10,000 down payment. The proportion of the gross profit to the total contract price is 25 percent (10,000/40,000 = 25 percent). Martin, by electing the installment method, need report as income in the year of sale only $2,500 (25 percent of $10,000 down payment) and $1,250 in each succeeding year (25 percent of $5,000).

Incidents of Legal Ownership

The land installment contract secures the payment of the buyer's indebtedness and gives the seller certain incidents of legal ownership. As discussed earlier, the seller may assign the property subject to the contract or mortgage the property up to the indebtedness. This is attractive to a seller who may reap the benefits of incidents of ownership while involved in a sale of the property.

Disadvantages to the Buyer

The land installment contract may present certain disadvantages to the buyer. These disadvantages may arise should the seller die, fail to transfer good title or neglect to record the contract.

Problems Created by the Death of the Seller

Although the land contract is enforceable against the seller's heirs upon death, as a practical matter enforcement may be very costly. The buyer may be forced to hire an attorney to accomplish the transfer. The beneficiaries may be difficult to locate, and the property may be tied up in probate for years. Should there be a large number of beneficiaries, the situation becomes more laden with concurrent ownership interests and difficulties. Since minor and incompetent beneficiaries may require the appointment of a guardian, resolution may be even further complicated and delayed. Similar problems are present when the seller assigns the installment contract to another who dies.

Unwillingness or Inability to Transfer Good Title

The seller might refuse to transfer the title to the buyer after fulfillment of the contract. The buyer, who is legally entitled to the deed, may be forced to institute suit seeking specific performance. Even worse, after the buyer pays the installments in conformity with the contract, the seller may not have good title. Normally, the seller has agreed to convey title to the buyer upon receiving the final payment. By prevailing authority the seller is not required to maintain marketable title during the pendency of the contract, although a few courts have taken a contrary view. The buyer could obtain protection by insisting upon a contract provision requiring the seller to maintain marketable title or by obtaining title insurance.

Failure to Record

As stated earlier, the installment contract should be recorded to protect the buyer's interest. Sellers may try to discourage buyers from recording because in the event of default less difficulty attends to quieting title in their name if there has been no recording. In fact, some contracts may contain *in terrorem* clauses that prohibit recording at the expense of forfeiture. Although their validity is dubious, they undoubtedly discourage some buyers from recording. Some states by statute require the installment contract to be recorded, and provide penalties for failure to do so, such as rescission of the contract.

If the installment contract is recorded, the majority of states give the buyer's contract priority over most subsequent purchasers and lienors since they are on constructive notice of the buyer's interest. Further, the land installment buyer usually has priority over subsequent purchasers and lienors who have knowledge of the buyer's interest, even if the contract is unrecorded. In many jurisdictions the fact that the buyer is in possession gives subsequent purchasers constructive knowledge of the buyer's interest, even if the contract is not publicly recorded.

Disadvantages to the Seller

From the seller's viewpoint the land installment contract is often a compromise sometimes negotiated as a result of an inability to sell the property for cash. Two reasons may exist for this inability. High market interest rates may make it impractical for purchasers to obtain conventional financing, or the purchaser's financial status may prevent him or her from obtaining a loan from a lending institution. Because the land contract does often attract buyers who are otherwise not able to purchase the property because of their financial status, risk of default is high. Default may result in the buyer's forfeiture of all rights in the property. The buyer's interest may revert to the seller, in which case the seller is burdened with the property once again and must reenter the real estate market, necessitating additional brokerage costs and attorney fees. In some jurisdictions forfeiture is not an available remedy. Instead, judicial foreclosure of the property is necessary to cut off the buyer's interest. The cost of foreclosure makes it a burdensome remedy for the seller.

Seller's Remedies

A seller possesses several remedies against a buyer who fails to pay or who otherwise defaults under the terms of the installment contract, including specific performance of the contract, damages, rescission, forfeiture and foreclosure. These remedies were covered generally in Chapter 13. Forfeiture and foreclosure remedies, however, deserve special attention as seller's remedies under the land installment contract.

Forfeiture

Often included within the terms of a land contract is a forfeiture clause, which provides that in the event the buyer fails to abide by the terms of the contract the seller has the right to terminate the contract, retake possession of the property and retain all prior payments. Traditionally, these forfeiture clauses have been upheld by the courts. When enforced, the defaulting buyer loses all equity in the property, and the seller often receives a substantial windfall. The forfeiture penalty may be very severe to a defaulting buyer.

Case Example

In 1971 Sellmer, the seller, entered into an installment sale contract with Donaldson, the buyer, for the purchase of a summer cottage on the Ohio River. The purchase price was $16,500 at the rate of eight percent per annum for ten years. The contract called for a $2,000 down payment, and the monthly payments were $175. Donaldson, on several occasions, failed to make timely payments and failed to make three monthly installments in 1973. Donaldson failed to keep the property insured, contrary to a provision in the installment contract to do so. Additionally, Donaldson failed to keep the property in repair and left the property in an uninhabitable condition. Sellmer sued Donaldson, seeking a forfeiture and termination of the contract. The court held that because "Donaldson had wholly failed to perform his obligation to acquire adequate insurance and had allowed the property to deteriorate to such an extent that substantial repair was necessary before the house would even be habitable," forfeiture was a proper remedy. Consequently, the court ordered that more than $7,000 in payments made by Donaldson be forfeited to Sellmer and that the contract be terminated. *Donaldson v. Sellmer, 166 Ind. App. 60, 333 N.E.2d 862 (1975).*

Most states have departed from automatic approval of the forfeiture remedy, and all states have mitigated its harshness by statute or judicial decision. Some states require a "grace period," within which the buyer may cure any breach. In those jurisdictions forfeiture is permitted only after compliance with procedural technicalities. The seller must notify the buyer of the intention to invoke forfeiture and of the grace period. If the buyer fails to correct the default within the specified period the statute permits, forfeiture is proper. The lengths of these grace periods vary from 30 days to a year. Some states graduate the grace period dependent upon the portion of the contract price the buyer has paid. In the event the seller affords the requisite statutory notice and there is no response by the buyer to cure the defect, some states permit forfeiture without judicial proceedings. Others require court action.

Another state statute eliminates forfeiture altogether by providing that the seller of a land installment contract shall be deemed to be a mortgagee and shall be subject to the same rules of foreclosure and to the same regulations, restraints and forms as are prescribed in relation to mortgages. Still, another statutory approach ameliorating the hardship of forfeiture is the elimination of forfeiture as a remedy under certain conditions. This type of statute is the subject of the next case.

Smith v. Blackburn
511 N.E. 132 (Ohio App. 1987)

Background: Doris Blackburn entered into a land installment contract with the Smiths. After several late payments by Blackburn, the Smiths served a notice that the contract would be forfeited and thereafter instituted a suit seeking forfeiture.

Decision: The trial court found in favor of Blackburn, holding that forfeiture was inappropriate. The court of appeals reversed the decision and remanded it to the trial court.

Judge Grey

The case raises an issue of statutory interpretation of [Revised Code] 5313.07. This section simply put, says

that when the vendee of a land contract has paid twenty percent of the purchase price, the vendor's remedy for default lies in foreclosure and not in forfeiture. The issue in this case is how is that twenty-percent figure to be calculated.

. . .

The land contract was executed on a printed form which did not contain the words "purchase price," but Blackburn agreed to pay $20,000, with $2,000 down and $204.85 per month at nine percent interest for twelve years. At the time of trial, it was stipulated that Blackburn had made the following payments: a down payment of $2,000;

twenty-three monthly payments of $204.85 ($4,711.55 total) as per the contract to cover principal and interest; insurance premiums for two years of $320; and real estate taxes for 1984 and part of 1983 in the amount of $571.61.

The trial court, in determining whether the Smith's action for forfeiture was properly brought . . . added together all the amounts paid by Blackburn, which totaled $7,603.16. The court ruled that since this amount was in excess of twenty percent of the purchase price, the Smiths had to bring an action in foreclosure and judicial sale. . . .

Blackburn asserts that she has paid $6,711.55—the cash down payment of $2,000, plus monthly payments totaling $4,711.55—which is in excess of twenty percent of $20,000 or $4,000. It must be stressed, however, that each monthly payment was to be applied under the terms of the contract, to *both* the principal amount *and* interest on the purchase price. The installment contract unambiguously describes the apportionment of each monthly payment to principal and interest. The new principal amount is calculated at the end of each month and interest on that amount is to be deducted from that month's payment. Whatever remains of the monthly payment is applied to reduce the principal amount.

. . .

The question is whether the statute contemplates interest payments being included in the "sum total" paid toward the purchase price. . . .

Since the term "purchase price" is not defined in [the statute] its meaning may be expressly determined by the parties to the contract or by implication, *i.e.,* using the word's meaning. It is apparent from the agreement, the actions, and the briefs of both parties that the purchase price was $20,000. This figure is the basis for all other payments: the ten-percent down payment, the monthly payments on the remaining $18,000, the insurance on the property and the real estate taxes and assessments. It was this figure which the parties agree to as the value of the premises in paragraph one, page two of the land installment contract.

Thus, with $20,000 being the "purchase price" pursuant to [the statute], the amounts paid toward it are to be determined in accordance with the terms of the contract. Under the agreement only a portion of each payment is to be applied toward the principal amount of the "loan," the balance of the purchase price. Under Blackburn's formulation, "purchase price," would include all payments, interest as well as principal. We reject this formulation. The interest was agreed to, but as *interest* on the remaining balance of $18,000 not as a part of the purchase price. . . .

. . .

The judgment of the [trial court] is reversed and the cause is remanded to that court with instructions to calculate twenty percent of the purchase price in accordance with this opinion. This court is aware that additional payments may have been made by the vendee during the pendency of this appeal and that these payments may have increased the total amount paid by the vendee to a sum that is in excess of twenty percent of the purchase price. In light of that possibility . . . we direct the [trial court] on remand to include in its calculations all payments made by the vendee during the pendency of this action.

Judgment reversed and the case remanded.

Even when there is no statutory modification, courts are reluctant to uphold a forfeiture clause and often employ various rationales to relieve the defaulting buyer from a harsh result. If, for example, a seller consistently accepts late payments from the buyer and thereafter seeks forfeiture for delinquent payment, a court may hold that the seller has waived any rights under the contract for forfeiture by failing previously to object to delinquent payment. Other jurisdictions analogize a defaulting buyer in a land installment contract to a defaulting mortgagor and recognize an "equity of redemption period." In those jurisdictions courts determine the period of grace through tests of fairness and reason.

Case Example

In April 1967, the Allens (purchasers) entered into a land installment contract with the Ulanders (sellers) for the purchase of real estate. Under the terms of the contract, the Ulanders agreed to convey the real estate to the Allens after payment of $9,700 at the rate of $85 or more per month at seven percent interest per annum. The contract further provided for forfeiture in the event the purchasers failed to make timely payments. Over a period of 7 1/2 years the Ulanders paid more than $7,500 in principal and interest and built up an equity of $1,583. They also made improvements to the property, adding two bedrooms, a bathroom and paneling. The Allens failed to make five payments in 1974 and 1975, and the Ulanders instituted an action in forfeiture. The court, applying equitable notions, allowed the purchasers 30 days to deposit with the court a sum equal to five months' payments to avoid forfeiture. The court held that "where a purchaser under an installment land contract has acquired a substantial equitable interest in the property, the court has discretion to utilize a remedy similar to that permitted in foreclosure actions." *Ulander v. Allen, 37 Colo. App. 279, 544 P.2d 1001 (1976).*

Still other equitable rationales may be invoked to support a refusal to recognize forfeiture. Some courts hold that, if the buyer would sustain a substantial net loss as a result of forfeiture, then forfeiture would be unconscionable; in that case the buyer is entitled to restitution. Under this view, if the seller's actual damages, based upon the fair market rental value of the property and other damages, are less than the buyer's payments, the buyer would be entitled to the difference.

Case Example

Mr. and Mrs. Hoyle, under an installment contract for the purchase of a motel, make total installment payments of $120,000 on a $345,000 purchase price. Additionally, they expend $30,000 on repairs and improvements to the premises. After four years the Hoyles default on their installment payments and vacate the premises. The reasonable rental value of the motel is $30,000 per year. Under an equitable approach, since the $150,000 expenditure on payments and improvements is substantial, the buyer is entitled to restitution in the amount of $30,000, computed as follows: Buyer's total expenditures are $150,000, consisting of payments in the amount of $120,000 and improvements in the amount of $30,000. The reasonable rental value of the property is $30,000 × 4 years (the period of time in which the Hoyles occupied the premises), or $120,000. The difference between the total payments and the reasonable rental value is $30,000 payable to the Hoyles.

Finally, some courts have struck down the forfeiture clause on the basis that it constitutes an unconscionable penalty.

Foreclosure

As noted, some states by statute provide for foreclosure as the proper remedy for a seller against a defaulting installment buyer. Only a few states have recognized foreclosure by judicial decision as a seller's remedy in the event of the buyer's default. Indiana is one such state. In Indiana the courts reserve the remedy of forfeiture for cases of absconding or abandoning buyers or where only a minimum amount has been paid by the buyer while the seller is making expenditures for taxes, insurance and maintenance. In all other cases in that jurisdiction and in some other jurisdictions the courts recognize judicial foreclosure as the proper remedy.

Case Example

Laura Virginia, seller, and Pam Osterholtz, purchaser, entered into a land contract for Whiteacre on the following terms: $10,000 down payment and $12,000 annually for five years, for a total of $70,000. Osterholtz paid $10,000 and made the first $12,000 installment but defaulted thereafter. Virginia instituted an action in forfeiture. The court held that foreclosure was the proper remedy. Under a foreclosure, if the property sold for $75,000 at a judicial sale, Virginia would receive $48,000 to satisfy the balance due on the contract and Osterholtz would receive the balance of $27,000. *See Sebastian v. Floyd, 585 S.W.2d 381 (Ky. 1979).*

Buyer's Remedies

The buyer possesses several possible remedies against a seller who fails to convey title or otherwise defaults under the terms of the contract. The remedies of specific performance, rescission, damages and foreclosure will be examined.

Specific Performance

When the installment buyer completes the requirements under the installment contract, including payment of the last installment, he or she is entitled to the deed. If the seller does not convey the deed, a court may award specific performance, mandating the seller to execute a deed in the buyer's favor. Refusal to abide by the decree may result in contempt of court and punishment. The court may also execute a deed in the buyer's favor, or the very decree may act as the instrument that results in passage of title to the buyer.

Rescission

Another remedy for an installment buyer upon a seller's default is to elect rescission—that is, to have the contract terminated and the contract payments returned. In this instance fairness often requires that a value for rental of the property be deducted from the amount due the buyer. The remedy of rescission is designed to return the parties to their original position. This remedy is especially desirable for the buyer when the subject of real estate has depreciated in value below the contract price.

Damages

The installment buyer in reliance upon the contract may have spent money to improve the property. If the seller breaches under these circumstances and is unable to convey a marketable title, the buyer may prefer to sue for damages. A judgment for damages becomes a general lien on all real property the seller owns until the judgment is satisfied. As a lienor, the buyer may foreclose on any of the seller's real property to satisfy the judgment. Other means of satisfying the judgment include attachment and sale of the seller's personal property and garnishment of the seller's wages.

Foreclosure

The installment buyer has an equitable interest in the property. As such, the buyer possesses an equitable lien on the property securing his or her interest. Consequently, the buyer may foreclose on the property in the event of the seller's default and recover the purchase payments.

Summary

The *land installment contract* provides for payments to be made in periodic installments. Under this type of contract, the seller extends financing to the buyer, who does not receive full title until the final payment is made. For the duration of the contract the buyer has the right to possession, although legal title is retained by the seller. To protect the buyer, the land contract should be recorded. In addition, the buyer should examine the title to make certain it is marketable.

The land installment contract has advantages for both buyer and seller. For the buyer, paying installments to the seller may be the only way to obtain affordable financing—when interest rates are high, for example. For the seller, this type of financing widens the market for the property and attracts buyers who would not otherwise have been able to buy. In addition, there is a significant tax advantage to the seller who reports gains from the sale of the property by the installment method.

Disadvantages may sometimes outweigh the advantages. One risk to the buyer is death of the seller and unwillingness of the heirs to perform under the contract; another is failure of the seller to maintain good title for the duration of the contract. One disadvantage to the seller is the risk of default by the buyer.

Remedies are available to the seller or buyer upon breach of the installment contract. Under some circumstances, foreclosure may be the seller's only remedy. This process is both time-consuming and inconvenient because it burdens the owner with the sale of the property once again. Remedies for the buyer against a seller who fails to convey the title may include specific performance, rescission, damages and foreclosure.

Review and Discussion Questions

1. Describe the differences between a land installment contract and an ordinary real estate purchase contract.

2. Who is helped by the doctrine of "after acquired title"? In what ways?

3. (a) What is the primary advantage to a buyer who buys property on a land installment contract? (b) What are the advantages to a seller?

4. (a) What is the primary disadvantage to the buyer who sells property on a land installment contract? (b) What are the disadvantages to the seller?

5. What are some acts that might be considered a buyer's breach of a land installment contract?

6. Describe the seller's remedy of forfeiture and explain how the states have softened the impact of that remedy.

7. Describe the buyer's remedies in the event the seller defaults on a land installment contract.

Case Problems

1. Donald Reed and LaVonne McAdow entered into a land installment contract for the sale of a parcel of land owned by Reed. The contract was never recorded. Subsequently, Reed assigned his entire interest in the land to Ohio Mortgage Company, which was unaware of the contract between Reed and McAdow. The assignment was not recorded. After the assignment of the land Kagey Lumber Company obtained a judgment against Reed and is now in the process of placing a lien on the property. (a) Will Kagey's judgment become a lien on the property? Why or why not? (b) What are Kagey's rights in the property? Describe. (c) Is Ohio Mortgage Company subject to the provisions of the contract between Reed and McAdow? Discuss. See *Butcher v. Kagey Lumber Company, 164 Ohio St. 85, 128 N.E.2d 54 (1955).*

2. Moorman and Whitman signed a land installment contract for the sale of real estate owned by Moorman. The contract stated that the land consisted of three tracts totaling 460 acres. Whitman assigned his interest in the contract to Maxwell. The assignment, expressly authorized by the contract, contained a description of the land similar to that in the land installment contract. After three years Maxwell paid Moorman the entire balance due under the land

installment contract and received the deed to the property. Maxwell then attempted to sell the property to Fentress. Before the deal was consummated, Fentress notified Maxwell that the property contained only 355.9 acres rather than 460 acres, as stated in their contract. Maxwell and Fentress agreed to a reduction in the purchase price, and the contract was signed. Maxwell then attempted to persuade Moorman to return to him approximately 23 percent of the purchase price he paid. Moorman refused. (a) Can Maxwell successfully maintain an action against Moorman for return of the disputed portion of the purchase price? Explain. (b) Does Moorman have a cause of action against Whitman? Explain. See *Maxwell v. Moorman, 522 S.W.2d 441 (Ky. Ct. App. 1975).*

3. Newman entered into a land installment contract with Mountain Park Land Company to purchase a tract of timberland. After Newman paid approximately half of the money due to the company under the contract, the company, without the consent of Newman, cut down trees from the land and sold a substantial amount of the timber. As a result of the actions of Mountain Park, the land decreased in value. (a) Does Newman have a cause of action against Mountain Park? (b) If so, what is that cause of action and what are his possible remedies? See *Newman v. Mountain Park Land Co., 85 Ark. 208, 107 S.W. 391 (1908).* (c) What if Newman harvested the trees and inflicted the damage to the property during the pendency of the installment contract? Would Mountain Park have a cause of action against Newman? Explain. See *Reynolds v. Lawrence, 147 Ala. 216, 40 So. 576 (1906).*

4. Ben Schottenstein and Jack J. Devoe entered into a land installment contract. The terms of the contract stipulated that certain property would be conveyed in fee simple absolute by Schottenstein to Devoe in return for $21,500 payable in installments over a ten year period. After signing the contract, Devoe learned that Schottenstein did not have legal title to the property at the time of the contract signing. Devoe therefore seeks to avoid the contract. (a) May he do so? Explain. (b) What is Schottenstein's counterargument? (c) What could Devoe have done if he knew of the state of Schottenstein's title prior to signing the contract? See *Schottenstein v. Devoe, 83 Ohio App. 193, 82 N.E.2d 552 (1948).*

5. Purchasers under a land installment contract made only four out of twelve monthly payments, failed to pay taxes and maintain insurance, and failed to pay sewer and water charges. In absence of a statute, what factors are relevant to determine the proper remedy available to the land installment seller? Explain. See *Grombone v. Krekel, 754 P. 2d 777 (Col. App. 1988).*

Part 5

Regulation of Ownership Interests

21

Land Use

The basic tenets of American property law can be traced back to feudal times in England. Between the king and the lowest serf was the great mass of landholders. The landholder was not an owner but had the right to use a parcel of land. In exchange for that right of use, certain duties were owed to the superior on the feudal scale. These duties might include providing military service or a portion of the crops grown on the land. Our system of private property has evolved from this scheme, in which each landholder owed certain obligations in exchange for the right of use, but the legal notion of private property in America took its own peculiar twist.

As in England, the landholder's *rights* gradually expanded into what we refer to as *ownership*. These rights eventually gave the owner almost absolute and unfettered control over his or her grant of land. William Blackstone, the great 18th-century authority on the common law, referred to a person's property right as "that sole and despotic dominion," thereby depicting the extensive freedom that accompanied land ownership. A person's ownership rights were never quite as absolute as Blackstone alleged, but the wide range of rights he connoted became indelibly etched in the minds of landowners in England and America.

The American difference applied not to the "rights" side of the equation but to the "duty" side. Almost from the inception of this country a landowner owed no duty to anyone except to refrain from acts on the property that would significantly interfere with another landowner's use of his or her property. Once the purchase price was paid, the buyer of land owed no additional duty to the seller. Our concept of property has always emphasized the landowner's rights over any duties arising from that ownership.

Though most Americans still cling tenaciously to the idea of absolute ownership rights in land, those rights have eroded sharply in the 20th century. The subdivider of land usually places a significant number of restrictions on use in the deed to the new homeowner. Municipal codes place an array of restraints on an owner's property rights. For instance, zoning laws limit an owner's use of the land. Other statutes or local ordinances require an owner to hook up to a sewer, to desist from playing loud music late at night, to refrain from keeping farm animals and to get a permit in order to build an addition to the house, to name only a few. This chapter will describe some of the traditional private restrictions on an owner's use of real property. It will then discuss constraints on government regulation of land: the Federal Constitution and the planning that must precede government regulation of land.

Private Restrictions on Land Use

Many limitations on the use of land are the result of agreements between buyers and sellers. These limitations are often referred to as *private restrictions*. The term *private restrictions* is also used to refer to limitations on land use imposed by the common law.

Restrictive Covenants

Private agreements, usually placed in the deed by the seller when conveying land to the buyer, that restrict future use of that land.

Parties to a real estate transaction are free to enter into any legal agreement that suits their particular situation. An agreement restricting the future use of the land is called a *restrictive* covenant.

A restrictive covenant is said to run with the land if it attaches to the land and is not dependent upon the continued ownership of the parties to the original deed. The buyer's successors in title would be bound by the covenant, and the seller's successors in title would continue to benefit from the covenant.

Case Example

Baum, as the original grantee of a subdivided parcel, covenanted in the deed to accept and pay for a seasonal water supply provided by the original grantor. Eagle Enterprises, the successor to the original grantor, sued Gross, the successor to the grantee Baum, to enforce the restrictive covenant relating to the supplying of water. Eagle Enterprises argues that the covenant attaches, or "runs with the land," thereby binding all subsequent owners to pay for supplying the water. Gross responds that the covenant bound only Baum and did not run with the land.

The court held that a restrictive covenant will run with the land if it meets three conditions: (1) the original parties must intend that it run with the land; (2) there must be privity of estate between the parties; and (3) the covenant must touch and concern the land. Although the court found that this particular covenant was personal and did not "touch and concern" the land, any covenant that meets the threefold test will be held to run with the land. *Eagle Enterprises, Inc. v. Gross, 39 N.Y.2d 505, 349 N.E.2d 816 (1976).*

Privity of estate is a phrase used to express the successive relationship of the parties to the land. For example, privity of estate exists between the grantor and grantee of an easement. The term *touch and concern the land* relates to the determination of whether the purported easement is peculiarly tied to the land itself or is rather a personal agreement between the parties and only incidentally concerns the land. The distinction between a personal covenant and one that touches and concerns the land is not always clear.

The restrictive covenant may carry a time limitation; for example, "This covenant shall run with the land and be in effect for 20 years from the date of the conveyance." Usually, however, no termination period is stipulated, and the covenant lasts indefinitely.

Over the years restrictive covenants have not been favored by the courts because they constituted an encroachment on the free transferability of land. Courts have never been enthusiastic about permitting land to be tied up in restrictions on use; when any doubt exists as to the meaning of the covenant, courts usually find against the party placing the restriction in the deed. Despite the clear intention of the parties in the *Eagle Enterprises* case described above, note the reluctance of the court to bind future parties where grounds existed for relieving the land from the restriction.

The use of restrictive covenants and the attitude of courts toward them may be shifting. Today a substantial amount of residential development takes place in the form of subdivisions. The developer usually places a broad range of restrictive covenants in the plat plan or the individual deeds of the homebuyers or both. The purpose of the restrictions is to protect other landowners in the subdivision from losing some of their property value because of the unorthodox activity of a neighbor in the subdivision. For example, a restrictive covenant might prohibit the landowners from raising pigs or other farm animals. To avoid conflicts caused by questionable land use during development or immediately after the subdivision is completed, developers are inclined to include restrictive covenants against everything not narrowly confined to normal single-family use. The developer thereby makes every subdivision owner the third-party beneficiary of the restrictive covenants in the deeds of the other homeowners in the tract. The covenants generally are part of the deed or are filed with the general plat plan for the development and then recorded, thereby giving notice to all parties having an interest in the land in the future. The covenant is now part of the chain of title and runs with the land indefinitely.

Traditionally, the person selling part of his or her land subject to restrictive covenants has the right to enforce the covenant in the courts. Similarly, any owner in the subdivision as the third-party beneficiary of the developer-homeowner contract has enforcement rights in the court. However, a modern practice is for the developer to create a group such as an architectural committee to administer the covenant procedure. The developer and some associates often comprise the committee. The committee is authorized to handle complaints and (sometimes) to permit deviations from the restriction in the covenants. For example, the restrictive covenant may bar all buildings from the land except the house and attached garage, unless approved by the architectural committee. Upon request, the committee may permit the homeowner to build a small toolshed on the property.

One problem may arise from this practice when the developer conveys all the parcels in the tract and does not provide for transfer of membership on the committee to the local subdivision residents, creating a hiatus. Theoretically, any homeowner *can* enforce the covenant. If the courts follow their traditional inclination of disfavoring restrictive covenants, however, enforcement may be impossible. It is arguable that the covenantor intended the *committee* to be the mechanism for enforcement, but the committee is now defunct.

An additional problem is that, when restrictive covenants proliferate, people tend to ignore them. County or local zoning and building codes reduce the need for restrictive covenants by controlling major use changes or construction on residential land.

Case Example

Rachel assembles a four- by six-foot metal shed on her property to store her lawn mower and garden tools. Although the building is prohibited (without permission) by the restrictive covenant in Rachel's deed, it is common in her subdivision to own these sheds; in other words, "everyone" ignores the covenant. The courts may not enforce the restrictive covenant upon request by a neighbor because the homeowners have acquiesced in this noncompliance.

However, there are instances where Rachel will clearly be subject to the restrictive covenant and probably to a building code. When Rachel decides to build a second house on her lot, the covenant is violated and a building permit is required. The building inspector, in order to offer some measure of protection to other residents, oversees her plans. The building code, rather than the restrictive covenant, will probably become the enforcement mechanism.

Nevertheless, the restrictive covenants still provide a mechanism for an unhappy neighbor to complain, even concerning minor alterations like the small metal storage shed.

Restrictive covenants can be terminated in several ways. *All* the concerned parties may agree in writing to the termination. This approach may prove infeasible where the number of parties to the covenant is large. The covenants can also be terminated through condemnation of the land by a public agency having the power of eminent domain.

A common method of extinguishing these covenants is through nonuse or misuse. The character of the neighborhood may change, making continuation of the restrictions meaningless.

Case Example

DeMarco brought an action against adjacent property owners to have restrictive covenants limiting use to residential purposes declared void. Due to the construction of the Edsel Ford Freeway, replacing a two-lane country road, all surrounding land on the parties' street was in commercial use.

The court voided the restrictive covenant because the four-lane freeway had completely changed the character of the area. *DeMarco v. Pallazzo, 47 Mich. App. 444, 209 N.W.2d 540 (1973).*

The longer the covenants are ignored or violated and the greater the number of people who participate in the violations, the less likely the court is to enforce the proscriptions in the deeds.

Easement

A nonpossessory interest in real property; the right to use another's real estate for a limited purpose.

Easements were discussed in detail in Chapter 6, and that discussion will not be repeated here. Easements run with the land and are a method of encumbering free use of the parcel by a subsequent taker.

A conservation easement is one type of easement that is gaining in popularity and constitutes a significant restriction on land use. A conservation easement is one that limits or prohibits development on real property for the purpose of maintaining the scenic or natural condition of the land. It is a negative easement.

In the past, the enforceability of conservation easements was questionable. The beneficiary of the easement was usually a private conservation organization or an arm of government. Such a beneficiary did not normally own adjoining land, so the easement was not appurtenant. The law generally requires an easement to be appurtenant in order for it to run with the land. If the easement did not run with the land, then it was enforceable only between the parties to the original agreement, and it would eventually be terminated.

In recent years, many states have adopted statutes declaring conservation easements to be enforceable and negating common law defenses against them, such as the lack of appurtenance. This statutory protection, along with an increased interest in preserving environmentally important lands, is likely to lead to increased use of conservation easements in the future.

Common Law Limitations

The restrictions discussed above are the result of specific covenants inserted in the deed by the grantor. In addition to these, there are limitations created by the common law itself. Such common law limitations are imposed by the law for the benefit of surrounding landholders.

Nuisance

An unreasonable interference by one party with another's use or enjoyment of his or her land.

The notion of nuisance is an ancient creation to protect landowners from unfettered and wrongful use of land by a neighbor. It does not require a physical invasion of the complainant's land, as does trespass. Such things as noise, dust, vibration and odors may constitute a nuisance. A party who is victimized by a nuisance will be able to get compensatory damages and may be able to enjoin the nuisance. Most states, however, will grant an injunction only after balancing the equities between the parties and determining that the benefit of the injunction will outweigh the ensuing detriment to the perpetrator of the nuisance. As a result of this balancing process, injunctions are not readily available to small landowners complaining about a nuisance created by a large industrial or commercial facility. For instance, in a case entitled *Boomer v. Atlantic Cement Co., 26 N.Y.2d 219, 257 N.E.2d 870 (1970),* New York's highest court was unwilling to enjoin the operation of the $45 million plant, though admitting that there was a substantial nuisance to several nearby landowners. Prior to this case, New York had been more liberal than most states in granting injunctions in nuisance cases.

Trespass
A wrongful, physical invasion of the property of another.

This common law remedy may be available to the landowner to put a stop to physical encroachments, whether they occur on the land's surface, in the air above or on the ground beneath.

Case Example

Pehrson brought an action in trespass for money damages against his neighbor, Saderup, for cutting down lilac bushes on Pehrson's land. The court decided that Saderup had committed a trespass by cutting the lilac bushes and awarded Pehrson money damages for the trespass based upon the difference between the fair market value before the cutting of the lilacs and that value afterward. *Pehrson v. Saderup, 28 Utah 2d 77, 498 P.2d 648 (1972).*

Actual damages need not be shown in order to recover for a trespass to land, but as a practical matter the landowner is likely to get only nominal damages where he or she does not actually show loss.

Public Restrictions in Land Use

In the twentieth century private restrictions were eclipsed in importance by public restrictions. Land use and development is controlled predominantly by legislation adopted at the state and local levels. Initially, control was by zoning codes; more recently, there have been a wide variety of other types of regulations.

Zoning and other regulatory legislation is examined in the next chapter. The remainder of this chapter is confined to three preconditions for a valid regulation. Any land use legislation must be a valid exercise of the police power, conform to federal and state constitutional limitations, and be preceded by a certain degree of planning.

The Police Power

The authority to regulate land use is almost exclusively provided by the police power. The police power is the inherent right of the state to regulate to protect the public health, safety or welfare of its citizens. The grant of authority under the police power is very broad, and it can be delegated to local governments.

To be a valid exercise of the police power, the legislative body must have a legitimate police power purpose, that is, a public health, safety or welfare reason for its enactment. It must prove also that there is a connection, or nexus, between the legislatively stated purpose and the regulation enacted. For instance, if the law's stated purpose is highway safety, it must substantially promote highway safety.

Unlike the exercise of the power of eminent domain, the legislature regulating under the public power does not take the regulated property nor does it pay just compensation to the property owner.

Constitutional Limitations

The most important constitutional limitation in the land use area pertains to eminent domain. Theoretically, the government has the inherent power to take land from private owners for its own use. The federal and state constitutions, however, place constraints on that power. They provide that a taking of property by government, or an exercise of eminent domain, must have a public purpose and that the government must pay just compensation. When the government exercises its power of eminent domain, it physically takes the land away from its former owner. It is not merely regulating use as it does when using the police power.

The government's power to *regulate* under the police power and its power to *take* land under eminent domain appear at first blush to be distinct and separate. The courts have found, however, that there can be conflict in the exercise of the two powers. A regulation under the police power may be so restrictive of the private owner's use of the land that a court may hold that it constitutes a "regulatory taking." In a regulatory taking, the court declares that the attempt to regulate went beyond the police power and crossed the constitutional line of the eminent domain clause. It requires the government therefore to withdraw the regulation or to pay the landowner just compensation.

The courts are clear that an attempted exercise of the police power can be found to be an unconstitutional regulatory taking. At this point, the clarity ends. Drawing the line between valid and invalid regulations has proven to be a struggle for courts. Some courts declare that a law that prevents a harm to the public is a valid regulation and one that confers a benefit on the public is an invalid regulatory taking. Is a regulation that requires a residential land developer to dedicate part of the land for parkland to serve the needs of future homeowners preventing harm (e.g., congestion) or conferring a benefit (e.g., giving them extra and unnecessary land without paying for it)? There is no inherently correct answer, and therein lies the frailty of the rule.

Some courts argue that a regulatory taking occurs when all reasonable use of the land is taken by the law. Is the "all reasonable use" test a purely economic analysis? If so, how much of the economic value of the land must be taken? Alternatively, when land has little economic value but significant natural resource value, such as a wetland, must the rule encompass more that the economic value of the land? No significant agreement exists among the federal and state courts as to how to perform the regulatory takings analysis.

The U.S. Supreme Court, while acknowledging the ad hoc nature of the analysis, has settled on a largely economic analysis. The Court makes clear, however, that a physical invasion of the land is a regulatory taking regardless of the economic implications.

Case Example

Teleprompter placed a one-foot-wide cable television box on the rooftop of a building owned by Loretto. The cable television company obtained the authority to do this from a state law permitting the placing of cable boxes and wires on private land. Loretto challenged the law as an unconstitutional regulatory taking of a part of her land.

The U.S. Supreme Court ruled for Loretto stating that a "permanent physical occupation authorized by government is a taking without regard to the public interest it may serve." It is noteworthy that the rule applies only to permanent physical occupations; it is a per se rule, however, applying regardless of the extent of the public interest served by the state law or the slight degree of economic injury to the landowner. *Loretto v. Teleprompter Manhattan CATV Corp., 458 U.S. 419 (1982)*.

Without a permanent physical occupation created by the regulation, the Court scrutinizes the full economic impact of the law on the value of the land, or the so-called diminution in value test. The Court has never defined where the diminution line should be drawn. Perhaps it is no more precise than being at the point at which all reasonable economic use is confiscated. The Court seldom finds regulatory takings under the diminution in value test.

A second economic-based test appears to be a modification of the diminution in value test, though both are applied in the same cases. The Court looks to see if the reasonable investment-backed expectations of the landowner are frustrated. If the landowner continues to obtain a reasonable return from the land despite the regulation, the Court is unlikely to find that the reasonable investment-backed expectations were frustrated. No significant clues beyond this have emerged from the Court as to how these reasonable expectations are determined.

Some courts have shied away from using a solely economic rationale in deciding regulatory takings cases. These courts contend that land is in part a public natural resource so fundamental to human existence on this planet that decisions about it cannot be made examining only a law's economic impact on its current owner.

The contrast between the U.S. Supreme Court's economic approach and the public natural resource approach may be best illustrated by the following two cases. The Penn Central case is the leading Supreme Court case, and the Just case is a landmark case for natural resource analysis.

Penn Central Transp. Co. v. New York City
U.S. Supreme Court
438 U.S. 104 (1978)

Background: In 1965 New York City adopted the Landmark Preservation Law. The law created a Commission which was to identify the criteria for determining a landmark, and then to designate specific landmarks that met the criteria. The designation as a landmark requires the owner to keep the exterior in good repair, and to obtain Commission approval prior to altering the exterior architectural features of the building. Owners of designated landmarks are restricted in their use, but may seek a permit to change a building's appearance. In addition, owners of parcels not developed to the fullest extent legally permissible can transfer development rights to contiguous parcels on the same city block.

Penn Central, the owner of Grand Central Terminal, a designated landmark, proposed to add more than 50 stories for offices atop the existing terminal. The Commission denied the application. Penn Central sued in New York State court to have the Landmark Preservation Law declared an unconstitutional taking as it applied to the terminal and for damages for the "temporary taking" resulting from the Commission's denial of the application.

The trial court granted the injunction. The intermediate appellate court reversed, and the reversal was affirmed by New York's highest court. Penn Central appealed to the U.S. Supreme Court on the constitutional issues.

Decision: The U.S. Supreme Court affirmed the decision of New York's highest court in favor of New York City.

J. Brennan

The [issue] presented by appellants [is] whether the restrictions imposed by New York City's law upon appellants' exploitation of the Terminal site effect a "taking" of appellants' property for a public use within the meaning of the Fifth Amendment, which of course is made applicable to the States through the Fourteenth Amendment. . . .

The question of what constitutes a "taking" for purposes of the Fifth Amendment has proved to be a problem of considerable difficulty. While this Court has recognized that the "Fifth Amendment's guarantee [is] designed to bar Government from forcing some people alone to bear public burdens which, in all fairness and justice, should be borne by the public as a whole," this Court, quite simply, has been unable to develop any "set formula" for determining when "justice and fairness" require that economic injuries caused by public action be compensated by the Government. Indeed, we have frequently observed that whether a particular restriction will be rendered invalid by the Government's failure to pay for any losses proximately caused by it depends largely "upon the particular circumstances [in that] case."

In engaging in these essentially ad hoc, factual inquiries, the Court's decisions have identified several factors that have particular significance. The economic impact of the regulation on the claimant and, particularly, the extent to which the regulation has interfered with distinct investment backed expectations are of course relevant considerations. So too is the character of the governmental action. A "taking" may more readily be found when the interference with property can be characterized as a physical invasion by Government, and this Court has accordingly recognized, in a wide variety of contexts, that Government may execute laws or programs that adversely affect recognized economic values.

Because this Court has recognized, in a number of settings, that States and cities may enact land use restrictions or controls to enhance the quality of life by preserving the character and desirable aesthetic features of a city, appellants do not contest that New York City's objective of preserving structures and areas with special historic, architectural, or cultural significance is an entirely permissible governmental goal. They also do not dispute that the restrictions imposed on its parcel are appropriate means of securing the purposes of the New York City law.

Apart from our own disagreement with appellants' characterization of the effect of the New York law, the submission that appellants may establish a "taking" simply by showing that they have been denied the ability to exploit a property interest that they heretofore had believed was available for development is quite simply untenable. "Taking" jurisprudence does not divide a single parcel into discrete segments and attempt to determine whether rights in a particular segment have been entirely abrogated. In deciding whether a particular governmental action has effected a taking, this Court focuses rather both on the character of the action and on the nature and extent of the interference with rights in the parcel as a whole, here, the city tax block designated as the "landmark site."

Secondly, appellants, focusing on the character and impact of the New York City law, argue that it effects a

"taking" because its operation has significantly diminished the value of the Terminal site. Appellants concede that the decisions sustaining other land use regulations, which, like the New York law are reasonably related to the promotion of the general welfare, uniformly reject the proposition that diminution in property value, standing alone, can establish a taking . . .

We now must consider whether the interference with appellants' property is of such a magnitude that "there must be an exercise of eminent domain and compensation to sustain [it]." That inquiry may be narrowed to the question of the severity of the impact of the law on appellants' parcel, and its resolution in turn requires a careful assessment of the impact of the regulation on the Terminal site.

. . . the New York City law does not interfere in any way with the present uses of the Terminal. Its designation as a landmark not only permits but contemplates that appellants may continue to use the property precisely as it has for the past 65 years: as a railroad terminal containing office space and concessions. So the law does not interfere with what must be regarded as Penn Central's primary expectation concerning the use of the parcel. More importantly, on this record, we must regard the New York City law as permitting Penn Central not only to profit from the Terminal but to obtain a "reasonable return" on its investment.

Appellants, moreover, exaggerate the effect of the Act on its ability to make use of the air rights above the Terminal . . . [I]t simply cannot be maintained, on this record, that appellants have been prohibited from occupying any portion of the airspace above the Terminal. While the Commission's actions in denying applications to construct an office building in excess of 50 stories above the Terminal may indicate that it will refuse to issue a certificate of appropriateness for any comparably sized structure, nothing the Commission has said or done suggests an intention to prohibit any construction above the Terminal.

Just v. Marinette County
Supreme Court of Wisconsin
201 N.W. 2d 761 (1972)

Background: Marinette County adopted a shoreland zoning ordinance. Its purpose is to prevent deterioration of the state's navigable waters. The county passed the law in response to a state mandate to do so. The state mandate was triggered by its role as public trustee of the state's navigable waters. The County ordinance prohibited filling or draining of wetlands in a "conservancy district" without obtaining a permit. Ronand and Kathryn Just owned land that was a designated wetland in a conservancy district. The Justs began to fill their land without applying for a permit. They were ordered to stop. The Justs sued the County, contending that the shoreland zoning ordinance created a regulatory taking of their land. The trial court dismissed the action. The Justs appealed to the state Supreme Court.

Decision: The Wisconsin Supreme Court affirmed the lower court's decision for Marinette County.

Chief Justice Hallows
To state the issue in meaningful terms, it is a conflict between the public interest in stopping the despoilation of natural resources, which our citizens until recently have taken as inevitable and for granted, and an owner's asserted right to use property as he wishes. The protection of public rights may be accomplished by the exercise of the police power unless the damage to the property owner is too great and amounts to a confiscation. The securing or taking of a benefit not presently enjoyed by the public for its use is obtained by the government through its power of eminent domain. The distinction between the exercise of the police power and condemnation has been said to be a matter of degree of damage to the property owner. In the valid exercise of the police power reasonably restricting the use of property, the damage suffered by the owner is said to be incidental. However, where the restriction is so great the landowner ought not to bear such a burden for the public good, the restriction has been held to be a constructive taking even though the actual use or forbidden use has not been transferred to the government so as to be a taking in the traditional sense. Whether a taking has occurred depends upon whether "the restriction practically or substantially renders the land useless for all reasonable purposes."

Many years ago, Professor Freund stated in his work on The Police Power, "It may be said that the state takes property by eminent domain because it is useful to the public, and under the police power because it is harmful. . . . From this results the difference between the power of eminent domain and the police power, that the former recognizes a right to compensation, while the latter on principle does not." Thus the necessity for monetary compensation for loss suffered to an owner by police power restriction arises when restrictions are placed on property in order to create a public benefit rather than to prevent a public harm.

This case causes us to re-examine the concepts of public benefit in contrast to public harm and the scope of an owner's right to use of his property. In the instant case we have a restriction on the use of a citizen's property, not to secure a benefit for the public, but to prevent a harm from the change in the natural character of the citizens' property. We start with the premise that lakes and rivers in their natural state are unpolluted and the pollution which now exists is man made. The State of Wisconsin under the trust doctrine has a duty to eradicate the present pollution and to prevent further pollution in its navigable waters. This is not, in a legal sense, a gain or a securing of a benefit by the maintaining of the natural status quo of the environment. What makes this case different from most condemnation or police power zoning cases is the interrelationship of the wetlands, the swamps and the natural environment of shorelands to the purity of the water and to such natural resources as navigation, fishing, and scenic beauty. Swamps and wetlands were once considered wasteland, undesirable, and not picturesque. But as the people became more sophisticated, an appreciation was acquired that swamps and wetlands serve a vital role in nature, are part of the balance of nature and are essential to the purity of the water in our lakes and streams. Swamps and wetlands are a necessary part of the ecological creation and now, even to the uninitiated, possess their own beauty in nature.

Is the ownership of a parcel of land so absolute that man can change its nature to suit any of his purposes? An owner of land has no absolute and unlimited right to change the essential natural characters of his land so as to use it for a purpose for which it was unsuited in its natural state and which injures the rights to others. The exer-

cise of the police power in zoning must be reasonable and we think it is not an unreasonable exercise of that power to prevent harm to public rights by limiting the use of private property to its natural uses.

This is not a case where an owner is prevented from using his land for natural and indigenous uses. The uses consistent with the nature of the land are allowed and other uses recognized and still others permitted by special permit. The shoreland zoning ordinance prevents to some extent the changing of the natural character of the land within 1,000 feet of a navigable river because of such land's interrelation to the contiguous water. The changing of wetlands and swamps to the damage of the general public by upsetting the natural environment and the natural relationship is not a reasonable use of that land which is protected from police power regulation. Nothing this court has said or held in prior cases indicated that destroying the natural character of a swamp or a wetland so as to make that location available for human habitation is a reasonable use of that land when the new use, although of a more economic value to the owner, causes a harm to the general public.

The Justs argue that their property has been severely depreciated in value. But this depreciation of value is not based on the use of the land in its natural state but on what the land would be worth if it could be filled and used for the location of a dwelling. While loss of value is to be considered in determining whether a restriction is a constructive taking, value based upon changing the character of the land at the expense of harm to public rights is not an essential factor or controlling.

The shoreland zoning ordinance preserves nature, the environment, and natural resources as they were created and to which the people have a present right. The ordinance does not create or improve the public condition but only preserves nature from the despoilage and harm resulting from the unrestricted activities of humans.

Affirmed.

Whichever theory is used, once a regulation is declared by a court to be a regulatory taking, the landowner is entitled to just compensation for the period the regulation was in effect.

Case Example

The Lutheran Church operated a campsite on land on Mill Creek. The site consisted of a retreat center and recreational area for handicapped children. A fire upstream denuded the hills of trees, making flooding a threat. The threat was realized in 1978 when rain caused a flood, wiping out all the buildings at the campsite. In 1979, the County passed a law prohibiting the Church from reconstructing their buildings on the site because of the threat to public health and safety from subsequent floods. The Church sued, contending the law constituted a regulatory taking.

The U.S. Supreme Court *assumed* that the lower courts found a regulatory taking and ruled for the Church. It held that the government must pay money damages for a regulatory taking, even if the taking is only temporary. The County may void the law after this Supreme Court ruling to avoid a permanent taking, but it must pay the Church for the damages suffered up to the time the law is voided. *First English Evangelical Church of Glendale v. County of Los Angeles, 107 S.Ct. 3141 (1987).*

By far the most important constitutional limitation in the land use area is the prohibition against regulatory takings. There are other constitutional limitations that have played a lesser role in land use litigation, such as the equal protection clause. Most regulations attacked in court with an equal protection argument were adopted for economic reasons. In economic-based equal protection cases, the courts permit a regulation to differentiate between classes of persons (e.g., married and unmarried), but the classification must be reasonable and bear a rational relationship to a permissible state objective (e.g., public safety). In short, regulators may differentiate between classes, but cannot discriminate against a group. It should be noted that this rational basis test does not apply in cases involving certain types of differentiations, such as those based on race or color. Differences based on race or color are subjected to a more rigorous test and are unlikely to survive judicial scrutiny.

Some state courts review land use regulations using a substantive due process standard. These courts examine the legislation under attack to see if in their view it is reasonable. So the courts actually second-guess the wisdom of the legislature in passing the law. The courts balance the benefit that the law can be expected to attain against the cost it will impose on society or individuals. Ideally, this is a repetition of the exact balancing process that the legislature carried out before adopting the law.

The federal courts and many state courts reject the notion of reviewing cases under a substantive due process standard. They contend that the wisdom of a law is within the purview of the legislative body and should not be overturned by a court unless it is arbitrary in nature. Whether these courts always refrain from reviewing the wisdom of land use laws despite what they say is a matter of some debate.

Planning

The cornerstone of any land use regulation is a plan. The law provides that regulations, especially zoning codes, must be based upon a comprehension plan. The regulator may organize, restrict or even prohibit development for public health, safety and welfare purposes, so long as the regulation is not arbitrary and is adopted pursuant to a plan.

There is no clear definition of what constitutes a comprehensive plan. Some state courts in zoning cases contend that the comprehensive plan need not be in writing, but may be inferred from the zoning map and the community's traditional land use patterns. In reality these courts pay only lip service to the planning requirement. It is rare a community that relies on a zoning map and past development patterns and develops in a truly planned fashion. Despite this fact, many states continue to minimize the planning requirement.

The Comprehensive Plan

Some states and municipalities take the planning requirement seriously and mandate the preparation and adoption of a bona fide comprehensive plan. A comprehensive, or master, plan has some standard characteristics. It deals with future physical development of the community, contains a textual statement of land use policies and has a set of descriptive maps. The plan and maps are general in nature. A zoning code and map are usually adopted to make the plan operational and to add precision to the broad policies and maps contained in the plan.

Generally, state legislation enables municipalities to enact zoning codes and other land use regulations, but makes comprehensive planning a precondition. In short, the planning and regulating are done locally under state authorization. There is a trend, however, for the states to become more involved in the land use planning and regulating process. During the 1970s, some state legislatures became dissatisfied with local planning and rescinded local power to do so. The rescission was usually for reasons of environmental protection and often applied to limited areas of the state. For example, New York placed land use control over the Adirondack Mountain region in the hands of a state-appointed regional agency, and California created the San Francisco Bay Conservation and Development Commission to plan and regulate future land use for the Bay Area.

This trend toward state control continues and is broadening. Some states have enacted comprehensive planning and land use systems applicable to the entire state, not confining it to environmental protection purposes.

Growth Management Systems: States

Several states have enacted comprehensive legislation setting up a system of growth management directed by the state. The leading state in this type of planning is Oregon. Oregon's system established a set of statewide planning goals and policies within which localities must operate. It established the state Land Conservation and Development Commission to oversee and guide the localities in this process. There are 19 goals with accompanying guidelines. The goals run the gamut from citizen involvement to land use planning to forest lands to energy conservation. Each locality must devise a land use plan and process consistent with these statewide goals.

Other states, including Florida, California, North Carolina, Vermont and New Jersey, have enacted similar legislation applying to a portion of the state, e.g., a coastal area, or to the entire state. Several other states are actively considering this type of legislation.

Growth Management Systems: Municipalities

Growth management plans have not been confined to state and regional activity. Some communities on the fringe of urban and suburban growth have enacted growth controls. These communities felt the financial pressures of a rapidly increasing population and saw their exurban style of life disappearing. They have reacted by trying to monitor future growth closely. These schemes can best be illustrated by describing three cases involving their use.

The town of Ramapo, New York, on the suburban edge of New York City's metropolitan growth, decided that the haphazard growth taking place under the existing zoning code could be better controlled. The town methodically went about getting the information and doing the planning to create a better community. It initiated an in-depth master plan, adopted a zoning code to implement the plan, made sewer and drainage studies to guide future growth and adopted a six-year capital budget for community services as well as a capital budget for community services as well as a capital budget program of capital expenditure for the following 12 years. Believing that a full range of community services could not be provided adequately wherever developers happened to acquire land, the town decided that it would systematically provide those services on a section-by-section basis. Sewers, water lines, firehouses, parks, schools and drainage facilities would be provided to those sections of the community as predetermined by the town and in accordance with the capital budgeting program adopted. At the end of 18 years—the capital budget period—the town would have a complete set of community services. Obviously, some sections of the town would not receive such services until the final years of the period. A developer who wished to build in those sections of the town that had not yet acquired services could agree to provide those services. A developer who could amass 15 points on a sliding-scale arrangement for providing community services could develop the land. Unstated, but obvious in the scheme, is that the developer's cost of providing these services would probably be financially prohibitive.

It did not take long for a landowner who was not to receive community services until late in the scheme to bring a suit asserting that the arrangement was illegal. The highest court of New York upheld the Ramapo growth management plan as within the town's police power. *Golden v. Town of Ramapo, 30 N.Y. 2d 350, 334 N.Y.S.2d 138 (1972).* The court asserted that, where restrictions are necessary to promote the ultimate good of the community and are within the bounds of reason, they are within the purview of the police power. The Ramapo scheme seemed consistent with good land planning and had as its purpose the systematic development of the town.

Two major warnings evolved from the Ramapo case and subsequent criticism of it. The Ramapo court noted that there was something "inherently suspect" about the scheme that restricted the free mobility of people, despite its professed altruistic purpose. Communities will have to balance closely the degree of public good that could ensue from a growth management plan against the level of restriction placed on the mobility of people. For instance, if the time taken by the town is longer than needed to provide the community services in a fiscally sound way, and the community is in the direct path of growth, the restraint on human mobility may be too great.

The second warning is that low- and middle-income people would be discriminated against. The Ramapo plan provided areas for low- and middle-income housing development, but there was no guarantee or community inducement for that type of development actually to take place. Since many of the state courts have become acutely interested in adequate provision for this type of housing, a community may have to take care to provide realistically for lower-cost housing to be built.

Two other communities have received notoriety after adopting a growth management plan. The City of Petaluma, California, also in the path of urban sprawl, adopted a comprehensive development plan that in essence limited growth to 500 units annually, well below anticipated unregulated growth levels. The U.S. Court of Appeals upheld the Petaluma Plan. *Constr. Indust. Ass'n of Sonoma County v. Petaluma, 522 F.2d 897 (1975), cert. denied, 424 U.S. 934 (1976).* The court noted that the plan had a rational relationship to a legitimate state interest and that was all that was required. The avowed purpose of the Petaluma Plan was to maintain the "small town character" of the city. Clearly, part of the plan was to limit, annually and ultimately, the city's growth. To this extent Petaluma is an extension of Ramapo, which overtly attempted only to regulate the pattern of growth to coincide with the temporary financial limitations of the town.

A third community was less fortunate. Boca Raton, Florida, placed a cap on population growth by limiting the number of residential units that could be constructed to 40,000. The court rejected the plan, however, because of the somewhat arbitrary way in which the number 40,000 was reached. Boca Raton did not methodically plan for the limitation, as had Ramapo and Petaluma. In fact, the court clearly stated that a population cap that *is* traditionally related to sound community planning and is not unduly restrictive of private property rights *would* be within the domain of the police power. *Boca Villas Corp. v. Pence, 45 Fla. Supp. 65 (1976).*

The key tests for the notion of growth management plans have been affirmative. It would seem that the important criteria to be met are comprehensive preplanning, a rational connection between the reasonable restrictions in the plan and the public-welfare-based goal of the scheme and a provision for low-income residential units where they are needed. The ultimate goal can be to maintain the existing character of the community or even to limit ultimate community growth, although the exact interpretation of these principles will have to evolve over time. It should also be noted that only a small number of states have made any pronouncement on growth management plans; therefore, we do not have assurance of their national acceptance at this time.

In addition, due to the building slump of the early 1980s, the communities of Ramapo and Petaluma have significantly modified their growth management plans. It is likely that the economic recovery of the building industry will revive interest in growth management plans similar to those discussed above.

Ecological Constraints on Development

Ecology is the science that deals with the relationship of organisms and their environment.

> "The basic insight of ecology is that all living things exist in inter-related systems; nothing exists in isolation. The world system is web-like; to pluck one strand is to cause all to vibrate; whatever happens to one part has manifestations for all the rest. Our actions are not indi-vidual but social; they reverberate throughout the whole ecosystem."[1]

Slowly, humans are coming to realize that they are part of the natural systems and that these systems have definable limits to their capacity to serve their needs. Thoughtless abuse of natural systems, such as the land, air and water, inevitably spread throughout the system, causing harm far beyond the source of the abuse.

In some measure, these ecological constraints differ from other constraints. Laws are usually the product of social value judgments made by government. For example, deciding that 55 miles per hour is the best speed limit on a highway is a value judgment. Arguably, some other number might have been selected at a different time, like 65 miles per hour. To a certain extent, ecologically based laws are the product of the natural and physical sciences, and not social policy determinations. For example, it is known that when the amount of oxygen in a stream is reduced due to pollution, certain residents (fish) of the stream ecosys-tem will die. There is no value judgment in that. If we make the value judgment that the fish must be protected, minimum oxygen levels in the water must be

---

[1]Science Action Coalition, with A. Fritsch, Environmental Ethics: Choices for Concerned Citizens, 3–4 (1980).

maintained. Whether it is the protection of fish or humans that concerns us, certain ecological imperatives must be met. The earth and its ecosystems have definable limits.

Development on land in the floodplain increases the chances of subsequent flooding destructive to human life and property and to their ecosystem. Filling a wetland for development reduces wildlife habitat and destroys major incubators for important food supplies for humans. Cutting of forests reduces the natural systems' ability to buffer against the build-up of carbon dioxide, causing global warming. The connection between land development and natural systems is significant and undeniable.

Today, a great deal of information about the impact of development on natural systems is known. Many jurisdictions mandate that an environmental assessment be done prior to development to assure that the ecological impacts are known to the decision maker.

Environmental Impact Assessment
A statement detailing environmental data and analyzing that data regarding a proposed land development action.

Twenty-five states now require some type of environmental impact review. Most of these state statutes and regulations are patterned after the National Environmental Policy Act (NEPA). NEPA requires the preparation of an environmental impact statement (EIS) for federal actions that may significantly affect the quality of the environment. The equivalent state laws, or little-NEPAs, require EISs for state actions. State action in many of these states includes private action requiring any type of state approval. In these states, significant development proposals, such as those large in size or those to be located in an environmentally sensitive area, must be accompanied by the preparation of an EIS.

An EIS is a detailed, analytical document that describes the action being proposed, portrays the state of the environment in the area where the action is proposed and analyzes the environmental impact that the proposal is likely to have on the existing environment. The purpose of the EIS is to provide the decision maker (government agency) and the public with all the relevant environmental data prior to making the decision to approve or disapprove the development.

In most states, the environmental impact law is a procedural law and cannot mandate a particular result. The law compels the agency to generate and analyze the environmental information, but does not compel the agency to disapprove the development proposal based on the bad environmental news. The decision maker must consider the environmental data along with the economic, technological, social and political data regarding the proposal. A few little-NEPAs create substantive law and can compel the agency to disapprove the development proposal.

The preparation of an EIS has become more manageable in recent years. Some communities have developed natural resource inventories that provide the scientific data to assist in preparing EISs. Many areas have private contractors available who specialize in preparing EISs.

Ultimate responsibility for preparing EISs lies with the government agency. The normal procedure is that the agency makes the threshold decision of whether to prepare an EIS. This decision may be facilitated by consulting the agency's EIS regulations, which will list projects necessitating EISs and those not requiring an EIS. For the types of actions not listed in its regulations, often called "unlisted actions," the agency prepares an environmental assessment. The environmental assessment (EA) is a mini-EIS whose purpose is to decide whether the proposed development action may have a significant affect on the quality of the environment. If the EA reveals that significant environmental impacts will not result, it terminates the process by issuing a "negative declaration." If the EA indicates that there may be significant environmental impacts, the agency must prepare an EIS. The preparation of the EIS is often preceded by a process called scoping. During scoping, the agency consults with all interested parties to determine what the significant impacts are likely to be (e.g., water pollution) and what the scope of those impacts are (e.g., the Black River watershed).

The EIS is initially prepared in draft form called a DEIS. The DEIS is circulated to relevant parties and is made available to the public. All parties have a specified period of time to respond to the DEIS. The agency then prepares a final EIS, known as an FEIS. The FEIS must address any shortcomings in the DEIS and respond to any reasonable comments made to the agency during the DEIS comment period. The FEIS is then considered by the agency decision maker along with other relevant information in determining whether to go ahead with the proposal.

Summary

An owner has a wide range of rights connected with property. Currently, however, an increasing number of restrictions are placed on land use by both individuals and public agencies. Private restrictions on land use include many types of *restrictive covenants* and other legal limitations such as *easements,* and the common law limitations of *nuisance* and *trespass.* Public restrictions on land use have developed in this century, beginning with the appearance of zoning codes.

Public regulation of land use has progressed far beyond simple zoning of land for a specific use, like residential or commercial. As these regulations become increasingly restrictive the question arises as to whether they create an unconstitutional regulatory taking. An important factor in making the constitutional determination is the economic impact on the private landowner.

A prerequisite for land use regulation is planning. The requirement to plan in a comprehensive fashion is gaining acceptance among an increasing number of states. Growth management plans are comprehensive plans for growth that facilitate the budgeting of public services to meet anticipated needs.

Part of modern comprehensive planning is an examination of the natural or ecological limitations of the land. A key to making land use decisions that recognize the ecological limitations of the land is the preparation of an *environmental impact assessment*. The assessment or statement discusses the proposed development, the existing environment and the impact that the proposed development will have on the existing environment.

Review and Discussion Questions

1. Explain the rationale used for permitting one homeowner in a subdivision to sue a neighbor asserting a restrictive covenant in the neighbor's deed.

2. Why are courts unfavorably inclined toward restrictive covenants?

3. At this time which is the more important land use control factor—restrictive covenants or zoning? Why?

4. Distinguish between the power of eminent domain and a police power regulation.

5. Why do many courts refuse to review cases under a substantive due process standard?

6. Distinguish between ecological constraints and social value judgments as used in this chapter.

7. Discuss the purpose behind environmental impact assessment.

Case Problems

1. Pursuant to a comprehensive plan, the City of Utica zoned an area "land conservation district." Within this district there were no automatically permitted uses. A special-use permit might be issued for several uses related to agriculture and recreation. Dur-Bar Realty Company sued to have the zoning ordinance declared unconstitutional. Discuss. *Dur-Bar Realty Co. v. City of Utica, 57 A.D.2d 52, 394 N.Y.S.2d 913 (1977)*.

2. Unlimited, Inc. applied for a building permit to construct a convenience store. Kitsap County granted the permit subject to two conditions: that Unlimited (1) provide an easement to owners of nearby commercially zoned property to facilitate the development of their land; and (2) dedicate, or give to the County, a strip of land for a county road extension. Unlimited sued the County contending that the conditions affected a taking of their property without due process of land. Discuss. *Unlimited v. Kitsap County, 30 Wash. App. 723, 750 P.2d 651 (1988)*.

3. The City of Seattle adopted a greenbelt ordinance that required landowners to preserve from 50 to 70 percent of their land in its natural state without paying them compensation. The City asserted a valid police power purpose for the law. What test must be applied to these facts to determine whether a

taking without due process of law has occurred? Discuss. *Allingham v. City of Seattle, 109 Wash.2d 947, 749 P.2d 160 (1988).*

4. A developer in New York City proposed to build a high-rise luxury condominium. New York State has a little-NEPA mandating the preparation of environmental impact statements (EISs) for some projects. The EIS examined the project's effects on the physical environment and found none that were significant. The EIS was challenged, however, because it did not discuss the impact that the project would have on the existing patterns of population concentration, distribution, growth or neighborhood character. The preparer of the EIS contended that these factors were not within the term environment. Discuss the pros and cons of the parties' positions in this case. *Chinese Staff and Workers Ass'n v. City of New York, 68 N.Y.2d 359, 502 N.E.2d 176, 509 N.Y.S. 449 (1986).*

22

Regulation of Land Development

Early in this century, state and local government strayed to some degree from their laissez-faire attitude toward private land ownership. Prior to this time, Americans took seriously the great 18th century authority on the common law, William Blackstone, who pronounced private property rights as "that sole and despotic dominion." Though landowners never had quite the absolute rights alluded to by Blackstone, little land regulation existed. This system of nonregulation faded as the congestion, noise, pollution and other urban ills manifested themselves to city dwellers.

The chief tool selected to address these problems early in the century was zoning. The adoption of zoning codes proliferated after the U.S. Supreme Court in the 1926 case *Village of Euclid v. Ambler 275 U.S. 365* found constitutional a system that divided the community into use zones. Zoning has retained its primacy as a land use regulatory mechanism. Many modern zoning codes are not confined to separating land uses, but address problems like protecting prime agricultural lands.

Zoning is no longer alone, whatever its form, in regulatory land use. Americans realized that zoning codes were not protecting the land from environmental degradation. Wetlands, prime agricultural lands, historical heritage and wildlife habitat were being lost at an alarming rate despite zoning. The result is legislation, in addition to zoning, addressing the special problems of environmental degradation.

This chapter discusses traditional zoning and its modern nuances. It describes some of the problems created by development for special types of land areas and discusses regulatory tools used to cope with these problems.

Zoning

The regulation by the public, usually a municipality, of structures and uses of land within designated zones.

In its simplest form traditional zoning divides the municipality into districts for residential, commercial and industrial uses. Within each of these districts limitations are placed on the size and height of buildings, the siting of the buildings on the parcel, the density of development in the area, the minimum size of the parcel and perhaps the type of structure permitted on the site. The purchaser of a parcel of land must be aware not only of the restrictions revealed by a title search but also of the limitations placed upon the land by the zoning code.

The power to zone is expressly given to each locality (municipality or county) by the state through *enabling legislation,* by which that state authorizes the locality to regulate in the area of land use control. That legislation requires that the zoning code adopted by the locality be consistent with a plan for development. The zoning districts are to be placed on a map pursuant to that plan, for the purpose of maintaining property values, matching designated use to the character of the land (low-density development in unsewered areas with relatively impermeable soil, for example) and promoting the environmental, cultural and economic welfare of the area in any other way.

The courts have been lenient in approving zoning codes when the question pertains to the existence of a plan. They have not required a truly comprehensive plan in the modern sense. Often a zoning code and map drawn up by a qualified firm and adopted by the town has met with judical approval, even through review of how to optimize local development or nondevelopment is lacking. One reason for this judicial leniency has been that sparsely populated localities cannot reasonably afford to develop a comprehensive plan. Thus, the economic ability of the locality to generate a more comprehensive plan becomes relevant. The courts are not explicit on this point, but this economic constraint seems to underlie many decisions.

The three basic zoning classifications of residential, commercial and industrial have tended to proliferate. It is not uncommon now for localities to have 15 to 20 or more zones. The use permitted within a zone is often more narrowly confined, with separate zones for single-family houses on one acre, single-family houses on one-half acre, condominiums, garden-type apartments, double houses and so on. Separate zones are designated for shopping centers, office buildings, personal service shops (beauty parlors) and gas stations. For industry, the developer has to select the correct zone from among heavy manufacturing, light manufacturing, warehousing and the like. With this multitude of zones the locality is able to exercise tighter control over the location of development.

One intrinsic problem with zoning that is magnified by the multiplication of zones is inflexibility. Theoretically, the municipality periodically studies the needs of the locality and develops a zoning code or makes amendments to the existing codes based upon those needs. Those needs may change before the municipality undertakes to assess them, so that zones may be outdated and discourage more appropriate development.

In some areas of the country where condominiums came into vogue, there were no appropriate zones to accommodate them, and their development was therefore hindered. Other localities acted promptly to create special districts for condominiums, only to find them a passing fad and economically infeasible for the area. The result was that districts zoned for condominiums were then classified inappropriately.

A major advantage of this inflexibility is that it tends to make land values more stable. Potential uses of the land are known, and within general limits the market value of the land is known. The apparent inflexibility of traditional zoning does not tell the entire story. There are several ways in which uses are permitted to exist despite their inconsistency with the zoning code restrictions.

Nonconforming Use

A legal use that was established prior to zoning or prior to the present zoning classification and is permitted to continue despite its non-conformance with the zoning code.

Most zoning codes are superimposed on partially developed localities. There is no guarantee that all development prior to zoning took place on optimal sites, as seen by the present drafters of the zoning code. These nonconforming uses present a problem. The owners cannot be ordered to discontinue their use immediately unless they are paid full value for their land. To do otherwise would constitute an unconstitutional taking of their land. The traditional solution was to permit the nonconforming use to continue and hope that it would eventually disappear.

The law regarding nonconforming uses has not left that disappearance purely to chance, however. The nonconforming user cannot enlarge that use. Whether the use has been enlarged will be a question for the fact finder (jury or judge). Similarly, a landowner who discontinues the nonconforming use will not be able to resume it later.

Case Example

In 1968, Patrick Gilbertie constructed a house on a one-acre parcel. He conducted a plumbing repair and supply business from his residence, which was a legal use under the town regulations in existence at that time. In 1972, the town regulations changed to prohibit the combined residential and business use. By 1988, Gilberti's business was booming, and the town ordered him to cease operations because his legal nonconforming use was now illegal because the amount of business being done had significantly increased.

Gilbertie sued and the Court found for him. The Court determined that the type of nonconforming use had not materially changed, and the fact that the amount of business had increased was not an illegal expansion of the nonconforming use. *Gilbertie v. Zoning Board of Appeals, 581 A.2d 7546 (1990).*

The nonconforming use is said to run with the land and not with the individual owner. The nonconforming user may convey his or her land to another, and the buyer can continue the nonconforming use. If the nonconforming building is substantially destroyed, it cannot be rebuilt in noncompliance.

Despite the precautions taken under the law to encourage the disappearance of nonconforming uses, they do not always fade away.

Case Example

Susan Wilson purchased a grocery store in an area subsequently zoned residential. As residential development occurs, Wilson will enjoy a virtual monopoly as a grocer because residential zoning has excluded grocery competition. Of course, Wilson will not be able to expand her store under current zoning.

Some localities have taken more direct steps to assure the discontinuance of nonconforming uses. Ordinances have been passed placing a limit on the length of time the nonconformity will be permitted. So long as the time limitation is reasonable, such ordinances will be upheld by the courts. An important factor in determining reasonableness will be the life expectancy of the nonconforming structure. However, even though there are many examples of ordinances limiting the time allowed for nonconformity of advertising signs, the authorities have been reluctant to apply similar time limitations to other structures.

Zone Change

A zoning amendment made by the legislative body that enacted the zoning code.

The apparent inflexibility of the zoning code is mythical in most localities, although the uses permitted in a given zone may be inflexible. As previously mentioned, the zoning code is created to implement a plan—master plan, comprehensive plan or some less specific plan—but none of these plans is intended or can be expected entirely to reflect the future needs of the community. The plan may soon become dated. In addition, some areas of the locality may be zoned not so much for the anticipated use but as a holding zone until more definite decisions can be made. For instance, the northern one-half of a community could be zoned A-1 for agricultural use. The reason for this zoning would not be that this part of the town would be used for agriculture indefinitely, but that since development in the area was years away, the A-1 classification would create a holding zone. This approach would permit the town to postpone its ultimate zoning decision until the time for development was closer and it could better perceive the community needs. In addition, any attempt to use the land for other than agriculture purposes would require a zone change, which would allow the town to monitor closely development in the interim.

The zone change technique employed by communities is a method for keeping their plans current and for reducing the inflexibility of the zoning code. Most jurisdictions treat zone changes as legislative matters requiring the legislature to act to change it. A few states contend that zoning is an administrative decision and zone changes can be made by the appropriate agency, e.g., planning board.

Although a local government can initiate a zone change, generally the moving party is a landowner or developer. He or she tries to convince the legislative body that the proposed use makes more sense that the use designated in the zoning code. When granting a zone change, the legislature must be careful to establish the reasons for the change. The change must be presented as being justified by the current needs of the community. In this way the zone change is assured of being consistent with the notion that the locality is continuing to plan for its land use.

In the *Sellon v. City of Manitou Springs* case, the City initiated a change of the existing zoning because of complaints received about the problems of living on the hills of the city.

Sellon v. City of Manitou Springs
Supreme Court of Colorado
745 P.2d 229 (1987)

Background: In May 1982, the City Council of Manitou Springs enacted a hillside zoning ordinance that restricted use in the hillside zone to low-density residential uses. The purpose of this special zone was to avoid problems of erosion, drainage and access in areas of hills and steep slopes. In January 1984, the City Council rezoned an area, called Crystal Hills, as a hillside zoning district. David Sellon and others owned the Crystal Hills land. Under the hillside zoning designation, Sellon was able to build up to sixty housing units. Under the prior zoning, Sellon was able to construct considerably more than sixty units. Sellon sued the City, claiming that the hillside zoning lacked an adequate police power purpose and that the ordinance violated the due process clause of the State and Federal Consti-

tutions. The lower court disagreed with Sellon.

Decision: The Colorado Supreme Court affirmed the lower court upholding the hillside zoning ordinance.

Justice Kirschbaum
The principles applicable to a determination of whether a particular municipal legislative enactment violates constitutional due process standards are well settled. A presumption of validity attaches to zoning decisions of municipal zoning authorities. Thus, a party challenging a zoning ordinance on constitutional grounds assumes the burden of proving the asserted invalidity beyond a reasonable doubt.

For purposes of the United States Constitution, an ordinance containing provisions that bear a rational relationship to legitimate state concerns satisfies due process requirements. The due process clause of article II, section 25, of Colorado's Constitution requires a reasonable relation between an ordinance and a valid interest, such as public health, safety, morals or general welfare. The hillside ordinance must be evaluated pursuant to these standards.

The record reflects that prior to the adoption of the hillside ordinance great attention had been directed by the City Council to problems that had developed after improvements were made to property containing relatively steep slopes. For example, the city manager testified that the development of single-family units on steeply graded plots of land continually forced the City to deal with erosion, drainage, maintenance and emergency access issues. The record also contains evidence that residents of various areas of the City historically had experienced significant difficulties with some or all of these problems. The adoption of the hillside ordinance reflected a considered effort by the City Council to deal with these very real problems. Viewed in light of these facts, the ordinance addresses significant issues directly affecting the health and welfare of the City's residents.

At the review hearing conducted by the district court the landowners introduced evidence to the effect that the hillside ordinance was not the best means available to address problems of erosion, drainage or emergency access associated with development of residential housing units in steep slope areas of the City. However, the question is not whether other solutions to a governmental problem are feasible or superior to the program actually adopted; the question is whether the decision made is itself reasonably and rationally related to the problem being addressed. In this case, it is abundantly clear that the provisions of the hillside ordinance are rationally and reasonably related to problems of erosion, drainage, maintenance and emergency access occurring on sloping terrain that effect the health and safety of the City's residents.

The landowners next contend that the hillside ordinance is confiscatory and therefore unconstitutional as applied to them because it, in effect, precludes the use of the Crystal Hills property for any reasonable purpose. It is true that a zoning ordinance that prohibits the use of property for any reasonable purpose will be deemed confiscatory and therefore violative of just compensation and due process protections afforded by Colorado's Constitution. However, our decisions have consistently emphasized the principle that a landowner is not entitled to obtain maximum profits from the use of property, and that so long as the zoning ordinance leaves some reasonable use for the property, the ordinance does not violate state constitutional standards.

The evidence establishes that the hillside ordinance does not render the Crystal Hills property devoid of any reasonable use, and the landowners may still build a minimum of sixty residential units on the land. They are not entitled to obtain maximum profits from the use of their land or to obtain the highest and best use for the property. The landowners failed to establish that as the result of the hillside ordinance they could not put their property to any reasonable use. They therefore failed to satisfy their burden of demonstrating beyond a reasonable doubt that the ordinance was confiscatory.

Variance

Permission obtained from the appropriate governmental authorities to deviate somewhat from the designations under the zoning code.

In contrast to a zone change, a variance is not actually a change in the law. A variance is generally a modest deviation from the requirements of the zoning code. For instance, a landowner may gain a variance to allow him to set his proposed house back only 25 feet from the street rather than the 30 feet required under the zoning law. His parcel of land would continue to be zoned R-1 as it was before the variance.

Use variances can also be granted. Since they could permit a commercial use in a residential zone, however, they are more destructive to the local plan and are less likely to be granted.

Variances are granted by an administrative body in the locality. It may be called a *zoning board of appeals*, a *board of adjustment* or some similar title. In order to obtain a variance, the applicant must prove that the failure to grant it will cause him or her unnecessary hardship. In addition, the applicant must show that the new use will not reduce the value of surrounding properties and that the granting of it is within the public interest and not contrary to the spirit of the zoning code.

Case Example

The Town of Hampstead's zoning ordinance prohibits residential buildings higher than 1 1/2 stories. The purpose of the regulation is to retain the view of and from the lake and to maintain the beauty and countrified atmosphere of the Town. Alexander applied for a variance to put an additional full story on his one-story home. His variance application was denied by the Town, and he sued to overturn the denial.

The Court held that the denial of the variance was based on protecting the lake view and was therefore not arbitrary. It went on to state that in order to obtain a variance, the applicant must prove the following: (1) no reduction in the value of surrounding properties would be suffered; (2) granting the permit would benefit the public interest; (3) denial of the variance would create unnecessary hardship for the applicant; (4) granting the permit would do substantial justice; and (5) the use must not be contrary to the spirit of the ordinance. *Alexander v. Town of Hampstead, 525 A.2d 276 (1987).*

The rule of law states that no one has a *right* to a variance, so courts will not overturn the administrator's decision to deny it unless the decision is arbitrary. This narrow scope of judicial review permits the zoning board wide latitude in approving and disapproving variances. Unless the zoning board strictly requires the applicant to meet the burden of proof mentioned above and unless it keeps foremost the goals intended to be accomplished in the zoning code, its wide latitude can lead to an undermining of the land use goals established for the locality.

Exceptions in Zoning

Permitted uses provided for in the ordinance that are inconsistent with the designated zone.

Unlike variances or zone changes, exceptions are built right into the zoning ordinance. For instance, an R-1 (residential) zone may permit by exception the construction of a church, school or park within that district. The uses by exception are different from the uses allowed by the zoning code but are considered to be compatible with those uses. No special administrative permission is necessary. So long as the proposed use coincides with the exception detailed in the zoning code, the landowner will be allowed to construct the excepted use.

Special-Use Permit

A system whereby special exceptions to the zoning ordinance are granted by the land use administrator under a permit arrangement set forth in the zoning ordinance.

It has become common in zoning codes to omit certain uses from any of the zoning classifications. These uses are allowed only by getting a permit, which entails obtaining the approval of local zoning officials. Hospitals, churches, schools, recreational facilities such as golf courses, and cemeteries are handled in this fashion. Some of these uses may not be offensive in any specific zone, but the permit process retains control for community officials over their location in those situations where they may be objectionable. The special-use permit provides for flexibility in locating these uses for the applicant and maintains public control at the same time.

The special-use permit can be attacked on the basis that it is spot zoning, that is, unplanned zoning. However, this approach can be distinguished in several ways. Generally special uses are enumerated as such in the zoning ordinance, giving rise to the notion that they may be appropriate uses in an array of zones, depending on surrounding conditions. Many of the uses are not intrinsically offensive; they are singled out for the special-use permit process so that they can be blended into the community in a planned way. This is the antithesis of spot zoning.

Even where the "permitted use" has greater potential for offending the area residents, such as a cemetery, jail or gas station, the purpose of segregating these uses in the zoning code is to ensure that they are placed on sites consistent with community needs.

Variations and Special Uses of Traditional Zoning

The original purpose of traditional zoning was to keep different uses of land separate so that, for instance, an industrial use did not become a nuisance for nearby residential homeowners. Communities discovered that separating uses alone did not eliminate all their problems, nor did it provide them with ideal living conditions. Zoning, and variations of it, are being used to attack a wide variety of urban and suburban ills.

Large-Lot Zoning

A zoning classification that requires a minimum of one acre or more of land for each single-family house that is constructed.

The selection of one acre as the minimum size for large-lot zoning and other zoning is somewhat arbitrary. Other writers may contend that it should be slightly larger or smaller. What size lot constitutes a questionable zoning classification may depend on the location of the property. For instance, city lots tend to be small, and rural lots tend to be much larger. In any event, at some point, depending on the environment, the minimum lot size may be so large that it raises a legal question as to whether or not the size can be justified under the police power.

Advantages

In many areas of the country it is not uncommon to have zoning classifications requiring a minimum lot size of one, two or even five acres. Several legitimate public policy reasons can be given for mandatory lots of that size. Where municipal sewers and water are not available, the soil and geologic conditions may necessitate sparse development for nature to function adequately in supplying water and for cleansing wastewater. In some states where it is recognized as a salient reason for zoning, and in other states where it may be used merely as an additive reason, aesthetics may be offered as a reason for large-lot zoning. Sparse development on large, generously landscaped lots is attractive to almost everyone.

Large-lot zoning, despite the language contained in the purpose clause of a local code, may have a hidden motivation. Wealthy people prefer to live on large lots, which give better assurance of privacy in tranquil surroundings. The greater the financial means of the owner, the larger the residential lot is likely to be. It is quite natural for someone who can afford it to select a dream home in suburbia. Similarly, the desire to have amenities as well as to retain the market value of their properties causes others to desire comparable high priced housing nearby.

A second purpose for this type of zoning is that sparse development on large lots tends to be less expensive in terms of the cost of public services. Though municipal sewer and water facilities, if available, may be more expensive, other community services, such as schools, fire and police, tend to be less expensive. A major share of municipal property taxes goes for schools, and taxpayers usually wish to keep these taxes down. Statistically, well-to-do people have relatively few children, and restricting developments to large lots enables residents to reduce school taxes.

Disadvantages

Hidden motivation may represent the negative side of large-lot zoning. The intent of such zoning, or at least a residual result, is discriminatory. Even when the intent of large-lot zoning is for the socially laudatory purpose of permitting people to enjoy the "fruits of their labor," one effect of such zoning is to exclude the poor and less financially advantaged.

Excluding the financially disadvantaged usually results in the exclusion of minority groups as well. A municipality that caters to the wealthy with large-lot zoning may be steering low- and middle-income housing and the resulting higher public service taxes into nearby communities. A community may feel that exclusive use of large-lot zoning will help prevent higher taxes, crime and congestion. These social ills do not go away, however; they are merely concentrated in communities that do not exclude through large-lot zoning.

Judicial Responses to Large-Lot Zoning

Though not yet widespread, there is a growing tendency among state courts to reject large-lot zoning as unconstitutional. The Pennsylvania and New Jersey courts have been leaders in this movement.

Case Example

The zoning ordinance in the Town of Concord required a minimum lot size of one acre along existing roads and three acres on the interior. Kit-Mar Builders were denied a request to rezone their property lots smaller than mandated by the code. Kit-Mar sued Concord, contending that the large-lot zoning was an unconstitutional taking of its property.

The Pennsylvania Supreme Court held that a zoning provision of this type is unconstitutional if either its purpose or its result is exclusionary. The only exception would be where the municipality can show some extraordinary justification for requiring large lots. An extraordinary justification would be where the natural conditions of the soil, for instance, cannot handle denser population and there is no other reasonable, nonexclusionary method of resolving the problem. *In re Kit-Mar Builders, Inc., 439 Pa. 466, 268 A.2d 765 (1970).*

Most Pennsylvania communities would be hard-pressed to satisfy the judicial burden of proving extraordinary justification.

The New Jersey courts have gone a step further. The New Jersey Supreme Court, in an opinion that has implications beyond large-lot zoning, has declared that developing communities must provide for their fair share of the low- and middle-income housing needs of their region. *South Burlington County N.A.A.C.P. v. Township of Mt. Laurel, 67 N.J. 151, 336 A.2d 713, appeal dismissed, 423 U.S. 808 (1975).* Taking a cue from the Pennsylvania courts, the opinion permits an exception when "peculiar circumstances" can be shown. *Peculiar circumstances* sounds very much like extraordinary justification. The legal basis of the court's ruling is that under state law citizens have a right to decent shelter, and rampant large-lot zoning could effect a denial of this right.

In short, large-lot zoning will be unacceptable where the community has not otherwise provided the housing, or potential for housing, for its share of the region's less financially advantaged people. The adoption of a regional approach to land use decision making has long been espoused by scholars and planners but had not previously received broad judicial approval.

The extent to which the Pennsylvania and New Jersey constraints on large-lot zoning will spread is uncertain at this time. See *Berenson v. Town of New Castle, 88 N.Y.2d 102, 378 N.Y.S.2d 672 (1975)*. If the New Jersey approach is broadly adopted, it will not sound the death knell for large-lot zoning. So long as a community is able to provide for its share of the regional housing needs elsewhere, it may continue to have large-lot zoning. In addition, there is nothing that prevents a developer from voluntarily building houses on large lots to satisfy a demand for such housing.

Planned Unit Development (PUD)

A concept involving a development larger than a traditional subdivision, generally permitting mixed uses within the development and attempting to provide a maximum amount of land for open space.

This definition of a PUD is necessarily vague. As it has evolved, the PUD has become many things. It is a term used to describe a development that clusters houses on undersized lots in order to provide more open space to the residents. The term is used to depict a development that permits various types of housing within the same tract, such as townhouses, apartments and single-family housing. In another community it may be flexible enough to allow mixed uses, such as residential, commercial and even light industry (such as warehouses). Some zoning maps designate areas of the community as PUD zones, while other communities adopt a *floating-zone* concept in which the PUD becomes affixed to a particular land area when an appropriate proposal for mixed use is made to the community officials. Whichever cloak PUD wears, it provides the land use decision maker with additional flexibility in planning for growth within the community.

Procedurally, the developer usually needs community approval for the total PUD at the inception of the project. This general approval both allows the PUD as such and sanctions the overall design or concept of the development presented. Since the PUD is a large development, it will be constructed in sections over several years. As the developer plans each section of the PUD, community approval will need to be obtained for the specifics of that section. A few years into the PUD construction, market conditions may change, causing the developer to seek an alteration of the general plan. For example, condominiums may not be selling in the community; the developer, seeking approval for Section 4 that was previously approved for condominiums, may seek to amend the PUD to put two-family homes in Section 4.

Since the floating PUD is more common than the fixed-zone approach, the PUD plan must obtain the approval of the planning board along with a zone change from the local legislative body. This dual clearance, added to the planning board's approval of each individual section, affords the community the opportunity for closely controlling the development. The key word is *opportunity*. The major criticism of PUDs is that this very flexibility offers too much chance for abuse by the developer. Sometimes a beautifully integrated PUD concept is undermined when the developer annually changes the proposal on the section-by-section approvals in order to take advantage of the short-run market for a given type of development. The result is a hodgepodge that gives the appearance of no planning. The antidote is a planning board, which presses the developer to retain the original plan unless there is an extraordinary reason for change or the change will enhance the overall design of the project.

The original PUD concept was intended to provide for large-scale, relatively self-sufficient development on the order of a new town. A large PUD has the potential for creating an integrated community. It provides for generous quantities of open space in exchange for an increase in density in the living areas, with total density remaining the same. Since the size of the project necessitates development over several years, it permits medium-range community planning with continuous updating through the section-by-section approvals. Where integrated multiple uses are permitted, it can provide for more proximity between residents and services and for a reduction in car miles and energy consumed. The major drawback, however, cannot be overemphasized. A PUD is only as good as the public administrators require it to be.

Performance Standards Zoning

One specialized zoning technique that is growing in popularity is performance standards zoning, which establishes certain standards that must be met by any user of land within the zone. Performance standards have been set for such things as noise, vibrations, odors, toxic wastes, signs and heat emanating from a site. For instance, a standard may provide that no odor is allowed beyond the property line. Most of these standards have been established to ensure that industrial operations do not interfere with surrounding land uses.

Performance standards are especially appropriate for multiple-use situations, such as exist in PUD developments. The concept of performance standards may also be useful for controlling adverse impacts in traditional, commercial and residential zones. For instance, they can be used to regulate impacts on drainage, visual sensitivity and traffic congestion.

Contract Zoning

Zoning in which an applicant will be granted a requested zone change only after contracting with the community to comply with certain covenants.

Contract zoning is a highly controversial concept. Under this approach the legislative body reviewing the zone change request may seek to obtain a contractual agreement from the developer that it will build in accordance with specifications more stringent than those required in the zoning code. For example, it may mandate a comprehensive landscaping plan for building and parking areas and less surface coverage by construction than allowed by the ordinance. The zoning contract provides the decision maker with needed flexibility; if not abused, it can serve the community welfare.

The controversy arises when the legislature insists that a zone change be contingent upon the meeting of certain conditions and the developer is unwilling to comply. Zoning is a legislative function, and must be adopted pursuant to a specific legislative process. Arguably, contract zoning is an attempt by the legislature to contract for a change in the zoning law, without following the legislative process.

The legality of contract zoning varies from state to state. Some states have approved restrictive covenants when placed upon the developer to ensure that a community benefit evolves from the project. Other states have reached the opposite conclusion, contending that the legislature is surrendering some of its lawmaking authority and thereby making an unconstitutional delegation. Still others have sanctioned contract zoning so long as the covenants are between the developer and other private citizens. One can only be a little skeptical of the latter approach, since the zone change will not occur unless the developer agrees to the private restrictive covenants.

Agricultural Lands Zoning

Lands that are actively being used for grazing and crop production.

Prime agricultural lands have been shrinking at an increasingly rapid rate, especially around the country's population centers. A report of the Council on Environmental Quality estimates that prime farmland is being lost at the rate of a million acres per year, or more than four square miles per day. People have become aware that regional shortages of farm crops are inevitable if farmlands continue to be lost to development and abandonment at this rapid rate.

Several factors have caused the shrinking of agricultural lands near metropolitan areas. Farmlands have been assessed for property taxes at development rates, which many farmers cannot pay out of profit from the farm operations, causing them to sell out. The inducement of high land prices has enticed many farmers to sell off their land for development. Further, the demands of farm life appeal to fewer and fewer young people as our society becomes more mobile and leisure-oriented.

Many states have undertaken measures to slow the decrease of farmland. Several states use a form of private contract to protect farmland. The farm owners agree to continue to use their land for agricultural purposes for a specific period of time (e.g., eight years, subject to renewal). The state agrees to fix real property tax assessments at agricultural land levels, rather than letting taxes increase as market values increase due to nearby development. This type of approach has been modestly successful in slowing farmland loss.

A technique with more long-run potential is zoning. Under traditional zoning, communities created a use zone for agricultural purposes. This agricultural zone in developing communities, however, is merely a holding zone awaiting a permanent classification when community leaders better understand its development needs for that area. This is not zoning for agricultural use.

Some communities now zone areas for farmland use and consider it to be the planned permanent use of that land. They determine that farm purposes are the highest and best use of the land, and sharply limit subdividing of agriculturally zoned land.

Subdivision Regulations

Restrictions on the division of a parcel of land into two or more units. A subdivision will require prior approval by an administrator such as a planning board.

The zoning code controls only the use and siting of construction on the land. Subdivision regulations control the size and location of streets and sidewalks, the placing of sewer and water lines and mandated drainage facilities and the location of parks and open spaces. When the subdivider presents a plat plan to the planning board, the board determines whether the streets, sewers and so forth meet the conditions necessary for maintenance of the public health, safety and welfare.

Subdivision regulations generally take the form of standards, specifications and procedures set for street signs, streetlights, street trees, fire hydrants, storm drains, sanitary sewers, curbs, gutters and sidewalks. The regulations may require the developer to post a performance bond to ensure compliance with these rules. The final plat, or subdivision map, submitted by the developer will illustrate in detail all the improvements required under the subdivision rules.

Case Example

Sowin Associates applied to the Planning and Zoning Commission for subdivision approval of a plan for 11 lots on a 10-acre parcel. The parcel was zoned residential. The Commission denied subdivision approval because the development could cause off-site traffic congestion, decrease property values and was in disharmony generally with the area. The Associates' plan was apparently in conformity with the Town's subdivision regulations. Sowin Associates sued to reverse the Commission's denial.

The Court reversed the Commission's denial because Sowin Associates' plan conformed to the Town's subdivision regulations. It stated that traffic congestion, decrease in property values and area disharmony are relevant considerations in a zoning matter determining the use of the land, but not in a subdivision matter. *Sowin Associates v. Planning and Zoning Commission, 23 Conn. App. 57c, 580 A.2d 91 (1990).*

Subdivision Exactions and Impact Fees

Subdivision exaction is a requirement that a subdivider dedicate part of its land, or an in-lieu-fee payment, to the community to serve site-specific needs created by the subdivision.

An impact fee is a device requiring a subdivider to fund major, off-site infrastructure expansion that serves the community at large as well as the subdivision residents.

Approval of the developer's plat plan usually coincides with the community's agreement to accept title to all streets, streetlights and so forth when completed. Herein lies the *quid pro quo*, the equal exchange that enables the community to regulate a subdivision closely. The developer agrees to comply with the various subdivision regulations and expects in return that the community will accept a *dedication*, or transfer of title, of the infrastructure facilities, including roads, sewers, hydrants, and drainage structures. The transaction relieves the developer of continuing responsibility for maintaining these facilities.

A dedication, or *subdivision exaction*, which is becoming common now is one for parks or open space. The planning board may insist that the developer dedicate a percentage of its land, or money in lieu of parkland, prior to granting approval of the final plat. This type of dedication has been approved as a reasonable extension of the transaction discussed above.

States take different approaches to how closely the need for the parkland must be tied to the demand created by the residents in the developer's subdivision. In states with a more flexible rule, the planning board can exact land based upon future, as well as present, needs of the subdivision residents; that is, ten years from now 15 acres of open space per thousand people will be the standard rather than the present 10 acres per thousand. The particular state rule should be investigated by interested parties.

As sources of funds for community improvement have disappeared over the past decade or so, communities are striving to create new tools to fund needed projects. The subdivision exaction tool addresses needs created by and within the subdivision. A new subdivision, along with other development in the area, generally creates the need for the construction or expansion of area-wide but off-site improvements. Many communities authorize the collection of user impact fees from subdividers for such improvements as widening of nearby highways, expansion of water and sewage treatement facilities and construction of landfills. The user impact fee resembles payment in lieu of land fees used in subdivision exactions. Some differences between the two are: in-lieu fees finance on-site improvements and user impact fees finance off-site projects; in-lieu fees are generally assessed based on the subdivision's acreage or number of lots, and user impact fees are based on the square footage of the proposed buildings or the number of bedrooms; and in-lieu fees are confined to residential subdivisions, while user impact fees are often applied to other types of development, too.

As with subdivision exactions, care must be taken to tie the size of the fee to the share of the cost of the improvement created by the subdivider. This caution is especially important in light of a recent U.S. Supreme Court case, *Nollan v. California Coastal Commission, 107 S.Ct. 3141 (1987)*. The Court decided that there must be a "substantial" connection between the government's stated purpose and the regulatory action. In this case, that means that there must be a substantial connection between the needs created by the subdivision and the specific subdivision's exaction or user impact fee. Insertion of the word *substantial* into the usual test for valid regulations provides the courts with the power to second-guess the regulators.

Land Ethic: Ecological Imperatives and Value Choices

As this century comes to a close, there is a growing awareness that humans are part of a larger community. This community includes not only the other humans who inhabit the planet, but the flora (plants) and fauna (animals) that share our living space. Human life and that of the plants and other animals cannot exist without certain essential ingredients, including clean air and water, sunlight, livable habitat and the ozone layer, to mention a few. Humans, other animals, plants and these essential ingredients are all bound together into an intricate and inseparable web of relationships called ecosystems. Humans are important, but not the sole participants in life on this planet.

The quality of life on the planet depends in large measure on the sensitivity and respect with which humans make decisions. No decisions are more important than those made about land. Land provides humans with their habitat, and it provides the habitat for the animals and plants that provide humans with the essential ingredients of existence, food and air.

During this century, humans have been less than sensitive and discrete in their decisions about land. In the long-view, this insensitivity threatens life itself. In the future, protectiom of some types of lands from development—like wetlands, prime agricultural lands, floodplains, coastal areas, and wildlife habitat—is an ecological imperative. Beyond these imperatives lie some important value choices about other types of land. The quality of human life seems to depend on retaining our history through preservation of landmarks and historical areas, protecting of aesthetically pleasing areas, and retaining diversity of land types.

The remainder of this chapter discusses some regulations aimed at protecting these ecological imperatives and environmental value choices. These regulations evidence an emerging land ethic that places future emphasis in land use decisions on environmental harmony. Protection of wetlands, the floodplain, the coastal zone and other critical areas, including prime farmland (discussed earlier), are ecological imperatives. Preservation of historical culture and scenic areas are community value choices.

Wetlands

Lands that have groundwater levels at or near the surface for much of the year or that are covered by aquatic vegetation.

Historically, wetlands, including treed swamps and grass-dominated marshlands, have been treated as wasteland. They were considered inaccessible areas whose major function was the breeding of pest insects. In recent years, however, we have begun to see wetlands in a different light. True, wetlands are breeding areas for mosquitoes, as is any depression that retains water, such as residential drain spouts. Nevertheless, wetlands are also an important natural resource.

Wetlands provide areas for storm waters to gather for their slow return to the groundwater and air. Therefore, they are important as flood control areas. High groundwater and storm waters do not disappear upon the development of a site or upon the laying of drainpipe. Drainpipe merely concentrates the water, shifting the wetness problem farther downstream in the watershed. Wetlands provide this retention function naturally.

In addition, wetlands provide highly productive wildlife habitats. Hunters, fishermen, bird-watchers, trappers and other recreationists find wetlands extremely important in supporting their leisure time habits. Wetlands provide an outdoor classroom for amateur and professional scientists and are aesthetically pleasant to many people. With public recognition of these resource values, and the setting aside of the traditional view of wetlands as areas to be filled and developed, legal methods for protecting these areas have evolved.

Many states passed legislation to control development in wetland areas. The technique generally adopted has been a permitting process. Prior to filling, dredging or otherwise substantially modifying a wetland area, the landowner must get a state, regional or local permit. Permits are not issued where development will cut deeply into the resource value of the wetland area, unless there is a strong counterbalancing reason for doing so. The state wetland protection systems vary, but they generally involve the preparation of wetlands inventories and maps and the issuance of guidelines or regulations for controlling the process of issuing permits. It should be realized that a permit process does not *automatically* curtail development on all wetlands but that it *may* result in a landowner's being unable to make full economic commodity use of his or her hand.

In 1990, the President announced a policy of "no net loss" of wetlands. The exact parameters of this policy are unknown at this time, but it clearly establishes an emphasis on protecting wetlands from development. In addition, the federal Clean Water Act of 1972, as amended, created a permit system administered by the U.S. Army Corps of Engineers for most dredging and filling activities in wetlands connected with navigable waters. The term *navigable waters* has been defined broadly under the statute to include any waters that have the capability of affecting interstate commerce. Prior to the issuance of any permit, the corps must prepare an environmental impact statement (EIS) that analyzes all environmental factors. One remedy the corps has utilized against landowners who fill without a permit is to compel the removal of the fill, and the restoration of the wetland, an undertaking that can be extremely expensive.

Some states and localities have used a zoning approach to control development in wetlands. These zones, which might be called *conservation and recreation districts*, allow only uses consistent with retaining the character of the wetland. Prior to 1970 the zoning approach, which lacked the flexibility of a permit system, was uniformly held to be an illegal taking without due process of law. The judicial rationale was that this type of zoning denied landowners all *reasonable* use of their land. Fishing, boating and hunting, which might have been allowed, were not "reasonable" uses.

More recently, most of the states' wetland measures, as well as the federal wetland permit procedures, have been upheld under judicial scrutiny. In addition, some life has been breathed into the zoning approach for controlling wetland development.

Traditional analysis states that the police power can be used to prevent public harm but not to grant a public benefit. In this case, as always with this type of analysis, whether the regulation involves a harm or benefit depends on who is doing the classifying. Today, most courts would find that protecting an ecologically important area like a wetland is preventing a public harm.

Another line of reasoning may bode well for the zoning approach to protecting wetland. The one constant in "takings" analyses is the rule that the landowner cannot be deprived of all reasonable use. A serious question is raised as to whether or not filling for development is a reasonable use of a wetland. Also, what is reasonable in this area is a time-related notion, so yesterday's unreasonable use may become a reasonable one day.

Wetlands are being controlled as special environments in most states where they are numerous. The techniques for control vary somewhat, but judicial approval for all the approaches seems to be growing.

Floodplains

Areas near waterways that are prone to flooding.

Human beings have always tended to settle near streams, lakes and other bodies of water. The body of water provided a drinking supply, fishing and a convenient means of transportation. The first permanent settlements were made with a wary eye toward the ravages that a flood-swollen stream could cause. High, sheltered places near the water were favored over lower-lying areas that were more susceptible to flooding.

People slowly seemed to lose this sensitivity to the forces of nature. Settlements became more numerous in low-lying, flood-prone river valleys. Floods were either tolerated or, in more recent history, controlled by capital construction projects such as dams, levees and dikes that alleviated the problem. In recent years it has become clear that, although dams and dikes may postpone or prevent some floods, sooner or later the dike weakens or the dam is not massive enough to handle a severe storm, and a flood ensues.

The cost of removing people from the floodplains throughout the world is prohibitive. Many people would not be willing to leave even if economic constraints did not prevail. In recent years, governments have undertaken measures to protect those living on the floodplain and to discourage others from building new structures or from repairing flood-damaged structures within the floodplain.

Some communities have used zoning as a method of controlling growth on the floodplain. A "floodplain district" would prohibit the building of new structures or filling or damming within the floodplain. It would prohibit any residential use. The purposes of this zoning would be to protect people who might choose to live on the floodplain unaware of the hazards of doing so, to protect those near the floodplain who would be injured by obstructions in the flow of floodwater and to protect the public at large, who must bear the cost of disaster relief when persons on the floodplains lose their property because of flooding.

The legal question raised again is whether this type of regulation, which permits very limited economic use, denies all reasonable use of the land and thereby constitutes a taking. What is a reasonable use must be looked at in the context of the land involved. Floodplain lands, with their vulnerability to massive flood destruction, are not reasonably usable for residential or other permanent types of construction. Although this line of reasoning has not been adopted uniformly to protect the floodplain, it probably represents the wave of the future.

Although this regulatory trend is aimed at keeping people out of the floodplain, the federal government is involved in protecting its residents. The national Flood Insurance Program makes flood insurance available to landowners in flood-prone communities, where such insurance was previously exorbitantly expensive or simply unavailable. In essence, unless an individual in a flood-prone area has flood insurance, he or she will not be able to get a mortgage from the bank. If a community does not participate in the flood insurance program, federal aid or loans for use within the federally described flood hazard area will not be made available. An additional regulatory hook in the system is that a community must agree to establish land use controls for the flood-prone area before it is able to participate in the insurance program. In short, insurance will replace disaster relief in some measure, and new construction on the floodplain will be discouraged.

Coastal Zone

The area including coastal waters and the adjacent shorelands.

The coastal zone environment is an extremely fragile area. It is an ecosystem of interconnected marshes, mudflats, beaches and dunes. Human activities that create pollution and siltation can destroy these fragile ecosystems and the quality of the coastal waters generally. To prevent this type of destruction, the federal and state governments have enacted regulatory schemes protecting the coastal zone.

The primary regulation in the area is the federal Coastal Zone Management Act of 1972 (CZMA). The purpose of the CZMA is to establish a fairly uniform system of state controls for coastal lands, including the Great Lakes. The program is administered by the National Oceanic and Atmospheric Administration. Participation in the program by the states is voluntary.

The CZMA requires the states to undertake coastal lands planning and to develop management programs for protection and development of these lands. The Act provides for annual grants of up to 80 percent of the cost of the development and implementation of coastal zone management programs. The state programs must identify the boundaries of the coastal zone, define the permissible uses within the zone and establish the regulatory agencies and controls that will implement the plan. The program must identify procedures for designating specific areas for preservation or restoration due to their "conservation, recreational, ecological and esthetic values."

The CZMA was broadened in several ways by legislation enacted in 1980. The Act expanded protection "to significant natural systems, including wetlands, floodplains, estuaries, beaches, dunes, barrier islands, coral reefs, and fish and wildlife habitat," within the coastal zone. The Act expands the CZMA purposes "to minimize the loss of life and property" in flood prone areas within the coastal zone.

This new law created Resources Management Improvement Grants, available to states for developing deteriorating urban waterfronts, for preserving and restoring of important natural areas and for providing public access to beaches and other coastal areas.

In addition to federal regulatory activity in coastal areas, several states are active in coastal zone protection separate from the CZMA program. For instance, under state legislation, New Jersey and Delaware regulate certain industrial activities in the coastal area. In a separate development, the New Jersey Supreme Court in *Matthews and Van Ness v. Bay Head Improvement Assoc., 471 A.2d 355 (1984)* held that the public has a right of access and use to the dry sand beach areas shoreward of the wet sand area generally recognized as public land.

Critical Areas

Areas legislatively identified as containing natural limitations, or ones that are important to maintaining the ecosystem.

Beyond zoning codes, the normal approach toward regulation is piecemeal one, that is, to adopt separate controls for wetlands, others for the flood prone areas and still others for prime agricultural lands. A more systematic approach is to regulate all sensitive areas under a single, comprehensive set of rules. Some communities have adopted critical area controls to accomplish this end.

The first task that must be undertaken by a community prior to enacting critical area controls is to make policy determinations as to what types of lands or resources have special value to the community. The legislature then adopts a critical area controls system aimed at protecting these lands and resources. Normally, these include lands that have natural limitations for development (floodplains, steep slopes), lands that are ecologically important (wetlands, habitat for endangered or threatened species of animals and plants) and lands that are prized by the community because of their economic value, scarcity or uniqueness (prime farmland, scenic vistas, historical sites). It should be noted that some of the areas identified as critical fit the category of ecological imperatives (wetlands), while others are products of community value choices (historical sites). The controls may contain a variety of types of regulations, including acquisition of some lands, zoning, and permits.

Once the types of lands to be protected are identified and the regulatory scheme is established, the specific geographic locations of the critical areas sites must be identified. Usually, these sites are mapped. The critical areas map can be overlayed onto the zoning map for use by the agency administering the critical area controls.

The advantages of critical area controls are that they are comprehensive and systematic. Prospective developers are put on notice as to those lands that are incompatible with development, thereby avoiding poor land investments and lost time.

The concept of critical area controls is not confined to local communities. Some states—including Florida, Maine, Maryland, Minnesota, Nevada, North Carolina, Oregon, Vermont and Wyoming—have enacted laws that make use of the concept. Other states—including New Jersey (Pinelands) and New York (Adirondack Mountains)—have singled out regions of the state for critical area controls. The Federal Land Policy and Management Act (1976) provides that the Bureau of Land Management identify critical environmental areas and promulgate regulations giving them special protection.

The use of critical area controls is growing, and they appear to provide a systematic addition to traditional land use regulations for protecting lands valued by the community.

Historic Preservation

The preservation of buildings, and perhaps archaeological sites, from destruction by new development.

Just as American culture deifies youth among people, it tends to favor new structures over those that are old. The crags and cracks of an aging building, despite its historical or architectural significance, seem to bring on a "replacement compulsion." Although some extraordinary historical sites have been preserved, the view that not enough preservation and renovation of these structures takes place has been growing. Under this view, replacement is relied upon too heavily.

Through the historical preservation concept is applied more broadly, it is usually applicable to buildings in urban areas. In some regions of the country communities have designated certain areas historic districts because of their economic and cultural significance. In effect, this is a type of zoning. Within historical districts, permits have to be obtained prior to making a significant change in the facade or structure of a building. Because the historical district usually enhances the economy of the affected area, and change is only controlled by a permit system rather than prohibited, the courts have been willing to support them.

Historically significant buildings do not normally comprise an entire district but are scattered among other urban developments. Many cities have designated landmarks in the community and have established a regulatory scheme for preserving their historical significance. The landmark designation differs from an historical district in that in the former the burden falls unevenly on a limited number of landowners. Also, the benefits of the landmark designation may accrue to the area in general and not solely to the landmark owner. In an historical district the burdens and benefits, at least theoretically, fall equally upon all landowners within the district.

One approach to landmark protection, adopted by New York City, utilizes a new concept known as *transferring development rights (TDRs)*. The TDR concept is somewhat variable and complex, so it will be oversimplified here. Each tract of land has a certain number or amount of development rights that attach to the land and are transferable. A landowner proposing to build a high-rise residential unit does not obtain enough development rights with the deed to develop to the maximum permitted by the zoning code. These rights, or TDRs have to purchased from other landowners—in this case, the ones who own the landmarks and are prohibited from fully utilizing the TDRs on their own property. In this fashion the economic burden of owning a landmark (or a wetland, a scenic vista or an archaeological site) does not fall solely on the shoulders of the landmark owner. Landowners simply go into a ready market to purchase or sell TDRs.

State and federal tax incentives exist to assist landmark preservation. Recent amendments to the Internal Revenue Code deny demolition expenses if an historic landmark is razed. Accelerated depreciation is also denied if a new structure replaces a landmark. If the landmark is preserved, accelerated depreciation of the acquisition costs and rehabilitation is available. The entrepreneur who preserves landmarks has the option of writing off the cost of improvements over five years. Investment tax credits are also available. In addition, states and local governments often make tax rebates available to assist in preservation efforts.

Historical preservation is a relatively new concern in this country, and the law pertaining to it is evolving. Reasonably designated historical districts seem secure from judicial consternation. Landmarks legislation is legal and has found a potentially useful tool in the use of TDRs, but questions as the their legality and as to whether a convenient market arrangement will evolve for their purchase and sale create some uncertainty at this time. Whatever the limitations, a growing number of communities are making the value choice to preserve the best of its historical heritage.

Aesthetics

Originally, regulation to retain visual and scenic beauty.

Traditionally, aesthetics is associated with a community's goal of maintaining its visual and scenic beauty. Regulation for aesthetic purposes may include a ban on billboards, set-back requirements in a zoning code, or fencing for junkyards. In recent years, two questions have occupied courts in reviewing aesthetic regulations. One is whether a regulation based solely on aesthetic purposes is a valid exercise of the police power and the second question pertains to the precise meaning of the term *aesthetics*, since it appears to be broadening from its initial definition.

The validity of aesthetic regulations has evolved over the course of the twentieth century. During the early part of this century, the courts indicated that a regulation based partially or exclusively on aesthetics was invalid. The main problem was that the courts perceived controls based on beauty and good taste to be too subjective for institutions that demanded objective standards. Toward the middle of the century, judicial attitudes shifted. Though aesthetics could not be the sole basis for a regulation, it was acceptable as a reason among other traditional reasons for regulating. If a community banned billboards because they threatened public safety and because they were ugly, an otherwise reasonable regulation was valid. Though the aesthetics-based part of the purpose was treated with suspicion and was referred to often as an unimportant makeweight, aesthetics clearly gained legitimacy as a regulatory purpose during this era.

Currently, another shift in judicial attitude toward aesthetics is occurring. It appears that a majority of state appellate courts are rapidly accepting aesthetics alone as a legitimate reason for exercising the community's police power, Communities can regulate billboards for the solitary purpose of improving the appearance of the area. The groundwork for the courts accepting aesthetics as a full-fledged regulatory purpose was laid by the U.S. Supreme Court in the case of *Berman v. Parker, 348 U.S. 26 (1954).* The Court declared that the concept of public welfare in the police power was broad enough to encompass aesthetic regulations. In regard to public welfare, it states that the "values it represents are spiritual as well as physical, aesthetic as well as monetary. It is within the power of the legislature to determine that the community should be beautiful as well as clean, well-balanced as well as carefully patrolled."

The New York Courts were among the earliest to accept the principle that aesthetics can stand alone as a basis for regulation.

Case Example

McCormick owned 39 acres of land on Oseetah Lake in the Adirondack Mountains. McCormick applied to the Adirondack Park Agency (APA) for a permit to develop 32 lots on the tract. The APA granted the permit subject to a restriction against placing any boat houses on the shoreline of the lake. The sole basis for the restriction was that boat houses would interfere with the rustic or aesthetic quality of the area. McCormick protested the restriction in court.

The court upheld the APA decision, affirming a previous position that aesthetics alone could substantiate a zoning regulation. The court noted that a "regulation in the name of esthetics must bear substantially on the economic, social and cultural patterns of the community or district." *Matter of McCormick v. Lawrence, 8 Misc.2d 64, 372 N.Y.S.2d 156 (1975).*

This latter language regarding community economic, social and cultural patterns may simply be recognizing that an aesthetics regulation must be supported by a public health, safety or welfare reason, or it may be an attempt to provide some criteria for reviewing the reasonableness of this type of regulation. Regardless, aesthetics as the primary reason for a regulation is an expansion of the limitations existing under prior law.

Now that the judicial mist is beginning to clear around the question of whether aesthetics can stand alone, the mist is reappearing on another front. The definition of aesthetics as used by communities in their regulations, and by the courts in validating those regulations, seems to be expanding. The aesthetics language being used by legislatures and courts is not confined to visual beauty. The courts continue to wince at the potential for abuse of such a subjective concept.

One writer who has analyzed the cases has opined that aesthetics is a concept referring to our "shared human values," and has nothing to do with visual beauty. Historical buildings and wetlands are not preserved because they are visually beautiful, but because the community cherishes them, beautiful or not. Another writer analyzing the recent cases suggests that aesthetics is being used to express the desire of humans to live in harmony with their physical environment. Protection of coastal areas and wildlife habitat is a reflection of the attitude that humans must share the planet by necessity with their fellow creatures.

Whatever its precise definition, the concept of aesthetics provides communities with significant latitude for adopting controls to protect and preserve the natural environment.

Summary

Zoning is by far the most widespread method for controlling land use. The basic zones are residential, commercial and industrial, but often communities have as many as 15 to 20 designated zones. Several bases exist for modifying zoning regulations, including *zone changes* and *variances,* and uses pre-dating the zoning ordinance are legal despite their being *nonconforming uses.*

Not all land use problems have been solved by traditional zoning. *Large-lot zoning,* for example, requires that building lots be one acre or more for one-family residences. This policy is defended by policymakers on grounds of environmental concerns and *aesthetics,* in addition to the reduction of costs of some public services. Criticisms relate to what may appear to be the intent of some communities to close the door on those considered "unacceptable." For this reason, among others, some courts have ruled that large-lot zoning is unconstitutional unless a community has also made some provision for low- and middle-income housing.

A trend that effectively mixes uses in one specific land area is the *PUD,* or *planned unit development.* Larger than a typical subdivision, the PUD provided a long-term plan for economic growth in an underused or vacant space. The plan might include various types of residences, stores and banks and perhaps even light industry or warehouses. The developer needs community approval for the plan at the outset and then must seek approval as each successive section is developed. This flexibility enables the builder to react and adapt to a changing marketplace. Unfortunately, it also provides opportunity for an unscrupulous builder to sabotage the plan by changing it frequently.

Contract zoning is one concept that permits controlled change in a community by requiring the builder or developer who requests a zone change to contract to build to certain standards of quality or aesthetics. It is not legal in all states and is often criticized for its requirement of restrictive covenants by the builder.

Subdivision regulations are a method of controlling the details of growth. Subdivision plans are drafted by the developer, builder or architect and must be approved by the local planning authority. Among other items, the subdivision plan should specify a percentage of land to be dedicated to parks and recreation and should allow for providing necessary public services.

Since the early 1970s environmental groups have been calling for preservation of various types of lands and buildings. *Wetlands, floodplains,* historical districts, landmark buildings, some archaeological sites, *coastal zones, critical areas* and *agricultural lands* have come to the attention of public-spirited citizens who point out the special value of these areas. Wholesale growth in the name of progress is no longer seen by everyone as desirable. Many people view land as a resource to be preserved with care.

Review and Discussion Questions

1. Large-lot zoning, requiring one or more acres per single-family dwelling, has not been popular with poor and minority groups. Why?

2. The courts that have rejected large-lot zoning have retained an exception to their declaration of illegality. They have said that large-lot zoning is all right if there is some "extraordinary justification." What would constitute such a justification?

3. Why have courts been reluctant to approve regulations that are based solely upon visual beauty or aesthetics?

4. If the floodplains are dangerous places to live, then we should have a policy against people living there. Discuss the implications of such a policy.

5. Contrast a zone change request with a variance request.

6. If a community wanted to permanently restrict the use of its prime farmland to agricultural use, can it legally do it? Support your answer.

7. What is meant by the term *ecologically imperative lands?*

8. What advantages does regulating under the "critical areas" approach have over the more traditional method of protecting wetlands, floodplains and the like, separately?

Case Problems

1. Rachel Karson's deed contained a clause that barred use of that land for purposes such as a "bar, tavern, alehouse or the like." Rachel would like to open a restaurant that serves alcoholic beverages. Will she be prohibited from doing so by the clause in her deed?

2. The Town of Preston passed a sign control ordinance. Section 8 of the ordinance stipulated that all existing signs within the town must conform to the sign ordinance within five years from the date of its enactment. Marvin Miller has a large, flashing, nonconforming sign that he does not wish to remove. What arguments should Marvin assert? Would he be successful?

3. S. Volpe & Company petitioned the board of appeals for a special permit to construct a golf course on its land. Golf courses were one of the specially permitted uses allowed under the Town of Wareham's zoning ordinance. The board denied the permit because the land included salt marshes and the golf course would destroy the ecology of the region and harm local fishing. What will be the result in court? *S. Volpe & Co. v. Board of Appeals of Wareham, 4 Mass. App. Ct. 57, 348 N.E. 2d 807 (1976).*

4. Rogers owns a large single-family house in the suburbs. She plans to move to a more expensive house in a nearby suburb. To afford the new house, Rogers wants to convert her present home into a two-family apartment. The zoning classification for her house is R-2, that is single-family house on a minimum lot size of 20,000 square feet. Advise Rogers on how to proceed. Is she likely to be successful under your suggested procedure?

5. Ima Nactivist, councillor for the Town of Riverview, introduced legislation at the town board meeting that, if enacted, would require the removal of all structures now existing on the floodplain in Riverview. The legislation included an array of dates upon which types of structures would have to be removed, ranging from one to 15 years. Older and less valuable structures would be removed earlier, and newer and more valuable ones would be eliminated later. Cyrus Caselaw, town attorney, informed Ima that the proposed law was clearly unconstitutional. Ima retorted that Cyrus was misinformed. Discuss.

6. Bayswater proposed a cluster subdivision of 115 units on smaller-than-required lots and proposed to dedicate 60 acres to open space. The Planning Board has the authority to allow clustering so long as the unit density does not exceed the site's legal capacity if not clustered, and so long as open space is dedicated to the town. The 60 acres was largely steep slopes and wetlands. The Town Planning Board approved Baywater's proposal as submitted, but required a $5,000 per unit subdivision exaction payment for parkland per another law. Bayswater refused to pay the in-lieu fee, contending that the 60 acres of open space in its proposal satisfies the parkland exaction portion of town law. Discuss. *Bayswater Realty and Capital Corp. v. Planning Board of the Town of Lewisboro, 544 N.S. 2d 613, 560 N.E.2d 1300 (1990).*

7. National Amusement proposed to build a shopping center. The proposal was opposed by local residents and businesses because they did not want the shopping center in their community and because existing businesses did not

want the competition. In response to the opposition, the City rezoned the area from general business to multiple-unit residential, though there had been no changes in the land use patterns in the vicinity. National Amusement charged the City with "spot zoning" its land. Discuss. *National Amusement, Inc. v. City of Boston, 29 Mass. App. 305, 560 N.E.2d 138 (1990).*

23

Environmental Law and Real Estate Transactions

Since the early 1970s, numerous federal laws have been enacted advocating protection of the physical environment. Several of these laws directly or indirectly affect real estate transactions. The impact of the Comprehensive Environmental Response, Compensation and Liability Act (CERCLA) is the most dramatic; however, the Clean Water Act, the Clean Air Act, the Resource Conservation and Recovery Act, the National Environmental Policy Act (discussed in Chapter 21), and several others affect real estate decisions. Each of these federal laws may be paralleled or complemented by similar state laws.

Comprehensive Environmental Response, Compensation and Liability Act (CERCLA)

A statute whose purpose is to provide a regulatory mechanism for cleaning up inactive waste sites that release hazardous substances to the environment.

The CERCLA, or Superfund Law, was enacted in 1980. It was significantly amended by the Superfund Amendments and Reauthorization Act, or SARA, in 1986. The purpose of CERCLA and SARA is to establish a regulatory mechanism for dealing with abandoned or inactive hazardous waste sites.

The public health and safety problem created by inactive hazardous waste sites was first brought to the public's attention by the discovery of significant health impacts of the Hooker Chemical site at Love Canal in New York. Since that time, literally thousands of inactive hazardous waste sites have been identified in every region of the country. Many of these sites leak hazardous materials into the water, air and soil in the surrounding area.

Superfund

CERCLA mandated that a national inventory of hazardous waste sites be made. The inventory identified some 30,000 inactive hazardous waste sites. The Environmental Protection Agency (EPA) identified those sites in the inventory that merited remedial action and placed them on the National Priority List (NPL). A site is listed on the NPL if it receives a minimum score, currently 28.5, under a technical listing procedure, called the Hazardous Ranking System (HRS). The major effect of being put on the NPL is that the site is eligible for Superfund monies to clean it up.

The Hazardous Substances Response Fund, or Superfund, was established to provide a source of funds for cleaning up hazardous waste sites. Under the law to date, Congress has made available over $10 billion to conduct cleanup activities. Approximately 87 percent of the Superfund monies come from taxes on industry, principally the petroleum and chemical industries, who are the major sources of hazardous waste. The remainder of Superfund monies comes from Congressional appropriations from other federal tax revenues. Superfund can be used to pay for expenses incurred in planning for site cleanup and for the cleanup itself. Many states have their own version of Superfund that may provide additional cleanup funds.

Implementing the Cleanup

Cleanup activities or response costs can be incurred by federal or state officials or private parties. If the party incurring the response costs wishes to be reimbursed by Superfund, by state funds or by the parties responsible for the hazardous waste, it must follow the National Contingency Plan (NCP).

The NCP originated in the Clean Water Act for cleaning up oil spills. Under CERCLA, it was adapted for use in cleaning up hazardous waste sites on land. The NCP provides a step-by-step procedure that must be followed in carrying out a removal action or a remedial action at the site. A removal action is immediate and interim measures used to neutralize an imminent threat from the site. For example, a removal action may involve removing barrels that are leaking waste into a stream, or putting up a security fence to protect the public from the hazardous nature on the site. A remedial action is the permanent action taken to eliminate the threat created by the site to public health or safety or to the environment.

A goal of CERCLA is to get the parties responsible for disposing of the hazardous waste to clean up the site. Unfortunately, the responsible parties may be unknown to the EPA, or be unwilling to clean up the site. The EPA determines, however, who will conduct the cleanup action. The EPA may choose to clean up the site itself using Superfund monies, or EPA may negotiate an agreement with the state by which the state will carry out the cleanup activities. The EPA may insist that the responsible parties clean up the site. Currently, responsible parties do about one-third of the cleanups, but the EPA is moving rapidly toward an agency goal of getting responsible parties to conduct 50 percent of the site cleanups.

Liability

Any party who has incurred response costs from either a removal action or a remedial action may recover all or part of those costs from potentially responsible parties. In order to succeed, the plaintiff must prove five elements:

1. that the place involved is a facility,

2. that the facility caused a release or threat of a release of a hazardous substance,

3. that the defendant is a potentially responsible party,

4. that the damages sought were incurred responding to a release, and

5. that the plaintiffs followed the NCP.

The party must prove that the place involved in incurring the costs is a "facility." The courts have broadly interpreted facility to be a typical hazardous waste disposal site, but also such places as horse stables and spraying trucks were held to be facilities.

Secondly, there must be a release or the threat of a release of a hazardous substance from the facility. CERCLA does not have its own definition of what substances are hazardous, but uses the hazardous definitions contained in the Clean Water Act and the Resource Conservation and Recovery Act. The release of the hazardous substance can be to any medium, including the soil, the groundwater or the wind.

Thirdly, the defendant from whom response costs are sought must be a person covered by the law, or a potentially responsible party (PRP). PRPs are broadly defined to include past or present owners or operators of the facility, past or present generators of the waste disposed at the facility, and past or present transporters of waste to the facility, if the transporter selected that facility. It should be noted that a PRP does not have to participate in, or even know about, the disposal of the hazardous waste. Merely being an owner or operator qualifies one as a PRP.

It is the broad definition of PRPs and the extent of their legal liability that has markedly changed real estate transactions in recent years. Owners may be lessors who knew nothing of the activities on the site, or lenders to the owners of the facility who have foreclosed on a defaulted mortgage and taken title to the land to protect their investment, or parent corporations who participated in the management of its subsidiary corporation who was facility-owner.

When a PRP is held liable for response costs under CERCLA, the liability is strict, and joint and several. Strict liability means that the plaintiff need not show fault on the part of the defendant, but only that they come within the definition of a PRP. Joint and several liability means that the plaintiff can sue any one or more of the PRPs without including all of them, and the PRPs sued are responsible for the total response costs. If the defendant PRPs know that other PRPs exist, it is up to them to bring them into the litigation. It is possible for a defendant PRP to prove that its waste is severable or divisible from all other waste at the facility. In the unlikely event that the defendant PRP can prove divisibility, it can only be held liable for the contribution of its waste to the response costs.

In order to hold a PRP liable for response costs, the plaintiff does not have to prove that the PRP's waste actually caused the release. With the broad definition of PRP, the restrictive nature of strict, and joint and several liability, and the requirement that the plaintiff does not have to prove causation, CERCLA casts a wide, almost impenetrable, net.

The fourth element that the plaintiff must prove is that costs it seeks to recover were reasonably necessary to remedy the threat created by release from the facility. Finally, the plaintiff must follow the National Contingency Plan in expending the funds to clean up the site.

The following case explores the remedies available to the current owner of a hazardous waste site against those who owned the site when the waste was actually deposited.

Cadillac Fairview/California Inc. v. Dow Chemical Co.
Ninth Circuit Court of Appeals
840 F.2d 691 (1988)

Background: In 1976, Cadillac Fairview purchased a site in Torrance, California. Later it learned that hazardous waste was deposited on the site and that it had migrated to the underlying soil and was a threat to cause substantial environmental and health problems. At the request of state officials, Cadillac Fairview hired engineers to do chemical testing at the site and to evaluate the hazards posed by the contamination. In addition, it erected a fence around the site and posted guards to keep trespassers off the site. It spent $70,000 on these activities.

The site had been purchased by the federal government in 1942 and a rubber-producing plant had been constructed on it. Dow Chemical operated the facility under a contract with the government; that contract authorized Dow to dump hazardous by-products of its production processes on the site. In 1955, Shell Oil purchased the site; it also deposited hazardous waste on the site until 1972. Cadillac Fairview pur-

chased the site from a successor in title of Shell Oil.

Cadillac Fairview sued the federal government, Dow and Shell to recover its response costs and for an injunction ordering that all remedial action and costs of that action were the responsibility of the federal government, Dow and Shell. The federal district court dismissed Cadillac Fairview's suit for failure to state a cause of action.

Decision: The Ninth Circuit Court of Appeals held that Cadillac Fairview was entitled to response costs for it removal action, but was not entitled to the injunction.

Circuit Judge Wallace
Section 107(a)(2)(B) of CERCLA expressly creates a private claim against any person who owned or operated a facility at the time hazardous substances were disposed of at the facility for recovery of necessary costs of responding to the hazardous substances incurred consistent with the national

contingency plan. Cadillac Fairview alleged that it incurred "necessary costs" of response within the meaning of section 107(a), and that Dow, Shell, and the federal defendants owned or operated the Site at the time that hazardous substances were deposited there. Despite these allegations, the district court dismissed Cadillac Fairview's suit against the private defendants for failure to state a claim under section 107(a).

The district judge based his decision to dismiss Cadillac Fairview's damages claims on its failure to await governmental action with respect to the Site before bringing suit. The court held that in order for a private response action to be "consistent with the national contingency plan," it must be "initiated and coordinated by a governmental entity, and not by a private individual acting alone." The court also stated that the costs incurred by Cadillac Fairview were not compensable response costs under section 107 because they did not constitute "cleanup costs" within the meaning of the national contingency plan.

Though the national contingency plan describes the role of lead agencies in examining information and determining appropriate responses to environmental hazards, we hold that such provisions do not constrain private parties seeking to recover response costs under section 107(a). We concluded that this reading of section 107(a) was supported both by "the lack of any procedure whereby a private party could seek to obtain prior governmental approval of a cleanup program" and by CERCLA's broad remedial purpose to promote private enforcement actions "independent of governmental actions financed by Superfund." In NL Industries, we reaffirmed our holding in *Wickland,* and rejected the argument that response costs cannot be deemed

"necessary" in the absence of lead agency approval of the cleanup.

Shell argues that although no federal involvement is necessary, some significant state or local governmental action must precede a response action for which recovery is possible under section 107(a).

Shell, however, cites no authority for the proposition that significant state or local governmental action is a necessary prerequisite to a private action under section 107(a). Nor is there any mention of such a requirement in either section 107 or in the national contingency plan. We are thus reluctant to read a state or local governmental action requirement into the statute absent some strong indication that Congress intended that private parties await action by a state or local government before commencing a response action. Our examination of CERCLA's provisions leads us to conclude that significant state or local governmental action need not precede a response action for that action to be either "necessary" or "consistent with the national contingency plan."

Dow argues that without preliminary governmental action, a defendant can be forced to pay for cleanup actions that are inadequate or ill-conceived. This argument ignores the plain language of the statute. Section 107(a) does not allow recovery of any and all costs of response that a private party incurs. To recover costs under section 107(a), the party undertaking the response action must prove that the costs it incurred were "necessary" and that it incurred those costs in a manner "consistent with the national contingency plan." A response action is consistent with the plan for purposes of section 107 only if it satisfies criteria set forth in pertinent regulations.

We conclude, therefore, that the district court erred in ruling that some governmental entity must authorize and initiate a response action for that action to be necessary and consistent with the national contingency plan.

As an alternative ground for the dismissal of Cadillac Fairview's damages claims, the district court held that Cadillac Fairview failed to allege that it incurred "cleanup" costs within the meaning of section 107(a). We rejected the distinction between investigatory costs and on-site cleanup costs in *Wickland.* Section 107(a)(2)(B) allows recovery of "costs of response," which includes costs incurred "to monitor, assess, and evaluate the release or threat of release of hazardous substances," and costs of actions "necessary to prevent . . . damage to the public health . . . [including] security fencing or other measures to limit access." The testing and security expenditures alleged by Cadillac Fairview fall within the ambit of those defined by the section. The district court thus erred in holding that Cadillac Fairview failed to state a claim for recovery of those costs under section 107(a)(2)(B).

Cadillac Fairview also pleaded a claim for injunctive relief ordering Dow, Shell, CC&F, and the federal defendants to undertake appropriate response actions with respect to the Site in a manner consistent with the national contingency plan. The district court examined CERCLA's provisions and found that the only private remedy provided in CERCLA is the private cause of action for response costs described in section 107(a). Under section 107(a), the United States, a State, an Indian Tribe, or any other person may recover necessary costs of response incurred consistent with the national contingency plan. There is no mention of a right to injunctive relief in section 107(a). In contrast, under section 106(a), the President may require the Attorney General to seek injunctive relief "when the President determines that there may be an imminent and substantial endangerment to the public health or welfare or the environment." The district court concluded that the failure to provide for injunctive relief in section 107(a), coupled with the absence of any provision for a private right of action under section 106(a), mandated the conclusion that Congress did not intend to create a private cause of action for injunctive relief under CERCLA.

We conclude, therefore, that CERCLA § 107(a) does not provide for a private right to injunctive relief against owners and operators as defined by section 107(a)(2). Section 106(a) and 107(a) indicate that when Congress wished to provide for injunctive relief under CERCLA, it knew how to do so and did so expressly. The district court's dismissal of Cadillac Fairview's claims for injunctive relief against Dow, Shell, CC&F, and the federal defendants is affirmed.

Defenses

The defenses for a PRP are few and narrow. The PRP may defend by proving that the release of a hazardous substance was caused by an act of God or of war. The law includes a "third party" defense, which is equally narrow. If the PRP can prove that the release was caused solely by a third party having no contractual relationship to the PRP and that the PRP used due care with respect to the hazardous substance, including taking adequate precautions to prevent harm, it is not liable under CERCLA. Proving the lack of any contractual relationship, such as a lease, a deed or a shipping contract is unlikely.

SARA added a defense, called the innocent purchaser defense, that is broader in nature. If the hazardous waste was placed on the site before the defendant PRP became the owner and the defendant did not know or have reason to know that the waste was on the site at the time of acquisition, or if the PRP is a government agency that obtained the land involuntarily (e.g., nonpayment of taxes), or is a person who acquired through inheritance or bequest, the defendant is not liable.

To meet the test "did not know or have reason to know," the defendant must undertake at the time of acquisition "all appropriate inquiry" into previous ownership and uses of the property consistent with good commercial and customary practice in an effort to minimize liability. All appropriate inquiry includes consideration of the specialized knowledge or experience of the defendant, the relationship of the actual purchase price to the market value of the property (if not contaminated), the obviousness of the presence of the hazardous waste and the ability to detect hazardous waste through appropriate inspection.

It appears that, at a minimum, the defendant at the time of acquisition must have visually inspected the property, checked government records concerning past ownership and uses of the property and made further inquiry if the purchase price was distinctly lower than the market prices of other property in the vicinity. Beyond these suggestions, it is unclear as to what steps are required to satisfy the "all appropriate inquiry" test. It is not unreasonable to expect that the standard necessary to meet the test will become higher with regard to commercial property as the awareness of CERCLA grows in the business world.

If the PRP cannot meet the "all appropriate inquiry" test, but is a minor contributor to the waste at the facility, the EPA may enter a de minimis settlement with the otherwise innocent purchaser. The statute authorizes a de minimis settlement when the purchaser did not know of, conduct or permit the generation, transportation, storage, treatment or disposal of any hazardous substance at the site, and did not otherwise contribute to the release of the hazardous substance. In the de minimis settlement, the PRP is required to pay a proportionately higher amount of the estimated response costs in exchange for avoiding the costs of litigation and the uncertainty of delay in settling the matter.

Damages

Any person can recover response costs, including costs of assessing and planning the cleanup. The government can get an injunction to halt a release of a hazardous substance, or insure an administrative order compelling a PRP to conduct the cleanup. If a PRP refuses to obey the administrative order to cleanup, the government can recover punitive damages up to three times the actual cost of the cleanup. The federal government may also assess civil penalties of up to $25,000 per violation.

CERCLA places an affirmative obligation on federal and state governments to seek to recover natural resource damages caused by the release of a hazardous substance. The term *natural resources* is broadly defined to include injury to public "land, fish, wildlife, biota, air, water, groundwater, drinking water supplies" and other natural resources owned or held in trust by the federal and state governments. The President and the Governor of the relevant state must identify a trustee for natural resources. The trustees must agree on the natural resource damage and seek recovery against the PRPs. Superfund monies cannot be used to pay natural resource damages.

State CERCLA-type Statutes

Several states—including California, Connecticut, Illinois, Iowa, Missouri, and New Jersey—have enacted CERCLA-type laws that often focus on real estate transactions. Many other states have very recently adopted or are considering laws to make the real estate transaction a trigger that sets off an inquiry into the possible existence of hazardous waste on the site. For example, the California Torres Act requires that an owner of nonresidential property who knows or has reasonable cause to believe that a release of a hazardous waste from the site has occurred must give written notice to the buyer or lessee prior to concluding a real estate transaction with them. Failure to do so may result in civil penalties.

The model that most states appear to be following is New Jersey's Environmental Clean-up Responsibility Act (ECRA), which went into effect in 1983. The law applies to any industrial establishment, including manufacturing firms, warehousing business, utilities, repair operations and transportation and communication services. It applies when the industrial establishment engages in any conveyance of real estate; changes in ownership or operation, mergers; is acquired or taken over; has a lease expire; or goes into bankruptcy or ceases or transfers operations.

If the industrial establishment engages in one of the above activities, it must undertake an environmental audit to determine if its site is contaminated by hazardous waste. If contamination is found, the firm must develop a cleanup plan, which is subject to review and approval by a state agency. The transaction cannot be concluded until the state agency signs off on the audit or the cleanup plan. The firm must provide financial assurances equal to the anticipated cost of the cleanup to guarantee that cleanup actually occurs.

Failure to comply with the statute makes the real estate or other transaction voidable by either the state or the transferee. The industrial establishment may be liable for up to $25,000 per day in fines and is strictly liable for all cleanup and related costs.

Notice that the New Jersey law has as its trigger a real estate or some other business transaction. Under federal CERCLA, the trigger is the release of a hazardous substance from the site.

Clean Water Act

A statute whose purpose is to cleanse, maintain and enhance the quality of the nation's water resources.

The Clean Water Act, adopted in 1972 and amended several times since then, uses a system of effluent and water quality standards to limit pollution in the nation's surface waters. The chief focus of the law through 1987 was on regulating point sources of pollution. A point source is a discrete conduit (pipe) used to dispose of wastes.

Statutory Structure: Industrial Dischargers

Effluent standards are technology-based standards imposed on major industrial sources of water pollution. Major industrial sources were categorized by industry (e.g., chemical) or subcategory of industry (e.g., chemical-sulfuric acid). Each source within the designated category of industry was to adopt "best practicable technology" by 1977, and a stricter "best available technology" or "best conventional technology" by 1983. In some cases, these dates were extended by subsequent amendments to the 1972 law.

Water quality standards are ambient standards based upon a use of the body of water designated by the state. The state determines that a stream, or portion of it, should be used to supply drinking water to a municipality or as a trout stream or for some other designated use. In order to use the stream for the state-designated purpose, certain types of pollution (e.g., fecal coliform) cannot exceed established levels. The established level is the water quality standard needed to maintain the quality of the receiving water.

A point source of water pollution must conform to the stricter of the effluent standard or water quality standard. In reality, the source must adopt the effluent standard, but if necessary, due to the high quality demanded by state-designated use (drinking water) or stream conditions (many other sources of mercury in the stream) or other factor, the source must adopt the stricter water quality standard. The enforcement mechanism is that each major pollution source must get a permit that states a specific number limitation on each type of effluent.

At this time, most industrial sources have adopted the technology necessary to meet the effluent standard. Two significant areas of water pollution are inadequately addressed by the point source, technology-based standard approach. Due to a lack of understanding and to limitations on existing technology, toxics dumped into the water are mostly unregulated. Nonpoint sources of pollution, those not emanating from a discrete conduit, are also by and large unregulated. Nonpoint sources of pollution come mainly from agricultural run-off, mining and timbering waste, and construction and road run-off.

In 1987, Congress, recognizing the continuing problems of toxic and nonpoint source pollution, amended the law in order to refocus attention on these pollution sources. The EPA must identify those waters that fail to meet water quality standards due to toxics and nonpoint sources of pollution. The states must then develop management programs to systematically eliminate the nonconformity of the identified waters to the water quality standards.

The effluent standards do not have a direct effect on land use, as they only designate the technology that must be used by a new industrial pollution source. However, the water quality standard, which concerns itself with the quality of the ambient water, may effect the location of water pollution sources. Industrial sources will have to be relatively clean in order to locate on a stream whose use is designated for drinking water or swimming. Others will be forced to locate on streams with lower water quality standards.

Statutory Structure: Municipal Dischargers

In addition to industrial point sources of water pollution, Congress recognized, in 1972, that no treatment, or rudimentary treatment, of municipal sewage was a major contributor to water pollution in surface waters. With the Clean Water Act, the country embarked on a major undertaking to provide secondary treatment for all municipal sewage. Secondary sewage treatment removes approximately 90 percent of all organic contaminants in the water.

Congress authorized the federal government to pay 75% of the cost of constructing publicly-owned sewage treatment works (POTWs). After spending over $40 billion in federal funds alone, it was reported in 1987 that 87 percent of all municipal sewage is receiving secondary treatment. The grants program has been changed to a revolving fund loan program. The revolving fund provides loans for up to 80 percent of the cost of construction of POTWs to complete the job of providing adequate treatment nationally. It should be emphasized that the current system is a loan arrangement, unlike the outright grants that were made by the federal government under the original law in 1972.

Real estate development can be curtailed if a community does not have a POTW capable of providing secondary treatment, or if the currently adequate POTW does not have the capacity to absorb the sewage from the new development.

Wetlands

The Clean Water Act regulates "waters of the United States," which include interstate waters, intrastate waters that have some connection to interstate commerce (e.g., for industrial waste disposal by firms that ship their goods in interstate commerce and wetlands that are connected to these bodies of water.

Under Section 404 of the statute, anyone wishing to dredge or fill in a wetland must obtain a permit from the Army Corps of Engineers (Corps). The Corps' permit program is overseen by the EPA, who can veto the issuance of any Corps permit. Before issuing a permit, the Corps must determine that its issuance will comply with all effluent and water quality standards, decide if the permit applicant has a practical alternative to using the wetlands, and take into account the "economics, aesthetics, effects on wetlands, historic preservation, fish and wildlife values, effects on floodplains, land use, navigation, recreation and energy needs" of the people.

Historically, the Corps has been lenient in granting §404 permits. Two recent developments are likely to change past Corps leniency. The EPA has taken an active role in reviewing Corps permit decisions and has shown a willingness to veto its decisions. Secondly, in 1990, President Bush announced a national policy of "no net loss" of wetlands.

The precise form of the regulations to implement the "no net loss" of wetlands policy is uncertain at this time. It seems, however, that the purchase of wetlands for the purpose of development is unwise environmentally and financially.

Clean Air Act

A statute whose purpose is to cleanse, maintain and enhance the quality of the nation's air resource.

The Clean Air Act, adopted in 1970 and amended in 1977 and 1990, mandates that the EPA regulate pollutants that are harmful to public health and welfare. The country is divided into air quality control regions for purposes of administering the Act. The EPA assembled the full body of relevant information about pollutants it chose to regulate and issued the information as a *criteria document*. Based on these criteria, the EPA promulgated national ambient air quality standards (NAAQS) for what came to be called the criteria pollutants. There are six criteria pollutants, including sulfur dioxide, nitrous oxide, carbon monoxide, ozone, particulates and lead.

There are two types of NAAQS. Primary standards are intended to protect public health. Secondary standards are stricter than primary standards and exist to protect public welfare. Public welfare includes protecting soil, water, vegetation, wildlife, visibility and the like.

The states were to formulate state implementation plans (SIPs) for meeting the NAAQS. Primary standards were to be met by 1975 and secondary standards within a reasonable time (1977 was designated by the EPA). These dates were extended, and 20 years later, approximately 100 regions continue to have trouble meeting one or more of the standards.

In the 1977 amendments to the Clean Air Act, Congress ordered the air quality control regions to be divided into those that attained and those that did not attain NAAQS. The regions are referred to as prevention of significant deterioration, or PSD, regions (attainment) and non-attainment regions. An industrial source of air pollution seeking to locate in an area needs to know whether it is a PSD region or a nonattainment region.

If the region is a clean air area, or PSD region, the law mandates that the air quality cannot be *significantly* deteriorated. The law divided PSD regions into three categories, based on the anticipated economic growth in the area. In the Class I region, little or no additional levels of a criteria pollutant is allowed. In a Class II region, moderate increases are allowed, and in Class III regions, greater increases are permitted. The regional increments, or allowed deterioration, are specific number limitations and are permanent. In no case, however, may the pollution exceed NAAQS, regardless of the allowed regional increment.

Any major industrial developer seeking to locate in a PSD region must obtain a permit, agree to use best available control technology as defined by the EPA to limit its emissions, and prove that the NAAQS and the PSD regional increment will not be exceeded. The industrial applicant for a permit to pollute the air is required to do a full year of site monitoring prior to construction to determine existing levels of the pollutants in the area, to assure that the PSD increment will not be exceeded.

To date, the EPA has established increments for sulfur dioxide and particulates, with an increment system for nitrous oxide apparently going into effect in the early 1990's. For the other three criteria pollutants, the PSD regulations are in limbo and need not concern the industrial developer at this time.

If the industrial source tries to locate in a nonattainment region, it must obtain a permit. Although pollution sources are permitted to locate in a nonattainment region it may be difficult to do so because the region must make regular progress toward achieving the NAAQS. Thus, the new source must find an offset for its pollution in the region, and must adopt control technology that achieves the lowest rate of emission required of any source of its type in the country (called LAER). The source also runs the risk that it will be required to achieve greater control in the future because the NAAQS must ultimately be met.

In 1990, Congress passed major amendments to the Clean Air Act. The amendments address four continuing problems: urban smog, motor vehicle emissions, acid rain, and toxic air pollutants. At least two of these areas of regulation may affect the industrial real estate developer. The urban smog provisions apply to the remaining nonattainment regions. These regions must make annual progress towards achieving the NAAQSs and must meet the standards within three to twenty years, depending on the severity of the current urban air pollution problems. A new industrial facility in a nonattainment region must show that its level of pollutants will be offset (and more) by reductions of other sources of pollution in the region in order to continue this region's progress toward meeting the NAAQS.

The acid rain provisions establish a permanent cap for sulfur dioxide emissions, which is less than one-half of the current level of emissions. The mechanisms chosen to achieve the necessary reductions are controls on electric generating power plants. It does not appear at this time that the acid rain provisions will directly affect industrial facilities, but may indirectly affect them by increasing the cost of energy or limiting its availability.

Other Legislation

There are many other statutes—federal, state and local—that directly or indirectly affect real estate transactions. The National Environmental Policy Act (NEPA) requires the preparation of environmental impact statements; the National Flood Insurance Act mandates protection for floodplain areas; and the Coastal Zone Management Act protects coastal regions from unwise development; these are discussed in Chapter 21 and 22. The Resource Conservation and Recovery Act (RCRA) regulates active hazardous waste sites, active solid waste sites and underground storage tanks. The Endangered Species Act protects the habitat of endangered or threatened species of plants and wildlife. The Federal Insecticide, Fungicide and Rodenticide Act (FIFRA) regulates the application of these substances to the land and to the environment generally. The Safe Drinking Water Act establishes minimum standards to protect the quality of municipal drinking water supplies. These and other federal environmental laws are often complemented by similar or more restrictive state laws. A careful review of the array of environmental legislation is necessary to safely conclude real estate transactions today.

Indoor Pollution

Pollution within buildings that may come from many sources and is now recognized as a serious health problem.

Indoor pollution sources release gases or particles into the air. Several recent studies point to indoor air pollution as the number one environmental human health risk. Inadequate ventilation, high temperature or humidity can increase concentrations of these pollutants. The sources of indoor pollution are many. Among the most prominent are radon, asbestos, tobacco smoke, formaldehyde, lead, pesticides and household products.

The health risks created by indoor pollution are magnified because people spend approximately 90 percent of their time indoors, and those likely to spend the most time indoors—the young, the elderly and the chronically ill—are the most susceptible. The adverse effects range from headaches and fatigue to cancer and heart disease.

As the case for indoor pollution is substantiated and the information regarding its risks is more widely communicated, the likelihood of builders, architects, employers and landlords incurring legal liability increases. The legal theories likely to be used are negligence, breach of express or implied warranties, strict product liability, fraud or misrepresentation, and a host of others.

Government regulation of indoor pollution is beginning to appear. The Safe Drinking Water Act was amended in 1986 to require the use of lead-free pipe, solder and flux in the installation of public water systems and in the plumbing of buildings connected to public water systems.

In 1988, Congress amended the Toxic Substances Control Act with an act called the Indoor Radon Abatement Law. Although the law specifically states that it does not create a legal cause of action, it brings nationwide attention to the radon problem. In addition, although it is the first venture into regulating radon, it is likely to be followed by more intrusive regulations. The law sets the long-term goal of reducing indoor radon levels to that of the outside ambient air. The EPA is ordered to publish periodic updates on radon health risks and information on the methods available to measure and reduce those risks. The EPA is to develop model construction standards and techniques for controlling radon levels. The statute provides money to assist states in developing programs to promote public awareness of radon risks and in developing feasible measures to mitigate the risk.

Other bills to regulate radon and asbestos are currently before Congress. Some states have begun to impose regulations on indoor pollution sources. Anyone involved in real estate transactions should seek the most up-to-date regulatory information; the pace of regulatory development is likely to be swift, and the risks may be high.

Summary

Laws aimed at protecting the physical environment are beginning to have a significant impact on real estate transactions. No statute is having a greater impact than the *Comprehensive Environmental Compensation and Liability Act (CERCLA)*, whose goal is to clean up inactive sites releasing hazardous waste into the environment. CERCLA makes all parties, with very narrow exceptions, who have had any interest in the site, potentially responsible for cleaning up the waste. Though the Superfund provides monies for government cleanup of sites, any monies expended can be recovered from the responsible parties.

CERCLA is supplemented in many states by statutes with goals similar to that of the federal statute. The state statutes often come into play at the time a real estate transaction is proposed. Prior to completion of the transaction, whether sale, lease or other ownership shift, the state must certify that the site is not contaminated by hazardous waste.

Major sources of water pollution must meet effluent and water quality standards to comply with the *Clean Water Act*. Though the effluent standard is the same wherever the firm locates, the water quality standard, or quality of the water receiving the pollutants, will vary and may limit where a firm can or should locate. If there are other pollution sources nearby or if the stream is small, the firm may have to choose another site. If the firm is planning to have its pollutants treated by the publicly owned treatment works (POTW), the existence of excess capacity at the POTW will decide whether it can locate in that area. A source of pollution must be careful to select a site where it will not be required to alter a wetland because there is a national policy of "no net loss" of wetlands.

All regions in the country are required to meet national ambient air quality standards (NAAQS) under the *Clean Air Act*. Whether locating in an area that meets the NAAQS, or one that does not, the air pollution's sources must obtain a permit to pollute. The types of conditions that must be met to get the permit will differ depending on whether the region is a "clean air" or "dirty air" area.

There are many other environmental statutes that may impinge upon real estate transactions. The National Environmental Policy Act (NEPA) mandates environmental planning if the proposed action is federally related. The National Flood Insurance Act and the Coastal Zone Management Act may limit development in floodplain and coastal areas.

The statutes discussed in the chapter are only a few of the most relevant ones; there are many more federal, state and local laws that may constrain real state transactions. It is likely that a new round of regulations will be adopted to protect public health against *indoor pollution*, especially indoor air pollution. Recent studies indicate that indoor pollution is a major public health threat. These regulations are likely to impose inspection and correction measures for indoor problems prior to the completion of real estate transactions.

Review and Discussion Questions

1. Discuss how the Hazardous Substances Response Fund, or Superfund, is used to pay for cleaning up hazardous waste sites.

2. If a business is going to purchase a site that was previously used by an industrial firm, what precautionary steps would you suggest to avoid CERCLA liability?

3. If a party wants to recover money spent on response costs under CERCLA, what must it prove to win in court?

4. Can an innocent landowner be held liable for response costs under CERCLA? Discuss.

5. What is the basic difference in approach between federal CERCLA and state hazardous waste cleanup statutes?

6. What are the chief problems left to be addressed in order to make the nation's water quality safe for public health and safety? Who is most likely to be affected by regulations addressing these problems?

7. How can air pollution controls affect real estate transactions?

8. What are the main sources of indoor pollution? Why is it critical that the problem of indoor pollution be remedied?

Case Problems

1. Idarado Mining Co. operated a mine for the extraction of several metals, including zinc, lead, silver and gold. The operation of the 16-square-mile site created hazardous waste in the form of tailings, mine drainage and waste rock. The State of Colorado submitted several alternative plans to a court for cleaning up the site under CERCLA. The Court approved one of the state's plans, stating that it was consistent with the National Contingency Plan and authorized the State to incur removal and remedial costs of nearly $2 million. The State completed the cleanup and sued Idarado for the response costs. Idarado contested some of the costs, including the costs of preparing the plans not approved by the Court and the cost of restocking a stream with fish. Idarado's waste previously destroyed the stream's fishery. Is Idarado likely to be successful in challenging these response costs? Explain. *Colorado v. Idarado Mining Co., 735 F. Supp. 368 (1990).*

2. Complaints by neighbors near a site formerly owned by Bell Petroleum Services, Inc. (Bell) about discolored drinking water caused an investigation by the Environmental Protection Agency (EPA). The investigation revealed that the aquifer from which the drinking water was drawn was contaminated by chromium, a hazardous waste. The State of Texas and the EPA cooperatively cleaned up the site and then sued Bell for response costs. Bell denies responsibility because it no longer owns the site and because the governments did not prove that it was their chromium waste that caused the contamination. Bell does not deny that it deposited chromium waste on the site. Discuss. *U.S. v. Bell Petroleum Services, Inc. 734 F., Supp. 771 (1989).*

3. Garden State Salvage, Inc. is proposing to lease a 146-acre site from Cooker Chemical Co. in Lockerbie, New Jersey. Garden State has been assured verbally by Cooker that the site is free of any pollutants. Under State law are the parties free to enter the lease agreement? If not, describe the actions that must be taken to avoid liability under State law.

4. Belvidere Steel Co. is seeking a site to expand its operations. It finds an apparently ideal site on the Little Lehigh River in northeastern Pennsylvania. The technical people have certified to the board of directors that the site is free of contamination from hazardous waste, has an excellent transportation system, and is otherwise ideally located for the manufacture of specialty steel. At this stage, you are called before the board to discuss the site as the technical expert on air and water pollution. What issues are you going to discuss with the Board?

5. Ruth Arones, a real estate broker, has an "exclusive right to sell" contract to sell a house owned by Karl and Nan Lipper. The Lippers tell Arones that the house is airtight and therefore extremely energy efficient. Arones notices that the inside of the house has not been painted in some time and that the paint is chipping badly. Arones knows also that some houses in the vicinity have shown high levels of radon when tested. Arones has a young couple, who have two small children, interested in buying the house. You are a senior broker in Arones' firm and she related these facts to you, seeking your advice on how to proceed. There are no applicable state statutes. How would you counsel Arones?

24

Fair Housing Laws

Fair Housing

The term used to describe a national policy against most types of discrimination in housing.

The second half of the 20th century has seen increasing involvement of government in housing in the United States. Types of housing regulations discussed elsewhere in the text include zoning and subdivision regulations, rent controls and mortgage regulations. During the same period government has exhibited an interest in assuring, through legislation, that no member of our society is refused an opportunity to obtain decent housing.

Segregation in Housing

The voluntary or enforced separation of one group from another in residential location based on religious association, ethnic background, race or a combination of these factors.

Until quite recently segregation was the American way of life. People were routinely segregated from one another on the basis of race, ethnic background and religious preference. Ethnic identity has traditionally been a source of pride among most people. This pride led to the Irish immigrants living in the Irish section of a city, the Germans in the German section and the Poles in the Polish section. Second- and third-generation descendants of these immigrants, however, began to drift away from their ethnic neighborhoods and become assimilated into the general population. The security provided by the support structure of the extended family in the ethnic community was no longer a necessity for the children and grandchildren of these immigrants. "Americanization" of language and customs along with ethnic intermarriages lessened their emotional and psychological bonds to their ethnic beginnings. Also, in most cities a parallel slow progression toward ethnic integration began in housing. Although this ethnic integration continues, it has by no means been uniformly successful for all ethnic groups.

Further, this assimilation and integration process did not occur in the area of racial segregation. Racial integration may have failed to parallel ethnic integration because of the highly visible differences among the races. Probably it also involves a host of social and cultural attitudes. Lack of integration among the races was seen in the housing market as well.

Racial segregation was institutionalized by the real estate industry. Developers, banks and realtors adopted practices that facilitated the continued separation of the races. For instance, it would not have been considered a good business practice for a realtor to negotiate the sale of a house to a black in a white neighborhood. Embittered whites would be likely to employ an embargo against the realtor because it was contended, sometimes accurately, that property values would become relatively depressed in such an integrated area. Lost business and depressed property values were negative inducements to realtors who relied on a percentage of the selling price for their commission.

"Separate but Equal" Facilities

A concept that permitted the states to enforce separation of the races so long as each race was provided with "equal" services or facilities.

In the late 19th century case of *Plessy v. Ferguson, 163 U.S. 537 (1896)*, the U.S. Supreme Court affirmed the doctrine that "separate but equal" was the law of the land. This concept was used to separate the races in many sectors of American life, including public transportation, education and accommodations. In housing, some state and local governments passed laws confining blacks and whites to separate sections of cities for residential living. This practice was considered constitutional as long as both black and white sections were provided. Economic and social pressures also were factors separating the races in residential areas.

The separate-but-equal interpretation of the federal constitution prevailed until the mid-20th century. Prior to that some erosion of the doctrine began to appear, especially in cases involving housing. In *Buchanan v. Warley, 245 U.S. 38 (1917)*, the Supreme Court struck down a city ordinance that prohibited blacks from moving to predominantly white streets and whites from migrating to predominantly black streets. The basis for the decision had nothing to do with the doctrine of separate but equal facilities. The legislation was held to be an undue restraint on a person's constitutionally protected right to *sell* property because it excluded an entire race from the available market.

The separate-but-equal doctrine played a more prominent role in a case decided 30 years later, in 1947.

Case Example

Shelley, a black man, pursuant to a contract, received a warranty deed to a parcel of land in the city of St. Louis. Unknown to Shelley, a former owner of the property had entered into an agreement with other property owners in the area restricting the sale of the property to members of the Caucasian race.

Kraemer and other property owners brought suit in the Missouri courts to prevent Shelley from occupying the premises. The lower courts in Missouri refused to enforce the agreement, but the Supreme Court of Missouri held the restrictive covenant enforceable. Shelley appealed to the U.S. Supreme Court.

The Supreme Court reversed the Missouri court, holding that "in granting judicial enforcement of the restrictive agreements . . . the States have denied petitioners the equal protection of the laws and that, therefore, the action of the state courts cannot stand." *Shelley v. Kraemer, 334 U.S. 1 (1947).*

In *Shelley v. Kraemer*, the court did not rule that the racially based restrictive covenants were unconstitutional, but only that the states, including their courts, must refrain from enforcing racial discrimination. Obviously, the effectiveness of a restrictive covenant is markedly reduced where enforcement in the courts is not available. Unless the party restricted by the covenant voluntarily complies with the limitation based on race, it is legally unenforceable.

The *Shelley* decision was quickly followed by several other cases that made it clear that courts could no longer be used as vehicles for enforcing racially discriminatory practices in housing. In 1950, the Chicago Real Estate Board, for example, amended a relevant section of its Code of Ethics. The board rewrote a section that advised realtors never to introduce members of a race or nationality into a neighborhood where the act would be detrimental to local property values. All reference to race or nationality was deleted from the Code of Ethics.

Equal Protection

The constitutional mandate that all people be treated equally under the law.

The separate-but-equal doctrine provided equality in theory, but it has been well documented that it had little relationship to equality in fact. Black and white schools were equal neither in physical plant nor in the quality of education children obtained in them. In housing as well, the quality and locations were not equal for blacks and whites.

In 1954, beginning with the school desegregation cases, the separate-but-equal doctrine was laid aside, and equal protection became the constitutional mandate. In these cases the plaintiffs were black children who, pursuant to statutes in Kansas, South Carolina, Virginia and Delaware, attended schools segregated on the basis of race. In each of these states, with the exception of Delaware, federal district courts had denied relief to the plaintiffs, citing the separate but equal doctrine of *Plessy v. Ferguson.* In the Delaware case, the state supreme court adhered to the doctrine, but ordered plaintiffs admitted to the white schools because of their superiority to the black schools. Plaintiffs appealed to the U.S. Supreme Court, which rejected the language of *Plessy v. Ferguson.* In an important decision the court stated:

We conclude that in the field of public education the doctrine of "separate but equal" has no place. Separate educational facilities are inherently unequal. Therefore, we hold that the plaintiffs and others similarly situated for whom the actions have been brought are, by reason of the segregation complained of, deprived of the equal protection of the laws guaranteed by the Fourteenth Amendment. *Brown v. Board of Education, 347 U.S. 483 (1954).*

After the decision in *Brown v. Board of Education,* the country began the slow process of racially integrating society. In the late 1950s and early 1960s, several states and cities enacted fair housing laws with varying degrees of coverage. These statutes were a prelude to the entry of the federal government into the fair housing arena. Since the federal government is now the focus for regulation of discrimination in housing. The remainder of this chapter will concentrate on several federal legislative enactments.

Federal Fair Housing Legislation

It was ten years after *Brown v. Board of Education* before Congress became active in the fair housing arena. It was not starting, however, with a clean legislative slate.

Civil Rights Act (1866)

Congress passed a civil rights act shortly after the conclusion of the Civil War. The act stated "[A]ll citizens of the United States shall have the same right, in every state and territory as is enjoyed by white citizens thereof to imperil, purchase, lease, sell, hold, and convey real and personal property."

The obvious intent of the statute is to prohibit discrimination based on race or color in real estate transactions. Despite the significant implications that this law would have had for elimination of racial discrimination, it lay dormant and unused until the case of *Jones v. Mayer,* which is discussed later in the chapter.

Civil Rights Act (1964)

The initial foray of Congress into fair housing was in Title VI of the Civil Rights Act of 1964. This law prohibited discrimination based on race, color, religion or national origin in most programs and activities in which the federal government rendered financial assistance. As a sanction for discrimination, the agency granting the financial aid could reject an application for money or terminate assistance already granted.

The 1964 law did not cover conventional mortgages because they did not involve federal aid. In addition, most FHA and DVA loans that required federal guarantees were excluded from coverage as well. One authority estimates that the statute applied to only about half of one percent of the houses purchased. Consequently, the impact of the 1964 Civil Rights Act upon racial discrimination in housing was far from dramatic.

The Civil Rights Act or the Fair Housing Act (1968)

Although a major effort was mounted in Congress in 1966 to get approval of more comprehensive fair housing legislation, the majority of the Congress was unwilling to go along. In 1968, however, Congress made its first comprehensive venture into fair housing by passing Title VIII of the Civil Rights Act of 1968, which is also called the Fair Housing Act.

The 1968 act prohibited discrimination based on race, color, religion, sex (in a later amendment) or national origin by someone either selling or leasing residential property. Residential property included any building occupied or designed for occupation, as well as any vacant land sold for the construction of a dwelling.

The act was amended in 1972 by a requirement that equal opportunity posters be displayed at brokerage houses, model home sites, mortgage lender offices and similar locations. The poster must contain the slogan "Equal Housing Opportunity" and must carry a brief equal housing opportunity statement. Failure to display such a poster will be treated as prima facie evidence of discrimination; that is, in the absence of evidence to the contrary it will be presumed that the broker discriminates in violation of the law.

Exceptions

The Fair Housing Act of 1968 does not apply to the sale or rental of commercial or industrial properties. In addition, the act creates several exceptions to the prohibited conduct stated above.

A person may discriminate in the sale or rental of a dwelling, providing he or she can meet all these criteria:

- The person does not own more than three houses at any one time.

- The person is living in the house or was the last person to live there. If this residency requirement is not met, then the exception applies to only one sale every 24 months.

- In addition, the exempt person may not use a broker, an agent, or a sales associate to facilitate the sale.

- The person also must refrain from discriminatory advertising.

Case Examples

Williams owns a house in town, one at the beach and another in the mountains. She lives in each during various parts of the year. She can discriminate in the sale of the beach house (or either of the others) so long as she sells it herself (without a broker) and does not advertise that there is a discriminatory preference or limitation.

Johnson also owns the same assortment of houses. He lives in the town house only and rents the other two. In addition to the restrictions mentioned above, Johnson is permitted to sell no more than one of the rental houses every two years if he wants to discriminate against buyers.

Another exception occurs when the owner of a multiple-family dwelling with no more than four units resides in one of the units and rents out the other units.

Occupancy of dwellings owned by religious organizations may be confined to the members of that organization, provided that membership in that organization is not based upon the categories protected by the Fair Housing Act.

Despite these exceptions, coverage of the act is comprehensive. Since most single-family homes are sold through the use of a broker and most multiple-family dwellings have more than four units, the bulk of sales and rentals would be covered by the statute.

Jones v. Mayer (1968)

The Civil Rights Act of 1866 lay largely dormant until resurrected by the Supreme Court in 1968, just prior to final approval of the Fair Housing Act of 1968. The Court, in *Jones v. Mayer, 392 U.S. 409 (1968),* raised this elderly statute to the status of a major factor in fair housing control.

At issue in the case was the following legislative language: "[A]ll citizens of the United States shall have the same right, in every state and territory, as is enjoyed by white citizens thereof to inherit, purchase, lease, sell, hold, and convey real and personal property." According to the Court in *Jones v. Mayer,* the intent of Congress was to prohibit any discrimination based on race or color in real estate transactions. It should be noted that, unlike the Fair Housing Act of 1968, this law applies only to race and color and not to religion, sex and national origin, but it does prohibit *all* discrimination based on race and color. In effect, the areas of discriminatory conduct excepted from coverage in the 1968 law are prohibited by the 1866 law where race or color is involved.

Also, the coverage of the 1968 statute is not confined to the real property transfer (sale, lease, and so on), as is the 1866 law, but encompasses discriminatory advertising, exaction of terms and brokerage activities. The two statutes are duplicative in some measure, but they also complement each other.

In summary, any discrimination in the transfer of real property based upon race or color is illegal. The exceptions of the 1968 statute continue to permit discrimination in limited circumstances noted above when that discrimination is based on religion, sex, or national origin.

The Fair Housing Amendments Act (1988)

Significant dissatisfaction developed with the Fair Housing Act of 1968. Some of these shortcomings are discussed as a preamble to the 1988 amendments. The statute is administered by the Department of Housing and Urban Development (HUD). Under the law, upon the receipt of a complaint contending that the complainant was the victim of a discriminatory practice, HUD was authorized to initiate a process of conciliation to resolve the dispute. HUD was without any power, however, to force the parties to reach an agreement. An alternative to the conciliation process was that the complainant could bring a private lawsuit in

Federal District Court to enjoin the practice and to get money damages. When the judicial approach was selected, however, damages were limited to actual damages and a maximum of $1,000 in punitive damages. The result was that damages recovered by parties complaining of discriminatory practices were notoriously low.

An alternative existed for those complaining of discrimination based on race or color. The *Jones v. Mayer* case, discussed earlier, provided a judicial remedy under the Civil Rights Act of 1866 and Section 1982 of the Federal Procedural Code. No specific remedies are provided by the law, but it was indicated under *Jones v. Mayer* that courts should frame effective equitable remedies. In practice, the Section 1982 suit had the benefit for complainants of no cap on the amount of punitive damages that can be recovered. A disadvantage of the Section 1982 is that complainants must prove that the discrimination is intentional and purposeful, a difficult burden of proof. Whatever its limitations, Section 1982 suits became a popular route for complainants to take.

To redress the shortcomings of the existing law, Congress passed the Fair Housing Amendments Act of 1988, amending its 1968 predecessor. Following is a description of the law as it now exists, integrating the two fair housing statutes. The prior discussion of the Fair Housing Act (1968) remains valid unless noted otherwise.

Conduct Prohibited by the Law

The Fair Housing Acts prohibit discrimination in all residential real estate transactions as defined in the act. For example, to *refuse* to sell or lease or to otherwise refuse to negotiate or to make a dwelling available is illegal. More over, *variation* in the terms of the sale or lease, as in provision of services or facilities in the sale or rental of a dwelling, is also prohibited.

Case Example

Filippo, a broker, refused to accept from a black person a purchase offer of $22,500, the price quoted to the buyer by Filippo's sales associate. Filippo instead told the black offeree that the selling price was $26,950. Later Filippo accepted a purchase order from a white buyer at $22,500 for the same property. As a result, Filippo's license was suspended for 45 days. Filippo appealed the suspension, but his appeal was rejected. *Filippo v. Real Estate Commission of District of Columbia, 223 A.2d 268 (D.C. 1966).*

Any *statement or advertisement* for the sale or lease of a dwelling, if it indicates a discriminatory preference or limitation based upon classifications defined in the law, is illegal.

Case Example

Cartwright and Lindsay visited a real estate firm where they indicated to a sales associate an interest in purchasing property in a certain section of Detroit. The sales associate stated that the section was fine "if you like a busted community." When asked what was meant by "busted community," the sales associate indicated that it was one that blacks had moved into. The sales associate also stated that housing values in that community are down and will continue to go down and that, while the schools are OK, "You know what will happen eventually." The sales associate then suggested another community.

Representation that a dwelling is not available for inspection sale or rental, when in fact it is available, is also illegal. Other discriminatory acts made illegal under the law include *denying membership* or *limiting participation* in real estate brokerage firms or their multiple listing pools, *blockbusting, redlining,* and steering. The *Asbury v. Brougham* case presents an example of a situation where the facts are misrepresented by the agent of the lessor to a minority person seeking housing.

Asbury v. Brougham
U.S. Court of Appeals, Tenth Circuit
866 F.2d 1276 (1989)

Background: Rosalyn Asbury tried to rent an apartment or a townhouse from Brougham Estates in Kansas City. The specific facts surrounding the refusal are discussed later in the case. Asbury charged that Brougham violated §1982 of the Federal Procedural Code and a section of the Fair Housing Act (1968) (FHA) by refusing to give her the opportunity to rent, to inspect, and to negotiate a rental of an apartment or townhouse because of her sex or race. Asbury was awarded $7,500 compensatory damages and $50,000 punitive damages by the jury at trial. Brougham contends that the evidence does not support the compensatory damages because Asbury failed to prove a discriminatory intent. Brougham challenged the punitive damages also because discriminatory motivation must be proven under §1982 to gain punitive damages. Brougham appealed to the Court of Appeals.

Decision: The Tenth Circuit Court of Appeals affirmed the trial court.

District Judge Parker
§1982 and the FHA both prohibit discrimination on the basis of race. In

order to prevail on a claim made under these statutes, plaintiff must prove a discriminatory intent. A violation occurs when race is a factor in a decision to deny a minority applicant the opportunity to rent or negotiate for a rental, but race need not be the only factor in the decision. In addition, the FHA specifically prohibits dissemination of false information about the availability of housing because of a person's race. Accordingly, failure to provide a minority applicant with the same information about availability of a rental unit or the terms and conditions for rental as is provided to white "testers" results in false information being provided and is cognizable as an injury under the FHA.

The three-part burden of proof analysis established in *McDonnell Douglas Corp. v. Green* has been widely applied to FHA and §1982 claims. Under the *McDonnell Douglas* analysis, plaintiff first must forward with proof of a prima facie case of discrimination. Second, if plaintiff proves a prima facie case, the burden shifts to defendants to produce evidence that the refusal to rent or negotiate for a rental was motivated by legitimate, non-racial considerations. Third, once defendants by evidence articulate non-discriminatory reasons, the burden shifts back to plaintiff to show that the proffered reasons were pretextual.

The proof necessary to establish a prima facie case under the FHA also establishes a prima facie case of racial discrimination under §1982. In order to establish her prima facie case, plaintiff had to prove that:

> (1) she is a member of a racial minority;
> (2) she applied for and was qualified to rent an apartment or townhouse in Brougham Estates;
> (3) she was denied the opportunity to rent or to inspect or negotiate for the rental of a townhouse or apartment; and
> (4) the housing opportunity remained available.

A review of the evidence in this case shows that plaintiff establishes her prima facie case. Defendants stipulated that Asbury is black. Plaintiff testified that on February 23, 1984, she went to Brougham Estates with her daughter to obtain rental housing. At the rental office at Brougham Estates, Asbury encountered Wanda Chauvin, the manager, and explained to Chauvin that she was being transferred to Kansas City and needed to rent housing. Asbury told Chauvin that she needed to secure housing by the middle of March or the beginning of April. In response, Chauvin said there were no vacancies, but told Asbury she could call back at a later time to check on availability. Chauvin provided no information concerning availability of rental units that would assist Asbury in her efforts to rent an apartment or townhouse at Brougham Estates. Asbury asked for the opportunity to fill out an application, but Chauvin did not give her an application, again stating that there were no vacancies and that

she kept no waiting list. Asbury also requested floor plans or the opportunity to view a model unit, and Chauvin refused. Instead, Chauvin suggested Asbury inquire at the Westminister Apartments, an apartment complex housing mostly black families. Although Chauvin did not ask Asbury about her qualifications, plaintiff was employed with the Federal Aviation Authority at a salary of $37,599. Based on her salary, defendants concede that Asbury would likely be qualified to rent an apartment or townhouse at Brougham Estates.

Defendants argue that Asbury was not rejected because Chauvin courteously invited her to call back. However, there is ample evidence in the record to support the jury's finding that defendant's failure or refusal to provide Asbury the opportunity to rent or inspect or negotiate for the rental of a townhouse or apartment constituted a rejection because of her race cognizable under §1982 and the FHA.

Defendants testified that families with a child are housed exclusively in the townhouses at Brougham Estates, and that there were no townhouses available on the date Asbury inquired. Asbury introduced evidence suggesting that both apartments and townhouses were available and, in addition, that exceptions previously had been created to allow children to reside in the apartments.

On February 24, 1984, the day after Asbury inquired about renting, Asbury's sister-in-law, Linda Robinson, who is white, called to inquire about the availability of two-bedroom apartments. The woman who answered the telephone identified herself as "Wanda" and invited Robinson to come to Brougham Estates to view the apartments. The following day, February 25, 1984, Robinson went to the rental office at Brougham Estates and met with Wanda Chauvin. Chauvin provided Robinson with four plans of one- and two-bedroom apartments at Brougham Estates. Robinson specifically asked Chauvin about rental to families with children, and Chauvin did not tell Robinson that children were restricted to the townhouse units. Robinson accompanied Chauvin to inspect a model unit and several available two-bedroom apartments. Upon inquiry by Robinson, Chauvin indicated that the apartments were available immediately and offered to hold an apartment for her until the next week.

Asbury also provided evidence indicating that townhouses were available for rent. On February 1, 1984, Daniel McMenay, a white male, notified Brougham Estates that he intended to vacate his townhouse. On April 4, 1984, Brougham Estates rented the town-house vacated by McMenay to John Shuminski, a white male.

Since Asbury met her burden of proving a prima facie case of racial discrimination, the burden shifted to defendants to prove a legitimate, non-discriminatory reason for denial of housing.

Defendants claimed their legitimate, non-discriminatory reasons for rejecting Asbury arose out of the policies at Brougham Estates that families with more than one child could rent townhouses but not apartments, and that families with more than one child were not permitted to move into Brougham Estates. Defendants contended that in accordance with these rental policies, no appropriate housing was available for Asbury when she inquired. However, plaintiff introduced evidence indicating that exceptions to these rules had been made on several occasions; families with children had rented apartments, and families with more than one child had been permitted to move into Brougham Estates. The jury could therefore find that defendants' reasons for denying Asbury the opportunity to negotiate for rental were not legitimate and non-discriminatory.

Defendants also argue that evidence of a high percentage of minority occupancy in Brougham Estates conclusively rebuts the claim of intentional racial discrimination. Although such statistical data is relevant to rebutting a claim of discrimination, statistical data is not dispositive of a claim of intentional discrimination. Moreover, there was other evidence from which the jury could have determined that race was a motivating factor in defendants' decision to refuse to negotiate with Asbury for a rental unit.

Having reviewed the record in this case, we find that there was substantial evidence supporting and a reasonable basis for the jury's verdict awarding both compensatory and punitive damages, and we affirm the district court's decision to deny defendants' motion for a new trial.

Affirmed and remanded.

Blockbusting
Inducing (for profit) the sale or rental of any dwelling indicating that a particular class of person (for example, nonwhite) has entered or will enter the neighborhood.

Case Example

Bowers and a number of other real estate firms in Northwest Detroit conducted solicitation campaigns in Northwest Detroit involving fliers, telephone calls and door-to-door canvassing. As part of their campaign, fliers were allegedly delivered to "Resident." One flier contained the legend "We think you may want a friend for a neighbor . . . know your neighbors." Another mailing also addressed to "Resident" purported to carry "neighborhood news." It announced that a real estate agency had just bought a house at a specific address in the recipient's neighborhood, that the named sellers had received cash and that the recipient might receive the same service. The recipients lived in changing neighborhoods. This conduct was judged to be illegal. *Zuch v. Hussey, 394 F. Supp. 1028 (D. Mich. 1975).*

Redlining

Denial of a loan by a lending institution or the exacting of harsher terms for loans in certain parts of a city.

Although this action is often a strictly economic decision by a lender, it has been found to be illegal in some cases because it results in discrimination.

Case Example

The Laufmans, a white couple, purchased a home in a predominately black neighborhood. When financing was denied by the Oakley Building and Loan Company, the Laufmans sued. They argued that the defendant had redlined areas in the community in which minority group families were concentrated.

The defendant moved for summary judgment. The court denied the motion. In denying the motion, the court stated that "although not altogether unambiguous, we read this [Sec. 3604 and 3605 of the Civil Rights Act of 1968] as an explicit prohibition of "redlining.' " *Laufman v. Oakley Building and Loan Co., 408 F. Supp. 489 (1976).*

The following case involves an allegation that a lending institution was engaged in redlining. Described within the arguments made by the plaintiff are several forms that redlining may take.

Cartwright v. American Savings and Loan Assoc.
U.S. Court of Appeals
Seventh Circuit
880 F.2d 912 (1989)

Background: On August 28, 1980 Mary Cartwright and her husband applied for a $90,000 home mortgage from American Savings and Loan Association (American Savings) to finance the construction of a home. American Savings' representative in this matter was Louis Green. There is a sharp disagreement between Cartwright and Green regarding what took place over the next few years, but the ultimate result was that Cartwright's application was not approved. Green contends that he could not find homes of comparable value so that he could get an accurate appraisal of the property prior to submitting the application to the bank's loan committee. Cartwright contends, among other things, that American Savings had redlined for racial reasons the area in which she proposed to build her house, thus being in violation of the Fair Housing Act (FHA) (1968). The trial judge found that Cartwright failed to prove her case, and she took her argument to the Court of Appeals.

Decision: The Seventh Circuit Court of Appeals affirmed the judgment in favor of American Savings.

Circuit Judge Coffey

The plaintiffs-appellants' statistical evidence of redlining from our review seems to rest upon two trial exhibits they prepared from information American Savings supplied revealing that American Savings granted two residential mortgage loans from January 1980 through January 1984 in substantially black, urban area of Hammond containing Mary Cartwright's Merrill Street property ("census tract" number 207). In contrast, American Savings granted, during the same period, thirty-six residental mortgage loans in census tract number 427, and twenty-five residential mortgage loans in census tract number 404, both of which according to the 1980 census, have a zero to one percent black population. The appellants maintain that the disparity in the number of the residential loans American Savings granted in a minority area is opposed to a nonminority area constitutes proof of redlining.

The obvious flaw in the appellants' "disparity" argument is their failure to identify any relevant statistical evidence of the number of residential loan applications American Savings received from financially qualified borrowers in any particular census tract or geographical area, and how many of those applications it rejected. Such proof lies at the very heart of any redlining allegation, as it is absurd to allege a discriminatory refusal to approve applications in a particular area without proof that qualified borrowers actually applied

and were rejected. We are unmoved by the fact that American Savings granted "only" two loan applications between January 1980 and January 1984 in census tract 207, because the appellants failed to present evidence of the number of applications American Savings received in that time frame for property located in that tract. It may be (for all we can determine from the record before us) that American Savings received only two loan applications for housing purchases in census tract 207, and granted them both. This evidence of a violation of §3605 (FHA) falls far short of establishing redlining.

Moreover, Louis Green's testimony supports the conclusion that the number of residential loan applications granted in census tract 207 was low because applications were few and far between, and not because American Savings practiced credit discrimination. Green (who served on American Savings' loan committee) testified that to his knowledge American Savings did not reject a single residential loan application from 1978 through the time of the trial relating to property located in census tract 207. In addition, Green testified that American Savings did not receive any loan applications for construction in the East Hammond urban renewal area (part of census tract 207) prior to the time the Cartwrights applied for their loan in August 1980, and that the number of mortgage loan applications was generally low in 1979 and 1980, probably or possibly due to extremely high interest rates. We fail to understand how American Savings can be considered as responsible for redlining a particular geographical area if in fact as the testimony reveals it granted every application submitted to it for homes located therein, and the appellants failed to demonstrate that that is not, in fact, what occurred.

At oral argument, the appellants' counsel conceded that there is no "raw data" in the record establishing the number of residential loan applications American Savings received and rejected in "census tract" number 207. However, counsel contended and speculated that—based on Louis Green's treatment of Mary Cartwright during their May 28, 1982, meeting—that American Savings has a policy of "discouraging" loan applications for property located in minority neighborhoods. As we discuss *infra*, Louis Green did not "discourage" Mary Cartwright from filing a new loan application in May 1982. Rather, Green provided information regarding the record high 17 1/2 percent interest rate and the availability of low interest loans through another institution participating in the Indiana Housing Authority's Bond Program. We find no evidence in the record that would tend to suggest, much less establish, that Green offered the information with a racially discriminatory motive. We therefore reject the appellants' contention that American Savings had a policy of discouraging mortgage loan applications for property located in substantially or predominantly black neighborhoods.

The appellants also contend that their claim of redlining finds support in Mary and Lawrence Cartwright's testimony that Louis Green told them during the initial August 28, 1980, meeting that the East Hammond urban renewal area could not "support" or "afford" a house as large as the one the Cartwrights wanted to build, but that

other communities could support it. We note that the district court's findings of fact are silent as to whether Louis Green actually told the Cartwrights that the urban renewal area could not "afford" their proposed home, and this court refuses to assume facts unsupported as findings in the district court record. Even assuming that Green told the Cartwrights that the urban renewal area could not "afford" their proposed residence, we are not persuaded that the evidence establishes redlining.

The Fair Housing Act's prohibition against denying a loan based upon the location of dwelling does not require that a lender disregard its legitimate business interests or make an investment that is not economically sound. It seems obvious that a lender must be concerned, for example, about financing a new, $90,000 home in a residential area comprised of homes valued at $60,000 or less. If the borrower defaults on the loan, the lender must foreclose and may be unable to recoup its investment, as potential buyers may be reluctant to pay $90,000 for the home (and other lenders may be unwilling to finance the purchase) in light of the surrounding property values. The regulations implementing the Fair Housing Act address this type of concern, stating lenders may legitimately consider "the present market value of the property offered as security . . . and the likelihood that the property will retain an adequate value over the term of the loan."

Steering

Channeling by a realtor or salesperson of prospective home buyers toward, or away from, certain areas either to maintain homogeneity or to change the character of that area, for the purpose of enhancing sales opportunities.

Case Example

The Village of Bellwood and six individuals brought suit against two real estate firms for steering black homebuyers to one area of the Village, and white homebuyers to another area. The REALTORS® argued that the Village and the individuals, who were admittedly testers and not prospective homebuyers, were not economically injured and could not sue under the Fair Housing Act.

The U.S. Supreme Court held the conduct of the real estate firms was illegal steering under the Fair Housing Act and that the plaintiffs contention that they were being denied the opportunity to live in an integrated community was adequate economic injury to bring the suit. *Gladstone Realtors v. Village of Bellwood, 441 U.S. 91 (1979).*

Aggrieved Parties

The Fair Housing Act allows any aggrieved party to file a complaint against discriminatory practices. The term *aggrieved party* is broadly defined to include a victim, corporations, fair houisng groups, testers, real estate professionals, local governments and the Secretary of HUD.

Prior to the Fair Housing Act Amendments of 1988, discrimination based on race, color, religion, sex or national origin was prohibited. The new law adds the handicapped and families with children as classes protected from discrimination. There is an exception for some senior citizen housing to the latter category. It defines intimidation as a discriminatory practice as well.

Statutory Remedies

It is in the area of remedies provided by the Fair Housing Act that the amendments of 1988 make their most significant changes. There are three distinct avenues open for redressing housing discrimination under the new law.

Administrative Enforcement

An aggrieved party may file a complaint of discrimination with HUD any time up to one year after its occurrence. The administrator will either transfer the complaint to a state or local agency, or begin an investigation. If the state or locality where the alleged discriminatory activity took place has a HUD approved "substantially equivalent" fair housing program, the complaint is assigned to the nonfederal authorities. Approximately 38 states and 84 local units of government have HUD approved programs.

If there is no "substantially equivalent" nonfederal program, HUD has 100 days to carry out an investigation of the complaint and to file a report of its findings. During the 100-day period, HUD must begin a process of conciliation attempting to obtain an agreement ending the dispute. Note that a state program must be substantially equivalent to the federal, so that when a complaint is referred to the state a similar procedure is followed.

If no conciliation agreement is reached during the 100-day investigatory period, HUD must dismiss the complaint or file charges. If HUD files charges, the aggrieved party has 20 days to exercise an election to take this matter to federal court for a jury trial. If the aggrieved party does not choose to go to federal court, the case stays in the administrative arena and is assigned to an administrative law judge.

The administrative law judge has 120 days to commence a hearing on the charges filed. At the conclusion of the administrative hearing, the judge will make recommendations to HUD for resolution of the dispute. It is highly likely that HUD will accept the recommendations. The administrative law judge can award the complainant actual damages, an injuction or other equitable relief, and/or assess substantial civil penalties. The judge can also award the complainant attorney's fees. Once HUD approves the ruling, the parties have 30 days to appeal the case to the appropriate Federal Court of Appeals.

Case Example

Blackwell, a white, refused to sell his house to a black couple (Herrons). Instead, Blackwell leased the house to a white couple. The Herrons filed a complaint with HUD. The administrative law judge (ALJ) found for the Herrons, granting them $40,000 in actual damages and granting $20,000 to the white couple who leased the house for their embarrassment and economic loss; he also assessed a civil penalty of $10,000 against Blackwell.

The Eleventh Circuit upheld the ALJ on all the relief granted. This is the first case decided by an ALJ under the 1988 Fair Housing Act Amendments enforcement procedures. Notice the flexibility the ALJ has in granting relief. *Secretary, HUD ex rel. Herron v. Blackwell, 908 F.2d 864 (1990).*

Attorney General Litigation

If, after HUD files a charge of discrimination, the aggrieved party exercises the election to have a jury trial, HUD will notify the Attorney General; the Attorney General has 30 days to file a civil action in federal court on behalf of the complainant.

In this type of litigation the court may grant any relief that is available in private litigation, (discussed in the next section), including actual and punitive damages, injuctions and other appropriate equitable remedies.

In addition to this type of civil action aimed at redressing a specific discriminatory action, the Attorney General may file suit where there is a pattern or practice of discrimination or there is a discriminatory denial of rights to a group of persons, raising issues of public importance.

Finally, the Attorney General has the authority to bring actions to enforce conciliation agreement reached by the parties under the administrative process of the Act.

Private Litigation

An aggrieved party may bring a private enforcement action in federal district court within two years of the discriminatory action. The private lawsuit can be filed even though an administrative complaint is filed with HUD. If a conciliation agreement is entered on the HUD-filed complaint, or if a hearing commences before the administrative law judge, the private lawsuit must be terminated.

There are several advantages to the private litigation avenue for the complainant. The judge can appoint an attorney for the complainant when he or she is unable to retain one and can waive statutory costs and fees if complainant is financially unable to bear them. More importantly, the court can grant unlimited actual and punitive damages and can more liberally require the defendant to pay the aggrieved parties' attorney's fees.

The removal of the prior $1,000 cap on punitive damages and the freer availability of attorney's fees is likely to make private litigation a favored route for complainants to take in the post-1988 period.

Summary

Fair housing is the term given to the national policy of abolishing *segregation in housing*. Segregation of one group from another has long been a characteristic of residential patterns. The civil rights movement, begun in the latter half of this century, however, has as its goal equal opportunity for members of all races to achieve adequate housing as well as employment.

Earlier in this century restrictive covenants in housing were upheld by the courts in most cases. More recently, however, those clauses forbidding sale of property to blacks have been held unenforceable, and in 1950 the Chicago Realtors Code of Ethics was rewritten to eliminate any justification of racial or ethnic segregation.

The doctrine of *equal protection* under the law provided by the Constitution started with the landmark school desegregation case of *Brown v. Board of Education* in 1954, thereby eliminating the prior *separate but equal* policy.

Ten years later Congress enacted the Civil Rights Act (1964), which refused federal assistance in the form of loans or mortgage guarantees to those who practice racial discrimination. This move had a limited impact on private housing, however. A more comprehensive venture into fair housing is found in the Fair Housing Act of 1968 and the Fair Housing Amendments Act of 1988. This act prohibits discrimination based on race, color, religion, sex, national origin, handicap or families with children in the sale or rental of a dwelling. An earlier Civil Rights Act, passed in 1866, had been largely ignored by the courts. In 1968 the U.S. Supreme Court gave new life to this old statute in the case of *Jones v. Mayer*.

Certain acts, when based on discrimination, are currently prohibited by law. These acts include refusal to sell or lease a dwelling, variation in terms of a sale or lease from one party to another, advertising that excludes certain groups and false representation that an available dwelling is no longer available. Also prohibited are the real estate practices of *blockbusting, redlining,* and *steering*.

Under the Fair Housing Acts, the party who suffers discrimination is entitled to bring a complaint to the Department of Housing and Urban Development (HUD). The party may also file suit in federal court. Legal remedies available to wronged parties may include collection of damages, both compensatory and punitive, and injunctions or other judicial orders.

Review and Discussion Questions

1. Compare the theory and the reality of the policies of "separate but equal" with "equal protection."

2. Which level of government is the most prominent in enforcing fair housing?

3. Compare the coverage of the Fair Housing Act (1968) with that of the Civil Rights Act (1866).

4. Using the rationale of *Shelley v. Kraemer*, explain how Congress can justify preventing individuals from using real estate brokers in a racially discriminatory sale of a residence, which would otherwise be exempt under the Fair Housing Act (1968). Would the same rationale pertain to the prohibition against discriminatory advertising?

5. How did the real estate profession play an active role in promoting racial segregation?

Case Problems

1. D. C. Williams and his wife, a black couple, wished to purchase lots in a subdivision being developed by the Matthews Company. The subdivision was not integrated. When they made an offer to purchase, a company official informed them that lots were sold only to builders. Although generally this was the case, some lots had been sold to individuals.

    Williams and his wife approached several white builders. Each of them refused to purchase and build for the Williams family, stating that they would get no more business in that area if they built for a black. Eventually Anderson, a black builder, agreed to purchase a lot and build the house that Williams and his wife wanted. The Matthews Company informed Anderson that it would not sell him the lot because he was not on the company's approved builder list. When Anderson attempted to find out what he had to do to become approved, he was informed that only the company president could do this and he was out of the country on a trip to the Orient for two months. The company had no policy for approval of builders but it did have an office memo indicating support for integration of the subdivision. The memo also indicated a belief that the issue was a sensitive one and should be handled at the level of company president.

    No public announcement had ever been made of the company's commitment to integration, and no black had ever acquired property in the subdivision. Has the Matthews Company violated any of the federal civil rights statutes? Discuss. *Williams v. Matthews Co., 499 F.2d 819 (8th Cir., 1974).*

2. Greenwood was a sales associate in an office visited by Bago, a prospective buyer. Bago expressed an interest in a property in a specific area of Detroit.

Greenwood told Bago that she had some nice property listed outside of the city. She stated, "The school system is poor in Detroit." Later she asked, "Do you read the newspapers? Even the police are afraid to live in the area, and they are supposed to protect us." Greenwood gave Bago several listings in Detroit and a suburb and suggested that he compare prices, indicating that prices were lower in Detroit because blacks lived there. Greenwood further indicated that she would sell him any property he was interested in, wherever it was located. What, if any, violation of fair housing legislation has Greenwood committed? Support your answer.

3. The Knights of Columbus, a Roman Catholic men's organization, maintains a community including 46 vacation homes. Only members can own a home, and members must be recommended by their parish priest based upon his finding that they are "practicing Catholics in good standing." Also, the bishop granted the Knights the right to have Mass said on the site and provided a priest to do so. The United States filed suit under the Fair Housing Act contending that the Knights discriminated based on religion. The Knights argued that they were exempt from the law under the "religious organization" exception. Discuss. *U.S. v. Columbus Country Club, 915 F.2d 877 (1990).*

4. Initially public officials in the city of Birmingham, Michigan, favored a senior citizens' housing project proposed by a church-sponsored citizens' group. The city worked with the citizens' group until it learned that a condition for obtaining state and federal funding was that one unit of low-income housing be provided for every two units of senior citizens' housing. When this condition became known to the public, there was a significant cry of opposition. The opposition complained about bringing "those people" into Birmingham and about lessening property values. The city owned the land proposed for the project and allowed an agreement for the sale of the land to lapse and refused to negotiate further with the citizens' group. Was there a violation of the Fair Housing Act (1968)? Discuss. *United States v. City of Birmingham, 538 F. Supp. 819 (D. Mich. 1982).*

5. The City of Parma, a suburb of Cleveland, had a policy rejecting any proposal for low-income housing, even if it meant losing unrelated federal funding. In addition, local ordinances made construction of low-income housing economically infeasible. Was the Fair Housing Act violated? Note that §3604 (a) of that Act makes it unlawful "to refuse to sell or rent . . . or otherwise make unavailable or deny, a dwelling to any person because of race, color, religion, sex, or national origin." Discuss. *United States v. City of Parma, 494 F. Supp. 1049 (D. Ohio 1980).*

Part 6

Leasehold
Interests and
Alternatives

25

The
Leasehold

Leasehold Estate

An estate created when the owner of property, known as the lessor or landlord conveys a possessory interest in the real property to another, known as the lessee or tenant for a specific period of time in exchange for the tenant's payment of rent.

An unusual aspect of a lease is that it is rooted firmly in two distinct areas of law: contract law and real property law. As a contract, the lease must contain the essential elements of any contract—offer, acceptance and consideration—in order to be enforceable. Since it relates to real property, the lease involves a conveyance of an estate in land, or a leasehold estate. The landlord surrenders his or her possessory rights to the premises for the duration of the lease. The tenant must pay for that possession during the term of the lease. Because the tenant is getting an estate in land, he or she is required by law to pay the rent even if there is no specific agreement regarding rent. Possession is exchanged for rent.

The granting of a leasehold estate gives to a tenant the *exclusive possession* of the premises for an agreed-upon term with a reversion at the end of the term to possession by the landlord. This exclusive right of possession deprives the owner of the premises during the lease. Even where tenants fail to comply with the leasehold bargain, landlords can remove them from the premises only by bringing formal eviction proceedings.

Four different kinds of leasehold estates can be created. They are term tenancy, periodic tenancy, tenancy at will and tenancy at sufferance.

Term Tenancy

An estate for a specified period of time that has a specific beginning date and a specific ending date. When the ending date arrives, the estate is terminated without notice by either party.

This tenancy, also known as an *estate for years,* terminates without any action by either party upon expiration of the term stated in the agreement. It should be noted that if the parties' lease stipulates notice or other conditions for termination of the tenancy, as written leases often do, then these conditions must be met. In the absence of a statute or an agreement to the contrary, the term tenancy is considered personal property and will pass as such to those entitled to take personal property from the estate of the deceased tenant.

If the parties fail to stipulate the amount of rent due, a reasonable rent is required. A reasonable rent is based on prevailing rental rates in the vicinity. Under the common law, however, the rent is not due until the end of the tenancy. By way of contrast, most modern leases require the rent to be prepaid since landlords are understandably unwilling to wait until the end of the term to receive payment of rent.

Periodic Tenancy

An estate from period to period, continuing from period to period until terminated by proper notice from one of the parties.

The periodic tenancy is normally from year to year or month to month but can be for any period up to a year. It can be created in several different ways. One way is by express agreement. If A leases her property to B "from month to month beginning April 1, 1990," a periodic tenancy is created. This estate or tenancy may also arise by implication.

This type of estate can also evolve from a term tenancy when the tenant remains, or "holds over," after the expiration of the term tenancy. The holdover tenancy will be discussed in more detail later in this section.

The periodic tenancy can be terminated by either party upon giving adequate notice. The parties may contractually agree on what will constitute adequate notice. Absent such an agreement, adequate notice will be one period's notice up to six months.

Case Example

Karen Kaiser leases Greenacre to Franks "from year to year beginning April 1, 1990." She leases Brownacre to Martin "from month to month beginning April 1, 1990." To terminate the lease to Greenacre, either Kaiser or Franks would have to give six months' notice unless they had an agreement to the contrary. The Brownacre lease could be ended by either party with one month's notice of termination, absent a contrary agreement.

These common law notice periods have been altered by statutes in many states. For example, the Uniform Residential Landlord and Tenant Act has been adopted in part in several states. This act provides that a week-to-week tenancy requires a written notice of ten days. A month-to-month tenancy requires a notice of at least 60 days. Year-to-year tenancies are not mentioned in the act because they almost inevitably apply only to agricultural lands and not to residential premises.

Notice given by the terminating party must reach the other party a full period early. The general rule is that the notice must be given one calendar period in advance, although some cases have held to the contrary.

Where there is uncertainty as to the period of the tenancy, a good indicator is the rent payments. If the rent is paid yearly or monthly, it is a good indication that the parties have a year-to-year or month-to-month periodic tenancy. An exception occurs when the yearly rent is stated in the lease but the payment is due monthly. This would be treated as a year-to-year period.

Case Example

The Smits, experienced dairy farmers, entered an oral agreement with the Prescotts to rent their farm. The parties agreed to a lease beginning May 1, for a period of three years, with an annual rental of $14,400 payable in equal monthly installments. The Smits moved onto the land and began paying rent before the written lease was prepared. By the time the written lease was ready, the Smits were having problems with some cows dying and others becoming sick. The problem was apparently a contaminated water supply. The Smits refused to sign the lease, and after several months stopped paying rent and abandoned the farm. The Prescotts sued for nonpayment of rent.

Among other things, the Court held that the lease was a term tenancy and that the term was year to year. The Court reasoned that it was a year-to-year term because the rent, though payable monthly, was stated in annual terms in their oral agreement. The conclusion was reinforced by the fact that it was a farm lease, and such leases are traditionally entered on a yearly basis. *Prescott v. Smits, 505 A.2d 1211 (1985).*

Tenancy at Will

A tenancy that exists until either party chooses to terminate it.

This type of estate may arise by express agreement. For example, a lease may state "to Franks at the will of Kaiser." This wording creates a tenancy at will. Despite this restrictive language, tenancies at will can be terminated by either party.

A tenancy at will is more likely to arise by implication.

Case Example

In the Prescott case discussed above, the Court had to decide whether the oral lease was an at will tenancy or a periodic tenancy. In the parties' state, an oral lease for a period longer than one year is unenforceable. Since the three-year term agreed to by the parties was not legally enforceable, the Court had to decide what type of tenancy had been created.

As stated above, the Court found that the lease was a year-to-year tenancy. If the situation had been altered so that the Smits had not yet moved onto the land, or the amount of the rent was left uncertain, the Court probably would have found that a tenancy at will arose by implication.

Under the common law no notice was required to end a tenancy at will. Many states now have statutes that require a minimum notice period, thereby softening the harshness of the common law rule. Although the estate exists wholly by permission, all the rights and duties of the landlord-tenant relationship exist. Unlike the previously mentioned leasehold estates, however, a tenancy at will is terminated by the death of either party or by the sale of the property to a third party.

Tenancy at Sufferance

Created when a person is wrongfully in possession of another's land without a valid lease.

The tenant at sufferance is similar to a trespasser. The major difference is that the tenant at sufferance entered the property legally. Usually he or she is the holdover tenant from a term tenancy. The landlord owes this tenant no duties, and the tenant can be evicted at any time. The classification of a person as a tenant at sufferance, not as a trespasser, actually works to the tenant's disadvantage. The tenant is unable to possess the property adversely against the landlord and eventually gain an ownership interest, although a trespasser could.

Holdover Tenant

One who failed to vacate or surrender possession of the premises on the ending date of a term tenancy.

The term *holdover tenant* is sometimes used in relation to a periodic tenancy, where the tenant stays on despite the landlord's adequate notice to vacate. Under these circumstances, a landlord who permits the tenant to remain has technically waived the notice and allowed the continuation of the periodic tenancy.

The term tenant who holds over after the expiration date of a lease temporarily becomes a tenant at sufferance. All options shift into the landlord's hands when the tenant holds over. The landlord has the option of evicting the tenant or of holding him or her for another term.

Case Example

Anton leases a house and lot to Glenn and Sarah Williams. The terms of the agreement stipulate that the lease commences on July 1, 1990, and terminates on June 30, 1991. On July 1, 1991, the couple is still living in the house. Anton has the option of beginning eviction proceedings against the Williamses, who are now tenants at sufferance, or of unilaterally extending their lease until June 30, 1992.

Once the landlord exercises the option to hold the tenant for an additional period, the estate becomes a periodic tenancy. The maximum length of the period will be one year, or more accurately year to year, even where the term tenancy was for a longer period. If the original term tenancy was for less than one year, the holdover tenant will be held to a periodic tenancy for that particular period, such as week to week or month to month.

The terms of the holdover tenant's new lease will be the same as those of the original lease except as to length of time, as noted above. One exception arises when the landlord notifies the tenant before the expiration of the lease that he or she is changing the terms (for example, raising the rent). The tenant is usually held to the altered terms.

If the holdover is involuntary and for a short period of time, courts will not hold the tenant for an additional term. For instance, if the holdover is caused by a tornado, a snowstorm, a death in the family or a one-day delay of the moving van, the court is not likely to hold the tenant for an additional period.

Lease

A contract, either written or oral, that transfers the right of possession of the premises to the lessee or tenant.

The relationship of lessor and lessee usually arises from an express contract on the part of the parties called a *lease*. As previously stated, the lease is firmly rooted in the law of contracts. The lease or contract normally includes terms giving the lessee the right to possession and entitling the lessor to a certain amount of rent. To this extent these contractual components overlap the possession-rent aspects that arise inherently from the real property notion of a conveyance of an estate in land. The lease-contract is likely to specify the terms of the possession and the amount of the rent, as well as many other factors that together compose the essence of the lessor and lessee's agreement.

Essential Elements of the Lease

The purpose of the lease is to detail the rights and duties of each of the parties in the contract. It is incumbent upon the parties to take great care in drafting the lease, especially if the terms of the agreement are complex or the duration of the lease is long. To do otherwise is to invite a lawsuit.

A Valid Contract

Since a lease is a contract, it must contain the essential elements of a contract. There must be a mutual consent to enter the agreement, and the agreement must be supported by consideration (rent in exchange for possession). The lease agreement will not require the use of any particular prescribed words. Essentially, it must be shown that it was mutually intended for the tenant to have possession and that the landlord retained a *reversionary* interest in the land (that is, the right to have the property back when the lease expired).

The consideration that supports the lease contract is usually the rent. Nevertheless, the periodic payment of rent is not necessary to have a valid contract. The requirement is merely that consideration, or something of value, be given at some time to the landlord.

The other elements of a valid contract, such as the capacity of the parties (both must be sane and of legal age) and legality of purpose, must be met as well.

Statute of Frauds

Prior to 1677, under the common law originally operating in England, leases did not have to be in writing. With the adoption of the Statute of Frauds, however, leases for a term in excess of three years had to be in writing to be enforceable beyond those three years. A few states have adopted the English version of the Statute of Frauds and require writings for leases in excess of three years. In most states, however, the Statute of Frauds provision necessitates a writing if the lease exceeds one year.

The intent of this requirement is to reduce fraud in the area of leases. It should be made clear that the statutory minimum, usually one year, does not indicate that leases for one year or less should not be in writing. The careful landlord and tenant will benefit if all terms of their agreement are reduced to writing in order to minimize the opportunity for misunderstanding or outright fraud.

It should be emphasized that an oral lease within the maximum term of the Statute of Frauds is every bit as valid as a written lease. If a dispute arises over an oral lease, however, the proof may be more difficult to derive. If a dispute arises over a lease that has gone beyond the allowable period under the Statute of Frauds, the estate is treated as a tenancy at will.

Parties

The lease must identify the parties as lessor and lessee, and both parties should sign the document. The signature of the lessor, the owner of the property, is normally mandatory. Under the Statute of Frauds, the signature of the party against whom the lease will be enforced is required.

The spouse of the lessor should sign the lease as well, if he or she has an outstanding interest or potential interest in the property. For example, if a married couple owns the premises jointly, both parties must sign the lease since the spouse is a concurrent owner. The wife should also sign the lease where the state recognizes a dower interest, inasmuch as her potential interest may come into effect during the term of the lease.

Under some contracts a lessee may have the power to sublease or to assign the property to a third party in which case the person signing as lessor of the property may not be the actual owner of the premises. For this reason a lessee should make certain that the nonowner lessor has the authority to sublet and convey all or part of the interest to another. Subleasing will be discussed in more detail in the following chapter.

If the lessor is an individual, he or she must have the *capacity* to contract—that is, be mentally competent and of legal age. If the lessor is a fiduciary, entering the lease for another as guardian, executor or trustee, for example, the lessee must be assured that the authority to lease is within the fiduciary's powers. Similarly, if the lessor is a corporation that is not in the business of leasing real estate, the lessee must verify the authorization of the corporation's board of directors to be assured that it is entitled to lease the premises.

Description of the Premises

In order to avoid a future dispute, the premises should be described clearly. If the landlord's entire conveyed premises are being leased, then the description as contained in the deed or deeds is satisfactory. A lot number or block number used for assessment purposes may be used if it is complete and accurate. A street number may not be adequate in itself because it relates only to the building and not to the land that is probably part of the leasehold as well.

When the lessor is leasing something less than all that he or she has, the lease should state clearly and exactly what is to be leased. In the absence of an agreement to the contrary, the lease of a building will be construed to include the use of everything reasonably necessary for the enjoyment of the land. It is up to the lessor expressly to exclude a use, or exclusive possession may pass to the lessee.

Case Example

Arthur leases one-half of an apartment house to Melanie, who has three small children. Unless the lease specifically excludes use of the fenced-in backyard, Melanie can use it for ingress and egress and as a play area for the children.

It is also to the lessee's benefit to have the precise nature of his or her use or possession spelled out in the lease, rather than to rely on the uncertain notion that he or she is entitled to certain unstated uses.

Statement of a Lease Term

The term of the lease should be stipulated clearly. Stating the beginning and ending dates as well as the length of the term will reduce doubt as to date of entry and the like. The lease should state, for example, "for one year beginning January 1, 1990, and terminating December 31, 1990." Where the beginning date is not spelled out, some doubt may exist as to whether the tenant began the term on the date the lease was signed, the first of the following month or some other date. If the beginning date is not stated, the commencement of the lease should be related to some event or ascertainable time so that the beginning of the lease is clear.

Case Example

Sanchez leased to Williams for one year beginning upon the surrender of possession by the present tenant or April 1, 1991, whichever comes first.

The courts do not favor leases of unlimited duration. If the time of termination is not fixed, the courts may interpret the agreement to be a tenancy at will, which is probably not what the parties intended. In a periodic tenancy, of course, the time of termination is fixed, although the tenancy is subject to automatic renewal upon the existence of certain conditions, such as failure to give notice of termination.

Some courts have been inclined to hold that leases that are too long—for instance, 100 years or more—are barred by statute. The theory behind the term limitation is that when the lease gets to be too long it defies the temporary aspect, or right of reversion, inherent in a leasehold estate. The result of these statutes and judicial rulings has been to popularize the 99-year lease. Similarly, in a few states, there is a restriction on the length of leases for agricultural lands.

There is a correlation between the length of the lease and the care with which the lease must be drawn. If the lease is as long as 75 years, the likelihood increases that the structures will need to be replaced. Some agreement should be reached to cover contingencies of this sort that will occur during the long period of the lease.

Rent

The compensation paid by the lessee for the possession of the leased property.

Normally, rent takes the form of a money payment. It could, however, take the form of a percentage of the crops harvested from the land or of relief for the lessor of an obligation owed to the lessee. A statement of the amount of rent is one of the essential terms of a lease; nevertheless, where it has been omitted, courts have declared that the landlord is entitled to a "reasonable rent," based on the area's prevailing rental rates.

The usual practice is to state in the lease that the rent will be paid in advance. If such a statement is lacking, the rent is due at the end of the period. The rationale behind this rule is that the lessee is paying for the possession that he or she has enjoyed, and nothing is due until he or she has had the enjoyment.

In addition to how much and when, the lease should indicate where the rent is to be paid. Absent such an indication, it is payable at the leasehold premises.

Unless stipulated to the contrary, the total rent is due on the date set for payment. The usual practice is to require in the lease monthly, quarterly or annual payments.

Case Example

Karen leases Greenacre to Frank for a rent of $2,400 annually, payable in advance and on the first of each month in installments of "$200, and presented at the residence of the lessor."

This wording covers each of the above considerations.

For short-term residential leases it is most common to have a straight rental fee, such as $200 per month. In commercial leases, however, a variety of methods are used for determining the rent. The net lease, percentage lease and ground lease will be discussed later. Another technique is to assess rent on a *graduated* basis. A lease might stipulate a rent of $2,400 the first year, $3,600 per year for the following two years and $4,800 per year for the last two years. If the lessee is operating a new business, under the graduated rental the amount of rent is smallest in the start-up period and increases as the business (theoretically) grows.

Other techniques include basing the rent on the consumer price index or on some other criterion that is particularly relevant to the parties, to the business or to the lease itself. In short, the days of the straight or flat rental fee as the sole method for calculating rent, especially in business leases, have long since passed.

Legal Use of the Premises

If the lease gives no indication as to the uses that can be made of the premises, the general rule is that the lessee can make any legal use of the land he or she wants. Some courts, however, would limit the lessee to "reasonable uses" where the agreement is silent on the matter. The question of reasonable use is a factual question that the court will examine in light of the type of premises involved and the prior uses of the property. If the building was constructed and has been used as a residence from its inception, for example, it would be unreasonable to use it now as a cheese factory.

Although it is appropriate for the lessor to limit the lessee's use by the agreement, careful drafting is warranted. If the lessor limits the use to a clearly designated purpose, courts will uphold that limitation. If the lessor indicates a *specific* purpose to which the premises can be put—for example, " . . . can be used for a beauty shop"—and nothing more, however, this wording will not prohibit the lessee from making other uses of the land than as a beauty shop. The rationale behind these rules is that the law favors unrestricted use of the land conveyed. In short, ambiguities will be construed against the lessor and toward maximizing the lessee's use. If the lessor's limitations on permitted uses are not designated clearly, the lease will be construed to favor the lessee. If the lessor, by permitting use as a beauty shop, has not clearly shown an intent to limit use to that purpose alone, the lessee will be able to make any other use as well. The careful drafter would have stated, " . . . for use as a beauty shop only."

Case Example

Ewing leased five acres of land to Adams for a five-year term. The lease contained a clause stating that the land was to be used for a drive-in movie theater. Adams used the land as an outdoor theater for a period of time, but then attempted to discontinue that use and to use it for other commercial purposes. Ewing objected, contending that Adams was confined to the use stipulated in the lease.

The Court found for the lessee, Adams. It stated that absent clear and specific words of limitation, the lease is strictly construed against the lessor. The clause confining use to a drive-in movie theater was merely descriptive and not intended to restrict the use of the premises to that sole purpose. *Ewing v. Adams, 573 So. 1364 (1990).*

Where the lessee's use of the property has been made illegal by a change in the law, the lease is not usually invalidated. If the lease permits other legal uses, the lessee can change the type of use. If, however, the lease limits the lessee to the now illegal use, the change in the law will invalidate the lease. The fact that the lessee's business has become unprofitable or that the property no longer suits him or her for a residence will not excuse performance under the lease contract.

A tenant who leases only part of a building for commercial purposes should be careful to reach some agreement with the lessor regarding the leasing of other parts of the building to competitors and use by the lessor as a competitor with the lessee. Without such an agreement, the lessor is free to put the remainder of the property to a competitive use.

Besides the terms of the lease, the tenant should also be careful to check the public regulation restrictions on his or her use. The zoning code may well prohibit uses that the lessor has not prohibited.

Right of Possession

In all jurisdictions the right of possession implicitly resides in the tenant; that is, no one will have possessory rights inconsistent with those granted to the tenant.

In a majority of jurisdictions the landlord covenants to give the right of possession and nothing more. If there is a wrongdoer in possession at the time the tenant's lease commences, the landlord has not violated his or her implied promise of giving the *right to possession*. The fact that the tenant may have to bring a lawsuit to obtain possession is an excellent reason why the tenant should be careful to see to it that the lease contains a provision ensuring that the landlord will give *possession* of the premises, not merely the right to possession. The possibility of the landlord's being unable to deliver actual possession is not terribly remote. Holding over by former tenants is not a rare incident.

In some jurisdictions the landlord implicitly covenants to deliver the possession of the premises. The onus then falls on the landlord to take necessary action (for example, eviction proceedings) to recover possession for the tenant.

It should be remembered that normally the tenant's possession is exclusive. Even the landlord, who may be the owner of the premises in fee simple, is not permitted to invade that exclusive possession without authorization. The landlord would be a trespasser, and the tenant could bring the appropriate legal action against him or her.

Recording the Lease

The practice of recording leases is permitted in most states since a lease is a conveyance of an interest in land. It is uncommon to record residential and other short-term leases, however, because actual possession by the tenant is notice to everyone of the tenant's interest in the land. Upon finding a tenant in possession, a potential taker of an interest in the land would have actual notice of the possession and would have the duty to inquire as to the possessor's right to be there. Failing to inspect the premises, he or she would still have constructive notice of the possession.

There is, however, more of an inclination to record leases that are for a longer period (three years or more). In about one-third of the states the rule holding that possession is constructive notice has been abolished where the lease exceeds a given period of time (usually either one year or three years). In these states it is very important that the tenant record the lease for his or her own protection.

Types of Leases

It was indicated earlier that several types of leases exist. Four of these will be discussed in more detail here. Most are used primarily in commercial applications.

Gross Lease

A lease in which a flat or fixed amount of rent is paid by the tenant.

Generally, under a gross lease the tenant pays the rent and the landlord is responsible for expenses incurred in operating the premises. The landlord pays the taxes, insurance, special assessments and the like. Responsibility for ordinary repairs may be bargained for separately. In residential leases the gross rental fee may or may not include heat and other utilities. It would seem to be to the benefit of both parties, and society as a whole, to exclude heat and utilities from the fixed rent in order to encourage the tenant to minimize the costs by reducing the consumption of energy.

Where long-term leases are desired, gross leases have gradually fallen from favor because of inflation and the fluctuation in the value of the dollar. Unless there is some provision in the lease to compensate the lessor for the gradually diminishing value of the periodic rent check, rental property becomes a questionable investment.

Net Lease

As contrasted with the gross lease, a type of lease in which the tenant agrees to pay the taxes, insurance, repairs and other operating expenses of the premises.

This type of lease assures the lessor of a steady income from the property and relieves him or her of the responsibility of overseeing the operations on the property. In short, the lessor has a real estate investment without most of the problems that usually accompany this type of investment.

Like the gross lease, the net lease does not necessarily take into account the loss of purchasing power due to inflation. Net leases can be drawn up that tie the amount of periodic rent that is payable to some recognized indicator, such as the consumer price index. In this way the lessor will have the same purchasing power at the end of a long-term lease that existed at the beginning.

Ground Lease

A specialized type of net lease in which the lessor leases a piece of vacant land to the lessee, usually with the stipulation that the lessee at his or her own expense will construct a building thereon.

The ground lease is a type of net lease in that the lessee agrees to assume the operating expense of the property. Once the building is constructed, it becomes part of the realty and title passes to the lessor. Therefore, several elements are common to the lease agreements in ground lease situations. The term of the lease is either for the life expectancy of the building or, at least, for a long period. When the term of the lease is not tied to the building's life expectancy, provisions must be made for the building at the expiration of the lease. The parties may agree that the lessor will have to pay the lessee the appraised value of the building at the time the lease expires. Of course the parties can write any agreement that suits them on this matter.

The rent agreement can be for a fixed rate but is often tied to the appraised value of the land. In this way the lessor retains the benefit of the land's appreciating value.

In most such leases the lessee needs financing to construct the building. If this is the case, provisions must be made to accommodate the mortgagee as well as the parties to the lease. The lessor will have to agree to permit the building to be mortgaged while excluding himself or herself from liability on that mortgage. Likewise, the mortgagee will insist upon the untrammeled right to sell the property in the case of a foreclosure. In addition, the mortgagee will usually insist that the term of the ground lease extend significantly beyond the duration of the mortgage so that the tenant does not lose the incentive to make mortgage payments during the latter years of the obligation.

Percentage Lease

A lease whose rental is based in part on the gross sales made by the tenant on the premises.

The lessee in such a lease is required to pay a fixed periodic rental, the amount of the rent to be less than the property's full rental value. In addition, the lessor is entitled to a percentage of the gross sales made by the lessee.

A common practice is to charge a flat minimum rent (perhaps $200 per month) plus a percentage of the gross sales over a stipulated figure (for example, $200 per month plus two percent of the gross sales over $30,000). If the lease has a long term, the percentage lease provides some hedge against inflation. As inflation grows, theoretically so do gross sales; once sales exceed $30,000, the rent increases proportionately. Since the flat minimum rent is usually lower than the maximum amount the landlord would expect, the percentage lease is a hedge for the commercial lessee against bad times.

Percentage leases have become very popular in the leasing of commercial property. The percentage may be very low (one or two percent) in the case of a supermarket or very high (70 to 80 percent) where a parking lot is involved. Regardless of the type of business or the percentage agreed upon, it is critical that the parties carefully draft their agreement. The lease should make clear exactly what is encompassed within the term *gross sales* and should establish the right of the lessor to examine records of the business. From the lessor's perspective, in addition to the protection of a carefully drafted lease, the lessee should be selected carefully to ensure a sound credit rating and good business history.

The Papa Gino's case deals with a percentage lease, and shows a court struggling with the meaning of the term *gross sales* used in the lease. The case speaks loudly for the premise that parties to a lease should be as precise as possible in drafting its terms.

Papa Gino's of America, Inc.
v.
Broadmanor Associates, Ltd.
Appellate Court of Conn.
500 A.2d 1341 (1985)

Background: In 1978, Papa Gino's entered into a written lease for the rental of commercial premises at the Manchester Shopping Parkade with Broadmanor Associates' predecessor in title. The lease was for a 10-year term with options to renew. The lease provided a fixed, monthly, minimum rental payment and additional rent equal to 5 percent of Papa Gino's "annual gross sales in excess of $285,000." Papa Gino's had a practice of providing meals free of charge or at a discount to employees and making discount coupons available to the public. When a discount coupon was presented by a purchaser, the face value of each coupon was deducted from the price of the food.

Broadmanor Associates purchased the parkade in 1981, and in 1982 notified Papa Gino's that it was deficient in its rental payments because under the percentage of gross sales provision, it had not included the value of the free and discounted meals to employees, or, the face value of the discount coupons. Papa Gino's paid the amount demanded under protest and sued Broadmanor Associates, seeking a declaration by the court that it was not deficient in the payment of its rent. The trial court held that the term "gross sales" in the lease included the face value of the discount coupons, but not the contested meals to employees.

Papa Gino's appealed the ruling on the discount coupons.

Decision: The Appellate Court of Connecticut reversed the ruling of the trial court on the issue of the discount coupons.

Judge Daly

The plaintiff has raised the following issues on appeal: (1) whether the trial court erred in failing to declare that the term "gross sales" in the lease does not include the face value of the discount coupons made available to the public, because the plaintiff receives no monetary compensation for the amount discounted in sales to coupon holders; and (2) whether the trial court erred in denying the return of the escrow fund to the plaintiff. We find that the trial court was in error on both points.

"A lease is a contract. In its construction, three elementary principles must be kept constantly in mind: (1) the intention of the parties is controlling and must be gathered from the language of the lease in the light of the circumstances surrounding the parties at the execution of the instrument; (2) the language must be given its ordinary meaning unless a technical or special meaning is clearly intended; and (3) the lease must be construed as a whole and in such a manner as to give effect to every provision, if reasonably possible.

A lease which provides for a percentage rent added to a fixed rent is a common arrangement for the rental of commercial premises. The percentage lease gears the landlord's return to the productivity of his location, such productivity being measured by the tenant's gross dollar volume in sales. In addition to a percentage lease arrangement, the lease in question defined "gross sales" to mean "the entire gross income from the use or occupancy of the leased premises (including advertising and demonstrations) and of all business thereat. These terms shall also include the full price of all sales made and services rendered at the lease premises.... There shall also be deducted, to the extent to which they shall be included in the sales price, the amount of sales or other taxes which may be imposed by law on the purchaser."

The definition of the term "gross sales" has no definitive judicial meaning, is imprecise, and depends principally upon the wording established by the parties in particular contract. The term "sale," as ordinarily defined and popularly understood, means the transfer of property for money *paid* or to be paid; this is the usage of the term in the lease with which we are here concerned. The term "receipts" indicates money received from a sale. Further, under the Connecticut sales tax laws, cash discounts are not included as taxable income and not considered as "gross receipts." In the hotel business,

total gross revenues from room rentals do not include credit card discounts. It would appear, then, that "gross sales" and "receipts" indicate money or cash that is actually received, and therefore would not apply to the discount coupons.

"The courts do not favor constructions in derogation of the course of conduct of the parties." The purpose of the coupons, presumably, is to lure customers into the plaintiff's restaurant with the expectation that they will purchase other items as well. By this method, the landlord receives a benefit from the gross sales. To give the landlord that value of the inducement as well (the coupon) would be to construe the lease as allowing the landlord an additional, uncontemplated kind of "double recovery." We conclude that this is unwarranted under the circumstances and, therefore, that the trial court incorrectly included the face value of the discount coupons offered to the restaurant patrons in the calculation of gross sales generated by the plaintiff's business.

The judgment is set aside and the case in remanded with direction to render judgment that the term "gross sales" shall not include the value of the subject discount coupons, and the amounts held in escrow shall be awarded to the plaintiff.

Reversed.

Other Types of Leases

Leases are as variable as the parties are creative. Some types of leases, such as the variety that relates rent to the consumer price index or some other index, may come into vogue temporarily as a reaction to unstable economic conditions. Others, such as the graduated lease, are tailored to meet the needs of a new business. Here the rent rises over time as the anticipated growth of the business takes place. Still others, such as the sale and leaseback arrangement, are attractive for large firms, which sell their real estate and lease it back from the new owner in order to release investment capital for future expansion. Partners under this type of lease are investors who have capital to invest in order to ensure an agreeable rate of return from the rents on the leased-back property. These examples represent only a few types of leases that have been adapted to the special needs of the parties.

Lease Renewal

Depending on the type of leasehold estate that was conveyed by the landlord, or upon the terms of the parties' agreement, the lease will terminate on its own or upon appropriate notice by either party. It is not unusual, however, to include in the lease a term that provides for the renewal of the lease. The renewal provision may be one that requires the tenant to give notice of renewal by a specified period of time prior to the termination of the lease. Alternatively, the renewal may be automatic, absent notice of nonrenewal by either party.

A renewal is a new lease. Unless otherwise stated, the renewal is under the same terms and conditions as the original lease. The parties may agree that the rent will be altered to reflect the present value of the land. For instance, each renewal may require a reappraisal of the land and a rent adjustment to reflect a specified percentage of the appraised value. Except where the agreement is for an automatic renewal of the lease, the parties should indicate whether the renewal clause will be operative in the second lease and in succeeding renewed leases.

Another method of renewal is by holding over. The legal implications for the holdover tenant were discussed in a preceding section.

Summary

A *lease* is both a contract and a conveyance. As a conveyance a lease creates a possessory interest in real property for a specified period of time. The owner of the real property conveys this estate to the tenant in exchange for *rent*. The tenant receives exclusive possession for the duration of the lease. As a lease is also contractual, it must contain the essential elements of any contract.

Four different types of *leasehold estates* may be created. They are the *term tenancy, periodic tenancy, tenancy at will* and *tenancy at sufferance*. The term tenancy and the periodic tenancy are the most common. They differ mainly in the manner in which they are terminated. A term tenancy ends automatically at the date specified in the lease. A tenant who fails to vacate upon termination of a term tenancy is a *holdover tenant*; this person may be held for an additional term. In a periodic tenancy, the party terminating the lease must notify the other party. The time of notification may be established in the lease. If no time is stated, the notice period is established by law.

Although an oral lease for a short term is valid, the Statute of Frauds requires leases for longer periods to be in writing. In most states a written lease is required if the term exceeds one year. In a few states only leases with terms exceeding three years must be in writing. Regardless, parties should insist that the lease be in writing, especially if the terms are complex or the value of the leasehold estate is high.

A lease should identify the parties as lessor and lessee, clearly describe the premises and stipulate the term of the lease and the rent, including how much is to be paid, when it is to be paid and where. Absent any stipulations provided in the agreement, the lessee may make any desired legal use of the premises. Though the *right of possession* implicitly resides in the tenant, tenants would be wise to make sure that the lease provides that the landlord will give not merely the right to possession but possession itself. For leases of three years or more, it is becoming common to record the lease.

Four kinds of leases are common for commercial use. In the *gross lease* a fixed amount of rent is paid periodically. The landlord is responsible for taxes, insurance and utilities. Often, payment of extraordinary expenses is negotiable between landlord and tenant. This type is not popular for long-term leases. In the *net lease* the tenant pays many of the operating expenses of the property such as taxes, utilities and insurance. The advantage to the landlord is obvious. The *ground lease*, another form, is a specialized type in which the lessee pays rent on vacant land, usually with the intent of constructing a building. This type of agreement can be very complex and is often of long duration. Finally, the *percentage lease* is another type widely used commercially. In a percentage lease rental is based in part on the tenant's gross sales. Like all leases, the agreement should clearly stipulate the terms; it should also establish the lessor's rights to examine the tenant's accounting records.

Provisions for renewal of leases are sometimes included in the original agreement. Nevertheless, a renewal constitutes a new lease and should conform to contractual requirements.

Review and Discussion Questions

1. Match the following:

    (a) Tenancy at sufferance
    (b) Term tenancy
    (c) Tenancy at will
    (d) Periodic tenancy

    (1) has a specific beginning and ending date.
    (2) exists as long as neither party chooses to terminate it.
    (3) continues from period to period until terminated by one of the parties giving proper notice.
    (4) exists when a person is wrongfully in possession of another's land without a valid lease.

2. Name two ways in which a periodic tenancy can be created.

3. Define the term *holdover tenant*.

4. List and briefly describe four terms that should be specified in a lease contract.

5. What risks are involved in entering an oral lease?

6. Why should the lessee insist on having the precise nature of his or her use or possession of the property explained in the lease contract?

7. Distinguish between "the landlord gives possession of the premises" and "the landlord gives the right of possession of the premises."

8. Match the following:

(a) net lease   (1) The rent is based in part on the gross sales made by
(b) gross lease   the lessee.
(c) percentage lease   (2) The lessor leases a piece of vacant land to the lessee,
(d) ground lease   usually with the stipulation that the lessee at his or
                                        her own expense will construct a building.
                           (3) The tenant agrees to pay taxes, insurance, repairs
                                        and other operating expenses of the premises.
                           (4) The rent is a fixed or flat amount.

9. Describe and discuss those rules of landlord-tenant law that no longer seem appropriate given present-day expectations of lay parties.

10. Describe the practical business situations in which the following types of leases would best satisfy the needs of the commercial lessor and lessee: (a) gross lease, (b) net lease, (c) percentage lease.

Case Problems

1. China Doll Restaurant, Inc., leased premises from Schweiger. China Doll agreed to pay a base rent of $600 per month and an amount equal to five percent of the restaurant's first $288,000 of gross sales. The owners of China Doll had considerable experience in operating a Chinese restaurant.

   The lease also contained a provision in which lessee agreed to use the premises "for conducting and operating a restaurant business." Before the expiration of the lease, China Doll moved to new and larger premises. At this time they stated that they intended to open a Mexican restaurant at the former China Doll location. Little was done to accomplish this, but they continued to pay the base rental of $600 per month. During this period the premises were unoccupied. Has China Doll violated the terms of the lease? *China Doll Restaurant, Inc. v. Schweiger, 19 Ariz. 315, 580 P.2d 776 (1978).*

2. Chapman rented farmland to Walker on a year-to-year basis beginning each year on January 1. Chapman sold the property to Gregory with a stipulation that Gregory was to have possession as of January 1, 1963. On July 1, 1962, Chapman gave Walker notice to vacate at the end of the year. Is this notice sufficient in a state following the traditional common law rule? *Gregory v. Walker, 239 Ark. 415, 389 S.W.2d 892 (1965).*

3. Regency Inn leased a rental office in the lobby of its hotel to Americar, a car rental agency. Wagner rented a car from Americar, and while walking through the hotel parking lot to reach her rental car, she was robbed and

raped. Wagner sued Regency Inn for damages alleging that they maintained a public nuisance. A clause in the lease held that Americar was responsible to indemnify Regency Inn for any damages suffered due to the operation of the car rental agency. At the time of assault on Wagner, Americar was a holdover tenant. Can Regency Inn claim indemnification under these conditions? *Wagner v. Regency Inn Corp., 463 N.W.2d 450 (1990).*

4. Doyle owed Byrne $5,000 for services performed in rewiring Doyle's house. After six months Doyle had paid nothing on the $5,000 bill and, upon being confronted by Byrne, admitted that it was unlikely that he could pay the bill in the near future. Byrne suggested that he would take a lease for a year on Doyle's camp on the lake. Doyle said "fine," and the conversation ended. In the spring Byrne moved into Doyle's camp and occupied it without incident until mid-July. At that time Doyle arrived at the camp and ordered Byrne to evacuate. Byrne refused, claiming that he had a one-year lease. Doyle retorted that there was nothing in writing, that no rent was stipulated and that the services for electrical work could not be used in lieu of cash payments for rent. Discuss the validity of Doyle's arguments.

26

The Landlord-Tenant Relationship

The signing of a lease creates obligations on the part of both the lessor and the lessee. Failure by either party to comply with obligations imposed either by contract or by law gives rise to the availability of certain legal remedies. The remedies available depend upon the nature of the obligation breached and upon the present circumstances of the parties. For example, did the lessee remain in possession, or were the premises abandoned? Some problems result from actions taken by one of the parties to the transaction—the lessee may have sublet the premises, for example—or actions involving not the parties but other persons, as when a visitor falls down the stairs of the leased premises. These occurrences lead to legal responsibilities on the part of the parties to the lease. Obligations imposed by the lease contract, by the relationship itself and by the law are the topics of this chapter.

Lessor's Security

Several techniques have evolved over time to protect landlords from tenants who mistreat the leased premises.

Landlord's Lien

Under common law, the lien known as the right of distress provided the landlord with a lien on the personal property of the tenant where there was a failure to pay rent.

This common law rule, which arose in feudal England, has not been viewed with favor by American courts because of the potential for abuse by the landlord. Under the right of distress the landlord can hold or even sell the personal property of the nonpaying tenant. The right, where it exists today, is limited to the personal property of the tenant that is on the leased premises. For the most part, states have statutorily eliminated the self-help notion of distress. It has been replaced with remedies such as actions for rent or the reclaiming of the premises for the landlord by public officials. Remedies currently available to the landlord, including eviction, are discussed later in this chapter.

Rent Paid in Advance

A normal requirement for modern leases is that rent payments are due prior to the beginning of the lease period.

Under common law where it is not otherwise specified, rent is due at the end of the rental period. The modern practice of requiring advance payment of the rent in the lease gives the landlord some additional assurance of stability. Where the rent is not forthcoming from the tenant by the first day of the rental period, the landlord is given some lead time in pursuing remedies for nonpayment. If the rent were not due until the end of the rental period, the landlord would lose additional time pursuing the remedies.

Security Deposit

Money deposited by the tenant for the security of the landlord, usually at the inception of the lease, over and above the advance payment of rent.

The security deposit is usually equivalent to one month's rent or more. Its purpose is to secure the landlord against damage done to the premises by the tenant or to clean or repair the premises, over and above normal wear and tear, when the tenant vacates. It may also provide a wider margin of security against a tenant who wrongfully abandons the premises. It has the practical effect of inducing the tenant who wants the security deposit returned to maintain the premises carefully during occupancy and to clean the premises thoroughly upon leaving. In some states, there is a limit on the amount the landlord can demand as a security deposit.

The security deposit is held by the landlord in trust for the tenant. The parties may agree that interest will be paid on this money. In some states, it is mandatory that the landlord of multiple-unit housing pay interest on any security deposit.

Because the security deposit is not a form of liquidated damages, the landlord can retain only as much as is necessary to pay for the damage done by the tenant. If the payment is a security deposit and not an advance rental, the tenant cannot use it in lieu of payment of rent for the last month. Whichever it is should be stipulated clearly by the parties.

Some states have adopted parts of the Uniform Residential Landlord and Tenant Act, which is geared toward promoting uniformity in landlord-tenant law. The act provides strict regulation of the security deposit. It would limit the amount deposited to one month's rent, require a written explanation of the purpose for and handling of the funds as well as an indication of the reasons for retaining any of the deposit and provide for the return of any unneeded funds to the tenant within 14 days after the termination of the lease. It also provides for penalties in case the landlord mishandles any of the security deposit funds. Most of the states have tailored these provisions to fit their needs.

Third-Person Guaranty of Rent

The landlord who has doubts about the capacity or reliability of the tenant in meeting the conditions of the lease may require a third person to guarantee performance.

In a commercial or industrial lease where the tenant is thinly capitalized, a personal guaranty by the individuals actually running the business under the corporate veil may be required. Also, where the tenant has a poor credit rating, the landlord may insist on the assurance of a more reliable third person. The guaranty would have to be in writing and signed by the guarantor. The guaranty agreement may be a part of the lease or a separate agreement usually appended to the lease.

Cognovit

A confession of judgment that permits the landlord, upon default by the tenant, to obtain a judgment against the tenant without the need for formal legal proceedings.

When this clause is present, the tenant has agreed in the lease that in case of his or her default the landlord can obtain a confession of judgment without the necessity of going to court to obtain the decree. Usually, the cognovit is executed by the landlord's attorney, who files an affidavit stating that the default occurred. Such a judgment, like any other, constitutes a lien on any real property in the jurisdiction of the leased premises.

The effect of a cognovit is to expedite the landlord's collection process after a default. It creates a situation ripe for abuse by the landlord, and in some states it is illegal for a tenant to execute such an agreement until after the default has taken place.

Lessor's Obligations

The landlord is bound by any promises made to the tenant in the lease. In addition, certain obligations have been imposed on the landlord by the law over and above the contractual understanding. The following covenants and warrants are the major ones with which the parties must be concerned.

Covenant of Quiet Enjoyment

A warrant by the landlord that the tenant will have the premises free from interference by the landlord or anyone claiming better right to the premises than the landlord.

There is no general guarantee by the landlord against wrongful intrusion by third persons. Should such an intrusion take place, the tenant will have satisfactory legal avenues through which to redress the interference. For centuries, however, the general common law rule has been that the tenant is protected from a wrongful intrusion by the landlord or someone claiming better rights than the landlord or tenant.

The covenant of quiet enjoyment is breached only upon eviction by the landlord or by a third person, either actual or constructive. Actual eviction consists of a physical removal of the tenant from the premises. Constructive eviction could occur when there is a substantial interference with the tenant's enjoyment of the premises.

Case Example

HTM leased commercial property from Goldman, Sachs and Company. Goldman failed to pay the mortgage, resulting in the mortgagee foreclosing on the property and ousting HTM from its lease. HTM sued for breach of implied covenant of quiet enjoyment.

The Court noted that in every lease of land there is, absent an agreement to the contrary, an implied covenant of quiet, peaceful enjoyment of the premises. Unfortunately for HTM, a clause in their lease stated that they accepted the premises subject to all mortgages. The mortgage preceded the HTM lease so that HTM had waived their implied convenant of quiet enjoyment by "agreeing to the contrary." *HTM Restaurants, Inc. v. Goldman, Sachs and Company, 797 S.W. 2d 326 (Texas, 1990).*

Generally, in the case of either an actual or a constructive eviction the tenant must have vacated the premises before asserting a breach of the covenant of quiet enjoyment.

Covenant to Deliver Possession

The landlord promises to deliver the right of possession to the tenant at the time the lease is scheduled to start.

This covenant is quite limited. It does not warrant against a wrongdoer being in possession of the premises at the time the lease commences, but only that the tenant will have the *right to possession.*

Case Example

Reichman leased premises from Emery for a term of five years. The lease was to commence on July 1. At the time the lease was executed the property was occupied by Drake, whose term expired on June 9. Drake, however, refused to vacate, and Reichman commenced an action to evict her. Several months later this suit was successful. After Drake was evicted, Reichman commenced a damage action against her as he had been unable to occupy the premises during the eviction proceeding. Drake argued that she had no liability to Reichman as she had no contractual relationship with him. An appellate court concluded that Drake's action violated Reichman's property rights and awarded damages. *Reichman v. Drake, 89 Ohio App. 222, 100 N.E.2d 533 (1951).*

Should a wrongdoer be in possession, the tenant has the obligation to evict him or her. A few jurisdictions have adopted the so-called English Rule, which requires the landlord to deliver *possession*, not merely the *right* to it. This interpretation is consistent with the usual expectancy of the parties upon entering the contract.

One aspect of this covenant that is sometimes misunderstood by residential landlords is that the tenant's right to possession is exclusive. This excludes the landlord as well as others.

Covenant of Fitness of the Premises

An assurance that the premises are fit for habitation.

The common law rule is that the landlord does not implicitly warrant that the premises are fit for habitation. Some jurisdictions still follow the dictate of this rule, but even in these a few exceptions have been created. Where the lease is for a furnished apartment or is intended for a short duration (a few days, weeks or months), there is an implied warranty that the premises are habitable upon entry. Similarly, when the landlord knew of latent defects—that is, defects that were unknown and not reasonably discoverable by the tenant—there is a breach of an implied covenant of fitness.

The general rule makes sense when placed in the context of the time of its creation. It arose during a period in which land was the predominant concern in a lease, and the tenant could readily discover what he or she needed to know about the land. In modern times the building is usually the chief concern of the parties, and often the building is to be used as a residence. The notion of *caveat emptor*—"let the buyer beware"—seems ill suited to a situation where the landlord is in a far superior position to know the condition of the premises and understands that the tenant wants to use it as a residence.

Implied Warranty of Habitability

A warranty imposed by law on the landlord by which he or she warrants that a residential property is safe and sanitary and fit for living at the time the tenant enters and during the period of tenancy.

In an effort to bring landlord-tenant law into modern times, many courts and legislatures have imposed an implied warranty of habitability. The reasons usually cited for changing the law is the inequality of bargaining position between the landlord and the tenant. Normally, the landlord drafts the terms of the lease and the tenant can accept them or look elsewhere for living accommodations. In addition, legislative action by state and municipal governments that created housing codes exhibited a concern for protecting tenants; these actions stiffened the backbone of the courts in finding the warranty of habitability.

Apparently the determination of what constitutes a breach of this warranty will be a question of fact. One court has noted that what constitutes a breach depends upon the nature of the deficiency, its effect on habitability, the length of time it persisted, the age of the structure, the amount of the rent, the area in which the premises are located and whether the tenant waived the defects or caused them through abnormal use of the premises. See *Kline v. Burns, 111 N.H. 87, 276 A.2d 248 (1971)*. An apartment leased for an amount substantially below local standards, for instance, may not have to be in as good a condition as other leased properties in the area. At least, rent will be one factor considered by the court in deciding whether the warranty of habitability has been breached.

In effect, this warranty imposes a duty upon the landlord to keep the premises in repair during the lease period. This would be true despite his or her failure to agree to perform repairs and contrary to the long-standing common law rule freeing either party of the duty to repair unless agreed to.

More than 50 percent of the states have adopted the theory of implied warranty of habitability for residential tenancies. However, the theory has rarely been applied to nonresidential situations. The Uniform Residential Landlord and Tenant Act makes void any provision in the lease waiving or otherwise negating the warranty of habitability.

Case Example

Mudusar, an infant, crawled up onto a table in his parents' bedroom in a second story apartment and fell through the screened window 25 feet to the concrete below. Mudusar was seriously injured, and brought suit against Murray, the landlord, for breach of implied warranty of habitability under a state statute. The statute requires that apartment windows be screened to prevent the instrusion of insects.

The Court held for Murray because the screen was adequate to keep out insects, the sole purpose for which it was mandated. The fact that it was inadequate to keep a small child from falling through it did not constitute a breach of implied warranty of habitability. *Mudusar v. V. G. Murray and Co., 369 S.E.2d 325 (1990)*.

Duty to Repair

Absent the existence of an implied warranty of habitability in a state, the landlord has no duty to repair the premises.

In addition to not covenanting that the premises are habitable upon entry, the common law rule does not require the landlord to repair during the habitation. However, where the landlord retains control over parts of the premises, he or she will be responsible for repairing those areas.

Case Example

Derman Rug Company leased the first floor and basement of a building from Ruderman. The lease contained a provision requiring the tenant to keep the premises in as good order and repair as they were at the beginning of the lease. A steam pipe embedded in the basement floor leaked and was repaired by the landlord, who sued the tenant for the cost of repairs.

The landlord's claim was rejected by the court. Two reasons were given for rejecting this suit. First, the court determined that pipes embedded in floors are within the landlord's exclusive control and as such are the landlord's sole responsibility. Second, the court was convinced that the tenant's duty to repair did not extend to the basement in a building in which upper floors were leased to other tenants, because the land under the building is not part of the leased premises. *Derman Rug Co. Inc. v. Ruderman, 4 Mass. App. Ct. 437, 350 N.E.2d 727 (1976).*

Because of the uncertainty in the law created by the spreading adoption of the warranty of habitability, the parties to a lease should be cautious and thorough in declaring their respective rights in relation to repairs.

In a significant number of states, statutes have been passed imposing a duty on the landlord to perform repairs. The parties should be careful, given the variability of the rules regarding repairs, to make the terms of their agreement clear. When the landlord has the duty to repair and fails to do so, the tenant may sue the landlord for damages or make the needed repairs and deduct the cost from the rent.

If the landlord agrees in the lease to perform repairs, there is a split of authority over the responsibility for rebuilding a structure destroyed by a fire or other catastrophe. Some courts hold that the obligation to repair includes rebuilding; others claim that "repairing" is narrower than "rebuilding." Under the latter rule, once the building is substantially destroyed, it would not be encompassed within the obligation to repair.

If the landlord has agreed to rebuild, whether expressly or by implication in consenting to repair, the failure to rebuild would terminate the tenant's obligation to pay rent, at least where the building is the major concern of the lease.

Duty to Pay Taxes

Absent a contrary agreement, the landlord has the duty to pay the property taxes.

As the owner of the fee interest in the premises, the landlord is responsible for paying the taxes. If the property is sold at a tax sale for nonpayment, the sale is subject to the existing lease. Where the tenant makes improvements to the property that cause the taxes to rise, the tenant will probably be liable to pay for the increase.

Building Code Compliance

Most cities have adopted building codes for the purpose of protecting the public health, safety and welfare by regulating building and construction standards.

Through the requirement of obtaining a building permit or a certificate of occupancy for new construction or substantial alteration of an existing structure, city officials inspect structures for violations of the building code. The code is usually divided into special areas, such as plumbing code, electrical code and fire code. As a result of the division, there may be several inspectors and a multitude of permits. Failure to comply with the building code may result in the landlord's being fined.

The codes are applicable to existing buildings as well, and the code process usually comes into play when there is a tenant complaint about a violation. Often the result of these complaints is that the tenant receives a notice to vacate the premises at the earliest legal opportunity. Naturally, this discourages tenant complaints. Due to this landlord reaction, some jurisdictions have created the affirmative defense of retaliatory eviction. Under this defense a tenant cannot be evicted for complaining, at least until a legislated period (sometimes 90 days) has lapsed after the complaint has been remedied. This provides only temporary protection to the tenant, and the landlord is free to terminate the tenancy after the time stated in the statute.

Lessor's Remedies

If the lease agreement is not complied with by one of the parties, the other party will have an array of potential remedies. The chief remedies of the landlord will be discussed here.

Eviction by the Landlord

The term usually associated with the legal procedure by which a landlord has the tenant removed from the premises because the tenant has breached the lease agreement.

Under the common law the covenants of a lease were mutually exclusive, and therefore the breach of a covenant by the tenant would not entitle the landlord to dispossess the tenant. The landlord would have a cause of action for damages resulting from the breach.

In the modern landlord-tenant situation, generally there is a provision in the lease, or the right may be provided by state statute, that the landlord can sue to regain possession of the premises in case of the tenant's failure to comply with the covenants in the lease. Though the agreement or the statute may not provide for dispossession in the case of *any* breach of a covenant, it normally applies to the failure to pay rent, the violation of the use provisions of the lease, the unlawful use of the premises or the violation of state and local health codes.

The eviction process will be used to dispossess a tenant who has received legal notice to vacate the premises and has failed to do so. Where the basis for the eviction is nonpayment of rent, the landlord will be required to notify the tenant of the possibility of eviction and make a demand for the rent prior to beginning the eviction proceedings.

The eviction of the tenant terminates the obligation to pay future rents. However, many business leases contain "survival clauses" under which the obligation to pay rent continues despite the eviction of the wrongdoing tenant. When it is a long-term lease, however, the right to sue accrues only at the termination of the lease, unless a clause in the lease indicates otherwise. It may be impractical to delay the suit for ten or more years until the lease period ends.

The term *eviction* is used to describe the wrongful dispossession of the tenant by the landlord as well as the legal action of the landlord described above. Wrongful eviction will be discussed under the lessee's remedies below.

Wrongful Abandonment

The tenant's vacating of the premises without justification and with the intention of no longer performing under the terms of the lease.

When the tenant wrongfully abandons the premises, the landlord has two options: either to do nothing until the lease period ends and then to bring an action for nonpayment of rent or to reenter the premises and reassert possessory rights.

The common law rule is that the landlord is free to do nothing and recover the full amount of unpaid rent at the termination of the lease. In some states, however, a duty arises to mitigate damages, thereby compelling the landlord to reenter and attempt to relet the premises. In all states the landlord can secure the right of reentry by including in the lease a survival clause permitting the entry but reserving the right to collect rent from the tenant. With this clause the landlord can minimize the damages by reletting the property while continuing to have the original tenant as a hedge against any losses caused by the wrongful abandonment.

When the landlord reenters after a wrongful abandonment and without the protection of a survival clause, he or she is said to accept the surrender of the premises. Upon acceptance of the surrender, the tenant's obligation to pay rent ends. In essence, by the force of the landlord's action of reentry, he or she has implicitly acquiesced to the abandonment of the tenant.

Action for Rent or Damages

The landlord may permit, or be required to permit, the wrongdoing tenant to retain possession of the property and seek money damages for the landlord's injury.

The usual action by the landlord for damages involves the recovery of unpaid rent. If no agreement exists to the contrary, the landlord will have to wait until the end of the lease to begin action for unpaid rent. However, most leases provide terms permitting an action for rent prior to termination, though these generally include the right to evict and are discussed above.

Should the tenant cause damage to the premises or otherwise violate the covenants of the lease over and above the value of the rent, the landlord has the right to sue for damages.

Lessee's Obligations

Obligations arise both from the lease contract and from modern real estate law.

Duty to Repair

The tenant's obligation to use the premises in a reasonable fashion and to deliver possession at the end of the lease in about the same condition as when received, reasonable wear and tear excluded.

Absent an agreement to the contrary, the tenant has no law-imposed duty to make substantial repairs to the premises. However, the tenant is obligated to maintain the property so as to protect it from the weather. This obligation is referred to as the tenant's responsibility to avoid waste.

Waste

Damage caused by the tenant including failure to protect the premises from decay and ruin caused by the natural elements.

The notion of waste can take two different forms. Voluntary waste results from the positive actions of the tenant, such as willfully breaking the windows or destroying the landscaping. Permissive waste results from an act of omission such as the failure to repair an accidentally broken window, thereby permitting injury to the premises from the weather.

The tenant may agree to perform repairs, just as the landlord might. Similarly, as previously noted under the landlord's obligations, there is a difference of opinion among jurisdictions as to whether the tenant is liable to rebuild the premises in the case of fire or other catastrophe where that tenant has agreed to repair. Since the parties would not normally intend the requirement of repairing to encompass rebuilding, they should expressly exclude this contingency from their agreement.

Whether or not the tenant agrees to repair, he or she will be liable in damages to the landlord for any injury, beyond normal wear and tear, caused to the premises.

Duty to Insure

Neither the tenant nor the landlord has an obligation to insure the premises against loss. However, the failure of the tenant to insure his or her interest may result in a continuing obligation to pay rent without enjoying the benefit of the property whose improvements have been destroyed by fire. Where the tenant leases both land and improvements, he or she is not relieved of the duty to pay rent despite the destruction of the premises. If the tenant leases only the improvements (such as an apartment in a multiple-family building), the obligation to pay rent will terminate when the improvements are substantially destroyed. If the destruction is only partial and the premises are still tenable, however, the tenant must continue to pay rent.

Where the tenant rents both land and buildings, the common law rule requiring the payment of rent after the buildings' destruction seems unduly harsh. In a few states the rule has been altered to provide for termination of the obligation to pay rent where the improvements have been substantially destroyed or become untenable through no fault of the tenant. The change in the rule seems equitable, given the fact that buildings are often the critical concern in modern leases.

Fixtures

Any personal property permanently affixed to the realty by the tenant; they become the property of the landlord at the termination of the lease.

The tenant can provide in the lease for removal of fixtures at the culmination of the tenancy; absent such an agreement, however, he or she will lose the right to those items attached to the realty that would otherwise be classified as fixtures. The common law created a harsh situation for the tenant.

This doctrine has been altered in some measure. To the extent that the tenant attaches items to the realty that enable him or her to carry on a commercial enterprise, for example, under the doctrine of trade fixtures the tenant will be able to remove the items up to the termination date of the lease.

Case Example

Lubin leases commercial shop space to Murphy. In order to sell her cards and gifts, Murphy installs shelves that are attached to brackets and the brackets affixed to the wall. Prior to the end of the lease Murphy can remove the shelves and brackets as long as the removal does not significantly or materially injure the shop.

The exception to the general rule is based upon the idea that it was the presumed intent of the parties to permit removal, and public policy supports rules that will encourage trade through flexibility.

Several things should be noted about trade fixtures. First, the question of whether an item is a trade fixture may be treated as one of fact and left up to the trier of fact (the jury). More certainty can be obtained by stipulating in the lease how these fixtures will be handled. Second, removal can be executed only where serious injury will not result to the premises. Finally, removal is not permitted after the termination of the lease. Upon termination of the lease, trade fixtures become the permanent property of the landlord.

Lessee's Remedies

The lessee has several remedies available when the lessor violates the conditions of the lease.

Wrongful Eviction

An act that occurs when the landlord without justification deprives the tenant of possession of the premises.

A tenant who has been wrongfully evicted (also referred to as an *actual eviction*) can sue for recovery of possession of the premises or for damages caused by the breach of covenant of quiet enjoyment. In a somewhat punitive aspect of this area of law, if the landlord wrongfully evicts the tenant from only part of the premises, the tenant may retain the remainder of the property but will have no obligation to pay any rent until the partial wrongful eviction ceases.

A wrongful eviction and breach of the covenant of quiet enjoyment will exist also where the tenant is ousted because a third person has proved rights superior to those of the landlord. In such a case the tenant will have an action for money damages.

Constructive Eviction

An occurrence that results when the actions of the landlord so materially interfere with the tenant's enjoyment as to make the premises untenable.

Theoretically at least, the right to assert a constructive eviction occurs when the tenant is forced by the condition of the premises to vacate. The tenant must notify the landlord of the conditions, where appropriate, and give the landlord a reasonable time to remedy the situation. Finally, the tenant must actually vacate the premises to be able to allege constructive eviction.

The concept of constructive eviction is a judicial construction. It is used to offset the fact that the landlord normally inserts in the lease a provision permitting the eviction of the tenant for failure to comply with the terms of the lease. Leases do not normally provide for comparable rights for the tenant. The Blackett case discusses the defense of constructive eviction.

Blackett v. Olanoff
Supreme Judicial Court of Massachusetts
358 N.E.2d 817 (1977)

Background: Jerrold Olanoff leased residential premises to Arthur Blackett. Olanoff leased other residential premises in the vicinity and also leased commercial premises to another for use as a bar and cocktail lounge. The noise emanating from the lounge in the late evening and early morning hours was substantial. Blackett complained about the noise to his landlord, who attempted unsuccessfully to control the noise from the lounge. After a reasonable time, Blackett vacated the premises contending that the noise made the premises untenable, thereby breaching his implied warranty of quiet enjoyment.

Olanoff brought this action against Blackett to recover unpaid rent. Blackett offered the defense of constructive eviction. Olanoff contended that he was not repsonsible for the noise created by the proprietors, employees and patrons of the lounge. Olanoff did not contend that the noise was not loud enough to cause a constructive eviction. The trial judge concluded that Blackett was constructively evicted.

Decision: The Supreme Judicial Court of Massachusetts affirmed the trial court's decision.

Justice Wilkins

Our opinions concerning a constructive eviction by an alleged breach of an implied convenant of quiet enjoyment sometimes have stated that the landlord must perform some act with the intent of depriving the tenant of the enjoyment and occupation of the whole or part of the leased premises. There are occasions, however, where a landlord has not intended to violate a tenant's rights, but there was nevertheless a breach of the landlord's covenant of quiet enjoyment which flowed as the natural and probable consequence of what the landlord did, what he failed to do, or what he permitted to be done. Although some of our opinions have spoken of particular action or inaction by a landlord as showing a presumed intention to evict, the landlord's conduct, and not his intentions, is controlling.

The judge was warranted in ruling that the landlords had it within their control to correct the condition which caused the tenants to vacate their apartments. The landlords introduced a commercial activity where they leased premises for residential purpose. The lease for the lounge expressly provided that entertainment in the lounge had to be conducted so that it could not be heard outside the building and would not disturb the residents of the leased apartments. The potential threat to the occupants of the nearby apartments was apparent in the circumstances. The landlords complained to the tenants of the lounge after receiving numerous objections from residential tenants. From time to time, the pervading noise would abate in response to the landlord's complaints. We conclude that, as matter of law, the landlords had a right to control the objectionable noise coming from the lounge and that the judge was warranted in finding as a fact that the landlords could control the objectionable conditions.

This situation is different from the usual annoyance of one residential tenant by another, where traditionally the landlord has not been chargeable with the annoyance. Here we have a case more like *Case v. Minot*, where the landlord entered into a lease with one tenant which the landlord knew permitted that tenant to engage in activity which would interfere with the rights of another tenant. There, to be sure, the clash of tenants' rights was inevitable, if each pressed those rights. Here, although the clash of tenants' interests was only a known potentiality initially, experience demonstrated that a decibel level for the entertainment at the lounge, acoustically acceptable to its patrons and hence commercially desirable to its proprietors, was intolerable for the residential tenants.

Because the disturbing condition was the natural and probable consequence of the landlords' permitting the lounge to operate where it did and because the landlords could control the actions at the lounge, they should not be entitled to collect rent for residential premises which were not reasonably habitable. Tenants such as these should not be left only with a claim against the proprietors of the noisome lounge. To the extent that our opinions suggest a distinction between nonfeasance by the landlord, which has been said to create no liability, and malfeasance by the landlord, we decline to perpetuate that distinction where the landlord creates a situation and has the right to control the objectionable conditions.

Judgments affirmed.

Damages, Reformation and Rescission

Actions a tenant may bring where an implied warranty of habitability exists and the landlord has failed to maintain the premises in a tenable condition.

The remedies made available to the tenant when the implied warranty of habitability is breached are of a complementary nature. That is, the tenant is afforded relief short of vacating the premises or withholding rent, both of which may be risky remedies.

The tenant may sue for damages measured by expenses incurred as a result of the landlord's refusal to perform the covenants in the lease. The tenant may seek reformation of the contract due to the conduct of the landlord in refusing to perform repairs. The reformation could take the form of reducing the amount of rent due in order to conform to the lessened value of the unrepaired premises. If the breach of covenant has reduced the value of the lease to the tenant significantly, prior to the tenant's entry he or she may seek to have a court rescind or negate the entire agreement.

Case Example

Laferty, the landlord, has agreed to provide repairs in his lease with Manne. The roof leaks into a small bedroom. Despite requests by Manne to Laferty to repair the roof prior to Manne's moving in, the roof remains unrepaired. Manne *needs* the bedroom for a child and seeks rescission of the lease. The tenant's attorney chooses this as a safer, albeit more time-consuming, remedy for the tenant than vacating after entry and contending constructive eviction. Under constructive eviction Manne would run the risk of the court's disagreeing with his contention that the premises are "untenable" and charge him for unpaid rent.

Rent Withholding

The practice, allowed in a few states under limited circumstances, in which the tenant withholds rent as an inducement to force the landlord to perform repairs.

It should be remembered that at common law the obligation to pay rent arises from the possession of the land and from the covenant to pay in the lease. Each covenant in the lease is independent. Therefore, the tenant normally has the duty to pay the rent despite the landlord's failure to perform some aspect of his or her obligation.

In some states, including New York, Illinois, Connecticut, Vermont and Michigan, tenants are legislatively authorized to withhold rent in cases where the landlord has failed to obtain a certificate of occupancy as required by the municipal housing code. Similarly, welfare agencies are authorized to withhold rent payments that they normally make directly to the landlord for the welfare tenant. A statute establishes the conditions for rent withholding and the procedures for utilizing the right. It affords protection to the tenant from being evicted.

It should be noted that rent withholding is not a broadly applicable remedy, and local and state law will have to be checked carefully to determine whether the right exists and to what extent.

Third-Party-Related Transactions

On occasion a person other than the landlord or tenant becomes involved with the leasehold agreement. Because of a job change, for example, a tenant may seek a substitute to complete the tenancy. Or a person visiting the tenant may fall down the hall stairway in the apartment due to poor lighting or a faulty railing. These and other third-party incidents affecting the lease are discussed next.

Sublease

A transfer of part of the leasehold interest of the tenant, with the tenant retaining a reversionary interest.

Case Example

Granville leases Hilltop Acres to Tomas under a term lease beginning January 1 and ending December 31 of the same year. On March 1, Tomas transfers her interest in Hilltop Acres to Nantes until November 30. This agreement is a sublease, since Tomas has retained a one-month reversionary interest.

Impact of a Sublease

When the tenant creates a sublease by conveying less than the entire interest in the land to a sublessee, there is no privity of estate or contract between the landlord and the sublessee. In short, the sublease does not alter in any respect the original landlord-tenant agreement. The sublessee will have an obligation to pay rent to the tenant, and the tenant will continue to have the obligation to pay rent to the landlord. Likewise, any restriction on limitations included in the original landlord-tenant agreement will pertain to the tenant-sublessee contract as well, since the tenant cannot give greater rights than he or she has. The tenant, despite not being in possession, will still have all the obligations arising from the initial landlord-tenant contract.

Assignment

A transfer in which the tenant gives the entire interest in the leasehold estate without retaining a reversionary interest.

Using the example above, if Tomas had transferred her interest until December 31, the agreement would have been an assignment; Tomas transferred her entire interest in the land. Unless otherwise agreed, the tenant is free either to sublet or to assign the premises. Often, however, the lease agreement includes wording that limits the tenant's right to sublet or assign. The permission of the landlord is the normal precondition to the transfer.

It is possible for a tenant to assign only *part of the premises*. The tenant can assign the second floor to an assignee, for example, retaining the first floor. This transfer would be treated as an assignment so long as the tenant gave the entire interest in the second floor to the assignee.

The distinction between assignment and sublease is not always simple. If the tenant transfers all that he or she has but retains the right to reenter the property in the case of nonpayment of the rent, the majority of courts hold that an assignment still exists. Several states, however, disagree. Courts in these states contend that the reservation of a right of reentry constitutes a reversion in the tenant/assignor, thereby making the transaction a sublease.

To create the proper interpretive environment, it should be noted that courts do not favor restrictions on a party's right to transfer real property. The landlord must be careful in drafting the limitation in the lease on the tenant's right to sublease or assign, or a court may undermine it. The courts' attitude is framed by their general objection to any restraint on the freedom to alienate or transfer property. This attitude has resulted in decisions that a landlord's prohibition against subleasing did not prohibit the tenant from assigning. Similarly, once the landlord consents to an assignment despite a prohibition in the lease, the leasehold is freely assignable thereafter. Even so, a single waiver of the limitation on subleasing does not allow the tenant to sublease later without the landlord's approval.

Impact of an Assignment

At the beginning of the preceding chapter some care was taken to describe a lease as a conveyance of an estate in land as well as a contractual obligation. In the area of assignment the dichotomy is important. Upon taking a transfer by lease, the tenant enters into a dual relationship. Under the estate-in-land aspect of the agreement, the landlord and the tenant are said to have *privity of estate*. Under the contractual side of the agreement, the parties have created *privity of contract*. As explained earlier, privity connotes the mutuality that binds parties to their agreement.

A tenant who assigns the lease to a third person surrenders possession and transfers the *privity of estate* to the assignee. The assignee literally stands in the legal shoes of the tenant, since he or she received all that the tenant has, and privity of estate now exists between the landlord and the assignee. The assignee's right to possession makes him or her liable directly to the landlord for payment of rent. Possession automatically gives rise to the obligation to pay rent.

By way of contrast, there is no *privity of contract* between the landlord and the assignee. There is no contract, or mutual agreement to be bound, created by the assignment. An outgrowth of this is that the tenant/assignor continues to be bound by the terms of the lease-contract to the landlord.

As the result of privity of estate existing between the landlord and the assignee, the landlord can sue the assignee for nonpayment of rent. If, when the assignment takes place, the assignee agrees to assume the obligations of the lease and to be bound to the lessor for rent, he or she will have privity of contract with the lessor as well as the privity of estate previously discussed.

Sale of the Leased Premises

The landlord is free to convey the leased premises at any time. The buyer takes subject to the leasehold interest of the tenant. The buyer has the right to collect all subsequent rents once the tenant has been notified of the sale.

The buyer is the successor in title to the lessor's land; the tenant has an obligation, arising out of the notion of a conveyance of real property, to pay the rent to the new owner. It would not, therefore, be necessary to have an assignment of the lease, or the lessor's contract rights to the buyer, in order to collect the rent. However, unless the lease or contract provides otherwise, the lessor would continue to be liable for covenants he or she made to the lessee in the lease.

Mortgage of the Leasehold

Absent an agreement to the contrary, the tenant can mortgage the leasehold interest. The tenant can subject only the interest that he or she has (for example, a lease for five years) to the mortgage. There may be a greater than usual risk for the mortgagee because the tenant may fail to make rent payments, thereby defaulting on the lease and causing the landlord to retake the premises. When a forfeiture takes place, the mortgage is terminated.

To avoid this consequence, the mortgagee may covenant with the lessor that notice be given to the mortgagee prior to any forfeiture, thereby preserving the mortgage and permitting the pursuit of remedies against the lessee/mortgagor.

In most jurisdictions the mortgage of a leasehold estate is subject to the recording statutes. Thus, the mortgagee will record the mortgage to protect his or her priority rights in the land from being depleted by future conveyances of the tenant.

Landlord's Mortgage of the Premises

The landlord is free to mortgage the premises that are the subject of a leasehold estate at any time. The mortgagee's rights will be subject to the rights of the existing lessee. The mortgagee will be able to foreclose on the mortgage upon the lessor's default, but a subsequent sale, whether to the mortgagee or to a third party, of the leasehold premises will be subject to the possessory rights of the lessee.

Parties' Tort Liability

In general, the person who has possession and control of the premises owes a civil duty to third parties to maintain the premises in a reasonably safe condition.

The leased premises are normally in the possession and under the control of the tenant, and the tenant must use reasonable care in maintaining those premises in a safe condition. Failure to do so is a civil wrong, or tort. As a consequence of this rule, and the rule that does not require the landlord to repair or make the property habitable, generally the landlord owes no duty to the tenant or to third parties when they are injured as the result of a defective condition of the premises. However, the general rule is under siege where jurisdictions have adopted a warranty of habitability. It should be kept in mind, however, that technically warranty is a contract theory and the extent of damages recoverable in case of a breach may be limited to contract damages (the cost of repair, not personal injury).

Even without the modern trend applying a warranty of habitability, there are exceptions to the rule holding that the landlord owes no duty in tort. When the landlord retains control over portions of the premises, such as stairways and halls, he or she will owe a duty to use reasonable care to maintain safe conditions. This is consistent with the general rule, since the landlord retains control of these areas.

In addition, where the landlord is aware of latent defects on the premises and fails to notify the unknowing tenant, he or she will owe a duty to the tenant and other third parties. Also, where the lease is for a furnished apartment and the tenant has no opportunity to inspect, the landlord will be liable in tort. Likewise, the landlord will be liable where he or she carelessly performs repairs.

Measure of Damages

Since the duty of the landlord to perform repairs grows out of the contractual understanding (the lease) or from a law-imposed contractual theory of warranty of habitability, the measure of damages owed is the cost of the repair; however, there is a trend to permit recovery for personal injury and property damages as well.

To hold that the injured tenant or third party can recover only for the cost of repairing the premises seems a bit conservative in this day and age. Nevertheless, the conclusion is consistent with the contract principle of permitting recovery to the extent of mending the breach but not for the ensuing personal injury. Much of the area of landlord-tenant law is in flux, and this measure of damages is no exception.

Some courts speak of warranty as being a tort remedy as well as a contract action. Other courts reject the utility of the concept of privity (one must be a party to a contract to allow recovery against the landlord) in a modern world of broader expectations. It is no surprise then that there is a distinct trend toward permitting the recovery of tort damages when the landlord fails to repair the premises. Under tort damages the tenant or third party can recover for the personal injury and property damage resulting from the landlord's wrongful conduct, along with the cost of repairing the premises. This trend is consistent with the broader movement toward protection of the tenant.

Exculpatory Clauses

A lease clause by which the landlord attempts to excuse himself or herself from liability for negligence in maintaining the leasehold premises.

Under the premise that the parties can reach any agreement they choose, landlords often include an exculpatory clause relieving themselves of liability for their negligence. At the present time there is a sharp split among the courts as to the enforceability of these clauses. Some courts permit the enforcement of the clause because of the notion that the parties have the right to contract freely. The incongruity in this conclusion is the erroneous assumption that the usual leasehold agreement involves equality of bargaining position. At least in residential leasing, the tenant seldom has the freedom to negotiate the terms of the lease.

Conversely, other courts have held that the position of the landlord in exculpating himself or herself from liability for negligence, in a typically unbargained-for lease, defies sound public policy. Sanctioning of these clauses would also lead to the demise of the warranty of habitability, since all form leases would incorporate a waiver clause. The trend in the courts is to prohibit the landlord from exculpating himself or herself from responsibility.

Summary

A lease creates obligations for both parties. These obligations arise both from the contract itself and from the law. Legal remedies vary according to the obligation breached and the relationships of the parties.

The *landlord's lien* is an early example of a legal means for providing security for the landlord in case of a tenant's nonpayment of rent. This device is not used widely today. The modern landlord almost always acquires the right to demand *rent paid in advance* by a provision in the lease. Another widely used protective device is the *security deposit,* usually an amount equivalent to one month's rent. It is normally returned to the tenant at the end of the lease term, but it may be used by the landlord to defray the cost of repairing damages caused by the tenant or as security against any rent owed by a vacating tenant. Laws in a number of states penalize a landlord who mishandles security deposit funds.

Among the obligations the landlord owes the tenant are the *covenant to deliver possession* (that is, to make the right of possession available to the tenant at the start of the lease period), the *covenant of quiet enjoyment* (protection from intrusion by someone claiming better rights than the landlord) and the *covenant of fitness of the premises* supplemented by the *implied warranty of habitability.* All of these obligations vary from state to state.

If the tenant fails to meet the contractual terms of the lease, the landlord has several remedies. *Eviction by the landlord* of the tenant, one example, is the legal procedure whereby the tenant is forced to vacate the leased premises. The landlord may also seek damages for unpaid rent or injury to the property.

Along with the duty to pay rent, the tenant's obligations include the *duty to repair,* keeping the premises in essentially as they were at the start of the lease, without causing *waste.* Although neither party is required to insure the premises, a tenant's failure to insure may result in an obligation to pay rent even after the leased space has been destroyed by fire or flood.

If the landlord violates the provisions of the lease, several remedies are available to the tenant. The tenant has recourse to the law when he or she suffers wrongful eviction—that is, put out by the landlord without justification. On the other hand, a tenant may claim *constructive eviction* and thus be released from the lease if forced to vacate because of the condition of the property. Since this remedy, as well as *rent withholding* may be risky and inconvenient for the tenant, other legal actions are available whereby the tenant may sue for correction of conditions.

The addition of a third party, either by a *sublease* arrangement or through an accident resulting in injury for a guest, further complicates the landlord-tenant relationship. Unless prohibited by the lease, a tenant may arrange to transfer all or part of his or her possessory rights to another party through sublease or *assignment*. Moreover, the premises may be sold to a new owner, in which case the tenant owes rent and other obligations to the new owner, who is legally bound by the terms of the lease. Finally, a tenant or guest can be injured on the premises. The extent of the landlord's financial responsibility depends upon many factors, including whether negligence can be proved, the laws and the attitudes of the courts in that state and the nature and extent of the injury.

Review and Discussion Questions

1. List and briefly describe four techniques implemented to protect landlords from tenants who mistreat leased premises.

2. State the purpose of the Uniform Residential Landlord and Tenant Act.

3. The covenant of quiet enjoyment is breached upon actual eviction or constructive eviction by the landlord. Define the terms *actual eviction* and *constructive eviction*.

4. (a) What is the *warranty of habitability?* (b) What environmental change has caused this warranty to come into vogue?

5. List and briefly describe three tenant's obligations arising either from his or her lease contract or by law.

6. When a lease agreement is not fulfilled by either of the parties, the injured party can seek several remedies. List the remedies that can be sought by (a) the landlord and (b) the tenant. Explain the situations that would prescribe the use of these various legal remedies.

7. Discuss the reasons why restricting an injured third person to contract damages may be impractical.

8. "The parties should be left to the bargain they made." Discuss the appropriateness of this position in lease situations.

9. As they relate to the area of assignment of leases, define *privity of estate* and *privity of contract*.

Case Problems

1. Keown leased a house from Housh. During the term of the lease Swanson, his girlfriend, moved in with tenant. The house had a second story deck on which Keown and Swanson sunned themselves. The deck had no railing, and had a cluster of television antenna wire connected to an unused antenna on the roof above. One night Keown and Swanson heard a noise and went to the deck to check for possible burglars. Swanson became tangled in the antenna wire and fell to the ground below. She sued Housh for injuries claiming that he was responsible for the "latent defect" created by the antenna wire. The house was rented unfurnished. Will Swanson recover? *Housh v. Swanson, 203 Ill. App. 377, 561 N.E.2d 321 (1990).*

2. Stefanik fails to vacate premises at the end of a term lease, holding over into a subsequent month. The owner has leased the property to Nunez. In the majority of American jurisdictions, would the owner or Nunez be obligated to remove Stefanik? Discuss.

3. Lubin owns an apartment in a college town. Many units in the building are rented to college students. Lubin retains keys to these apartments. From time to time she visits the tenants. Although she always phones first, if the tenants are not available she will use her duplicate key to enter. The main purpose of Lubin's visit is to ensure that the utilities, appliances and plumbing are functioning properly. If she does not interfere with the tenants' occupancy, is Lubin's conduct legally proper? Discuss.

4. Stankiewicz was a tenant in an apartment rented to her by Hawkes. She was forced to vacate the apartment because its physical condition was a health hazard. Many items were left behind when she moved. Hawkes entered the apartment and concluded that the items were abandoned. He instructed his workers to put them in a pile in the yard. As a result, the items were seriously damaged. Would the landlord's argument that the property had been abandoned be successful? *Stankiewicz v. Hawkes, 4 Mass. App. Ct. 437, 350 N.E.2d 727 (1974).*

5. Addison leased a unit in an apartment building from Seikely. He tripped over a loose board on an exterior stairway and was injured. He sued Seikely, claiming negligent maintenance of the common stairway. Seikely offers as a defense that a clause in the lease excuses him from liability for any injury incurred on the premises. Discuss the validity of Seikely's defense.

6. Gokey rented a mobile home (part of the realty) to the Bessettes at a monthly rent of $400. During the tenancy, the Bessettes complained of numerous problems, including a leak in the roof, a broken furnace and a break in the sewer line. The Bessettes complained to code enforcement officials about the sewer line because noxious liquids lay under the trailer for up to four months, causing foul odors to fill their home. Should the Bessettes move out? Should they stop paying rent? Explain. *Gokey v. Bessette, 580 A.2d 488 (1990).*

27

Condominiums, Cooperatives, Time Shares and Real Estate Investments

The condominium and the cooperative afford techniques for obtaining an ownership interest in a dwelling or office. They are in many ways similar, but they also have marked differences. This chapter will focus initially on the condominium and will then describe and contrast the cooperative.

The chapter also discusses various types of time share agreements and real estate syndications.

Condominium

The fee simple ownership of one unit in a multiple-unit structure, combined with an ownership of an undivided interest in the land and all other parts of the structure held in common with the owners of the other individual units in the structure.

The concept of condominium ownership has blossomed in the United States since the mid-1960s. The notion of fee ownership, coupled with a release from the repair and maintenance chores of home ownership, made condominiums attractive to many people, especially to the elderly and to single-person households.

Condominiums did not present any fundamental legal problem. The common law had long recognized separate ownership of individual rooms or floors in a structure, which in essence is the nature of a condominium. Common or joint ownership of land and building was equally well established. Condominium ownership as a specific form, however, not only was new but also was a complex form of residential ownership. Describing the co-ownership, joint management, cross-easements and enforcement of individual responsibilities was part of the complexity. To provide some clarity and uniformity for this new area, states quickly began to adopt permissive condominium legislation. By 1968 all the states had adopted some form of condominium law. Although the terminology differs, there is a great deal of similarity in the statutes adopted by the various states.

This chapter discusses condominium ownership as it applies to residential units. The condominium form is also being used in commercial and some industrial property. The legal principles are the same, regardless of the use to which the condominium unit is put.

Formation of a Condominium

The developer may purchase an existing multiple-family apartment building for conversion into a condominium. Alternatively, he or she may purchase land and obtain a construction mortgage for erecting the condominium structure. The completed condominium units are then sold to individuals. The individual purchasing the condominium unit attains a fee simple interest in the apartment unit. In addition, the individual becomes a tenant in common with the other unit owners of the land and all structures outside the walls of the individual apartments. These are known as the *common elements*.

The condominium owner, if necessary, obtains a mortgage on his or her individual unit. Payment at the time of purchase is made to the condominium developer, who in turn pays off the construction mortgage as it pertains to that individual unit and its appropriate share of the common elements and has them released from the lien of the construction mortgage.

Case Example

Greg and Helene Burnside purchase a condominium unit from Condo Developers Inc. for $128,000. They obtain a mortgage on the unit for $110,000 from Security Bank, provide $18,000 of their own cash and deliver a check for $128,000 to Condo in exchange for a deed to the unit. Condo pays its mortgagee an amount sufficient to obtain a release for the Burnsides' unit and for one percent of the common elements. (There are 100 units of equal value in the development.)

Declaration

A document required by state law, which must accompany and be recorded with the master deed for the condominium development.

The declaration, one of three documents commonly mandated by state law, contains a description of the property, restrictions on use and the detailed legal requirements that attach to ownership of a condominium unit. The other two documents are the bylaws and the deed to each individual unit.

The declaration is required for both new construction and for conversion of an existing building. It is filed in the county where the property is located, and it is maintained by the county clerk in the condominium records for the county. The declaration must contain a legal description of the property; a general description of each unit, including square footage and identification by floor and unit number; a description of any area that is subject to limited control, such as carports and garages; a description of the common areas and each apartment's fractional interest in the entire condominium regime. Any changes or alterations to these declarations must be filed with the county clerk.

Declarations can also contain other matters, such as restrictive covenants. Restrictive covenants are discussed in Chapter 8, and the law discussed there is as applicable to condominiums as it is to other types of real property. Sometimes the condominium declaration will state that the association has a *right of first refusal* so that it can screen potential buyers of condominium units. When the existing owner of a unit has a willing buyer, the association is given a limited time in which to determine whether the prospective owner is satisfactory to them. If not, the association can purchase the unit under the same terms as offered by the buyer.

In addition, provisions are made for the contingency that the buildings might be substantially destroyed by fire or some other disaster. The declaration usually provides for its own amendment by a majority of the unit owners.

Bylaws

The rules governing the internal operation of the condominium development.

The bylaws of a condominium development are not unlike the bylaws of any organization. They provide for the selection of the board of directors of the association, meetings, regulations for the common elements, rights and responsibilities of unit owners, assessment and collection of monthly charges and other relevant matters.

The bylaws are very important to the property owners because they establish the rights and responsibilities of each with respect to the condominium regime. Prior to the purchase of a unit, the bylaws as well as the declaration should be read carefully. The courts strictly enforce the bylaws and will uphold action taken by the council of owners pursuant to the bylaws.

Individual Unit Deed

The deed for each individual condominium unit in the development.

Since the interior of each condominium apartment, along with a share of the common element, is owned in fee simple by the unit owner, the deed must be recorded to protect the unit owner from a fraudulent conveyance by the seller. In addition, it provides a chain of title that can be relied upon by a subsequent purchaser to ensure the marketability of the title. Each individual unit owner is entitled to apply for a mortgage in order to help finance the purchase.

Common Elements

The parts of the development property that are necessary or convenient for the residents of the condominium and are owned in common by all the condominium residents.

Each condominium unit owner has a tenancy in common in the land and buildings and other structures not constituting the interior of his or her individual condominium unit. This ownership interest is undivided; that is, all unit owners have an equal right to all the common elements.

The common elements generally include hallways, elevators, recreational facilities, land, stairways, exterior of the buildings and so on. Most state statutes specifically designate what items are included in the common elements. Where not so provided, they should be described carefully in the declaration.

The percentage of the common elements ascribed to each apartment unit may be equal where the units are quite similar. Where significant differences exist among the units, however, the percentage may be based upon the differing values of the individual units. In any event, the amount attributable to each unit is designated in the declaration.

The high-rise condominium has caused a distinction to be created between two kinds of common elements. *General common elements* are those previously described, in which all the unit owners share. In a condominium made up of townhouses all the common elements are usually general. *Limited common elements* that are shared by more than one unit owner but less than all of them may include stairways, balconies and elevators in divided sections of a high-rise condominium.

The state statutes generally provide that the expenses of administering, maintaining, repairing and replacing the common elements be paid for by an assessment of the unit owners made by the board of directors of the association. The board of directors is then responsible for repairing and operating the common elements. Unit owners are bound by the terms of the declaration to pay their shares of the assessment. Payment of the expenses cannot be avoided by waiving the right to use certain parts of the common elements. For example, a nonswimmer cannot reduce the monthly assessment by deducting an amount that would cover maintenance of the swimming pool.

If the association that administers the common elements is unincorporated, the individual unit owners are liable as principals for all authorized and apparently authorized acts of the association. Incorporation of the association, however, limits the unit owners' liability to the assets of the corporation.

Condominium Association

The organization stipulated by statute to administer the operation of the common elements of the condominium.

The association, and its board of directors on a day-to-day operational level, carries out the business of caring for the condominium. Members of the board of directors are the representatives of the unit owners and bear a fiduciary relationship to those owners. Their responsibility to the unit owners is multifaceted. For instance, their fiduciary duty to the unit owners requires that the board deal fairly and carefully with the business interests of the unit owners. It must avoid participation in decisions that present conflicts of interest for individuals. In short, board members can be held legally liable for mismanagement or for secretly profiting from that management. Board members are not relieved of liability merely because they are "volunteer" or unpaid.

Since the association is generally mandated by state law, it is quasigovernmental in nature. Its actions may be treated as "state action" and thus subject to the proscriptions in the constitution. For instance, when a unit owner is subjected to sanctions provided in the declaration for nonpayment of an assessment, the unit owner is entitled to due process (notice and hearing). Similarly, the right of first refusal cannot be utilized by the association to exclude prospective purchasers on the basis of race, creed, color, sex or national origin. Although the boundaries of constitutional responsibility of associations are unclear at this time, it appears certain that some restrictions such as those mentioned above will be imposed.

Assessments

The regular monthly payments for upkeep of the common elements, as well as payments required for special expenses or improvements to those common elements.

State legislation generally provides that the bylaws establish the rules for regular and special assessments. The association's board of directors, or a project manager appointed by the board, normally collects the assessments and uses them in maintaining the condominium property. The original setting of the amount of the regular assessment, the changing of that amount and the imposition of a special assessment are determined by the terms of the bylaws. The bylaws are likely to place responsibility for establishing these assessments with the association or its board of directors.

Case Example

The newly elected board of directors of a high-rise condominium discovered that the building had serious structural defects and that the association was in debt. The board of the Tower West Condominium discussed the woes at length and then levied a $100,000 special assessment to be paid proportionately by the unit owners. Papalexion and several other unit owners refused to pay the assessment contending that according to the bylaws a vote of the full association was necessary unless there was "an extreme emergency." They argued that this was not such an emergency.

    The court held that the unit owners had to pay the assessment. Based upon the structural problem and the poor financial condition of the condominium association, the board acted reasonably in concluding that this was an extreme emergency as intended under the bylaws. *Papalexion v. Tower West Condominium, 167 N.J. Super. 516, 401 A.2d 280 (1979).*

When a unit owner refuses or is unable to pay an assessment, he or she is subject to enforcement procedures that are usually stated in the bylaws. In at least two states the statute permits the association to cut off utilities ten days after notice of delinquency is given. The normal route, however, makes any unpaid assessment a lien on the property with priority over all other liens except those designated in the statute. Generally, the liens designated in the statute are the most common forms: tax liens, prior mortgages, mechanic's liens and the like.

The procedure for foreclosing on this lien is the same as followed under the state's mortgage foreclosure law, unless otherwise stated. At the foreclosure sale the association is permitted to purchase the delinquent unit unless the practice is proscribed by the declaration. The main disadvantage of the foreclosure procedure is that the other unit owners must bear the expense of the delinquency during what may be a protracted foreclosure action.

The association also has the option of bringing an action for money damages, and this action does not preclude the subsequent lien foreclosure action described above. If delinquency is caused by a unit owner's shortage of funds, generally an action for money damages is not advisable.

In states that have homestead laws, seizure of the place of residence may be prohibited. Often the residential condominium qualifies as the homestead. A second lien method that circumvents these laws is the trust and lien upon sale technique. This technique permits recovery of the delinquent amount from the proceeds at the time the delinquent unit is sold. Because the proceeds are considered to be in trust, the assessment lien must be satisfied prior to any distribution to the seller of the condominium unit. The legal implications for the buyer are unclear. A cause of action may lie against the buyer who receives the proceeds prior to a satisfaction of the assessment lien.

Again, this technique may force the other unit owners to bear the burden of the delinquency for an extended period of time. However, it should circumvent the difficulty under the homestead laws existing for the previously described lien technique.

The *Beachwood Villas* case which follows provides a good insight into the roles that the state condominium statute, the declaration, and the Board of Directors play in regulating condominium use.

Beachwood Villas Condominium v. Poor
District Court of Appeal of Florida
448 So.2d 1143 (1984)

Background: The Board of Directors of Beachwood Villas Condominium adopted two rules regulating unit rentals and the occupancy of units by guests during the owner's absence. Earl and Iris Poor, owners of a condominium unit, were unhappy with the rules and sued to have them declared invalid because they exceeded the scope of the Board's authority. The trial court agreed with the Poors', deciding that the Board exceeded its authority.

Decision: The District Court of Appeals reversed the judgment of the trial court.

Judge Hurley

Rule 31, the rental rule, requires that: (1) the minimum rental period be not less than one month, (2) the number of rentals not exceed a specified number which is calculated to the size of the unit, (3) tenants not have pets without the approval of the board, and (4) a processing fee of $25.00 be paid. Rule 33, the guest rule, requires: (1) board approval for the "transfer" of a unit to guests when the guests are to occupy the unit during the owner's absence, (2) the number of transfers (either by rental or guest occupancy) not exceed six per year, and (3) that the occupancy rate not exceed a specified number which is calculated to the size of the unit.

Hidden Harbour Estates, Inc. v. Basso, (1981), suggested that condominium rules falling under the generic heading of use restrictions emanate from one of two sources: the declaration of condominium or the board of directors. Those contained in the declaration "are clothed with a very strong presumption of validity . . . ," because the law requires their full disclosure prior to the time of purchase and, thus, the purchaser has adequate notice. Board rules, on the other hand, are treated differently. When a court is called upon to assess the validity of a rule enacted by a board of directors, it first determines whether the board acted within its scope of authority and, second, whether the rule reflects reasoned or arbitrary and capricious decision making.

The reasonableness of rules 31 and 33 was not questioned below and, therefore, we are concerned only with the scope of the board's authority. Inquiries into this area, begin with a review of the applicable statutes and the condominium's legal documents, i.e., the declaration and by-laws.

By express terms in the statute and in the declaration the association has been granted broad authority to regulate the use of both the common element and limited common element property.

In general, that power may be exercised as long as the exercise is reasonable, is not violative of any constitutional restrictions, and does not exceed any specific limitations set out in the statutes or condominium documents.

Since there has not been any suggestion that either rule violates the Condominium Act, Section 718, Florida Statutes (1983), we begin by viewing the Beachwood Villas declaration of condominium. Article X provides that "[t]he operation of the condominium property shall be governed by the By-Laws of the Association which are . . . made a part hereof." In turn, Article IV of the by-laws states that "[a]ll of the powers and duties of the Association shall be exercised by the board of directors . . . ." More specific is Article VII, Section 2, which states that "[t]he Board of Directors may, from time to time, adopt or amend previously adopted rules and regulations governing and restrictiong the use and maintenance of the condominium units. . . . "

It is obvious from the foregoing that the board of directors is empowered to pass rules and regulations for the governance of the condominium. The question remains, however, whether the topics encompassed in rules 31 and 33 are legitimate subjects for board rulemaking. Put another way, must regulations governing rental of units and occupancy of units by guests during an owner's absence be included in the declaration of condominium? At least one court has held that "[u]se restrictions to be valid, must be clearly inferrable [sic] from the Declaration." This test is rooted in the concept that declarations of condominium are somewhat like covenants running with the land. Even so, we believe that this test is too stringent. A declaration of condominium is "the condominium's constitution." Often, it contains broad statements of general policy with due notice that the board of directors is empowered to implement these policies and address day-to-day problems in the condominium's operation through the rulemaking process. It would be impossible to list all restrictive uses in a declaration of condominium. Parking regulations, limitations on the use of the swimming pool, tennis court and card room—the list is endless and subject to constant modification. Therefore, we have formulated the appropriate test in this fashion: provided that a board-enacted rule does not contravene either an express provision of the declaration or a right reasonably inferable therefrom, it will be found valid, wihtin the scope of the board's authority. This test, in our view is fair and functional; it safeguards the rights of unit owners and preserves unfettered the concept of delegated board management.

Inasmuch as rules 31 and 33 do not contravene either an express provision of the declaration or any right reasonably inferable therefrom, we hold that the board's enactments are valid and plainly within the scope of its authority. Accordingly, we reverse the order on appeal and remand the cause for further proceedings consistent with this opinion.

Reversed and Remanded.

Cooperative

A form of ownership in which the land and buildings are (usually) owned by a corporation; individual unit residents own stock in the corporation and have a proprietary lease in a specific unit or apartment.

Unlike the condominium unit owner, the cooperative owner or tenant does not have a fee simple interest in the apartment. Instead, the owner has shares of stock in the corporation that owns the land and building, along with a long-term *proprietary lease*. Occasionally, the cooperative ownership is in a trust or partnership form rather than a corporate form.

The notion of a proprietary lease connotes that, unlike typical tenants, the cooperative tenants participate in the running of the cooperative through their stock interest in the corporation. The participation may be direct, when an individual is elected as a member of the board of directors, or indirect, when voting for directors or giving opinions to the elected directors. Despite the proprietary nature of the lease, however, it continues to be a lease and is governed by landlord-tenant law. One must be cautious, however, because the state may choose to treat cooperatives differently than a traditional lease.

Case Example

Drew Associates, a cooperative developer, challenged the New Jersey Cooperative Recording Act as unconstitutional. One of Drew's grounds was that the statute created an illegal restraint on the alienation of land by requiring that all transfer documents be recorded, and that it contain the consent of the board of managers of the cooperative. These conditions are not placed on other leases or even condominium transfers.

The Court upheld the statute stating that cooperative ownership is a "hybrid" form of property and does not fall within traditional notions of either realty or personalty. It is reasonable, therefore, for the state to impose conditions on cooperative transfers not imposed on other forms of transfer. *Drew Associates of N.J. v. Travisano, 122 N.J. 249, 584 A.2d 807 (1991).*

Financing a Cooperative

In a typical situation an investor purchases a multiple-unit dwelling to convert it into a cooperative. To finance the conversion, the investor takes out a mortgage with a bank for 80 percent of the dwelling's value. The remaining 20 percent is paid initially by the investor but is recouped through the issuance of stock in the cooperative corporation to the future tenants. Future tenants pay their share of the 20 percent by purchasing stock when they enter the cooperative. In addition, each makes monthly payments that cover his or her share of the mortgage payment as well as operating expenses.

In addition to the mortgage share, each tenant as part of the monthly rent will pay a share of any other debt, taxes and operating expenses. As in a condominium, the share of these expenses may be on a per-unit basis or may vary with the relative value of the apartment. The amount of the annual or monthly assessment is determined by the board of directors of the corporation.

Differences Between Condominiums and Cooperatives

One difference between a cooperative and a condominium is the type of mortgage obtained. In the condominium each unit owner arranges for his or her own mortgage; in the cooperative there is a *blanket mortgage* for the entire building. The blanket mortgage may be more difficult to obtain.

In the cooperative there are restrictions on the ability of the tenants to sell their interest. Generally, the tenant needs the approval of the board of directors for the proposed new tenant. This procedure is a little more stringent than the right of first refusal used in the condominium area. These restrictions on the cooperative go beyond the outright sale and may prevent a tenant from assigning or subletting his or her share of the premises. The purpose behind these restrictions is to assure that a compatible group of tenants is assembled in the cooperative.

The cooperative form of ownership has advantages for the tenant compared to the usual landlord-tenant situation. The tenant is not subjected to annual rent increases and does not risk having the lease terminated arbitrarily. The cooperative tenant has a long-term lease and participates in any decision to raise the rent.

Like the condominium owner, the cooperative owner or tenant is subject to an extensive set of rules and regulations governing the cooperative. Failure to comply with the terms of the regulations may permit the board of directors to cancel the tenant's lease or to take some other action provided in the rules for redressing the violation.

Upon the death of the tenant, any successor—an heir under the tenant's will or by law—must clear the screening of the board of directors. There is no automatic right on the part of successors to be able to continue the cooperative lease. This differs from a condominium, where the unit is owned in fee and can freely be passed on to successors.

There are some distinct advantages to fee simple ownership, of which the condominium owner is the beneficiary. The notion of fee ownership itself carries a certain feeling of security and psychological confidence that is not matched by the lease of the cooperative arrangement. Many of these advantages are tangible and specific.

The condominium owner is responsible for his or her own mortgage and is not as vulnerable to default as the cooperative owner, who shares a blanket mortgage with everyone else in the cooperative. The condominium owner can directly take advantage of certain tax benefits, such as property tax deduction, interest deductions, casualty loss deductions and depreciation allowance if the unit is rented, that are not available individually to the cooperative owners, although residential cooperatives may be able to take advantage of some federal tax benefits, such as property tax and interest deductions, if the cooperative is formed properly. Under Section 528 of the Internal Revenue Code, however, a condominium owner is permitted to make a tax-free contribution to the association for capital expenses, maintenance and operating expenses provided the association meets the requirements of Section 528. Thus, a condominium owner can make a tax-free payment to the association for a new roof or for the pool lifeguard. A payment for similar expenses to a cooperative would not qualify.

Upon the sale of a condominium unit, the owner can sell at market value and pay the reduced capital gains rate on his or her gain, subject to postponement and rollover provisions. The cooperative owner generally must sell the stock back to the cooperative at a stipulated price. Often the stipulated price is the original price.

Cooperatives can be troublesome during difficult economic times. Initially, it may be more difficult to get a blanket mortgage loan than to get a mortgage loan on an individual condominium unit. Given the nature of the interdependence created by the blanket mortgage, the default of one or several cooperative owners can cause a default on the mortgage. Upon default all cooperative owners stand to lose their investments, even those who can afford to keep up their share of expenses. In a condominium, on the other hand, the default on an individual mortgage does not affect the other condominium owners. Nevertheless, the financial straits that caused the mortgage default are likely to prevent payment of condominium assessments; in this respect, delinquencies can place a financial strain on the other condominium owners.

One advantage the cooperative has over the condominium is that it is relatively easy to get rid of an incompatible tenant. A tenant who refuses to comply with the rules of the cooperative can be evicted in summary proceedings in most instances. Although a condominium owner who is in default on assessments can be ousted through a lien foreclosure, the procedure is likely to be more prolonged and expensive.

Time Shares

Time-sharing has become a popular marketing device for resort developments in the United States. Time-sharing includes several very different types of ownership. Some of these forms include ownership of some type of interest in the real property, and other forms are mere rights of use with no interest in the property itself.

Time-sharing arrangements can be built upon several different legal principles. In some instances the arrangement is a variation of the tenancy in common. In others it is a variation of a cooperative. It could also be a lease. When it is built upon one of these types of legal ownership of property, it always includes a limitation as to the time of use. For example, a tenancy in common is an estate that includes more than one owner, with each co-owner owning an undivided interest. A time-sharing arrangement based upon the legal principles of the tenancy in common would introduce the characteristic of time with respect to possession of the property. An ordinary tenant in common has an equal right to possession with the other co-tenants. The time-share agreement limits the right to possession to a specific time period each year.

The time-sharing arrangement can also include principles of contract, partnership, license or corporate law. For example, a time-sharing arrangement based in contract would include the right to use a specific piece of property at a definite time each year for a certain number of years. At the expiration of that period the property would be owned by the developer, not the owner of the time-share.

Much of the criticism of time-sharing arrangements is a result of misleading marketing practices. The legal rights associated with time-sharing arrangements can vary significantly from development to development. The variety of legal rights that are being marketed as time-shares coupled with deceptive and misleading information by salespersons has prompted some states to enact legislation dealing specifically with time-shares.

Real Estate Securities

Any syndication whereby a person invests money in a common enterprise involving real estate with the expectation of attaining profits from the efforts of a promoter or some other third party.

A normal transaction for the sale or lease of real property is not a security within the context of federal and state security laws. When a person or promoter offers an interest in the arrangement to the public, however, it may become a security. On other occasions, a person will sell a business, and the assets include real property. Real estate securities and business opportunity sales have separate and distinct control schemes from the usual real estate transactions.

If the transaction constitutes the issuance of a security, unless exempted, the promoter must comply with federal and (probably) state regulations.

Case Example

Fafner offers a group of his friends and neighbors an opportunity to be investors with him in a piece of mountaintop property he is about to acquire. The property has multiple-unit housing on it, and the investors will share in the profits. This purchase is a real estate security and must be registered as described later in this section.

One of the chief federal regulations in the area of securities is the 1933 Securities Act. The language of Section 2 of the act covers any investment contract or profit-sharing arrangement and is therefore broad enough to encompass almost any real estate syndication. The key factors are that transactions be a common enterprise and that there be management of the investment by a third party for the benefit of a passive investor. When an agency or court makes the decision as to whether or not a transaction involves a security, the emphasis is on the substance and economic reality rather than on the form the transaction takes. In defining what is a security, or any other regulation hereinafter discussed, the investor must take care to research the provisions of the state "blue-sky" laws, which regulate security transactions as well.

Condominiums as Securities

The offering of a condominium unit is not normally treated as a security, but as a sale of real estate. Thus, the sale is not subject to the regulation of the Securities and Exchange Commission (SEC) or to similar state laws.

Case Example

Joyce entered a purchase agreement for a condominium unit, which he planned to use for his personal residence. Joyce sued the condominium project owner, contending that his contract was an "investment contract" and subject to federal securities laws. The security had not been registered, nor had Joyce received a prospectus as required by federal securities law.

The federal district court held that a condominium purchase does not fall within the definition of an investment contract. An investment contract presumes that the investor hopes to realize a profit from the investment due to the activity of a third party. This is not the case where a typical condominium is purchased as a personal residence. *Joyce v. Ritchie Tower Properties, 417 F. Supp. 53 (D. Ill. 1976).*

Nevertheless, several states have extensive regulations of condominiums as securities. In California, for example, all condominium sales are regulated as securities because the common areas are not under direct control of the unit owner. It is clear, however, that in any state if condominium advertisements or other documents make any reference to providing rental services for the buyer for the period the buyer is not using the condominium, the purchase will be treated as an investment contract and the above-mentioned security regulations will apply. For more detail, SEC Release No. 33-5347 (January 4, 1973) provides guidelines for determining when condominium offerings are securities.

If the security regulations apply, registration of the entire offering must be made with the SEC. About half the states follow the disclosure rule: the prospect must be fully informed so that an intelligent decision can be made. In the other states full disclosure as well as minimum standards of "fairness" apply to the condominium offering when treated as an investment contract.

Exemptions

Transactions that would otherwise meet the definition of a security but that have been statutorily excused from the law's restrictions.

Exemptions from registration are made in the case of two types of transactions: intrastate sales and private offerings.

Intrastate Offerings

This exemption is provided in Section 3(a)(11) of the statute and applies to offerings that are made *solely* to residents of the state where the offerer or issuer is a resident and doing business. A key word in this exemption is *solely*. If one sale is made to a single nonresident of the relevant state, or if the issue is not wholly owned by residents up to nine months after the distribution of the issue is complete, the exemption will not apply.

Case Example

Referring back to the earlier example, Fafner, using the intrastate offering exemption, sells a share in his mountaintop venture to Thorsen. It takes six months to sell the full interest in the investment. If Thorsen, prior to completion of the sale, sells her share to her brother-in-law who lives out of state, Fafner's offering would no longer qualify under the intrastate offering exemption.

To use this exemption, therefore, the promoter must have assurances that the purchasers do not intend to resell. The burden of proving this exemption is upon the promoter. For a sizable issuance it is very risky to rely on this exemption in light of its restrictive character. Note that, despite its exemption under the federal statute, the issue may have to comply with the state law regarding securities. An array of remedies is available against an issuer who has relied on the intrastate exemption but who has failed to meet all the requirements of the exemption. Recovery of damages for the price paid for the security, plus interest, is among those remedies. For further clarification of the meaning of this exemption, see SEC Rule 147.

Private Offering

This exemption applies to offerings that are made to knowledgeable investors who have adequate information to evaluate fully the risks entailed in the transaction. It is the intent of this exemption that the offering be made to investors who are adequately informed so that they do not need the protective umbrella of the SEC disclosure rules. The purpose behind the exemption is to exclude such issues from expensive and time-consuming regulations.

Case Example

When the SEC challenged an offering made to employees under the private offering exemption by Ralston Purina Company, the Supreme Court adopted a several-fold test in determining the availability of the exemption.

The court stated that these questions should be asked: Were the offerees the type of persons who could fend for themselves? Did the offerees have access to the same type of information that would appear in a registration statement? Were the securities purchased for the investor's own account? *Securities and Exchange Commission v. Ralston Purina Co., 346 U.S. 119 (1953).*

The determination of whether or not an offering is private is based on numerous factors, including the number of offerees, the sophistication of the offerees, the number of units in the issue and their denomination and the manner of the offering, that is, personal contact or public advertising. There are no hard and fast rules, but the SEC will weigh the above factors in deciding whether or not the issue is a private one.

The SEC has adopted Regulation D, SEC Release No. 6389 (1982) as a "safe harbor" for those seeking to take advantage of the private offering exemption. If Regulation D is adhered to it exempts the issue from registration requirements, but not the antifraud, civil liability or other provisions of the SEC Act. The exemption applies only to the original issuer of the security. The requirements of Regulation D are complex and detailed, and are not amenable to a brief summary here. The regulation should be followed closely to assure compliance and the protection of the "safe harbor."

Registration of Securities

The listing of an issuance that meets the definition of a security—and is not otherwise exempted—with the SEC and (perhaps) with state officials.

Prior to making any offering of a nonexempt security, the promoter must register the issuance with the SEC. No sales can take place before the SEC declares the *registration statement* to be effective. During the period between the filing with the SEC and its approval, the promoter can make oral offers or even written offers by way of a preliminary prospectus, but no investor can be bound and no sale concluded until the registration is declared effective by the SEC.

Case Example

MacLeish has filed a prospectus and supporting documents with the SEC. While waiting approval, he begins to contact potential investors, providing them with a copy of the preliminary prospectus explaining the benefits of the investment. MacLeish asks for no commitments from these prospects. There would be nothing illegal about MacLeish's conduct.

If the promoter makes any sale prior to SEC approval, all investors have the right to rescind the transaction and get their money back, plus interest.

Prospectus

A written document containing all the information necessary for an investor to make an independent and intelligent decision regarding a securities offering.

The prospectus must be filed with the SEC registration and must be provided to prospective investors. The registration also will include the financial statements for the promoter's operation and the operating statements for the property (for example, statements indicating the income received from the property for the past five years). Any publicity regarding the offering should be avoided prior to filing with the SEC.

The SEC, in examining the proposed registration, compares the annual earnings history to the yearly cash distributions proposed by the issuer. The SEC attempts to see that the information alleged in the prospectus is complete and accurate; it does not pass upon the merits of the issue.

For example, the SEC examiner explores the registration documents to determine whether the six percent annual return in investment asserted in the prospectus is realistic in light of past performance. The examiner does not comment on the fact that a six percent return, given existing market conditions, is a poor investment.

Under federal law the offeror is required to give full and fair disclosure and is not permitted to give advice on the wisdom of the investment opportunity. In some states the state regulatory agency also evaluates the merits of the offering.

Forms of Ownership

The modes of ownership or ways of setting up a real estate syndication are varied. A simple vehicle such as concurrent ownership (tenancy in common), discussed in Chapter 5, can be used. Traditional forms of doing business—partnerships, limited partnerships and corporations—are utilized. Less common techniques such as trusts, particularly the real estate investment trust (REIT), have gained popularity.

Each method of ownership has its intrinsic advantages and disadvantages. Tenants in common retain direct individual control over their investment fates, but the death of a tenant can suddenly propel an heir into the ownership picture as an unwanted tenant. Partners can retain control over decision making, but, as with tenants in common, operational rules must be clearly provided or chaos may ensue. Partners avoid the dual taxation that exists in a corporate form but do not enjoy the limited liability of corporate shareholders. Limited partners enjoy some of the best of both the partnership world and the corporate world since they generally avoid dual taxation and have limited liability. Nevertheless, tax risks exist in the limited partnership technique in the form of income tax recapture penalties that may be imposed on the investor above the loss of the initial investment capital. Because of the additional risks, the limited partnership form has been confined largely to sophisticated investors by choice of both the promoters and the investors.

Each of these techniques is used broadly within and outside the real estate investment area. A complete explanation of them would require an entire textbook; they are usually covered in a separate course of study. It may be useful, however, to discuss in more detail the trust device and the real estate investment trust in particular.

Trust

A legal relationship in which a grantor transfers legal title to property to a trustee who manages the property for the benefit of third parties, or beneficiaries.

By creating a trust, the grantor in essence splits the title to the property into legal title and equitable title. The trustee holds legal title to the real property that forms the corpus of the trust, and the beneficiaries are the possessors of the equitable ownership of the corpus. The grantor may become a beneficiary.

Case Example

The five McKuen brothers have received a devise of a mountain resort property from their recently deceased uncle. Having no desire to manage the property or acumen for doing so, they create a trust by conveying the property to a trustee, a successful resort owner and person of high integrity, to manage the resort for their benefit. The brothers remain as beneficial owners of the resort property.

The trustee should be selected carefully and be a highly trustworthy individual. The trustee owes a fiduciary duty to the beneficiaries of the trust and so may not have a personal financial interest in the trust. The trustee must use a high degree of skill and care in activity for the beneficiaries and cannot treat them as arm's-length business adversaries. Despite the availability of legal remedies against a bad trustee, careful selection in the first place can prevent substantial grief and financial loss in the future. Trustees are confined to individuals and banks, since other corporations are generally prohibited from serving as trustees.

The duties, powers and other responsibilities should be spelled out carefully in the trust agreement. Because of the trustee's high level of responsibility, he or she will probably have to be well paid. But there are some distinct advantages to the trust arrangement. For instance, the trustee owns the land "as trustee" and, as such, can convey as trustee when necessary. This avoids having all the beneficiaries, who could number in the hundreds, sign the deed. Additionally the trustee is the "front person," the one known to the public, whereas the beneficiaries are not generally known. This may be advantageous in some situations.

For tax purposes a trust is treated like a separate entity. As in a corporation, the trust income may be subject to dual taxation, first as income to the trust and again as income to the beneficiaries. To avoid this extra tax bite the trust can be structured so as to pay out all income to the beneficiaries. In this way the trust is treated like a partnership for tax purposes, and the tax falls solely on the beneficiaries.

Real Estate Investment Trust (REIT)

A tax shelter that exempts certain qualified real estate investment syndications from corporate taxes where 90 percent or more of the ordinary income is distributed annually to the beneficiaries or investors.

The Real Estate Investment Trust Act was passed by Congress in 1960. The rules governing these statutory trusts are very complex and must be strictly adhered to by those attempting to take advantage of the form. The real estate investment trust can exist only where it is permissible under state law.

The REIT is a conduit for getting income to certificate holders while avoiding the taxation of the trust as a corporation that would normally occur. For example, a group of friends invest some funds by purchasing certificates in a REIT. The trustee of the REIT, an independent manager, uses their money to purchase an apartment complex for the purpose of attaining a return on that investment through rental income from the units. The net profits from the rentals are distributed to the group of friends (and any fellow investor in the REIT). These profits are taxed as ordinary income to all the investors, but the trust does not pay tax on the distributed portion of the profits.

The major conditions for creating a REIT are:

- There must be 100 or more certificate holders.

- A minimum of 90 percent of the gross income of the REIT must be derived from passive investments, such as rents, dividends and interest.

- At least 75 percent of the gross income of the REIT must be derived from transactions connected to real estate, such as rents from real estate mortgage interest, gains on the sale of real property and the like.

- The trustees must have centralized authority over the trust.

- At least 90 precent of the earned income from the trust business must be distributed to the certificate holders.

- There are additional restrictions on income produced by assets held for less than four years.

There are some distinct advantages to using the REIT form, in addition to the avoidance of dual corporate taxation. Other factors include centralized management, limited liability to the investors and the availability of real estate experts to do the investing. Nevertheless, the investments are limited to passive ones, and these may not provide the highest return on the investment dollar. Because of the size of trust distribution (100 or more certificate holders), the trust must generally register with the SEC, which is an expensive procedure.

Due to the complexity of the REIT qualifications, this simplified description of the procedure should not be relied upon by anyone interested in forming this type of trust. State laws may proved further restrictions on REITs.

Summary

The *condominium* and the *cooperative* are devices by which owners acquire rights in individual units of a multiunit residential or office building. Many factors have combined to make the condominium popular, although until fairly recently condominium ownership was unusual in the United States. As a result of this new popularity the states have had to develop new laws and procedures for purchase of condos and for the protection of owners. For example, the *declaration*, a document now required by law in most states, must accompany the master deed for condominium development and must be officially recorded with it. The law also requires condominium *bylaws* and *individual unit deeds* to condominium owners.

The declaration contains the legal description and lists restrictions on uses and legal requirements for each unit. The bylaws are the rules governing the internal operation of the condominium development. The deed to each unit is similar to the deed to any real property.

Each owner, in addition to fee simple ownership of a unit, has part ownership in the *common elements* of the structure. These include areas such as hallways, staircases, lobby and grounds. To administer these common elements, the *condominium association* is formed. Each owner is assessed a prorated amount of the total expense for operation of the common elements. Methods for measuring and collecting these *assessments* are established in the bylaws. Remedies in case of nonpayment are stipulated by state statutes.

Another form of joint ownership is the cooperative. Individual owners in this form do not own their respective units; each owns a portion of stock in a corporation that owns the land and buildings. Instead of the fee simple interest enjoyed by condominium owners, the cooperative owner has a long-term proprietary lease, which is governed by landlord-tenant law.

A major difference between the condominium and the cooperative is the type of mortgage obtained: each owner in a condominium obtains his or her own mortgage, while the cooperative usually carries a blanket mortgage on the entire complex. Taxation and liquidity benefits vary accordingly.

Some real estate transactions are subject to securities regulation. To qualify as a security, the real estate investment must involve a common enterprise and the expectation of profits through the efforts of a third party. The federal agency that regulates these sales is the Securities and Exchange Commission (SEC), created by legislation in 1934. Unless exempt, all sales that qualify as securities under the law must be registered with the SEC. Each investor must be furnished a written *prospectus* that contains all the information needed to make an independent decision.

Several types of ownership are available to the real estate investor who wishes to pool resources with others. A popular form is the *real estate investment trust* (REIT). This *trust* has tax benefits as well as other business advantages.

Review and Discussion Questions

1. Match the following terms with their correct definitions:

    (a) declaration
    (b) bylaws
    (c) individual unit deed

    (1) document prepared for each individual condominium unit in the development
    (2) document, required by state law, that must accompany and be recorded with the master deed for condominium development
    (3) document outlining the rules governing the internal operation of a condominium development.

2. What are the common elements in a condominium arrangement? Distinguish between general common elements and limited common elements.

3. A condominium unit owner surrenders in writing her right to use the swimming pool, one of the common elements. Does that action relieve her of the responsibility of sharing the cost of maintaining the pool?

4. Describe the usual decision-making arrangements made for the operation of condominium units.

5. Compare and contrast condominiums with cooperatives.

6. Roberta Geist is undertaking to promote a shopping center construction project. To obtain the necessary capital, Geist is considering offering shares in the venture to 20 business associates and friends.

    (a) Geist and all the offerees live in Nebraska. Discuss with Geist the pros and cons of not registering with the SEC and utilizing the intrastate offerings exemption.

    (b) All of Geist's proposed offerees are experienced businesspersons. Would you advise her to take advantage of the private offerings exemption? Why?

7.   What advantages accrue to investors entering a joint real estate venture who use the real estate investment trust form?

Case Problems

1.   Lynne Voyant inherited $50,000 upon the death of her rich uncle. Voyant is exploring investment possibilities and is considering investing in a real estate venture promoted by a friend, Percy Shifter. Shifter has assured Voyant that the investment is an excellent opportunity to make her money grow since the offering is registered with the SEC. Voyant has a premonition that there is more to consider than this. Clarify the situation for her.

2.   Jon Chai sued Support, Inc., the corporate owner of the cooperative in which he was a resident and stockholder. Chai contended that issuance of the stock was a security within the definition of federal security laws. What would be the result? Why? See *United Housing Foundation v. Forman, 421 U.S. 837 (1974).*

3.   Enterprise, Inc., purchased an existing shopping center and converted the commercial rentals into commercial condominium units. Jack Jackson, owner and operator of Jackson's Drug Store, tenant in the shopping center, sued to enjoin the conversion, contending that (1) condominium formulation is illegal for commercial units; (2) the conversion requires the issuance of a prospectus; and (3) it is illegal to deny him a vote since the day-to-day operation of the common elements will be done by the board of directors and not all the members of the condominium association. Was Jackson correct? Why?

4.   The original officers and directors of Avila S. Condominium Association contracted with Kappa Corp. to provide the association with recreational facilities. These officers and directors were also officers and directors of Kappa Corp. Other members of the condominium association sued the original officers and directors, contending that they were unjustly enriched as a result of their involvement with the Kappa Corp. Discuss. *Avila S. Condominium Ass'n. v. Kappa Corp., 347 So.2d 599 (Fla. 1977).*

5.   Kellogg owned an individual unit within a condominium. He decided that he wanted to put an additional story onto his unit and to expand the width of the existing story. He got the approval of the town zoning officials, but did not get the consent of the other condominium owners. The bylaws of the condominium indicate that unanimous consent of the owners is necessary for a unit owner to make a private use of the common elements. Kellogg claims that he is not using the common elements, but only unused air space. What do you think of Kellogg's argument as to (a) the horizontal expansion? (b) the vertical expansion? *Grey v. Coastal States Holding Co., 22 Conn. App. 497, 578 A.2d 1080 (1990).*

Glossary

abstract of title A summary of all the recorded transactions, including deeds, mortgages, judgments and the like, that affect the title to a specific parcel of land.

acceleration clause A provision in a mortgage giving the mortgagee the right to declare the entire debt due and payable upon default.

acceptance Assent to the terms of an offer.

accession Gradual increase in riparian or littoral property as a result of deposits of sediment made by a body of water.

accretion The rights and principles the law uses to deal with changes in the size and shape of land due to natural causes.

accord An agreement to substitute a different kind of performance for that originally contracted for.

acknowledgment In conveyancing, the act by which a person who has executed an instrument goes before an authorized officer, usually a notary public, and declares that the instrument is genuine and executed voluntarily.

action for rent or damages The landlord may permit, or be required to permit, the wrongdoing tenant to retain possession of the property and seek money damages for the landlord's injury.

actual notice Title information that is acquired personally by the interest holder.

adjudicated insane Has been declared insane by a court.

adjustable-rate mortgage (ARM) A type of flexible-rate mortgage.

administration of estates A general term used to describe the management and settlement of decedent's estate by a person appointed by the courts.

administrative remedies Remedies provided by the administrative agencies based on power granted in enabling act.

administrator A person charged with administering the estate of an intestate decedent.

adverse possession Acquisition of title to real estate by means of wrongful occupancy for a period of time established by statute.

aesthetics Regulation to retain visual and scenic beauty.

affidavit of title A sworn statement verifying facts that satisfy certain objections to title.

after acquired title Title acquired by a grantor after the grantor attempts to convey good title.

agency A legal relationship in which one party, called the *principal*, authorizes another, called the *agent*, to act in the principal's behalf.

agency coupled with an interest An agency that cannot be revoked by the principal.

agricultural lands Lands that are actively being used for grazing and crop production.

alienation Transferring ownership, title or interest in real estate from one person to another.

allodial system A system in which land is owned without obligations to pay rents.

alluvion Land created by sediment left by a body of water.

amortization Repayment of a debt in periodic installments of interest and principal over a period of time.

annual percentage rate (APR) As defined in the "Truth-in-Lending" Act, the percentage that the total finance charge calculated on an annual basis bears to the amount of the loan or credit.

anticipatory breach A breach of contract that occurs as a result of repudiating a contract before the date due for performance.

appeal Process in which a higher court reviews alleged legal errors made by a lower court or an administrative agency.

architect A professional person to prepare the plans and specifications for the construction of a house.

assessments The regular monthly payments for upkeep of the common elements, as well as payments required for special expenses or improvements to those common elements.

assignee A party to whom a right is transferred.

assignment Transfer of property right from one person (the assignor) to another (the assignee).

assignor A party who transfers a right.

assumption A contract between a grantor/mortgagor and a grantee in which the grantee agrees to assume responsibility for the mortgage debt.

attachment (1) the process by which a secured party acquires a security interest in collateral; (2) the act of seizing a defendant's property by legal process to be held by a court to ensure satisfaction of a judgment that might be awarded.

attestation The act of witnessing the execution of an instrument and subscribing as a witness.

authority Term used in the law of agency denoting the agent's power to perform acts authorized by the principal. (See also express authority and implied authority.)

balloon payment The final payment under a contract, which is substantially larger than the previous installment payments.

bargain and sale deed A deed that conveys title but makes no warranties.

bilateral contract A contract involving a promise in exchange for a promise.

blockbusting Inducing (for profit) the sale or rental of any dwelling by indicating that a particular class of person (for example, non-white) has entered or will enter the neighborhood.

breach of contract The unexcused failure to perform an obligation under a contract.

broker An agent who facilitates a transaction between parties.

builder See contractor.

building code compliance Protects the public health, safety and welfare by regulating building and construction standards.

buyer's broker A broker who has contracted to locate real estate for a buyer.

bylaws The rules governing the internal operation of the condominium development.

call Term used to refer to the different monuments, courses and distances that make up a metes-and-bounds description.

capacity The legal ability to enter into a contract.

caveat emptor Let the buyer beware.

caveat venditor Let the seller beware.

certificate of title A statement of opinion by an attorney that describes the status of the title to a parcel.

certiorari, writ of A legal document in which a higher court orders a lower court to supply the record of a case that the higher court wishes to review.

chain of title The recorded history of events that affect the title to a specific parcel of land, usually beginning with the original patent or grant.

Clean Air Act A statute whose purpose is to cleanse, maintain and enhance the quality of the nation's air resource.

Clean Water Act A statute whose purpose is to cleanse, maintain, and enhance the quality of the nation's water resources.

closing The final state of the real estate purchase transaction, when the deed and the purchase money are exchanged.

coastal zone Area including coastal waters and the adjacent shorelands.

codification Collection and organization of judge-made law into a code or statute.

cognovit A confession of judgment that permits the landlord, upon default by the tenant, to obtain a judgment against the tenant without the need for formal legal proceedings.

commitment Used in mortgage financing to designate the lender's promise to loan a specified amount of money at an agreed upon rate of interest.

common elements The parts of the development property that are necessary or convenient for the residents of the condominium and are owned in common by all the condominium residents.

common law (1) law based upon written opinions of appellate courts (see judge-made law); (2) the traditional nonstatutory law of England and the United States.

community property A form of co-ownership between husband and wife in which each has a one-half interest in property acquired through the labor of either during marriage.

Comprehensive Environmental Response, Compensation and Liability Act (CERCLA) A statute providing for clean up of inactive waste sites that release hazardous substances to the environment.

comprehensive plan A prerequisite for regulating land use. Its contents can range from a thorough master plan to a zoning code and map.

condemnation Legal action by which government acquires private property for a public use. Based upon the right of eminent domain.

condominium The fee simple ownership of one unit in a multiple-unit structure, combined with an ownership of an undivided interest in the land and all other parts of the structure held in common with the owners of the other individual units in the structure.

condominium association The organization stipulated by statute to administer the operation of the common elements of the condominium.

consideration A promise, act or forbearance bargained for and given in exchange for a promise, act or forbearance.

construction mortgage A mortgage given to secure funds advanced to construct or improve a building.

constructive eviction An occurrence that results when the actions of the landlord so materially interfere with the tenant's enjoyment as to make the premises untenable.

constructive notice The knowledge of certain facts that might be discovered by a careful inspection of public records, provided that such information is within the history of title, or discovered by an inspection of the premises.

contingency clause A provision within a contract that makes performance under the contract conditional upon the occurrence of a stated event.

contract A promise or an agreement that the law will enforce.

contractor The person or firm that undertakes to construct a house at a given price.

contract for a deed See land installment contract.

contract zoning Zoning in which an applicant will be granted a requested zone change only after contracting with the community to comply with certain covenants.

cooperative A form of ownership in which the land and buildings are (usually) owned by a corporation; individual unit residents own stock in the corporation and have a proprietary lease in a specific unit or apartment.

co-ownership Ownership of real estate in which two or more people have undivided interests.

correlative right, doctrine of A legal doctrine that prohibits depletion of a common pool of oil or gas. Sometimes applied to water.

co-tenancy See co-ownership.

counteroffer A new offer made as a response to a person who has made an offer.

covenant of fitness of the premises An assurance that the premises are fit for habitation.

covenant of quiet enjoyment A warrant by the landlord that the tenant will have the premises free from interference by the landlord or anyone claiming better right to the premises than the landlord.

covenant to deliver possession The landlord promises to deliver the right of possession to the tenant at the time the lease is scheduled to start.

critical areas Areas legislatively identified as containing natural limitations, or ones that are important to maintaining the ecosystem.

curtesy A common law estate that provided a husband with a life interest in all his wife's real property at the time a child was born of the marriage.

damages Money recoverable by one suffering a loss or injury due to breach of the contract.

decisional law Law that evolves from published opinions of appellate courts (see judge-made law).

declaration A document required by state law, which must accompany and be recorded with the master deed for the condominium development.

dedication The grant of real property such as a public street to a governmental unit for public use.

deed A legal instrument that conveys title to real property upon delivery and acceptance by the grantee.

deed in lieu of foreclosure A deed in which a mortgagor conveys mortgaged real estate to the mortgagee, who promises in return not to foreclose on the mortgage debt, which is in default.

deed of trust A legal instrument in which a borrower transfers real property to a trustee as security for a debt. The lender is the beneficiary of the trust.

default Nonperformance of a duty or obligation as part of the mortgage transaction.

defeasible fee See fee simple defeasible.

deficiency judgment A money judgment awarded to the mortgagee when funds obtained as a result of a foreclosure sale are insufficient to pay the debt.

delivery Surrender of possession and control of a document to a third party.

Department of Veterans Affairs loan guarantees Guarantees provided by DVA to lenders that finance housing construction and purchases by veterans.

developer The person or firm that subdivides a parcel of land and prepares the site for construction.

disavow Avoid a contract.

discharge The release of contractual obligations.

diversity jurisdiction Power of federal courts to hear cases involving citizens of different states.

dominant estate The parcel of land that benefits from an easement appurtenant; also called *dominant tenement.*

dower Life estate of a widow in one third of any real estate to which her husband had legal title during marriage. (See also inchoate dower.)

dual agency A transaction in which an agent represents both principals.

due-on-sale clause A provision found in some mortgages requiring the mortgagor to pay off the mortgage debt if he or she sells the property.

duty to repair Tenant's obligation to leave premises in about the same condition as when received, reasonable wear and tear excluded.

earnest money A cash deposit evidencing a good-faith intention to complete a transaction.

easement A nonpossessory interest in real property; the right to use another's real property for a particular purpose.

easement appurtenant The right of an owner of a parcel of land to benefit from the use of another's land. (See also dominant estate and servient estate.)

easement by necessity An easement that permits the owner of a landlocked parcel to cross a parcel of land of which the landlocked parcel formerly was a part.

easement in gross An easement that exists as a personal right apart from a dominant estate.

ejectment A legal action to recover possession of real property.

elective share The share of a deceased spouse's property that the surviving spouse may claim if the decedent left no will or the surviving spouse did not receive the minimum specified by law.

eminent domain Right of the state to take private property for public use. Just compensation must be paid to the owner.

enabling legislation State statutory authorization granting a local government the right to regulate in a specific area.

environmental impact assessment A statement describing and analyzing the environmental impacts of a proposed action.

Equal Credit Opportunity Act Federal statute prohibiting discrimination in an applicant's credit transaction.

equal protection The constitutional mandate that all people be treated equally under the law.

equitable title The buyer's right to obtain ownership of real property upon payment of the purchase price.

equity of redemption The right of a mortgagor or another person with an interest in real estate to reclaim it after default but before foreclosure.

escheat Reversion to the state of title to property of a person dying without heirs or leaving a will.

escrow A process by which money and/or documents are held by a third party until the terms and conditions of an agreement are satisfied.

escrow agent The third party who is the depository in an escrow transaction.

escrow agreement An agreement that directs the escrow agent regarding terms and conditions under which the deed or other instruments are to be delivered to the parties and the disposition of the deed or other instruments on default.

estate The extent and character of a person's ownership interest in real property. (See also future estate and life estate.)

estoppel certificate A statement by a mortgagor that he or she has no defense against paying the mortgage debt; also indicates the amount that remains unpaid.

eviction by the landlord The term usually associated with the legal procedure by which a landlord has the tenant removed from the premises because the tenant had breached the lease agreement.

evidence of title A document verifying ownership of property.

exceptions in zoning Permitted uses provided for in the ordinance that are inconsistent with the designated zone.

exclusive agency A listing in which the seller gives one broker authority to procure a buyer for property but also retains the right for himself or herself.

exclusive right to sell A listing in which the seller gives one broker authority to procure a buyer for property, but the broker is entitled to a commission if the seller procures the buyer.

exculpatory clauses A lease clause by which the landlord attempts to excuse himself or herself from liability for negligence in maintaining the leasehold premises.

executed A promise that has been performed.

executor Person appointed to administer the estate of a decedent who died testate.

executory An unperformed promise.

exemptions Transactions that would otherwise meet the definition of a security but that have been statutorily excused from the law's restrictions.

express authority Authority a principal confers upon an agent explicitly and distinctly. May be conferred orally or in writing.

express grant An easement created by an owner expressly granting in a deed a specific right to another to use the owner's property.

express reservation Property owner conveys title to another by deed specifically reserving an easement for himself or a third party within the deed.

fair housing The term used to express a national policy against most types of discrimination in housing.

federal question A legal dispute that involves the U.S. Constitution, a treaty, or a federal statute. Federal question cases are heard by federal courts.

fee simple (absolute) The most extensive estate in real property that an owner can possess.

fee simple defeasible A fee simple estate that terminates upon the occurrence of a specified condition; also called a *qualified fee*.

fee simple determinable A defeasible fee that terminates automatically if a stated act or event occurs.

fee simple subject to condition subsequent A fee that may be terminated by the grantor when a certain condition is fulfilled.

feudal system A system in which landowners pay rents to a superior.

FHA insurance Insurance provided lenders under Title II of the National Housing Act of 1943.

fiduciary duty A trustee's responsibility to act solely in the best interests of the owner or beneficiary of the trust.

finance charge Defined in the "Truth-in-Lending" Act as the monetary total of all charges a borrower must pay the lender for credit or a loan.

fixture An item that was personal property but has been permanently affixed to real property.

fixture filing A section of the UCC that allows a security interest to persist in goods (personal property) that later become fixtures.

flexible-rate mortgage A mortgage that contains a provision permitting the mortgagee to adjust the interest rate upward or downward in a manner specified in the mortgage.

floodplains Areas near waterways that are prone to flooding.

foreclosure A procedure in which property used as security for a debt is sold in the event of default to satisfy the debt.

foreclosure of mortgage Legal procedure by which a lender who has advanced funds with real property as security recovers in the event of default. (See also judicial foreclosure, power-of-sale foreclosure and strict foreclosure.)

forfeiture The loss of the right to a down payment or real estate as a result of a breach of contract.

fraud A deceptive act or statement deliberately made by one person in an attempt to gain an unfair advantage over another.

freehold estate An interest in real property created to last for an uncertain period of time.

future estate An interest in real property that will become possessory in the future.

general lien A lien that applies to all property that a person owns.

grantee Person who acquires title to real property by deed.

grantor Person who transfers title to real property by deed.

gross lease A lease in which a flat or fixed amount of rent is paid by the tenant.

ground lease A specialized type of net lease in which the lessor leases a piece of vacant land to the lessee, usually with the stipulation that the lessee at his or her own expense will construct a building thereon.

growth management plans Comprehensive growth plans that dictate both when and where growth will occur.

historic preservation The preservation of buildings, and perhaps archaeological sites, from destruction by new development.

holdover tenant One who failed to vacate or surrender possession of the premises on the ending date of a term tenancy.

homestead laws Provide heads of families some exemptions from creditor's claims.

implied authority An agent's authority to do those acts necessary and proper to accomplish the express terms of the agency.

implied notice Legal notice that is imposed by the law when conditions exist that would lead a reasonable person to inquire further into the condition of the title.

implied warranty of habitability A warranty imposed by law on the landlord by which he or she warrants that a residential property is safe and sanitary and fit for living at the time the tenant enters and during the period of tenancy.

in pari delicto At equal fault.

in terrorem clause A clause in an installment contract that prohibits recording at the expense of forfeiture.

inchoate dower The expectant interest of a wife to dower.

indemnification The act of compensating another in the event of loss.

independent contractor A person who is retained to do a job, using his or her own judgment as to how the work will be done.

individual unit deed The deed for each individual condominium unit in the development.

indoor pollution Pollution within buildings and is recognized as a health problem.

innocent misrepresentation An unintentional misstatement of a material fact that induces justifiable reliance to the detriment of a party.

inter vivos trust A trust that takes effect during the life of the creator.

interpleader A legal procedure whereby a party deposits money into court so that the court can distribute it to the rightful owner.

intestate A person who dies without leaving a will.

intestate succession Distribution of property of a person who dies without leaving a will or whose will is invalid.

intrastate offering An exemption from registration under federal securities law where the offering is made solely to residents of the state by a resident offeror doing business in the same state.

involuntary alienation The transfer of title to land against the owner's wishes.

joint tenancy Co-ownership in which the entire estate passes to the survivor upon the death of the other joint tenant or tenants.

joint venture A business entity in which two or more persons agree to carry out a single undertaking for profit.

judge-made law Law based upon the written opinions of appellate courts, called *precedent.*

judgment creditor A plaintiff who has won a monetary judgment that has not yet been paid.

judgment lien A lien that attaches to real property of a defendant when a plaintiff wins a judgment in the jurisdiction in which the property is located.

judicial foreclosure A foreclosure ordered by a court.

judicial remedies Remedies provided by the courts.

jurisdiction The power of a court to hear a case.

just compensation The award to the owner when property is taken by the government through eminent domain.

land installment contract A contract in which the buyer pays the purchase price on an installment basis. The seller/owner retains title until the purchase price is paid; also called *contract for a deed.*

landlord's lien Under common law, the lien known as the right of distress provided the landlord with a lien on the personal property of the tenant where there was a failure to pay rent.

large-lot zoning A zoning classification that requires a minimum of one acre or more of land for each single-family house that is constructed.

lease A contract, either written or oral, that transfers the right of possession of the premises to the lessee or tenant.

leasehold estate An estate created when the owner of property, known as the *lessor* or *landlord,* conveys a possessory interest in the real property to another, known as the *lessee* or *tenant,* for a specific period of time in exchange for the tenant's payment of rent.

legal description A description of a parcel of land complete enough to locate and identify the premises.

legal notice A knowledge of another's interest in real property sufficient to make the adverse interest legally binding to the prospective purchaser or any other party acquiring interest in the property.

license A personal privilege to enter another's property for a specific purpose.

licensing laws State laws that require a person to obtain a license in order to act as a real estate broker or sales associate and regulate the conduct of those who act as brokers or sales associates.

lien A claim against another's property securing either payment of a debt or fulfillment of some other monetary charge or obligation. (See also general lien and specific lien.)

life estate An ownership interest in real property created to last for a person's life.

limited partnership A partnership formed according to the provisions of a state limited partnership act. The liability of a limited partner is limited to the amount he or she has invested.

limited warranty deed A deed in which the seller warrants against acts that he or she has done that might affect title; also called *special warranty deed.*

lis pendens, notice of A notice filed for the purpose of warning people that legal action has been taken that might affect title or possession of specified real property.

listing A contract between a seller and a broker authorizing the broker to find a buyer for real property upon specified terms in return for a fee if the broker is successful. (See also open listing.)

littoral lands Lands that border on an ocean, a sea or a lake.

long-term escrow A financing device that combines the land installment contract and the escrow.

marketable title Title that is free of liens or other encumbrances that interfere with the peaceful enjoyment of the property.

mechanic's lien The right of one who renders services or supplies materials in connection with improvements to real property to seek a judicial sale of the realty to satisfy unpaid claims.

memorandum A writing that contains essential terms in satisfaction of the Statute of Frauds.

metes and bounds A method of describing land using compass directions, monuments or landmarks, and linear measurements.

mistake Unintentional error.

mistakes in recording Errors made by the recorder.

mistakes in the instrument Errors made in the preparation of the instrument to be recorded.

mobile home A transportable structure built on a chassis and designed for year-round living.

mortgage A document that uses real property to secure payment of a debt.

mortgagee A lender who acquires an interest in a borrower's real property as security for repayment of the loan.

mortgage insurance Insurance provided by government agencies or private corporations protecting mortgage lenders against loss caused by a borrower's default.

mortgagor A borrower who gives a lender an interest in the borrower's real property to secure payment of a loan.

multiple listing service An organization among brokers who have contracted to agree to share listings with each other.

negative amortization When periodic payments on an amortized loan do not cover all the interest that is due, the unpaid amount is added to the principal. This is referred to as *negative amortization.*

NEPA Statute requiring the preparation of a document detailing environmental data and analyzing that data regarding a proposed government action.

net lease As contrasted with the gross lease, a type of lease in which the tenant agrees to pay the taxes, insurance, repairs and other operating expenses of the premises.

nonconforming use A legal use that was established prior to zoning or prior to the present zoning classification and is permitted to continue despite its nonconformance with the zoning code.

note The borrower's written promise to repay a loan according to its terms.

notice statutes Statutes that provide that the subsequent buyer prevails over all interested parties who have not recorded their interest at the time the buyer accepts the conveyance and pays consideration for the land without notice of the preexisting conveyance.

novation An agreement in which a creditor agrees to discharge an existing debt and to substitute a new obligation and a new debtor in its place.

nuisance An unreasonable interference by one party with another's use or enjoyment of his or her land.

offer A proposal intended to create a contract upon acceptance by the person to whom it is made.

open-end mortgage A mortgage that permits the mortgagor to borrow additional funds, usually up to the original amount of the debt.

open listing A brokerage agreement that entitles the broker to a fee only if his or her activities bring about the sale. The property may be listed with several brokers.

option contract A contract that gives a person a designated period of time to buy or lease real property at a specified price.

optionor One who agrees not to revoke an offer.

optionee One who is the recipient of an option.

package mortgage A mortgage debt secured by both personal and real property.

parol evidence Oral or other evidence extraneous to a written contract.

parties' tort liability A civil duty to third parties to maintain premises in a reasonably safe condition.

partition A legal action in which a co-owner obtains a division of real property, terminating any interest of other co-owners in the divided portion. Each former co-owner's share is now owned individually.

partnership An association of two or more persons to organize a business venture and divide the profits.

party wall A single wall on the boundary of adjoining properties; it serves as a common support for buildings on each of two parcels.

per capita Distribution of an intestate's property in equal shares to persons who have the same relationship to the decedent without reference to the share an ancestor would have taken.

per stirpes Distribution of an intestate's property to persons who take only the share that an ancestor would have taken.

percentage lease A lease whose rental is based in part on the gross sales made by the tenant on the premises.

percolating water Water that passes through the ground, not flowing in a clearly defined underground stream or supplied by streams flowing on the surface.

perfection (1) Legal steps necessary to establish a valid mechanic's lien; (2) acts by which a secured party establishes priority in collateral over claims of third parties.

performance standards zoning Standards set to limit the adverse off-site impact of an owner's use. For example, standards can be established for odors, noise and signs.

periodic tenancy An estate from period to period, continuing from period to period until terminated by proper notice from one of the parties.

personal property Property that is not real property; generally characterized as having substance and being movable.

planned unit development (PUD) A concept involving a development larger than a traditional subdivision, generally permitting mixed uses within the development and attempting to provide a maximum amount of land for open space.

plat A map of a subdivision indicating boundaries of individual properties. Also includes details such as lot numbers, blocks, streets, public easements and monuments.

possession The right to occupy and control real estate to the exclusion of all others.

possibility of reverter A possibility that an estate based upon a condition may revert to the grantor if the grantee or those who take through the grantee breach the condition.

power of attorney A document authorizing a person, the attorney-in-fact, to act as agent on behalf of another as indicated in the instrument.

power-of-sale foreclosure Foreclosure based on terms in a mortgage giving a mortgagee or third party the power to sell the security if the borrower defaults.

power of termination The future interest that a grantor of an estate on condition subsequent has to terminate the estate if the condition occurs; also called *right of reentry*.

precedent A published opinion of an appellate court that serves as authority for determining a legal question in a later case that has similar facts.

prescription Acquisition of an easement through wrongful use of another's land for a period of time designated by statute.

prior appropriation Water rights doctrine giving primary rights to first users of water.

private offering An exemption from registration under federal securities law for offerings made to knowledgeable investors who have adequate information to evaluate fully the risks in the transaction.

probate The legal proceeding that establishes the validity of a will.

profit à prendre A nonpossessory interest in real property permitting the holder to remove part of the soil or produce of the land.

promissory estoppel A doctrine that prevents a party from denying that a promise is supported by consideration.

property Legal rights that a person possesses with respect to a thing; rights that have economic value.

prorate To divide or allocate proportionately.

prospectus A written document containing all the information necessary for an investor to make an independent and intelligent decision regarding a securities offering.

public use A use that benefits the community.

puffing Statements of opinion made by a seller to induce the purchaser to buy.

punitive damages Damages awarded as a punishment to the wrongdoer. Punitive damages are added to damages actually incurred.

purchase money mortgage A mortgage given to a buyer to secure part of the purchase price of real property and delivered contemporaneously with the transfer of title to the buyer.

quitclaim deed An instrument that conveys whatever title the grantor has.

race-notice statutes Statutes that provide that a subsequent buyer will prevail only if he or she has no notice of the prior transaction at the time of conveyance.

ratify Approve a contract.

ready, willing and able Capable of present performance.

real estate escrow See escrow.

real estate investment trust (REIT) A tax shelter that exempts certain qualified real estate investment syndications from corporate taxes where 90 percent or more of the ordinary income is distributed annually to the beneficiaries or investors.

real estate purchase contract An agreement whereby a seller promises to sell an interest in realty by conveying a deed to the designated estate for which a buyer promises to pay a specified purchase price.

real estate sales associate A person employed by a real estate broker who lists and sells real estate.

real estate securities Any arrangement whereby a person invests money in a common enterprise involving real estate with the expectation of attaining profits from the efforts of a promoter or some other third party.

Real Estate Settlement Procedures Act (RESPA) A federal law that requires lending institutions to disclose certain information to purchasers of residential real estate and prohibits those institutions from engaging in certain fraudulent activities.

real propery Land, buildings and other improvements permanently affixed to land.

real property rights Ownership or proprietary rights in land and anything permanently affixed to land.

recording statutes Laws that require the entry into books of public record the written instruments affecting the title to real property.

rectangular survey system System of land description that applies to most of the land in the United States.

redlining Denial of a loan by a lending institution or the exacting of harsher terms for loans in certain parts of a city.

reformation Change in lease agreement due to landlord's refusal to make repairs.

registration of securities The listing of an issuance that meets the definition of a security—and is not otherwise exempted—with the SEC and (perhaps) with state officials.

regulatory taking A regulation that deprives the owner of all reasonable use of the land constitutes a de facto taking of the property without due process of law under the Fifth and Fourteenth Amendments to the Constitution.

rejection An offeree's refusal or failure to accept an offer.

relation back A legal doctrine whereby the title acquired by a deed relates back to the moment of the first delivery to an escrow agent.

release of mortgage See satisfaction of mortgage.

reliction Land created when water recedes.

remainder A future interest in real estate created when a grantor conveys less than fee simple and by the same instrument directs another estate to arise immediately upon the termination of the prior estate.

rent The compensation paid by the lessee for the possession of the leased property.

rent paid in advance Rent payments due prior to the beginning of the lease period.

rent withholding The practice, allowed in a few states under limited circumstances, in which the tenant withholds rent as an inducement to force the landlord to perform repairs.

rescission A cancellation of a contract that results in the parties being restored to the position they were in before the contract was made.

respondeat superior, doctrine of The legal doctrine that an employer is liable for the wrongful acts of employees done within the scope of their employment.

restrictive covenant A provision in a deed limiting the uses that may be made of the property.

reversion A future interest in real estate created by operation of law when a grantor conveys a lesser estate than he or she possesses.

revocation An offeror's act of withdrawing an offer.

right of reentry See power of termination.

right of possession In all jurisdictions the right of possession implicitly resides in the tenant; that is, no one will have possessory rights inconsistent with those granted to the tenant.

right of survivorship A characteristic of some forms of co-ownership by which the surviving co-tenant acquires the entire estate.

riparian lands Lands that border on a stream or watercourse.

riparianism Water rights doctrine based on the idea that all owners of riparian lands are entitled to share equally in the use of water.

rollover mortgage A mortgage that must be refinanced every few years in order to adjust the interest rate up or down in response to prevailing market conditions.

rule of capture A legal principle of oil and gas law allowing a land owner the right to all oil and gas from wells on his or her land, including oil and gas migrating from the land of others.

run with the land Rights in real property that pass to successive owners are said to run with the land.

S corporation A corporation that has elected to be treated as a partnership for tax purposes.

satisfaction The performance of an agreement to substitute a different kind of performance for that originally contracted for.

satisfaction of mortgage A written statement by the mortgagee that the debt secured by the mortgage has been paid, also called a *release of mortgage*.

scienter In fraud action, knowingly making a false statement or asserting that something is true without actual knowledge.

section An area of land approximately one mile square, containing as nearly as possible 640 acres.

secured transaction A transaction in which the parties agree that personal property or fixtures will secure a loan or the purchase of an item on credit.

security deposit Money deposited by the tenant, usually at the inception of the lease, over and above the advance payment of rent for the security of the landlord.

segregation in housing The voluntary or enforced separation of one group from another in residential location based on religious association, ethnic background, race or a combination of these factors.

seisin Ownership of real property.

"separate but equal" facilities A concept that permitted the state to enforce separation of the races so long as each race was provided with "equal" services or facilities.

separate property In community property jurisdictions, property owned by either spouse prior to marriage and property acquired during marriage by gift, inheritance or will.

servient estate The parcel of land that is subject to an easement appurtenant; also called *servient tenement*.

settlement See closing.

settlement clerk The person who is designated to coordinate the exchange of documents at the closing.

special-use permit A system whereby special exceptions to the zoning ordinance are granted by the land use administrator under a permit arrangement.

specific lien A lien that applies only to a designated property.

specific performance A court decree mandating a party to perform according to the contract.

spot zoning A zone change permitted by the local legislature that is not in harmony with the comprehensive plan for that area.

Statutes of Descent and Distribution Provide for the distribution of an intestate's personal property; patterned after the English Statute of Distribution.

Statute of Frauds A statute that necessitates that certain contracts, in order to be enforceable, be supported by a written memorandum and signed by the party against whom enforcement is sought.

statutory law Law enacted by local and state legislative bodies and by Congress.

statutory right of redemption The right of a mortgagor to redeem the property after a foreclosure sale.

steering Channeling of prospective home buyers to or away from certain areas.

strict foreclosure A judicial procedure that terminates the mortgagor's equity of redemption and establishes the mortgagee's absolute title to mortgaged real property.

subdivision regulations Restrictions on the division of a parcel of land into two or more units. A subdivision will require prior approval by an administrator such as a planning board.

subject to As used in financing the purchase of real property, a sale in which an existing mortgage on the property is not paid off. The buyer paying only for the seller's equity.

sublease A transfer of part of the leasehold interest of the tenant, with the tenant retaining a reversionary interest.

subordination agreement As used in mortgage financing, an agreement in which a mortgage surrenders a priority lien and accepts a junior position in relationship to other liens or claims.

substantial performance The amount of compliance under the terms of a contract that discharges a party from further obligation although failing to perform totally under the contract.

syndicate A group of investors who pool their resources to develop, manage or purchase real estate.

tax lien A lien imposed against real property for payment of taxes.

tenancy at sufferance Created when a person is wrongfully in possession of another's land without a valid lease.

tenancy at will A tenancy that exists until either party chooses to terminate it.

tenancy by the entirety Co-ownership of real property by husband and wife. The right of survivorship is a characteristic of a tenancy by the entirety.

tenancy in common A form of co-ownership in which each owner possesses an undivided right to the entire property. Shares of co-owners need not be equal, and no right of survivorship exists.

tenancy in partnership A form of co-ownership in which each partner owns partnership property along with all other partners.

tender An offer of money or property as required by the contract.

tenure An historic system of holding lands, a characteristic of which was the possessor's subordination to some superior to whom the possessor owed certain duties.

term tenancy An estate for a specified period of time that has a specific beginning date and a specific ending date. When the ending date arrives, the estate is terminated without notice by either party.

testamentary trust A trust that does not take effect until the death of the creator.

testate succession Transfer of property when a person dies leaving a will.

testator A person who dies leaving a will.

third-party beneficiary A person who is allowed to enforce a contract although not a party to it.

third-person guaranty of rent The landlord who has doubts about the capacity or reliability of the tenant in meeting the conditions of the lease may require a third person to guarantee performance.

title The totality of rights and obligations possessed by an owner; evidence of ownership.

title insurance The comprehensive indemnity contract that insures the titleholder against title defects and encumbrances that may exist at the time the policy is issued.

Torrens certificate A document issued under the Torrens system, a type of land title registration.

township An area of land approximately six miles square, containing as nearly as possible 23,040 acres and divided into 36 sections.

trade fixtures Items added to land or buildings by a tenant to be used in the tenant's trade or business.

traditional zoning Zoning based on classifying land into use districts, such as residential, commercial and industrial uses.

transferring development rights A system of land controls that permits the transfer of the right to develop from sites that are desired to be preserved to sites on which maximum development is desirable.

trespass A wrongful, physical invasion of the property of another.

trust A legal relationship in which a person transfers legal title to property to a trustee who manages it for the benefit of third parties, the beneficiaries of the trust. (See also inter vivos trust and testamentary trust.)

trustee The person responsible for managing a trust.

Truth-in-Lending Federal statute that requires lenders to disclose the cost of consumer credit.

unconscionable contract A contract that a court may render unenforceable because it is grossly unfair.

underground streams Subterranean waters that flow in clearly defined channels discoverable from the earth's surface.

undivided interest Interest of a co-owner that gives him or her the right to possession of the entire property along with other co-owners (See co-ownership).

undue influence The exertion of dominion over another person that destroys that person's ability to exercise independent judgment.

Uniform Partnership Act A model act that establishes the legality of the partnership form of ownership.

uniform settlement statement A closing statement required for all federally related residential first mortgages.

unilateral contract A contract involving a promise in exchange for an act.

usury The practice of charging interest on a loan in excess of a rate allowed by law.

variable-rate mortgage A type of flexible-rate mortgage.

variance Permission obtained from the appropriate governmental authorities to deviate somewhat from the designations under the zoning code.

vendor's lien The right of a seller to a lien against land conveyed for any unpaid or unsecured portion of the purchase price.

voidable A contract that may be voided or validated at the option of a party.

waiver Intentional surrender of a known right or privilege.

warranty deed A deed that conveys title and warrants that title is good and free of liens and encumbrances. (See also limited warranty deed.)

waste Damage caused by the tenant, including failure to protect the premises from decay and ruin caused by the natural elements.

wetlands Lands that have groundwater levels at or near the surface for much of the year or that are covered by aquatic vegetation.

will A written instrument that permits distribution of an owner's property after death.

wraparound mortgage A second mortgage covering an existing mortgage that the lender agrees to service.

wrongful abandonment The tenant's vacating of the premises without justification and with the intention of no longer performing under the terms of the lease.

wrongful eviction An act that occurs when the landlord without justification deprives the tenant of the possession of the premises.

zone change A zoning amendment made by the legislative body that created the zoning code.

zoning The regulation by the public, usually a municipality, of structures and uses of land within designated zones.

Alphabetical Index
of Cases

Subject Index
of Cases

Index